50,001 best Baby names

Diane Stafford

NAPERVILLE, ILLINOIS

Published by Sourcebooks, Inc.
P.O. Box 4410, Naperville, Illinois 60567-4410
(630) 961-3900
FAX: (630) 961-2168
www.sourcebooks.com

Library of Congress Cataloging-in-Publication Data

Stafford, Diane.
50,001 best baby names / by Diane Stafford.
p. cm.
Includes bibliographical references (p.   ).
ISBN 1-4022-0498-1
1. Names, Personal—Dictionaries. I. Title: Fifty thousand and one best baby names. II. Title.
CS2377.S57 2003
929.4'4'03—dc21
2003007137

Printed and bound in the United States of America
VHG   10 9 8 7 6 5 4 3

Dedication

To my wonderful daughter, Jennifer, whose loving ways have brought me happiness every day of her life— and to my darling grandson, Ben, whose sweetness and charm are constant joys.

Acknowledgments

Sincere thanks to: Ed Knappman of New England Publishing Associates, for giving me the opportunity to write this book—and to Elizabeth Frost Knappman, literary agent and friend, who has made my dreams come true.

Hillel Black of Sourcebooks, for his patience, support, direction, and kindness. To Bethany Brown, Kelly Barrales-Saylor, Dan Bulla, Kristin Esch, Samantha Raue, and Morgan Hrejsa for their hard work on *50,001 Best Baby Names*.

Dana Chandler, Slavek Rotkiewicz, Camilla Pierce, Gabriela Baeza Ventura, and Jennifer Shoquist San Luis, for their help with this book.

And special thanks to my wonderful family and friends, whose names will always be tops on my list of favorites:

Jennifer, Benjamin, Robert, Clinton, Belle, Allen, Christina, Austin, Xanthe, Richard, Camilla, Britt, Gina, Curtis, Lindsay, Cameron, Josh, Jake, David, Amber, Dan, Fletcher, Russ, Martin, Dinah, Chris, Donna, Annie, Angela, Jami, Lucy, Tessie, Bob, Lily, Carolyn, Beth, Dot, Laurens, Cynthia, Laura, Jeffrey, Dana, Clarence, Eddi, Jay, Jim, Martha, Carrie, Natasha, Kathleen, Rachel, Renee, Wendy, Kristina, Jennifer, Liz, Elizabeth, Christy, Shannon, John, Shari, JoAnn, Alice, Gary, C.D., Bernice, Karla, Karen, Doug, Michael, Tom, Joanne, Mark, Fred, Spiker, Scott, Dominique, Russell, Evin, Dennis, Patrick, Cari.

Table of Contents

Introduction

Your name. Those two words should make you smile.

Nothing is more personal. Whether one-of-a-kind (Shawnikwaronda) or most-popular-of-the-century (Jennifer), your name gives you an identity that sets you apart from the twenty other kids in kindergarten and labels you the first day of a new job. If your name is memorable or a perfect fit, people say it more often. But if yours is hard to pronounce or difficult to remember, chances are good that you will go through life rarely hearing your "Daphinola" at all.

Indeed, a name can affect the ebb and flow of your entire existence. That's exactly why parents-to-be often give the baby-naming process numerous hours of list-perusing, head-scratching, and poll-taking.

For a kid who feels "stuck" with an albatross name, life can be long and bumpy. While people with better names seem to glide through social encounters effortlessly, the name-challenged types are more likely to stumble and bungle their way through the jungle.

If you have any doubt, note the baby-naming efforts of a person who grew up as Nyleen or Hortense, Huelett or Drakeston, and you'll probably find that this individual will have offspring named John or Ann. Just having a sibling with a tough moniker will nudge us in the direction of plain when it comes to naming a tiny, innocent baby.

What's the significance of all of this for you, the parent-in-waiting? You are dead-on right in thinking that finding the "right" name constitutes a major responsibility. This occasion is momentous enough to merit lots of discussion and lots of thumbing through the baby-naming book until you finally hit on it—The Right Name.

Whether or not you want to admit it, you really and truly want your child to like his name. No wonder you feel awed by the job! Most parents fret and falter, marvel and malinger, worry and wonder—sometimes for the entire nine months of pregnancy.

And that's because authors and songwriters immortalize names. People in love grow misty-eyed just thinking of them. Names are glorified and mocked, loved and loathed.

You're looking for a name that resonates, one that's memorable and perfect—but not *frighteningly* memorable or overly perfect. You're out to locate a name that is absolutely sure, 100 percent guaranteed, to have a positive effect on your little tyke's life. For that reason alone, you're willing to give the baby-naming gig quite a few hours of overanalysis.

We all want great names. We all struggle with the thousands of contenders.

Couldn't that little embryo give us a hint as to what name he would prefer? Is it better to be one of ten Davids in your class at school, or is it more of a challenge to try to pull off a quirky Ringo?

Maybe you're already submitting name-nominees to the acid tests: Is it too cute? Overly hip? Brutally boring? And, what's wrong with just going with your gut? This is your baby, after all. So why not tag that little biscuit with the way-cool name you've had squirreled away since your Barbie-and-Ken days!

Have fun with the name game. Approach it with wackiness, high spirits, and good insider information. Stay on message, and don't let yourself get sidetracked by relative-schmoozing or movie-star-mimicking. Carefully assess the pros and cons of your finalists, and you're bound to come up with a winner.

And while you're at it, do weigh the fact that a name can shape personality, career, and self-esteem. (How could a girl named Buzzie be anything other than a cheerleader?) And just as clearly, a person's name can be a lifelong drawback, as in the guy whose parents reversed the letters of their surname, and came up with an unpronounceable humdinger that made kids laugh at the boy all the way through school. So what happens to this kind of nuisance-name? When the man turns twenty-one, he goes to the courthouse and banishes that kookiness forever. What used to be "Enord" becomes the benign letter "E."

Also, consider any nasty connotations. Erica took on a whole new and scary feel after thirty years of being kicked around by the malevolent Erica Kane on the soap *All My Children.* And, by a different, somewhat slatternly yardstick, who could in good conscience name an innocent baby girl Monica in the post–Bill Clinton era?

At the same time, names can be an asset, a source of pride and distinction. Who would bet on anything other than a promising future for a Theodore or a Saul, a Grace or a Claire?

Some parents get so confused that they throw up their hands and pick a generic name. That way, the child can make what he wants of it. (Think how many times you've met Anne, Patricia, Carol, Michael, Richard, David, and Mark.)

Everyone knows what his own name did for him growing up (and what it didn't do). Maybe your parents envisioned a man being sworn in for President and chose Adlai,

John, Roosevelt, or George. Or, perhaps, your mother had warm, fuzzy feelings about a good old boy she knew growing up, so you were christened Billy Bob, certainly well suited for country-western singing (or for tattooing Angelina Jolie). Or your aunt loved the "artist formerly known as Prince" and made sure your birth certificate registered the eccentric "Purple Rain."

Boggled by mega-input, many parents toss around names for the entire nine months. And adding to the confusion is the steady stream of names offered by well-meaning grandparents, aunts, uncles, cousins, coworkers, employees, repairmen, and friends.

Baby-naming can even become so daunting that perplexed parents-to-be waffle daily. And then after they have identified a few winners, a couple faces the key issue that often comes into play—finding a name they can agree on. Usually, the result is a rush to judgment on delivery day, when Mom and Dad are finally forced to choose a name in the maternity ward.

Basic attitudes toward baby-naming can range from frivolous and cavalier to serious and tradition-laden. One Houston mother with the surname Palms named her African-American son White so that each time he introduced himself, "I'm White Palms," he was greeted with a grin or a look of disbelief. The same goes for a Texan named King Solomon, whose name is so memorable that this author was introduced to him at age fifteen, and decades later can still remember the shock of meeting a very confident kid who actually managed to pull off that spectacular name. (Some children can make a traffic-stopping name a big asset. But, some can't.) A friend of mine named Jeffrey wore her boy-name like a badge of honor, growing up to be both funny and popular. But, another girl whose parents chose a masculine name (Christopher) struggled with the name lifelong, forced to live with kids' ridicule.

That brings up a major trend going strong currently, the meshing of names to come up with something brand new. The U.S. Social Security Administration shows growing numbers of "creations" such as Tamikas and Rayshons, but don't mistake the proliferation for anything resembling approval by the kids so named. Most children don't appreciate their parents' inventiveness because teachers either mispronounce or avoid made-up names (as they have through the ages), and classmates make a hobby of terrorizing kids with odd names.

Some folks consider the practice of giving an old name a new spelling—Genefur for Jennifer, for example—a very cool way to go, while others scoff at this as downright laughable. By the same token, plenty of parents contend that giving new spellings to old names lends a fresh and splashy feel.

In some ethnic groups, a baby's name reflects the mother's pregnancy impressions. One book titled *Narco* tells of a Spanish mother who had a complicated process for naming seven sons. Each long name was a three-pronged affair consisting of a number for the birth order, a word that represented the mother's main obsession during the nine months, and the name of a famous writer. Cuatro Conrad Confabulation was the fourth son—Cuatro, meaning fourth son; Conrad, for the writer Joseph Conrad; and Confabulation, indicating that she spent her pregnancy gossiping with other pregnant women. Cinco Cervantes Cirrus, by the same token, was the fifth child, named for the writer Miguel Cervantes, and Cirrus, a cloud name that represents the mother's daydreaming pregnancy.

On the other end of the spectrum from those parents who dream up bizarre, fanciful names are the families who view baby-naming as a holy act, right up there with baptism. Some societies believe that names hold spiritual and prophetic significance, and that a child's name is sure to have an enormous impact on his future. The people of Ghana, for instance, think that a name is a mark of religious identification that carries honor and respect. A good name is highly treasured in Ghanaian society, and each baby is honored with a naming ceremony.

Obviously, no science has ever been devised to pinpoint the whys and hows of choosing a name. But, in this book, we give you 50,001 names, tips on the selection process, and, most importantly, clues as to how our names affect us. Be sure to read Part II, which features anecdotes from people who reflect on their names and how they were shaped (or weren't) by their names.

part one

Tips for Naming Your Baby

What do most people do? Some of the baby-naming approaches frequently used include the following:

- Mesh two names together to form a new one.
- Pick a name you've always loved.
- Find a name that bodes well for a promising career.
- Go with a name that connotes a trait—honesty, friendliness, *savoir faire*.
- Use the mother's maiden name for the first name.
- Honor a beloved relative by using his name.
- Stick with something time-honored and safe.
- Make up a name, a practice that some people consider *tres gauche*, and others rate high on the creativity scale.

And while you are dabbling in the name game, be sure to remember these naming taboos:

- Avoid a name that's carrying baggage equivalent to Amtrak, as in Cher, Michael Jackson, Richard Simmons, Billy Joel, or Sting.
- Don't let family members talk you into a "junior" unless you don't mind your child being called "Little John" or "Junior" lifelong. Listen to all the suggestions relatives fling your way, but you make the call.
- Don't be too bothered by existing connotations that you associate with a name ("I knew a Margaret in school, and she was the meanest person in our class," "I sat next to a Stone in college, and he had a million moles," or "I dated a Morgan, and she was the most boring girl I've ever known"). The reason you shouldn't let old associations trip you up is that once you name your child Tasha or Truman, there isn't another person in the world with that name who matters. *Trust me on this.*

Ten Great Tips for Successful Baby-Naming

A "set of rules" can ratchet up your confidence. If you don't really need a framework, just read the following tips as a fun diversion.

Here are ten steps for naming your baby:

1. Consider the sound—does it work with your last name?
When the full name is said aloud, you want something that has a nice ring, not a tongue-twister or a rhyme. You may find that a long last name jibes best with a short first name; by the same token, put a long first name with a short last name, and you may have a winner.

   The union of a first name ending in a vowel paired with a last name that starts with a vowel is not the greatest choice. For example: Ava Amazon. It's just hard to say. Puns aren't good omens for a happy life, either. Look at the infamous Ima Hogg name of a Houston philanthropist. If the poor woman wasn't burdened enough, she also had to deal with life-long rumors of a sister named Ura.

2. Know exactly what happens when you give your baby a crowd-pleaser name.
Give your kid a common name, and she'll probably end up Sarah B. in a classroom with six Sarahs. She may be comfortable with the anonymity that a plain-Jane name lends her—considering it far better than being the class Brunhilda, who gets ridiculed daily. Or, she may ask you every other day of her childhood why you weren't more original in naming her: "Why did you give me the same name fifty million other kids have? Why couldn't you have come up with something better? Why didn't you take more time?"

3. Think seriously about the repercussions of choosing a name that's over-the-top in uniqueness.
You are definitely sticking your neck out by giving your child the name Rusty if your last name is Nail. Sure, he may muster up enough swagger to pull it off, but what if he doesn't? Lots of people with unusual or hard-to-spell last names will purposely opt for a simple first name for their child, just to ease the load of having two names to spell over and over. Some research suggests that kids with odd names get more taunting from peers and are less well socialized. You can be sure that junior-high kids will make fun of a boy named Stone, but later, as an adult, he may enjoy having an unusual name.

Just make sure you don't choose a "fun" name simply because you like the idea of having people praise your creativity—instead, ask yourself how your child will feel about being a Bark or a Lake.

4. Ponder the wisdom of carrying on that family name.
Aunt Priscilla did fine with her name, but how will your tiny tot feel in a classroom full of Ambers and Britneys? Extremely old-fashioned names sometimes make their way back into circulation and do just fine, but sometimes they don't. (Will we really ever see the name Durwood soar again?)

5. Consider the confusion that is spawned by a namesake.
A kid named after a parent won't like being "Junior" or "Little Al." Ask anyone who has been in that position about the amount of confusion it generates in regard to credit cards and other personal I.D. information. You'll spend half your life unraveling the mix-ups. Psychiatrists (many of them juniors themselves) will tell you that giving a child his very own name is a much better jumpstart than making him a spin-off or a mini-me.

At the same time, we have all run across someone who absolutely loves being Trey or a III because the name represents tradition and history.

6. Make your family/background name an understudy (the middle name).
Let's say you want your baby's name to reflect his heritage or religion, but you strongly prefer more mainstream names. You can fill both bills by using the ancestry name as a middle name.

7. Ponder whether the name's meaning matters to you.
For some people, knowing a name's meaning is extremely important, often much more so than its Greek or German origin. And your child could turn out to be the type who loves investigating such things. So what happens when that offspring of yours finds out that her name Delilah means "whimpering harlot guttersnipe"? She may wish you had taken a longer look at the name's baggage.

8. Look at shortened versions of a name and check out initials.
Don't think your child's schoolmates will fail to notice that his initials spell out S.C.U.M. And, you can be sure that Harrison will become "Harry" or, occasionally, "Hairy." View the teasing as being as much a given as school backpacks, and think twice about whether you want to give your child's peer group something they can really grab onto. Tread lightly. Naming always starts with good intentions, but you can do your kid a favor by considering each name-candidate's bullying potential.

9. After you've narrowed your list, try out each name and see how it feels.
Say, "Barnabus Higgins, get yourself over here!" Or, "Harrison Higgins, have you done your homework?" Or, "Hannibal Higgins, would you like some fava beans?"

10. Once you and your mate have decided on a name, don't broadcast it.
You may want to keep your name choice a secret, otherwise relatives and friends are likely to share all of their issues with the name and a long string of other, "better" options. Another possibility is that people will start calling the unborn baby that name, which will be unfortunate if you happen to find one you like better.

Bottom line: take the Name Game seriously, but don't be afraid to go with the one that just *feels right*. That precious infant who will change your life dramatically is sure to be the best thing that has ever happened to you—give him or her a name that you will love singing and saying every single day, a million times over.

Baby Ben (Jen), I'm so glad you're mine.

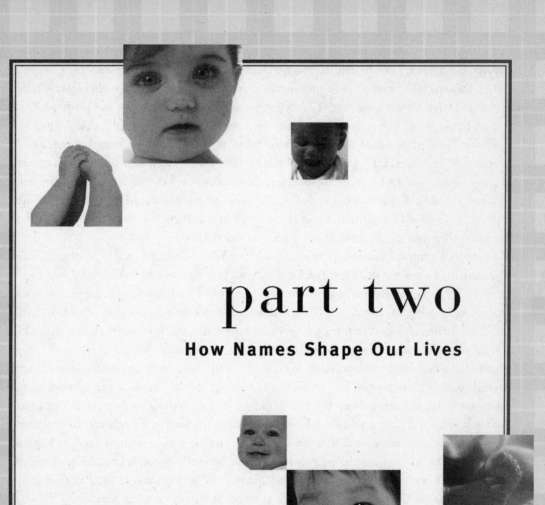

part two

How Names Shape Our Lives

Here, twenty-one people share their thoughts on their names:

Camilla Shirley Pierce, homemaker and mother, Houston: "Although I was named for a beloved great aunt, I always felt that carrying around such an unusual name was not great. When I was a child, no one could pronounce it or spell it. It was a source of embarrassment and aggravation. Now, at age sixty-two, when people read my name they still mispronounce it, and I always feel like saying, 'How hard can it be? I could pronounce it at age three!' "

David Nordin, proposal writer: "I always liked my name because it had more character than other names. David has Biblical history, and it's more elegant and regal than your average name. On the flip side, my odd middle name caused me years of embarrassment. Teachers would call out that name during roll call, and people would laugh and make fun of me...As soon as I was grown, I had it legally changed. Parents should never name their kids anything that could make them objects of ridicule."

Clarence Raymond Chandler, President of Marshall & Winston, Inc., in Midland, Texas: "I was named after my dad's favorite brother, who was a great guy I admired. I was raised in south Texas (Benavides), where my friends were named Roberto, Jose, Ricardo, Jesus, and Francisco, so being a George, Bill, Jerry, Charles, or Roger never really came up on my 'wish list.' I was content! Today, technology has caused the minor inconvenience of not being able to find enough room on forms to print out my long name, much less my signature." Chandler adds: "I had it easy compared to my dad, who was born in an era when children were named after famous people; he got incessant ribbing, not to mention playground fights, when he was growing up, because his challenge was answering to Napoleon Bonaparte Chandler, which is right up there with the ranks of Johnny Cash's 'how do you do, my name is Sue.' In school, it was common knowledge that you only picked on him once, or you had a real dogfight on your hands. To avoid 'you gotta be kidding' comments, he adopted the name 'Nap' Chandler. He was a great dad, patriot, WWII veteran, ethical businessman, champion for the little guy, and a loving and tough SOB—he was my hero!"

Jennifer Wright, a psychiatrist in Atlanta, Georgia: "I've always liked my name. Some of my best friends have been named Jennifer also, and I think it suits our personalities. The benefit of having a 'common' name is that I never have difficulty finding personalized items. Plus, I like the nicknames 'Jen' and 'Jenny.' "

Kristina Kaczmarek Holt, a graphic artist in Canada: "I have always liked my name because it was unique. I had never come across a Kristina with a 'K' until I was a teenager, and then it was usually a Kristy or Kristine. I liked the sound of my first and last name together (the two Ks)—that seemed to work. My name was a heck of a thing to learn to spell in kindergarten, but it was all mine. They used to tape your name to those thick green pencils you learned to write with, and I was always sharpening my pencil down into my name. It wasn't until I recently had a child of my own (Noah) that my dad told me where he got my name. I assumed he picked it because it was a Polish name, and his family was half-Polish. But instead, he named me after a woman who was especially nice to him when he was young, who must have made a strong impression because the name stuck with him until I was born."

Homemaker Dana Huggins Chandler: "I like to be just a little different from everyone else around me, so I always loved my name. There are now many people named Dana, but most don't have the same pronunciation. My name rhymes with Anna and Lana. I always tell people I was named after my dad—Dan—which isn't true, but it does help people remember how to pronounce my name."

Houston TV anchor Dominique Sachse: "Considering you can't pick your name at birth, I'm quite pleased with the one my parents chose for me. I think it has a level of sophistication, and it's unique and European, which I am. I've never considered changing it, shortening it, or going by a nickname. It's a name I feel I've had to live up to."

Cari LaGrange, Internet business owner: "I liked my name growing up, but like most kids, I went through a phase when I wished I could change it, the way girls with straight hair want curly hair and vice versa. Thankfully, my name and its spelling were unique in the town where I grew up, so there was no other girl by my name to compare my identity to."

Jane Vitrano, homemaker in Midland, Texas: "My mother named my sister Linda and me Jane because she hated her own name, Lula Mae, and said she would never want her daughters to have anything but plain names—and no middle names."

Donna Pate, technical writer: "I was neutral about my name. It was okay but not too exciting or interesting. At least it didn't lend itself to juvenile humor. There was the chance of being labeled 'Prima Donna,' but that was beyond the vocabulary of most kids. I liked my name better after I learned what it meant, but that wasn't until I was an adult."

Natasha Graf, acquisitions editor for Wiley Publishing, New York: "My name is pretty special because I was named after a very important woman in my father's life. When I was young and wanted to be like every other girl with an American name, I didn't always like my name because it was unusual at the time, being Russian and all. However, when my father shared with me who I was named after, I came to love it because I feel like I am connected to her somehow. She was a professor at my father's college, and she spoke seven languages—a brilliant woman who had emigrated from Russia. She was his mentor—the first really intellectual person he met during college, and they stayed friends after he went to medical school. It was not an affair—more a meeting of the minds. They wrote to each other. He saved every letter she wrote, and he let me read them. It was so interesting to see my father as a young person through these letters. She died before I was born, before my father was married. I wish I could have met her; I wonder what she would have thought of me. As you can tell, I wouldn't want my name to be anything else."

JoAnn Roberson, fifth-grade teacher in Edna, Texas: "I didn't like my name because it reminded me of a boy's name—Joe. My dad said they were going to name me Jacquelyn, but an uncle said that was too long a name for a little baby, and I would never learn to spell it. I always wished that was my name."

Trey Speegle, art director for *US Weekly*, New York City: "I've always appreciated my name, although when I was very young and wanted to fit in, I wished I had a more normal name, like Chris, or a cool name like Skip. My great-grandmother named me; I was born on her birthday, April 13, and I was her thirteenth great-grandson. Her son (my grandfather) was John Hugh Speegle Sr., and my father is John Hugh Speegle Jr., so she named me Trey John—'the third' John."

Angela Theresa Clark, co-owner of Court Record Research, Inc.: "My mother named me Angela Theresa after two of her favorite Carmelite nuns. I was known as Theresa until sixth grade, when I tired of telling teachers that I didn't go by Angela and just surrendered to being called that. I thought it was stupid to be named something so close to the word 'angel.' Angels are imaginary, soft, and I saw them as easy prey. I was also afraid people might think I was angelic. I thought I had to be tough in my family, with five brothers and two big (mean) older sisters (ha!). I was tomboyish, and Theresa just fit better. Some family members still call me Theresa, although it doesn't fit me anymore because now I'm softer and much more vulnerable. I love my name."

Spiker Davis, dentist, Houston, Texas: "I really liked my name because people always remembered it, and there's no one to get confused with. Also, with a last name like Davis (seventh most common name in the U.S.), you need something to separate you from the crowd."

Cristy Ann Hayes, journalist and mother of two: "My name became a primary focus when I was young and searching for a sense of self, like other preteens. I was disappointed when people would ask what Cristy was short for, and I had to reply 'nothing.' I would wish my mom had taken more time to give me a name as substantial as Christina or Christian. My name also worked well as a taunt for my brother, who insisted I was the only one of the three siblings whose name didn't start with W, so I was not part of the family. Will and Wendy could be rascals that way. My mom thought it was clever to give my name an unconventional spelling, so I have, my entire life, had to take special care in spelling my name, and often people will add an *h*. My driver's license is incorrect because of this, and many of my in-laws still spell it wrong. But after years of frustration regarding the spelling, I now appreciate the measuring tool it has become for me, showing how attuned someone is to me. I hold in high regard those who actually take the time to recognize the unique spelling and write it correctly. I believe it says something about one's character and approach to life when you take care to get a name right!"

Frank Vitrano, retired petroleum engineer in Midland, Texas: "I was born in Waco, Texas, of a Sicilian father, and I was named for my grandfather, Frank Anthony, which is the Italian custom for the first-born son. You get your grandfather's name."

Jennifer Colwell, commercial property management, Midland, Texas: "Since I'm in my fifties, there were not very many Jennifers when I was growing up, and I always loved my name. I thought it was pretty and considered it an asset."

Christopher (Chris) Fleming, female computer consultant, Houston, Texas: "Growing up, I hated my name, Christopher Anne. I was called Christopher Columbus, was sent a draft notice, and was labeled 'effeminate' on an aptitude test in high school. I finally told my mother how much I had hated my name, and she was surprised. In my opinion, parents should choose a name that indicates the child's sex (not one that's androgynous), and that's easy to spell. I don't think it's good to give a baby a name that's bizarre or made up from several words."

Wendy Schnakenberg Corson, EMT: "I have always hated my name. There were never any other Wendys, and if there were, they certainly weren't popular. My parents said they also liked the name Robin, which is a name I love; I told them how mad I was that they chose such a terrible name for me. Also, my middle name, Anne, is just boring. I was never teased about my name, so I suppose that is a positive. But, of course, kids had my last name—Schnakenberg—to tease me with!"

Carey Layne Davis, male landscape architect: "I have always liked my name and never wanted to be called anything else. It was somewhat unique, and I was never teased."

part three

Changing Your Name

Typically, U.S. hospital officials require parents to name their child before leaving the hospital. Other places, such as Canada, give a couple ten days to make their decision.

If you want to change your name, you can hire a lawyer to give you all of the specifics and forms, or you can go to LawGuru.com on the Internet. The latter route gives you, for a fee, the legal forms your state requires.

For your money, you get a name-change package that has forms and instructions for circulating your name-change to government agencies and other groups such as employers, the Social Security Administration, post offices, banks, clubs, the driver's license bureau, insurance companies, the IRS, and the state tax commission, as well as forms for changing your legal documents, including your will.

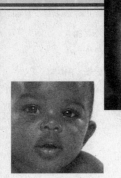

part four

230 Fun Lists

Powerful Names

Boys	Girls
Andrew	Anna
Angus	Blake
Anthony	Campbell
Charles	Candace
Cole	Elizabeth
Colin	Evan
Easton	Grace
Ford	Greta
Grant	Harper
Harrison	Honor
Heath	Hope
Jacob	Jessica
James	Julia
Jon	Lauren
Justice	Madison
Lamar	Margaret
Louis	Olivia
Michael	Pace
Nash	Parker
Nolan	Pilar
Quentin	Quinn
Reagan	Reeve
Solomon	Rhea
Thomas	Sarah
William	Wylie

Names That Get Shortened

Boys	Girls
Alexander	Abigail
Augustus	Alexandra
Barnabus	Anastasia
Bradford	Angelina
Christopher	Cassandra
Cornelius	Charmaine
Donovan	Constance
Emmanuel	Deborah
Enrique	Elizabeth
Franklin	Evangeline
Frederic	Gabrielle
Gregory	Guadalupe
Jonathon	Gwendolyn
Nathaniel	Jacqueline
Nicholas	Jennifer
Randolph	Josephine
Roberto	Kimberly
Roderick	Lucretia
Roosevelt	Magdalena
Salvador	Nanette
Samuel	Penelope
Solomon	Rebecca
Timothy	Rosalinda
Wilfredo	Roxanna
Woodrow	Susannah

To Give You a Leg Up in Life

Boys	Girls
Barrett	Anna
Benjamin	Ashley
Blake	Bella
Burke	Caroline
Daniel	Celeste
David	Claire
Ethan	Danielle
Graham	Dominique
Gus	Elizabeth
Julian	Emma
Kyle	Grace
Lance	Isabella
Liam	Jennifer
Logan	Julia
Mason	Kim
Matt	Margaret
Max	Marion
Michael	Merit
Nathaniel	Michelle
Patrick	Natalie
Ralph	Nicole
Samuel	Rose/Rosa
Tremayne	Sadie
Tyler	Sidney
Will	Sophie

Tomorrow's Slackers

Boys	Girls
Bacchus	Abilene
Bo	Aspen
Chauncey	Barbie
Diego	Birdie
Eden	Callie
Edsel	Chesney
Gino	DeeDee
Kato	Dodie
Kyd	Empress
Link	Eve
Loki	Felicity
Longo	Fluffy
Magni	Happy
Mohican	Jethra
Montana	Lark
Ojay	Lotus
Pluto	Marvel
Rio	Precious
Rip	Roseanne
Somers	Sissy
Sonny	Soleil
Taos	Summer
Tavaris	Sunny
Tino	Tea
Tyson	Trixie

part
four

23

Reality TV Stars

Boys	Girls
Adam	Aimie
Alvie	Azalea
Amadeo	Babette
Art	Becky
Bart	Bella
Bonnard	Breanna
Carlos	Carmen
Chyrell	Chanina
Danton	Dyana
Deno	Estella
Diego	Grace
Ellison	Isra
Fabrizio	Janaye
Gabe	Janelle
Gabino	Lauren
Garrick	Lisel
Joke	Liliana
Lonzo	Lilly
Mario	Maryann
Pierre	Marva
Ransom	Natalie
Rory	Nicole
Tab	Renee
Zach	Roxanne
Zennie	Tabla

Achievers

Boys	Girls
Andrew	Addison
Butler	Emma
Chason	Blythe
Dennis	Bonnie
Doug	Brittney
Ewan	Camille
Gavin	Christina
Hank	Cindy
John	Delisa
Jeff	Emerey
Kaufman	Emma
Keane	Erin
Kent	Gaynor
Kevin	Gina
Mitchell	Hollyn
Norton	Janiqua
Patton	Jessalyn
Rance	Leanne
Robert	Mallory
Schultz	Phoebe
Scott	Rebecca
Skip	Roxanne
Teague	Shae
Thorne	Taylor
Usher	Tonya

Cool Names for Athletes

Althea (Gibson)
Arnold (Palmer)
Babe (Ruth)
Ben (Hogan)
Bill (Russell)
Billie Jean (King)
Bo (Jackson)
Bonnie (Blair)
Carl (Lewis)
Craig (Biggio)
Cy (Young)
Deion (Sanders)
Evander (Holyfield)
Gale (Sayers)
George (Foreman)
Gordie (Howe)
Greg (Louganis)
Hakeem (Olajuwon)
Hank (Aaron)
Jack (Nicklaus)
Jackie (Robinson)
Jeff (Bagwell)
Jerry (Rice)
Jesse (Owens)
Jim (Brown, Thorpe)
Joe (DiMaggio)
Johnny (Unitas)

Julius (Erving)
Kareem (Abdul-
  Jabbar)
Lance (Armstrong)
Larry (Bird)
Lou (Gehrig)
Magic (Johnson)
Mark (Spitz)
Martina (Navratilova)
Michael (Jordan)
Mickey (Mantle)
Muhammad (Ali)
Picabo (Street)
Red (Grange)
Sandy (Koufax)
Serena (Williams)
Stan (Musial)
Sugar Ray (Robinson)
Ted (Williams)
Tiger (Woods)
Ty (Cobb)
Venus (Williams)
Walter (Payton)
Wayne (Gretzky)
Willie (Mays)
Wilma (Rudolph)
Wilt (Chamberlain)

Future "Most Dependable"

Boys	Girls
Aaron	Amica
Alton	Amy
Barry	Bethany
Brent	Carrie
Chris	Chandra
Clint	Deb
Cole	Elle
Demarris	Heather
Derek	Hope
Devin	Juliet
Elmer	Larsen
Forrest	Lemuela
Gary	Lynn
Hunter	Olena
Jack	Otilie
Jeston	Penthea
Keller	Randie
Leo	Siaka
Mack	Sofie
Manny	Trella
Overton	Tucker
Radu	Varina
Scott	Weslee
Werner	Ximena
Will	Zore

Children of Lesbians and Gays

Boys	Girls
Alex	Amber
Anson	Annabelle
Avery	April
Bevan	Bianca
Brett	Brianna
Caleb	Candace
Carson	Celeste
Casey	Chloe
Clay	Daisy
Derek	Darcy
Ethan	Feo
Forrest	Gloria
Jake	Hilary
Kyle	Ingrid
Logan	Jessica
Marco	Kirsten
Matt	Lara
Noel	Lola
Owen	Maura
Ray	Mia
Silas	Molly
Spencer	Noele
Yale	Pia
Zack	Ramona
Zeke	Sharon

Charmers

Boys	Girls
Brad	Ajana
Bret	Bead
Chance	Bridget
David	Chandi
Deryn	Coco
Devean	Dancy
Duncan	Denise
Fernando	Dionne
Jaret	Gidget
Jase	Ginzi
Jeremy	Halea
Kobe	Jen
LeBron	Joanna
Lorenzo	Kimana
Luke	Laya
Nissan	Maryann
Rasheed	Mia
Rob	Nicolae
Russ	Rita
Sage	Robin
Santino	Roxy
Slater	Shauna
Tolbert	Sierra
Tolfe	Tanisha
Viggo	Torry

Celebrity Names

Boys
Antonio
Ashton
Ben
Booker
Brad
Burt
Casey
Casper
Damon
Denzel
Fabrice
Fernando
Goran
Griffin
Hudson
Keenan
Kiefer
Liam
Marc
Matthew
Mel
Patrick
Russell
Ryan
Tom

Girls
Charlize
Demi
Drea
Drew
Fiona
Halle
Isabella
Jennifer
Jessica
Julia
Kate
Lara
Liv
Natasha
Oprah
Portia
Reese
Renee
Rosanna
Sela
Selma
Sheena
Simone
Thora
Uma

Names Celebrities Give Their Babies

Boys
Aaron (Robert DeNiro and Toukie Smith)
Bailey (Anthony Edwards and Jeannine Lobell)
Blanket (Michael Jackson)
Boston (Kurt Russell and Season Hubley)
Chance (Larry King and Shawn Southwick)
Chester (Tom Hanks and Rita Wilson)
Connor (Tom Cruise and Nicole Kidman)
Elijah Blue (Cher and Gregg Allman)
Giacomo (Sting and Trudie Styler)
Gib (Connie Selleca and Gil Gerard)
Griffin (Brendan Fraser and Afton Smith)
Hughie (Marg Helgenberger and Alan Rosenberg)
Jett (John Travolta and Kelly Preston)
Joaquin (Kelly Ripa and Mark Consuelos)
Miles (Eddie and Nicole Murphy)
Pedro (Frances McDormand and Joel Coen)
Prince Michael (Michael Jackson)
Rafferty (Jude Law and Sadie Frost)
Roman Caruso (Dee Dee and Dan Cortese)
Satchel (Woody Allen and Mia Farrow)
Theo (Kate Capshaw and Steven Spielberg)
Zachary (Robin Williams and Valerie Velardi)

Names Celebrities Give Their Babies

Girls

Beige Dawn (Don Adams)

Bria (Eddie and Nicole Murphy)

Brielle Nicole (Desiree and Blair Underwood)

Cassidy (Kathy Lee and Frank Gifford)

Ella Bleu (John Travolta and Kelly Preston)

Eulala (Marcia Gay Harden and Thaddeus Scheel)

Giovanna (Vanna White and George Santo Pietro)

Gracie (Faith Hill and Tim McGraw)

Greta (Phoebe Cates and Kevin Kline)

Ireland (Kim Basinger and Alec Baldwin)

Kenya (Natassja Kinski and Quincy Jones)

Maggie (Faith Hill and Tim McGraw)

Mary Willa (Meryl Streep and Donald Gummer)

Paris (Michael Jackson)

Prima (Connie Sellecca and John Tesh)

Rumer Glenn (Demi Moore and Bruce Willis)

Sailor (Christie Brinkley and Peter Cook)

Scarlett (Mick Jagger and Jerry Hall)

Scout LaRue (Demi Moore and Bruce Willis)

Shayne (Eddie and Nicole Murphy)

Starlite Melody (Marisa Berenson)

Wylie Quinn (Richard Dean Anderson and Apryl Prose)

Zola (Eddie and Nicole Murphy)

Pistols, Wild Things, and Pieces-Of-Work

Boys	Girls
Ajay	Ambelu
Alec	Aundrea
Brush	Brynne
Corbin	Callie
Cuca	Caralyn
Demetrie	Cawana
Derant	Charner
Drake	Concetta
Dyron	Dandra
Enrico	Dorshea
Erold	Dracy
Flint	Emmagene
Harold	Harley-Jane
Kin	Heydee
Lynus	Jacquier
Mandrake	Kisha
Mashawn	Krysia
Rockney	Mallory
Sean	Mireya
Shamone	Moti
Slim	Nevelyn
Steve	Pariann
Storm	Sharell
TeRez	Tangie
Teshombe	Trenna

Future Fashionistas

Boys	Girls
Ant	Anoushka
Barkan	Ardythe
Blevin	Austene
Calum	Chiara
Clarke	Corianna
Clay	Divine
Dario	Dori
Harding	Elkie
Kamal	Emge
Jean-Luc	Evette
Kelvin	Fabulia
Kenji	Joonypur
Kirklin	Kisha
Laranz	Mare
Lear	Misti
Leon	Roquina
Robin	Sasa
Ruben	Selia
Massimo	Shawnda
Mustafa	Shaytella
Rage	Siva
Rainier	Tammy
Tayshaun	Tanis
Wash	Tirsa
Worth	Viviana

Names that Are So Over

Boys	Girls
Al	Bertie
Bob	Betty
Dennis	Carla
Donald	Delores
Douglas	Edith
Ernie	Faye
Frank	Frances
Garland	Gail
Gary	Hilary
Glanville	Judy
Harold	Loretta
Harvey	Louise
Jaden	Marilyn
Jason	Maureen
Jerry	Minnie
Juwon	Myrna
Ken	Nancy
Leon	Nina
Marvin	Priscilla
Morey	Stacy
Oscar	Tiffany
Ottis	Tracy
Randy	Veronica
Rick	Wanda
Todd	Winona

Future Truck Drivers

Boys	Girls
Butch	Clara
Carl	Cora
Cash	Davette
Derrell	Edna
Derlin	Ethelene
Earl	Flo
Hal	Gretchen
Harlan	Irma
Henry	Jody
Herb	Lacresha
Hugh	Lataisha
Joe-Eddy	Latrice
Johnny	Makula
Lonnie	Nadine
Mace	Nerline
Marvin	Pearlie
Milton	Sonequa
Nate	Sherlene
Norman	Sue
Otis	Wanda
Otto	Usha
Revill	Vatoya
Rylance	Veva
Scatman	Virgia
Sorlie	Zennida

Future Computer Techies

Boys	Girls
Alcazar	Anna
Alexandre	Arye
Boleslav	Brana
Brian	Devane
Challen	Eva-Marie
Cornel	Gert
Dan	Glenne
Dickey	Jules
Don	Kala
Emeril	Kate
Gray	Keira
Gurinder	Kim
Jayon	Kitty
Jensen	Margot
Jim	Megan
Lon	Nell
Marshall	Rachel
Matthieu	Ramonda
Ned	Ravada
Randolph	Shannon
Saginaw	Skylar
Timothy	Sonora
Todd	Stephanie
Warren	Talisa
Zero	Tania

Burdensome Names

Boys	Girls
Ambrose	Alfre
Ankoma	Antigone
Archibald	Bathsheba
Bartholomew	Chastity
Boaz	Clotilde
Bouvier	Columbine
Cord	Cornelia
Dakarai	Cricket
Durwood	Edna
Gershom	Elspeth
Godfrey	Flannery
Hercules	Henrietta
Humphrey	Indiana
Ignatius	Keturah
Kalunga	Majidah
Lafayette	Millicent
Lazarus	Minerva
Marmaduke	Muriel
Mortimer	Priscilla
Percy	Prudence
Reginald	Purity
Thelonius	Thomasina
Vladimar	Ursula
Wolfgang	Zona
Zacharias	Zuwena

Future Veterinarians

Boys	Girls
Blaine	Apple
Chazz	Amybeth
Cheech	Anouk
Clancy	Barb
Dave	Caterina
Dolph	Char
Errol	Christy
Gregor	Clarice
Gurinder	Dotty
Jayle	Genevive
Kurt	Jade
Marty	Lendora
Merlin	Linal
Monty	Livia
Morly	Lizanne
Reagan	Mia-Sara
Reginald	Monie
Richard	Pauline
Spence	Rosalind
Taye	Sheanne
Tate	Spectra
Truman	Stella
Toll	Tanica
Ugo	Tianna
Vally	Tico

Derived from Literature

Boys	Girls
Ahab	Alice
Ali Baba	Austen
Boswell	Bronte
Cervantes	Browning
Chaucer	Cale
Cummings	Charlotte
Cyrano	Colette
Dickens	Daisy
Don Quixote	Godiva
Dryden	Grisham
Emerson	Harper
Foster	Jane
Grimm	Kipling
Hunter	Lara
Keats	McMurtry
Lowell	Meg
Milton	Melanie
Norman	Millay
Pope	Patricia
Rhett	Sadie
Sherman	Scarlett
Spenser	Scout
Swift	Simone
Wordsworth	Stella
Yeats	Whittier

Future Morticians

Boys	Girls
Aladdin	Anita
Blackie	Angel
Canyon	Angelita
Cecil	Cloudy
Charles	Deatrice
Coffin	Demona
Diaz	Edith
Dyer	Electra
Fahren	Elsa
Fritz	Francika
Hutch	Justine
Marvin	Honor
Mervyn	Jenice
Night	Kalisha
Patch	Ladonia
Paul	Malanda
Phillipe	Melrose
Sharky	Misti
Spidey	Morticia
Stephan	Rose
Stone	Suganda
Taber	Susannah
Talmadge	Tina
Von	Tonetta
Walter	Vivica

Nerd/Dork/Wallflower Names

Future Gymnasts

Boys	Girls
Antone	Berit
Bendell	Chaley
Bourne	Colleen
Brandon	Dimitra
Cam	Emma
Chad	Erica
Costa	Fabiana
Costello	Goldie
Eric	Grisham
Fahren	Jamie
Harve	Mary Lou
Kifney	Nadia
Lohan	Natasha
Markie	Nasha
Plato	Marissa
Roddick	Olympia
Ryan	Oxana
Silver	Pamela
Taber	Shannon
Tony	Shonna
Varden	Summer
Wash	Tynisha
Whip	Winter
Zatuichi	Zina
Zhano	Zooey

Nerd/Dork/Wallflower Names:

Barney
Bruce
Cheryl
Chester
Dabney
Dudley
Durwood
Edgar
Edward
Elwood
Emory
Engelbert
Estes
Ethelbert
Eugene
Eustace
Ewan
Fagan
Fairfax
Gomer
Pembroke
Percy
Priscilla
Ted
Warren

Place Names

Boys	Girls
Aberdeen	Asia
Albany	Bali
Aleppo	Bonn
Alps	Cairo
America	Cambay
Beaumont	Capri
Bexley	China
Billings	Dallas
Bradford	Dayton
Carson	Easter
Cuba	Egypt
Cyprus	Flanders
Dodge	Georgia
Elam	India
Gobi	Indiana
Gwent	Ireland
Hollywood	Jordan
Hull	Kansas
Logan	Kentucky
Macon	Kenya
Orlando	Lansing
Rainier	Odessa
Sydney	Persia
Texas	Savannah
Yukon	Venice

Mr. Perfect and Ms. Perfect

Boys	Girls
Alex	Alexandra
Anthony	Allison
Ben	Bailey
Blake	Brittney
Brent	Celeste
Christian	Christiane
Christopher	Courtney
Clint	Danielle
Fletcher	Elizabeth
Giancarlo	Hollyn
Harrison	Jennifer
Hunter	Jill
James	Leah
Joaquin	Lexi
Justin	Marissa
Kirk	Meredith
Kyle	Merit
Monty	Mia
Reese	Miranda
Riley	Natalie
Robert	Nia
Rory	Riley
Ryan	Shara
Wells	Sloan
Zack	Trina

Future Cops

Boys	Girls
Arlen	Anne
Artie	Becky
Bold	Bristol
Bruno	Carni
Buck	Cricket
Cody	Darla
Doug	Darlyn
Frank	Donella
Gary	Holly
George	Jana
Gray	Janet
Guard	Jessie
Justice	Kathy
Ken	Kim
Ladden	Kyla
Law	Lori
Mace	Lydia
Mark	Marg
Matt	Micah
Mike	Moira
Rocko	Paige
Seno	Raquel
Stu	Serena
Tom	Tiawanna
Wayne	Tully

Future Televangelists

Boys	Girls
Abbott	Alma
Adam	Amanze
Alf	April
Aleksey	Ariel
Brendon	Athena
Carl	Autumn
Cedric	Beate
Ceph	Bernadette
Coley	Blynthia
Cordell	Capricia
Cornelius	Cherlyn
Darius	Danyelle
Dayne	Darice
Dayton	Dinah
Deangelo	Eunicetine
Erfan	Irma
Felix	Jardene
Hamilton	Karolyn
Hardman	Palmira
Hardy	Sharonda
Jim	Sondra
Malcolm	Tabitha
Sean	Tammy
Sumpter	Trish
Wyatt	Valorie

Tomorrow's Justin Timberlake and Britney Spears

Justin Timberlake	Britney Spears
Amadeo	Adora
Angus	Becca
Arturo	Blondelle
Bart	Bonita
Bonnard	Breanna
Carlos	Caitlin
Chyre	Dyana
Diego	Emma
Fabrizio	Grace
Francisco	Janelle
Gabe	Jasmine
Gabino	Julia
Giancarlo	Kiki
Heath	Liliana
Jair	Lily
Jude	Lisa
Lonzo	Lourdes
Mario	Maryann
Pierre	Marva
Ransom	Natalie
Rory	Nicole
Ruben	Renee
Sly	Roxanne
Zach	Shae
Zennie	Shyla

Future Crooked Politicians

Boys	Girls
Ave	Annaca
Bradlee	Amarosa
Brew	Ceidy
Chant	Consuell
Colt	Danal
Deshan	Donna
Elmo	Erica
Gagan	Floweret
Hec	Ganine
Hermanse	Heidel
Howie	Hillario
Jerrell	Jillianeo
Kib	Kanique
Nixon	Kishey
Lobby	Lanetta
Mazime	Luzey
Ogery	Mavis
Owelie	Monda
Real	Ranika
Rich	Sabrine
Silverio	Shawna
Theodorist	Starret
Ty	Yania
Wilbret	Veronica
Zekel	Vernissha

Names for Daredevils

Boys	Girls
Andre	Alyx
Avery	Anatasia
Beau	Ardythe
Blevin	Austin
Colombo	Bead
Dagan	Della
Emrys	Elkie
Fernando	Emge
Fico	Kiera
Fitz	Kita
Geronimo	LaSonya
LeBron	L'Ann
Matt	Latona
Hector	Lena
Hughey	Mare
Mustafa	Paradise
Nissan	Priss
Owen	Raven
Rick	Rocket
Rossano	Seneca
Santino	Swan
Sergio	Tirsa
Slater	Yelana
Tayshaun	Zabrina
Tassos	Ziz

Names that Make You Feel Weird

Boys	Girls
Arno	Breezy
Bloo	Charm
Butler	Chastity
Car	Cherish
Delete	Delite
Elmo	Fashion
Elmore	Glory
Ervin	Harmony
Excell	Lake
Fabio	Leaf
Fable	Liberty
Fergus	Michelin
Fife	Misty
Forester	Oceana
Geronimo	Panther
Gomer	Peace
Maverick	Pity
Oswald	Precious
Paris	Promise
Prince	Purity
Rebel	Rain
Stone	Sweetpea
Stormy	Tree
Welcome	True
Ziggy	Vixen

Bad-to-the-Bone, Death-Row Names

Boys	Girls
Adolph (Hernandez)	Aileen Carol
Clydell (Coleman)	(Wuomos)
David (Hammer, Long)	Ana (Cardona)
Excell (White)	Andrea (Jackson)
Henry Lee (Lucas)	Antoinette (Frank)
Jeffrey (Dahmer,	Betty (Beets)
Lundgren)	Blanche (Moore)
Jemarr (Arnold)	Caroline (Young)
Jessie (Patrick)	Christa Gail (Pike)
John (Baltazar)	Darlie Lynn (Routier)
John Wayne (Gacy)	Debra (Milke)
Leonard (Rojas)	Delores (Rivers)
Mack (Hill)	Faye (Copeland)
Markum (Duff-Smith)	Frances (Newton)
Napoleon (Beazley)	Gail Kirsey (Owens)
Randy (Knese)	Jaqueline (Williams)
Reginald (Reeves)	Karla Faye (Tucker)
Richard (Ramirez,	Kerry (Dalton)
Speck, Kutzner)	Latasha (Pulliam)
Ricky (McGinn)	Maria (del Rosio
Robert (Atworth)	Alfaro)
Rodolfo (Hernandez)	Marilyn (Plantz)
Stanley (Baker)	Mary Ellen (Samuels)
Ted (Bundy)	Maureen (McDermott)
Timothy (McVeigh)	Nadine (Smith)
Toronto (Patterson)	Pamela (Perillo)
Windell (Broussard)	Vernice (Ballenger)

Party Animals

Boys	Girls
Bucky	Cat
Corlon	Chili
Cuca	Donica
Derant	Dorshea
Derrick	Dracy
Deshon	Fantasia
Darnell	Ginzi
Dyron	Gleam
Erold	Infinity
Flex	Janina
Guido	Jaquier
Kev	Jersey
Lynus	Larhonda
Nashawn	Maisha
Rage	Neva
Ryder	Paisley
Shale	Paris
Shamone	Rujena
Sparky	Sand
Spiker	Sharell
Stevan	Shinika
Tabor	Sonequa
TeRez	Tangie
Ugo	Toranda
Zorro	Vatoya

Hyper Kids

Boys	Girls
Ace	Armey
Dezi	Bianca
Dino	Brandi
Demeet	Chris
Eddie	Dottie
Grasshopper	Fawn
Jarrup	Gia
Jaquan	Jama
Jehan	Kawana
Jerome	KayKay
Jovan	Kendra
Kayotae	Pammy
Kerry	Rochelle
Lance	Sheilia
Levi	Sherin
Mikey	Suzy
Rambabu	Latoya
Rocky	Mandy
Rosheon	Tara
Tajuan	Tonie
Troy	Tyna
Thad	Vicki
Tony	Vida
Vito	Yvette
Willie	Zorina

Future TV Anchors

Boys	Girls
Audon	Bai
Carland	Calliope
Carr	Cerah
Chazz	Dominique
Chaffee	Grisham
Cornel	Kelly
Doran	Jorja
Gavin	Julia
Judson	Kanye
Karcher	Kaley
Kwame	Lea
Landon	Livia
Long	Marianela
Lundy	Meryl
Montgomery	Meloni
Ran	Phia
Ronan	Pfeiffer
Roly	Shanahan
Seth	Sheanne
Sammon	Star
Seaton	Tana
Tassilo	Taft
Taye	Tessa
Trev	Tru
Vane	Wyoming

Names for Playful Personalities

Babe
Bebe
Bliss
Bunny
Buzzie
Chica
Dusky
Fluffy
Happy
Jandy
Jinx
Lily
Merrilee
Miranda
Pal
Pixie
Poppy
Precious
Queenie
Rabbit
Schmoopie
Skip
Sunny
Trixie
Viveca

Names for Vegetarians

Boys	Girls
A'Dhron	Analisa
Biondi	Alula
Binyon	Anita
Bruce	Beatrice
Clyde	Bonita
Dorian	Cassie
Germain	Connie
Jerrell	Daphne
Jovan	Detra
Kemper	Donnette
Kent	Kimber
Lari	Fara-Lynn
Loring	Gerrita
Marquis	Jaslynne
Nolan	Jini
Norm	Jeannie
Ocy	Jenette
Rex	Jolyn
Riquee	Joyce
Rhys	Justine
Rumford	Kelsi
Silas	Rita
Todd	Sarita
Trav	Talonna
Vince	Zhyra

Old-Fashioned Names that Are Cute Again

Boys	Girls
Atticus	Abby
Barney	Alma
Casper	Annette
Charlie	Arden
Chester	Arlene
Clem	Ava
Curtis	Belle
Dexter	Betsy
Duane	Beulah
Duke	Corinna
Elmer	Ethel
Gill	Flo
Harvey	Hazel
Homer	Inez
Luke	Irene
Mitchell	Isabel
Monty	Kay
Mort	Kyra
Myron	Laverne
Ned	Loretta
Norm	Lorraine
Oscar	Lydia
Stanley	Mabel
Wilbur	Polly
Wyatt	Trudy

Good Dancers

Boys	Girls
Brice	Annice
Brody	Anora
Canyon	Blessing
Cobin	Cabot
Dai	Callidora
Dale	Caresse
Dominic	Carys
Drew	Charm
Farley	Dagny
Garrick	Delaney
Gavin	Frenchelle
Hollis	Gia
Kalo	Ingrid
Keary	Kiki
Landon	Kelby
Lionel	Mamie
Mose	Marg
Nagel	Neci
Nash	Poni
Nate	Posala
Renny	Rayna
Rigsby	Romey
Ronno	Shantel
Spencer	Waverly
Tellis	Yancy

Future Inventors

Boys	Girls
Arnold	Amira
Brody	Cate
Cain	Clea
Chew	Connery
Clever	Crisiant
Deems	Cyd
Dov	Delfina
Gif	Drea
Grail	Fia
Hadwin	Gaudi
Halston	Greer
Inder	Isolde
Isaac	JoBeth
John	Joie
Jute	Juanita
Kelvis	LaTanya
Kobi	Madelon
Laphonso	Nicollette
Lee	Novela
Lucan	Olwen
Marvell	Pandora
Ola	Robin
Pirney	Romola
Thanos	Rhonwen
Tinker	Wendy

Future Life Strategists

Boys	Girls
Aldous	Adele
Booker	Brie
Clayton	Camara
Darth	Cardine
Davis	Cynda
Edward	Dionara
Garreth	Donica
Ham	Hallie-Kate
Heston	Jordan
Jackal	Judy
Jennings	Kaley
Kester	Kaven
Kojo	Lilia
Macdowell	Linda
Madden	Lizzie
Mariner	Mahowny
Phil	Mackenzie
Pippin	Mel
Ridge	Mina
Rudy	Mirren
Sagan	Muni
Shep	Piper
Teo	Robin
Thurlos	Romola
Zane	Susanna

Names for Smart Kids

Boys	Girls
Adam	Allene
Allen	Beth
Barry	Carolyn
Benjamin	Carrie
Brent	Colby
Byron	Dana
Clarence	Dominique
Curtis	Donna
David	Elizabeth
Eric	Jamie
Gray	Jennifer
Guy	Karen
Hillel	Kathleen
Jack	Kristina
Kent	Leticia
Laurens	Maude
Martin	Micheline
Maximilian	Natasha
Peter	Page
Philip	Shannon
Richard	Shari
Russell	Shaune
Scott	Suzanne
Trevor	Tessie
William	Zoann

Future Models

Boys	Girls
Adebayo	Alessandra
Alim	Anise
Anka	Bovary
Canyon	Camara
Carswell	Carles
Dagan	Cinda
Daly	Donella
Eaves	Estelle
Faxan	Heather
Fabron	Imogene
Faldo	Gabi
Flea	Grazia
Franchot	Jonica
Friso	Katrine
Gabor	Lily
Hagan	Lizzie
Jory	Madchen
Kipp	Majandra
Tyee	Mirren
Tymon	Monet
Umar	Paulina
Vachel	Rue
Walmond	Rylance
Yudel	Sloan
Xenos	Zim

Future Doctors

Boys	Girls
Bryant	Ann
Charles	Athena
Dimitri	Brenda
Frazier	Bryce
George	Catrice
Herbert	Claire
James	Dana
John	Donna
Judd	Elaine
Lister	Elizabeth
Mark	Freda
Martin	Greta
Mason	Jane
Murray	Jennifer
Newell	Linda
Nick	Lydia
Niles	Lynn
Peter	Marianne
Philip	Mary
Ralph	Maureen
Randall	Miriam
Reagan	Sarah
Rell	Suzanne
Russell	Tina
Sabin	Victoria

Last Names as First Names

Boys	Girls
Afton	Abery
Besley	Briley
Bevil	Campbell
Bolin	Childers
Brandt	Cortland
Cawley	Fields
Chatwin	Gilmore
Coben	Gray
Corbitt	Garson
Deagan	Harrison
Given	Holiday
Greer	Keaton
Halliwell	Jennings
Hutter	Lane
Kentlee	Lancaster
Laskey	Mackenzie
Mackeane	Maclaine
Orton	O'Brien
Prescott	Pace
Rollins	Payton
Stadler	Pfeiffer
Tomlin	Rainey
Trivett	Reeve
Vane	Somers
Wingate	Taylor

Future Republicans

Boys

Alan (Keyes)
Ambrose (Evans-Pritchard)
Ari (Fleischer)
Arnold (Schwarzenegger)
Bill (O'Reilly)
Calvin (Coolidge)
Charlton (Heston)
Colin (Powell)
David (Limbaugh)
Dennis (Hastert)
Gary (Aldrich)
Gerald (Ford)
Jack (Kemp)
J.C. (Watts)
Mitt (Romney)
Newt (Gingrich)
Norm (Schwartzkopf)
Orrin (Hatch)
Richard (Nixon)
Rudy (Giuliani)
Rush (Limbaugh)
Sean (Hannity)
Spiro (Agnew)
Tony (Snow)
Trent (Lott)

Girls

Angie (Harmon)
Barbara (Bush & Olson)
Bo (Derek)
Condoleezza (Rice)
Diane (Thompson)
Elaine (Chao)
Erika (Harold)
Gale (Norton)
Heather (Whitestone)
Jeane (Kirkpatrick)
Jenna (Bush)
Jennette (Bradley)
Jill (Jackson)
Katherine (Harris)
Laura (Bush & Ingraham)
Lilibet (Hagel)
Linda (Chavez)
Lynne (Cheney)
Lindsey (Graham)
Mary (Matalin)
Michelle (Malkin)
Mona (Charon)
Nancy (Reagan)
Peggy (Noonan)
Tammy (Bruce)

Future Democrats

Boys

Al (Gore & Sharpton)
Barack (Obama)
Bill (Clinton)
Blythe (William J. B. Clinton)
Carter (Jimmy)
Howard (Dean)
Delano (Franklin D. Roosevelt)
Evan (Bayh)
Bob (Graham)
Thomas (Jefferson)
Jesse (Jackson)
Joseph (Lieberman)
Kent (Conrad)
Lloyd (Bentsen)
Lyndon (Johnson)
Max (Bauscus)
Michael (Moore)
Robert (Rubin)
Tim (Robbins)
Theodore (Roosevelt)
Harry (Truman)
Walter (Mondale)
Warren (Christopher)
Wesley (Clark)
Zell (Miller)

Girls

Barbara (Mikulski)
Bess (Truman)
Carol (Moseley-Braun)
Chelsea (Clinton)
Claudia ("Lady Bird" Johnson)
Debbie (Stabenow)
Donna (Shalala)
Edith (Kermit Roosevelt)
Eleanor (Roosevelt)
Geraldine (Ferraro)
Gloria (Steinem)
Jacqueline (Kennedy)
Janeane (Garofalo)
Janet (Reno)
Joycelyn (Elders)
Kim (Gandy)
Madeleine (Albright)
Molly (Ivins)
Patricia (Ireland)
Rosalynn (Carter)
Ruth (Bader Ginsberg)
Sandra (Day O'Connor)
Susan (Sarandon)
Teresa (Heinz-Kerry)
Tipper (Gore)

Patriotic Names

America
Amerigo
Asia
Blue
Cherokee
Cheyenne
Columbus
Eagle
Flag
Free
Liberty
Librada
Lincoln
Loyalty
Nation
Pacifika
Patriot
Peace
Red
Sailor
Salute
Spirit
Starr
Utopia
Victory

Overpowering Names

Boys	Girls
Abbott	Antoinette
Axelrod	Aunjanue
Baldridge	Bjork
Balthazar	Calista
Domenico	Colemand
Don Quixote	Deja-Marie
Dontrell	Gwyneth
Esmond	Illeana
Gabbana	Ione
Galbraith	Jowannah
Huntley	Kallioppe
Hyde	Karalenae
Kensington	Madonna
Lothario	Mariangela
Montague	Oprah
Napoleon	Perabo
Ottway	Penelope
Pluto	Philomena
Quintavius	Russo
Reginald	Sahara
Rochester	Siphronia
Ronford	Stockard
Roosevelt	Teah
Thor	Thora
Wyclef	Winifred

Soap Opera Names

Future Racecar Drivers

Boys	Girls	
Blake	Allura	A.J. (Foyt)
Carson	Amanda	Al (Unser)
Cyrano	Amber	Alex (Tagiliani)
Dag	Bianca	Arie (Luyendyk)
Dante	Brandy	Bruno (Junqueira)
Dario	Brisa	Buddy (Lazier)
Dax	Candy	Dale (Earnhardt, Jr.)
Dean	Carmen	Danny (Sullivan)
Deone	Charmaine	Dario (Resta)
Destin	Cocoa	Eddie (Cheever, Jr.)
Diego	Dakota	Helio (Castroneves)
Dom	Desiree	Hermie (Sadler)
Duke	Fawn	Jacques (Villeneuve)
Fabio	Madonna	Jeff (Gordon)
Harley	Monica	Johnny (Rutherford)
Keller	Renee	Juan (Montoya)
Maximilian	Salome	Jules (Goux)
Rico	Samantha	Kenny (Brack)
Rip	Sasha	Leo (Kinnunen)
Romeo	Simone	Mario (Andretti,
Ryan	Tatiana	Dominguez)
Sebastian	Tawny	Mauri (Rose)
Shiloh	Tish	Oriol (Servia)
Thor	Treece	Rick (Mears)
Wells	Yolie	Rusty (Wallace)
		Sam (Hanks)

Future Olympians

Boys

Aaron (Piersol)
Alexei (Yagudin)
Andre (Ward)
Apollo (Ono)
Bart (Conner)
Bruce (Jenner)
Dan (Jansen)
David (Pelletier)
Derek (Parra)
Dwight (Phillips)
Gary (Hall)
Greg (Louganis)
Jeremy (Wariner)
Justin (Gatlin)
Matthew (Emmons)
Michael (Phelps)
Paul (Hamm & Wylie)
Phil (Ford)
Rulon (Gardner)
Scott (Hamilton)
Shawn (Crawford)
Steven (Lopez)
Timothy (Mack)
Todd (Eldredge)
Tyler (Hamilton)

Girls

Amanda (Beard)
Carly (Patterson)
Chris (Witty)
Dorothy (Hamill)
Fanny (Blankers-Koen)
Jill (Bakken)
Joanna (Hayes)
Katarina (Witt)
Kimberly (Rhode)
Kelly (Clark)
Kerri (Walsh)
Kristi (Yamaguchi)
Mariel (Zagunis)
Mia (Hamm)
Michelle (Kwan)
Misty (May)
Nadia (Comaneci)
Nancy (Kerrigan)
Natalie (Coughlin)
Peggy (Flemming)
Sarah (Hughes)
Sasha (Cohen)
Sonja (Henie)
Tristan (Gale)
Vonetta (Flowers)

Future Mechanics

Brewster
Bunard
Carl
Chubby
Ernie
Fred
Gary
Glen
Hal
Hank
Harry
Jake
Joey
Leon
Max
Merle
Moey
Ralph
Red
Rusty
Sonny
Spanky
Terry
Toby
Zeke

Future Lawyers

Boys	Girls
Atticus	Ann
Bryan	Brianna
Caleb	Campbell
Carlson	Carlisle
Dick	Charlotte
Gary	Dana
Jack	Emily
Jacob	Haley
John	Joanna
Josh	Kate
Lawrence	Kendra
Noble	Lane
Preston	Madison
Price	Mariel
Quinn	Mason
Reese	Meg
Roark	Parker
Robert	Rachel
Rush	Sally
Rusty	Sarah
Ryder	Serena
Samuel	Sloan
Sander	Taylor
Sandford	Tekla
Tom	Terese

Future Cowboys and Cowgirls

Cowboys	Cowgirls
Austin	Abilene
Beau	Angeline
Chaparro	Annie
Cody	Arizona
Cole	Cassidy
Cooper	Cheyenne
Dallas	Conroe
Dobie	Cydell
Doc	Dacey
Dustin	Daisy
Earp	Dakota
Emmett	Denton
Gene	Dixie
Jesse	Dobie
Jimmydee	Dusty
Justin	Harlee
Kyle	Jessie
Maverick	Johanna
Rusty	Luella
Shane	Montana
Stetson	Oakley
Sudbury	Rosita
Sutter	Ruby
Wadell	Sierra
Wyatt	Suellen

Future Nobel Prize Winners

Boys

Archer (Martin, 1952, Chemistry)

Baruch (Blumberg, 1976, Medicine)

Boyd (Lord John Boyd Orr of Brechinm 1949, Peace)

Cordell (Hull, 1945, Peace)

Dario (Fo, 1997, Literature)

Desmond (Tutu, 1984, Peace)

Emil (Fischer, 1902, Chemistry)

Giulio (Natta, 1963, Chemistry)

Hamilton (Smith, 1978, Medicine)

Jacinto (Benavente, 1922, Literature)

Kenichi (Fukui, 1981, Chemistry)

Kenzaburo (Oe, 1994, Literature)

Linus (Pauling, 1954, Chemistry, 1962, Peace)

Niels (Bohr, 22, Physics)

Peyton (Rous, 1966, Medicine)

Renato (Dulbecco, 1975, Medicine)

Roald (Hoffman, 1981, Chemistry)

Romain (Rolland, 1915, Literature)

Seamus (Heaney, 1995, Literature)

Simon (Kuznets, 1971, Economics)

Sinclair (Lewis, 1930, Literature)

Susumu (Tonegawa, 1987, Medicine)

Sydney (Brenner, 2002, Medicine)

Werner (Arber, 1978, Medicine)

Winston (Churchill, 1953, Literature)

Girls

Alva (Myrdal, 1982, Peace)

Barbara (McClintock, 1983, Medicine)

Bertha (Baroness...Sophie Felicita Von Suttner, 1905, Peace)

Betty (Williams, 1976, Peace)

Christiane (Nüsslein-Volhard, 1995, Medicine)

Dorothy (Crawfoot Hodgkin, 1964, Chemistry)

Emily (Greene Balch, 1946, Peace)

Gabriela (Mistral, 1945, Literature)

Gerty (Cori, 1947, Medicine)

Grazia (Deledda, 1926, Literature)

Irene (Joliot-Curie, 1935, Chemistry)

Jane (Addams, 1931, Peace)

Jody (Williams, 1997, Peace)

Mairead (Corrigan, 1976, Peace)

Marie (Curie, 1911, Chemistry)

Nadine (Gordimer, 1991, Literature)

Pearl (Buck, 1938, Literature)

Rigoberta (Menchu Tum, 1992 Peace)

Rita (Levi-Montalcini, 1986, Medicine)

Rosalyn (Yalow, 1977, Medicine)

Selma (Ottilia Lovisa Lagerlof, 1909, Literature)

Shirin (Ebadi, 2003, Peace)

Sigrid (Undset, 1928, Literature)

Teresa (Mother Teresa, 1979, Peace)

Toni (Morrison, 1993, Literature)

TV Character Names

Boys

Aidan (*Sex & the City*)
Balki (*Perfect Strangers*)
Bo (*Days of Our Lives*)
Chachi (*Happy Days*)
Conan (*Late Night with Conan O'Brien*)
Cory (*Boy Meets World*)
Dante (*The Sopranos*)
Elliot (*Law & Order: SVU, The Sopranos*)
Elvin (*The Cosby Show*)
Gil (*CSI*)
Grady (*Murder, She Wrote*)
Gunther (*Friends*)
Jack (*Three's Company, Alias, Will & Grace*)
Jordan (*My So-Called Life*)
Kramer (*Seinfeld*)
Maxwell (*M*A*S*H*)

Mork (*Mork & Mindy*)
Niles (*Frasier*)
Odafin (*Law & Order: SVU*)
Raymond (*Everybody Loves Raymond*)
Ricky (*I Love Lucy*)
Sam (*Cheers*)
Simon (*Seventh Heaven*)
Vinnie (*Blossom*)
Wilson (*Home Improvement*)

Girls

Blossom (*Blossom*)
Calleigh (*CSI: Miami*)
Carla (*Cheers*)
Daphne (*Frasier*)
Dharma (*Dharma & Greg*)
Elaine (*Seinfeld*)
Fran (*The Nanny*)
Jeannie (*I Dream of Jeannie*)
Laverne (*Laverne & Shirley*)
Lorelai (*Gilmore Girls*)
Krissie (*Three's Company*)
Lucy (*I Love Lucy, Seventh Heaven*)
Mallory (*Family Ties*)
Marissa (*The O.C.*)
Meadow (*The Sopranos*)
Miranda (*Sex & the City*)
Phoebe (*Friends, Charmed*)
Prue (*Charmed*)

Rayanne (*My So-Called Life*)
Rhoda (*The Mary Tyler Moore Show*)
Rudy (*The Cosby Show*)
Scully (*The X Files*)
Sidney (*Alias*)
Tabitha (*Bewitched*)
Topanga (*Boy Meets World*)

Future Architects

Unforgettable Names

Boys	Girls	
Aaron	Adrianna	Allegra
Alan	Alana	Aura
Alexander	Annie	Bai
Art	Beata	Cocoa
Ed	Candace	Hyacinth
Jack	Deandra	Jumbe
Jay	Diana	King
Lawrence	Ernestine	Lake
Liam	Fawn	Leelee
Paul	Fortune	Lindberg
Rafael	Grace	Madonna
Robert	Hannah	Momo
Ron	Janna	Montague
Royce	Joann	Pink
Sage	Justine	Prince
Sam	Katy	Rivers
Sebastian	Kelly	Santeene
Seth	Landa	Schmoopie
Shaw	Marianne	Spirit
Smith	Olga	Sting
Sterling	Penelope	Symphony
Taylor	Queen	Talent
Theo	Stella	Tame
Victor	Susannah	Trocky
Walt	Treece	Wyclef

Future Chef

Boys
Alton (Brown)
Baker
Basil
Bobby (Flay)
Cary (Neff)
Charlie (Trotter)
Coriander
Cook
Delmonico
Dweezil (Zappa)
Emeril (Lagasse)
Francis (Anthony)
George (Foreman)
Herb
Hiroyuki
Lawson
Martin (Yan)
Jamie (Oliver)
Rick (Bayless)
Al (Roker)
Tamarind
Tarragon
Ted (Allen)
Tyler (Florence)
Wolfgang (Puck)

Girls
Angelica
Betty (Crocker)
Candy
Caraway
Cassia
Ceci (Carmichael)
Cicely
Crescent
  (Dragonwagon)
(Little) Debbie
Genievre
Ginger
Honey
Ina (Garten)
Jenny (Craig)
Julia (Child)
Marjolaine
Martha (Stewart)
Nigella (Lawson)
Poppy
Rosemary
Saffron
Sandra (Lee)
Sarriette
Seattle (Sutton)
Verbena

Season/Weather Names

Autumn
Cloudy
Dusky
Easter
Equinox
Fog
Frosty
Grey
Holly
Misty
Noel
Rain
Rainbow
Season
Sky
Snow
Soleil
Spring
Storm
Summer
Sunny
Sunshine
Typhoon
Windy
Winter

Scary/Creepy Names

Boys	Girls
Bigram	Adelaide
Brick	Agnes
Bruno	Arlette
Butcher	Beatrix
Delete	Crispy
Dweezil	Denz
Elmo	Earlene
Graven	Edna
Gruver	Hortense
Horatio	Lakeesha
Izzy	Nunu
Modred	Nyleen
Nada	Peta
Napoleon	Phyllida
Narcissus	Quinceanos
Nellie	Randelle
Neptune	Scylla
Nero	Sharama
Percival	Swoosie
Pontius	Tashanee
Seymour	Uzbek
Sindbad	Winnie
Sisyphus	Wyetta
Socrates	Zeb
Zero	Zulemita

Names for the Handsome and Beautiful

Boys	Girls
Allen	Addison
Austin	Anabelle
Benjamin	Annie
Cal	Ashley
Cameron	Ava
Chad	Belle
Cooper	Catrice
Dax	Dominique
Dylan	Eden
Ethan	Gina
Fletcher	Jade
Gus	Jennifer
Hudson	Jessica
Ian	Jinx
Jan-Erik	Jolie
Jude	Jordan
Julian	Liz
Kyle	Marisol
Logan	Miranda
Owen	Natasha
Riley	Petra
Ryan	Rachel
Sebastian	Renee
Shiloh	Sheyn
Will	Trista

Mythological and Astrological	Macho Men	Sweetie-Pies
Ajax	Bucko	Alicia
Alala	Butch	Angie
Argus	Buzz	Annabelle
Aries	Cal	Bay
Bacchus	Cash	Brook
Bran	Duke	Darcy
Cadmus	Esteban	Dolce
Cressida	Evander	Dove
Evander	Hud	Faith
Galatea	Hugo	Goldie
Gawain	Jock	Greta
Gemini	Judd	Honey
Kalliope	Mack	Jenny
Lake	Ram	Julianna
Lancelot	Rebel	Kate
Merlin	Reem	Laurel
Nestor	Rip	Lisa
Ocean	Rocco	Marina
Penelope	Sam	Robin
Phoenix	Santiago	Rosa
Tane	Spike	Roseanne
Terra	Stone	Sarah-Jessica
Thor	Trocky	Tammy
Venus	Waylon	Wylie
Zeus	Zoom	Yolie

Made-Up Names

Boys	Girls
Bryton	Alexakai
Damarcus	Amberkalay
Dantrell	Bryelle
Daquan	Dalondra
Dashawn	Danelle
Derlin	Darlonna
Devonte	Darshell
Donyell	Dashawn
Jabari	Dashika
Jaquawn	Dasmine
Jashon	Davelyn
Javaris	Dawntelle
Juwon	Jaleesa
Keshon	Jameka
Kyan	Kaneesha
Leeron	Keoshawn
Markell	Latasha
Quintavius	Noemi
Raekwon	Quanisha
Roshaun	Shalonda
Shaquille	Shanique
Shawnell	Shawanna
Tevin	Tamika
Tre	Tamyrah
Tyree	Tearah

Make Your Baby Popular

Boys	Girls
Britt	Ava
Cam	Britney
Cody	Clancy
Dylan	Coby
Ethan	Coco
Evan	Emma
Fletch	Gina
Gino	Lauren
Gus	Lexi
Heath	Lily
Hunter	Lindsay
Ian	Lola
Jake	London
Jason	Lyla
Jeremy	Mackenzie
Jerod	Madison
Joshua	Morgan
Julian	Nicole
Justin	Piper
Kyle	Reese
London	Samantha
Max	Skye
Morgan	Sophie
Nick	Tara
Tyler	Taylor

Future Artists

Boys	Girls
Ballard	Alexis
Blaze	Ashantia
Ceron	Azure
Eduardo	Caramia
Francesco	Chantal
Francoise	DeeDee
Frederic	Emelle
Gansta	Eve
Graham	Janice
Hector	Jenna
Jean-Claude	Kavita
Jose	Lace
Laurent	Lanee
Lionel	Lavonne
Maximilian	Margina
Michael	Mary-Catherine
Octavio	Michaele
Oscar	Mona
Paulo	Neva
Pash	Prema
Pedro	Regine
Ronnie	Sisteene
Sancho	Skyler
Sebastian	Tallulah
Stephan	Zora

Lyrical Names

Boys	Girls
(You Can Call Me) Al	Allison (My Aim is True)
Alfie	Angie (You're Beautiful)
Ben	
Billy (Don't Be a Hero)	Barbara Ann
Bobby (McGee)	Betty Lou's (Gettin' Out Tonight)
Chuckie's (in Love)	
Daniel	Billie Jean
Denis	(Sweet) Caroline
Floyd (the Barbara)	Cecelia
Frederick	Clementine
(Hit the Road) Jack	(Sweet) Jane
Jeremy	Janie ('s Got a Gun)
Jesse ('s Girl)	Layla
(Don't Mess Around With) Jim	Lola
Johnny (B. Goode)	Maggie May
(Hey) Jude	Mandy
(What's the Frequency) Kenneth	(Proud) Mary
Leroy (Brown)	Michelle
Mack (the Knife)	Peggy Sue
Mickey	Penny Lane
(Tall) Paul	(Help Me) Rhonda
(Roll 'em) Pete	(My) Sharona
(Doctor) Robert	(Sweet Little) Sheila
Vincent	(Run-around) Sue
	(Wake up little) Susie
	(Oh) Susannah

World's Strangest Names

Adjanys
Bego
Blue
Bucko
Bukola
Car
Dix
Dweezil
Edju
Idarah
Kermit
Kiwa
Lovella
Moon Unit
Nimrod
Oak
Obey
Pity
Rudow
Swell
Tiago
Tilla
Zap
Zip
Zone

Future Workaholics

Boys

Aneel (Bhusri)
Archie (W. Dunham)
Bill (Gates)
Charles (F. Knight)
David (R. Goode & Mott)
D.J. (Mimran)
Douglas (Becker)
Edward (Brennan & Hagenlocker)
Franklin (A. Thomas)
Fred (L. Krehbeil)
Ivan (G. Seidenberg)
James (A. Johnson)
Jerry (Yang)
Lawrence (Sonsini)
Louis (W. Sullivan)
Matthew (D. Walter)
Michael (Andretti, Miles, & Morgan)
Pierre (Omidyar)
Promod (Haque)
Roger (McNamee)
Seth (Neiman)
Ted (Turner)
Thomas (J. Usher)
Vernon (E. Jordan Jr.)
William (H. Gray III)

Girls

Abigail (Smith Adams)
Andrea (Jung)
Belva (Lockwood)
Bette (Midler)
Brenda (Barnes)
Carol (Bartz)
Carleton (Fiorina)
Catherine (Elizabeth Hughes)
Christa (McAuliffe)
Clara (Barton)
Dale (Evans)
Dawn (Lepore)
Emma (Willard)
Judith (Regan)
Lucille (Ball)
(Anne Sullivan) Macy
Marjorie (Scardino)
Mary Kay (Ash)
Meg (Whitman)
Muriel (Siebert)
Nadia (Boulanger)
Oprah (Winfrey)
Shelly (Lazarus)
Shirley (A. Jackson)
Valentina (Tereshkova)

Wimpy names	Girlie-girl Names	Exotic names	
		Boys	**Girls**
Babe	Bebe	Desiderio	Cherokee
Barney	Bubbles	Destin	Cheyenne
Bobo	Buffy	Diego	Chiara
Brownie	Bunny	Enrique	Kia
Brucie	Cherry	Enzo	Kimone
Byrd	Cinderella	Esme	Lakesha
Chubby	Cinnamon	Francesco	Lani
Clydell	Cookie	Franco	Laurent
Corky	Darlie	Frederic	Pax
Denny	Debbie-Jean	Gabriel	Pepita
Dewey	Deedee	Gaston	Phaedra
Dudley	Dolly	Genaro	Philomena
Dusty	Fluffy	Giancarlo	Phyllida
Dwight	Melrose	Hamlet	Quanda
Feo	Poppy	Hansel	Rania
Fergie	Posy	Hawke	Rasheeda
Fuddy	Precious	Heinz	Rhiannon
Perry	Primrose	Helio	Saffron
Skeeter	Princess	Hermes	Santana
Skippy	Prissy	Honorato	Sasha
Spanky	Sissy	Jacques	Sequoia
Terry	Sugar	Janus	Sheba
Timmy	Sweetpea	Javier	Shoshana
Tippy	Tippie	Jean-Paul	Simone
Wendell	Trixiebelle	Johann	Solange

Names Teachers Can't Pronounce

Boys	Girls
Artemus	Aisha
Declan	Aleithea
Dionysus	Camilla
Flody	Carenleigh
Gyth	Chesskwana
Hamif	Deighan
Hermes	Falesyia
Hieronymos	Gisbelle
Honorato	Gresia
Iago	Madchen
Ignatius	Maromisa
Ioannis	Mayghaen
Isidro	Meyka
Jetal	Naeemah
Jovan	Nissie
Larrmyne	Nunibelle
Mihow	Rhonwen
Mischa	Ruthemma
Moey	Sade
Raoul	Shaleina
Revin	Sharrona
Seth	Shawneequa
Sladkey	Tanyav
Slavek	Tierah
Takeya	Twyla

Alternative Spellings for Names You Can't Pronounce

Boys	Girls
Adolfus (Adolphus)	Afrodytee (Aphrodite)
Amadayus (Amadeus)	Alaygrah (Allegra)
Booveeay (Bouvier)	Alaytheea (Aleithea)
Breeahno (Briano)	Anewk (Anouk)
Byorn (Bjorn)	Dafnee (Daphne)
Dalanee (Delaney)	Dayna (Dana)
Dameetree (Dmitri)	Duhnell (Danelle)
Dolf (Dolph)	Egzanth (Xanthe)
Eve (Yves)	Elkie (Elke)
Flavean (Flavian)	Felisha (Felicia)
Gweedo (Guido)	Hiah (Heija)
Jordahno (Giordano)	Kamela (Camilla)
Keyohtee (Quixote)	Katelyn (Kaitlin)
Klev (Cleve)	Margo (Margot)
Loocho (Lucho)	Mazie (Maisie)
Lukah (Luca)	Maxeeme (Maxime)
Makale (Mikhail)	Moneek (Monique)
Malla-Ki (Malachi)	Q-malee (Cumale)
Odisius (Odysseus)	Sade (Sharday)
Playtoh (Plato)	Salowmee (Salome)
Preemoh (Primo)	Shanade (Sinead)
Shawn (Sean)	Sheelyah (Shelia)
Sonteeahgo (Santiago)	Shivan (Siobhan)
Ulissus (Ulysses)	Skyler (Schulyer)
	Tateeahna (Tatianna)

Future Sports Fanatics

Boys

A.J. (Foyt)
Al (Oerter)
Barry (Sanders)
Dick (Butkus)
Eddie (Arcaro)
Edwin (Moses)
Elgin (Baylor)
Gale (Sayers)
Gordie (Howe)
Honus (Wagner)
Jack (Dempsey)
Lawrence (Taylor)
Man (O'War)
Mario (Andretti & Lemieux)
Maurice (Richard)
Oscar (Robertson)
O.J. (Simpson)
Otto (Graham)
Rafer (Johnson)
Roberto (Clemente)
Rocky (Marciano)
Rogers (Hornsby)
Sammy (Baugh)
Satchel (Paige)
Willie (Shoemaker)

Girls

Annika (Sorenstam)
Cammi (Granato)
Carol (Heiss)
Chamique (Holdsclaw)
Charlotte (Dod)
Cheryl (Haworth)
Chris (Evert)
Donna (Lopiano)
Florence (Griffith Joyner)
Glenna Collett (Vare)
Hazel (Hotchkiss Wightman)
Ingrid (Kristiansen)
Janet (Evans & Guthrie)
Jeannie (Longo)
Julie (Krone)
Lisa (Wagner)
Manon (Rheaume)
Mickey (Wright)
Paula (Newby-Fraser)
Senda (Berenson)
Sheryl (Swoopes)
Steffi (Graf)
Susan (Butcher)
Tamara (McKinnie)
Tracy (Austin)

Future Authors

Boys

Albert (Camus)
Antoine (de Saint-Exupery)
Anton (Chekhov)
Bertolt (Brecht)
Miguel (de Cervantes)
Conrad (Richter)
Derek (Walcott)
T.S. (Eliot)
Ernest (Hemingway)
(James) Fenimore (Cooper)
Isaac (Asimov)
Italo (Calvino)
James (Joyce)
Jean-Paul (Sartre)
Jorge (Luis Borges)
Kurt (Vonnegut)
Raymond (Carver)
Samuel (Beckett)
John (Steinbeck)
Thomas (Pynchon)
Umberto (Eco)
John (Updike)
Upton (Sinclair)
Vladimir (Nabokov)
William (Faulkner)

Girls

Alice (Munro & Walker)
Amy (Tan)
Anais (Nin)
Bobbi Ann (Mason)
Doris (Lessing)
Djuna (Barnes)
Edith (Wharton)
Eudora (Welty)
Flannery (O'Connor)
Harper (Lee)
Helen (Vendler)
Isabel (Allende)
Jamaica (Kincaid)
Judy (Blume)
Kate (Chopin)
Louisa May (Alcott)
Maeve (Binchy)
Margaret (Atwood & Fuller)
Marguerite (Duras)
Maryse (Conde)
Sandra (Cisneros)
Simone (de Beauvoir)
Virginia (Woolf)
Willa (Cather)
Zora (Neale Hurston)

Famous Mob Names

Angelo "Docile Don" Bruno

Aniello Dellecroce

Antonio "Tony Bananas" Caponigro

Dominick "Little Dom" Curra

Frank "Frankie Fap" Fappiano

James J. "Whitey" Bulger

John "Jackie Nose" D'Amico

John Gotti

Joseph "Skinny Joey" Merlino

Louis "Big Louie" Vallario

Lucky Luciano

Michael "Mikey Scars" DiLeonardo

Nicky "The Little Guy" Corozzo

Paul Castellano

Paulie Cimino

Peter "The Crumb" Caprio

Ralph Natale

Salvatore "Sammy the Bull" Gravano

Sonny Visconti

Stephen "The Rifleman" Flemmi

Vincent "The Chin" Gigante

Vincent Palermo

Hippie-Sounding Names

Apple

Breezy

Cloud

Dune

Free

Gypsy

Happy

Maverick

Oceana

Peace

Peaches

Rain

Rainbow

River

Sea

Serenity

Sierra

Spring

Star

Summer

Sunny

Tree

True

Willow

Winner

Plain Jane and Joe Schmoe

Joe Schmoe	Plain Jane
Bill	Annabelle
Bob	Betty
Buddy	Carol
Claude	Cindy
Fred	Dana
Ed	Dawn
Floyd	Doris
Guy	Edith
Henry	Jane
Jack	Janet
Joe	Jill
John	Martha
Kevin	Mary
Larry	Nancy
Lloyd	Norma
Mark	Patty
Max	Pauline
Paul	Sally
Ralph	Sarah
Rick	Shirley
Sam	Sue
Scott	Thelma
Tom	Velma
Wally	Vera
Wayne	Wilda

Names That Spawn Nasty Nicknames

Boys	Girls
Adolf	Christopher
Aldred	Cocoa
Alec	Dusky-Dream
Alfonso	Earlene
Apple	Feather
Ash	Fortune
Asher	Gay
Ashley	Harriet
Ashton	Haute
Babe	Hedy
Boris	Hermione
Bucky	Hodge
Butler	Hortense
Byrd	Lesbia
Clement	Monica
Dominic	Rainey
Farley	Romona
Farnham	Ruta
Farr	Scarlett
Flabia	Sesame
Ferdinand	Sigrun
Harry	Sweetpea
Haywood	Taffy
Jericho	Teddi
Titus	Winifred

Names to Make You Smile

Angel
Bambi
Bitsie
Boots
Buffalo
Buffy
Bunny
Champagne
Cheer
Cherry-Sue
Coco
Cookie
Corky
Dusty
Fluffy
Galaxy
Harmony
Honey
Peach
Poppy
Ritz
Snooks
Sundancer
Sunny
Tweetie

Activists

Boys

Andrei (Sakharov)
Bayard (Rustin)
Bienvenido (Santos)
Bill (Wilson)
Cesar (Chavez)
Che (Guevara)
Christopher (Reeve)
Chuck (Rowland)
David (McTaggert)
Eldridge (Cleaver)
Frederick (Douglass)
Harry (Hay)
Harvey (Milk)
Jesse (Jackson)
John James (Audubon)
Julian (Bond)
Mahatma (Gandhi)
Malcolm (X)
Martin (Luther King, Jr.)
Medgar (Evers)
Nelson (Mandela)
Noam (Chomsky)
Rutherford (Hayes)
Telford (Taylor)
Whitney (Young)

Girls

Angelina Emily
  (Grimke)
Betty (Friedan)
Carrie (Chapman Catt)
Charlotte (Perkins
  Gilman)
Ella Cora (Hind)
Coretta (Scott King)
Diane (Nash)
Dorothea (Dix)
Elizabeth (Cady
  Stanton)
Ella (Baker)
Evangeline (Booth)
Fannie Lou (Hamer)
Harriet (Beecher
  Stowe & Tubman)
Ida (Wells-Barnett)
Jane (Addams)
Jeannette (Rankin)
Linda (Chavez-
  Thompson)
Lucretia (Mott)
Lydia Maria (Child)
Margaret (Brown)

Myrlie (Evers-
  Williams)
Prudence (Crandell)
Rosa Lee (Parks)
Sojourner (Truth)
Susan (B. Anthony)

Androgynous Names

Andy/Andi
Bailey
Cameron
Carol, Carroll
Chris
Corey
Dakota
Dale, Dell
Darcy
Darryl
Dylan
Gail/Gale
Jamie
Jean, Gene
Jordan
Kat
Kelly
Kerry/Carrie
Lane
Lee
Leslie
Morgan
Pat
Shawn, Sean
Terry

Names that Sound Presidential

Boys	Girls
Abraham	Andrea
Adam	Ann
Adlai	Carolyn
Andrew	Claire
Benjamin	Elizabeth
Blake	Ella
Calvin	Emily
Charles	Emma
Daniel	Evan
Dwight	Helen
Earnest	Hillary
George	Isabel
Hamilton	Julia
Hampton	Kay
Harrison	Kelly
Henry	Kyle
Hudson	Lauren
James	Madison
John	Mia
Reagan	Miriam
Robert	Parker
Roger	Rachel
Ronald	Rose
Winston	Stella
Zachary	Taylor

Names for Future Poets

Boys	Girls
Billy (Collins)	Adrienne (Rich)
Carl (Sandburg)	Amy (Lowell)
Charles (Baudelaire, Wright)	Anne (Sexton)
David (Lehman)	Audre (Lorde)
Dylan (Thomas)	Barbara (Guest)
Edgar Allan (Poe)	Brigit (Pegeen Kelly)
Ezra (Pound)	Christina (Rossetti)
Gary (Snyder)	Denise (Levertov)
Gerard (Manley Hopkins)	Dorothy (Parker)
Henry David (Thoreau)	Edna (St. Vincent Millay)
John (Ashbery)	Elizabeth (Barrett Browning, & Bishop)
Kahlil (Gibran)	Emily (Dickinson)
Langston (Hughes)	Gertrude (Stein)
Ogden (Nash)	Gwendolyn (Brooks)
Pablo (Neruda)	Hilda (Doolittle)
Percy (Bysshe Shelley)	Jorie (Graham)
Philip (Levine)	Louise (Gluck)
Ralph Waldo (Emerson)	Marianne (Moore)
Robert (Pinsky)	Marge (Piercy)
Seamus (Heaney)	Maxine (Kumin)
Sherman (Alexie)	Maya (Angelou)
Stanley (Kunitz)	Nikki (Giovanni)
(Lord Alfred) Tennyson	Rita (Dove)
Theodore (Roethke)	Sara (Teasdale)
William (Blake, Carlos Williams)	Sylvia (Plath)

Comfy Names

Boys	Girls
Allen	Allison
Ben	Amber
Brent	Annie
Brian	Ashley
Casey	Becca
Chad	Callie
Daniel	Carrie
Dave	Danielle
Ethan	Diane
Gavin	Emily
Jack	Hailey
Jake	Heather
Jason	Isabel
Jesse	Jessica
Josh	Jordan
Justin	Justine
Logan	Kim
Matt	Lauren
Max	Liz
Mike	Maggie
Nicholas	Nicole
Rob	Rachel
Ryan	Samantha
Sam	Sarah
Tyler	Selena

Over-the-Top Names to Avoid

Boys	Girls
Achilles	Aphrodite
Adonis	Asp
Amadeus	Bijou
Aristotle	Birdie
Attila	Blaze
Bark	Bless
Beauregard	Blossom
Brando	Blush
Caesar	Butter
Eagle	Chantilly
Goliath	Chastity
Hamlet	Cher
Jock	Cleopatra
Lancelot	Desire
Laramie	Fantasia
Lobo	Fashion
Lord	Fawn
Lothario	Fluffy
Rambo	Honesty
Rip	Jezebel
Rocco	Loyalty
Rod	Ophelia
Stormy	Psyche
Sylvester	Purity
Titan	Tempest

Colors

Boys	Girls
Amarillo	Amber
Auburn	Azura
Brinley	Blanche
Brown	Bionda
Cyan	Burgundy
Forest	Carmine
Hazel	Cerise
Hunter	Ciara
Jet	Crimson
Kuper	Crystal
Laban	Cyanetta
Loden	Fuchsia
Odhran	Henna
Phoenix	Indigo
Red	Iona
Ross	Jade
Rudd	Jetta
Russet	Kelly
Rusty	Lavender
Sable	Melina
Sand	Peridot
Slate	Saffron
Stone	Scarlet
Tyrian	Sienna
Umber	Xanthe

Names of Rich Americans

Abigail (Johnson)
Amy (Brinkley)
Andre (Agassi)
Ann (Moore), Anne (Mulcahy)
Betsy (Holden, Bernard)
Bobby (Kotick)
Brad (Pitt)
Colleen (Barrett)
Dan (Snyder)
David (Filo, Hitz)
Elon (Musk)
Halsey (Minor)
Jeff/Jeffrey (Skoll, Bezos, Citron, Mallett, Zients)
Jerry (Yang, Greenberg)
Joe (Liemandt)
Judy (McGrath, Lewent)
Julia (Roberts)
Karen (Katen)
Lois (Juliber)
Marc (Andreessen, Ewing)

Michael (Dell, Jordan, Robertson)
Oprah (Winfrey)
Pat (Woertz, Russo)
Paul (Gauthier)
Percy (Miller)
Raul (Fernandez)
Scott (Blum)
Sean (Combs— P. Diddy)
Shaquille (O'Neal)
Sherry (Lansing)
Stacey (Snider)
Ted (Waitt)
Tiger (Woods)
Vinny (Smith)
Will (Smith)

Future Country-Western Singers

Boys

Alan (Jackson)
Billy Ray (Cyrus)
Brad (Paisley)
Buck (Owens)
Cash (Moline)
Chance (Martin)
Charley (Pride)
Chet (Atkins)
Clay (Walker)
Clint (Black)
Conway (Twitty)
Dwight (Yoakum)
Garth (Brooks)
George (Strait)
Hank (Williams)
Kenny (Rogers)
Lyle (Lovett)
Merle (Haggard)
Tex (Ritter)
Tim (McGraw)
Toby (Keith)
Travis (Tritt)
Vince (Gill)
Waylon (Jennings)
Willie (Nelson)

Girls

Allison (Krauss)
Anne (Murray)
Barbara (Mandrell)
Brenda (Lee)
Carlene (Carter)
Cristy (Lane)
Dolly (Parton)
Emily (Robison)
Faith (Hill)
Jo Dee (Messina)
Kitty (Wells)
LeAnn (Rimes)
Lee Ann (Womack)
Loretta (Lynn)
Martie (Maguire)
Martina (McBride)
Maybelle (Carter)
Natalie (Maines)
Pam (Tillis)
Patsy (Cline)
Reba (McIntire)
Shania (Twain)
Tamara (Walker)
Trisha (Yearwood)
Wynonna (Judd)

Brand-Name Babies

Boys
(Uncle) Ben
(Mercedes) Benz
Brooks (Brothers)
Calvin (Klein)
Carter (Carter's baby
  clothes)
Duncan (Hines)
Gianni (Versace)
Giorgio (Armani)
Hamlet (Cigars)
Hiram (Walker)
Hugo (Boss)
Isaac (Mizrahi)
Jack (Daniels)
Jimmy (Dean)
John (Deere)
Johnnie (Walker)
Kenneth (Cole)
Merrill (Lynch)
Morton (Salt)
Samuel (Adams)
Scott (Tissue)
Thomas (Cooke)
T.J. (Maxx)
Todd (Oldham)
Tommy (Hilfiger)

Girls
Anna (Sui)
Anne (Klein)
(Aunt) Jemima
Betsey (Johnson)
Betty (Crocker)
Campbell (Soup)
Carolina Herrera
Charmin (bath tissue)
Cristal (champagne)
Del Monte
Delia
Donna (Karan)
Elizabeth (Arden)
Ellen (Tracy)
Fanta
Gloria (Vanderbilt)
Harley (Davidson)
Kimberly (Clark)
Lexus
(Little) Debbie
Liz (Claiborne)
Mercedes (Benz)
Sara (Lee)
Stella (Artois)
Wendy ('s restaurant)

Old Maids and Grumpy Old Men

Grumpy Old Men
Adolf
Ambrose
Amos
Clifford
Cyrus
Diedrich
Ebenezer (Scrooge)
Edwin
Elmer (Fudd)
Engelbert
Felix
Gaylord
Godfrey
Gomer
Henry
Herb
Leander
Lester
Maurice
Maynard
Mortimer
Oscar
Otis
Percival
Sigmund

Old Maids
Amelia
Baptista
Bertha
Clemence
Clotilde
Corliss
Eldora
Ernestine
Estelle
Geraldine
Gladys
Heloise
Hildegard
Hortense
Mabel
Matilda
Mavis
Maude
Mildred
Millicent
Phyllis
Solange
Thelma
Winifred
Zelda

Future Middle Management

Boys	Girls
Bob	Celeste
Brent	Ceil
Buddy	Connie
Chalmers	Darla
Davey	Fay
Deke	Fern
Dewey	Florence
Dick	Gayle
Duane	Ingrid
Fabian	Jo-Dee
Gareth	Kay
Gene	Lauralee
Howard	Leeanne
Irv	Leonora
Leonard	Luna
Myron	Marge
Newt	Marisol
Ronnie	Mitzi
Rosco	Myrtle
Sal	Pearl
Sanford	Ruth
Skip	Shirley
Terrance	Trudy
Ward	Velma
Wyatt	Yvonne

Future Composers

Aaron (Copland)
Antonin (Dvorak)
Antonio Lucio (Vivaldi)
Belle (Van Zyulen)
Dimitri (Shostakovich)
Domenico (Scarlatti)
Elisabetta (de Gambarini)
Ellen (Taaffe Zwilich)
Felix (Mendelssohn)
Francesca (LeBrun)
Franz Peter (Schubert)
Fryderyk Franciszek (Chopin)
George (Gershwin)
Gustav (Holst or Mahler)
Johann Sebastian (Bach)
Joseph (Haydn)
Leo (Sowerby)
Ludwig (van Beethoven)
Maria (Agnesi)
Melinda (Wagner)
Paul (Moravec)
Pyotr (Ilyich Tchaikovsky)
Rebecca (Clarke)
Robert Alexander (Schumann)
Wolfgang Amadeus (Mozart)

From Music and Instruments	Eccentric Names	Future Class Clowns	
		Boys	**Girls**
Allegra	Antigone	Adam (Sandler)	Brett (Butler)
Aria	Balfour	Ashton (Kutcher)	Carol (Burnett & Channing)
Baird	Bark	Ben (Stiller)	
Bongo	Beetle	Billy (Crystal)	Cheri (Oteri)
Cadence	Bird	Bob (Hope)	Elayne (Boosler)
Canon	Chantilly	Chris (Rock)	Ellen (Degeneres)
Chantal	Cloudy	Conan (O'Brien)	Gilda (Radner)
Citare	Echo	Dana (Carvey)	Goldie (Hawn)
Giritha	Ecstasy	Dave (Chappelle)	Gracie (Allen)
Gloria	Flirt	Jamie (Foxx)	Jane (Curtin)
Harmony	Free	Jay (Leno & Mohr)	Jean (Smart)
Harper	Fudge	Jeff (Foxworthy)	Joan (Cusack)
Kalliope	Galatea	Jerry (Seinfeld)	Joy (Behar)
Kyrie	Gawain	Jim (Carrey)	Julia (Louis-Dreyfus & Sweeney)
Lydia	Goliath	Johnny (Knoxville)	
Lyra	Lady	Lenny (Bruce)	Kirstie (Alley)
Melody	LaRue	Gene (Wilder)	Lily (Tomlin)
Nicola	Lazarus	George (Burns & Carlin)	Margaret (Cho)
Octavia	Obedience		Molly (Shannon)
Odele	Orson	Phil (Hartman)	Paula (Poundstone)
Pitch	Oz	Richard (Pryor)	Rita (Rudner)
Sonata	Rambo	Robin (Williams)	Roseanne (Barr)
Tune	Stoli	Rodney (Dangerfield)	Rosie (O'Donnell)
Viola	Webb	Steve (Martin)	Sandra (Bernhard)
Whistler	Zeus	Will (Farrell)	Tina (Fey)
		Woody (Allen)	Tracey (Ullman)
			Whoopi (Goldberg)

International Treasures

Alexandria (Lighthouse)

Amazon (rainforest, Brazil)

Artemis/Artemesia (Temple, Sardis)

Asmara (capital city of Eritrea)

Ben (Clock Tower, England)

(Magna) Carta

Damascus (capital city of Syria)

Delphi

Dover (Cliffs)

Easter (Island)

Euphrates (River)

Giza (pyramid)

(Mount St.) Helen

Hope (Diamond)

Limoges (French China)

Niagara (Falls)

Nicosia (capital city of Cyprus)

(city of) Olympia

Petra (Ancient City, Jordan)

(The Colossus of) Rhodes

Santorini (Greece)

Saffron (Spice)

Sistine (Chapel, Vatican City)

Victoria (Falls, border of Zambia and Zimbabwe)

(Statue of) Zeus (Ancient Greece)

Works of Art

Adam, Michelangelo

Ambroise Vollard, Picasso

Beatrice, Tiepelo

Cana, Gerard David

Cindy, Robert Longo

Danae, Gustav Klimt

David, Donatello, also Michelangelo

Fanny, Chuck Close

Francesco Clemente Pinxit, Francesco Clemente

Hyacinth, Alphonse Mucha

Irene, Renoir

Jackie, Andy Warhol

Jacob, Gaugin

Jeremiah, Rembrandt

Joseph Roulin, Van Gogh

Madonna, Sanzio Raffaello

Magdalen, La Tour

Marie, Rubens

Marcus Aurelius, unknown (sculpture)

Mona Lisa, Leonardo da Vinci

Olympia, Manet

Salome, Beardsley

Sarah Bernhardt, Nadar

Theresa, Bernini

Venus, Botticelli

Future Royalty

Boys

Alexander (the Great)
Alois (Prince of Liechtenstein)
Charles (Prince of Wales)
Christian (King of Denmark)
Constantine (King of Greece)
Ermias (Prince of Ethiopia)
Fahd (King of Saudi Arabia)
Felipe (Crown Prince of Spain)
Geoffrey (King of Batwa)
Hamad (King of Bahrain)
Hussein (King of Jordan)
Juan Carlos (King of Spain)
Louis (King of France)
Maha Mongut (King of Siam)
Midas (King of Phrygia)
Mswati (King of Swaziland)
Napoleon Bonaparte (Emperor of France)
Naruhito (Crown Prince of Japan)
Rainer (King of Morraco)
Richard (King)
Saul (King of Israel)
Tutankhamen (King Tut)
Vlad (Prince Dracula)
Wenceslas ("Good King" of Bohemia)
William (Prince of England)

Girls

Anastasia (Grand Duchess of Russia)
Anne (Bolyn)
Boadicea (Warrior Queen of Iceni)
Catherine (the Great)
Cleopatra (Queen of Egypt)
Diana (Princess of Wales)
Eleanor (of Aquataine)
Elizabeth (Queen of England)
Esther (Queen of Persia)
Grace (Kelly, Princess of Monaco)
Haya (Princess of Jordan)
Jane (Grey)
Josephine (Empress of France)
Lalla (Princess of Morocco)
Liliuokalani (last Hawaiian Monarch)
Louise (Princess of Belgium)
Marie (Antoinette)
Mary (Queen of Scots)
Mumtaz Mahal ("Jewel of the Palace")
Ranavalona (Queen of Madagascar)
Sarah (Ferguson, Duchess of York)
Sonja (Queen of Norway)
Tzu His (China's Dowager Empress)
Victoria (Crown Princess of Sweden)

Jewish/Hebrew Names

Boys	Girls
Aaron	Anne
Abe	Claire
Barry	Esther
Benjamin	Golda
Daniel	Hannah
David	Ilana
Eli	Jenny
Esau	Johanna
Ethan	Judith
Gabriel	Leah
Harrison	Lena
Ira	Lillian
Isaac	Linda
Jake	Mary
Jay	Miriam
Joshua	Naomi
Levi	Rachel
Marvin	Rebekah
Milton	Ruth
Nathan	Sadie
Sam	Sarah
Saul	Shara
Sheldon	Sophie
Solomon	Sylvia
Stanley	Tovah

Arabic/Islamic Names

Boys	Girls
Abdul-Jabbar	Aisha
Ahmad, Ahmed	Almira
Ali	Asma
Amir	Bathsira
Dawud	Cala
Fariol	Dhelal
Ghassan	Fatima
Habib	Habibah
Hakim, Hakeem	Hadil
Hamid	Hajar, Hagir
Hasan	Hayfa
Ibrahim	Ihab
Jabir, Jabbar	Jamila
Jamal	Kalila
Kamal, Kamil	Karima
Kareem	Laila
Khalid	Leila
Mahmud	Malak
Muhammad, Mohammad	Nada
Nuri	Nima
Rafi	Rashidah
Rashid	Rida
Salim	Sabah
Sharif	Salima
Yasir	Zulema

Biblical and Saintly Names

Boys	Girls
Abel	Anna
Adam	Bathsheba
Benjamin	Deborah
Daniel	Delilah
David	Dinah
Elijah	Esther
Ezekiel	Eve
Isaiah	Joanna
Jacob	Judith
Jesus	Julia
Job	Leah
John	Magdalene
Jonah	Martha
Joseph	Mary
Joshua	Miriam
Lazarus	Naamah
Luke	Naomi
Mark	Phoebe
Matthew	Rachel
Moses	Rebekah
Noah	Ruth
Paul	Salome
Peter	Sarah
Samuel	Tamar
Solomon	Zipporah

Scandinavian Names

Boys	Girls
Aksel	Astrid
Anders	Birgit
Anton	Bonnevie
Bjorn	Dufvenius
Christian	Elsa
Claus	Erika
Dirk	Fia
Erik	Frida
Gustav	Gudrun
Hendrik	Gunilla
Ingmar	Inge
Isak	Ingrid
Johannes	Janna
Karl	Johanna
Knut	Kristina
Krister	Liv
Lars	Lotta
Matts	Mini
Mikael	Sabina
Niels	Sanna
Niklas	Sigrid
Oskar	Sofia
Per	Sonya
Rudolf	Ursula
Stellan	Wilhelmina

Italian Names

Boys	Girls
Aldo	Annamaria
Alessandro	Bella
Angelo	Cara
Arturo	Caramia
Carlo	Carissa
Carmine	Carlotta
Ciro	Chiara
Cosmo	Donna
Dante	Elda
Emilio	Elena
Enrico	Eliana
Franco	Elisa
Gianni	Elletra
Gino	Faustina
Giorgio	Fidelia
Guido	Gina
Leonardo	Isabella
Lorenzo	Maria
Luciano	Melania
Marco	Nicola
Mario	Paulina
Salvatore	Pia
Tomasso	Rosa
Vincenzo	Rosamaria
Vito	Sophia

French Names

Boys	Girls
Alain	Aimee
Charles	Amelie
Claude	Anais
Francois	Angelique
Frederic	Antoinette
Gaston	Arianne
Gerard	Chantal
Germain	Claire
Gregoire	Colette
Guy	Daniele
Henri	Desiree
Isidore	Dominique
Jacques	Eliane
Jean	Elisabeth
Jean-Claude	Emmanuelle
Jean-Michel	Esmee
Jean-Paul	Gabrielle
Laurent	Genevieve
Louis	Giselle
Luc	Maria
Marcel	Michele
Maxime	Monique
Phillipe	Simone
Robert	Yvette
Yves	Yvonne

German Names

Boys	Girls
Claus, Klaus	Ada
Erik	Anke
Folker	Anneliese
Freiderich	Annemarie
Garrick	Beata
Gerhard	Clotilda
Gunther	Constanze
Gustaf	Cordula
Heinrich	Ebba
Helmut	Elisabeth
Hendrik	Elsa
Karl	Emma
Konrad	Felicie
Kurt	Gudrun
Leopold	Heidi
Max	Hilda
Norbert	Juliana
Oswald	Karoline
Otto	Katharina
Ralph	Kristina
Roger	Margarite
Rudy	Maria
Stefan	Martina
Wilhelm	Rosa
Wolfgang	Ursula

Polish Names

Boys	Girls
Aleksander	Anna
Andrzej	Barbara
Aniol	Cecilia
Anzelm	Celestyna
Bogdan	Gabriela
Boleslaw	Gizela
Czeslaw	Grazyna
Dobromir	Hanna
Helmut	Honorata
Jacek	Iwona
Jozef	Jadwiga
Karol	Kamilia
Kazimierz	Karolina
Krzysztof	Krysta
Marek	Krystyna
Pawel	Lucja
Ryszard	Maria
Slawomir	Marusya
Waclaw	Matylda
Walenty	Mirka
Witold	Monika
Wladymir	Otylia
Wladyslaw	Roksana
Wojtek	Waleria
Zbigniew	Wiktoria

Russian Names

Boys	Girls
Adya	Anastasiya
Alek	Anninka
Aleksei	Dariya
Denis	Dasha
Dmitri	Duscha
Grigori	Elena
Igor	Evelina
Ivan	Inessa
Karl	Irene/Irina
Maksimilian	Ivanna
Mikhail	Kira
Misha	Lara
Nikita	Lia
Nikolai	Masha
Oleg	Nadya
Pavel	Natalia
Sasha	Natasha
Sergei	Oksana
Sidor	Olga
Stanislav	Polina
Valentin	Sasha
Valeri	Sofya
Vlad	Sonya
Vladimir	Svetlana
Vladja	Tatiana

Irish Names

Boys	Girls
Aidan	Aileen
Art	Amanda
Bran	Annie
Brendan	Brenda
Brian	Briana
Colin	Catherine
Curran	Cathleen
Devin	Ciara
Farris	Deirdre
Fergus	Dorren
Finn	Eavan
Ian	Eliza
James	Emma
Jamie	Ethnea
John	Karen
Kevin	Kate
Kieran, Keiran	Kathy
Killian	Maggie
Liam	Molly
Lochlain	Nancy
Owen	Nessa
Patrick	Polly
Rowan	Riona
Sean	Sally
Shay	Sinead

Scottish Names

English Names

Boys	Girls	Boys	Girls
Ainsley	Alexandra	Arthur	Agnes
Alan	Alison	Charles	Alexandra
Angus	Annella	Clinton	Althea
Bean	Christy	Clive	Amanda
Bennett	Dina	Colin	Andie
Cally	Fiona	Earl	Angie
Cameron	Heather	Edward	Anna/Anne
Charles	Jeanie	George	Becky
Clement	Jenny	Harry	Betty
Conall	Lexine	Henry	Carla
Donald	Lexy	Jay	Connie
Fergus	Lindsay	Jeff	Cynthia
Gregor	Lucy	Max	Elizabeth
Harry	Maidie	Michael	Esther
Iagan	Maisie	Nicholas	Georgina
Ian	Margaret	Nigel	Hayley
James	Nan	Norman	Ida
Jock	Netta	Peter	Jennifer
Jon	Nora	Philip	Jill
Kenneth	Peigi	Roger	Katherine
Peader	Robina	Roland	Margaret
Roddy	Rona	Ronald	Moira
Scott	Rowena	Toby	Pippa
Stewart	Sandy	William	Rhonda
Walter	Tory	Winston	Wendy

African Names

Boys	Girls
Addae	Aamori
Adio	Abayomi
Ayo	Adia
Bakari	Aisha
Bomani	Asabi
Dalila	Bayo
Dumisani	Eshe
Hamidi	Fatima
Harun	Femi
Hasani	Habiba
Hondo	Hasina
Jaja	Jumoke
Kamal	Kibibi
Kamau	Kissa
Muhhamad	Lateefa
Rudo	Maudisa
Runako	Nailah
Saeed	Nomble
Salehe	Omorose
Salim	Oni
Sekani	Rufaro
Themba	Salama
Umi	Taliba
Zikomo	Tisa
Zuberi	Zahra

Spanish Names

Boys	Girls
Adonis	Angela
Alejandro	Beila
Alfonso	Beilarosa
Angel	Bonita
Benito	Caliopa
Carlos	Carlotta
Damaso	Carmen
Diego	Clementina
Emilio	Consuelo
Enrique	Delicia
Esteban	Delfina
Fiero	Destina
Francisco	Elena
Hector	Flora
Isidoro	Graciela
Javier	Guadalupe
Jorge	Honoria
Jose	Juanita
Juan	Maria
Julio	Mariposa
Miguel	Odelita
Mundo	Paloma
Raoul	Primalia
Roberto	Soledad
Tomas	

Greek Names

Boys	Girls
Alexandros	Aggie
Andreas	Andrianna
Ari	Ariadne
Basil	Athena
Cletus	Calista
Demetri	Calla
Demetrios	Chloe
Demos	Damalla
Flavian	Delos
Hilarion	Diona
Jason	Filia
Lucas	Gillian
Markos	Helena
Nikos	Iona
Paul	Isadora
Sander	Kali
Seth	Kalidas
Socrates	Kori
Stephanos	Kynthia
Theo	Leandra
Theodoros	Nia
Theophilos	Phyllis
Tito	Pia
Verniamin	Theodora
Zeno	Zoe

Asian Names

Boys	Girls
An (Chinese)	Bao (Chinese)
Chang (Chinese)	Bay (Vietnamese)
Dong (Chinese)	Cai (Chinese)
Hiro (Japanese)	Connie-Kim (Vietnamese)
Huang (Chinese)	De (Chinese)
Ibu (Japanese)	Fang (Chinese)
Ji (Chinese)	Ha (Vietnamese)
Jin (Chinese)	Lei (Chinese)
Jing (Chinese)	Li (Chinese)
Ju-Long (Chinese)	Lian (Chinese)
Kang (Korean)	Ling (Chinese)
Li (Chinese)	Mai (Japanese)
Liang (Chinese)	Min (Chinese)
Pin (Vietnamese)	Ming (Chinese)
Quon (Chinese)	Niu (Chinese)
Shen (Chinese)	Nu (Vietnamese)
Sheng (Chinese)	Pang (Chinese)
Shuu (Japanese)	Tam (Japanese)
So (Vietnamese)	Thim (Thai)
Tan (Japanese)	Veata (Cambodian)
Tung (Chinese, Vietnamese)	Yu (Chinese)
Yen (Chinese)	Zan (Chinese)
Yu (Chinese)	Zhi (Chinese)
Yuan (Chinese)	Zhong (Chinese)
Zhong (Chinese)	Zi (Chinese)

Most Popular Names of the 1950s

Boys

1. Michael
2. James
3. Robert
4. John
5. David
6. William
7. Richard
8. Thomas
9. Mark
10. Charles
11. Steven
12. Gary
13. Joseph
14. Donald
15. Ronald
16. Kenneth
17. Paul
18. Larry
19. Daniel
20. Stephen
21. Dennis
22. Timothy
23. Edward
24. Jeffrey
25. George

Girls

1. Mary
2. Linda
3. Patricia
4. Susan
5. Deborah
6. Barbara
7. Debra
8. Karen
9. Nancy
10. Donna
11. Cynthia
12. Sandra
13. Pamela
14. Sharon
15. Kathleen
16. Carol
17. Diane
18. Brenda
19. Cheryl
20. Elizabeth
21. Janet
22. Kathy
23. Margaret
24. Janice
25. Carolyn

Most Popular Names of the 1960s

Boys

1. Michael
2. David
3. John
4. James
5. Robert
6. Mark
7. William
8. Richard
9. Thomas
10. Jeffrey
11. Steven
12. Joseph
13. Timothy
14. Kevin
15. Scott
16. Brian
17. Charles
18. Daniel
19. Paul
20. Christopher
21. Kenneth
22. Anthony
23. Gregory
24. Ronald
25. Donald

Girls

1. Lisa
2. Mary
3. Karen
4. Susan
5. Kimberly
6. Patricia
7. Linda
8. Donna
9. Michelle
10. Cynthia
11. Sandra
12. Deborah
13. Pamela
14. Tammy
15. Laura
16. Lori
17. Elizabeth
18. Julie
19. Jennifer
20. Brenda
21. Angela
22. Barbara
23. Debra
24. Sharon
25. Teresa

Most Popular Names of the 1970s

Boys	Girls
1. Michael	1. Jennifer
2. Christopher	2. Amy
3. Jason	3. Melissa
4. David	4. Michelle
5. James	5. Kimberly
6. John	6. Lisa
7. Robert	7. Angela
8. Brian	8. Heather
9. William	9. Stephanie
10. Matthew	10. Jessica
11. Daniel	11. Elizabeth
12. Joseph	12. Nicole
13. Kevin	13. Rebecca
14. Eric	14. Kelly
15. Jeffrey	15. Mary
16. Richard	16. Christina
17. Scott	17. Amanda
18. Mark	18. Sarah
19. Steven	19. Laura
20. Timothy	20. Julie
21. Thomas	21. Shannon
22. Anthony	22. Christine
23. Charles	23. Tammy
24. Jeremy	24. Karen
25. Joshua	25. Tracy

Most Popular Names of the 1980s

Boys	Girls
1. Michael	1. Jessica
2. Christopher	2. Jennifer
3. Matthew	3. Amanda
4. Joshua	4. Ashley
5. David	5. Sarah
6. Daniel	6. Stephanie
7. James	7. Melissa
8. Robert	8. Nicole
9. John	9. Elizabeth
10. Joseph	10. Heather
11. Jason	11. Tiffany
12. Justin	12. Michelle
13. Andrew	13. Amber
14. Ryan	14. Megan
15. William	15. Rachel
16. Brian	16. Amy
17. Jonathan	17. Lauren
18. Brandon	18. Kimberly
19. Nicholas	19. Christina
20. Anthony	20. Brittany
21. Eric	21. Crystal
22. Adam	22. Rebecca
23. Kevin	23. Laura
24. Steven	24. Emily
25. Thomas	25. Danielle

Most Popular Names of the 1990s

Boys	Girls
1. Michael	1. Ashley
2. Christopher	2. Jessica
3. Matthew	3. Emily
4. Joshua	4. Sarah
5. Jacob	5. Samantha
6. Andrew	6. Brittany
7. Daniel	7. Amanda
8. Nicholas	8. Elizabeth
9. Tyler	9. Taylor
10. Joseph	10. Megan
11. David	11. Stephanie
12. Brandon	12. Kayla
13. James	13. Lauren
14. John	14. Jennifer
15. Ryan	15. Rachel
16. Zachary	16. Hannah
17. Justin	17. Nicole
18. Anthony	18. Amber
19. William	19. Alexis
20. Robert	20. Courtney
21. Jonathan	21. Victoria
22. Kyle	22. Danielle
23. Austin	23. Alyssa
24. Alexander	24. Rebecca
25. Kevin	25. Jasmine

Most Popular Names in 2001

Boys	Girls
1. Jacob	1. Emily
2. Michael	2. Madison
3. Matthew	3. Hannah
4. Joshua	4. Ashley
5. Christopher	5. Alexis
6. Nicholas	6. Samantha
7. Andrew	7. Sarah
8. Joseph	8. Abigail
9. Daniel	9. Elizabeth
10. William	10. Jessica
11. Anthony	11. Olivia
12. David	12. Taylor
13. Tyler	13. Emma
14. John	14. Alyssa
15. Ryan	15. Lauren
16. Zachary	16. Grace
17. Ethan	17. Kayla
18. Brandon	18. Brianna
19. James	19. Anna
20. Alexander	20. Megan
21. Dylan	21. Victoria
22. Justin	22. Destiny
23. Jonathan	23. Sydney
24. Christian	24. Rachel
25. Austin	25. Jennifer

Most Popular Names of 2002

Boys
1. Jacob
2. Michael
3. Joshua
4. Matthew
5. Ethan
6. Joseph
7. Andrew
8. Christopher
9. Daniel
10. Nicholas
11. William
12. Anthony
13. David
14. Tyler
15. Alexander
16. Ryan
17. John
18. James
19. Zachary
20. Brandon
21. Jonathan
22. Justin
23. Christian
24. Dylan
25. Samuel

Girls
1. Emily
2. Madison
3. Hannah
4. Emma
5. Alexis
6. Ashley
7. Abigail
8. Sarah
9. Samantha
10. Olivia
11. Elizabeth
12. Alyssa
13. Lauren
14. Isabella
15. Grace
16. Jessica
17. Brianna
18. Taylor
19. Kayla
20. Anna
21. Victoria
22. Megan
23. Sydney
24. Chloe
25. Rachel

Most Popular Names of 2003

Boys
1. Jacob
2. Michael
3. Joshua
4. Matthew
5. Andrew
6. Joseph
7. Ethan
8. Daniel
9. Christopher
10. Anthony
11. William
12. Ryan
13. Nicholas
14. David
15. Tyler
16. Alexander
17. John
18. James
19. Dylan
20. Zachary
21. Brandon
22. Jonathan
23. Samuel
24. Christian
25. Benjamin

Girls
1. Emily
2. Emma
3. Madison
4. Hannah
5. Olivia
6. Abigail
7. Alexis
8. Ashley
9. Elizabeth
10. Samantha
11. Isabella
12. Sarah
13. Grace
14. Alyssa
15. Lauren
16. Kayla
17. Brianna
18. Jessica
19. Taylor
20. Sophia
21. Anna
22. Victoria
23. Natalie
24. Chloe
25. Sydney

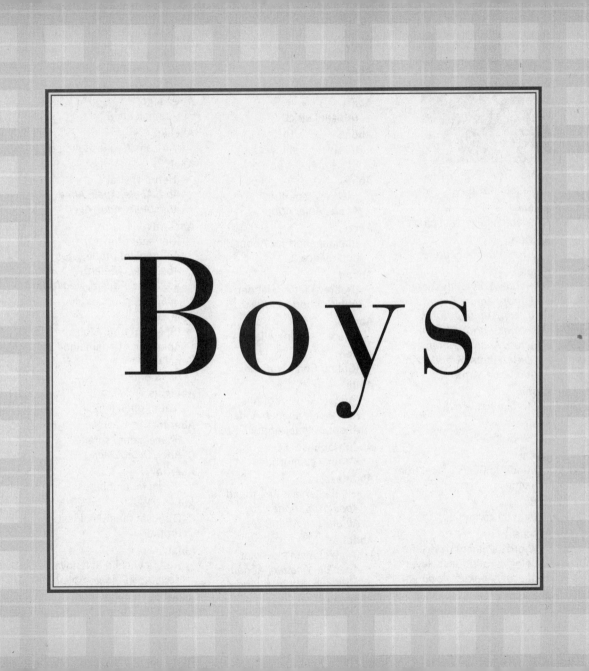

Boys

A

Aabid
(Arabic) loyal

Aalam
(Arabic) universal spirit

Aarcuus
(Greek) rambunctious

Aaron
(Hebrew) revered; sharer
Aahron, Aaran, Aaren,
Aareon, Aarin, Aarone,
Aaronn, Aarron, Aaryn,
Aeron, Aharon, Ahran,
Ahren, Ahron, Aranne, Aren,
Arin, Aron, Arron

Aashiq
(Arabic) fights evil

Aasif
(Hindi) brash

Aasim
(Hindi) in God's grace; from
Aamin

Aatiq
(Arabic) caring

Abacus
(Word as name) device for
doing calcalutions; clever
Abacas, Abakus, Abba

Abaddon
(Hebrew) knows God

Abahu
(Hindi) hopeful

Abanobi
(Mythology) water lover

Abasi
(African) strict

Abbas
(Arabic) harsh
Ab, Abba

Abbey
(Hebrew) spiritual
Abbie, Abie, Abby

Abbo
(Italian) short for Abbondio;
abundance

Abbott
(Hebrew) father; leader
Abbitt, Abott, Abotte

Abdiel
(Arabic) serving Allah

Abdon
(Greek) God's worker

Abdul
(Arabic) servant of Allah
Ab, Abdal, Abdeel, Abdel,
Abdoul, Abdu, Abdual, Abul

Abdul-Jabbar
(Arabic) comforting

Abdulaziz
(Hindi) servant of a friend
Abdelazim, Abdelaziz,
Abdulazaz, Abdulazeez

Abdullah
(Arabic) Allah's servant
Abdalah, Abdalla, Abdallah,
Abdualla, Abdulah, Abdulla,
Abdulahi

Abe
(Hebrew) short for
Abraham; father of many
Abey, Abie

Abednego
(Aramaic) faithful

Abeeku
(African) Wednesday-born

Abel
(Hebrew) vital
Abe, Abele, Abell, Abey,
Abie, Able, Adal, Avel

Abelard
(German) firm
Ab, Abalard, Abbey, Abby,
Abe, Abel, Abelerd,
Abelhard, Abilard, Adalard,
Adelard

Abelino
(Spanish) from Biblical
Abel, son of Adam and Eve;
naïve
Abel, Able

Abercius
(Latin) open mind

Aberdeen
(Place name) serene
Aber, Dean, Deen

Aberlin
(German) ambitious

Abi
(Turkish) family's oldest
brother

Abiah
(Hebrew) child of Jehovah
Abia, Abiel, Abija, Abijah,
Abisha, Abishai, Aviya,
Aviyah

Abidla
(Arabic) worshipping

Abiezer
(Hebrew) father's light

Abijah
(Hebrew) God's gift
Abish

Abilene
(Place name) town in Texas; good-old-boy
Abalene, Abileen

Abimbola
(African) destined for riches

Abimelech
(Hebrew) believer

Abinadab
(African) Tuesday-born

Abioye
(African) he loves God

Abir
(Hebrew) strong
Abeer

Abisia
(Hebrew) God's gift; gifted child
Abixah, Absa

Abner
(Hebrew) cheerful leader
Ab, Abnir, Abnor, Avner, Ebner

Aboo
(African) father; wise

Abosi
(African) remembered

Abraham
(Hebrew) fathering multitudes
Abarran, Abe, Aberham, Abey, Abhiram, Abie, Abrahim, Abrahm, Abram, Bram, Ibrahim

Abram
(Hebrew) short for Abraham
Abe, Abrams, Avram, Bram

Abraar
(Hebrew) fathers many

Abraxas
(Spanish) bright
Aba

Abrasha
(Hebrew) father

Abs
(Hebrew) short for Absalom; muscular
Abe

Absalom
(Hebrew) peaceful; handsome
Abe, Abs, Absalon, Avshalom

Abundio
(Spanish) living in abundance
Abun, Abund

Acacius
(Latin) blameless

Ace
(Latin) one; unity
Acer, Acey, Acie

Achard
(Last name as first name) dark mind

Achilles
(Greek) hero of *The Iliad*
Achill, Achille, Achillea, Achillios, Ackill, Akil, Akili, Akilles

Acisclo
(Spanish) frantic

Acisclus
(Greek) from Achelous; river god

Acker
(American) oak tree
Aker

Ackerley
(English) born of the meadow; nature-loving
Accerley, Ackerlea, Ackerleigh, Ackersley, Acklea, Ackleigh, Ackley, Acklie

Acton
(English) sturdy; oaks
Acten, Actin, Actohn, Actone

Adael
(Hebrew) decorated by God

Adair
(Scottish) negotiator
Adaire, Adare, Ade

Adal
(German) noble man
Adall, Adel

Adalberto
(Spanish) bright; dignified
Adal, Berto

Adalai
(Hebrew) my witness

Adalard
(German) brave

Adam
(Hebrew) first man; original
Ad, Adahm, Adama, Adamo,
Adas, Addam, Addams,
Addie, Addy, Adem, Adham

Adomas
(African) blessed

Adamson
(Hebrew) Adam's son
Adams, Adamsen,
Adamsson, Addamson

Adan
(Irish) bold spirit
Aden, Adin, Adyn, Aidan,
Aiden

Adar
(Hebrew) fire; spirited
Addar

Adaucus
(Latin) from Daucus;
audacious

Addae
(African) the sun

Addis
(English) short for Addison;
masculine
Addace, Addice, Addy, Adis

Addison
(English) Adam's son
Ad, Addis, Adison, Adisson

Addy
(German) awesome;
outgoing
Addey, Addi, Addie, Adi

Ade
(German) short form of
Adel; noble man

Adebayo
(African) joyfully born

Adeeb
(African) twelfth son

Adel
(German) royal
Adal, Addey, Addie, Addy

Adelaido
(Latin) adorned

Adelard
(German) brave
Adalar, Adalard, Addy, Adel,
Adelar, Adelarde

Adelmo
(German) protects others

Adelpho
(Greek) breathes
Adelfo

Adeone
(Welsh) royal
Addy, Adeon

Adeoye
(Latin) God-given

Adewale
(Welsh) in flight; soars

Adigun
(American) distinctive

Adin
(Hebrew) good-looking
Adan

Adio
(African) devout

Adir
(Hindi) lightning

Adlai
(Hebrew) ornamented
Ad, Addy, Adlay, Adley, Adlie

Adler
(German) eagle-eyed
Ad, Addler, Adlar

Adlay
(Hebrew) God's haven
Adlei, Adley

Adna
(Hebrew) physical

Adnee
(English) loner
Adni, Adny

Ado
(American) respected
Ad, Addy

Adolf
(German) sly wolf
Ad, Adolfe, Adolph

Adolfus
(German) form of Adolphus
Adulphus

Adom
(African) blessed

Adonaldo
(Spanish) baby of hope

Adonijah
(Hebrew) believer

Adonis
(Greek) gorgeous
(Aphrodite's love in
mythology)
Addonis, Adon Adones,
Adonnis, Adonys, Andonice

Adrian
(Latin) wealthy; dark-
skinned
Adarian, Ade, Addie,
Adorjan, Adrain, Adreeyan,
Adreian, Adreyan, Adriaan,
Adriane, Adriann, Adrien,
Adrion, Adron, Adryan,
Adryon, Aydrien, Aydrienne

Adriano
(Italian) wealthy
Adriannho, Adrianno

Adriel
(Hebrew) God's follower
Adrial, Adryel

Adrien
(French) form of Adrian
Ade, Adriene, Adrienn

Adya
(Russian) man from Adria

Adyn
(Irish) manly
*Adann, Ade, Aden, Aidan,
Ayden*

Aedan
(Welsh) fire; fiery
temperament

Aeneas
(Greek) worthy of praise
*Aineas, Aineias, Eneas,
Eneis*

Aeolus
(Greek) ruler of the winds

Afan
(Russian) short for Afansi;
forever

Afanasy
(Russian) forever
Afanasi

Afdhaal
(Arabic) quiet

Afililio
(Hispanic) commentator

Afton
(English) dignified
Affton, Aftawn, Aften

Agamemnon
(Greek) slow but sure
Agamem

Agapito
(Spanish) loving

Agapius
(Greek) love

Agnar
(Irish) purity

Agricola
(Irish) farms

Agripino
(Hispanic) grieves

Agueleo
(Greek) wise one

Agustin
(Latin) dignified
Aguste, Auggie, Augustin

Ahab
(Hebrew) father's brother;
sea captain in *Moby Dick*

Ahaziah
(Hebrew) beloved

Ahearn
(Irish) horsetender
*Ahearne, Aherin, Ahern,
Aherne, Hearn*

Aherin
(Hebrew) held on high
Aharon, Ahern, Aherne

Ahimelech
(Biblical) religious support

Ahmad
(Arabic) praised man
*Achmad, Achmed, Ahamad,
Ahamada, Ahamed,
Ahmaad, Ahmaud, Amad,
Amahd, Amed*

Ahmoz
(African) praised

Ahsan
(Hindi) gracious

Aidan
(Irish) fiery spirit
*Adan, Aden, Adin, Aiden,
Aydan, Ayden, Aydin*

Aided
(Irish) spirited, fiery

Aigars
(Russian) content

Aignan
(Greek) pure

Aiken
(English) hardy; oak-hewn
Aicken, Aikin, Ayken, Aykin

Ailbhe
(Irish) saint, noble

Ailred
(Last name as first name)
spiritual

Aimery
(German) leader
*Aime, Aimerey, Aimeric,
Amerey, Aymeric, Aymery*

Ainsley
(Scottish) in a meadow
*Ainsleigh, Ainslie, Ansley,
Ainslee, Ainsli, Aynslee,
Aynsley, Aynslie*

Ainsworth
(Last name as first name)
joyful

Aiwar
(Arabic) from Anwar; bright

Aiyetoro
(African) destined for a
peaceful life

Ajani
(African) victorious

Ajax
(Greek) daring
Ajacks

Ajay
(American) spontaneous
A.J., Aj, Ajah, Ajai

Ajmal
(African) depressed

Akar
(Hindi) lightning
Akara

Akbar
(Hindi) Muslim king; giving

Akeem
(Arab) form of Hakeem;
skilled; introspective
*Ackeem, Ackim, Akieme,
Akim, Hakeem, Hakim*

Akevy
(Hebrew) from Akiva;
replacing

Aki
(Scandinavian) blameless

Akil
(Arabic) intelligent
*Ahkeel, Akeel, Akeyla,
Akhil, Akiel, Akili*

Akilles
(Greek) form of Achilles;
heroic

Akim
(Russian) loved by God
*Achim, Ackeem, Ackim,
Ahkieme, Akeam, Akee,
Akeem, Akiem, Akima,
Arkeem*

Akinori
(Japanese) from Aki; born in
the fall

Akins
(African) brave

Akira
(Japanese) intellectual

Akiva
(Hebrew) cunning,
replacement
Akiba, Kiva

Akram
(Arabic) kind

Aksel
(Scandinavian) calm

Akwasi
(African) hopes

Akwete
(African) second-born twin

Al
(Irish) short for Alexander
and Alan; attractive

Aladdin
(Arabic) believer
*Al, Ala, Alaa, Alaaddin,
Aladdein, Aladean, Aladen*

Alain
(French) form of Alan and
Allen
*Alaen, Alainn, Alayn, Allain,
Alun*

Alair
(Gaelic) happy
Alaire

Alan
(Irish) handsome boy
*Ailin, Al, Aland, Alen, Allan,
Allen, Alley, Allie, Allin,
Allyn, Alon, Alun*

Alander
(American) argumentative;
cogitative

Alando
(Spanish) form of Alan;
attractive
*Al, Alaindo, Alan, Aland,
Alano, Allen, Allie, Alun,
Alundo, Alyn*

Alanson
(Last name as first name)
son of Alan; handsome
Alansen, Alenson, Allanson

Alaric
(German) ruler
*Alarick, Alarik, Aleric,
Allaric, Allarick, Alric, Alrick*

Alasdair
(Scottish) form of Alistair;
highbrow
*Al, Alaisdair, Alasdaire,
Alasdare, Alisdair, Allysdair*

Alastair
(Scottish) strong leader
*Alaistair, Alasteir, Alastere,
Alastaire, Alastor, Aleistere,
Alester, Alistair, Allaistar,
Allastair, Allastir, Alystair*

Alaster
(American) form of Alastair;
staunch advocate
Alaste, Alester, Allaster

Alban
(Latin) white man; from
Alba's white hill
*Abion, Albain, Albany,
Albean, Albee, Albein,
Alben, Albi, Albie, Albin,
Alby, Auban*

Albanse
(Invented) from the place name Albany, New York; white
Alban, Albance, Albanee, Albany, Albie, Alby

Albany
(Place name) town in New York; restless
Albanee, Albanie

Albe
(Latin) from Alba; white hill

Alberic
(German) ruler; tough
Albric

Albert
(German) distinguished
Al, Alberto, Alberts, Albie, Albrecht, Alby, Ally, Aubert

Alberto
(Italian) distinguished
Al, Albert, Bertie, Berto

Albie
(German) short for Albert; smart
Albee, Albi, Alby

Albion
(Greek) old-fashioned
Albionne, Albyon

Alcordia
(American) in accord with others
Alcord, Alkie, Alky

Alcott
(English) cottage-dweller
Alcot, Alkokt, Alkott, Allcot, Allcott, Allkot, Allkott

Alden
(English) wise
Al, Aldan, Aldin, Aldon, Elden

Alder
(English) revered; kind

Aldo
(Italian) older one; jovial
Aldoh

Aldorse
(American) form of Aldo; old
Al, Aldo, Aldorce, Aldors

Aldous
(German) wealthy
Aldis, Aldus, Aldas

Aldred
(English) advisor; judgmental
Al, Aldrid, Aldy, Alldred, Eldred

Aldren
(English) old friend
Al, Aldran, Aldie, Aldrun, Aldy, Aldryn

Aldrich
(English) wise advisor
Aldie, Aldric, Aldrick, Aldridge, Aldrige, Aldrish, Aldritch, Alldric, Alldrich, Alldrick, Alldridge, Eldridge

Alec
(Greek) high-minded
Al, Aleck, Alek, Alic

Alejandro
(Spanish) defender; bold and brave
Alejandra, Alejo, Alex, Alexjandro

Alek
(Russian) short for Aleksei; brilliant
Aleks

Aleksander
(Greek and Polish) defender
Alek, Sander

Aleksei
(Russian) defender; brilliant
Alek, Alik, Alexi

Aleksey
(Russian) smart

Alemet
(African) world leader

Aleppo
(Place name) easygoing
Alepo

Aleric
(Scandinavian) rules all
Alarik, Alerick, Alleric, Allerick

Aleron
(French) the knight's armor; protected

Alessandro
(Italian) helpful; defender
Allessandro, Alessand

Alessio
(Italian) defensive

Alex
(Greek) short for Alexander; leader
Alax, Alecs, Alix, Allax, Allex

Alexander
(Greek) great leader; helpful
*Al, Alec, Alecsander,
Aleksandar, Aleksander,
Aleksandur, Alex,
Alexandar, Alexandor,
Alexandr, Alexis,
Alexsander, Alexxander,
Alexzander, Alisander,
Alixander, Alixandre*

Alexandros
(Greek) form of Alexander;
helpful
Alesandros, Alexandras

Alexis
(Greek) short for Alexander
*Alexace, Alexei, Alexes,
Alexey, Alexi, Alexie,
Alexius, Alexiz, Alexy, Lex*

Alf
(Italian) short for Alfonso;
noble

Alfalfa
(Botanical) sprite

Alfeus
(Hebrew) follower
Alpheus

Alfie
(English) short for Alfred;
friendly
Alf, Alfi, Alfy

Alfonso
(Spanish) bright; prepared
*Alf, Alfie, Alfons, Alfonsin,
Alfonso, Alfonsus, Alfonz,
Alfonza, Alfonzo, Alfonzus,
Alphonsus, Fons, Fonzie,
Fonzy*

Alford
(English) wise

Alfred
(English) counselor
*Al, Alf, Alfeo, Alfie, Alfrede,
Alfryd*

Alfredo
(Italian, Spanish) advisor
Alf, Alfie, Alfreedo, Alfrido

Alfredrick
(American) combo of Alfred
and Fredrick; pretentious
*Al, Alf, Alfred, Freddy,
Fredrik*

Alger
(German) hardworking
Algar, Allgar

Algernon
(English) man with facial
hair
*Al, Algenon, Alger, Algie,
Algin, Algon, Algy*

Algia
(German) prepared; kind
Alge, Algie

Ali
(Arabic) greatest
Alee, Aly

Ali-Baba
(Literature) *A Thousand and
One Nights*

Alicio
(Spanish) noble; dignified

Alim
(Arabic) musical

Alipi
(Spanish) calm

Alireza
(Hebrew) joyful

Alisander
(Greek) form of Alexander
*Alisander, Alissander,
Allisandre, Alsandair,
Alsandare, Alsander*

Alisen
(Irish) honest

Allan
(Irish) form of Alan
Allane, Allayne

Allard
(English) brave man
Alard, Ellard

Allegheny
(Place name) mountains of
the Appalachian system;
grand
*Al, Alleg, Alleganie,
Alleghenie*

Allen
(Irish) handsome
*Al, Alen, Alley, Alleyn,
Alleyne, Allie, Allin, Allon,
Allyn, Alon*

Allward
(Polish) brave

Almagor
(Hebrew) courageous

Almar
(German) form of Almarine;
strong
Al, Almarr, Almer

Almere
(American) director
Almer

Almo
(American) form of Elmo;
easygoing

Almund
(Botanical) form of almond; wise

Alois
(Czech) famous warrior
Aloysius, Aloisio

Alonzo
(Spanish) enthusiastic
Alano, Alanzo, Alon, Alonso, Alonza, Alonze, Elonzo, Lon, Lonnie

Aloysius
(German) famed
Alaois, Alois, Aloisius, Aloisio

Alpar
(Hindi) champions downtrodden

Alpheus
(Hebrew) form of Alfeus; follower
Alphaeus

Alphonse
(German) distinguished
Alf, Alfonse, Alphons, Alphonsa, Alphonso, Alphonzus, Fonsi, Fonsie, Fonz, Fonzie

Alpin
(Scottish) man from alpine area

Alps
(Place name) climber
Alp

Alquince
(American) old; fifth
Al, Alquense, Alquin, Alquins, Alquinse, Alqwence

Alrick
(German) leader
Alrec, Alric

Alroy
(American) combo of Al and Roy; sedate
Al, Alroi

Alston
(English) serious; nobleman
Allston, Alsten, Alstin

Alsworth
(English) from a manor; rich

Altair
(Scottish) defender

Altarius
(African American) from Altair; shining star
Altare, Altair, Altareus, Alterius, Alltair, Al

Alter
(Hebrew) old; will live to be old

Altman
(German) wise
Altmann, Atman

Alto
(Place name) town in Texas; alto voice; easygoing
Al

Alton
(English) excellent; kind
Allton, Altawn, Alten, Altyn

Altus
(Latin) form of Alta; high
Al, Alta

Alula
(Latin) winged

Alva
(Hebrew) intelligent; beloved friend
Alvah

Alvado
(Spanish) fair

Alvar
(Spanish) careful
Alvaro, Alver

Alvarado
(Spanish) peacemaker
Alvaradoh, Alvaro, Alvie, Alvy

Alvaro
(Spanish) just
Alvaroh, Alvarro, Alvey, Alvie, Alvy

Alvern
(English) old friend
Al, Alverne, Alvurn

Alvin
(Latin) light-haired; loved
Alv, Alvan, Alven, Alvie, Alvy, Alvyn

Alvincent
(American) combo of Alvin and Vincent; giving friend
Alvin, Alvince, Vin, Vince, Vincent, Vinse

Alvis
(American) form of Elvis; old friend
Al, Alviss, Alvy

Alvord
(Greek) cautious

Alwin
(German) variant of Alvin; loved
Allwyn, Alwyn, Alwynn, Aylwin

Alzado
(Arabic) forlorn

Amaan
(African) loyal
Aman, Amman

Amadayus
(Invented) form of Amadeus
Amadayes

Amadeo
(Italian) blessed by God; artistic

Amadeus
(Latin) God-loving
Amad, Amadayus, Amadeaus, Amadei, Amadio, Amadis, Amado, Amador, Amadou, Amedeo, Amodaos

Amado
(Spanish) loved
Amadee, Amadeo, Amadi, Amadis, Amadus, Amando

Amadour
(French) loved
Amador, Amadore

Amadus
(Latin) adores God
Amandus

Amal
(Hebrew) hardworking; optimistic
Amahl, Amhall

Amancio
(Spanish) faithful

Amandeep
(Hindi) light of peace
Amandip, Amanjit, Amanjot, Amanpreet

Amar
(Arabic) making a home
Amari, Amario, Amaris, Ammar, Ammer

Amaramto
(Latin) beauty does not fade

Amarillo
(Place name) town in Texas; in Spanish, it means yellow; renegade
Amarille, Amarilo

Amasa
(Hebrew) carries a heavy load

Amato
(Italian) loving
Amahto, Amatoh

Amazu
(Hebrew) burdened

Ambert
(Arabic) golden boy

Ambrose
(German) everlasting
Amba, Ambie, Ambroce, Ambrus, Amby

Ameer
(Arabic) rules

America
(Place name) patriotic

Americo
(Spanish) patriotic
Ame, America, Americus, Ameriko

Amerigo
(Italian) ruler; name of Italian explorer
Amer, Americo, Ameriko

Amery
(Arabic) regal birth
Amory

Ames
(French) friendly
Aims

Amias
(Latin) devoted to God
Amyas

Amichai
(Hebrew) my nation lives

Amiel
(Hebrew) my people's God
Ameal, Amheel, Ammiel

Amin
(Arabic) honorable; dependable
Aman, Ameen

Amir
(Arabic) royal; ruler
Ameer, Amire

Amit
(Hindi) forever; (Hebrew) truth
Amitan, Amreet, Amrit

Amiti
(Japanese) endless friend

Ammon
(Irish) hidden
Amnon

Amor
(Latin) love
Amerie, Amoree, Amori, Amorie

Amory
(German) home ruler
Amery, Amor

Amos
(Hebrew) strong
Amus

Ampah
(African) certainty

Ampy
(American) fast
Amp, Ampee, Ampey, Amps

Amund
(Scandinavian) fearless

Amyas
(Latin) lovable
Aimeus, Ameus, Amias, Amyes

An
(Chinese) peaceful; safe
Ana

Anan
(Irish) outdoorsy
An, Annan

Anand
(Hindi) delightful
Ananda, Anant, Ananth

Ananias
(Biblical) pious

Anarolio
(Spanish) called forth

Anas
(Czech) born again

Anastasius
(Greek) reborn
Anas, Anastagio, Anastas, Anastase, Anastasi, Anastasio, Anastastios, Anastice, Anasticius, Anastisis, Athanasius

Anatole
(French) exotic
Anatol, Anatoli, Anatolijus, Anatolio, Anatoly, Anitolle

Ancel
(French) creative
Ance, Ancell, Anse, Ansel, Ansell

Andel
(Scandinavian) honored

Ander
(English) form of Andrew; masculine

Anders
(Swedish) masculine
Ander, Andersen, Anderson, Andirs, Andries, Andy

Andras
(French) form of Andrew; masculine
Andrae, Andres, Andrus, Ondrae, Ondras

André
(French) masculine
Andra, Andrae, Andre, Anrecito, Andree, Aundré, Andrei

Andreas
(Greek) masculine
Andrieas, Andries Adryus, Andy

Andrere
(Greek) from Andreios; manly

Andres
(Spanish) macho
Andras, Andrés, Andrez, Andy

Andretti
(Italian) speedy
Andrette, Andy

Andrew
(Greek) manly and brave
Aindrew, Anders, Andery, Andi, Andie, Andreas, Andres, Andrews, Andru, Andrue, Andy, Audrew

Andronicus
(Greek) clever

Andros
(Polish) masculine
Andris, Andrus

Andru
(Greek) form of Andrew; masculine
Andrue

Andrzej
(Polish) manly

Andy
(Greek) short for Andrew; masculine
Andee, Andie

Aneurin
(Welsh) golden child
Aneirin

Anfanio
(Spanish) secretive

Anferny
(American) variation of Anthony
Andee, Anfernee, Anferney, Anferni, Anfernie, Anfurny

Angel
(Greek) angelic messenger
Ange, Angele, Angell, Angie, Angy

Angelberto
(Spanish) shining angel
Angel, Angelbert, Bert, Berto

Angelo
(Italian) angelic
Ange, Angelito, Angeloh,
Angelos, Anglo, Anjelo

Angits
(Celtic) divine, exceptional

Angle
(Invented) word as name;
spin doctor
Ange, Angul

Anglin
(Greek) angelic
Anglen, Anglinn, Anglun

Angus
(Scottish) standout;
important
Ange, Angos, Aonghas

Anh
(Vietnamese) smart

Anibal
(Spanish) brave noble

Aniello
(Italian) risk-taker

Anil
(Hindi) air
Aneel, Anel, Aniel, Aniello

Aniol
(Polish) angel
Ahnjol, Ahnyolle

Anka
(Polish) gracious; stems
from Anna

Ankoma
(African) last-born child

Annan
(African) second; from Annar

Annatto
(Botanical) tree; tough
Annatta

Annibale
(Phoenician) from Hannibal;
bold

Anniel
(Biblical) angel

Anolus
(Greek) masculine
Ano, Anol

Anrue
(American) masculine
Anrae, Anroo

Anscom
(English) awesome man
Anscomb

Ansel
(French) creative
Ancell, Ansa, Anse, Ansell

Anselm
(German) protective
Anse, Ansehlm, Ansellm

Anselmo
(Spanish) protected by God
Ancel, Ancelmo, Anse, Ansel,
Anselm, Anzelmo, Selmo

Anshel
(Hindi) blessed
Anshel, Anshl

Anskar
(German) brusque

Ansley
(English) loner
Anslea, Anslee, Ansleigh,
Anslie, Ansly, Ansy

Anson
(German) divine male
Anse, Ansonn, Ansun

Antal
(Latin) princely

Antero
(Greek) moves with grace

Anthony
(Latin) outstanding
Anathony, Anothony, Anth,
Anthawn, Anthey, Anthoney,
Anthoni, Anthonie,
Anthonio, Anthyonny,
Anton, Antony, Tony

Antipas
(Greek) father

Antoan
(Latin) variant of Anthony;
priceless

Antoine
(French) worthy of praise
Antone, Antons, Antos,
Antwan, Antwon, Antwone

Anton
(Latin) outstanding
Antan, Antawn

Antonce
(African American) form of
Anthony; valued
Antawnce

Antonio
(Spanish) superb
Antinio, Antonello, Antoino,
Antone, Antonino,
Antonioh, Antonnio,
Antonyio, Antonyo,
Antonyia, Tony

Antony
(Latin) good
Antawny, Antini, Antonah,
Antone, Antoney, Antoni,
Antonie, Anty, Tone, Tony

Antrinell
(African American) valued
Antrie, Antrinel, Antry

Antroy
(African American) form of Anthony; prized
Antroe, Antroye

Antwan
(American) form of Antoine; achiever
Antawan, Antawn, Anthawn, Antowine, Antowne, Antown, Antwain, Antwaine, Antwaion, Antwane, Antwann, Antwanne, Antwaun, Antwen, Antwian, Antwine, Antwion, Antwoan, Antwoin, Antwoine, Antwon, Antwonn, Antwonne, Antwuan, Antyon, Antywon

Antwone
(American) variant of Antoine; achiever
Antwonn

Anwar
(Arabic) shining
Anour, Anouar, Anwhour

Anwyl
(Welsh) beloved
Anwyll, Anwell

Anyon
(Latin) from Anthony; priceless

Anzelm
(Polish) protective
Ahnzselm

Apolinar
(Spanish) manly and wise
Apollo

Apollo
(Greek) masculine; a god in mythology
Apolloh, Apolo, Apoloniah, Applonian, Appollo

Apolonio
(Greek) from Apollo, god of music, poetry, prophesy

Apostle
(Greek) follower; disciple
Apos

Apostolos
(Greek) disciple
Apos

Apple
(American) favorite; wholesome
Apel

Aquan
(Native American) tranquil

Aquila
(Spanish) eagle-eyed
Acquilla, Aquil, Aquilas, Aquile, Aquilla, Aquillino

Aquileo
(Spanish) warrior
Akweleo, Aquilo

Aram
(Syrian) noble; honorable
Ara, Aramia, Arra

Aramis
(French) clever
Airamis, Arames, Aramith, Aramys, Aramyse, Arhames

Aracin
(Latin) ready; heaven's gate

Araldo
(German) army leader

Aralt
(Irish) army leader

Arber
(American) from arbor; adorned

Arbet
(Last name as first name) high
Arb, Arby

Arbogast
(German) covered

Arceneaux
(French) friendly; heavenly
Arce, Arcen, Arceno

Arch
(English) short for Archie and Archibald; athletic
Arche

Archard
(English) bold

Archer
(English) athletic; bowman
Arch, Archie

Archibald
(German) bold leader
Arch, Archibold, Archie

Archie
(English) short for Archibald; bold
Arch, Archi, Archy

Ardan
(Latin) passion; eagle

Ardee
(American) ardent
Ard, Ardie, Ardy

Ardell
(Latin) go-getter
Ardel

Arden
(Latin) ball of fire
*Ard, Arda, Ardie, Ardin,
Ardon, Arrden*

Ardley
(English) with dedication

Ardmohr
(Latin) more ardent than
others
Ard, Ardmoor, Ardmore

Ardolph
(German) ardent

Areeb
(Arabic) passionate

Arelus
(Latin) form of Aurelius;
golden son

Aren
(Dutch) from Arnold; form
of Aaron

Arenda
(Spanish) eager

Aristeo
(Spanish) best
Aris, Aristio, Aristo, Ary

Argan
(American) leader
*Argee, Argen, Argey, Argi,
Argie, Argun*

Argento
(Spanish) silver
Arge, Argey, Argi, Argy

Argus
(Greek) careful; bright
Agos, Arjus

Argyle
(English) diamond pattern;
planning
Argile

Ari
(Greek) best
*Ahree, Aria, Arias, Arie, Arih,
Arij, Arri*

Aribert
(German) holy

Aribold
(German) holy

Aric
(English) leader
*Aaric, Arec, Areck, Arick,
Arik, Arric, Arrick, Arrik*

Ariel
(Hebrew) God's spirited lion
*Airel, Arel, Arell, Ari, Arie,
Ariele, Arielle, Ariya, Ariyel,
Arrial, Arriel*

Aries
(Greek) god of war;
mythology
Arees, Arie, Ariez

Arik
(German) leads

Arild
(Hebrew) God's lion

Ario
(Spanish) warring
Ari, Arrio

Arion
(Greek) enchanted man
*Ari, Arian, Ariane, Arien,
Arrian, Arie, Ariohn*

Aristides
(Greek) son of the
outstanding
Ari, Aris, Aristidis

Aristophanes
(Greek) playwright

Aristotle
(Greek) best man
*Ari, Aris, Aristie, Aristito,
Aristo, Aristokles,
Aristotelis, Aristottle*

Arjan
(Hindi) one Pandavas
Arjun

Arkady
(Russian) revered

Arki
(Greek) ruler

Arkyn
(Scandinavian) royal
offspring
*Aricin, Ark, Arkeen, Arken,
Arkin*

Arle
(Irish) sworn
Arlee, Arley, Arly

Arledge
(English) lives by a lake
*Arleedj, Arles, Arlidge,
Arlledge*

Arleigh
(Irish) sworn
Arly

Arlen
(Irish) dedicated
*Arl, Arlan, Arland, Arle,
Arlend, Arlin, Arlyn, Arlynn*

Arley
(English) meadow-loving; outdoorsy
Arleigh, Arlie, Arly

Arlis
(Hebrew) dedicated; in charge
Arlas, Arles, Arless, Arly

Arlo
(German) strong
Arloh

Arlonn
(Irish) sworn; cheerful
Arlan, Arlann, Arlen, Arlon

Arlys
(Hebrew) pledged
Arlis

Arm
(English) arm
Arma, Arman, Arme

Arman
(German) also Armand; army man; defender
Armaan

Armand
(German) strong soldier
Armad, Armanda, Armando, Armands, Armanno, Armaude, Arme, Armenta, Armond, Ormand

Armando
(Spanish) entertainer
Armand, Arme, Armondo

Armani
(Italian) army; disciplined talent
Amani, Arman, Armanie, Armon, Armoni

Armen
(Spanish) from the name Armenta; soldier
Arme, Arment, Armenta

Armitage
(Last name as first name) safe haven
Armi, Armita, Army

Armon
(Hebrew) strong as a fortress
Arman, Arme, Armen, Armin, Armino, Armoni, Armons

Armro
(Italian) from Armino; warrior

Armstrong
(English) strong-armed
Arme, Army

Arnaud
(French) strong
Arnaldo, Arnauld

Arnborn
(Scandinavian) eagle-bear; animal instincts
Arn, Arne, Arnborne, Arnbourne

Arndt
(German) strong
Arne, Arnee, Arney, Arni, Arnie

Arne
(German) short for Arnold; ruler
Arn, Arna, Arnel, Arnell

Arnette
(Dutch) little eagle
Arnat, Arnet, Arnot, Arnott

Arnie
(German) short for Arnold; ruler
Arne, Arney, Arni, Arnny, Arny

Arnithan
(African American) form of Arnie and Jonathan; eagle-eyed
Arnee, Arnie, Nithan

Arno
(German) far-sighted
Arn, Arne, Arnoh, Arnou, Arnoux

Arnold
(German) ruler; strong
Arnald, Arne, Arndt, Arnie, Arnoll, Arny

Arnome
(Invented) powerful
Arnom

Arnon
(German) eagle

Arnot
(French) from Arnold; eagle-eyed
Arnott, Arnart, Arnett

Arnst
(Scandinavian) eagle-eyed (arn means eagle)
Arn

Arnulfo
(Spanish) strong
Arne, Arnie, Arny

Aroldo
(German) eagle; strong

Aron
(Hebrew) generous
Aaron, Arron, Erinn

Arpad
(Hungarian) prince; sunny

Arrigo
(Italian) ruler

Arsenio
(Greek) macho; virile
*Arne, Arsen, Arsenius,
Arseny, Arsinio, Arsonio*

Arshad
(Iranian) revered

Arshaq
(Arabic) supports

Art
(English) bear-like; wealthy
Arte, Artie

Artemus
(Greek) gifted
*Art, Artemas, Artemio,
Artemis, Artie, Artimas,
Artimis, Artimus*

Arthisus
(Origin unknown) stuffy
Arth, Arthi, Arthy

Arthur
(English) distinguished
*Art, Arth, Arther, Arthor,
Artie, Artor, Artur, Arty,
Aurther, Aurthur*

Artie
(English) short for Arthur;
wealthy
Art, Artee, Arty

Arturo
(Italian) talented
*Art, Arthuro, Artur, Arture,
Arturro*

Arun
(Hindi) the color of the sky
before dawn
Aruns

Arundel
(English) lives with eagles;
soars

Arvai
(Hebrew) roams
Arve

Arvel
(German) friendly

Arvid
(Hebrew) full of wanderlust
*Arv, Arvad, Arve, Arvie,
Arvind, Arvinder, Arvydas*

Arvin
(German) friendly
*Arv, Arven, Arvie, Arvind,
Arvinder, Arvon, Arvy*

Arwen
(German) friend
*Arwee, Arwene, Arwhen,
Arwy*

Ary
(Hebrew) lion; fierce
Ari, Arye

Asa
(Hebrew) healer
Ase, Aza

Asád
(Arabic) happy
*Asaad, Asad, Asid, Assad,
Azad*

Ascot
(English) cottage-dweller

Asgar
(Scandinavian) God's home

Ash
(Botanical) tree; bold
Ashbey, Ashby, Ashe

Asharious
(Mythology) Ashur, god of
war; combative boy

Ashbel
(Hebrew) fiery god

Ashby
(Scandinavian) brash
*Ashbee, Ashbey, Ashie,
Ashy*

Asher
(Hebrew) joyful
Ash, Ashar, Ashor, Ashur

Ashfaaq
(Arabic) honorable

Ashford
(English) spunky
Ash, Ashferd, Ashtin

Ashley
(English) smooth
*Ash, Asheley, Ashelie,
Ashely, Ashie, Ashlan,
Ashlee, Ashleigh, Ashlen,
Ashlie, Ashlin, Ashling,
Ashlinn, Ashlone, Ashly,
Ashlyn, Ashlynn, Aslan*

Ashlin
(English) from Ashley; lives
in a forest

Ashraf
(Arabic) honors others

Ashton
(English) handsome
Ashteen, Ashtin

Ashur
(Hebrew) happy

Asifa
(Hebrew) gathers

Aslan
(Literature) lion-like

Asmus
(German) well-known

Asner
(Hebrew) giving

Aspah
(Greek) from Aspar; leader; welcomed

Asriel
(Hebrew) praised

Aston
(English) eastern
Asten, Astin

Aswin
(English) from the land of ash trees

Atam
(American) form of Adam; tough
Atame, Atom, Atym

Atanacio
(Spanish) everlasting
Atan, Atanasio

Ateeq
(Arabic) affectionate

Athanasius
(Greek) from Athanasios; immortal
Atanasio, Atanas

Athar
(English) lives on a farm

Atherton
(English) coming from a farm

Atilano
(Greek) strong

Atinuwa
(African) aware

Atkins
(Last name as first name) linked; known
Atkin

Atlas
(Greek) courier of greatness
Atlass

Atley
(English) from the meadow
Atlea, Atlee, Atleigh, Atli, Attley

Atsu
(African) second-born twin

Atticus
(Greek) ethical
Aticus, Attikus

Attila
(Gothic) powerful
Atalik, Atila, Atilio, Atiya, Atlya, Att

Atwater
(English) living by the water

Atwell
(English) place name; the well; full of gusto

Atwood
(English) place name; the woods; outdoorsy

Atworth
(English) farmer

Atyab
(Arabic) cultivated

Auberon
(German) like a bear; highborn
Aube, Auberron, Aubrey

Aubert
(German) leader
Auber, Aubey

Aubin
(French) ruler; elfin
Auben

Aubrey
(English) ruler
Aubary, Aube, Aubery, Aubree, Aubry, Aubury, Bree

Auburn
(Latin) brown with red cast; tenacious
Aubern, Aubie, Auburne

Auden
(English) old friend
Aude, Audie

Audencio
(Spanish) companion
Auden

Audie
(German) strong man
Aude, Audee, Audi, Audiel, Audley

Audley
(English) rich
Audlea, Audlee, Audleigh, Audly

Audon
(Scandinavian) alone

Audelon
(French) wealthy

Audras
(Scandinavian) having wealth
Audres

Audric
(French) wise ruler

Audun
(Scandinavian) form of
Audon; alone

Audwin
(English) rich

Augie
(Latin) short for Augustus
Aug, Auggie, Augy

August
(Latin) determined
Auge, Augie

Augustine
(Latin) serious and revered
*Agostino, Agoston, Agustin,
Aug, Augie, August,
Augustene, Augustin*

Augusto
(Spanish) respected; serious
*Agusto, Augey, Auggie,
Austeo*

Augustus
(Latin) highly esteemed
Aug, Auge, Augie, August

Aulie
(English) form of Audley
Awlie

Aurek
(Latin) golden

Aurelius
(Latin) golden son
*Arelian, Areliano, Aurel,
Aurey, Aurie, Auriel, Aury*

Aust
(American) from Austin; kind

Austin
(Latin) capital of Texas;
ingenious; southwestern
*Astin, Aust, Austen,
Austine, Auston, Austyn*

Auther
(American) form of Arthur;
brave and smart
Authar, Authur

Autry
(Latin) golden

Avan
(Hindi) short for Avanidra;
lord of earth

Avenall
(English) from the woods;
calm
Avenel, Avenell

Avent
(French) up-and-coming
Aventin, Aventino

Averill
(French) April-born child
*Ave, Averel, Averell, Averiel,
Averil, Averyl, Averyll, Avrel,
Avrell, Avrill, Avryl*

Avrylle
(French) hunter
Avryll

Avery
(English) soft-spoken
*Avary, Ave, Aveary, Averey,
Averie, Avry*

Avi
(Hebrew) springlike
*Avian, Avidan, Avidor, Aviel,
Avion*

Aviaz
(Hebrew) believer

Avinoam
(Biblical) pleasant brother

Avion
(French) flyer
Aveonn, Avyon, Avyun

Aviv
(Hebrew) spring

Avner
(Hebrew) father of light
Avneet, Avniel

Avniel
(Hebrew) God is my rock

Avram
(Hebrew) almighty father
*Arram, Avraham, Avrom,
Avrum*

Axel
(German) peaceful;
contemporary
*Aksel, Ax, Axe, Axil, Axill,
Axl*

Awet
(Welsh) from Awst; great

Axton
(German) town of peace;
peacemaker

Aydin
(Irish) masculine

Ayers
(Last name as first)
industrious

Aylmer
(English) of noble birth

Aylward
(English) guards best

Aylwin
(Welsh) elf friend

Ayo
(African) happy

Ayson
(Origin unknown) lucky
Aison

Azad
(Arabic) lucky

Azael
(Spanish) God-loved

Azariah
(Biblical) aided by Jehovah

Azeem
(Arabic) cherished
Aseem, Asim

Azeez
(Arabic) also Aziz; strong

Azhar
(Arabic) flourishes

Azi
(African) a child

Azim
(Arabic) grandiose

Aziz
(Arabic) powerful

Azizi
(African) beloved

Azrae
(Mythology) Azrael, angel of
God

Azriel
(Hebrew) the Lord's angel

Azuriah
(Hebrew) aided by God
Azaria, Azariah, Azuria

Babar
(Turkish) lion
Baber

Babe
(American) athlete

Babu
(Hindi) fierce

Bacchus
(Greek) reveler; jaded
Baakus, Bakkus, Bakus

Bach
(Last name as first name)
talented
Bok

Bachir
(Hebrew) oldest son; reliable
Bachur

Bacon
(English) literary;
outspoken
Baco, Bake, Bakon

Badar
(Hindi) full moon

Baden
(German) bathes; cleansed

Badger
(Last name as first name)
difficult
*Badge, Badgeant, Bage,
Bagent*

Badr
(African) full moon; lucky

Badru
(African) full moon; lucky

Baha
(Arabic) splendid

Bahir
(Arabic) magnificent

Bailey
(French) attentive
Baile, Baily, Baley, Baylie

Bainbridge
(Irish) bridge; negotiator
Bain, Banebridge, Beebee

Baines
(Last name as first name)
pale
Baine, Baynes

Bainlon
(American) form of Bailey;
pale
Bailey, Baily

Baird
(Irish) singer/poet; creative
Bard, Bayrde

Bakari
(African) promising

Baker
(English) cook
Baiker, Baykar

Bal
(Hindi) strong

Bala
(Hindi) young

Baldemar
(Spanish) form of
Balthasar; brave and wise
Baldy

Balder
(Scandinavian) good prince
Baldur, Baudier

Baldev
(Hindi) strong God

Baldie
(German) nickname for
Baldwin; brave friend

Baldric
(German) leader
Baldrick, Baledric, Bauldric

Baldridge
(English) persuasive

Baldwin
(German) steadfast friend
Baldwinn, Baldwynn, Bally

Balendin
(Place name) Balen,
Belgium; sylvan

Baley
(American) form of Bailey
Baleye

Balfour
(Scottish) landowner
Balf, Balfore

Balfre
(Spanish) brave

Balin
(Hungarian) from Balint;
healthy

Ballance
(American) courageous
Balance, Ballans

Ballard
(German) brave
Ballerd

Balraj
(Hindi) strong king

Balthasar
(Greek) God save the king
Bath, Bathazar

Balu
(Hindi) young

Balwin
(Last name as first name)
friendly; brave
Ball, Winn

Banan
(Irish) white

Bancroft
(English) bean field;
gardener
Banc, Bankie, Bankroft

Bandy
(Origin unknown)
gregarious
Bandee, Bandi

Banks
(Last name as first name)
focused
Bank

Banning
(Irish) fair-haired
Bannie, Banny, Bannyng

Bao
(Chinese) prized boy

Baptist
(Latin) one who has been
baptized

Barak
(Hebrew) lightning; success
Barrak, Barack

Baram
(Hebrew) son of the people

Barclay
(Scottish) audacious man;
birch tree meadow
*Bar, Barclaye, Bark, Barklay,
Barky*

Bard
(Irish) singer
Bar, Barr

Barden
(English) peaceful; valley-
dweller
Bardon

Bardolf
(German) wily hero

Bardrick
(English) sings ballads
Bardric

Barend
(Scandinavian) bearlike

Bargo
(Last name as first name)
outspoken
Barg

Bark
(English) short for Barker;
outgoing
Birk

Barker
(English) handles bark;
lumberjack
Bark, Barkker

Barlow
(English) hardy
Barloe, Barlowe

Barman
(Last name as first name)
bright; blessed
Barr

Barn
(American) word as name; works in barns
Barnee, Barney, Barny

Barnabas
(Hebrew) seer; comforter
Barn, Barnaby, Barnebus, Barney, Barnie, Barny

Barnaby
(Hebrew) companionable
Barn, Barnabee, Barnabie, Barnie, Barny

Barner
(English) mercurial
Barn, Barnerr, Barney, Barny

Barnes
(English) powerful; bear

Barnett
(English) leader of men
Barn, Barnet, Barney

Barney
(English) short for Barnett
Barn, Barni, Barnie, Barny

Barnum
(German) safe; barn
Barnham, Barnhem, Barnie

Baron
(English) noble leader
Bare, Baren, Barren, Baryne

Barra
(Irish) fair-haired

Barrett
(German) strong and bearlike
Bar, Baret, Barett, Barette, Barry

Barrington
(English) dignified
Bare, Baring, Berrington

Barry
(Irish) candid
Barre, Barrie, Bary

Bart
(Hebrew) persistent
Bartee, Bartie, Barty

Bartley
(Last name as first name) rural man
Bart, Bartle, Bartlee, Bartli, Bartly

Barth
(Hebrew) protective
Bart, Barthe, Barts

Bartholomew
(Hebrew) friendly; earthy
Bart, Barthlolmewe, Bartie

Bartlett
(Last name as first name) motivated

Barto
(Spanish) form of Bartholomew; upward
Bartelo, Bartol, Bartoli, Bartolo, Bartolomeo

Barton
(English) persistent man; Bart's town
Bart, Barty

Bartram
(English) intelligent
Bart, Barty

Baruch
(Hebrew) most blessed
Barry

Baruti
(African) teaches

Basant
(Arabic) smiling

Basford
(American) charming; low-profile
Bas, Basferd, Basfor

Bash
(American) party-loving
Bashi, Bashey, Bashy

Basil
(Greek) regal
Basel, Basey, Basile, Bazil

Basim
(Arabic) smiles
Bassam

Basir
(Turkish) smart

Bass
(Last name as first name) fish; charmer
Bassee, Bassey, Bassi, Bassy

Bassett
(English) small man
Baset, Basett, Basey, Basse

Bastian
(Greek) respected
Bastien, Bastyun

Basye
(American) home-based; centered
Base, Basey

Batch
(French) short for bachelor; unmarried man
Bat, Bats, Batsh

Bates
(English) romantic
Bate

Baudoin
(Latin) winning

Baul
(Gypsy) slow-moving

Baurice
(African American) from Maurice; dark man

Bavol
(Gypsy) windblown

Baxley
(English) from the meadow; outdoorsy
Bax, Baxlee, Baxli

Baxter
(English) tenacious
Bax, Baxey, Baxie, Baxther

Bay
(English) hair of russet; vocal
Baye, Bayie

Bayard
(English) russet-haired
Bay, Baye, Bayerd

Baylon
(English) from the bay; outdoorsman

Bazzy
(American) loud
Bazzee, Bazzi, Bazzie

Bazooka
(American) fun-loving; unusual
Bazookah

Beacan
(Irish) small boy
Beag, Bec, Becan

Beach
(English) fun-loving
Bee, Beech

Beacher
(English) pale-skinned; beech tree
Beach, Beachie, Beachy, Beecher

Beagan
(Irish) small
Beagen, Beagin

Beale
(French) attractive
Beal, Beally

Beaman
(English) tends bees
Beamann, Beamen, Beeman

Beamer
(English) musician
Beam, Beamy, Beemer

Bean
(Scottish) lively
Beann

Beanon
(Irish) good boy
Beinean, Beineon, Binean

Bearach
(Irish) spearing
Bearchan, Bercnan, Bergin

Beasley
(English) nurturing; pea field
Beas, Beasie, Beesly

Beate
(German) serious
Bay, Baye, Bayahtah, Beahta, Beahtae

Beattie
(Irish) happy

Beau
(French) handsome man
Beaubeau, Bo, Boo, Bow

Beauford
(French) attractive
Beau, Beauf, Beaufort

Beaumont
(French) attractive and strong
Bo, Bomont, Bowmont, Beau

Beauregard
(French) a face much admired
Beau, Beauregarde, Beaurigard, Bobo

Beaver
(French) tenacious
Beav, Beever, Bevoh, Beave

Bebe
(Spanish) baby
Be-Be

Becher
(Hebrew) firstborn
Bee

Beck
(English) stream; laid-back
Bec, Becc, Becke, Becker, Bek

Becker
(English) calm
Bekker

Beckett
(English) methodical
Beck, Beket, Bekette

Bede
(English) prayerful
Bea, Bead, Beda, Bedah

Bedford
(Last name as first name) laid-back

Bedrich
(Czech) rules peacefully

Bedro
(Spanish) form of Pedro; surprising
Bed

Beebe
(English) tending bees; tenacious
B.B., Bee-be, Beebee

Beeson
(Last name as first name) son of beekeeper; wary
Bees

Beggs
(Last name as first name) admired
Begg, Begs

Beige
(American) calm
Bayge

Beinish
(Latin) from Benedict; blessed

Beircheart
(Welsh) spears

Bela
(Hawaiian) beauty

Belden
(English) plain-spoken
Beld, Beldene, Beldon, Bell, Bellden, Belldon

Belen
(Greek) following the arrow's straight path

Bell
(French) handsome man

Bellamy
(French) beautiful friend
Belamie, Bell, Bellamie, Bellmee, Belmy

Bellindo
(German) ferocious; attractive
Balindo, Belindo, Belyndo

Bello
(African) advocates Islam

Belmount
(French) gracious
Belmon, Belmond, Belmonde, Belmont, Belmonta

Belton
(English) from a lovely town of bells
Beltan, Belten

Belvin
(American) form of Melvin; attractive
Belven

Bem
(African) peaceful

Ben
(Hebrew) short for Benjamin; wonderful
Benjy, Bennie, Benno, Benny

Benaiah
(Hebrew) God-built; wars
Benaya, Benayahu

Bence
(American) short for Benson; good
Bens, Bense, Binse

Bend
(American) word as name; lithe

Bendell
(Last name used as first name) loving
Ben

Benedict
(Latin) blessed man
Ben, Benedik, Benne, Bennie, Benny

Bender
(American) tweaker; diplomatic
Ben, Bend

Bendo
(American) soothing
Ben, Bend

Benes
(Czech) blessed

Beniah
(Hebrew) articulate
Benia, Benyah

Benicio
(Spanish) adventurous
Benecio, Benito

Benito
(Italian) blessed
Benedo, Beni, Beno

Benjamin
(Hebrew) son of right hand; wonderful boy
Behnjamin, Ben, Benjamen, Benjamine, Benjie, Benjy, Benni, Bennie, Benny, Benyamin

Benjiro
(Japanese) promotes peace

Bennett
(French) blessed
Ben, Benet, Benett,
Bennett, Bennette, Benny

Benno
(Italian) form of Ben;
wonderful; best
Beno

Benny
(Hebrew) short for
Benjamin
Benge, Benjy, Benni, Bennie

Benoit
(French) growing and
flourishing
Ben, Benoyt

Benoni
(Hebrew) sorrow

Bensey
(American) easygoing; fine
Bence, Bens, Bensee

Benson
(Hebrew) son of Ben; brave
heart
Bensahn, Bensen

Bent
(English) short for Benton
Bynt

Bentley
(English) clever
Bent, Bentlee, Leye

Benton
(English) formidable
Bentan, Bentawn, Bentone

Benvenuto
(Italian) welcomed child
Ben

Benz
(German) from carmaker
Mercedes-Benz; upscale
Bens

Benzi
(Hebrew) blessed

Beowulf
(Literature) warrior

Ber
(Hebrew) bear

Berdy
(German) bright

Beresford
(English) place of spears
Berresford

Berfit
(Origin unknown) farming;
outdoorsman
Berf

Berg
(German) tall; mountain
Bergh, Berj, Burg, Burgh

Bergen
(Irish) little spear man
Bergin, Birgin

Berger
(French) watchful; shepherd
Bergher, Bergie

Bergin
(Swedish) loquacious; lives
on the hill
Bergan, Berge, Bergen,
Berger, Bergin, Birgin

Berk
(Turkish) rough-hewn

Berkeley
(English) idolized; (Place
name) town in California
Berk, Berkeley, Berki,
Berkie, Berklee, Berkley,
Berklie, Berkly, Berky

Berko
(Hebrew) bear
Ber

Berks
(American) adored
Berk, Berke, Berkelee,
Berkey, Berkli, Berksie,
Berkslee, Berky, Birklee,
Birksey, Burks, Burksey

Berman
(German) steady
Bermahn, Bermen, Bermin

Bernabe
(German) bold
Bernabee, Bernabey,
Bernaby, Bernby, Bernebe,
Berns, Bernus, Burnby

Bernal
(German) bearlike
Bern

Bernard
(German) brave and
dependable
Bern, Bernarde, Bernee,
Bernerd, Bernie, Berny,
Burnard

Bernardo
(Spanish) brave; bear
Berna, Bernardo,
Barnardoh, Berny

Bernave
(American) form of Bernard; smart
Bernav, Bernee, Berneve, Berni

Bernd
(German) bear-like
Bern, Berne, Bernee, Berney, Berny

Berne
(German) courageous
Bern, Berni, Bernie, Bernne, Berny

Bernie
(German) brave boy
Bern, Berni, Berny, Birnie, Burney

Berry
(English) botanical; flourishing

Bert
(English) shining example
Berti, Bertie, Berty, Birt, Burt

Berthold
(German) bold ruler
Bert, Berthol, Berthuld, Berty, Bertolt

Berthrand
(German) form of Bertram; strong; raven
Bert, Berthran, Bertie, Bertrand, Berty

Bertil
(Scandinavian) bright
Bertel

Bertin
(English) form of Burton; dramatic
Berton, Burtun

Bertoldo
(Spanish) ruler
Bert

Berton
(American) form of Burton; brave; dramatic
Bert, Bertan, Berty

Bertram
(German) outstanding
Bert, Bertie, Bertrem, Bertrom, Berty

Bertrand
(German) bright
Bert, Bertie, Bertran, Bertrund, Birtryn

Berty
(English) form of Bert; shining
Bert, Bertie, Burty

Bervick
(American) upwardly mobile; brave
Bervey

Berwyn
(English) loyal friend
Berrie, Berwin, Berwynd, Berwynne

Besley
(Last name as first name) calm
Bes, Bez

Best
(American) word as name; quintessential man
Beste

Bethel
(Hebrew) loves the house of God
Bethell

Bettis
(American) vocal
Bettes, Bettus, Betus

Beuford
(Last name as first name) form of Buford; country boy
Beuf, Bu, Bueford

Beval
(Welsh) vivacious

Bevan
(Welsh) beguiling
Bev, Bevahn, Beven, Bevin

Bever
(English) form of Bevis; sophisticated

Beverly
(English) from a stream of beavers; natural

Bevil
(English) form of Bevis; dignified

Bevis
(French) strong-willed
Bev, Bevas, Beves, Bevvis, Bevys, Bevyss

Bexal
(American) studious
Bex, Bexlee, Bexly, Bexy

Bexley
(Place name) distinguished

Bhakati
(Hindi) devoted man

Bhanu
(Hindi) sun-loving

Bharat
(Hindi) fire

Bhaskar
(Hindi) shining

Biaggio
(Italian) stutters; unsure
Biage, Biagio

Bialas
(Polish) white-haired
Bialy

Bickford
(English) wields an ax; chops

Biffy
(American) popular
Bibbee, Biff

Bigram
(Origin unknown)
handsome
Bigraham, Bygram

Bijou
(French) jewel

Bilal
(Arabic) selected one

Bill
(German) short for William;
strong; resolute
Billi, Billie, Billy

Billings
(Place name) sophisticated

Billy
(German) short for William;
strong
Bilie, Bill, Billee, Billi, Billie,
Bily

Billybob
(American) combo of Billy
and Bob
B.B., Billibob, Billiebob,
BillyBob, Billy Bob

Billy-Dale
(American) from William
and Dale; countrified
Billidell, Billydale

Billyjoe
(American) combo of Billy
and Joe
Billiejoe, Billijo, Billjo,
BillyJoe

Billymack
(American) combo of Billy
and Mack
Billiemac, Billimac, Billy,
BillyMack, Mackie

Billyray
(American) combo of Billy
and Ray
Billirae, Billy Ray

Bing
(German) outgoing
Beng

Bingo
(American) spunky
Bengo, Bingoh

Binh
(Vietnamese) a part of the
whole

Binkie
(English) energetic
Bink, Binki, Binky

Birch
(English) white and shining;
birch tree
Berch, Bir, Burch

Bird
(American) soaring
Byrd

Biren
(American) form of Byron
Biran

Birger
(Scandinavian) helpful

Birkett
(English) living in birches;
calming
Birk, Birket, Birkie, Birkitt,
Burkett, Burkette, Burkitt

Birkey
(English) from the birch tree
isle
Birkee, Birkie, Birky

Birley
(English) outdoorsy;
meadow
Berl, Birl, Birlee, Birly

Birney
(English) single-minded;
island
Birne, Birni, Birny, Burney

Birtle
(English) from the hill of
birds; natural

Bish
(Hindi) universal

Bishamon
(Mythology) Japanese god
of war and luck

Bishop
(Greek) supervisor; serving
the bishop
Bish, Bishie, Bishoppe

Bix
(American) hip
Bicks, Bixe

Bjorn
(Swedish) athletic
Bjarn, Bjarne, Bjonie,
Bjorne, Bjorny

Black
(Scottish) dark
Blacke, Blackee, Blackie

Blackburn
(Scottish) lives by a brook; dark

Blade
(Spanish) prepared; knife
Bladie, Blayd

Blagden
(English) likes the dark valley

Blaine
(Irish) svelte
Blain, Blane, Blayne

Blair
(Irish) open
Blaire, Blare, Blayree

Blaise
(French) audacious
Blasé, Blayse, Blaze

Blake
(English) dark and handsome
Blaike, Blakey, Blakie

Blakeley
(English) outdoorsy; meadow
Blake, Blakelee, Blakely, Blakie

Blame
(American) sad
Blaim, Blaime

Blanchard
(Last name as first name) white
Blan

Blanco
(Spanish) light
Blancoh, Blonco, Blonko

Blanford
(English) from the gray ford
Blandford

Blank
(American) word as name; blank slate; open
Blanc

Blanket
(Invented) security
Blank, Blankee, Blankett, Blankey, Blankie, Blanky

Blanton
(English) mild-mannered
Blanten, Blantun

Blasio
(Spanish) stutterer
Blaseo, Blasios, Blaze

Blaze
(English and American) daring
Blaase, Blaise, Blazey, Blazie

Blazej
(Czech) stutters; insecure

Bleddyn
(Welsh) heroic

Bliss
(English) happy
Blice, Blyss

Blithe
(English) merry
Bly, Blye, Blythe

Blitzer
(German) adventurous
Blitz, Blitze

Blocker
(Last name as first name) block
Bloc, Block, Blok

Bloo
(American) zany

Blue
(Color name) hip
Bleu, Blu

Blye
(American) joyful
Blie

Bo
(Scandinavian) lively
Beau

Boat
(American) word as name; sea-loving
Bo

Boaz
(Hebrew) strong; swift
Bo, Boase, Boaze, Boz

Bob
(English) short for Robert; bright; outstanding
Bobbi, Bobbie, Bobby

Bobby
(English) short for Robert; bright; outstanding
Bob, Bobbie, Bobi

Bobbydee
(American) combo of Bobby and Dee; country boy
Bobbidee, Bobby D, Bobby Dee, Bobby-Dee

Bobbymack
(American) combo of Bobby and Mack; jovial
Bobbimac, Bobbymac, Bobby-Mack

Bobby-Wayne
(American) combo of Bobby and Wayne; small-town boy
Bob, Bobbiwayne, Bobbi-Wayne, Bobby, Bobby Wayne, Bobbywayne, Wain, Wayne

Bobo
(African) Tuesday-born

Bodaway
(Native American) fire maker

Boden
(French) communicator
Bodin, Bodun, Bowden

Bodhi
(Buddhist) founder of Ch'an Buddhism in China
Bodhee

Bodil
(Scandinavian) living

Bodua
(African) last one

Bogart
(German) bold, strong man
Bo, Bobo, Bogardte, Boge, Bogert, Bogey, Bogie

Bogdan
(Polish) God's gift

Bogdari
(Polish) gift from God
Bogdi

Boggle
(American) confusing
Bogg

Bogumil
(Polish) loves God

Bojan
(Czech) fighter

Bojesse
(American) comical
Boje, Bojee, Bojeesie, Bojess

Bola
(American) careful; bold
Bolah, Boli

Bolden
(American) bold man
Boldun

Boleslaw
(Polish) in glory
Boleslav

Bolin
(Last name as first name) bold
Bolen

Bolivar
(Spanish) aggressive
Bolley, Bollivar, Bolly

Bolley
(American) strong
Bolly

Bolton
(English) town of the bold

Bomani
(African) fighter
Boman

Bon
(French) good
Bonne

Bonar
(French) gentle
Bonarr, Bonnar, Bonner

Bonaventura
(Spanish) good fortune
Bona, Bonavento, Buenaventura, Buenaventure, Ventura

Bonaventure
(Latin) humble
Bonaventura, Bonnaventura, Buenaventure

Bond
(English) farmer; renegade
Bondee, Bondie, Bondy

Bongo
(American) type of drum; musical
Bong, Bongy

Boni
(Latin) fortunate
Bonne

Bonifacio
(Spanish) benefactor
Bona, Boni, Boniface

Bono
(Spanish) good
Bonno

Booker
(English) lover of books
Book, Booki, Bookie, Booky

Boone
(French) blessed; good
Boon, Boonie, Boony

Booth
(German) protective
Boot, Boothe, Boothie, Bootsie

Boots
(American) cowboy
Bootsey, Bootsie, Bootz

Booveeay
(Invented) form of Bouvier; elegant
Boo

Bordan
(English) secretive; of the boar
Borde, Bordee, Borden, Bordi, Bordie, Bordy

Border
(American) word as name; fair-minded; aggressive
Bord

Borg
(Scandinavian) fortified; castle
Borge, Borgh

Borges
(Last name as first name) labyrinthine

Boris
(Russian) combative
Boras, Bore, Bores

Bornami
(Asian) conflicted

Borr
(Russian) contentious

Bos
(English) woodsman
Boz

Boscoe
(English) woodsman

Boseda
(African) Sunday-born

Bosley
(English) thriving; grove
Bos, Boslee, Boslie, Bosly

Bost
(Place name) from Boston, Massachusetts; audacious
Bostt

Boston
(Place name) distinctive
Boss, Bost

Boswell
(English) well near woods; dignified
Bos, Bosswell, Boz, Bozwell

Botan
(Japanese) long-living

Botolf
(English) wolf; standoffish
Botof

Bour
(English) loves the stream

Bourbon
(Place name) jazzy
Borbon, Bourbonn, Bourbonne

Bourey
(Vietnamese) countryman

Bourne
(French) planner; boundary
Bourn, Bourney, Bournie, Byrn, Byrne, Byrnie

Bouvier
(French) elegant; sturdy; ox
Bouveah, Bouveay, Bouviay

Bowen
(Welsh) shy
Bowie, Bowin

Bowie
(Irish) brash; western
Booie, Bowen

Boyce
(French) defender
Boice, Boy, Boyce

Boyd
(Scottish) fair-haired
Boide, Boydie

Boyne
(Irish) cow; grows

Bovo
(Last name as first name) macho
Bovoh

Bowing
(Last name as first name) blond and young
Beau, Bo, Bow, Bowen

Bowman
(Last name as first name) young; archer
Bow

Bowry
(Irish) form of Bowie; able; young
Bowy

Boy
(American) boy child of the family

Boydine
(French) from the woods
Boyse

Boyer
(French) woodsman

Bozidar
(Polish) God's precious
Bovza, Bovzek

Brack
(English) from the plant bracken; fine
Bracke

Bracken
(English) plant name; debonair
Brack, Brackan, Brackin, Brackun

Brad
(English) short for Bradley;
expansive
Braddie, Braddy

Bradan
(English) open-minded
Braden, Bradin, Brady,
Bradyn, Braedyn, Braid

Bradford
(English) mediator
Brad, Brady

Bradley
(English) prosperous;
expansive
Brad, Bradie, Bradlee,
Bradlie, Bradly

Bradshaw
(English) broad-minded
Brad, Brad-Shaw, Bradshie

Brady
(Irish) high-spirited
Brade, Bradee, Bradey

Brahma
(Hindi) worshipful

Brain
(Invented) word as name;
brilliant
Brane

Brainard
(English) princely
Brainerd

Bram
(Hebrew) short for
Abraham; great father
Brahm, Bramm

Bran
(Irish) raven; blessed
Brann

Branch
(Latin) growing
Bran, Branche

Branco
(Last name as first name)
authentic
Brank, Branko

Brand
(English) fiery
Brandd, Brande, Brandy,
Brann

Brandeis
(Czech) has a charitable
nature

Brando
(American) talented
Brand

Brandon
(English) hill; high-spirited
Bradonn, Bran, Brandan,
Brandin, Branny

Brandt
(English) dignified
Bran, Brandtt, Brant

Brandy
(English) firebrand; bold;
brandy drink
Brand, Brandee, Brandey,
Brandi, Brandie

Brannon
(Irish) bright-minded
Bran, Brann, Brannen,
Branon

Branson
(English) persistent
Bran, Brans, Bransan,
Bransen

Brant
(English) hothead
Brandt

Brasil
(Irish) disagrees
Brazil, Breasal, Bresal

Brashier
(French) brash
Brashear, Brasheer

Bratcher
(Last name as first name)
aggressive
Bratch

Bratumil
(Polish) brother's love

Bravillo
(Spanish) brave
Braville

Bravo
(Italian) top-notch
Bravoh, Bravvo

Brawley
(English) meadow man

Braxton
(English) worldly
Brack, Brackston, Brax,
Braxsten, Braxt

Bray
(English) vocal
Brae

Brayan
(Origin unknown) to yell out
Brayen

Braydon
(English) effective
Braedan, Braedon, Brayden,
Braydun

Brecht
(Last name as first) playwright

Breck
(Irish) fair and freckled
Breckie, Breckle, Brek

Brede
(Scandinavian) glacier; cold heart

Breeahno
(Invented) form of Briano

Breeon
(American) strong

Breeson
(American) strong
Breece, Breese, Bresen

Breeze
(American) happy
Breese, Breez, Breezy

Brencis
(Russian) sad

Brendan
(Irish) armed
Brend, Brenden, Brendie, Brendin, Brendon

Brennan
(English) pensive
Bren, Brenn, Brennen, Brennon, Brenny

Brenson
(Last name as first name) disturbed; masculine
Brens, Brenz

Brent
(English) prepared; on the mountain
Bren, Brint

Brenton
(English) forward-thinking
Brent, Brenten, Brintin

Brett
(Scottish) man from Britain; innovative
Bret, Breton, Brette, Bretton, Britt

Brettson
(American) manly man; Briton
Brett

Brewster
(English) creative; brewer
Brew, Brewer

Breyen
(Irish) strong; aggressive
Brey, Breyan

Brian
(Irish) strong man of honor
Bri, Briann, Brien, Brienn, Bry, Bryan

Briander
(American) inquisitive; rider of waves

Briareus
(Mythology) giant with one hundred arms; strong

Brice
(Welsh) go-getter
Bryce

Brick
(English) alert; bridge
Bricke, Brik

Brickle
(American) surprising
Brick, Brickel, Brickell, Bricken, Brickton, Brickun, ·Brik

Bridgely
(English) coming from the bridge
Bridgeley

Bridger
(English) makes bridges
Bridge

Bridon
(English) bright-eyed

Brigdo
(American) leader
Brigg, Briggy

Brigham
(English) mediator
Brigg, Briggie, Briggs, Brighum

Brighton
(English) from the shining town

Briley
(English) calm
Bri, Brilee, Brilie, Brily

Brinley
(English) also Brinlee; of the joyful meadow; sweet
Brindley, Brinly, Brynley, Brynly

Briscoe
(Last name as first name) forceful
Brisco, Brisko, Briskoe

Brishen
(English) craftsman

Britt
(English) humorous; from Britain
Brit, Britts

Britton
(English) loyal; from Britain

Brock
(English) forceful
Broc, Brocke, Brockie, Brocky, Brok

Brockly
(English) place name; aggressive
Brocklee, Brockli, Broklee, Broklie, Brokly

Brockton
(English) badger; stuffy
Brock

Brod
(English) short for Broderick
Broddie, Broddy

Broder
(Scandinavian) true brother
Brolle, Bror

Broderick
(English) broad-minded; brother
Brod, Broddee, Broddie, Broddy, Broderic, Broderik, Brodric, Brodrick

Brodie
(Irish) builder
Brode, Brodee, Brody

Brodny
(Irish) falling aside; brash

Brogan
(Irish) sturdy shoe; dependable
Brogann

Bromley
(English) meadow of shrubs; unpredictable
Brom, Bromlee, Bromlie, Bromly

Bron
(Irish) sadness

Bronc
(Spanish) wild; horse
Bronco, Bronk, Bronko

Bronco
(Spanish) wild; spirited
Broncoh, Bronko, Bronnco

Brondo
(Last name as first name) macho
Bron, Brond

Brone
(Irish) sorrow

Bronson
(English) Brown's son
Bron, Brondson, Bronni, Bronnie, Bronny, Bronsan, Bronsen

Bronto
(American) short for brontosaurus; thunderous
Bront, Brontee, Brontey, Bronti, Bronty

Bronze
(Metal) alloy of tin and copper; brown
Bronz

Brook
(English) easygoing
Brooke, Brookee, Brookie

Brooks
(English) easygoing
Brookes, Brooky

Broughton
(English) from a protected place

Brow
(American) snob
Browy

Brown
(English) tan
Browne, Brownie, Browny

Brownie
(American) brown-haired
Brown

Bruce
(French) complicated; from a thicket of brushwood
Bru, Brucie, Brucy, Brue

Brumley
(French) smart; scattered
Brum

Bruno
(German) brown-skinned
Brune, Brunne, Brunoh

Brunon
(Polish) brown-haired

Bruiser
(American) tough guy
Bruezer, Bruser, Bruzer

Brush
(American) confident

Brutus
(Latin) aggressive; a bully

Bryan
(Irish) ethical; strong
Brye, Bryen

Bryant
(Irish) honest; strong
Bryan, Bryent

Bryce
(Welsh) spunky
Brice, Bry, Brye

Brychan
(Welsh) speckled

Brydon
(American) magnanimous
Bridon, Brydan, Bryden, Brydun

Bryn
(Welsh) hill-dweller

Brynmor
(Welsh) big hill

Bryson
(Welsh) Bryce's son; smart
Briceson, Bry, Bryse

Bryton
(Welsh) hill town

Bu
(Irish) winner; short for Buagh

Bubba
(German) a regular guy
Bub, Buba, Bubb, Bubbah

Buck
(English) studly; buck deer
Buckey, Buckie, Bucko, Bucky

Buckley
(English) outdoorsy; a meadow for deer
Buckey, Buckie, Bucklee, Bucklie, Bucks, Bucky

Bucko
(American) macho
Bukko

Bucky
(American) warm-hearted
Buck, Buckey, Buckie

Bud
(English) courier
Budd, Buddie, Buddy, Budi, Budster

Buddy
(American) courier
Bud, Buddi, Buddie, Budi

Budington
(English) awakened

Buell
(German) upward; hill
Bue

Buffalo
(American) tough-minded
Buff, Buffer, Buffy

Buford
(English) diligent
Bueford, Bufe, Buforde

Bulgara
(Slavic) hardworking
Bulgar, Bulgarah, Bulgaruh

Bulldog
(American) rough-and-tough
Bull, Dawg, Dog

Bullock
(Last name as first name) practical

Bumpus
(Last name as first name) humorous
Bump, Bumpey, Bumpy

Bunard
(English) good
Bunerd, Bunn

Bunyan
(English) good and burly
Bunyan, Bunyen

Buran
(American) complex
Burann, Burun

Burchard
(English) tree trunks; sturdy
Burckhardt, Burgard, Burgaud, Burkhart

Burditt
(Last name as first name) shy
Burdett, Burdette, Burdey

Burford
(Last name as first name) from the water

Burge
(English) form of Burgess; middle-class
Burges, Burgis, Burr

Burgess
(English) businessman
Berge, Burge, Burges, Burgiss

Burhan
(Last name as first name) complex

Burke
(German) fortified
Berk, Berke, Burk, Burkie

Burl
(German) homespun

Burley
(English) nature-lover; wooded meadow
Burl, Burlea, Burlee, Burli, Burly, Burr

Burnaby
(English) brook man

Burne
(English) lives by the brook
Bourn, Bourne, Burn, Byrn, Byrne, Byrnes

Burnell
(English) of the brook
Burnel

Burnett
(English) by the small brook
Burnet, Burnitt

Burnis
(English) by the brook
Burn, Burnes, Burney, Burr

Burr
(English) prickly; brusque
Burry

Burrick
(English) townsman
Bur, Burr, Burry

Burney
(English) loner; island
Burn, Burne, Burnie, Burny

Burris
(English) sophisticated; living in the town
Berris, Buris, Burr, Burres

Burt
(English) shining man
Bert, Bertee, Burtie, Burty

Burton
(English) protective; town that is well fortified
Burt, Burty, Brutie

Busby
(Scottish) artist; village
Busbee, Busbi, Buzbie, Buzz, Buzzie

Busher
(Last name as first name) bold
Bush

Buster
(American) fun
Bustah

Butcher
(English) worker
Butch, Butchy

Butler
(English) directing the house; handsome
Butler, Butlir, Butlyr, Buttler

Buxton
(Last name as first name) kind

Buzz
(Scottish) popular
Buzy, Buzzi, Buzzie, Buzzy

Byford
(English) leaving the cottage; forever young

Byorn
(American) form of Bjorn

Byram
(English) stealthy; yard that houses cattle
Bye, Byrem, Byrie, Byrim

Byrd
(English) birdlike
Bird

Byrne
(English) loner
Birn, Birne, Byrn, Byrni, Byrnie, Byrny

Byrnett
(Last name as first name) stable
Burn, Burnett, Burney, Burns, Byrne, Byrney

Byron
(English) reclusive; small cottage
Biron, Biryn, Bye, Byren, Byrom, Byrone, Byryn

Cab
(American) word as name
Cabby, Kab

Cabell
(Last name as first name) spontaneous

Cable
(French) rope-making boy; crafty
Cabel

Cabot
(French) loves the water
Cabbott

Cabrera
(Spanish) able
Cabrere

Cack
(American) laughing
Cackey, Cackie, Cacky, Cassy, Caz, Kass, Kassy, Khaki

Cactus
(Botanical) plant as name; prickly
Cack, Kactus

Cadby
(Norse) spirited heritage

Caddock
(Last name as first name) high spirits

Cade
(English) stylish; bold; round
Cadye, Kade

Cadel
(Welsh) fierce

Caden
(English) spirited
Cadan, Cade, Cadun, Caiden, Kaden, Kayden

Cadman
(Irish) fighter
Cadmann

Cadmar
(Greek) fiery
Cadmarr

Cadmus
(Greek) one who excels; prince
Cad, Cadmuss, Kadmus

Cady
(American) forthright
Cadee, Cadey, Cadie

Caesar
(Latin) focused leader
Caeser, Caez, Caezer, Cesaro, Cezar, Seezer

Cage
(American) dramatic
Cadge

Cailen
(American) gentle
Kail, Kailen, Kale

Cain
(Hebrew) aggressive
Caine, Cainen, Cane, Kain, Kane

Cairn
(Welsh) stone; sturdy
Cairne

Cal
(Latin) short for Calvin; kind
Callie, Kal

Calbert
(American) cowboy
Cal, Calbart, Calberte, Calburt, Callie, Colbert

Calder
(English) stream; flowing
Cald, Kalder

Calderon
(Spanish) stream; flowing
Cald, Kald, Kalder, Kalderon

Caldwell
(English) refreshing; cold well

Cale
(Hebrew) slim; good heart
Kale

Caleb
(Hebrew) faithful; brave
Cal, Calab, Cale, Caley, Calie, Calub, Kaleb

Calek
(American) fighter; loyal
Calec, Kalec, Kalek

Calen
(Irish) slim
Cailun

Caley
(Irish) slender

Calf
(American) cowboy
Kalf

Calhoun
(Irish) limited; from the narrow woods
Cal, Calhoon, Calhoune, Callie

Calixto
(Spanish) handsome
Calex, Calexto, Cali, Calisto, Calix, Callie, Cally, Kalixto

Callahan
(Irish) spiritual
Cal, Calahan, Calihan, Callie

Callie
(American) short for Calvin; kind
Cal, Calley, Calli, Cally

Callo
(American) attractive
Cal, Cally, Kallo

Cally
(Scottish) peacemaker

Calman
(Last name as first name) caring
Cal

Calum
(Irish, Scottish) peaceful; (American) calm
Cal, Callum, Calym, Calyme

Calvary
(American) word as name; herding all
Cal, Kal, Kalvary

Calvert
(English) respected; herding
Cal, Calber, Calbert, Calver, Kal, Kalvert

Calvin
(Latin) bold
Cal, Calvie, Kal

Cam
(Scottish) short for Cameron; loving
Camm, Cammey, Cammie, Cammy, Kam

Cambell
(American) form of Campbell; reliable; irregular mouth
Cam, Cambel, Cammy, Kambell

Camberg
(Last name as first name) valley man
Cam

Cambridge
(Place name) twisting; mover
Cambrydge

Camden
(Scottish) conflicted
Cam, Camdan, Camdon

Camerero
(Last name as first name) charismatic

Cameron
(Scottish) mischievous; crooked nose
Cam, Camaron, Camerohn, Cami, Cammy, Camren, Camron

Camilo
(Latin) helpful; (Italian) free
Cam, Camillo

Campbell
(Scottish) bountiful; crooked mouth
Cambell, Cammie, Camp, Campie, Campy

Camrin
(American) form of Cameron; kind

Camron
(Scottish) short for Cameron
Camren

Canaan
(Biblical) spiritual leanings
Cane, Kanaan, Kanan

Canal
(Word as name) waterway
Kanal

Candelario
(Spanish) bright and glowing
Cadelario

Cander
(American) candid
Can, Candor, Candy, Kan, Kander, Kandy

Candido
(Spanish) pure; candid
Can, Candi, Candide, Candy

Candle
(American) bright; hip
Candell

Cannon
(French) courageous
Canney, Canni, Cannie, Canny, Canon, Canyn, Kannon, Kanon

Canute
(Scandinavian) great
Knut, Knute

Canyon
(Nature) hip

Capote
(Italian) bright

Cappy
(French) breezy; lucky
Cappey, Cappi

Caractacus
(Latin) bold

Carad
(American) wily
Karad

Caravaggio
(Italian) painter

Card
(English) short for Carden; crafty
Kard

Cardan
(English) crafty; carder
Card, Cardon, Carden

Cardew
(Welsh) dark, sturdy

Cardwell
(English) craftsman
Kardwell

Carel
(Dutch) free

Carew
(Latin) runner
Carrew

Carey
(Welsh) masculine; by the castle
Care, Cari, Cary, Karey

Cari
(English) masculine
Care, Carie, Cary

Carino
(Last name as first name)
strong

Carl
(Swedish) kingly
Karl

Carlfred
(American) combo of Carl
and Fred; dignified
Carl-Fred, Carlfree

Carlin
(Irish) winning
*Carlan, Carle, Carlen, Carlie,
Carly*

Carlisle
(English) strengthens
Carl, Carly, Carlyle

Carlo
(Italian) sensual; manly
Carl, Carloh

Carlon
(Irish) form of Carl; winning
Karlon, Carlonn

Carlos
(Spanish) manly; sensual
Carl, Carlo

Carlson
(English) son of a manly
man
Carls, Carlsan, Carlsen

Carlton
(English) leader; town of
Carl
*Carleton, Carltan, Carlten,
Carltown, Carltynne*

Carmel
(Hebrew) growing; garden
Carmell, Karmel

Carmello
(Italian) flourishing
*Carm, Carmel, Carmelo,
Karmello*

Carmichael
(Scottish) bold; Michael's
follower
Car, Kar, Karmichael

Carmine
(Italian, Latin) dear song
*Carmane, Carmin, Carmyne,
Karmen, Karmine*

Carmody
(French) manly; adult
Carmodee

Carnell
(Irish) victor
*Car, Carny, Kar, Karnell,
Karney*

Carney
(Irish) winner
*Carn, Carnay Carnee,
Carnie, Carny*

Carol
(Irish) champion
Carroll, Carrol, Carroll

Carr
(Scandinavian) outdoorsy
Car, Kar

Carrew
(Latin) runner

Carrick
(Irish) lives on rocky place

Carroll
(German) masculine;
winner
*Carall, Care, Carell, Caroll,
Carrol, Carrolle, Carry, Caryl*

Carson
(English) confident
Carr, Cars, Carsan, Carsen

Carsten
(German) a Christian

Carswell
(English) diligent

Cart
(American) word as name;
practical
Cartee, Cartey, Kart

Carter
(English) insightful
Cart, Cartah, Cartie

Carland
(Last name as first name)
land of free men

Cartrell
(English) practical
*Car, Cartrelle, Cartrey,
Cartrie, Cartrill, Kar, Kartrel,
Kartrell*

Cartwright
(English) creative
*Cart, Cartright, Kart,
Kartwright*

Caruso
(Italian) musically inclined
Karuso

Carvell
(English) innovative
*Carvel, Carvelle, Carver,
Karvel*

Carver
(English) carver
Carve, Carvey, Karver, Karvey

Cary
(English) place name; pretty brook; charming
Carey

Casdeen
(American) assertive; ingenious
Kassdeen

Case
(Irish) highly esteemed
Casey

Casey
(Irish) courageous
Case, Casey, Casi, Casie, Kacie, Kacy, Kase, Kaysie

Cash
(Latin) conceited
Casha, Cashe, Cazh

Cashmere
(American) smooth; soft-spoken
Cash, Cashmeer, Cashmyre, Kashmere

Cashone
(American) cash-loving
Casho

Casiano
(Latin) empty

Casimir
(Polish) peace-loving
Casmer, Casmir

Casimiro
(Spanish) famous; aggressor
Casmiro, Kasimiro

Casper
(German) secretive
Caspar, Casper, Caspey, Caspi, Caspie, Cass

Caspian
(Place name) daring

Cass
(Irish) short for Cassidy; funny
Cash, Caz, Kass

Cassidy
(Irish) humorous
Casidy, Cass, Cassadie, Cassidee, Cassidie, Kasidy, Kass, Kassidy

Cassie
(Irish) short for Cassidy; clever
Casi, Cass, Cassy

Cassius
(Latin) protective
Cass, Casseus, Casshus

Cast
(Greek) form of Castor; fiery star
Casta, Caste, Kast

Castellan
(Spanish) adventurer

Casto
(Mythology) from Castor, a Gemini twin
Cass, Kasto

Castor
(Greek) eager protector
Cass, Caster, Castie

Castulo
(Spanish) aggressor
Castu, Kastulo

Cata
(American) form of Catarino

Cathal
(Irish) leader

Cathmor
(Irish) brave warrior

Cato
(Latin) zany and bright
Catoe, Kato

Catarino
(Spanish) unflawed; perfect
Catrino

Cavan
(Irish) attractive man
Cavahn, Caven, Cavin

Cavance
(Irish) handsome
Caeven, Cavanse, Kaeven, Kavance

Cavell
(Last name as first name) opinionated
Cavil, Cavill

Cawley
(Last name as first name) brash

Cayce
(American) form of Casey; brave
Cace, Case, Kayce

Cayetano
(Spanish) feisty

Caynce
(Invented) form of Cayce; daring
Caincy, Cainse, Kaynse

Cazare
(Last name as first name)
daring
Cazares

Cecil
(Latin) unseeing; hard-
headed; blind
*Cece, Cecel, Cecile, Cecilio,
Cicile*

Cedar
(Botanical) tree name;
sturdy
Ced, Sed, Sedar

Cedric
(English) leader
Ced, Ceda, Cedrick

Ceferino
(Spanish) careful

Celedonio
(Spanish) heavenly

Celso
(Italian) heavenly
*Celesteno, Celestino,
Celesto, Celestyno, Celsus,
Selso*

Celumiel
(Spanish) of the heavens
Celu

Centola
(Spanish) tenth child
Cento

Century
(Invented) remarkable
Cen, Cent

Cerf
(French) buck

Cerone
(French) serene; creative
Serone

Cervantes
(Literature, Spanish)
original
Cervantez

Cesar
(Spanish) leader
Cesare, Cezar, Zarr

Chad
(English) firebrand
Chadd, Chaddy

Chadburn
(English) spirited

Chadwick
(English) warrior
Chad, Chadwyck

Chaffee
(Last name as first name)
bold adventurer

Chaggy
(American) cocky
Chagg, Shagg, Shaggy

Chaika
(Hebrew) life
*Chaikeh, Chaikel, Chaiki,
Chai*

Chaim
(Hebrew) life
*Chai, Chayim, Haim, Hy,
Hyman, Hymie, Khaim,
Manny*

Chaise
(French) chases
Chayse

Challen
(American) variant of Allen;
well-liked

Chalmer
(Scottish) the lord's son
Chall, Chally, Chalmers

Chalmers
(French) chambers;
surrounded
Chalm

Chamblin
(American) easygoing
Cham

Chan
(Chinese) bright;
(Vietnamese) truthful

Chanan
(Hebrew) filled with God's
compassion

Chanina
(Hebrew) compassionate by
virtue of God

Chance
(English) good fortune;
happy
*Chancey, Chanci, Chancy,
Chanse, Chanz, Chauncey*

Chancellor
(English) book keeper
Chance, Chancey

Chandell
(African American)
innovator
*Chandelle, Chandey,
Chandie, Shandel, Shandell*

Chandler
(English) ingenious;
(French) maker of candles
Chand, Chandey, Chandlor

Chaney
(French) strong
*Chane, Chanie, Chayne,
Chaynee*

Chang
(Chinese) free; flowing

Channing
(English) brilliant
Chann, Channy

Chanoch
(Hebrew) dedicated; loyal

Chason
(French) hunts
Chansen

Chante
(French) singer
Chant, Chanta, Chantay, Chantie

Chapa
(Last name as first name) merchant; spirited
Chap, Chappy

Chaparro
(Spanish) from chaparral (southern landscape); cowboy
Chap, Chaps

Chapell
(Hindi) spiritual

Chapen
(French) clergyman
Chapin, Chapland, Chaplin

Chapman
(English) businessman
Chap, Chappy

Charilaos
(Greek) giving

Charles
(German) manly; well-loved
Charl, Charley, Charli, Charlie, Charly, Chas, Chaz, Chazz, Chuck

Charleston
(Place name) Charles's town; confident
Charlesten

Charles-Wesley
(German) combo of Charles and Wesley; strong and sensitive
Charles Wes, Charles Wesley

Charlie
(German) manly
Charl, Charley, Charli, Charly

Charlton
(English) leader
Charles, Charley, Charlie, Charlt

Charome
(American) masculine
Char, Charoam, Charom, Charrone, Charry

Charon
(Greek) mythological ferryman of the underworld

Charro
(Spanish) wild-spirited cowboy
Charo, Charroh

Chas
(American) short for Charles; happy boy

Chase
(French) hunter
Chace, Chass

Chaskel
(Hebrew) strong

Chat
(American) happy
Chatt

Chatham
(Last name as first name) serious

Chatwin
(Last name as first name) thoughtful

Chaucer
(Literature, English) distinguished
Chauce, Chauser

Chauncey
(English) fair-minded
Chance, Chancey, Chanse, Chaunce

Chavakuk
(Hindi) from Charvaka; jaded

Chavivi
(Hebrew) beloved

Chayne
(Scottish) swagger
Chane, Channe, Chay

Chaz
(German) short for Charles; manly
Chas, Chazz, Chazzie, Chazzy

Ché
(Spanish) short for José; aggressive
Chay, Shae, Shay

Chee
(American) high-energy
Che

Chekhov
(Russian) playwright; genius

Chen
(Chinese) great

Cheney
(French) outdoorsman
Chenay, Cheney

Cheramy
(American) form of Jeremy; excitable
Cheramee, Charamie, Chermy

Chermon
(French) my dear

Chesley
(American) patient
Ches, Cheslee, Chez, Chezlee

Chester
(English) comfy-cozy
Ches, Chessie, Chessy

Chet
(English) creative
Chett

Chetwin
(English) winding road

Chevalier
(French) gallant
Chev, Chevy

Chevalle
(French) dignified
Chev, Chevi, Chevy

Cheven
(Invented) playful
Chevy

Chevery
(French) from Chevy; elegant
Chev, Shevery

Cheves
(American) from liquor name Chivas; jaded
Chevez, Shevas

Chevy
(French) clever
Chev, Chevi, Chevie, Chevv

Chew
(Chinese) mountain

Chiamaka
(African) God is good

Chibale
(Hebrew) loving

Chick
(English) short for Charles; friendly
Chic, Chickie, Chicky

Chico
(Spanish) boy
Chicoh, Chiko

Chiel
(Hebrew) God lives

Chijoke
(African) talented

Chikosi
(African) the ruins

Chili
(American) appetite for hot food

Chilton
(English) serene; farm
Chill, Chillton, Chilly, Chilt

Chimanga
(African) grain

Chin
(Korean) precious boy

Chip
(English) chip off the old block; like father, like son
Chipp, Chipper

Chiram
(Hebrew) held in high esteem

Chisholm
(Place name) Chisholm Trail; pioneer spirit
Chis, Chishom, Chiz

Chiura
(Italian) light; textured

Chiztam
(Hebrew) imbued with God's strength

Chovev
(Hebrew) companion, admirer

Chow
(Chinese) everywhere

Chris
(Greek) short for Christopher; close to Christ
Cris, Chrissy, Chrys

Christer
(Norwegian) religious
Krister

Christian
(Latin) follower of Christ
Chris, Christen, Christiane, Christyan, Cristian, Kris, Krist, Kristian

Christodoulous
(Greek) filled with sweet love for Christ

Christophe
(French) beloved of Christ
Cristoph, Kristophe

Christopher
(Greek) the bearer of Christ
Chris, Christofer, Crista, Cristopher, Cristos, Kit, Kristopher

Christopherson
(English) son of Christopher; religious
Christophersen, Cristophersen, Cristopherson

Christos
(Greek) form of Christopher
Chris, Kristos

Chito
(American) fast-food eater; hungry
Cheetoh, Chitoh

Choicey
(American) word name; picky
Choicie, Choisie

Chonito
(Spanish) friend
Chonit, Chono

Chopo
(American) cowhand
Chop, Choppy

Choto
(Spanish) kid
Shoto

Chotto
(Last name as first name) child

Chubby
(American) oversized
Chubbee, Chubbey, Chubbi, Chubbie

Chuck
(German) rash
Chuckee, Chuckey, Chuckie, Chucky

Chucky
(German) impulsive
Chuckey, Chucki, Chuckie

Chuhei
(Japanese) shy

Chuna
(Hebrew) warm

Chuneh
(Hebrew) with the Lord's grace

Chunky
(American) word name; large
Chunk, Chunkey, Chunki

Churchill
(English) bright
Church

Chutar
(Spanish) aiming for goals
Chuter

Cian
(Irish) old soul

Cicero
(Latin) strong speaker
Cice

Cicil
(English) shy
Cecil, Cice

Cid
(Spanish) leader; lord
Ciddie, Ciddy, Cyd, Sid

Cimarron
(Place name) cowboy
Cimaronn

Cinco
(Spanish) fifth child
Cinko, Sinko

Ciprian
(Latin) from the island of Cyprus
Cipriano

Ciriaco
(Italian) lordly

Cirill
(English) form of Cyril; lord

Cirillo
(Spanish) lordly
Cirilo

Ciro
(Italian) lordly
Ciroh, Cirro, Cyro

Cirrus
(Latin) thoughtful; cloud formation
Cerrus, Cirrey, Cirri, Cirrie, Cirry, Cirus, Serrus, Serus

Cisco
(American) clever
Sisco, Sysco

Citronella
(American) oil from fragrant grass; pungent
Cit, Citro, Cytronella, Sitronella

Civille
(American) form of place name Seville

Claiborn
(English) born of earth
Claiborne

Clance
(Irish) form of Clancy; redhead; aggressive
Clancy, Clanse, Klance, Klancy

Clair
(English) renowned
Claire, Clare

Clancy
(Irish) lively; feisty redhead
Clance, Clancey, Clancie

Claran
(Latin) bright
Clarance, Claransi, Claranse, Clare, Claren, Clarence, Clary, Klarense

Clarence
(Latin) intelligent
Clarance, Clare, Clarens, Clarense, Clarons, Claronz, Clarrence, Klarence, Klarens

Clarinett
(Invented) plays the clarinet
Clare, Clarinet, Clary, Klare, Klari

Clark
(French) personable; scholar
Clarke

Claude
(Latin) slow-moving; lame
Claud, Claudey, Claudie, Claudy, Klaud, Klaude

Claus
(Greek) victorious
Klaas, Klaus

Claven
(English) endorsed
Klaven

Clavero
(Spanish) lame

Clawdell
(American) form of Claudell
Clawd

Claxton
(English) townie
Clax, Klax

Clay
(English) firm; short for Claybrook and Clayton; reliable
Claye, Klae, Klay

Claybey
(American) southern; earthly
Claybie, Klaybee

Clayborne
(English) earthly
Clabi, Claybie, Claybourne, Clayborn, Klay

Claybrook
(English) sparkling smile
Claibrook, Clay, Claybrooke, Clayie

Clayton
(English) stodgy
Clay, Claytan, Clayten

Cleary
(Irish) smart
Clear, Clearey, Clearie

Cleavon
(English) daring
Cheavaughn, Cleavaughn, Cleave, Cleevaughan, Cleevon

Clem
(Latin) casual
Cleme, Clemmey, Clemmie, Clemmy, Clim

Clement
(Scottish) gentle
Clem, Clemmyl

Clemente
(Spanish) pleasant
Clemen, Clementay

Clements
(Latin) forgiving man
Clem, Clement, Clemmants, Clemment

Clemer
(Latin) mild
Clemmie, Clemmy, Klemer, Klemmie, Klemmye

Clemmie
(Latin) mild
Clem, Klem, Klemmee, Klemmy

Clenzy
(Spanish) forgiving; cleansed
Clense, Clensy, Klenzy

Cleofas
(African American) brave lion

Cleopatrick
(African American) combo of Cleopatra and Patrick
Cleo, Cleopat, Kleo, Kleopatrick, Pat, Patrick

Cleophas
(Greek) seeing glory; known
Cle, Cleofus, Cleoph, Klee, Kleofus, Kleophus

Cleon
(Greek) famed man
Clee, Cleone, Kleon

Clete
(Greek) from Cletus; wanted
Cleet, Cleete

Cletus
(Greek) creative; selected
Clede, Cledus, Cletis

Cleve
(English) precarious
Clive

Cleveland
(English) daring
Cleavelan, Cleve, Clevon, Clevy, Cliveland

Clevis
(Greek) prolific
Cleviss, Clevys, Clevyss

Cliff
(English) short for Clifford; dashing
Clif, Cliffey, Cliffie, Cliffy

Clifford
(English) dashing
Cleford, Cliff, Cliffy, Clyford

Clift
(American) cliff-dweller
Clifte

Clifton
(English) risk-taker
Cliff, Clifftan, Clifften, Cliffy

Cline
(Last name as first name) musical

Clint
(English) short for Clinton; bright
Clent, Clynt, Klint

Clinton
(English) curious; bright; cliff in town
Clenton, Clint, Clinten, Clynton, Klinten, Klinton

Clive
(English) daring; living near a cliff
Cleve, Clyve

Clooney
(American) dramatic
Cloone, Cloonie, Cloony, Clune, Cluney, Clunie, Cluny

Clotaire
(French) famous
Clotie, Klotair, Klotie

Clovis
(German) famed warrior
Clove, Cloves, Clovus, Klove, Kloves, Klovis

Cloyd
(American) form of Floyd; cloying
Cloy, Cloye, Kloy, Kloyd

Clske
(Dutch) dark

Cluny
(American) dramatic

Clwe
(Dutch) face of a mountain

Clyde
(Welsh) adventurer
Clide, Clydey, Clydie, Clydy, Clye, Klyde, Klye

Clydell
(American) countrified
Clidell, Clydel

Clydenestra
(Spanish) form of Clyde
Clyde

Coal
(American) word as a name
Coale, Koal

Cobb
(English) cozy
Cob, Cobbe

Coben
(Last name as first name) creative
Cob, Cobb, Cobe, Cobee, Cobey, Cobi, Coby, Kob, Kobee, Koben, Kobi, Koby

Coby
(American) friendly
Cob, Cobe, Cobey, Cobie

Coca
(American) excitable
Coka, Cokey, Cokie, Koca, Koka

Cochise
(Native American) warrior
Cocheece, Cochize

Cocinero
(Italian) slippery

Coco
(French) brash
Coko, Koko

Cody
(English) comforting
Coday, Code, Codee, Codey, Codi, Codie

Cog
(American) short for Cogdell; necessary
Kog

Cogdell
(Last name as first name) needed
Cogdale

Cohn
(American) winner
Kohn

Cokie
(American) bright
Cokey, Coki, Cokie, Cokki, Kokie

Colbert
(English) cool and calm
Colbey, Colbi, Colbie, Colburt, Colby, Cole

Colborn
(English) intimidating; cold brook
Colbey, Colborne, Colburn, Colby, Cole

Colby
(English) bright; secretive; dark farm
Colbey, Colbi, Colbie, Cole, Colie

Colden
(English) haunting
Coldan, Coldun, Cole

Cole
(Greek) lively; winner
Coal, Coley, Colie, Kohl, Kole

Coleman
(English) lively; peacemaker
Cole, Colemann, Colman, Kohlman

Colgate
(English) passway
Colgait, Colgaite, Kolgate

Colier
(Last name as first name) sophisticated

Colin
(Irish) young and quiet; peaceful; the people's victor
Colan, Cole, Colen, Collin, Collyn

Colis
(English) he who delights others

Colley
(English) dark-haired
Col, Colli, Collie

Collier
(English) hard-working; miner
Colier, Collie, Colly, Colyer

Collin
(Scottish) shy
Collen, Collie, Collon, Colly

Collins
(Irish) shy; holly
Collens, Collie, Collons, Colly, Kolly

Colm
(Irish) dove; peaceful

Colorado
(Place name) state; outdoorsy

Colson
(English) precocious; son of Nicholas
Cole, Colsan, Colsen

Colt
(English) frisky; horse trainer
Colty, Kolt, Koltt

Colten
(English) dark town; mysterious
Cole, Collton, Colt, Coltan, Coltawn, Colton, Kol

Colter
(English) keeping the colts
Colt, Coltor, Colty

Colum
(Latin) peaceful; dove
Colm, Kolm, Kolum

Columbus
(Latin) peaceful (discovered America)
Colom, Colombo, Columbe

Colwen
(Irish) peaceful
Colwin, Colvin

Comanche
(Native American) tribe; wild-spirited; industrious
Comanch, Komanche

Commodore
(French) commander

Como
(Place name) handsome
Comoh

Comus
(Greek) humorous
Comes, Comas, Commus, Komus

Conall
(Scottish) highly regarded
Conal

Conan
(Irish) worthy of praise
Conen, Connie, Conny, Conon

Conant
(Irish) top-notch
Conent, Connant

Concord
(English) agreeable
Con, Concor, Conny, Koncord, Konny

Conde
(Last name as first name)
driven

Cong
(Chinese) bright

Coniah
(Irish) pure
Conias, Conah

Conlan
(Irish) winner
Con, Conland, Conlen, Conleth, Conlin, Connie, Conny

Conk
(Invented) from conch (mollusk of the ocean); jazzy
Conch, Conkee, Conkee, Conkey, Conky, Konk, Kanch, Konkey, Konkey

Connaughton
(American) sapient

Connell
(Irish) strong
Con, Conal, Connall, Connel, Connelle, Connie, Conny

Connery
(Scottish) daring
Con, Conery, Connarie, Connary, Connie, Conny

Connie
(Irish) short for Connor
Connery, Conrad, Con, Conn, Connee, Conney, Conni, Conny

Connor
(Scottish) brilliant
Con, Conn, Conner, Conor, Kon, Konnor

Conrad
(German) optimist
Con, Connie, Conny, Conrade, Konrad

Conrado
(Spanish) bright advisor
Conrad, Conrod, Conrodo

Conridge
(Last name as first name) advisor
Con, Conni, Connie, Conny, Ridge

Conroy
(Irish) wise writer
Conrie, Conroye, Conry, Roy, Roye

Constant
(French) devotee; loyal

Constantine
(Latin) consistent
Con, Conn, Consta, Constance, Constant, Constantin Constantyne, Konstantin

Conway
(Irish) vigilant
Con, Connie, Kon, Konway

Cooke
(Latin) cook
Cook, Cookie, Cooky

Coolidge
(Last name as first name) wary
Cooledge

Cooney
(Last name as first name) giving

Cooper
(English) handsome; maker of barrels
Coup, Couper, Koop, Kooper, Kouper

Cope
(English) able
Cape

Corbell
(Latin) raven; dark
Corbel

Corbet
(Latin) dark
Corb, Corbett, Corbit, Corbitt, Korb, Korbet

Corbin
(Latin) dark and brooding
Corban, Corben, Corby

Corbitt
(Last name as first name) brooding
Corbet, Corbett, Corbie, Corbit, Corby

Corby
(Latin) dark
Corbey, Korbee, Korby, Korry

Corcoran
(Irish) ruddy-skinned
Corkie, Corky

Cord
(Origin unknown) soap opera hunk
Corde, Kord

Cordaro
(Italian) roped

Cordel
(French) practical
Cordel, Cordell, Cordelle, Cordie, Cordill, Cordy

Cordell
(Latin) bound; rope

Cordero
(Spanish) gentle
Cordara, Cordaro, Cordarro, Kordarro, Kordero

Corey
(Irish) laughing
Core, Corie, Corry, Cory, Korey, Korrie, Kory

Corin
(Latin) combative
Coren, Dorrin, Koren, Korrin

Cork
(Place name) city in Ireland
Corkee, Corkey, Corki, Corky, Kork

Corky
(American) casual
Corkee, Corkey, Korky

Corlon
(American) tasteful

Cormac
(Irish) the raven's offspring; watchful
Cormack, Cormak

Cormick
(Last name as first name) old-fashioned
Cormac, Cormack

Corn
(Latin) form of Cornelius; horn; yellow-haired
Korn

Cornall
(Irish) from Cornelius; horn; loquacious

Cornelio
(Spanish) hornblower

Cornelius
(Greek) a temptation
Coarn, Conny, Corn, Corni, Cornie, Corny, Kornelius, Neel, Neely, Neil, Neiley

Cornell
(French) fair
Corne, Cornelle, Corny, Kornell

Corodon
(Greek) lark

Corrado
(Italian) worthy advisor

Corrigan
(Irish) aggressive
Coregan, Corie, Correghan, Corrie, Corry, Koregan, Korrigan

Cort
(German) eloquent
Corte, Court, Kort

Cortazar
(Last name as first) creative

Cortez
(Spanish) victorious; explorer
Cortes

Corvin
(English) friend
Corwin, Corwynn, Korry, Korvin

Corwin
(English) heart's delight
Corrie, Corry, Corwan, Corwann, Corwyn, Corwynne

Cory
(Latin) humorous
Coarie, Core, Corey, Corrie, Kohry, Kori

Coryell
(Greek) lark; devious

Cosell
(French) outgoing

Cosgrove
(Irish) winner
Cosgrave, Cossy, Kosgrove, Kossy

Cosma
(Greek) universal
Cos, Kosma

Cosmas
(Greek) universal
Cos, Kosmas, Koz

Cosmo
(Greek) in harmony with life
Cos, Cosimo, Cosimon, Cosme, Cosmos, Kosmo

Cosner
(English) organized; handsome
Cosnar, Kosner

Costas
(Greek) constant
Costa, Costah

Cotton
(Botanical name) casual
Cottan

Coty
(French) comforter
Cotey, Coti, Cotie, Koty

Coug
(American) short for cougar; fierce
Cougar, Koug, Kougar

Coulter
(English) dealing in colts;
horseman
Colter, Coult, Kolter, Koulter

Counsel
(Latin) advisor
*Consel, Council, Kounse,
Kounsell*

Country
(Word as name) cowboy

Court
(English) royal

Courtland
(English) born in the land of
the court; dignitary

Courtnay
(English) sophisticated
*Cort, Corteney, Court,
Courtney, Courtny*

Covell
(English) warm
Covele, Covelle

Covet
(American) word as name;
desires
Covett, Covette, Kovet

Covington
(English) distinctive
*Covey, Coving, Kovey,
Kovington*

Cowan
(Irish) cozy
Cowen, Cowie, Cowy

Cowboy
(American) western

Cowell
(English) brash; frank
Kowell

Cowey
(Irish) reclusive
Cowee, Cowie, Kowey

Coye
(English) outdoorsman
Coy, Coyey, Coyie

Coyle
(English) in the woods

Coylie
(American) coy
Coyl, Koyl, Koylie

Coystal
(American) bashful
Coy, Koy, Koystal

Crad
(American) practical
Cradd, Krad, Kradd

Craddock
(Last name as first name)
practical

Crago
(Last name as first name)
macho
Crag, Craggy, Krago

Craig
(Irish) brave climber
*Crai, Craigie, Cray, Craye,
Crayg, Creg, Cregge, Kraig*

Crandal
(English) open
*Cran, Crandall, Crandell,
Crane*

Crandale
(English) from the land of
cranes
Crandall, Crandell

Cranley
(English) lives in a field of
cranes

Cranston
(English) from the town of
cranes

Crawford
(English) flowing
Crafe, Craford, Craw, Fordy

Crayton
(English) substantial
Craeton, Cray, Creighton

Creed
(American) believer
Crede, Creede, Creyd, Kreed

Creighton
(English) sophisticated
Criton

Crenshaw
(Last name as first name)
good intentions

Crescin
(Latin) expansive

Crey
(English) short for
Creighton; slight
Craedie, Cray, Creigh, Creydie

Creshaun
(African American) inspired
Creshawn, Kreshaun

Cresp
(Latin) man with curls
*Crisp, Crispen, Crispun,
Crispy, Cryspin, Kresp,
Krisp, Krispin, Krispyn*

Crew
(American) word as name;
sailor
Krew

Cris
(Welsh) short for Crisiant;
crystal-like

Crisanto
(Spanish) anoint

Crisoforo
(Spanish) bearing Christ;
form of Christopher

Crispin
(Latin) man with curls
*Chrispy, Crespen, Crispo,
Crispy, Krispin, Krispo*

Crispo
(Latin) curly-haired
Crisp, Krispo

Crist
(Spanish) Christian

Cristo
(Place name, Spanish) from
Count of Monte Cristo
Kristo

Cristian
(Greek) form of Christian
Kristian

Cristobal
(Spanish) bearing Christ

Criten
(American) shortened
version of Critendon;
faultfinding
Critan, Kriten

Critendon
(Last name as first name)
critical
Crit, Criten, Krit, Kritendon

Crofton
(Irish) comforter
Croft, Croften

Crompton
(Last name as first name)
giving

Cromwell
(Irish) giving
Chromwell, Crom, Crommie

Cronus
(Greek) reigning

Crosby
(Irish) easygoing
*Crosbee, Crosbie, Cross,
Krosbie, Krosby*

Croston
(English) by the cross
Cro, Croton, Kroston

Cruze
(Spanish) cross
Cruise, Cruse, Kruise, Kruze

Csaba
(Hungarian) shepherd

Ctirad
(Czech) long-suffering

Cuba
(Place name) distinctive;
spicy
Cubah, Cueba, Kueba, Kuba

Cubbenah
(Jamaican) Wednesday

Cuchulain
Cuchulainn, Cu Chulainn

Cucuta
(Place name) city in North
Colombia; sharp
Cucu

Cudjo
(Jamaican) Monday

Cuernavaca
(Place name) city in Mexico;
cowhorn
Vaca

Cuffy
(Jamaican) Friday
Cuffee, Cuffey

Cuke
(American) zany
Kook, Kooky, Kuke

Culbert
(Last name as first name)
practical

Culkin
(American) child actor
Culki, Kulkin

Cull
(American) selective
Cullee, Cullie, Cully, Kulley

Cullen
(Irish) attractive
*Culen, Cull, Cullan, Cullen,
Cullie, Cully, Kullen, Kully*

Culley
(Irish) secretive
Cull, Cullie, Cully, Kull, Kully

Culver
(English) peaceful
*Colver, Cull, Culley, Culli,
Cully*

Culverado
(American) peaceful
*Cull, Cullan, Culver, Culvey,
Kull*

Cummings
(Literature) poetic; creative
Cumming, Kummings

Cuney
(Last name as first name)
serious
Cune, Kune, Kuney

Cunning
(Irish) from surname Cunningham; wholesome
Cuning

Cunningham
(Irish) milk-pail town; practical
Cuningham

Curb
(American) word as a name; dynamic
Kurb

Curbey
(American) form of Kirby; high-energy
Curby

Curley
(American) cowboy
Curly, Kurly

Curran
(Irish) smiling hero
Curan, Curr, Curren, Currey, Currie, Curt

Currey
(English) messenger; calm

Currie
(English) messenger; courteous
Kurrie

Curt
(French) short for Curtis; kind
Kurt

Curtis
(French) gracious; kind-hearted
Curdi, Curdis, Curt, Curtey, Curtice, Curtie, Curtiss, Curty, Kurt

Custer
(Last name as first name) watchful; stubborn
Cust, Kust, Kuster

Cuthbert
(English) intelligent

Cutler
(English) wily
Cutlar, Cutlur, Cuttie, Cutty

Cutsy
(English) from Cutler; knife-man
Cutlar, Cutler, Cuttie, Cutty, Kutsee, Kutsi, Kutsy

Cutter
(English) man who cuts gemstones

Cuttino
(African American) athletic
Kuttino

Cuyler
(American) form of Schuyler; protective
Kuyler

Cy
(Greek) shining example
Cye, Si

Cyler
(Irish) protective chapel
Cuyler, Cyle

Cyll
(American) bright
Syll, Cyl

Cynric
(Greek) thorn

Cyprien
(French) religious
Cyp, Cyprian

Cyprus
(Place name) outgoing

Cyrano
(Greek) shy heart
Cyranoh, Cyre, Cyrie, Cyrno, Cyry

Cyril
(Greek) regal
Ciril, Cyral, Cyrell, Cyrille

Cyrus
(Persian) sunny
Cye, Syrus

Cyrx
(American) conniving
Cyrxie

Czeslaw
(Polish) honorable
Slav, Slavek

Dabney
(Place name) careful; funny
Dab, Dabnee, Dabnie, Dabny

Dacey
(Irish) southerner
Dace, Dacian, Dacius, Dacy, Daicey, Daicy

Dacias
(Latin) brash
Dace, Daceas, Dacey, Dacy, Dayce, Daycie

Dada
(African) curly-haired

Dade
(Place name) county in Florida; renegade
Daide, Dayde

Daedalus
(Greek) father of Icarus; inventor
Daidalos, Dedalus

Dag
(Scandinavian) sunny
Dagg, Dagget, Daggett, Dagny

Dagan
(Hebrew) earthy
Dagon

Daggan
(Scandinavian) day

Dagny
(Scandinavian) day
Dag

Dagoberto
(Spanish) day
Dagbert, Dagobert

Dagwood
(English) comic
Dag, Dawood, Woody

Dahy
(Irish) lithe
Dahey

Dai
(Japanese) great man

Dailey
(English) from Dale; valley
Daley, Daly, Daily

Dainard
(Irish) loved
Danehard, Danehardt, Daneard, Daneardt, Dainehard, Dainhard, Daynard

Dairus
(Invented) daring
Daras, Dares, Darus

Daithi
(Irish) speedy

Daivat
(Hindi) powerful man

Dakarai
(African) happy
Dakarrai, Dakk

Dakota
(Native American) friendly
Daccota, Dack, Dak, Dakoda, Dakodah, Dakoetah, Dakotah, Dekota, Dekohta, Dekowta, Kota

Dakote
(Place name) from Dakota (states North and South Dakota)
Dako

Dalai
(Indian) peaceful
Dalee

Dalanee
(Invented) form of Delaney
Dalaney, Dalani

Dalbert
(English) man who lives in the valley
Del, Delbert

Dale
(English) natural
Dail, Daile, Daley, Dallan, Dalle, Dallin, Day, Dayl, Dayle

Dalen
(English) up-and-coming
Dalan, Dalin, Dallen, Dallin, Dalyn

Daley
(Irish) organized
Dailey, Daily, Dale

Dalgus
(American) loving the outdoors

Dalhart
(Place name) city in Texas
Dal

Dallas
(Place name) good old boy; city in Texas
Dal, Dall, Dalles, Dallice, Dallis, Dallus, Delles

Dallin
(English) valley-born; fine
Dal, Dallan, Dallen, Dallon

Dalsten
(English) smart
Dal, Dalston

Dalt
(English) abundant
Dall, Daltt, Daltey

Dalton
(English) farmer
Daleton, Dall, Dallton, Daltan, Dalten

Dalvis
(Invented) form of Elvis;
sassy
Dal, Dalves, Dalvus, Dalvy

Daly
(Irish) together
Daley, Dawley

Dalziel
(Scottish) from the field

Damacio
(Spanish) calm; tamed
*Damas, Damasio, Damaso,
Damazio*

Damarcus
(African American) confident
*D'Marcus, Damarkes,
Damarkus, Demarcus*

Damario
(Spanish) tamer of wild
things
*Damarios, Damarius,
Damaro, Damero*

Damary
(Greek) tame
Damaree, Damarie

Damascus
(Place name) capital of
Syria; dramatic
Damas, Damask

Damaskenos
(Greek) of Damascus; life-
changing
Damascus, Damaskinos

Damaso
(Spanish) taming
Damas

Damean
(American) form of Damian;
tamed
*Dama, Daman, Damas,
Damea*

Dameetre
(Invented) form of Dmitri;
audacious
Dimitri

Damek
(Czech) earth
*Adamec, Adamek, Adamik,
Adamok, Adha, Damick,
Damicke*

Damian
(Greek) fate; (Latin) demon
*Daemon, Daimen, Daimon,
Daman, Dame, Damean,
Damen, Dameon, Damey,
Damiano, Damianos,
Damianus, Damien,
Damion, Damon, Damyan,
Damyean, Damyen,
Damyon, Damyun, Dayman,
Daymian, Daymon, Demyan*

Damon
(Greek) dramatic; spirited
Damonn, Damyn

Dan
(Hebrew) short for Daniel;
spiritual
Dahn, Dannie, Danny

Dana
(Scandinavian) light-haired
Danah, Dane, Danie, Dayna

Danar
(English) from Denmark; dry

Danaus
(Mythology) king of Argos
Denaus, Dinaus

Dandre
(American) light
*Dan, Dandrae, Dandray,
AeAndrae, DeAndray,
Aiondrae*

Dandy
(Hindi) from Dandin;
spiritual

Dane
(English) man from
Denmark; light
*Dain, Daine, Daney, Danie,
Danyn, Dayne, Dhane*

Daneck
(American) well-liked
*Danek, Danick, Danik,
Danike, Dannick*

Danely
(Scandinavian) Danish
Dainely, Daynelee

Dang
(Vietnamese) worthy

Dangelo
(Italian) angelic
Danjelo

Danger
(American) word as a name;
dangerous
Dang, Dange, Dangery

Daniel
(Hebrew) judged by God;
spiritual
*Da, Danal, Dane, Daneal,
Danek, Dani, Danial,
Daniele, Danil, Danilo,
Danko, Dann, Dannel,
Danney, Danni, Dannie,
Danniel, Danny, Danyal,
Danyel, Danyell, Danyyell,
Deiniol*

Danne
(Biblical) form of Daniel; faithful
Dann

Danner
(Last name as first name) rescued by God
Dan, Dann, Danny

Danno
(Hebrew) kind
Dannoh, Dano

Danny
(Hebrew) short for Daniel; spiritual
Dan, Dann, Dannee, Danney, Danni, Dannie

Danon
(French) remembered
Danen, Danhann, Dannon, Danton

Dante
(Latin) enduring
Dan, Danne, Dantae, Dantay, Dantey, Dauntay, Dayntay, Dontae, Dontay, Donté

Danton
(Last name as first name) Dan's town

Dantre
(African American) faithful
Dantray, Dantrae, Dontre, Dantrey, Dantri, Dantry, Don, Dont, Dontrey, Dontri

Dantrell
(African American) spunky
Dantrele, Dantrill, Dantrille

Danube
(Place name) flowing; river
Dannube, Danuube, Donau

Daphnis
(Greek) attractive; from Daphne

Daquan
(African American) rambunctious
Dakwan, Daquanne, Dequan, Dequanne, Dekwan, Dekwohn, Dekwohnne

Dar
(English) deerlike

Darbrie
(Irish) free man; light-hearted
Dar, Darb, Darbree, Darbry

Darby
(Irish) free spirit
Dar, Darb, Darbee, Darbey, Darbie, Darre, Derby

Darce
(Irish) dark
Darcy, Dars, Darsy, D'Arcy

Darcel
(French) dark
Dar, Darce, Darcelle, Darcey, Darcy, Darsy

Darcy
(French) slow-moving
Darce, Darse, Darsey, Darsy

Dardanos
(Greek) adored
Dar, Dardanio, Dardanios, Dardanus

Dare
(Irish) short for Darroh; dark
Dair, Daire, Darey

Darian
(American) inventive
Dari, Darien, Darion, Darrian, Darrien, Darrion, Derreynn

Darin
(Irish) great
Daren, Darren, Darrie, Daryn

Dario
(Spanish) rich
Darioh, Darrey

Darion
(Irish) great potential
Dare, Darien, Darrion, Daryun

Darius
(Greek) affluent
Dare, Dareas, Dareus, Darias, Ariess, Dario, Darious, Darrius, Derrius, Derry

Dark
(Slavic) short for Darko; macho
Dar, Darc

Darko
(Slavic) macho
Dark

Darlen
(American) darling
Darlan, Darlun

Darnell
(English) secretive
Dar, Darn, Darnall, Darnel, Darnie, Darny

Darnley
(English) sly

Darold
(American) clever
Dare, Darrold, Darroll, Derold

Daron
(Irish) great
Darren, Dayron

Darrah
(Irish) dark, strong
Darach, Darragh

Darrel
(Aboriginal) blue sky
*Darral, Darrell, Darrill,
Darrol, Darroll, Darry,
Darryl, Darryll, Daryl, Derrel,
Derrell, Derril, Derrill, Deryl,
Deryll*

Darrell
(French) loved man
*Darel, Darol, Darrel, Darrey,
Daryl, Derrel, Derrell*

Darren
(Irish) great man
*Daren, Darin, Daron,
Darran, Darrin, Darring,
Darron, Darryn, Derrin,
Derron, Derry*

Darrett
(American) form of Garrett;
efficient
Dare, Darry

Darrien
(Greek) with riches
*Darian, Darion, Darrian,
Darrion, Darryan, Darryen*

Darroh
(English) armed; bright
*Dare, Daro, Darrie, Darro,
Darrohye, Darrow*

Darrti
(American) fast; deer
Dart, Darrt

Darryl
(French) darling man
*Darrie, Daryl, Derrie, Deryl,
Deryll*

Darshan
(African American) pious

Dart
(Place name) decisive
Darte, Dartt

D'Artagnan
(French) leader;
ostentatious

Darton
(English) swift; deer

Darwin
(English) dearest friend
*Dar, Darwen, Darwinne,
Darwon, Darwyn, Derwin,
Derwynn*

Daryn
(American) form of Darren
Darynn, Deryn

Dash
(American) speedy; dashing
Dashy

Dashawn
(African American) unusual
*D'Sean, D'Shawn, Dashaun,
Deshaun, Deshawn*

Dashell
(African American) dashing
Dashiell

Dasher
(American) dashing; fast
Dash

Dathan
(Biblical) fountain of hope

Davao
(Place name) city in the
Philippines; exotic
Davo

Dave
(Hebrew) short for David;
loved
Davey, Davi, Davie, Davy

Daven
(American) form of Dave;
dashing
Davan

Davenport
(Last name as first name) of
the old school; sea-loving

Davey
(Hebrew) short for David;
loved
*Dave, Davee, Davi, Davie,
Davy*

Davian
(Hebrew) dear one
*Daivian, Daivyan, Daveon,
Davien, Davion, Davyan,
Davyen, Davyon*

David
(Hebrew) beloved
*Daffy, Daffyd, Dafydd, Dai,
Davad, Dave, Daved, Davee,
Daven, Davey, Davi, Davide,
Davie, Davies, Davin, Davis,
Davon, Davy, Davyd, Davydd*

David-Drue
(American) combo of David
and Drue; sweet and loved
*David-Drew, David-Dru,
David Drue*

Davidpaul
(American) beloved
David-Paul

Davidson
(English) son of David
Davidsen, Davison

Davin
(Scandinavian) smart
Dave, Daven, Dayven

Davins
(American) from David; smart
Davens

Davis
(Welsh) David's son; heart's child
Dave, Daves, Davidson, Davies, Davison, Daviss, Davy

Davon
(American) sweet
Davaughan, Davaughn, Dave, Davone, Devon

Davonnae
(African American) from David; loved
Davawnae, Davonae

Davonte
(African American) energetic
D'Vontay, Davontay, Devonta

Daw
(English) quiet
Dawe, Dawes

Dawber
(Last name as first name) funny
Daw, Dawb, Dawbee, Dawbey, Dawby, Daws

Dawk
(American) spirited
Dawkins

Daws
(English) dedicated
Daw, Dawsen, Dawz

Dawson
(English) David's son; loved
Daw, Dawe, Dawes, Dawsan, Dawse, Dawsen, Dawsey, Dawsin

Dax
(French) unique; water-loving
Dacks, Daxie

Day
(English) calm
Daye

Dayanand
(Hindi) a loving man

Daymond
(Invented) compassionate

Dayton
(English) the town of David; planner
Daeton, Day, Daye, Daytan, Daytawn, Dayten, Deytawn, Deyton

Deacon
(Greek) giving
Deakin, Decon, Deecon, Deekon, Dekawn, Deke, Dekie, Dekon, Diakonos

Deagan
(Last name as first name) capable
Degan

Deal
(Last name as first name) wheeler-dealer
Deale

Dean
(English) calming
Deane, Deanie, Deany, Deen, Dene, Deyn, Dino

DeAndré
(African American) very masculine
D'André, DeAndrae, DeAndray, Diandray, Diondrae, Diondray

Deangelo
(Italian) sweet; personable
D'Angelo, Dang, Dange, DeAngelo, Deanjelo, Deeanjelo, DiAngelo, Di-Angelo

Deans
(English) sylvan; valley
Dean, Deaney, Deanie

Deanthony
(African American) rambunctious
Deanthe, Deanthoney, Deanthonie, Deeanthie, Dianth

Deanza
(Spanish) smooth
Denza

Dearborn
(Last name as first name) endearing; kind from birth
Dearbourn, Dearburne, Deerborn

Dearing
(Last name as first name) endearing
Dear

Dearon
(American) dear one
Dear

Deason
(Invented) cocky
Deace, Deas, Dease, Deasen, Deasun

Debonair
(French) with a beautiful air; elegant and cultured
Debonaire, Debonnair, Debonnaire

Debythis
(African American) strange
Debiathes

Decatur
(American) place name; special
Dec, Decatar, Decater, Deck

Deccan
(Place name) region in India; scholar
Dec, Dek

Decimus
(Latin) tenth child
Decio

Deck
(Irish) short for Declan; strong; devout
Decky

Declan
(Irish) strong; prayerful
Dec, Deck, Dek, Deklan, Deklon

Deddrick
(American) form of Deidrich; substantial
Dead, Dedric, Dedrick, Dedrik, Dietrich

Dedeaux
(French) sweet
Dede, Dee

Dedric
(German) leader
Dedrick, Deidrich

Dee
(American) short for names that start with D
D, De

Deek
(American) short for Deacon; leader
Deke

Deems
(English) merits

Deepak
(Sanskrit) light of knowledge
Depak, Depakk, Dipak

Deeter
(American) friendly
Deter

DeForest
(French) of the forest
Defforest

DeFoy
(French) child of Foy
Defoy, Defoye

Degraf
(French) child of Graf
DeGraf

Deidrich
(German) leader
Dedric, Dedrick, Deed, Deide, Deidrick, Diedrich

Deinol
(Greek) form of Daniel; judged by God

Deinorus
(African American) vigorous
Denorius, Denorus

Deion
(Greek) form of Dion/Deone (god of wine); fun-loving; charismatic
Dee

Dejuan
(African American) talkative
Dajuan, Dajuwan, Dejuane, Dejuwan, Dewaan, Dewan, Dewaughan, Dewon, Dewonn, Dewuan Dwon, Dwonn, Dwonne

Deke
(Hebrew) from Dekel; brilliant; sturdy tree
Deek, Dekel

Del
(English) valley; laid-back and helpful
Dail, Dell, Delle

Delaney
(Irish) challenging
Del, Delaine, Delainey, Delainie, Delane, Delanie, Delany, Dell

Delano
(Irish) dark
Del, Delaynoh, Dell

Delbert
(English) sunny
Bert, Bertie, Berty, Dalbert, Del, Delburt, Dell, Dilbert

Delete
(Origin unknown) ordinary
Delette

Delfino
(Spanish) dolphin; sealoving
Define, Fino

Delgado
(Spanish) slim

Delius
(Greek) from Delos
Deli, Delia, Delios, Delos

Dell
(English) from the country;
sparkles

Delling
(Norse) shines

Delmar
(Last name as first name)
friendly
Delm

Delmer
(American) country
Del, Delmar, Delmir

Delmis
(Spanish) friend
Del, Delms

Delmore
(French) seagoing
*Del, Delmar, Delmer,
Delmor, Delmoor, Delmoore*

Delmy
(American) from French
Delmore; seagoing
Delmi

Delphin
(French) dolphin
*Delfin, Delfino, Delfinos,
Delfinus, Delphino,
Delphinos, Delphinus,
Delvin*

Delroy
(French) royal; special
*Del, Dell, Dellroy, Delroi,
Roi, Roy*

Delsi
(American) easygoing
*Delci, Delcie, Dels, Delsee,
Delsey, Delsy*

Delt
(American) fraternity boy
Delta

Delton
(English) friend
Delt, Deltan, Delten

Delvan
(English) form of Delwin;
friend
*Del, Dell, Delly, Delven,
Delvin, Delvun, Delvyn*

Delwin
(English) companion
*Dalwin, Dalwyn, Delavan,
Delevan, Dellwin, Delwins,
Delwince, Delwen,
Delwinse, Delwy, Delwyn*

Demarco
(Italian) daring
*D'Marco, Deemarko,
Demarkoe, Demie, Demmy,
Dimarco*

Demarcus
(American) zany; royal
*Damarcus, DaMarkiss,
DeMarco, DeMarcus,
Demarkes, Demarkess,
DeMarko, DeMarkus,
Demarkus, DeMarquess,
DeMarquez, Demarquiss,
DeMarquiss*

Demario
(Italian) bold
*D'Mareo, D'Mario,
Demarioh, Demarrio,
Demie, Demmy, Dimario*

Demarques
(African American) son of
Marques; noble
*Demark, Demarkes,
Demarquis, Demmy*

Demas
(Greek) well-liked
Dimas

Demete
(American) from Greek
Demetrius; a saint
Deme, Demetay

Demetrice
(Greek) form of Demetrius;
fertile

Demetrick
(African American) earthy
Demetrik, Demi, Demitrick

Demetrios
(Greek) earth-loving
*Demeetrius, Demetreus,
Demetri, Demetrious,
Demetris, Demi, Demie*

Demetrius
(Greek) form of Demeter,
goddess of fertility
*Dametrius, Dem, Demetri,
Demetrice, Demetris,
Demitrios, Demmy, Demos,
Dhimitrios, Dimetre, Dimitri,
Dimitrios, Dimitrious,
Dimitry, Dmitri, Dmitrios,
Dmitry*

Demitri
(Greek) fertile; earthy
*Demetrie, Demetry, Demi,
Demie, Demitry, Dmitri*

Demond
(African American) worldly
Demonde

Demos
(Greek) of the people
Demas, Demmos

Demosthenes
(Greek) orator; eloquent
Demos

Demps
(Irish) form of Dempsey;
sturdy
Demps, Dempse, Dempz

Dempsey
(Irish) respected; judge
*Dem, Demi, Demps,
Dempsie, Dempsy*

Den
(Greek) short for Dennis;
reveler

Denali
(Hindi) great

Denard
(Last name as first name)
envied
*Den, Denar, Denarde,
Denny*

Denby
(Scandinavian) place name;
adventurous
*Danby, Denbee, Denbey,
Denbie, Denney, Dennie,
Denny*

Dene
(Hungarian) reveler

Denham
(Scandinavian) hamlet of
Danes

Denholm
(Scandinavian) house of
Danes

Deni
(English) form of Dionysius,
god of revelry and wine;
festive
Denni

Denis
(Greek) reveler
Den, Denese, Dennis

Denk
(American) sporty
Denky, Dink

Denley
(English) dark
Denlie, Denly

Denman
(English) dark; valley-
dweller
*Den, Deni, Denmin, Denney,
Denni, Dennie, Dennman,
Denny, Dinman*

Denmark
(Scandinavian) place as
name; from Denmark

Dennis
(Greek) reveler
*Den, Denes, Deni, Denies,
Denis, Deniss, Dennes,
Dennet, Denney, Denni,
Dennie, Dennies, Dennison,
Denniz, Denny, Dennys,
Deno, Denys, Deon, Dino,
Dion, Dionisio, Dionysius,
Dionysus, Diot*

Dennisen
(English) Dennis's son;
partier
*Den, Denison, Dennison,
Dennizon, Dennyson,
Tennyson*

Denny
(Greek) short for Dennis;
fun-loving
*Den, Denee, Deni, Denney,
Denni*

Denton
(English) place name; valley
settlement; happy
*Denny, Dent, Dentan,
Denten, Dentie, Dentin*

Denver
(Place name) capital of
Colorado; climber
Den, Denny

Denzel
(English) sensual
*Den, Denny, Densie, Denz,
Denze, Denzell, Denzelle,
Denziel, Denzil, Denzill,
Denzille, Denzyl, Denzylle,
Dinzie*

Deodar
(Sanskrit) cedar

Deondray
(African American) romantic
*Deandre, Deeon, Deondrae,
Deondrey, Deone*

Deone
(Greek) short for Dionysius,
god of wine; fun-loving;
charismatic
*Deion, Deonah, Deonne,
Dion*

Deonté
(French) outgoing
*De'On, Deontae, Deontay,
Deontie, Diontay, Diontayye*

Deordre
(African American) outgoing
Deordray

Deotis
(African American) combo of De and Otis; scholar
Deo, Deoh, Deotus

Depp
(American) movie-star surname; theatrical
Dep

Derald
(American) combo of Harold and Derrell; content
Deral, Dere, Derry, Deruld

Derby
(Irish) guileless
Derbey, Derbie

Derek
(German) ruler; bold heart
Darrick, Darriq, Derak, Dere, Dereck, Deric, Derick, Derik, Deriq, Deriqk, Derk, Derreck, Derrek, Derrick, Derrik, Derryck, Derryk, Deryk, Deryke, Dirk, Dirke, Dyrk

Derland
(English) from the land of deer
Durland

Derlin
(English) from Derland, deer land; sly
Derl, Derlan, Derland, Derlen, Derlyn, Durland, Durlin

Dermod
(Irish) from Dermot; guileless; thoughtful
Dermud

Dermond
(Irish) unassuming
Dermon, Dermun, Dermund, Derr

Dermot
(Irish) unabashed; giving
Der, Dermod, Dermott, Derree, Derrey, Derri, Diarmid, Diarmuid

Deron
(African American) variation on Darren; smart
Dare, Daron, DaRon, Darone, Darron, Dayron, Dere, DeRronn

Derrell
(French) another form of Darrell; loved
Dere, Derrel, Derrill

Derri
(American) breezy
Derree, Derry

Derrick
(German) bold heart
Derak, Derick

Derry
(Irish) red-haired
Dare, Darry, Derrey, Derri, Derrie

Derward
(Last name as first name) clunky
Der, Derr, Derwy, Dur, Durr, Ward

Derwent
(Last name as first name) of deer

Derwin
(English) bookish
Darwin, Darwyn, Derwyn, Derwynn, Durwen, Durwin

Des
(Irish) short for Desmond; delightful

Deseo
(Spanish) desire
Des, Desi, Dezi

Deshan
(Hindi) patriot
Deshad, Deshal

Deshawn
(African American) brassy
D'Sean, D'Shawn, Dashaun, Dashawn, Desean, Deshaun, Deshaune, Deshawnn, Deshon

Deshea
(American) confident
Desh, DeShay, Deshay, Deshie

Deshon
(African American) bold; open
Desh, Deshan, Deshann

Desiderio
(Italian, Spanish) desirable
Deri, Derito, Des, Desi, Desideratus, Desiderios, Desiderius, Desie, Diderot, Didier, Dizier

Desire
(American) word as name; desirable
Des, Desi, Desidero

Desmee
(Irish) form of Desmond;
from Munster, Ireland
*Desi, Dessy, Dezme,
Dezmee, Desmey, Dezmie,
Dezmo, Dezzy*

Desmond
(Irish) from Munster, Ireland
profound
*Des, Desi, Desmon,
Desmund, Dezmond,
Dizmond*

Desmun
(Irish) form of Desmond;
wise
Dez, Dezmund

Desperado
(Spanish) renegade
*Des, Desesperado, Dessy,
Dezzy*

Destin
(Place name) city in Florida;
destiny; fate
*Desten, Destie, Deston,
Destrie*

Detleff
(Germanic) decisive
Detlef, Detlev

Detroy
(African American) outgoing
Detroe

Detton
(Last name as first name)
determined
Deet, Dett

Deuce
(American) two in cards;
second child
Doos, Duz

DeUndre
(African American) child of
Undre
*Deundrae, DeUndray,
Deundry*

Dev
(Irish) short for Devlin; from
Dublin; poetic
Deb, Deo

Deval
(Hindi) godlike
Deven

Devann
(American) divine child
DeVanne, Deven

Devaughan
(American) bravado
Devan, Devaughn, Devonne

Devdan
(Hindi) God's gift
Debdan, Deodan

Devender
(American) poetic
Devander, Deven, Devendar

Deverell
(American) special
*Dev, Devee, Deverel,
Deverelle, Devie, Devy*

Devereux
(French surname) divine
Deveraux

Devin
(Irish) poetic; writer
*Dev, Devan, Deven, Devinn,
Devon, Devvy, Devyn,
Devynn*

Devine
(Latin) divine
Dev, Devinne

Devinson
(Irish) poetic
*Dev, Devan, Devee, Deven,
Davin, Devy*

Devland
(Irish) courageous
*Dev, Devlend, Devlind,
Devvy*

Devlin
(Irish) fearless
*Devlan, Devlen, Devlon,
Devlyn, Devy*

Devo
(American) quirky; fun
Divo

Devon
(Irish) writer
*Deavon, Dev, Deven, Devin,
Devohne, Devond, Devonn,
Devy, Devyn*

Devonte
(African American) variation
on Devon; outgoing
Devontae, Devontay

Dewayne
(American) spirited
*Dewain, Dewaine, Duwain,
Dwain*

Dewey
(Welsh) valued
*Dew, Dewi, Dewie, Dewy,
Duey*

Dewitt
(English) fair-haired
*Dewie, DeWitt, Dwight,
Witt, Wittie, Witty*

DeWittay
(African American) witty
Dewitt, De Witt, Witt, Witty

Dewon
(African American) clever
Dejuan, Dewan

Dex
(Latin) from Dexter; right-handed; hearty
Dexe

Dexee
(American) short for Dexter; lucky
Dex, Dexey, Dexi, Dexie

Dexter
(Latin) skillful; right-handed
Decster, Dex, Dext, Dextah, Dextar, Dextor

Dezi
(Irish) form of Desi; from S. Munster, Ireland

Diablo
(Spanish) devil

Diamon
(American) luminous
Dimon, Dimun, Diamund

Diamond
(English) bright; gem
Dimah, Dime, Dimond, Dimont

Diarmid
(Irish) happy for others' successes
Diarmaid, Diarmait, Diarmi

Diaz
(Spanish) rowdy
Dias, Diazz

Dice
(English) risk-taking
Dicey, Dies, Dize, Dyce, Dyse

Dick
(German) short for Richard; ruler who dominates
Dickey, Dicki, Dickie, Dicky, Dik

Dickens
(Literature) articulate

Dickinson
(Last name as first name) poetic

Dickon
(Last name as first name) strong king

Didier
(French) desirable

Diedrich
(German) form of Dedrick; ruler
Dedric, Dedrick, Deed, Died, Dietrich

Diego
(Spanish) untamed; wild
Dago, Deago, Deagoh, Dee, Diago

Diesel
(American) movie-star name
Dees, Deez, Desel, Dezsel, Diezel

Dieter
(German) prepared
Dedrick, Deke, Derek, Detah, Deter, Diederick, Dirk

Dietmar
(German) famous

Digby
(Irish) man of simplicity

Diggory
(French) lost
Diggery, Diggorey, Digory

Dijon
(Place name) France; mustard
Dejawn

Dilip
(Hindi) protests; royal
Duleep

Dill
(Irish) faithful
Dillard, Dilly

Dillion
(Irish) from Dillon; loyal

Dillon
(Irish) devoted
Dill, Dillan, Dillen, Dilly, Dilon, Dylan, Dylanne, Dyllon, Dylon

Dimas
(Spanish) frank

Dimitri
(Russian) fertile; flourishing
Demetry, Demi, Demitri, Demitry, Dmitri

Dinesh
(Hindi) day lord

Dingo
(Animal) wild spirit

Dino
(Italian) short for Dean; little sword
Dean, Deanie, Deano, Deinoh, Dinoh

Dinos
(Greek) short for Constantine; proud
Dean, Dino, Dinohs, Dynos

Dinose
(American) form of Dino; joyful
Denoze, Dino, Dinoce, Dinoz, Dinoze

Dins
(American) climber
Dinse, Dinz

Dinsdale
(English) hill protector; innovator

Dinsmore
(Irish) guarded
Dinnie, Dinnsmore, Dinny, Dins

Diogenes
(Greek) honest man
Dee, Dioge, Dioh

Dion
(Greek) short for Dionysius, god of wine; reveler
Deion, Deon, Deonn, Deonys, Deyon, Dio, Dionn

Dionisio
(Spanish) from Dionysius, god of wine and revelry; reveler
Dionis, Dioniso, Dionysio

Dionysus
(Greek) joyous celebrant; god of wine
Dee, Deonysios, Dion, Dionio, Dioniso, Dionysios, Dionysius, Dionysos, Dionysus

Dirk
(Scandinavian) leader
Derk, Dierck, Dieric, Dierick, Dirck, Dirke, Dirky, Durk,

Diron
(American) form of Darren; great
Diran, Dirun, Dyronn

Dit
(Hungarian) short for Ditrik

Dix
(American) energetic
Dex

Dixie
(American) southerner
Dix, Dixee, Dixey, Dixi

Dixon
(English) Dick's son; happy
Dickson, Dix, Dixie, Dixo

Doan
(English) hills; quiet
Doane, Doe

Dobbs
(English) fire

Dobes
(American) unassuming
Dobe, Doe

Dobie
(American) reliable; southern
Dobe, Dobee, Dobey, Dobi

Dobromir
(Polish) good
Dobe, Dobry, Doby

Dobry
(Polish) good
Dobe, Dobree, Dobrey

Doc, Dock
(American) short for doctor; physician
Dok

Dodd
(English) swaggering; has a small-town sheriff feel
Dod

Dodge
(English) swaggering
Dod, Dodds, Dodgson

Dody
(Greek) God's gift
Doe

Dog
(American) animal as name; good buddy
Daug, Dawg, Dogg, Doggie, Doggy

Doherty
(Irish) rash
Docherty, Doh, Doughertey, Douherty

Dolan
(Irish) dark
Dolen

Dolf
(German) short for Rudolph; wolf
Dolfe, Dolfie, Dolfy, Dolph, Dophe

Dolgen
(American) tenacious
Dole, Dolg, Dolgan, Dolgin

Dolon
(Irish) brunette
Dole, Dolen, Dolton

Dolph
(German) noble wolf
Dolf, Dollfus, Dollfuss, Dollphus, Dolphus

Dom
(Latin) short for Dominic,
saint; of the Lord
Dome, Dommie, Dommy

Domenico
(Italian) confident
Dom, Domeniko

Domingo
(Spanish) Sunday-born boy
*Demingo, Dom, Domin,
Dominko*

Dominic
(Latin) child of the Lord;
saint
*Demenico, Demingo, Dom,
Domenic, Domenico,
Domenique, Domingo,
Domini, Dominick, Dominie,
Dominik, Dominique,
Domino, Dominy, Nick*

Dominique
(French) spiritual
*Dom, Dominick, Dominike,
Domminique*

Domino
(Latin) winner
Domeno, Dominoh, Domuno

Don
(Scottish) short for Donald;
powerful
*Dahn, Doni, Donn, Donney,
Donni, Donnie, Donny*

Donaciano
(Spanish) dark
*Dona, Donace, Donae,
Donase*

Donahue
(Irish) fighter
*Don, Donahoe, Donohue,
Donohue*

Donald
(Scottish) world leader;
powerful
*Don, Donal, Donaldo,
Donall, Donalt, Donaugh,
Donel, Doneld, Donelson,
Donild, Donn, Donnel,
Donnell, Donney, Donni,
Donnie, Donny*

Donatello
(Italian) giving
*Don, Donatelo, Donetello,
Donny, Tello*

Donatien
(French) generous
*Don, Donatyen, Donn,
Donnatyen*

Donato
(Italian) donates

Donder
(Dutch) thunder

Dong
(Chinese) from the east

Donnan
(Irish) brown-haired;
popular

Donnell
(Irish) courageous
*Dahn, Don, Donel, Donell,
Donhelle, Donnie, Donny*

Donnelly
(Irish) righteous
*Donalee, Donally, Donelli,
Donely, Donn, Donnell
Donnellie, Donnie*

Donnis
(American) from Donald;
dark; regal
Don, Donnes, Donnus

Donny
(Irish) fond leader
Donney, Donni, Donnie

Donovan
(Irish) combative
*Don, Donavan, Donavon,
Donavaughn, Donavyn,
Donevin, Donevon, Donivin,
Donny, Donoven, Donovon*

Don Quixote
(Literature) an original

Dont
(American) dark; giving
Don, Dontay

Dontae
(African American)
capricious
Dontay, Donté

Dontave
(African American) wild
spirit
Dontav, Donteve

Dontavious
(African American) giving
*Dantavius, Dawntavius,
Dewontavius, Dontavious*

Donté
(Italian) lasting forever
*Dantae, Dantay, Dohntae,
Dontae, Dontay, Dontey*

Donton
(American) confident
Don, Donnee, Dont, Dontie

Dontrell
(African American) jaded
*Dontray, Dontree, Dontrel,
Dontrelle, Dontrey, Dontrie,
Dontrill*

Donyale
(African American) regal; dark
Donyel, Donyelle

Donyell
(African American) loyal
Donny, Danyel, Donyal

Donzell
(African American) form of Denzel
Dons, Donsell, Donz, Donzelle

Doocey
(American) clever
Dooce, Doocee, Doocie, Doos

Dooley
(Irish) shy hero
Doolee, Dooli, Dooly

Dor
(Aboriginal) energetic
Doram, Doriel, Dorli

Doran
(Irish) adventurer
Dore, Dorian, Doron, Dorran, Dorren

Dorian
(Greek) the sea's child; mysterious; youthful forever
Dora, Dore, Dorean, Dorey, Dorie, Dorien, Dorrian, Dorrien, Dorryen, Dory

Dorman
(Last name as first name) practical
Dor, Dorm

Doron
(Greek) unlimited passion
Doran, Doroni

Dorral
(Last name as first name) vain
Dorale, Dorry

Dorset
(Place name) county in England
Dorsett, Dorzet

Dorsey
(French) sturdy as a fortress
Dorsee, Dorsie

Dotan
(African) hardworking
Dotann

Dotson
(Last name as first name) loquacious; son of Dot
Dotsen, Dottson

Dov
(Hebrew) bear

Doug
(Scottish) short for Douglas; strong
Dougie, Dougy, Dug, Dugy

Dougal
(Irish) dark, mysterious
Doyle, Dougall, Dugal, Dugald, Dugall

Douglas
(Scottish) powerful; dark river
Doug, Douggie, Dougie, Douglace, Douglass, Douglis, Dugaid

Dovie
(American) peaceable
Dove, Dovee, Dovey, Dovi, Dovy

Dow
(Irish) brunette
Dowan, Dowe, Dowson

Dowd
(American) serious
Doud, Dowdy, Dowed

Doyal
(American) form of Doyle; dark and unusual
Doile, Doyl, Doyle

Doyle
(Irish) deep; dark
Doil, Doy, Doyal, Doye, Doyl

Doylton
(Last name as first name) pretentious
Doyl, Doyle

Dracy
(American) form of Stacy; secretive
Dra, Drace, Dracee, Dracey, Draci, Drase, Drasee, Drasi

Dradell
(American) serious
Drade, Dray

Drake
(English) dragonlike; fire-breathing
Drago, Drakie, Drako

Draper
(English) precise; maker of drapes
Draiper, Drape

Dravey
(American) groovy
Dravee, Dravie, Dravy

Drew
(Welsh) wise; well-liked
Dru, Druw

Drexel
(American) thoughtful
Drex

Dries
(Dutch) brave
Dre

Driscoll
(Irish) pensive
Driscol, Drisk, Driskell

Dru
(English) wise; popular
Drew, Drue

Drummond
(Scottish) practical
Drum, Drumon, Drumond

Drury
(French) loving man
Drew, Drewry, Dru, Drure, Drurey, Drurie

Dryden
(English) writer; calm
Driden, Drydan, Drydin

Drystan
(Welsh) form of Tristan; mourning
Drestan, Dristan, Drystyn

Duane
(Irish) dark man
Dewain, Dewayne, Duain, Duwain, Duwaine, Duwayne, Dwain, Dwaine, Dwayne

Dub
(Irish) short for Dublin; friendly
Dubby

Dublin
(Place name) city in Ireland; trendy

Duc
(Vietnamese) honest

Dude
(American) cool guy

Dudley
(English) compromiser; rich; stuffy
Dud, Dudd, Dudlee, Dudlie, Dudly

Dueart
(American) kind
Art, Duart, Due, Duey

Duff
(Scottish) dark
Duf, Duffey, Duffie, Duffy

Dugan
(Irish) dark man
Doogan, Dougan, Douggan, Duggan, Duggie, Duggy, Dugin

Duke
(Latin) leader of the pack
Dook, Dukey, Dukie

Dumisani
(African) leader

Dumont
(French) monumental
Dummont, Dumon, Dumonde, Dumonte, Dumontt

Dunbar
(Irish) castle-dweller
Dunbarr

Dunbaron
(American) dark
Baron, Dunbar

Duncan
(Scottish) spirited fighter
Dunc, Dunk, Dunkan, Dunn, Dunne

Dundee
(Australian) spunky

Dunham
(Last name as first name) dark

Dunia
(American) dark
Dunya

Dunk
(Scottish) form of Duncan; dark; combative
Dunc, Dunk

Dunlavy
(English) sylvan
Dunlave

Dunley
(English) meadow-loving
Dunlea, Dunlee, Dunleigh, Dunli, Dunlie, Dunly, Dunnlea, Dunnleigh, Dunnley

Dunlop
(English) sylvan

Dunmore
(Scottish) guarded
Dun, Dunmohr, Dunmoore

Dunn
(Irish) neutral
Dun, Dunne

Dunphy
(American) dark; serious
Dun, Dunphe, Dunphee, Dunphey

Dunstan
(English) well-girded
Dun, Duns, Dunse, Dunsten, Dunstin, Dunston

Dunstand
(English) form of Dunstan; protected
Dunsce, Dunse, Dunst, Dunsten, Dunstun

Duran
(Last name as first name) lasting; musical
Durann, Durante, Durran

Durand
(Latin) from Durant; dependable
Duran, Durayn

Durant
(Latin) lasting; alluring
Dante, Duran, Durand, Durante, Durr, Durrie, Durry

Durban
(Place name) city in South Africa
Durb, Durben

Durham
(Last name as first name) supportive
Duram

Duro
(Place name) Palo Duro Canyon; enduring
Dure

Durrell
(English) protective
Durel, Durell, Durr, Durrel, Durry

Durward
(English) gatekeeper

Durwin
(English) dear friend
Derwin, Derwyn, Durwen, Durwinn, Durwyn

Durwood
(English) vigilant; home-loving
Derrwood, Derwood, Durr, Durrwood, Durwould, Durward

Duryea
(Hindi) invincible

Duster
(American) form of Dusty; deliberate
Dust, Dustee, Dustey, Dusti, Dusty

Dustin
(German) bold and brave
Dust, Dustan, Dusten, Duston, Dustie, Dusty, Dustyn

Dusty
(German) short for Dustin; brave
Dust, Dustee, Dustey, Dusti, Dustie

Dusty-Joe
(American) cowboy
Dustee, Dusti, Dusty, Dustyjoe, Joe

Dutch
(Dutch) from Holland; optimistic
Dutchie, Dutchy

Duval
(French) valley; peaceful
Dovahl, Duv, Duvall, Duvalle

Dwain
(American) form of Dwayne; country; dark
Dwaine

Dwan
(African American) fresh
D'wan, D'Wan, Dewan, Dwawn, Dwon

Dwanae
(African American) dark; small
Dwannay

Dwayne
(American) country
Duane, Duwain, Duwane, Duwayne, Dwain, Dwaine

Dweezel
(American) creative
Dweez, Dweezil

Dwight
(English) intelligent; white
Dwi, Dwite

Dwyer
(Irish) wise
Dwire, Dwyyer

Dyer
(English) creative
Di, Dier, Dyar, Dye

Dylan
(Welsh) sea god; creative
Dill, Dillan, Dillon, Dilloyn, Dilon, Dyl, Dylahn, Dylen, Dylin, Dyllan, Dylon, Dylonn

Dynell
(African American) seaman; gambler
Dinell, Dyne

Dyron
(African American) mercurial; sea-loving
Diron, Dyronn, Dyronne

Dyson
(English) sea-loving
Dieson, Dison, Dysan, Dysen, Dysun, Dyzon

Dyvet
(English) worker; dyes
Dye

Eagan
(Irish) form of Egan; intense
Egan, Egon

Eagle
(Native American) sharp-eyed
Eagal, Egle

Eamon
(Irish) form of Edmund; thriving; protective
Amon, Eamen, Emon

Earl
(English) promising; noble
Earle, Earley, Earlie, Early, Eril, Erl

Early
(English) punctual
Earl, Earlee, Earley

Earnest
(English) genuine
Earn, Earnie, Ern, Ernie

Earon
(American) form of Aaron
Earonn

Earvin
(English) sea-loving
Dervin, Ervin

Easey
(American) easygoing
Easy, Ezey

East
(English) from the east
Easte

Easton
(English) outdoorsy; east town
Easten

Eaton
(English) wealthy
Eaten, Etawn, Eton

Eaves
(English) edges by

Eb
(Hebrew) short for Ebenezer; helpful man

Ebby
(Hebrew) short for Ebenezer; rock; reliable
Ebbey, Ebbi

Eben
(Hebrew) helpful; loud
Eban

Ebenezer
(Hebrew) base of life; rock
Eb, Ebbie, Ebby, Eben, Ebeneezer, Ebeneser

Eberhardt
(German) brave
Eb, Eber, Eberhard

Ebo
(African) Tuesday-born

Eckhardt
(German) iron-willed
Eck, Eckhard, Eckhart, Ekhard

Ed
(English) short for Edward
Edd, Eddie, Eddy, Edy

Edan
(Scottish) fiery
Edon

Edbert
(German) courageous
Ediberto

Edcell
(English) focused; wealthy
Ed, Edcelle, Eds, Edsel

Eddie
(English) short for Edward
Eddee, Eddey, Eddy

Edel
(German) of noble birth
Adel, Edelmar, Edelweiss

Eden
(Hebrew) delight
Eadon, Edin, Edon, Edye, Edyn

Edenson
(Hebrew) son of Eden; delight
Edence, Edens, Edensen

Edgar
(English) success
Ed, Eddie, Edghur, Edgur

Edgard
(English) spear thrower
Ed, Eddie, Edgarde

Edgardo
(English) successful
Edgar, Edgard, Edgardoh

Edge
(American) cutting edge;
trendsetter
Eddge, Edgy

Edilberto
(Spanish) noble
Edilbert

Edison
(English) Edward's son;
smart
Ed, Eddie, Edisen, Edyson

Edmond
(English) protective
Ed, Edmon, Edmund

Edmund
(English) protective
Ed, Eddie, Edmond

Edrick
(English) rich leader;
(American) laughing
Ed, Edri, Edrik, Edry

Edsel
(English) rich
Ed, Eddie, Edsil, Edsyl

Eduardo
(Spanish) flirtatious
Ed, Eddie, Edwardo

Edward
(English) prospering;
defender
*Ed, Eddey, Eddi, Eddie,
Eddy, Edwar, Edwerd*

Edwin
(English) prosperous friend
Ed, Edwinn, Edwynn

Efrain
(Hebrew) fertile
Efren

Efrim
(Hebrew) short for Ephraim
Ef, Efrem, Efrum

Efton
(American) form of
Ephraim; (Hebrew) fruitful
Ef, Eft, Eften, Eftun

Egan
(Irish) spirited
Eggie, Egin, Egon

Egbert
(English) bright sword
Egber, Egburt, Eggie, Eggy

Egborn
(English) ready; born of
Edgar
*Eg, Egbornem, Egburn,
Eggie*

Egerton
(English) town of a
spearman
*Edgarton, Edgartown,
Edgerton, Egeton*

Eghert
(German) smart
Eghertt, Eghurt

Egil
(Scandinavian) the sword's
edge
Eigil

Egmon
(German) protective
*Egmond, Egmont, Egmun,
Egmund, Egmunt*

Egeus
(American) word as name;
protective
Aegis, Egis

Egon
(Irish) passionate

Egypt
(Place name)mysterious;
majestic

Ehren
(Hebrew) form of Aaron;
aware

Eikki
(African) strong

Einar
(Scandinavian) lone fighter

Ekon
(African) muscular

El
(English) old friend

Elam
(Hebrew) from Eliam; God-
centered; distinctive

Elan
(French) finesse
Elann, Elen, Elon, Elyn

Elbis
(American) exalted
Elb, Elbace, Elbase, Elbus

Elbridge
(American) presidential
Elb, Elby

Elder
(English) older sibling
El, Eldor

Eldon
(English) place name; charitable
Edwin, El, Elden, Eldin

Eldorado
(Place name) city in Arkansas (El Dorado)
El, Eld, Eldor

Eldread
(English) wise advisor
El, Eldred, Eldrid

Eldridge
(English) supportive
Eldredge

Eleazar
(Hebrew) helped by God
Elazar, Eleasar, Eliasar, Eliazar, Elieser, Elizar

Elger
(German) also Alger; of noble birth
Elger, Ellgar, Ellger

Elgin
(English) elegant
Elgen

Elegy
(Spanish) memorable
Elegee, Elegie, Elgy

Elendor
(Invented) special
Elen, Elend

Eli
(Hebrew) faithful man; high priest
El, Elie, Eloy, Ely

Elian
(Spanish) spirited
Eliann, Elyan

Elias
(Greek) spiritual
El, Eli, Eliace, Elyas

Eliezer
(Origin unknown) of God
Elieser, Elyeser

Elighie
(American) form of Elijah; sophisticated, classy

Elihu
(Hebrew) true believer
Elih, Eliu, Ellihu

Elijah
(Hebrew) religious; Old Testament prophet
El, Elie, Elija

Elijah-Blue
(American) combo of Elijah and Blue; devout
Elijah-Bleu, Elijah-Blu

Eliseo
(Spanish) daring
Elizeo

Elisha
(Hebrew) of God's salvation
Elishah, Elysha, Elyshah

Ellard
(German) brave man
Ell, Ellarde, Ellee, Ellerd

Ellery
(English) dominant
El, Ell, Ellary, Ellerie, Ellie

Elliott
(English) God-loving
Elie, Elio, Ell, Elliot

Ellis
(English) form of Elias; devout
Ellice, Ells

Ellis-Marcelle
(American) combo of Ellis and Marcelle; achiever
Ellis, Ellismarcelle, Marcelle

Ellison
(English) circumspect
Ell, Ellason, Ellisen, Ells, Ellyson

Ellkan
(Hawaiian) saved by God
Elkan, Elkin

Ellory
(Cornish) graceful swan
Elory, Elorey, Ellorey

Ellsha
(Hebrew) saved by the Lord
Elljsha, Elisee, Elish, Elishia, Elishua

Elman
(American) protective
El, Elle, Elmen, Elmon

Elmer
(English) famed
Ell, Elm, Elmar, Elmir, Elmo, Elmoh

Elmo
(Greek) gregarious
Ellmo, Elmoh

Elmore
(Last name as first name) sassy; royal

Elmot
(American) lovable
Elm

Elmore
(English) radiant
Elm, Elmie, Elmoor, Elmor

Elsworth
(Last name as first name)
pretentious
Ells, Ellsworth

Elof
(Swedish) the one heir
Loff

Eloi
(French) chosen one
Eloie, Eloy

Elonzo
(Spanish) sturdy; happy
El, Elon, Elonso

Elrad
(Hebrew) God rules his life

Elroy
(French) giving
Elroi, Elroye

Elsden
(English) spiritual
Els, Elsdon

Elson
(English) from Elston;
affluent
Elsen

Elston
(English) sophisticated
Els, Elstan, Elsten

Elton
(English) settlement;
famous
Ell, Ellton, Elt, Eltan, Elten

Elvin
(English) friend of elves
El, Elv, Elven

Elvind
(American) form of
Elvin/Alvin; friend of elves
Elv

Elvis
(Scandinavian) wise;
musical
El, Elvyse, The King

Elvy
(English) elfin; small

Elwell
(English) born in the old-
well area

Elwen
(English) friend of elves
*Elwee, Elwin Elwy, Elwyn,
Elwynn, Elwynt*

Elwond
(Last name as first name)
steady
Ellwand, Elwon, Eldwund

Elwood
(English) old wood;
everlasting
*Ell, Elwoode, Elwould,
Woodie, Woody, Woodye*

Ely
(Hebrew) lifted up
Eli

Emanuel
(Hebrew) with God
Em, Eman, Emanuele

Emberto
(Italian) pushy
Berty, Embert, Emberte

Emerson
(German) Emery's son; able
Emers, Emersen

Emery
(German) hardworking leader
*Em, Emeri, Emerie,
Emmerie, Emory, Emrie*

Emil
(Latin) ingratiating
Em, Emel, Emele

Emilio
(Italian) competitive;
(Spanish) excelling
Emil, Emile, Emilioh, Emlo

Emjay
(American) reliable
Em-J, Em-Jay, M.J., MJ

Emmanuel
(Hebrew) with God
*Em, Eman, Emmannuel,
Emmanuele, Manny*

Emmett
(Hebrew) truthful; sincere
*Emit, Emmet, Emmit,
Emmitt, Emmyt, Emmytt*

Emory
(German) industrious
leader
*Emery, Emmory, Emorey,
Emori, Emorie*

Emre
(Turkish) bond of brothers
Emra, Emrah, Emreson

Emrick
(German) form of Emergy;
ruler
Emryk

Emuel
(Hebrew) form of Emmanuel
(God with us); believer
Emanuel, Imuel

Eneas
(Hebrew) much-praised
Ennes, Ennis

Engelbert
(German) angel-bright
*Bert, Bertie, Berty,
Engelber, Inglebert*

Enlai
(Chinese) thankful

Ennis
(Irish) reliable

Enoch
(Hebrew) dedicated
instructor
En, Enoc, Enok

Enos
(Hebrew) mortal
Enoes

Enrick
(Spanish) cunning
Enric, Enrik

Enrico
(Italian) ruler
Enrike, Enriko, Enryco

Enrique
(Spanish) charismatic ruler
*Enrika, Enrikae, Enriqué,
Enryque, Quiqui*

Enver
(Turkish) brightest child

Enzi
(African) strong boy

Enzo
(Italian) fun-loving

Ephraim
(Hebrew) fertile
*Eff, Efraim, Efram, Efrem,
Ephraime, Ephrame,
Ephrayme*

Erasmus
(Greek) beloved
Eras, Erasmas, Erasmis

Erastus
(Greek) loved baby

Erazmo
(Spanish) loved
Erasmo, Eraz, Ras, Raz

Erbert
(German) from Herbert;
famed fighter
Ebert, Erberto

Ercole
(Italian) glorious God's child

Erebus
(Greek) nether darkness

Erhardt
(German) strong-willed
Erhar, Erhard, Erhart, Erheart

Eric
(Scandinavian) powerful
leader
*Ehrick, Erek, Erick, Erik,
Eryke*

Erie
(Place name) a Great Lake
in the U.S.

Erikson
(Scandinavian) Erik's son;
bold man
*Ericksen, Eriksen, Erycksen,
Eryksen, Erykson*

Erin
(Irish) peace-loving
Aaron, Arin, Aron, Eryn

Erlan
(English) aristocratic
*Earlan, Earland, Erland,
Erlen, Erlin*

Ernest
(English) sincere
*Earnest, Ern, Ernie, Erno,
Ernst, Erny, Ernye*

Ernesto
(Spanish) sincere
Ernie, Nesto, Nestoh

Ernie
(English) short for Ernest
Ernee, Erney, Erny

Erol
(American) noble
Eral, Eril, Errol

Eros
(Greek) sensual
Ero

Erose
(Greek) from the word eros;
sensual; resolute
Eroce

Errol
(German) noble
Erol, Erold, Erroll, Erryl

Erskine
(Scottish) high-minded
Ers, Ersk, Erskin

Erv
(English) good-looking

Ervin
(English) sea-loving
*Earvin, Erv, Ervan, Erven,
Ervind, Ervyn*

Ervine
(English) sea-lover
Ervene, Ervin

Erving
(Scottish) good-looking

Erwin
(English) friendly
Erwyn

Esau
(Hebrew) rough-hewn
Es, Esa, Esauw, Esaw

Esaul
(American) combo of Esau and Saul; hairy
Esau, Esaw, Esawle, Saul

Eskil
(Scandinavian) divine

Esmé
(French) beloved
Es, Esmae, Esmay

Esmond
(French) handsome
Esmand, Esmon, Esmund

Esmun
(American) kind
Es, Esman, Esmon

Espen
(German) bear of God

Espn
(American) form of Espen; sports enthusiast
ESPN

Esperanza
(Spanish) from esperance; (English) hopeful
Esper, Esperance, Esperence

Essex
(Place name) dignified
Ess, Ez

Este
(Spanish) short for Esteban; crowned

Esteban
(Spanish) royal; friendly
Estabon, Estebann, Estevan, Estiban, Estyban

Estes
(Place name) eastern; open
Estas, Este, Estis

Estevan
(Spanish) crowned
Estivan, Estyvan

Estridge
(Last name as first name) fortified
Es, Estri, Estry

Etereo
(Spanish) heavenly; spiritual
Etero

Ethan
(Hebrew) firm will
Eth, Ethen, Ethin, Ethon

Etheal
(English) of good birth
Ethal

Ethelbert
(German) principled
Ethelburt, Ethylbert

Ettore
(Italian) loyal
Etor, Etore

Euclid
(Greek) brilliant
Euclide, Uclid

Eugene
(Greek) blue-blood
Eugean, Eugenie, Ugene

Eural
(American) from Ural Mountains; upward
Eure, Ural, Ury

Eurby
(Last name as first name) sea
Erby, Eurb

Eurskie
(Invented) dorky
Ersky

Eusebio
(Spanish) devoted to God
Eucebio, Eusabio, Eusevio, Sebio, Usibo

Eustace
(Latin) calming
Eustice, Eustis, Stace, Stacey, Ustace

Eustacio
(Spanish) calm; visionary
Eustacio, Eustase, Eustasio, Eustazio, Eustes, Eustis

Evagelos
(Greek) form of Andrew; strong character
Evaggelos, Evangelo, Evangelos

Evan
(Irish) warrior
Ev, Evann, Evanne, Even, Evin

Evander
(Greek) manly; champion
Evand, Evandar, Evandir

Evans
(Welsh) believer in a gracious God
Evens, Evyns

Evanus
(American) form of Evan; heroic
Evan, Evin, Evinas, Evinus

Evaristo
(Spanish) form of Evan; heroic
Evariso, Evaro

Eve
(Invented) form of Yves
Eeve

Evelyn
(American) writer
Ev, Evlinn, Evlyn

Everard
(German) tough
Ev, Evrard

Everest
(Place name) highest mountain peak in the world

Everett
(English) strong
Ev, Everet, Everitt, Evret, Evrit

Everhart
(Scandinavian) vibrant
Evhart, Evert

Everly
(American) singing
Everlee, Everley, Everlie, Evers

Everton
(English) from the town of boars; fearless

Evetier
(French) good

Evett
(American) bright
Ev, Evatt, Eve, Evidt, Evitt

Evon
(Welsh) form of Evan; warrior
Even, Evin, Evonne, Evonn, Evyn

Ewald
(Polish) fair ruler

Ewan
(Scottish) youthful spirit
Ewahn, Ewon

Ewand
(Welsh) form of Evan; warrior
Ewen, Ewon

Ewanell
(American) form of Ewan; hip
Ewanel, Ewenall

Ewart
(English) shepherd; caring
Ewar, Eward, Ewert

Ewing
(English) law-abiding
Ewin, Ewyng

Excell
(American) competitive
Excel, Exsel, Exsell

Exia
(Spanish) demanding
Ex, Exy

Eza
(Hebrew) from Ezra; helpful
Esri

Ezekiel
(Hebrew) God's strength
Eze, Ezek, Ezekhal, Ezekial, Ezikiel, Ezkeil, Ezekyel, Ezikiel, Ezikyel, Ezykiel, Zeke

Ezequiel
(Spanish) devout

Ezer
(Hebrew) also from Ezra; helpful boy

Ezira
(Hebrew) helpful
Ezirah, Ezyra, Ezyrah

Ezra
(Hebrew) helpful; strong
Esra, Ezrah

Ezri
(Hebrew) my help
Ezrey, Ezry

Ezzie
(Hebrew) from the name Ezra; helpful
Ez

Faakhir
(Arabic) proud

Faber
(German) grower
Fabar, Fabir, Fabyre

Faberto
(Latin) form of Fabian; grower; deals in beans
Fabe, Fabey, Fabian, Fabien, Fabre

Fabian
(Latin) grower; singer
Fab, Fabe, Fabean, Fabeone, Fabie, Fabien, Fabiano

Fabio
(Italian) seductive; handsome
Fab, Fabioh

Fable
(American) storyteller
Fabal, Fabe, Fabel, Fabil

Fabrice
(French) skilled worker
Fabriano, Fabricius, Fabritius, Fabrizio, Fabrizius

Fabrizio
(Italian) fabulous

Fabron
(French) blacksmith

Fabryce
(Latin) crafty
Fab, Fabby, Fabreese, Fabrese, Fabrice

Fabulous
(American) vain
Fab, Fabby, Fabu

Fachan
(Last name as first name) precocious

Factor
(English) entrepreneur

Facundo
(Last name as first name) profound

Faddis
(American) loner; deals in beans
Faddes, Fadice, Fadis

Faddy
(American) faddish
Fad, Faddey, Faddi

Fadi
(Arabic) saved by grace

Fadil
(Arabic) giving

Fagan
(Irish) fiery
Fagane, Fagen, Fagin, Fegan

Fahd
(Arabic) fierce; panther; brave
Fahad

Fahim
(Arabic) intelligent

Faheem
(Arabic) brilliant

Fahren
(American) variant of Faron; direct

Fairbanks
(English) place name; forceful
Fairbanx, Farebanks

Fairbairn
(Scottish) fair-haired child

Fairchild
(English) fair-haired child

Fairfax
(English) full of warmth
Fairfacks, Farefax, Fax, Faxy

Faisal
(Arabic) authoritative
Faisel, Faizal, Fasel, Fayzelle

Faizon
(Arabic) understanding

Fakhr
(Arabic) proud

Faladrick
(Origin unknown) variation of Frederick
Faldrick, Faldrik

Falcon
(American) bird as name; dark; watchful
Falk, Falkon

Faldo
(Last name as first) brassy

Faline
(Hindi) fertile

Falk
(Hebrew) falcon
Falke

Falkner
(French) handles falcons
Fowler, Faulkner

Fallows
(English) inactive
Fallow

Fam
(American) family-oriented
Fammy

Famous
(American) word as name; ambitious
Fame

Fane
(English) exuberant
Fain, Faine

Fannin
(English) happy
Fane

Faolan
(Irish) wolf; sly
Felan, Phelan

Far
(English) traveler
Farr

Faraji
(African) he who comforts others

Faramond
(English) protected
Faramund, Farrimond, Farrimund, Pharamond, Pharamund

Faran
(American) sincere
Fahran, Faren, Faron, Feren, Ferren

Fareed
(Arabic) special

Fargo
(American) jaunty
Fargouh

Farkas
(Last name as first name) strong man

Farley
(English) open
Farl, Farlee, Farleigh, Farlie, Farly, Farlye

Farmer
(English) he farms

Farnall
(Last name as first name) strong man
Farnell, Fernald

Farnham
(English) windblown; field
Farnhum, Farnie, Farnum, Farny

Farnley
(English) from a place of ferns

Farold
(Invented) lively

Farouk
(Arabic) knowing what's true
Faruq, Faruqh

Farquar
(French) masculine

Farr
(English) adventurer
Far

Farrar
(French) distinguished
Farr

Farrell
(Irish) brave
Farel, Farell, Faryl

Farren
(English) mover
Faran, Faron, Farrin, Farron

Farris
(Arabic) rider; (Irish) rock; reliable
Fare, Farice, Faris

Farro
(Italian) grain
Farron, Faro

Fasta
(Spanish) offering

Fattah
(Arabic) conquerer

Faulkner
(English) disciplinarian
Falcon, Falconner, Falkner, Falkoner

Faunus
(Latin) god of nature
Fawnus

Faust
(Latin) lucky
Fauston

Favian
(Latin) knowing
Fav, Favion

Fawad
(Arabic) victorious

Fawcett
(American) audacious
Fawce, Fawcet, Fawcette, Fawcie, Fawsie, Fowcett

Faxan
(Anglo-Saxon) outgoing
Faxen, Faxon

Fay
(Irish) raven-haired
Faye, Fayette

Faysal
(Arabic) judgmental

Febronio
(Spanish) bright

Fedde
(Italian) true

Federico
(Spanish) peaceful and affluent
Federik

Fedor
(German) form of Theodore; romantic
Faydor, Feodor, Fyodor

Fedrick
(American) form of Cedrick; wandering
Fed, Fedric, Fedrik

Feibush
(Last name as first name)
particular

Feivel
(Hebrew) bright

Felimy
(Irish) good

Felipe
(Spanish) horse-lover
Felepe, Filipe, Flippo

Felix
(Latin) joyful
Felixce, Filix, Phelix, Philix

Fellini
(Last name as first)
carnivalesque

Felman
(Last name as first name)
smart
Fel, Fell

Felton
(English) farming the field

Fenimore
(Last name as first name)
creative

Fenner
(English) capable
Fen, Fenn, Fynner

Fenris
(Scandinavian) fierce

Fenton
(English) nature-loving
Fen, Fenn, Fennie, Fenny

Fentress
(English) natural
Fentres, Fyntres

Fenwick
(English) from the marsh
village; able

Feo
(Native American) confident
Feeo, Feoh

Ferdinand
(German) adventurer
*Ferdie, Ferdnand, Ferdy,
Fernand*

Ferenc
(Hungarian) free

Fergall
(Irish) bravest man
Fearghall, Forgael

Fergus
(Irish, Scottish) topnotch
*Feargus, Ferges, Fergie,
Fergis, Fergy*

Ferguson
(Irish) bold; excellent
*Fergie, Fergs, Fergus,
Fergusahn, Fergusen, Fergy,
Furgs, Furgus*

Ferlin
(American) countrified
Ferlan

Fermin
(Spanish) strong-willed
Fer, Fermen, Fermun

Fernando
(Spanish) bold leader
*Ferd, Ferdie, Ferdinando,
Ferdy, Fernand*

Fernley
(English) from the fern
meadow; natural
*Farnlea, Farnlee, Farnleigh,
Farnley, Fernlea, Fernlee,
Fernleigh*

Ferrand
(French) gray-haired
Ferrant, Farrand, Farrant

Ferrell
(Irish) hero
Fere, Ferrel, Feryl

Ferris
(Irish) rock
Farris, Farrish, Ferriss

Festatus
(Irish) raven; dark

Festive
(American) word as name;
joyful
Fest, Festas, Festes

Festus
(Latin) happy
Festes

Fhoki
(Japanese) discriminating

Fiachra
(Irish) raven; watchful

Fico
(Italian) form of Frederick;
dedicated

Fidel
(Latin) faithful
Fidele, Fidell, Fydel

Fidencio
(Spanish)
Fidence, Fidens, Fido

Field
(English) outdoorsman
Fields

Fielding
(English) outdoorsman;
working the fields

Fien
(American) elegant
Fiene, Fine

Fiero
(Spanish) fiery

Fife
(Scottish) bright-eyed
Fyfe, Phyfe

Fiji
(Place name) Fiji Islands;
islander
Fege, Fegee, Fijie

Fikry
(American) industrious
Fike, Fikree, Fikrey

Filbert
(English) genius
Fil, Filb, Bert, Phil

Filip
(Greek) horse-lover;
(Belgium) form of Philip
Fil, Fill

Filmer
(English) from Filmore;
famed
Fill, Filmar

Filmore
(English) famed
*Fill, Fillie, Fillmore, Filly,
Fylmore*

Filomelo
(Spanish) friend

Finbar
(Irish) blond

Finch
(Last name as first name)
birdlike

Fineas
(Egyptian) dark

Finian
(Irish) fair
Fin, Finean, Finn, Fynian

Finlay
(Irish) blond soldier
Finley, Findlay, Findley

Finley
(Irish) magical
Fin, Finny, Fynn, Fynnie

Finn
(Scandinavian) fair-haired;
from Finland
Fin, Finnie, Finny

Finnegan
(Irish) fair
*Finegan, Finigan, Finn,
Finny*

Fintan
(Irish) small blond man

Finton
(Irish) magical, fair
Finn, Finny, Fynton

Fiorello
(Italian) flowering

Firman
(French) also Firmin; loyal
*Firmin, Farman, Farmann,
Fermin*

Fishel
(Hebrew) fish
Fish, Fysh

Fisher
(English) he fishes
*Fish, Fischer, Fisscher,
Visscher*

Fisk
(Scandinavian) also Fiske;
fisherman
Fiske

Fitch
(French) throws spears

Fitz
(French) bright young man;
son
Fitzy

Fitzgerald
(English) bright young man;
Gerald's son

Fitzhugh
(French) Hugh's son; big-
hearted

Fitzmorris
(Last name as first name)
son of Morris
Fitz, Morrey, Morris

Fitzpatrick
(French) Patrick's son; noble

Fitzroy
(French) son of Roy; lively

Fitzsimmons
(English) bright young man;
Simmons's son

Flabia
(Spanish) light-haired
Flavia

Flag
(American) patriotic
Flagg

Flaminio
(Spanish) priest; thoughtful
Flamino

Flann
(Irish) red-haired
Flainn, Flannan, Flannery

Flannan
(Irish) red-haired

Flavean
(Flavian) variant of Flavian

Flavian
(Greek) blond
Flovian

Flavio
(Italian) shining
Flav, Flavioh

Fleada
(American) introvert
Flayda

Fleetwood
(English) from the woods

Flemming
(English) from Flanders;
confident
Fleming, Flyming

Fletcher
(English) kind-hearted;
maker of arrows
*Fletch, Fletchi, Fletchie,
Fletchy*

Flint
(English) stream; nature-
lover
Flinn, Flintt, Flynt, Flynnt

Flip
(English) loves horses; wild
movements

Florentin
(Italian) blooming
Florencio

Florian
(Latin) flourishing
Florean, Florie

Floyd
(English) practical; hair of
gray
Floid

Flux
(Middle English) flowing

Flynn
(Irish) brash
*Flin, Flinn, Flinnie, Flinny,
Flyne*

Flynt
(English) flowing; stream
Flint, Flinte, Flinty, Flynte

Foley
(Last name as first name)
creative
Folee, Folie

Folke
(German) of the people

Folker
(German) watchful
Folke, Folko

Fontayne
(French) giving; fountain
*Font, Fontaine, Fontane,
Fountaine*

Fonzie
(German) short for
Alphonse
Fons, Fonsi, Fonz, Fonzi

For
(American) word as a name
Fore

Foran
(American) derivative of
foreign; exotic
Foren, Forun

Forbes
(Irish) wealthy
Forb

Ford
(English) strong
Feord, Forde, Fyord

Fordan
(English) river crossing;
inventive
Ford, Forday, Forden

Foreign
(American) word as name;
foreigner
Foran

Forend
(American) forward
Fore, Foryn, Forynd

Forest
(French) nature-loving
Forrest, Fory, Fourast

Forester
(English) protective; of the
forest
Forrester, Forry

Fortney
(Latin) strength of character
*Fortenay, Forteney, Forteny,
Fortny, Fourtney*

Fortune
(French) fortunate man
Fortounay, Fortunae

Fortuno
(Spanish) lucky man
Fortunio

Fost
(Latin) form of Foster;
worthwhile
Foste, Fostee, Fosty

Foster
(Latin) worthy
Fauster, Fostay

Fouad
(Arabic) good heart
Fuad

Fowler
(English) hunter; traps fowl
Fowller

Fraime
(Anglo-Saxon) newcomer

Fraine
(English) ash tree; tall
Frayne, Freyne

Francesco
(Italian) flirtatious
Fran, Francey, Frankie, Franky

Franchot
(French) free

Francis
(Latin) free spirit; from France
Fran, Frances, Franciss, Frank, Franky, Frannkie, Franny, Frans

Francisco
(Spanish) free spirit; from Latin Franciscus; Frenchman
Chuco, Cisco, Francisk, Franco, Frisco, Paco, Pancho

Francista
(Spanish) Frenchman; free
Cisco, Cisto, Francisco, Franciscus, Fransico

Franco
(Spanish) defender; spear
Francoh, Franko

Francois
(French) smooth; patriot; Frenchman
Frans, Franswaw, French, Frenchie, Frenchy

Frank
(English) short for Franklin; outspoken; landowner
Franc, Franco, Frankee, Frankie, Frankey, Frankie, Franko, Franky

Franklin
(English) outspoken; landowner
Francklin, Franclin, Frank, Frankie, Franklinn, Franklyn, Franklynn, Franky

Frantisek
(Czech) free man

Franz
(German) man from France; free
Frans

Frasier
(English) attractive; man with curls
Frase, Fraser, Fraze, Frazer

Frayne
(English) foreigner
Fraine, Frayn, Frean, Freen, Freyne

Fred
(German) short for Frederick; plainspoken leader
Fredde, Freddo, Freddy, Fredo

Freddie
(German) short for Frederick; plainspoken leader
Freddee, Freddey, Freddi, Freddy

Freddis
(German) from the name Frederick; friendly
Freddus, Fredes, Fredis

Frederic
(French) peaceful king
Fred, Freddy

Frederick
(German) plainspoken leader; peaceful
Fred, Freddy, Frederic, Fredrich, Fredrik, Fryderyk

Freeborn
(English) born free

Freed
(English) free boy
Fried

Freedom
(American) loves freedom

Freeman
(English) free man
Free, Freedman, Freman

Fremont
(German) protective; noble

French
(English) boy from France

Frewen
(Anglo-Saxon) free
Frewin

Frey
(Scandinavian) fertility god

Frick
(English) brave man

Fridmann
(Last name as first name) free man

Fridolf
(Scandinavian) relishes peace
Freydolf, Freydulf, Friedolf, Fridulf

Fridolin
(German) free

Frieder
(German) peaceful leader
Frie, Fried, Friedrick

Friederich
(German) form of Frederick; leader of peace
Fridrich, Friedrich

Friedhelm
(German) peaceful helmet
Friedelm

Frisco
(American) short for Francisco; free
Cisco, Frisko

Friso
(Anglo-Saxon) best self

Fritz
(German) short for Frederick and Friedrich
Firzie, Firzy, Frits, Fritts, Fritzi, Fritzie, Fritzy

Frode
(Scandinavian) intellectual

Fromel
(Hebrew) outgoing

Frost
(English) cold; freeze

Froyim
(Hebrew) kind

Fructuoso
(Spanish) fruitful
Fru, Fructo

Fry
(English) new sprout; growing
Frye, Fryer

Fu
(Japanese) from Fudo, god of wisdom and fire

Fuddy
(Origin unknown) bright-eyed
Fuddie, Fudee, Fudi

Fukuda
(Japanese) field

Fulbright
(German) brilliant; full of brightness
Fulbrite

Fulgentius
(Latin) full of kindness; shines
Fulgencio

Fulke
(English) folksy
Fulk, Fawke, Fowke

Fuller
(English) tough-willed
Fuler

Fullerton
(English) strong
Fuller, Fullerten

Fulton
(English) fresh mind; field by the town

Funge
(Last name as first name) stodgy
Funje, Funny

Furlo
(American) macho
Furl

Fursey
(Irish) spiritual

Fyfe
(Scottish) craftsman
Fife, Fyffe, Phyfe

Furman
(German) form of Firman; runs a ferry
Fuhrman, Fuhrmann, Furmann

Fyodor
(Russian) divine
Feodor, Fyodr

Gabbana
(Italian) creative
Gabi

Gabe
(Hebrew) short for Gabriel; devout
Gabbee, Gabbi, Gabbie, Gabby, Gabi, Gabie, Gaby

Gabino
(Spanish) strong believer
Gabby, Gabi

Gable
(French) dashing

Gabor
(Last name as first name)
believer; colorful

Gabriel
(Hebrew) God's hero;
devout
*Gabby, Gabe, Gabi, Gabreal,
Gabrel, Gabriele, Gabrielle,
Gabryel*

Gad
(Hebrew) lucky; audacious
Gadd

Gaddiel
(Hebrew) fortunate
Gadiel

Gaddis
(American) hard to please;
picky
Gad, Gaddes, Gadis

Gadi
(Hebrew) short for Gaddiel;
lucky
Gadish

Gael
(English) speaks Gaelic;
independent

Gaetano
(Italian) from the city of
Gaeta; Italian
Gaetan, Geitano, Guytano

Gagan
(French) form of Gage;
dedicated
Gage

Gage
(French) dedicated

Gahuj
(African) hunts

Gailen
(French) healer; physician
Galan, Galen, Galun

Gaines
(Last name as first name)
rich
Ganes, Gaynes

Gair
(Irish) little boy
Gaer, Geir

Gaius
(Latin) joyful
Gal

Galbraith
(Irish) sensible
Gal

Galbreath
(Irish) practical man
Galbraith, Gall

Gale
(English) cheerful
*Gael, Gail, Gaile, Gaille,
Gayle*

Galegina
(Native American) lithe; deer

Galen
(Greek) calming; intelligent
*Gaelin, Gailen, Gale,
Galean, Galey, Gaylen*

Galfrid
(Last name as first name)
uplifted
Galfryd

Galileo
(Italian) from Galilee;
inventor
Galilayo

Gallagher
(Irish) helpful
*Galagher, Gallager, Gallie,
Gally*

Gallant
(American) word as a name;
savoir-faire
Gael, Gail, Gaila, Gaile, Gayle

Gallman
(Last name as first name)
lively
Galman, Gallway, Galway

Galo
(Spanish) enthusiastic
Gallo

Galloway
(Irish) outgoing
*Gallie, Gally, Galoway,
Galway*

Galt
(German) empowered

Galton
(English) landowner;
reclusive

Galvin
(Irish) sparrow; flighty
*Gallven, Gallvin, Galvan,
Galven, Galway*

Gamal
(Arabic) camel; travels long
distances

Gamaliel
(Hebrew) rewarded by God
Gamaleel, Gamalyel

Gamba
(African) warring

Gamberro
(Spanish) hooligan
Gami

Gamble
(Scandinavian) mature wisdom
Gam, Gamb, Gambel, Gambie, Gamby

Gamel
(Hebrew) God rewards him

Gamliel
(Arabic) camel; wanders
Gamaliel

Gammon
(Last name as first name) game
Gamen, Gamon, Gamun

Gan
(Chinese) wanders wide

Gandy
(American) adventurer

Ganesh
(Hindi) Lord of all

Ganon
(Irish) fair-skinned
Gannon, Ganny

Ganso
(Spanish) goose; goofy
Gans, Ganz

Ganya
(Russian) strong

Garai
(African) settled

Garbhan
(Irish) rough boy

Garvan
(English) throws spears; athletic

Garcia
(Spanish) strong
Garce, Garcey, Garsey

Gard
(English) guard
Garde, Gardey, Gardi, Gardie, Gardy, Guard

Gardner
(English) keeper of the garden
Gar, Gard, Gardener, Gardie, Gardiner, Gardnyr, Gardy

Garek
(Polish) brave boy
Garreck, Garrik, Gerek

Gareth
(Irish) kind, gentle
Gare

Garfield
(English) armed
Gar, Garfeld

Gariana
(American) form of Gary; wild heart

Garin
(American) form of Darin; kind
Gare, Gary

Garland
(French) adorned
Gar, Garlan, Garlend, Garlind, Garlynd

Garmon
(German) man who throws spears
Garmen

Garn
(American) prepared
Gar, Garnie, Garny, Garr

Garner
(French) guard
Gar, Garn, Garnar, Garnir

Garnett
(English) armed; spear
Gar, Garn, Garnet, Garny

Garnock
(Welsh) from alder-tree place; outdoor spirit

Garon
(American) gentle
Garonn, Garonne

Garonzick
(Last name as first name) secure
Gare, Garon, Garons, Garonz

Garp
(German) form of Garbo

Garr
(English) short for Garnett and Garth; giving
Gar

Garreth
(German) brave
Gareth, Garryth, Garyth

Garrett
(Irish) brave; watchful
Gare, Garet, Garitt, Garret, Garritt, Gary, Gerrot

Garrick
(English) ruler with a spear; brave
Garey, Garic, Garick, Garik, Garreck, Gary, Gerrick, Gerrieck

Garridan
(English) form of Gary; quiet

Garrison
(French) prepared
Garris, Garrish, Garry, Gary

Garroway
(English) throws spears;
physical presence
Garraway

Garson
(English) son of Gar; fort
home; industrious

Garth
(Scandinavian) sunny;
gardener
*Gar, Gare, Garry, Gart,
Garthe, Gary*

Garthay
(Irish) from Gareth; gentle
Garthae

Garton
(English) place of spear
man; rowdy

Garv
(English) peaceful
Garvey, Garvy

Garvy
(Irish) peacemaker
Garvey

Garwood
(English) natural
*Garr, Garwode, Garwoode,
Woody*

Gary
(English) strong man
Gare, Garrey, Garri

Gaspard
(French) holds treasure
Gaspar, Gasper

Gaspare
(Italian) treasure-holder
Casper, Gasp, Gasparo

Gaston
(French) native of Gascony;
stranger
Gastawn, Gastowyn

Gate
(English) open
Gait, Gates

Gatsby
(Literature) ambitious; tragic

Gaudy
(American) word as name;
colorful
Gaudin, Gaudy

Gaurav
(Hindi) proud

Gautier
(French) form of Walter;
distinctive
Gauther, Gauthier

Gavard
(Last name as first name)
creative
Gav, Gaverd

Gavin
(English) alert; hawk
*Gav, Gaven, Gavinn, Gavon,
Gavvin, Gavyn*

Gavriel
(Herbew) filled by God's
strength
Gavryel

Gavril
(Hebrew) strong
Gavrill, Gavryl, Gavryll

Gawain
(Hebrew) archangel
Gawaine, Gawayne, Gwayne

Gawath
(Welsh) white falcon; from
Gawain, knight

Gawin
(Scottish) watchful; wise
Gawyn

Gaylin
(Greek) calm
*Gaelin, Gayle, Gaylen,
Gaylon*

Gaylord
(French) high-energy
*Gallerd, Galurd, Gaylar,
Gayllaird, Gaylor*

Gaynor
(Irish) spunky
Gainer, Gaye, Gayner

Gayton
(Irish) fair
Gayten, Gaytun

Geary
(English) flexible
Gearey

Gedaliah
(Hebrew) great in Jehovah's
love
*Gedalia, Gedaliahu,
Gedalya, Gedalyahu*

Geer
(German) spearman
Geere

Gefaniah
(Hebrew) vineyard of the
Lord; grows
*Gefania, Gefanya,
Gephania, Gephaniah*

Gemini
(Astrology) zodiac twins;
intelligent

Genaro
(Latin) dedicated
Genaroe, Genaroh

Gene
(Greek) noble
Geno, Jene, Jeno

General
(American) military rank as name; leader

Geno
(Italian) spontaneous

Genoah
(Place name) city in Italy
Genoa, Jenoa, Jenoah

Genovese
(Italian) spontaneous; from Genoa, Italy
Genno, Geno, Genovise, Genovize

Gent
(American) short for gentleman; mannerly
Gynt, Jent, Jynt

Gentil
(Spanish) charming
Gentilo

Gentry
(American) high breeding
Genntrie, Gent, Gentree, Gentree, Gentrie

Genty
(Irish) man of snow; changes

Geo
(Greek) form of George; good
Gee

Geoff
(English) short for Geoffrey; peaceful
Jeff

Geoffrey
(English) peaceful
Geffry, Geoff, Geoffie, Geoffry, Geoffy, Geofry, Jeff

Georg
(German) works with the earth

George
(Greek) land-loving; farmer
Georg, Georgi, Georgie, Georgy, Jorg, Jorge

Georgio
(Italian) earth-worker
Giorgio, Jorgio, Jorjeo, Jorjio

Georgios
(Greek) land-loving

Georgy
(Greek) short for George
Georgee, Georgi, Georgie

Geraint
(English) old

Gerald
(German) strong; ruling with a spear
Geralde, Gerrald, Gerre, Gerry

Gerard
(French) brave
Gerord, Gerr, Gerrard

Gerber
(Last name as first name) particular
Gerb

Gerbold
(German) bold with a spear
Gerbolde

Gere
(English) spear-wielding; dramatic
Gear

Gerhard
(German) forceful
Ger, Gerd

Gerlach
(German); athlete with spears; musical

Germain
(French) growing; from Germany
Germa, Germaine, Germane, Germay, Germayne, Jermaine

German
(German) from the country of Germany

Gerod
(English) form of Gerard; brave
Garard, Geraldo, Gerard, Gerarde, Gere, Gererde, Gerry, Gerus, Giraud, Jerade, Jerard, Jere, Jerod, Jerott, Jerry

Gerold
(Danish) rules with spears
Gerrold, Gerry

Geronimo
(Italian, Native American) wild heart
Geronimoh

Gerry
(English) short for Gerald
Gerr, Gerre, Gerree, Gerrey, Gerri, Gerrie

Gersh
(Biblical) short for Gershon; unwanted
Gershe, Gursh, Gurshe

Gershom
(Biblical) exile

Gervaise
(French) man of honor
Gerv, Gervase, Gervay

Gervasio
(Spanish) aggressive
Gervase, Gervaso, Jervasio

Gervis
(German) honored
Jervis, Gerv, Gervace, Gervaise, Gervey, Jervaise

Gerwyn
(Welsh) fair and lovely

Geshem
(Hebrew) raining

Geter
(Origin unknown) hopeful
Getterr, Getur

Gethin
(Welsh) dark skin

Gevariah
(Hebrew) strength
Gevaria, Gevarya, Gevaryah, Gevaryahu

Ghalby
(Origin unknown) winning
Galby

Ghalib
(Arabic) wins

Ghassan
(Arabic) in the prime of life

Ghayth
(Arabic) victor
Ghaith

Ghoshal
(Hindi) the speaker
Ghoshil

Gi
(Italian) form of John; short for Gian; live wire

Giacomo
(Italian) replacement; musical
Como, Gia

Giancarlo
(Italian) combo of Gian and Carlo; magnetic
Carlo, Carlos, Gia, Gian, Giannie, Gianny

Giann
(Italian) believer in a gracious God
Ghiann, Giahanni, Gian, Gianni, Giannie, Gianny

Gianni
(Italian) calm; believer in God's grace
Giannie, Gianny

Gibbs
(English) form of Gibson; spunky
Gib, Gibb, Gibbes

Gibbon
(Scottish) strong
Gibben, Gibbons

Gibor
(Hebrew) short for Giborah; strong boy

Gibson
(English) smiling
Gib, Gibb, Gibbie, Gibbson, Gibby, Gibsan, Gibsen, Gibsyn

Gid
(Hebrew) form of Gideon; warrior; Bible distributor
Gidd, Giddee, Giddi, Giddy

Gideon
(Hebrew) power-wielding
Giddy, Gideone, Gidion, Gidyun

Gidney
(English) strong
Gidnee, Gidni

Gif
(English) giver
Giff

Giffin
(English) giving
Giffyn

Gifford
(English) generous-hearted
Giford

Gig
(English) man in the carriage

Giglio
(Italian) form of the word gigolo
Gig

Gifford
(English) generous-hearted
Giff, Gifferd, Giffie, Giffy

Gil
(Hebrew) for Gilam; joyful
Gill

Gilad
(Hebrew) testimonial hill; outspoken
Giladi, Gilead

Gilam
(Hebrew) joyful people

Gilbert
(English) intelligent
Gil, Gilber, Gilburt, Gill, Gilly

Gilberto
(Spanish) bright
*Bertie, Berty, Gil, Gilb,
Gilburto, Gillberto, Gilly*

Gilby
(Irish) blond
Gilbie, Gill, Gillbi

Gilchrist
(Irish) open
Gill

Gildea
(Irish) God's servant

Gildo
(Italian) macho
Gil, Gill, Gilly

Giles
(French) protective
Gile, Gyles

Gilford
(English) kind-hearted
Gill, Gillford, Guilford

Gill
(Hebrew) happy man
Gil, Gilli, Gillie, Gilly

Gillanders
(Scottish) serves

Gillean
(Scottish) able server
Gillan, Gillen, Gillian

Gilles
(French) miraculous
Geal, Zheal, Zheel

Gillespie
(Irish) humble
Gilespie, Gill, Gilley, Gilli, Gilly

Gillett
(French) hospitable
Gelett, Gelette, Gillette

Gilley
(American) countrified
Gill, Gilleye, Gilli, Gilly

Gillian
(Irish) devout
Gill, Gilley, Gilly, Gillyun

Gilman
(Irish) serving well
*Gilley, Gilli, Gillman,
Gillmand, Gilly, Gilmand,
Gilmon*

Gilmer
(English) riveting
Gelmer, Gill, Gillmer, Gilly

Gilmore
(Irish) riveting
Gill, Gillmore, Gilmohr

Gilo
(Hebrew) joyful

Gilon
(Hebrew) joyful
Gill

Gilroy
(Irish) king's devotee
*Gilderoy, Gildray, Gildrey,
Gildroy, Gillroy*

Gilson
(Irish) devoted son

Gilus
(Scottish) Jesus's servant

Ginder
(American) form of gender;
vivacious
Gin, Gind, Gindyr, Jind, Jinder

Gino
(Italian) of good breeding;
outgoing
Geeno, Geino, Ginoh

Ginton
(Hebrew) garden

Giona
(Italian) for John; form of
Giovanni; believer

Giordano
(Italian) delivered
Giorgie, Jiordano

Giorgio
(Italian) earthy; creative
*George, Georgeeo, Georgo,
Jorge, Jorgio*

Giovanni
(Italian) jovial; happy
believer
*Geovanni, Gio, Giovani,
Giovannie, Giovanny,
Vannie, Vanny, Vonny*

Gipsy
(English) travels widely

Girioel
(Welsh) lord

Girvin
(Irish) tough-minded
Girvan, Girven, Girvon

Gitel
(Hebrew) good

Giulio
(Italian) youth

Giuseppe
(Italian) capable
Beppo, Giusepe, Gusepe

Given
(Last name as first name) gift
Givens, Gyvan, Gyven, Gyvin

Givon
(Hebrew) boy of heights

Gizmo
(American) playful
Gis, Gismo, Giz

Glad
(American) happy
Gladd, Gladde, Gladdi, Gladdie, Gladdy

Gladstone
(English) cheering

Gladus
(Welsh) lame; rueful

Gladwyn
(English) friend who has a light heart
Glad, Gladdy, Gladwin, Gladwynn

Glaisne
(Irish) serene
Glasny

Glancy
(American) form of Clancy; ebullient
Glance, Glancee, Glancey, Glanci

Glanville
(French) serene

Glasgow
(Place name) city in Scotland

Glenard
(Irish) from a glen; nature-loving
Glen, Glenerd, Glenn, Glennard, Glenni, Glennie

Glen
(Irish) natural wonder
Glenn

Glendon
(Scottish) fortified in nature
Glen, Glend, Glenden, Glenn, Glynden

Glendower
(Welsh) water valley boy

Glenn
(Irish) natural wonder
Glen, Glenni, Glennie, Glenny, Glynn, Glynny

Glennon
(Last name as first name) living in a valley
Glenen, Glennen, Glenon

Gloster
(Place name) form of Gloucester, city area in England

Glyndwr
(Welsh) water valley life
Glyn, Glynn, Glynne

Glynn
(Welsh) lives in a restful glen
Glyn, Glin, Glinn

Gobi
(Place name) audacious
Gobee, Gobie

Gobind
(Sanskrit) the name of a Hindi deity
Govind

Gockley
(Last name as first name) peaceful
Gocklee

Goddard
(German) staunch in spirituality
Godard, Godderd, Goddird

Godfrey
(Irish) peaceful
Godfree, Godfrie, Godfry

Godfried
(German) imbued with God's peace
Godfreed

Godric
(English) man of God
Godrick, Godrik, Godryc, Godryck, Godryk

Godridge
(Last name as first name) place of God

Godwin
(English) close to God
Godwinn, Godwyn, Godwynn

Goel
(Hebrew) redeemed

Goethe
(Last name as first name) poet, playwright; genius

Gofraidh
(Irish) God's peace child
Gothfraidh, Gothraidh

Gohn
(African American) spirited
Gon

Golding
(English) golden boy

Goldo
(English) golden
Golo

Goliath
(Hebrew) large
Goliathe

Gomda
(Native American) wind's moods

Gomer
(English) famed fighter
Gomar, Gomher, Gomor

Gong
(American) forceful

Gonz
(Spanish) form of Gonzalo; wild wolf
Gons, Gonz, Gonza, Gonzales, Gonzalez

Gonzales
(Spanish) feisty
Gonzalez

Gonzalo
(Spanish) feisty wolf
Gonz, Gonzoloh

Goodman
(Last name as first name) a good man
Goodeman

Goodrich
(Last name as first name) giving; good
Goodriche

Goode
(English) good
Good, Goodey, Goody

Goran
(Croatian) good

Gordo
(American) jovial guy

Gordon
(English) nature-lover; hill
Gord, Gordan, Gorden, Gordi, Gordie, Gordy

Gordy
(English) short for Gordon
Gordee, Gordi, Gordie

Gore
(English) practical; pie-shaped land

Gorgon
(Place name) form of Gorgonzola, Italy
Gorgan, Gorgun

Gorham
(English) sophisticated; name of a silver company
Goram

Gorky
(Place name) Russian amusement park in the novel *Gorky Park*; mysterious
Gork, Gorkee, Gorkey, Gorki

Gorman
(Irish) small man
Gormann, Gormen

Goro
(Japanese) fifth son

Gosheven
(Native American) leaps well; athletic

Gotam
(Hindi) best cow; cherished
Gautam, Gautoma

Gottfried
(German) form of Godfried; peaceful god

Gotzon
(German) angel

Gower
(Welsh) unblemished

Gowon
(African) rainmaking

Gozal
(Hebrew) baby bird; trying his wings

Grady
(Irish) hardworking
Grade, Gradee, Gradey

Graem
(Scottish) homebody
Graeme

Graham
(English) wealthy; grand house
Graeham, Graeme, Grame

Grail
(Word as name) desired; sought after
Grale, Grayle

Gram
(American) form of Graham; homeloving

Granbel
(Last name as first name) grand and attractive
Granbell

Granderson
(Last name as first name) grand
Grand, Grander

Grange
(French) lonely; on the farm
Grainge, Granger, Grangher

Granison
(Last name as first name) son of Gran; grandiose
Gran, Grann

Granite
(American) rock; hard
Granet

Grant
(English) expansive
Grandt, Grann, Grannt

Grantly
(French) tall; lithe
Grantlea, Grantleigh, Grantley

Granville
(French) grandiose
Grann, Granvel, Granvelle, Gravil

Gravette
(Origin unknown) grave
Gravet

Gray
(English) hair of gray
Graye, Grey

Graylon
(English) gray-haired
Gray, Grayan, Graylan, Graylin

Grayson
(English) son of man with gray hair
Gray, Grey, Greyson

Graz
(Place name) city in Austria

Graziano
(Italian) dearest
Graciano, Graz

Greenlee
(English) outdoorsy
Green, Greenlea, Greenly

Greeley
(English) careful
Grealey, Greel, Greely

Greenwood
(English) untamed; forest
Greene, Greenwoode, Greenwude, Grenwood

Greer
(Last name as first name) sly
Greere, Grier

Greg
(Latin) short for Gregory; vigilant
Gregg, Greggie, Greggy

Gregoire
(French) watchful
Gregorie

Gregor
(Greek) cautious
Greger, Gregors, Greig

Gregorio
(Greek) careful

Gregory
(Greek) cautious
Greg, Greggory, Greggy, Gregori, Gregorie, Gregry

Gregson
(Last name as first name) son of Greg; careful
Greggsen, Greggson, Gregsen

Grenville
(New Zealand) outdoorsy
Granville, Gren

Gresham
(English) of pasture village; sylvan
Grisham

Greville
(English) thoughtful

Grey
(Last name as first name) quiet; grey-haired
Greyson

Griffin
(Latin) unconventional
Greffen, Griff, Griffee, Griffen, Griffey, Griffie, Griffon, Griffy

Griffith
(Welsh) able leader
Griff, Griffee, Griffey, Griffie, Griffy

Grigg
(Welsh) vigilant

Grigori
(Russian) watchful
Grig, Grigor

Grimbald
(Last name as first name) dark
Grimbold

Grimm
(English) grim; dark
Grim, Grym

Grimshaw
(English) from a dark forest; quiet

Gris
(German) gray
Griz

Griswald
(German) bland
Greswold, Gris, Griswold

Grosvenor
(French) hunts well

Grover
(English) thriving
Grove

Gruver
(Origin unknown) ambitious
Gruever

Guard
(American) protects

Guerdon
(English) combative

Guido
(Italian) guiding
Guidoh, Gwedo, Gweedo

Guilford
(English) from a ford with
yellow flowers; nature-lover
Gilford, Guildford

Guillermo
(Spanish) attentive
Guilermo, Gulermo

Gullet
(Latin) throat

Gulshan
(Hindi) gardener; flourishes

Gulzar
(Arabic) thrives

Gundy
(American) friendly
Gundee

Gunn
(Scandinavian) macho;
gunman
Gun, Gunner

Gunnar
(Scandinavian) bold
Gunn, Gunner, Gunnir

Guntersen
(Scandinavian) macho;
gunman
Gun, Gunth

Gunther
(Scandinavian) able fighter
*Funn, Gunnar, Gunner,
Guntar, Gunthar, Gunthur*

Gunyon
(American) tough; gunman
Gunn, Gunyun

Gur
(Hindi) from guru; teacher

Gurpreet
(Hindi) devoted follower

Guryon
(Hebrew) lionlike
Garón, Gorion, Gurion

Gus
(Scandinavian) short for
Gustav
Guss, Gussi, Gussy, Gussye

Gustachian
(American) pretentious
Gus, Gussy, Gust

Gustaf
(German) armed; vital
*Gus, Gusstof, Gustav,
Gustovo*

Gustav, Gustave
(Scandinavian) vital
*Gus, Gussie, Gussy, Gusta,
Gustaf, Gustaff, Gusti,
Gustof, Gustoff*

Gustavo
(Spanish) vital; gusto
Gus, Gustaffo, Gustav

Gusto
(Spanish) pleasure
Gusty

Gustus
(Scandinavian) royal
*Gus, Gustaf, Gustave,
Gustavo*

Guth
(Irish) short for Guthrie; in
the wind
Guthe, Guthry

Guthrie
(Irish) windy; heroic
Guthree, Guthry

Gutierre
(Spanish) from Walter;
distinguished

Guy
(French) assertive;
(German) leader
Guye

Guwayne
(American) combo of Guy
and Wayne
*Guwain, Guwane, Guy,
Gwaine, Gwayne*

Guzet
(American) bravado
Guzz, Guzzett, Guzzie

Gwandoya
(African) miserable fate

Gwynedd
(Welsh) fair-haired
*Gwyn, Gwynfor, Gwynn,
Gwynne*

Gweedo
(Invented) form of Guido

Gwent
(Place name) city in Wales

Gwill
(American) dark-eyed
Gewill, Guwill

Gwynn
(Welsh) fair
Gwen, Gwyn

Gyan
(Hindi) knowledgeable
Gyani

Gyasi
(African) terrific man

Gylfi
(Scandinavian) king;
stealthy

Gyth
(American) capable
Gith, Gythe

Haadee
(Arabic) leader

Haafiz
(Arabic) protector

Haakon
(Scandinavian) chosen son

Haaris
(Arabic) good man

Haas
(Last name as first name)
good

Habakkuk
(Hebrew) embrace

Habib
(Arabic) well loved
Habeeb

Habie
(Origin unknown) jovial
Hab

Habimama
(African) believer in God

Hachiro
(Japanese) eighth son

Hachman
(Last name as first name)
chops
Hachmann, Hachmin

Hackett
(Last name as first name)
chops

Hackman
(German) fervent; hacks
wood
Hackmann

Hadar
(Hebrew) respected
Hadaram, Hadur, Heder

Hadden
(American) bright; natural
*Haddan, Haddon, Haddin,
Haden, Hadon*

Haddy
(English) short for Hadley;
sylvan
Had, Haddee, Haddey, Haddi

Hadad
(Arabic) calm

Hades
(Mythology) Greek god of
the dead

Hadi
(Arabic) guide

Hadley
(English) lover of nature;
meadow with heather
*Haddleye, Hadlee, Hadlie,
Hadly*

Hadrian
(Roman) from Hadria

Hadriel
(Hebrew) blessed

Hadwin
(Last name as first name)
natural man
Hadwyn

Hafiz
(Arabic) guards others
Hafeez, Hapheez, Haphiz

Hagan
(German) defender
Hagen, Haggan, Haggin

Hagar
(Hebrew) wanders

Hagen
(German) chosen one
Hagan, Haggen

Hagley
(Last name as first name)
defensive

Haidar
(Hindi) lionlike
Haider, Haydar, Hyder

Haig
(Last name as first name)
authoritative

Haike
(Asian) of the water

Haim
(Hebrew) alive
Hayim, Hayyim

Haines
(Last name as first name)
confident
Hanus, Haynes

Hakan
(Arabic) fair

Hakim
(Arabic) brilliant
Hakeam, Hakeem, Hakym

Hako
(Japanese) honorable

Hakon
(Scandinavian) chosen son
*Haaken, Haakin, Haakon,
Hacon, Hagan, Hagen,
Hakan, Hako*

Hal
(English) home ruler

Haland
(Last name as first name)
island
Halland

Halbert
(Last name as first name)
island
Hal, Bert

Haldane
(German) fierce; person
who is half Danish
Haldayn, Haldayne

Haldas
(Last name as first name)
dependable

Halden
(German) man who is half
Dane
*Haldin, Haldane, Haldan,
Halfdan*

Haldor
(Scandinavian) thunderous
rock

Hale
(English) heroic
Hal, Halee, Haley, Hali

Halen
(Swedish) portal to life
*Hailen, Hale, Haley, Hallen,
Haylen, Haylin*

Haley
(Irish) innovative
*Hail, Hailee, Hailey, Hale,
Halee, Hayley*

Halford
(Last name as first name)
kind

Hali
(Greek) loves the sea

Hall
(English) solemn

Hallam
(African) gentle

Hallberg
(English) comes from a
town of valleys
Halberg, Halburg, Hallburg

Halle
(Scandinavian) rocklike
dependability

Halley
(English) holy man

Halliwell
(Last name as first name)
sea-loving

Hallward
(English) guards the hall;
wily
Halward, Halwerd, Hawarden

Halmer
(English) robust

Halse
(English) on the island
*Halce, Halsi, Halsy, Halzee,
Halzie*

Halsey
(English) isolated; island

Halstead
(Last name as first name)
home on the rock
Halsted

Halston
(Origin unknown)
fashionable

Halton
(English) town on a hill;
country boy
Halten, Hallton, Halton

Halvard
(Scandinavian) staunch
Halvor, Hallvard

Halwell
(English) special
Hallwell, Halwel, Halwelle

Ham
(Last name as first name)
praising

Hamaker
(Last name as first name)
industrious
Ham

Hamal
(Arabic) lamb

Hamar
(Scandinavian) hammer

Hamid
(Arabic) grateful
Hameed

Hamidi
(Arabic, African)
praiseworthy
Ham, Hamedi, Hameedi,
Hamm, Hammad

Hamil
(English) rough-hewn
Hamel, Hamell, Hamill,
Hamm

Hamilton
(English) benefiting
Hamelton, Hamil,
Hammilton

Hamish
(Irish) form of James;
supplanting

Hamlet
(German, French)
conflicted; small village;
Shakespearean hero
Ham, Hamlette, Hamlit,
Hamm

Hamlin
(German) homebody
Hamaline, Hamelin,
Hamlen, Hamlyn

Hammer
(German) works with a
hammer; able
Hammar, Hammur

Hammond
(English) ingenious
Ham, Hamm, Hammon,
Hamond

Hamon
(Scandinavian) leader
Hamo

Hamor
(Hebrew) organized

Hamp
(American) fun-loving
Ham, Hampton

Hampden
(English) distinctive; valley
home

Hampton
(English) distinctive
Ham, Hamm, Hamp, Hampt

Han
(Arabic) from Hani;
happiness

Hanani
(Arabic) merciful

Hancock
(English) has a farm;
practical

Haneef
(Arabic) believer

Hanford
(Last name as first name)
forgiving
Hamford

Hani
(Arabic) happy

Hanif
(Arabic) Islam believer

Hanisi
(African) Thursday-born

Hank
(English) short for Henry;
ruler; cavalier
Hankey, Hanks, Hanky

Hanley
(English) natural; meadow
high
Han, Hanlee, Hanleigh, Hanly

Hannes
(Scandinavian) short form
of Johannes; giving
Hahnes

Hannibal
(Slavic) leader
Hanibal, Hanibel, Hann

Hanoch
(Hebrew) loyal

Hans
(Scandinavian) believer;
warm
Hahns, Hanz, Hons

Hansa
(Scandinavian) traditional;
believer in a gracious Lord
Hans

Hansel
(Scandinavian) gullible;
open
Hans, Hansie, Hanzel

Hansen
(Scandinavian) warm;
Hans's son
Han, Handsen, Hans,
Hansan, Hanson, Hanssen,
Hansson, Hanz

Hansraj
(Hindi) king of swans;
smooth

Haqq
(Arabic) truth

Harbin
(English) optimist

Harcourt
(English) loves nature

Hardin
(English) lively; valley of hares
Hardee, Harden

Harding
(English) fiery
Harden, Hardeng

Hardwick
(English) castle boy
Harwyck

Hardwin
(English) keeps hares

Hardy
(American) fun-loving; substantial
Hardie, Hardey, Harday, Harding

Harean
(African) aware

Harel
(Scandinavian) ruler

Harence
(English) swift

Harford
(English) jolly
Harferd

Hargrove
(English) fruitful

Harim
(Arabic) above all

Hark
(American) word as name; behold
Harko

Harkin
(Irish) red-faced
Harkan, Harken

Harlan
(English) army land; athletic
Hal, Harl, Harlen, Harlon, Harlynn

Harlemm
(African American) from Harlem; dancer
Harl, Harlam, Harlem, Harlems, Harlum, Harly

Harley
(English) wild-spirited
Harl, Harlee, Harly

Harlow
(English) bold
Harlo, Harloh

Harmon
(German) dependable
Harm, Harman, Harmen

Harmony
(Mythology) from Harmonia; in harmony with life
Harmonio

Harod
(Biblical) king
Harrod

Harold
(Scandinavian) leader of an army
Hal, Harald, Hareld, Harry

Harper
(English) artistic and musical; harpist
Harp

Harpo
(American) jovial
Harpoh, Harrpo

Harrell
(Hebrew) likes the mountain of God; religious

Harrington
(English) comes from the town of Harry; old-fashioned

Harris
(English) dignified
Haris, Harriss

Harrison
(English) Harry's son; adventurer
Harrey, Harri, Harrie, Harris, Harrisan, Harrisen, Harry

Harrod
(Hebrew) victor
Harod, Harry

Harry
(English) home ruler
Harree, Harrey, Harri, Harrie, Harye

Harshad
(Hindi) evokes joy

Harsho
(Hindi) joy

Hart
(English) giving
Harte

Hartley
(English) wilderness wanderer
Hartlee, Hartleigh, Hartly

Hartman
(German) strong-willed
Hart, Hartmann, Harttman

Hartsey
(English) lazing on the meadow; sylvan
Harts, Hartz

Hartwell
(English) good-hearted
Harwell, Harwill

Hartwig
(German) strong

Haruki
(Japanese) child of the spring

Harun
(Arabic) highly regarded

Harv
(German) able combatant
Har

Harvey
(German) fighter
Harv, Harvi, Harvie, Harvy

Harwin
(American) safe
Harwen, Harwon

Harwood
(English) from the deer wood; artistic
Harewood

Hasan
(Arabic) attractive

Hasani
(African) good

Hashim
(Arabic) force for good
Hasheem

Hashum
(African) crushes
Heshum

Hasin
(Arabic) handsome
Hassin, Hasen

Hask
(Hebrew) from Haskell, form of Ekekial; smart
Haske

Haskell
(Hebrew) ingratiating
Hask, Haskel, Haskie, Hasky

Haslett
(English) land of hazel trees; worthy
Haslit, Haslitt, Hazel, Hazlett, Hazlitt

Hassan
(Arabic) good-looking
Hasan

Hasso
(German) sun
Hasson

Hastings
(English) leader
Haste

Haswell
(English) dignified
Has, Haz

Hattan
(Place name) from Manhattan; sophisticate
Hatt

Havard
(American) form of Harvard; guardian
Hav

Havelock
(Czech) form of Paul; prudent

Haven
(English) sanctuary
Haiv, Hav

Haward
(English) guards the hedge; border man
Hawarden

Hawes
(English) stays by the hedges
Haws

Hawke
(English) watchful; falcon
Hauk, Hawk

Hawthorne
(English) observer

Hayden
(English) respectful
Haden, Hadon, Hay, Haydon, Haydyn, Hayton

Haye
(English) open

Hayes
(English) open
Haies, Hay, Haye

Hayman
(English) hedging
Hay

Haymo
(Last name as first name) good-natured

Hayne
(English) working outdoors
Haine, Haines, Haynes

Hayward
(English) creative; good work ethic
Hay, Heyward

Hayword
(English) open-minded
Haword, Hayward, Haywerd

Hazael
(Old English) hazel tree

Hazaiah
(Hebrew) believes God's decisions

Hazard
(Origin Unknown)
Hazzard

Hazen
(English) form of Hayes; hedges; indecisive
Hazin

Hazleton
(English) from woods of hazel trees

Hazlewood
(English) from woods of hazel trees

Hearn
(English) optimistic
Hearne, Hern

Heath
(English) place name; open space; natural
Heathe, Heith, Heth

Heathcliff
(English) mysterious

Heaton
(English) high-principled
Heat, Heatan, Heaten

Heber
(Greek) from Hebe; youthful goddess
Hebor

Hector
(Greek) loyal
Hec, Heck, Heco, Hect, Hectar, Hecter, Hekter, Tito

Heddwyn
(Welsh) peaceful; fairhaired
Hedwin, Hedwyn, Hedwynn

Hedley
(English) natural

Hedeon
(Russian) woodsman

Heimdall
(Scandinavian) white; god
Heiman, Heimann

Hein
(German) advising
Heiiri, Heiner, Heini, Heinlich

Heinrich
(German) form of Henry; leader
Hein, Heine, Heinrick, Heinrik

Heinz
(German) advisor
Heinze

Heladio
(Spanish) boy born in Greece; ingenious
Eladio, Elado, Helado

Helgi
(Scandinavian) happy
Helge

Helio
(Hispanic) bright

Heller
(German) brilliant

Hellerson
(German) brilliant one's son; smart
Helley

Helmand
(German) helmet; protected

Helmar
(German) protected; smart
Helm, Helmer, Helmet, Helmut

Helmut
(German, Polish) brave

Heman
(Last name as first name) direct

Hender
(German) ruler; illustrious
Hend

Henderson
(English) reliable
Hender, Hendersen, Hendersyn

Hendrik
(German) home ruler
Heinrich, Hendrick, Henrick, Hindrick

Henech
(Last name as first name) leading the pack
Henach

Henley
(English) surprising
Henlee, Henly, Henlye, Hinley

Henning
(Scandinavian) ruler

Henrik
(Norwegian) leader
Henric, Henrick

Henry
(German) leader
Hal, Hank, Harry, Henny, Henree, Henri

Henson
(Last name as first name) son of Hen; quiet

Heraldo
(Spanish) divine

Herb
(German) energetic
Herbi, Herbie, Herby, Hurb

Herbert
(German) famed warrior
Bert, Herb, Herbart, Herberto, Herbie, Herbirt, Herby, Hurb, Hurbert

Hercule
(French) strong
Hercuel, Harekuel, Herkuel

Hercules
(Greek) grand gift
Herc, Herk, Herkules

Heriberto
(Spanish)
Herbert, Heribert

Herman
(Latin) fair fighter
Heremon, Herm, Hermahn, Hermann, Hermie, Hermon, Hermy

Hermes
(Greek) courier of messages
Hermez

Hermod
(Scandinavian) greets and welcomes

Hernando
(Spanish) bold
Hernan

Herndon
(English) nature-loving
Hern, Hernd

Herne
(English) from bird heron; inventive
Hearne, Hern

Hernley
(English) from the heron meadow; easygoing
Hernlea, Hernlee, Hernlie, Hernly

Herodotus
(Greek) the father of history

Herrick
(Last name as first name) never alone

Herrod
(Biblical) king
Herod

Hershall
(Hebrew) from Hershel; deer; swift
Hersch, Herschel, Hersh, Herzl, Heshel, Hirschel, Hirsh, Hirshel

Herschel
(Hebrew) fast; deer
Hersch, Hersh, Hershel, Hershell, Hershelle, Herzl, Hirchel, Hirsch, Hirshel

Hershey
(Hebrew) deer; swift; sweet
Hersh, Hershel, Hirsh

Hertzel
(Hebrew) form of Herschel; deer; swift
Hert, Hertsel, Hyrt

Herve
(French) ready for battle

Hervey
(American) form of Harvey; ardent and studious
Herv, Herve, Hervy

Herzon
(American) from Hershel; fast
Herz, Herzan, Herzun

Hesed
(Hebrew) sweet

Hesperos
(Greek) evening star
Hesperios, Hespers

Hess
(Last name as first name) bold
Hes, Hys

Hessel
(Dutch) bold man

Heston
(Last name as first name) star quality

Hewitt
(German) smart
Hew, Hewet, Hewett, Hewie, Hewit, Hewy, Hugh

Hewney
(Irish) smart
Owney

Hewson
(Irish) son of Hugh; smart; giving

Hevel
(Hebrew) alive, breathing

Heywood
(Last name as first name) thoughtful
Haywood

Hezekiah
(Biblical) strong man
Hezeklah, Zeke

Hiawatha
(Native American) Iroquois chief
Hia

Hickok
(American) Wild Bill Hickok, U.S. marshal

Hidalgo
(Literature) westerner

Hidde
(Japanese) excellent

Hideaki
(Japanese) cautious

Hideo
(Japanese) excellent
Hideyo

Hieremias
(Greek) God lifts him up

Hieronymos
(Greek) alternate of Jerome
Heronymous

Hifz
(Arabic) memorable

Higinio
(Hispanic) forceful

Hilarion
(Greek) cheery; hilarious
Hilary, Hill

Hilary
(Latin) joyful
Hilaire, Hill, Hillarie, Hillary, Hillery, Hilly, Hilorie

Hildebrand
(German) combative; sword
Hill, Hilly

Hill
(English) lives on a hill; dreamy

Hillard
(German) wars; diligent
Hilliard, Hillier, Hillyer

Hillel
(Hebrew) praised; devout
Hilel, Hill

Hillery
(Latin) form of Hilary; pleasant
Hill

Hilliard
(German) brave; settlement on the hill
Hill, Hillard, Hillierd, Hilly, Hillyerd, Hylliard

Hilton
(English) sophisticated
Hillten, Hillton, Hiltan, Hiltawn, Hiltyn, Hylton

Himesh
(Hindi) snow king

Hines
(Last name as first name) strong
Hine, Hynes

Hippocrates
(Greek) philosopher
Hipp

Hippolyte
(Greek) frees horses
Hippolit, Hippolitos, Hippolytus, Ippolito

Hiram
(Hebrew) most admired
Hi, Hirom, Hirym

Hiramatsu
(Japanese) exalted

Hiro
(Japanese) giving

Hirsh
(Hebrew) deer; swift
Hersh, Hershel, Hirschel, Hirshel

Hirza
(Hebrew) lithe; deer

Hitchcock
(English) creative; spooky
Hitch

Hjalmar
(Scandinavian) protective warrior
Hjalamar, Hjallmar, Hjalmer

Ho
(Chinese) good

Hoashis
(Japanese) God

Hobart
(German) haughty
Hobb, Hobert, Hoebard

Hobbes
(English) from Robert; famed, intelligent
Hob, Hobbs

Hobert
(German) studious

Hobson
(English) helpful backer
Hobb, Hobbie, Hobbson, Hobby, Hobsen

Hockley
(English) high meadow boy
Hocklea, Hocklee, Hocklie, Hockly

Hockney
(English) from a high island, a spirited boy
Hockny

Hodge
(English) form of Roger;
vibrant
Hodges

Hodgie
(English) nickname for
Hodge
Hodgy

Hodgson
(English) boy born to Roger;
up-and-coming
Hodge, Hodges

Hoffman
(Last name as first name)
sophisticated

Hogan
(Irish) high-energy; vibrant
Hogahn, Hoge, Hoghan

Hogue
(Last name as first name)
youth
Hoge

Hojar
(American) wild spirit
Hobar, Hogar

Hoke
(Origin unknown) popular

Holbert
(German) capable
Hilbert

Holbrook
(English) place name;
educated
*Brooke, Brookie, Brooky,
Holb, Holbrooke*

Holcomb
(Last name as first name)
bright

Holden
(English) quiet; gracious
Holdan, Holdin, Holldun

Holder
(English) musical
Hold, Holdher, Holdyer

Holegario
(Spanish) superfluous
Holegard

Holger
(Last name as first name)
devoted

Holiday
(English) born on a holy day
Holliday

Hollis
(English) flourishing
*Holl, Hollace, Hollice,
Hollie, Holly*

Holloway
(Last name as first name)
jovial
Hollo, Hollway, Holoway

Hollywood
(Place name) cocky;
showoff
Holly, Wood

Holm
(English) natural; woodsy
Holms

Homain
(Last name as first name)
homebody
Holman, Holmen

Holmes
(English) safe haven
Holmm, Holmmes

Holmfrid
(Last name as first name)
prefers home-and-hearth

Holt
(English) shaded view
Holte, Holyte

Homer
(Greek) secure
*Hohmer, Home, Homere,
Homero*

Honchy
(American) form of honcho;
leader
*Honch, Honchee, Honchey,
Honchi*

Honda
(African) from Hondo;
warrior

Hondo
(African) warring

Honesto
(Spanish) truthful
Honesta, Honestoh

Hong
(Vietnamese) pink; tasteful

Honorato
(Spanish) full of honor
Honor, Honoratoh

Honoré
(Latin) man who is honored
Honor, Honoray

Hood
(Last name as first name)
easygoing; player
Hoode, Hoodey

Hooker
(English) shepherd

Hoolihan
(American) hooligan
Hool, Hoole, Hooli

Hoop
(American) ball player
Hooper, Hoopy

Hopkins
(Welsh) Hopkin; Robert's
son; famous
*Hopkin, Hopkinson,
Hopkyns, Hopper, Hoppner*

Hopper
(Last name used as first
name) creative

Horace
(Latin) poetic
Horaace, Horase, Horice

Horatio
(Latin) poetic; dashing
Horate, Horaysho

Horsley
(English) calm field of
horses; keeper
*Horslea, Horsleigh, Horslie,
Horsly*

Horst
(German) deep; thicket
Hurst

Horstman
(German) profound
Horst, Horstmen, Horstmun

Horston
(German) thicket; sturdy
Horst

Horton
(English) brash
Horten, Hortun

Hosaam
(Arabic) handsome

Hosea
(Hebrew) prophet

Hosie
(Hebrew) from Hosea;
prophet
Hosaya, Hose

Hosni
(Arabic) excellent

Hosty
(Literature) musical

Houghton
(Last name as first name)
bravado

Houston
(English) Texas city; rogue;
hill town
Houst, Hust, Huston

Hovannes
(Hebrew) believer in a
gracious God; form of
Johannes

How
(American) word as a name
Howe, Howey, Howie

Howard
(English) well-liked
*How, Howerd, Howie,
Howurd, Howy*

Howart
(Origin unknown) admired
Howar

Howe
(German) high-minded
How, Howey, Howie

Howell
(Welsh) outstanding
*Howel, Howey, Howie,
Howill*

Howlan
(English) living on a hill; high

Howland
(American) well-known
Howlend, Howlond, Howlyn

Hoyt
(Irish) spirited
Hoit, Hoye

Hrothgar
(Literature) king

Huang
(Chinese) rich

Hubbard
(German) fine
Hubberd, Hubert, Hubie

Hubert
(German) intellectual
*Bert, Bertie, Burt, Hubart,
Huberd, Hue, Huebert,
Hugh*

Hubie
(English) short for Hubert
Hube, Hubee, Hubey, Hubi

Huckleberry
(American, Literature)
glossy black berry;
mischevious

Hud
(English) charismatic cowboy
Hudd

Hudson
(English) Hugh's son;
charismatic adventurer
Hud, Hudsan, Hudsen

Hudya
(Arabic) going the right way

Huelett
(American) bright; southern
Hu, Hue, Huel, Hugh, Hulette

Huey
(French) hearty

Hugh
(English) intelligent
Hue, Huey, Hughey, Hughi,
Hughie, Hughy

Hughdonald
(American) combo of Hugh
and Donald; southern
Huedonald, Hughdon,
Hughdonal, Hughdonn

Hughie
(English) intelligent; lucky
in parentage
Hughee, Hughi, Hughy

Hugo
(Latin) spirited heart

Huland
(English) bright
Hue, Huel, Huey, Hugh

Hulbard
(Last name as first name)
singing; bright
Hulbert, Hulburt

Hull
(Place name) spirited;
confident

Humberto
(Spanish) brilliant
Hum, Humb, Humbert,
Humbie

Hume
(Last name as first name)
daunting

Humphrey
(German) strong
peacemaker
Hum, Humfry, Hump,
Humphry, Humprey

Hunn
(German) combative
Hun

Hunt
(English) active

Hunter
(English) hunter; adventurer
Hunt

Hunting
(English) hunter
Huntyng

Huntington
(Last name as first name)
town of hunters

Huntler
(English) hunter
Huntt

Huntley
(English) hunter
Hunt, Hunter, Huntlea,
Huntlee, Huntlie, Huntly

Huon
(Hebrew) form of John;
believer

Hurd
(Last name as first name)
tends the herd

Hurlbert
(English) shining army man
Hulbert, Hurlburt, Hurlbutt

Hurley
(Irish) the tide; flowing
Hurlea, Hurlee, Hurli, Hurly

Hurst
(Last name as first name)
entrepreneurial

Husky
(American) big
Husk, Huskee, Huskey, Huski

Hussein
(Arabic) attractive man
Husain, Husane, Husein,
Hussain

Hutch
(American) safe haven;
unique
Hut, Hutchey, Hutchie,
Hutchy

Hutter
(Last name as first name)
tough
Hut, Hutt, Huttey, Huttie,
Hutty

Hutton
(English) sophisticated
Hutt, Huttan, Hutten, Hutts

Huxford
(Last name as first name)
outdoorsman

Huxley
(English) outdoorsman
Hux, Huxel, Huxle, Huxlee,
Huxlie

Hwang
(Japanese) yellow

Hyacinthe
(French) flowering
Hyacinthos, Hyacinthus,
Hyakinthos

Hyatt
(English) secure
Hy, Hye, Hyett, Hyut

Hyde
(English) special; a hyde is
120 acres
Hide, Hy

Hyghner
(Last name as first name)
lofty goals
High, Highner, Hygh

Hyll
(Origin unknown) open-minded
Hy, Hye, Hyell

Hyman
(Hebrew) life
Hy, Hymen, Hymie

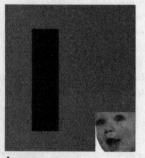

Iagan
(Scottish) fire

Iago
(Spanish) feisty villain
Iagoh, Jago

Iain
(Scottish) believer

Ian
(Scottish) believer; handsome
Iain, Ean, Eon, Eyon

Ib
(Arabic) joy

Ibrahim
(Arabic) fathering many
Ibraham, Ibrahem

Ibu
(Japanese) creative

Icarus
(Mythology) ill-fated
Ikarus

Ich
(Hebrew) short for Ichabod; has-been
Ick, Ickee, Ickie, Icky

Ichabod
(Hebrew) glory in the past; slim
Ich, Icha, Ickabod, Ika, Ikabod, Ikie

Idi
(African, Arabic) born during Idd Festival

Idris
(Welsh) impulse-driven
Idriss, Idriys

Idwal
(Welsh) known

Iefan
(Welsh) form of John; believer in God's grace

Ieuan
(Welsh) form of Ivan; grace

Ifan
(Welsh) form of John; believer

Ifor
(Welsh) archer

Iggy
(Latin) short for Ignatius; spunky
Iggee, Iggey, Iggi, Iggie

Ignace
(French) fiery
Iggy, Ignase

Ignatius
(Latin) firebrand
Ig, Iggie, Iggy, Ignacius, Ignashus, Ignatious, Ignnatius

Igor
(Russian) warrior

Ihsan
(Arabic) charitable

Ike
(Hebrew) short for Isaac and Eisenhower; friendly
Ika, Ikee, Ikey, Ikie

Ilan
(Hebrew) tree
Illan

Illtyd
(Welsh) from well-populated homeland
Illtud

Ilom
(Welsh) happy

Immanuel
(Hebrew) honored
Emmanuel, Imanuel

Imran
(Arabic) host

Inder
(Hindi) lord of sky gods is Indra; ethereal
Inderjeet, Inderjit, Inderpal, Indervir, Indra, Indrajit

Indiana
(Place name) U.S. state; rowdy; dashing
Indio, Indy

Indore
(Place name) city in India
Indor

Indra
(Hindi) lord of sky gods

Ing
(Scandinavian) he who is foremost
Inge

Ingelbert
(German) combative
Ing, Inge, Ingelbart, Ingelburt, Inglebert

Inger
(Scandinavian) fertile
Ingemar, Ingmar

Ingmar
(Scandinavian) fertile
Ing, Ingamar, Ingamur, Inge, Ingemar, Ingmer

Ingmer
(Scandinavian) short for Ingemar; famed
Ing, Ingamar, Ingemar, Ingmar

Ingra
(English) short for Ingram; kind-hearted
Ingie, Ingrah, Ingrie

Ingram
(English) angelic; kind
Ing, Ingraham, Ingre, Ingrie, Ingry

Ingvar
(Scandinavian) fertility god
Ingevar

Inigo
(Spanish) from Ignatius; eager

Iniko
(Japanese) serves

Innis
(Irish) isolated
Ines, Inis, Innes, Inness, Inniss

Innocencio
(Spanish) innocent

Inteus
(Native American) proud, unashamed

Ior
(Welsh) short for Iorworth; attractive

Iorgos
(Greek) outgoing

Ira
(Hebrew) cautious
Irae, Irah

Iram
(English) smart
Irem, Irham, Irum

Iranga
(Sri Lanken) special

Irv
(English) short for Irving

Irvin
(English) attractive
Irv, Irvine

Irving
(English) attractive
Irv, Irve, Irveng, Irvy

Irwin
(English) practical
Irwen, Irwhen, Irwie, Irwinn, Irwy, Irwynn

Isa
(African) saved

Isaac
(Hebrew) laughter
Isaak, Isack, Izak, Ize, Izek, Izzy

Isadore
(Greek) special gift
Isador, Isedore, Isidore, Issy, Izzie, Izzy

Isai
(Hebrew) believer

Isaiah
(Hebrew) saved by God
Isa, Isay, Isayah, Isey, Izaiah, Izey

Isak
(Scandinavian) laughter
Isac

Isam
(Arabic) protector

Isas
(Japanese) worthwhile

Isham
(Last name as first name) athletic

Ishan
(Hindi) sun

Ishmael
(Hebrew) outcast son of Abraham in the Bible
Hish, Ish, Ishmel, Ismael

Isidore
(Greek, French) gift
Isi, Izzie

Isidoro
(Spanish) gift
Cedro, Cidro, Doro, Izidro, Sidro, Ysidor

Isidro
(Greek) gift
Isydro

Israel
(Hebrew) God's prince;
conflicted
Israyel, Issy, Izzy

Israj
(Hindi) king of gods

Issa
(Hebrew) laughing

Isser
(Slavic) creative

Itzak
(Hebrew) form of Isaac
Itzik

Ivan
(Russian) believer in a
gracious God; reliable one
Ivahn, Ive, Ivey, Ivie

Ivar
(Scandinavian) Norse god

Ive
(English) able
Ivee, Ives, Ivey, Ivie

Ives
(American) musical
Ive

Ivo
(Polish) yew tree; sturdy
Ivar, Ives, Ivon, Ivonnie, Yvo

Ivor
(Scandinavian) outgoing;
ready
Ifot, Ivar, Ive, Iver, Ivy

Izaak
(Polish) full of mirth

Izacz
(Slavic) spicy; happy
Isaac, Izak, Izie, Izze, Izzee

Izador
(Spanish) gift
*Dorrie, Dory, Isa, Isador,
Isadoro, Isidoros, Isodore,
Iza, Izadoro*

Izzy
(Hebrew) friendly
Issie, Issy, Izi, Izzee, Izzie

Ja
(Korean) gorgeous

Jaan
(Scandinavian) from John;
believes in the Lord

Jabal
(Place name) short for
Japalpur (city in India);
attractive

Jabari
(African American) brave

Jabbar
(Arabic) comforting

JaBee
(American) combo of Jay
and B
J.B., Jabee, Jaybe, Jaybee

Jaber
(American) form of Arabic
Jabir; comforting
Jabar, Jabe, Jabir

Jabez
(Hebrew) sorrow
Jabezz

Jabin
(Hebrew) God's own

Jabir
(Arabic) supportive
Jabbar

Jabon
(American) wild
Jabonne

Jabot
(French) shirt ruffle

Jace
(American) audacious
Jase, Jhace

Jacee
(American) combo of Jay
and C
*J.C., Jacey, JayC, Jaycee,
Jaycie, Jaycy*

Jacek
(Polish) hyacinth; growing
Jack, Yahcik

Jacett
(Invented) jaunty
Jaycett

Jachym
(Hebrew) from Jacob;
supplants; helpful
Jach

Jacinto
(Spanish) hyacinth; fragrant
Jacint

Jack
(Hebrew) believer in a gracious God; personality-plus
Jackee, Jackie, Jacko, Jacky, Jax

Jackal
(Sanskrit) wild dog; betrays
Jackel, Jackell, Jackyl, Jackyll

Jackie
(English) personable
Jackee, Jackey, Jacki, Jacky, Jaki

Jackson
(English) Jack's son; full of personality
Jackee, Jackie, Jacks, Jacsen, Jakson, Jax, Jaxon

Jacksonville
(Last name as first name) town of Jack's son; sturdy
Jacsonville, Jaksonville

Jacob
(Hebrew) replacement; best boy
Jaccob, Jacobe, Jacobee, Jake, Jakes, Jakey, Jakob

Jacobo
(Spanish) warm
Jake, Jakey

Jacobs
(Biblical) replacing
Jakobs, Jakey

Jacobus
(Latin) from Jacob
Jakobus

Jacoby
(Hebrew) from Jacob
Jacobey, Jakobey, Jakoby

Jacquard
(French) class act
Jackard, Jackarde, Jacquarde, Jaqard, Jaquard, Jaquarde

Jacques
(French) romantic; ingenious
Jacquie, Jacue, Jaques, Jock, Jok

Jacy
(American) from Jacob; replacement

Jadaan
(Last name as first name) content
Jada, Jadan, Jade, Jay

Jadall
(Invented) punctual
Jada, Jade

Jade
(Spanish) valued (jade stone)
Jadee, Jadie, Jayde

Jadee
(American) combo of Jay and D
J.D., Jadee, JayD, Jaydy

Jadney
(Last name as first name)
Jad

Jadon
(American) devout; ball-of-fire
Jade, Jadin, Jadun, Jadyn, Jaeden, Jaiden, Jaydie, Jaydon

Jadrien
(Invented) combo of Jaden and Adrien; audacious

Jaegel
(English) salesman
Jaeg, Jaeger, Jael

Jaeger
(German) outdoorsman
Jaegir, Jagher, Jagur

Jael
(Hebrew) climber

Jaequon
(African American) combo of Jae and Quon; outgoing
Jaequan, Jayquon, Jayquan

Jaewon
(African American) form of Juwon
Jaewan, Jaywan, Jaywon

Jafar
(Arabic) from the stream
Gafar, Jafari

Jaffey
(English) form of Jaffe
Jaff

Jagan
(English) confident
Jagen, Jagun

Jagger
(English) brash
Jagar, Jager, Jaggar, Jagir

Jaggerton
(English) brash
Jag, Jagg

Jagit
(Invented) brisk
Jaggett, Jaggit, Jagitt

Jago
(English) self-assured

Jaguar
(Spanish) fast
Jag, Jagg, Jaggy, Jagwar, Jagwhar

Jahan
(Sanskrit) worldly

Jahi
(African) runs well; dignity

Jahmal
(Arabic) beautiful
Jahmaal, Jahmall

Jahmil
(Arabic) beautiful
Jahmeel, Jahmyl

Jai
(American) adventurer
Jay

Jaidev
(Hindi) God's victory

Jaime
(Spanish) follower
Jaimey, Jaimie, Jamee, Jaymie

Jaimini
(Hindi) winner

Jair
(Hebrew) teacher
Jairo

Jairaj
(Hindi) Lord's victor

Jairo
(Spanish) God enlightens
Jaero, Jairoh

Jairus
(Biblical) faithful

Jaison
(American) form of Jason
Jaizon

Jaja
(African) praise-worthy

Jajuan
(African American) combo of Ja and Juan; loves God

Jakar
(Place name) from Jakarta, Indonesia
Jakart, Jakarta, Jakarte

Jake
(Hebrew) short for Jacob
Jaik, Jakee, Jakey, Jakie, Jayke

Jakeem
(Arabic) has been lifted

Jakey
(American) nickname for Jake; friendly
Jaky

Jakob
(Hebrew) form of Jacob
Jakab, Jake, Jakeb, Jakey, Jakie, Jakobe, Jakub

Jal
(Arabic) from Jalal; great; travels

Jaleel
(Arabic) handsome
Jalil

Jalen
(American) vivacious
Jalon, Jaylen, Jaylin, Jaylon

Jamail
(Arabic) good-looking
Jahmil, Jam, Jamaal, Jamahal, Jamal, Jamil, Jamile, Jamy

Jamaine
(Arabic) good-looking

Jamar
(American) from Jamal; attractive
Jamarr, Jemar, Jimar

JaMarcus
(African American) combo of Jay and Marcus; attractive
Jamarcus, Jamark, Jamarkus

Jamari
(African American) attractive

Jamarr
(African American) attractive; formidable
Jam, Jamaar, Jamar, Jammy

Jamel
(Arabic) form of Jamal
Jameel, Jamele, Jimelle

James
(English) dependable; steadfast
Jaimes, Jamsey, Jamze, Jaymes, Jim, Jimmy

Jameson
(English) able; James's son
Jamesan, Jamesen, Jamesey, Jamison, Jamsie

Jamie
(English) short for James
Jaimey, Jaimie, Jamee, Jamey, Jay, Jaymey, Jaymsey

Jamil
(Arabic) beautiful
Jameel, Jamyl

Jamin
(Hebrew) favored son
Jamen, James, Jamie, Jamon, Jaymon

Jamisen
(American) form of James/Jamie; lively
Jami, Jamie, Jamis, Jamison

Jan
(Dutch) form of John; believer
Jaan, Jann, Janne

Jan-Erik
(Slavic) combo of Jan and Erik; reliable
Jan-Eric

Janesh
(Hindi) thankful

Janson
(Scandinavian) Jan's son; hardworking
Jan, Janne, Janny, Jansahn, Jansen, Jansey

Jantz
(Scandinavian) short for Jantzen
Janson, Janssen, Jantzon, Janz, Janzon

Janus
(Latin) Roman god of beginnings and endings; optimistic; born in January
Jan, Janis

Japheth
(Hebrew) grows
Japhet

Jaquawn
(African American) rock
Jacquon, Jakka, Jaquan, Jaquan, Jaquie, Jaqwen, Jequon, Jock

Jarah
(Hebrew) sweet

Jard
(American) form of Jared; longlasting
Jarra, Jarrd, Jarri, Jerd, Jord

Jareb
(Hebrew) contender
Jarib, Yarev, Yariv

Jared
(Hebrew) descendant; giving
Jarad, Jarod, Jarode, Jarret, Jarrett, Jerod, Jerrad, Jerrod

Jarek
(Slavic) fresh
Jarec

Jarell
(Scandinavian) giving
Jare, Jarelle, Jarey, Jarrell, Jerrell

Jaren
(Hebrew) vocal
Jaron, Jayrone, J'ron

Jarenal
(American) form of Jaren; long-lasting
Jaranall, Jaret, Jarn, Jaronal, Jarry, Jerry

Jareth
(American) open to adventure
Jarey, Jarith, Jarth, Jary

Jarman
(German) stoic
Jerman

Jaromil
(Czech) spring love
Jarmil

Jarred
(Hebrew) form of Jared
Jared, Jere, Jerod, Jerred, Jerud

Jarrell
(English) jaunty
Jare, Jarell, Jarrel, Jarry, Jerele, Jerrell

Jarrett
(English) confident
Jare, Jaret, Jaritt, Jarret, Jarrit, Jarritt, Jarry, Jarryt, Jarrytt, Jerot, Jerret, Jerrett, Jurett, Jurette

Jarrod
(Hebrew) form of Jared
Jare, Jarod, Jarry, Jerod

Jarvey
(German) celebrated
Garvey, Garvy, Jarvee, Jarvi, Jarvy

Jarvis
(German) athletic
Jarv, Jarvee, Jarves, Jarvey, Jarvhus, Jarvie, Jarvus, Jarvy

Jary
(Spanish) form of Jerry; leader
Jaree

Jase
(American) hip

Jashon
(African American) combo of Jason and the letter h

Jason
(Greek) healer; man on a quest
Jace, Jacey, Jaisen, Jase, Jasen, Jasey, Jasyn, Jayson, Jaysun

Jason-Joel
(American) combo of Jason and Joel; popular
Jasonjoel, Jason Joel

Jaspal
(Pakistani) pure

Jasper
(English) guard; country boy
Jasp, Jaspur, Jaspy, Jaspyr

Jaster
(English) form of Jasper; vigilant
Jast

Jathan
(Invented) combo of Jake and Nathan; attractive
Jae, Jath, Jathe, Jathen, Jathun, Jay

Javan
(Biblical) righteous
Javin, Javon

Javaris
(African American) ready
Javares, Javarez

Javas
(Sanskrit) bright eyes

Javier
(Spanish) affluent; homeowner
Havyaire, Javey, Javiar

Javon
(Hebrew) hopeful
Javan, Javaughn, Javen, Javonn, Javonte

Javonte
(African American) jaunty
Javaughantay, Javawnte, Ja-Vonnetay, Ja-Vontae

Javy
(American) short for Javaris; prepared
Javey, Javie

Jawdat
(Arabic) excellent
Gawdat

Jawhar
(Arabic) gem

Jawon
(African American) shy
Jawan, Jawaughn, Jawaun, Jawuane, Jewan, Jewon, Jowon

Jax
(American) form of Jackson; fun
Jacks, Jaxx

Jay
(English) short for a name starting with J; colorful
Jai, Jaye

Jaya
(American) jazzy
Jay, Jayah

Jayant
(Hindi) winner

Jaydon
(American) bright-eyed
Jayde, Jayden, Jaydey, Jaydi, Jaydie, Jaydun, Jaydy

Jaylin
(American) combo of Jay and Lin

Jaymes
(American) form of James
Jaimes, James

JayR
(American) actor
J.R.

Jayson
(Greek) form of Jason

Jazeps
(Latvian) God will increase

Jazon
(Polish) heals

Jazz
(American) jazzy
Jazze, Jazzee, Jazzy

Jean
(French) form of John; kind
Jeanne, Jeannie, Jene

Jean-Baptiste
(French) combo of Jean and Baptiste; John the Baptist; religious
John-Baptiste

Jean-Claude
(French) combo of Jean and Claude; gracious

Jean-Francois
(French) combo of Jean and Francois; smooth

Jean-Michel
(French) combo of Jean and Michel; godly

Jean-Paul
(French) combo of Jean and Paul; small and giving

Jean-Philippe
(French) combo of Jean and Philippe; handsome

Jean-Pierre
(French) combo of Jean and Pierre; giving and dependable

Jeb
(Hebrew) jolly
Jebb, Jebby

Jebediah
(Hebrew) close to God
Jeb, Jebadiah, Jebby,
Jebedyah

Jecori
(American) exuberant
Jekori

Jed
(Hebrew) helpful
Jedd, Jeddy, Jede

Jediah
(Hebrew) God's help
Jedi, Jedyah

Jedidiah
(Hebrew) close to God
Jed, Jeddy, Jeddyah, Jedidyah

Jedrek
(Polish) virile
Jedrick, Jedrus

Jeevan
(African American) form of
Jevon; lively
Jevaughn, Jevaun

Jeff
(English) short for Jeffrey or
Jefferson
Geoff, Jeffie, Jeffy

Jefferson
(English) dignified
Jeff, Jeffarson, Jeffersen,
Jeffursen, Jeffy

Jeffery
(English) alternate for
Jeffrey; peaceful
Jeffrey, Jeffrie, Jeffry, Jefry

Jeffrey
(English) peaceful
Geoffrey, Jeff, Jeffree, Jeffrie,
Jeffry, Jeffy, Jefree

Jehan
(French) for John; spiritual

Jehu
(Hebrew) true believer

Jela
(African) honors

Jelani
(African American) trendy
Jelanee, Jelaney, Jelanne

Jem
(English) short for James
Jemmi, Jemmy, Jemmye,
Jemy

Jemarr
(African American) worldly
Jemahr

Jemonde
(French) man of the world
Jemond

Jenda
(Czech) form of John;
humble

Jenkins
(Last name as first name)
God is gracious
Jenkin, Jenks, Jenky,
Jenkyns, Jenx, Jinx

Jennett
(Hindi) heavenly
Jennet, Jennit, Jennitt,
Jennyt, Jennytt, Jinnat

Jennings
(Last name as first name)
attractive
Jennyngs

Jensi
(Hungarian) also Jenci;
noble
Jenci, Jens

Jenson
(English) son of Jen;
blessed
Jensen, Jenssen, Jensson

Jep
(American) easygoing
Jepp

Jephtha
(Biblical) judges others;
outgoing

Jerald
(English) form of Gerald;
merry
Jere, Jereld, Jerold, Jerrie,
Jerry

Jeramy
(Hebrew) exciting
Jeramah, Jeramie, Jere,
Jeremy

Jerard
(French) confident
Jerrard

Jere
(Hebrew) short for Jeremy
Jeree, Jerey

Jeremiah
(Hebrew) prophet uplifted
by God; far-sighted
Jeramiah, Jere, Jeremyah,
Jerome, Jerry

Jeremie
(Hebrew) loquacious
Jeremee, Jeremy

Jeremy
(English) talkative
Jaramie, Jere, Jeremah,
Jereme, Jeremey, Jerrey, Jerry

Jeriah
(Hebrew) uplifted; from Jeremiah

Jericho
(Arabic) nocturnal
Jerako, Jere, Jerico, Jeriko, Jerycho, Jerycko, Jeryco, Jeryko

Jerick
(American) form of Jericho; tenacious
Gericho, Jereck, Jerik, Jero, Jerok, Jerrico

Jeril
(American) form of Jarrell; leader
Jerill, Jerl, Jerry

Jerma
(American) form of Germain; man of Germany
Jermah, Jermane, Jermayne

Jermain,
(French) from Germany
German, Germane, Germanes, Germano, Germanus, Jermaine, Jerman, Jermane, Jermayn, Jermayne

Jermaine
(German) form of Germaine
Germain, Germaine, Jere, Jermain, Jermane, Jermene, Jerry

Jermey
(American) short for Jermaine; friendly
Jermy

Jermon
(African American) dependable
Jermonn

Jerney
(Slavic) from Greek, Jerome; funny

Jernigan
(Last name as first name) spontaneous
Jerni, Jerny

Jero
(American) jaunty
Jeroh, Jerree, Jerri, Jerro, Jerry

Jerod
(Hebrew) form of Jerrod and Jarrod

Jerold
(English) merry
Jerrold, Jerry

Jerome
(Latin) holy name; blessed
Jarome, Jere, Jerohm, Jeromy, Jerree, Jerrome, Jerry, Jirome

Jerone
(English) hopeful
Jere, Jerohn, Jeron, Jerrone

Jeronimo
(Italian) form of Gerome; Geronimo, Apache Indian chief; excited
Gerry, Jero, Jerry

Jerral
(American) form of Gerald/Jerald; exciting
Jeral, Jere, Jerry

Jerram
(Hebrew) God has uplifted
Jeram, Jerem, Jerrem, Jerrym, Jerym

Jerrell
(American) exciting
Jarell, Jerre, Jerrel, Jerrie, Jerry

Jerrett
(Hebrew) form of Jarrett
Jeret, Jerete, Jerod, Jerot, Jerret

Jerrick
(American) combo of Jerry and Derek (Derrick); lively
Jerick, Jerrie

Jerry
(German) strong
Gerry, Gery, Jerre, Jerri, Jerrie, Jerrye

Jerse
(Place name) calm; rural
Jerce, Jercey, Jersey, Jersy, Jerzy

Jervis
(Greek) honorable
Gervase

Jesmar
(American) from Jesse; Biblical
Jess, Jessie, Jezz, Jezzie

Jesper
(American) easygoing
Jesp, Jess

Jess
(Hebrew) wealthy
Jes

Jesse
(Hebrew) wealthy
Jess, Jessee, Jessey, Jessi, Jessie, Jessye

Jessup
(Last name as first name) rich
Jesop, Jesopp, Jess, Jessa, Jessie, Jessopp, Jessy, Jesup, Jesupp, Jessupp

Jesuan
(Spanish) devout

Jesus
(Hebrew) saved by God
Hesus, Jesu, Jesuso, Jezus

Jesus-Amador
(Spanish) combo of Jesus
and Amador; loving the
Lord
Jesusamador, Jesus Amador

Jesus-Angel
(Spanish) combo of Jesus
and Angel; angel of God
Jesusangel, Jesusangelo

Jet
(English) black gem

Jetal
(American) zany
*Jetahl, Jetil, Jett, Jettale,
Jetty*

Jethro
(Hebrew) fertile
Jeto, Jett, Jetty

Jeton
(French) a chip for
gamblers; wild spirit
Jet, Jetawn, Jets, Jett, Jetty

Jett
(American) wild spirit
Jet, Jets, Jetty, The Jet

Jettie
(American) from mineral
name Jett; wild spirit
Jette, Jettee, Jetti

Jetty
(American) from the mineral
name Jett; wild spirit
Jettey

Jevan
(African American) spirited
*Jevaughn, Jevaun, Jevin,
Jevon*

Jevon
(African American) spirited
Jevaun

Jex
(American) form of Jack;
personable

Jhonatan
(African) spiritual
Jhon, Jon

Ji
(Chinese) organized; orderly

Jibben
(American) form of Jivan;
Hindi for alive

Jibri
(Arabic) angel

Jie
(Chinese) wonderful

Jim
(Hebrew) short for James
*Jem, Jihm, Jimi, Jimmee,
Jimmy*

Jimbo
(American) cowhand;
endearment for Jim
*Jim, Jimb, Jimbee, Jimbey,
Jimby*

Jimbob
(American) countrified
*Gembob, Jim Bob, Jim-Bob,
Jymbob*

Jimmy
(English) short for James
*Jim, Jimi, Jimmey, Jimmi,
Jimmye, Jimy*

Jimmydee
(American) combo of Jimmy
and Dee; southern boy
*Jimmy D, Jimmy Dee, Jimmy-
Dee*

Jimmy-John
(American) country boy
*Jimmiejon, Jimmyjohn,
Jimmy-Jon, Jymmejon*

Jimoh
(African) Friday's child

Jin
(Chinese) golden

Jinan
(Place name) city in China
Jin

Jindrich
(Czech) ruling
*Jindra, Jindrik, Jindrisek,
Jindrousek*

Jing
(Chinese) unblemished;
capital

Jiri
(Czech) working the earth
Jira, Jiricek

Jiro
(Japanese) second boy born

Jivon
(Hindi) living; vibrant

Joab
(Hebrew) praising God;
hovering
Joabb

Joachim
(Hebrew) a king of Judah;
powerful; believer
Akim, Jakim, Yachim, Yakim

Joah
(Greek) form of Jonah; unfortunate

Joaquin
(Spanish) bold; hip
Joakeen, Joaquim, Joaquin, Juakeen, Jwaqueen

Job
(Hebrew) patient
Jobb, Jobe, Jobi, Joby

Jobson
(English) son of Job; patient

Joby
(Hebrew) patient; tested
Job, Jobee, Jobi

Jock
(Hebrew) grace in God; athlete
Jockie, Jocky

Jody
(Hebrew) believer in Jehovah; (American) combo of Joe and Dee
Jodee, Jodey, Jodie, Jodye, Joe

Joe
(Hebrew) short for Joel and Joseph
Jo, Joey, Joeye, Joie

Joebob
(American) combo of Joe and Bob
J.B., Jobob, Joe-Bob

Joedan
(American) combo of Joe and Dan
Jodan, Jodin, Jodon, Joe-Dan, Joedanne

Joel
(Hebrew) prophet in the Bible
Joelie, Joell, Jole, Joly

Joemac
(American) combo of Joe and Mac
J.M., Joe-Mac, Joe-Mack, Jomack

Joergen
(Scandinavian) earth worker

Joey
(Hebrew) short for Joel and Joseph
Joee, Joie

Joffre
(German) form of Jeffrey; bright star

Johann
(German) spiritual musician
Johan, Johane, Yohann, Yohanne, Yohon

Johannes
(Hebrew) form of John, the Biblical name
Johan, Jon

Johar
(Hindi) gem

John
(Hebrew) honorable; Biblical name
Jahn, Jhan, Johne, Johnne, Johnni, Johnnie, Johnny, Johnnye, Jon

Johnnie
(Hebrew) endearment for John; honorable man
Gianni, Johnie, Johnny, Jonni, Jonny

Johnny-Dodd
(American) country sheriff
Johnniedodd, Johnny Dodd

Johnpaul
(American) combo of John and Paul
John Paul, John-Paul, Jonpaul

Johnny-Ramon
(Spanish) renegade
Johnnyramon, Johnny Ramon

Johnson
(English) John's son; credible
Johnsen, Johnsonne, Jonsen, Jonson

Joji
(Japanese) form of John; believes

JoJo
(American) friendly; popular
Jo-Jo

Jolon
(Native American) oak valley dweller

Jomar
(African American) helpful
Joemar, Jomarr

Jomei
(Japanese) lightens

Jon
(Hebrew) alternative for John
Jonni, Jonnie, Jonny, Jony

Jonah
(Hebrew) peacemaker
Joneh

Jonas
(Hebrew) capable; active
Jon

Jonathan
(Hebrew) gracious
Johnathan, Johnathon, Jonathon

Jones
(American) saucy

Jonte
(American) from John; loves God
Johatay, Johate, Jontae

Jon-Eric
(American) combo of Jon and Eric
Joneric, Jon Eric, John-Eric

Jon-Jason
(American) combo of Jon and Jason
Johnjace, John-Jaison, John-Jazon, Jon Jason, Jonjason, Jon-Jayson

Jonjay
(American) combo of Jon and Jay; jaunty; believer
Jonjae, Jon Jay, Jon-Jay

Jonmarc
(American) combo of Jon and Marc
Jon Marc, Jon-Marc, John Mark

Jonnley
(American) form of Jon; believer
Jonn, Jonnie

Joplin
(Place name) city in Montana; sings
Joplyn

Jordahno
(Invented) form of Giordano

Jordan
(Hebrew) descending
Jorden, Jordon, Jordun, Jordy, Jordyn

Jordane
(Hebrew) form of Jordan; down-flowing river

Jordison
(American) son of Jordi; glowing
Jordisen, Jordysen, Jordyson

Jordy
(Hebrew) from Jordan
Jordie, Jordey

Jorge
(Spanish) form of George; farmer
Jorje, Quiqui

Jorgen
(Scandinavian) farmer
Jorgan

Jory
(Hebrew) descendant
Jorey

Jos
(Place name) city in Nigeria

José
(Spanish) asset; favored
Joesay, Jose, Pepe, Pepito

Josef
(Hebrew) asset; supported by Jehovah
Jodie, Joe, Joey, Josep, Joseph, Josephe, Jozef, Yusif

Josh
(Hebrew) saved by the Lord; devout
Joshua, Joshuam, Joshyam, Josue, Jozua

Josha
(Hebrew) variant of Joshua;

Joshuah
(Hebrew) devout

Josia
(Hebrew) form of Josiah; supported by the Lord
Josea

Josiah
(Hebrew) Jehovah bolsters
Josyah

Joss
(English) form of Joseph; cool
Josslin, Jossly

Josue
(Spanish) devout

Jotham
(Biblical) a king of Judah; believer in perfect Jehovah
Jothem, Jothym

Jourdain
(French) flowing
Jordane, Jorden

Jovan
(Slavic) gifted
Jovahn, Jovohn

Jovani
(Italian) Roman god Jove; jovial
Jovani, Jovanni, Jovanny, Jovany

Jove
(Mythology) Roman sky god

Juanantonio
(Spanish) combo of Juan and Antonio; believer in a gracious God
Juan Antonio, Juan-Antonio

Joza
(Czech) from Joseph; he adds to life

Jozef
(Polish) supported by Jehovah; asset
Joe, Joze

Juan
(Spanish) devout; lively
Juann, Juwon

Juancarlos
(Spanish) combo of Juan and Carlos; debonair

Juan-Fernando
(Spanish) combo of Juan and Fernando; believer in a gracious God
Juanfernand, Juanfernando, Juan Fernando

Juanjose
(Spanish) combo of Juan and Jose; active
Juan-Jose

Juanmiguel
(Spanish) combo of Juan and Miguel; hopeful
Juan-Miguel

Juanpablo
(Spanish) combo of Juan and Pablo; believer
Juan Pablo, Juan-Pablo

Jubal
(Hebrew) celebrant

Jubilo
(Spanish) rejoicing; jubilant
Jube

Judah
(Biblical) praised
Juda

Judas
(Latin) Biblical traitor

Judd
(Latin) secretive
Jud

Jude
(Latin) form of Judas; disloyal
Judah

Judge
(English) judgmental
Judg

Judson
(Last name as first name) mercurial
Juddsen, Juddson, Judsen, Judssen

Judule
(American) form of Judah; judicious
Jud, Judsen, Judsun

Jules
(Greek) young Adonis
Jewels, Jule

Julian
(Greek) gorgeous
Juliane, Julien, Julyon, Julyun

Julio
(Spanish) handsome; youthful
Huleeo, Hulie, Julie

Julius
(Greek) attractive
Juleus, Jul-yus, Jul-yuz

Ju-Long
(Chinese) powerful

Jumaane
(African) Tuesday-born

Jumah
(African) from Jumapili; Sunday-born
Juma

Jumbe
(African) strong
Jumbey, Jumby

Jumoke
(African) beloved

Jun
(Japanese) follows the rules

Juneau
(Place name) capital of Alaska
Juno, Junoe

Junior
(Latin) young son of the father, senior
Junnie, Junny, Junyer

Junius
(Latin) youngster
Junie, Junnie, Junny

Jupiter
(Roman) god of thunder and lightning; guardian
Jupe

Jura
(Place name) mountain range between France and Switzerland
Jurah

Jurass
(American) from Jurassic period of dinosaurs; daunting
Jurases, Jurassic

Jurgen
(Scandinavian) working the earth

Juri
(Slavic) farms

Jus
(French) just
Just, Justice, Justis

Juste
(French) law-abiding
Just, Zhuste

Justice
(Latin) just
Jusees, Just, Justice, Justiz, Justus, Juztice

Justie
(Latin) honest; fair
Jus, Justee, Justey, Justi

Justin
(Latin) fair
Just, Justan, Justen, Justun, Justyn, Justyne

Justinian
(Latin) ruler; Roman emperor
Justinyan

Justino
(Spanish) fair
Justyno

Justiz
(American) judging; fair
Justice, Justis

Justus
(German) fair

Jute
(Botanical) practical

Juvenal
(Latin) young
Juve

Juventino
(Spanish) young
Juve, Juven, Juvey, Tino, Tito

Juwon
(African American) form of Juan; devout; lively
Jujuane, Juwan, Juwonne

Kabir
(Hindi) spiritual leader
Kabar

Kabonero
(African) symbol

Kabonesa
(African) born in hard times

Kacancu
(Rukonjo) firstborn

Kacy
(American) happy
K.C., Kace, Kacee, Kase, Kasee, Kasy, Kaycee

Kadar
(Arabic) empowered
Kader

Kade
(American) exciting
Cade, Caden, K.D. Kadey, Kaid, Kayde, Kydee

Kadeem
(Arabic) servant
Kadim

Kaden
(American) exciting
Cade, Caden, Caiden, Caidin, Caidon, Caydan, Cayden, Caydin, Caydon, Kadan, Kadon, Kadyn, Kaiden

Kadir
(Hindi) talented
Kadeer, Qadeer, Qadir

Kadmiel
(Hebrew) God-loving

Kado
(Japanese) through life's gate

Kaelan
(Irish) strong
Kael, Kaelen, Kaelin, Kaelyn

Kaemon
(Japanese) happy

Kaeto
(American)
Cato, Cayto, Caytoe, Kato

Kahale
(Hawaiian) homebody

Kahil
(Turkish) ingénue; (Arabic) friend; (Greek) handsome
Cahill, Kaleel, Kalil, Kayhil, Khalil

Kaholo
(Hawaiian) boy who runs

Kai
(Hawaiian, African) attractive
Kay, Keh

Kaid
(English) round; happy
*Caiden, Cayde, Caydin,
Kaden, Kadin, Kayd*

Kaihe
(Hawaiian) spear

Kailin
(Irish) sporty
*Kailyn, Kale, Kalen, Kaley,
Kalin, Kallen, Kaylen*

Kaipo
(Hawaiian) embraces

Kairo
(Arabic) from Cairo; exotic

Kaiser
(German) title that means
emperor

Kaj
(Scandinavian) earthy

Kala
(Hawaiian) sun boy

Kalama
(Hawaiian) source of light
Kalam

Kalani
(Hawaiian) of one sky
Kalan

Kale
(American) healthy;
vegetable
*Kail, Kayle, Kaylee, Kayley,
Kaylie*

Kaleb
(American) form of Caleb
Caleb

Kalgan
(Place name) city in China
Kal

Kali
(Polynesian) comforts

Kalil
(Arabic) best friend
*Kahil, Kahleel, Kahlil,
Kaleel, Khaleel, Khalil*

Kalkin
(Hindi) tenth child

Kallen
(Greek) handsome
*Kallan, Kallin, Kallon,
Kallun, Kalon, Kalun, Kalyn*

Kalogeros
(Greek) beautiful in aging

Kalunga
(African) watchful; the
personal god of the
Mbunda of Angola

Kalvin
(Latin) form of Calvin;
blessing
Kal

Kamaka
(Hawaiian) pretty face

Kamal
(Arabic) perfect
Kameel, Kamil

Kamau
(African) quiet soldier
Kamall

Kameron
(Scottish) form of Cameron
*Kameren, Kammeron,
Kammi, Kammie, Kammy,
Kamran, Kamrin, Kamron*

Kamon
(American) alligator, (Place
name) Cayman Islands
alligator
*Cayman, Caymun, Kame,
Kammy, Kayman, Kaymon*

Kana
(Japanese) strength of
character

Kance
(American) combo of Kane
and Chance; attractive
*Cance, Cance, Cans, Kaince,
Kans, Kanse, Kaynce*

Kane
(American, English) sterling
spirit
*Cahan, Cahane, Cain, Kain,
Kaine, Kaney, Kanie, Kayne*

Kang
(Korean) healthy

Kaniel
(Hebrew) confident;
supported by the Lord;
hopeful
*Kane, Kan-El, Kanel, Kanelle,
Kaney*

Kano
(Place name) city in Nigeria
Kan, Kanoh

Kant
(German) philosopher
Cant

Kantu
(Hindi) joyous

Kanye
(American) unbreakable

Kaori
(Japanese) scented

Kaper
(American) capricious
Cape, Caper, Kahper, Kape

Kapila
(Hindi) foresees
Kapil

Kapono
(Hawaiian) anointed one

Kapp
(Greek) short for the surname Kaparos
Kap, Kappy

Karcher
(German) beautiful blond boy

Kare
(Scandinavian) large
Karee

Kareem
(Arabic) generous
Karehm, Karem, Karim, Karreem, Krehm

Karey
(Greek) form of Cary or Carey
Karee, Kari, Karrey, Karry

Kari
(Scandinavian) hair curls

Karif
(Arabic) fall-born
Kareef

Kareem
(Arabic) generous
Karam, Karim

Karl
(German) manly; forceful
Carl, Kale, Karel, Karll, Karlie, Karol, Karoly

Karmel
(Hebrew) red-haired
Carmel, Carmelo, Karmeli, Karmelli, Karmelo, Karmello, Karmi

Karney
(Irish) wins
Carney

Karolek
(Polish) form of Charles; grown man
Karol

Karr
(Scandinavian) curly hair
Carr

Karsten
(Greek) chosen one

Karu
(Hindi) cousin
Karun

Kaseem
(Arabic) divides
Kasceem, Kaseym, Kasim, Kazeem

Kaseko
(African) ridiculed

Kasem
(Asian) joyful

Kasen
(Spanish) helmet; protected

Kasey
(Irish) form of Casey
Kasi, Kasie

Kasi
(African) short for Kasiya; leaving
Kasee, Kasey, Kasie

Kasim
(Hindi) shining

Kasimir
(Arabic) serene
Kasim Kazimir, Kazmer

Kasper
(German) reliable
Caspar, Casper, Kasp, Kaspar, Kaspy

Kass
(German) standout among men
Cass, Kasse

Kassidy
(Irish) form of Cassidy
Kass, Kassidi, Kassidie, Kassie

Kato
(African) second of twins

Katzir
(Hebrew) reaping
Katzeer

Kauai
(Place name) Hawaiian island; breezy spirit
Kawai

Kaufman
(Last name as first name) serious
Kauffmann, Kaufmann

Kavan
(Irish) good-looking
Cavan, Kaven, Kavin

Kavi
(Hindi) poetic

Kay
(Greek) joyful
Kai, Kaye, Kaysie, Kaysy, Keh

Kayin
(African) desired baby

Kayle
(Hebrew) faithful
Kail, Kayl

Kaylen
(Irish) form of Kellen;
laughing
*Kaylan, Kaylin, Kaylon,
Kaylyn*

Kayven
(Irish) handsome
Cavan, Kavan, Kave

Kazan
(Greek) creative
Kazann

Kazimierz
(Polish) practical
Kaz

Kazuo
(Japanese) peaceloving

Kealoha
(Hawaiian) bright path

Keandre
(American) combo of Ke
and Andre; grateful
Keondre

Keane
(German) attractive
Kean, Keen, Keene, Kiene

Keanu
(Hawaiian) cool breeze over
mountains
Keahnu

Kearn
(Irish) outspoken
Kearny, Kern, Kerne, Kerney

Kearney
(Irish) sparkling
*Karney, Karny, Kearns,
Kerney, Kirney*

Keary
(Irish) form of Kerry; dark

Keaton
(English) nature-lover
Keaten, Keatt, Keatun, Keton

Keats
(Literature) poetic
Keatz

Keawe
(Hawaiian) lovable

Keb
(Egyptian) loves the earth

Kecalf
(American) inventive
Keecalf

Kechel
(African American)
Kach, Kachelle

Kedar
(Hindi) powerful
Kadar, Keder

Kedem
(Hebrew) old soul

Kedrick
(American) form of Kendrick
Ked, Keddy, Kedric, Kedrik

Kee-Bun
(Taiwanese) good news
Keebun

Keefe
(Irish) handsome
Keaf, Keafe, Keef, Keeffe, Kief

Keegan
(Irish) ball-of-fire
*Keagan, Keagin, Kegan,
Kege, Keghun*

Keelan
(Irish) slim
*Kealan, Keallan, Keallin,
Keilan, Keillan, Kelan*

Keeley
(Irish) handsome
*Kealey, Kealy, Keelee,
Keelie, Keely, Keilie*

Keen
(German) smart
*Kean, Keane, Keene,
Keeney, Kene*

Keenan
(Irish) bright-eyed
Kenan

Keeney
(American) incisive
*Kean, Keane, Keaney,
Keene, Kene*

Kefir
(Hebrew) young lion; high
spirits

Keir
(Irish) brunette

Keirer
(Irish) dark
Kerer

Keiron
(Irish) dark
Keiren, Keronn

Keitaro
(Japanese) blessed baby
Keita

Keith
(English) witty
Keath, Keeth, Keithe

Keithen
(Scottish) gentle
Keith

Kekoa
(Hawaiian) one warrior

Kel
(Irish) fighter; energetic
Kell

Kelby
(English) snappy; charming
Kel, Kelbey, Kelbi, Kelbie, Kelbye, Kell, Kellby, Kelly

Kelcy
(English) helpful
Kelci, Kelcie, Kelcye, Kelsie

Kele
(Hawaiian) watches like a hawk

Kelle
(Scandinavian) springlike

Kelemen
(Hungarian) softspoken

Kell
(English) fresh-faced
Kel, Kelly

Kellagh
(Irish) hardworking
Kellach

Kellen
(Irish) strong-willed
Kel, Kelen, Kelin, Kell, Kellan, Kellin, Kelly, Kelyn

Keller
(Last name as first name) bountiful
Kel, Keler, Kelher, Kell, Kylher

Kelly
(Irish) able combatant
Keli, Kellee, Kelley, Kelli, Kellie

Kelmen
(Hungarian) form of Kelemen; softspoken

Kelsey
(Scandinavian) unique among men
Kel, Kells, Kelly, Kels, Kelsi, Kelsie, Kelsy, Kelsye, Kelzie, Kelzy

Kelton
(Irish) energetic
Keldon, Kelltin, Kellton, Kelten, Keltin, Keltonn

Kelts
(Origin unknown) energetic
Kel, Kelly, Kelse, Kelsey, Keltz

Kelvin
(English) goal-oriented
Kelvan, Kelven, Kellven, Kelvon, Kelvun, Kelvynn, Kilvin

Kelvis
(Invented) combo of K and Elvis; ambitious
Kellvis, Kelviss, Kelvys

Kemal
(Turkish) honored infant; generous

Kemp
(English) champion

Kemper
(American) high-minded
Kemp, Kempar

Kempton
(American) takes the high road

Kemuel
(Hebrew) God's advocate

Ken
(Scottish) short for Kenneth; cute
Kenn, Kenny, Kinn

Kendall
(English) shy
Ken, Kend, Kendahl, Kendal, Kendoll, Kendy, Kenney, Kennie, Kenny, Kindal

Kendan
(English) strong; serious
Ken, Kend, Kenden

Kendrick
(English) heroic
Kendricks, Kendrik, Kendryck, Kenric, Kenrick, Kenricks, Kenrik

Kenel
(Invented) form of Kendall; hopeful
Kenele

Kenelm
(English) handsome boy
Kenhelm, Kennelm

Kenlee
(American) combo of Ken and Lee

Kenley
(English) distinguished
Kenlea, Kenlee, Kenleigh, Kenlie, Kenly

Kenn
(English) river; flowing

Kennard
(English) courageous;
selfless
*Ken, Kenard, Kennaird,
Kennar, Kenny*

Kennedy
(Irish) leader
*Canaday, Canady,
Kennedey, Kennedie,
Kennidy*

Kenner
(English) capable
Kennard

Kennet
(Scandinavian) good-
looking
Kenet, Kennete

Kenneth
(Scottish) handsome; (Irish)
good-looking
*Ken, Keneth, Kenith,
Kennath, Kennie, Kenny*

Kenny
(Scottish) short for Kenneth
*Kennee, Kenney, Kenni,
Kennie*

Kenrick
(English) heroic boy

Kent
(English) fair-skinned
Kennt, Kentt

Kentaro
(Japanese) large baby boy

Kentlee
(Last name as first name)
dignified
*Ken, Kenny, Kent, Kentlea,
Kentleigh, Kently*

Kenton
(English) from Kent
Kentan, Kentin, Kenton

Kentrell
(English) white

Kenward
(Last name as first name)
bold

Kenway
(Last name as first name)
bold

Kenyatta
(African) from Kenya;
patriotic

Kenyon
(Irish) dear blond boy
*Ken, Kenjon, Kenny,
Kenyawn, Kenyun*

Kenzie
(Scottish) form of Kinsey;
leads
Kensie

Keola
(Hawaiian) vibrant

Keon
(American) unbridled
enthusiasm
*Keion, Keonne, Keyon,
Kion, Kionn*

Keontay
(African American)
outrageous
Keon, Keontae, Keontee

Kepler
(German) loves astrology;
starry-eyed
*Kappler, Keppel, Keppeler,
Keppler*

Kerel
(African) forever young

Kerem
(Hebrew) works in vineyard

Kerey
(Irish) dark

Kerm
(Irish) form of Kermit;
guileless
Kurm

Kermit
(German) droll
*Kerm, Kermee, Kermet,
Kermey, Kermi, Kermie,
Kermy*

Kern
(Irish) dark; musically
inclined
*Curran, Kearn, Kearne,
Kearns*

Kernaghan
(Last name as first name)
dark
Carnahan, Kernohan

Kernis
(Invented) dark; different
Kernes

Kerr
(Scandinavian) serious
Karr, Kerre, Kurr

Kerrick
(English) rules

Kerry
(Irish) dark
*Keary, Kere, Keri, Kerrey,
Kerrie*

Kers
(Todas) an Indian plant

Kersen
(Indonesian) cherry bright

Kerstie
(American) spunky
Kerstee, Kersty

Kerwyn
(Irish) energetic
Kerwen, Kerwin, Kerwun, Kir, Kirs, Kirwin

Keshawn
(African American) friendly
Kesh, Keshaun, Keyshawn, Shawn

Keshet
(Hebrew) rainbow; bright hopes

Keshon
(African American) sociable
Kesh

Keshua
(African American) form of the female name Kesha
Keshe

Kesin
(Hindi) needy

Kesley
(American) derivative of Lesley; active
Keslee, Kesli, Kezley

Kesse
(American) attractive
Kessee, Kessey, Kessi, Kessie

Kester
(Scottish) form of Christopher; Christ-loving

Kestrel
(English) soars

Ketchum
(Place name) city in Idaho
Catch, Ketch, Ketcham, Ketchim

Kettil
(Scandinavian) self-sacrificing
Keld, Kjeld, Ketil, Ketti

Keung
(Chinese) universal spirit

Kevin
(Irish) handsome; gentle
Kev, Kevahngn, Kevan, Keven, Kevvie, Kevvy

Key
(English) key
Keye, Keyes

Keyohtee
(Invented) form of Quixote

Keyshawn
(African American) clever; believer

Khadim
(Hindi) forever
Kadeem, Kadeen, Kahdeem, Khadeem

Khalid
(Arabic) everlasting
Khalead, Khaled, Khaleed

Khalil
(Arabic) good friend

Khaliq
(Arabic) ingenious
Kaliq, Khalique

Khambrel
(American) articulate
Kambrel, Kham, Khambrell, Khambrelle, Khambryll, Khamme, Khammie, Khammy

Khan
(Turkish) shares; prince

Khayru
(Arabic) giving
Khiri, Khiry, Kiry

Khevin
(American) form of Kevin; good-looking
Khev

Khouri
(Arabic) spiritual
Couri, Khory, Khourae, Kori

Khyber
(Place name) pass on border of Pakistan and Afghanistan
Kibe, Kiber, Kyber

Kibbe
(Nayas) nocturnal bird

Kibo
(Place name) mountain peak (highest peak of Kilimanjaro); spectacular
Kib

Kidd
(Last name as first name) adventurous

Kiel
(Place name) city in North Germany

Kieran
(Irish) handsome brunette
Keiran, Kier, Kieren, Kierin, Kiers, Kyran

Kidder
(Last name as first name)
brash; confident

Kiefer
(Irish) loving
*Keefer, Kieffer, Kiefner,
Kieffner, Kiefert, Kuefer,
Kueffner*

Kieran
(Scottish) dark-haired
*Keiran, Keiren, Keiron, Kern,
Kernan, Kiernan, Kieron,
Kyran*

Kier
(Icelandic) large vat or tub

Kiet
(Asian) respected

Kiev
(Place name) capital city of
Ukraine

Kiho
(Hawaiian) moves carefully

Killi
(Irish) form of Killian;
fighter
Killean, Killee, Killey, Killyun

Killian
(Irish) effervescent
*Kilean, Kilian, Killean,
Killee, Killi, Killie, Killyun,
Kylian*

Kim
(Vietnamese) gold
(English) enthusiastic
Kimmie, Kimmy, Kimy, Kym

Kimball
(Greek) inviting
*Kim, Kimb, Kimbal, Kimbie,
Kimble, Kymball*

Kimberly
(English) bold
*Kim, Kimbo, Kimberleigh,
Kimberley*

Kin
(Japanese) gold

Kincaid
(Scottish) vigorous
Kincaide, Kinkaid

Kinch
(Last name as first) knife
blade

King
(English) royal leader

Kingman
(Last name as first name)
gracious man

Kingsley
(English) royal nature
*King, Kings, Kingslea,
Kingslee, Kingsleigh,
Kingsly, Kins*

Kingston
(English) gracious
King, Kingstan, Kingsten

Kingswell
(English) royal; king

Kinnard
(Last name as first name)
leaning
Kinnaird

Kinnel
(Place name) from
Kinnelon, New Jersey

Kinsey
(English) affectionate;
winning
Kensey, Kinsie

Kinton
(Hindi) adorned

Kioshi
(Japanese) thoughtful
silence

Kip
(English) focused
Kipp, Kippi, Kippie, Kippy

Kipling
(Literature) adventurous
Kiplen, Kippling

Kipp
(American) hill; upward
bound
Kip, Kyp

Kiral
(Greek) lord

Kiran
(Hindi) light

Kirby
(English) brilliant
*Kerb, Kirb, Kirbee, Kirbey,
Kirbie, Kyrbee, Kyrby*

Kiri
(Vietnamese) like
mountains, everlasting

Kiril
(Russian) lord
*Cyril, Cyrill, Kirill, Kirillos,
Kyril, Kyrill*

Kirk
(Scandinavian) believer
Kerk, Kirke, Kurk

Kirkland
(Last name as first name)
church land

Kirkley
(Last name as first name)
church wood
Kirklea, Kirklee, Kirklie, Kirkly

Kirkwell
(Last name as first name)
wood; giving of faith

Kirkwood
(English) heavenly
Kirkwoode, Kurkwood

Kirton
(English) from town of
churches

Kirvin
(American) form of Kevin;
good-looking
*Kerven, Kervin, Kirv, Kirvan,
Kirven*

Kit
(Greek) mischievous
Kitt

Kito
(African) precious

Kiva
(Hebrew) from Akiva;
replacement

Kizza
(African) child born after
twins' birth

Klaus
(German) wealthy
Klaas, Klaes, Klas, Klass

Klay
(English) form of Clay;
reliable
Klaie, Klaye

Kleber
(Last name as first name)
serious
Klebe

Kleef
(Dutch) boy from the cliff;
daring

Klein
(Last name as first name)
bright
Kleiner, Kleinert, Kline

Klemens
(Latin) gentle
Klemenis, Klement, Kliment

Kleng
(Scandinavian) claw;
struggles

Klev
(Invented) form of Cleve
Kleve

Knight
(English) protector
Knighte, Nighte

Knightley
(English) protects
*Knight, Knightlea, Knightlee,
Knightlie, Knightly, Knights*

Knoll
(American) flamboyant
Noll

Knowles
(English) outdoorsman
Knowlie, Knowls, Nowles

Knox
(English) bold

Knud
(Scandinavian) ruler

Knut
(Scandinavian) aggressive
Canute, Cnut, Knute

Kobe
(Hebrew) cunning
Kobee, Kobey, Kobi, Koby

Kobi
(Hebrew) cunning; smart
*Cobe, Cobey, Cobi, Cobie,
Coby, Kobe, Kobey, Kobie,
Koby*

Kodiak
(American) bear; daunting

Kody
(English) brash
*Kodee, Kodey, Kodi, Kodie,
Kodye*

Kofi
(African) Friday-born

Kohana
(Hawaiian) best

Kohler
(German) coal

Kojo
(African) Monday-born

Koka
(Hawaiian) man from
Scotland; strategist

Kolby
(American) form of Colby;
congenial
Kelby, Kole, Kollby

Kolton
(English) coal town

Komic
(Invented) funny
Com, Comic, Kom

Konane
(Hawaiian) spot of moonlight

Kondo
(African) fights

Kong
(Chinese) heavenly

Konnor
(Irish) another spelling of Connor; brilliant
Konnar, Konner

Kono
(African) industrious

Konrad
(German) bold advisor
Khonred, Kon, Konn, Konny, Konraad, Konradd, Konrade, Kord, Kort

Konstantin
(Russian) forceful
Kon, Konny, Kons, Konstance, Konstantine, Konstantyne

Konstantinos
(Greek) steadfast
Constance, Konstance, Konstant, Tino, Tinos

Koren
(Greek) strong-willed

Koresh
(Hebrew) farms
Choresh

Korey
(Irish) lovable
Kori, Korrey, Korrie

Kornel
(Czech) horn; communicator
Kornelisz, Kornelius, Kornell

Kornelius
(Latin) another spelling of Cornelius
Korne, Kornellius, Kornelyus, Korney, Kornnelyus

Korrigan
(Irish) another spelling of Corrigan
Koregan, Korigan, Korre, Korreghan, Korri, Korrigon

Kort
(German) talkative

Kory
(Irish) hollow
Kori, Korre, Korrey, Korrye

Kosey
(African) temperamental; lionlike

Koshy
(American) jolly
Koshee, Koshey, Koshi

Kosmo
(Greek) likes order
Kosmy, Cosmos

Kostas
(Russian) from Kostyn and Konstantin; loyal

Koster
(American) spiritual
Kost, Kostar, Koste, Koster

Kosumi
(Native American) fishes with a spear; smart

Kovit
(Asian) talented

Kraig
(Irish) another spelling for Craig
Krag, Kragg, Kraggy

Kramer
(German) shopkeeper; humorous

Kricker
(Last name as first name) reliable
Krick

Kris
(Greek) short for Kristian and Kristopher
Krissy, Krys

Krishna
(Hindu) pleasant
Krishnah

Krispin
(Irish) form of Crispin; curly hair

Krister
(Scandinavian) religious

Kristian
(Greek) another form of Christian
Kris, Krist, Kristyan

Kristo
(Greek) short for Kristopher

Kristopher
(Greek) bearer of Christ
Kris, Krist, Kristo, Kristofer

Kruz
(Spanish) also Cruz; delight

Krystyn
(Polish) Christian
Krys, Krystian

Krzysztof
(Polish) bearing Christ
Kreestof

Kubrick
(Last name as first name)
creative
Kubrik

Kueng
(Chinese) of the universe;
fine

Kugonza
(African) in love

Kumar
(Hindi) boy

Kuper
(Hebrew) copper, red hair

Kurt
(Latin) wise advisor
Curt, Kurty

Kurtis
(Latin) form of Curtis
*Kurt, Kurtes, Kurtey, Kurtie,
Kurts, Kurtus, Kurty*

Kutty
(English) knife-wielding
Cutty

Kwako
(African) Wednesday-born

Kwame
(African) Saturday's child
Kwamee, Kwami

Kwan
(Korean) bold character

Kwasi
(African) born on Sunday
Kweisi, Kwesi

Kwintyn
(Polish) fifth child
Kwint, Kwintin, Kwynt

Kyan
(Place name) village in Japan
Kyann

Kyle
(Irish) serene
*Kiel, Kiyle, Kye, Kyl, Kyley,
Kylie, Kyly*

Kyle-Evan
(American) combo of Kyle
and Evan
Kyle Evan

Kyler
(English) peaceful
Cuyler, Kieler, Kiler, Kye, Kylor

Kylerton
(American) form of Kyle
Kylten

Kynan
(Welsh) leads

Kynaston
(English) serene

Kyne
(English) blue-blooded

Kyrone
(African American) combo
of K and Tyrone; brash
*Keirohn, Keiron, Keirone,
Keirown, Kirone, Kyron*

Kyros
(Greek) masterful

Kyzer
(American) wild spirit
Kaizer, Kizer, Kyze

Laban
(Hebrew) white
Lavan

Labarne
(American) form of Laban;
(Hebrew) white
Labarn

Labaron
(French) the baron
LaBaron, LaBaronne

Labhras
(Irish) form of Lawrence;
introspective
Lubhras

LaBryant
(African American) son of
Bryant; brash
*Bryant, La Brian, La Bryan,
Labryan, Labryant*

Lachlan
(Scottish) feisty
*Lachlann, Lacklan, Lackland,
Laughlin, Lock, Locklan*

Lachtna
(Irish) gray; aging with grace

Lacy
(Scottish) also Lachie;
warlike
Lacey

Ladan
(Hebrew) having seen; aware

Ladarius
(Origin unknown) combo of La and Darius

Ladd
(English) helper; smart
Lad, Laddee, Laddey, Laddie, Laddy

Ladden
(American) athletic

Laddie
(English) youthful
Lad, Ladd, Laddee, Laddey, Laddy

Ladisiao
(Spanish) helpful
Laddy

Lado
(Spanish) artistic

Lael
(Hebrew) belonging to Jehovah
Lale

Laertes
(Literature) from Shakespeare; action-oriented

Lafaye
(American) cheerful
Lafay, Lafayye, Laphay, Laphe

Lafayetta
(Spanish) from the French name Lafayette; bold
Lafay

Lafayette
(French) ambitious
Lafayet, Lafayett

Lafe
(American) punctual
Laafe, Laife, Laiffe

Lafi
(Polynesian) shy

Lagos
(Place name) city in Nigeria
Lago

Lagrand
(African American) the grand
Grand, Grandy, Lagrande

Lahahana
(Hawaiian) warm as sunshine

Laionela
(Hawaiian) lion boldness

Laird
(Scottish) rich
Layrd, Layrde

Lais
(Indian) leonine

Lake
(English) tranquil water

Lakista
(African American) bold man

Lakshman
(Hindi) promising

Lal
(Slavic) from Lala; tulip; colorful

Lalo
(Latin) singer of a lullaby
Laloh

Lamalcom
(African American) son of Malcolm; kingly
LaMalcolm, LaMalcom, Mal, Malcolm, Malcom

Lamar
(Latin) renowned
Lamahr, Lamarr, Lemar, Lemarr

Lamber
(German) form of Lambert; ingratiating
Lambur

Lambert
(German) bright
Lamb, Lamber, Lambie, Lamburt, Lammie, Lammy

Lamond
(French) worldly
Lammond, Lamon, Lamonde, Lemond

Lamont
(Scandinavian) lawman
Lamon

Lamonte
(French) mountain; also LaMonte

Lance
(German) confident
Lanse, Lantz, Lanz

Lancelot
(French) romantic
Lance, Lancelott, Launcelot, Launcey

Landan
(English) from the plains; quiet

Lander
(English) landed
Land, Landor

Landers
(English) wealthy
Land, Landar, Lander, Landor

Landis
(English) owning land; earthy
Land, Landes, Landice, Landise, Landly, Landus

Lando
(American) masculine
Land

Landon
(English) plain; old-fashioned
Land, Landan, Landen

Landry
(French) entrepreneur
Landré, Landree

Lane
(English) secure
Laine, Laney, Lanie, Lanni, Layne

Lang
(English) top
Lange

Langdon
(English) long-winded
Lang, Langden, Langdun

Langford
(English) healthy
Lanford, Langferd

Langham
(Last name as first name) long
Lang

Langilea
(Polynesian) loud as thunder

Langiloa
(Polynesian) stormy; moody

Langley
(English) natural
Lang, Langlee, Langli, Langly

Langston
(English) long-suffering
Lang, Langstan, Langsten

Langton
(English) long
Lange

Langundo
(Polynesian) graceful

Langward
(Last name as first name) long

Langworth
(Last name as first name) of long worth

Lani
(Hawaiian) lithe

Lanny
(American) popular
Lann, Lanney, Lanni, Lannie

Lansing
(Place name) city in Michigan
Lance, Lans

Lanty
(Irish) lively
Laughun, Leachlainn, Lochlainn, Lochlann

Lanu
(Native American) circular

Laoghaire
(Irish) caretaker of cows

Laoiseach
(Irish place name) from the county Leix

Lap
(Vietnamese) independent

Laphonso
(African American) prepared; centered

Lapidos
(Greek) cologne
Lapidus

Laquintin
(American) combo of La and Quintin

Laramie
(French) pensive
Laramee

Lare
(American) wealthy
Larre, Layr

Largel
(American) intrepid
Large

Lariat
(American) word as name; roper
Lare, Lari

Larkin
(Irish) brash
Lark, Larkan, Larken, Larkie, Larky

Larndell
(American) generous
Larn, Larndelle, Larndey, Larne

Larne
(Place name) district in Northern Ireland
Larn, Larney, Larny

Larnell
(American) giving
Larne

Laron
(American) outgoing
Larron, Larrone

Larrimore
(Last name as first name)
loud
Larimore, Larmer, Larmor

Larrmyne
(American) boisterous
*Larmie, Larmine, Larmy,
Larmyne*

Larry
(Latin) extrovert
*Lare, Larrey, Larri, Larrie,
Lary*

Lars
(Scandinavian) short for
Lawrence and Laurens
Larrs, Larse, Larsy

Lashaun
(African American)
enthusiastic
*Lashawn, La-Shawn,
Lashon, Lashond*

Laskey
(Last name as first name)
jovial
Lask, Laski

Lassen
(Place name) a peak in
California in the Cascade
Range
Lase, Lasen, Lassan, Lassun

Lassit
(American) broad-minded
Lasset, Lassitte

Lassiter
(American) witty
*Lassater, Lasseter, Lassie,
Lassy*

Laszlo
(Hungarian) famous leader
Laslo, Lazuli

Lateef
(Arabic) a gentle man

Latham
(Scandinavian) farmer;
knowing
Lathe, Lay

Lathrop
(English) home-loving
*Lathe, Lathrap, Latrope,
Lay, Laye, Laythrep*

Latimer
(English) interprets;
philanthropic
Latymer

Latorris
(African American) notorious
LaTorris

Latravious
(African American) healthy
Latrave

Latty
(English) giving
Lat, Latti, Lattie

Laughlin
(Irish) servent

Laurence
(Latin) glorified
*Larence, Laurance, Laurans,
Laure, Lorence*

Laurens
(German) brilliant
*Larrie, Larry, Laure, Laurins,
Lorens, Lors*

Laurent
(French) martyred
Laurynt

Lavan
(Latin) pure

Lavaughn
(African American) perky
*Lavan, Lavon, Lavonn,
Levan, Levaughn*

Lavaughor
(African American) laughing
Lavaugher, Lavawnar

Lavesh
(Hindi) little piece; calm

Lavi
(Hebrew) uniter

Lawford
(English) dignified
Laford, Lauford, Lawferd

Lawler
(Last name as first name)
honoring; teacher
Lawlor, Lollar, Loller

Lawrence
(Latin) honored
*Larrie, Larry, Laurence,
Lawrance, Lawrunce*

Lawrie
(Latin) form of Lawry;
anointed
Lowrie

Lawson
(English) Lawrence's son;
special
Law, Laws, Lawsan, Lawsen

Lawton
(Last name as first name)
honored town

Layshaun
(African American) merry
Laysh, Layshawn

Laysy
(Last name as first name)
sophisticated
Lay, Laycie, Laysee

Layt
(American) fascinating
Lait, Laite, Late, Layte

Layton
(English) musical
Laytan, Laytawn, Layten

Laz
(Spanish) short for Lazaro;
God-loved

Lazar
(Hebrew) from Lazarus;
helped by God
Lazare, Lazaro, Lazear, Lazer

Lazarus
(Greek) renewed
*Eleazer, Lasarus, Lazerus,
Lazoros*

Leal
(Greek) self-assured

Leamon
(American) powerful
Leamm, Leamond, Leemon

Leand
(Greek) from Leander;
leonine
Leander

Leander
(Greek) ferocious; lion-like
Anders, Leann, Leannder

Lear
(Greek) royal
Leare, Leere

Learly
(Last name as first name)
terrific
Learley

Leary
(Irish) herds; high goals

Leather
(American) word as name;
tough
Leath

Leavery
(American) giving
*Leautree, Leautri, Leautry,
Levry, Lo, Lotree, Lotrey,
Lotri, Lotry*

Leben
(Last name as first name)
small; hopeful

Lebna
(African) soulful

Lebron
(French) form of Lebrun

Lechoslaw
(Polish) glorious Pole; envied
Lech, Leslaw, Leszek

Lectoy
(American) form of Lecter
and Leroy; good-old-boy
Lec, Lecto, Lek

Lee
(English) loving
Lea, Lee, Leigh

Leeander
(Invented) form of Leander

Leenoris
(African American) form of
Lenore; respected
Lenoris

Leeodis
(African American) combo
of Lee and Odis; carefree
Lee-Odis, Leotis

Leeron
(African American) combo
of Lee and Ron
Leerawn

Leggett
(Last name as first name)
able
Legate, Leggitt, Liggett

Lei
(Hawaiian) wreath;
decorative

Leibel
(Hebrew) lion

Leif
(Scandinavian) loved one
Laif, Leaf, Leife

Leigh
(English) smooth

Leighton
(Last name as first name)
hearty
*Laytan, Layton, Leighten,
Leightun*

Leith
(Scottish) broad

Lel
(Gypsy) taker

Leland
(English) protective
*Leeland, Leighlon, Leiland,
Lelan, Lelond*

Leldon
(American) form of Eldon;
bookish
Leldun

Lem
(Hebrew) from Lemuel; loves God

Lemar
(American) form of Lamar; famed landowner
Lemarr

Lemetrias
(African American) form of Lemetrius
Lem

Lemon
(American) fruit; tart
Lemonn, Lemun, Limon

Lemuel
(Hebrew) religious
Lem, Lemmie, Lemmy, Lemy

Len
(German) short for Leonard
Lennie, Lynn

Lenard
(American) form of Leonard; heart of a lion
Lenerd

Leni
(Polynesian) lives for today

Lennan
(Irish) gentle

Lennart
(Scandinavian) brave
Lenn, Lenne

Lenno
(Italian) brave

Lennon
(Irish) renowned; caped
Lenn, Lennan, Lennen

Lennor
(Last name as first name) brave

Lennox
(Scottish) authoritative
Lennix, Lenocks, Lenox, Linnox

Lenny
(German) short for Leonard
Lenn, Lenney, Lenni, Lennie, Leny, Linn

Lensar
(English) stays with parents

Lenton
(American) religious
Lent, Lenten, Lentun

Lenvil
(Invented) typical
Lenval, Level

Leo
(Latin) lionlike; fierce

Leocadio
(Spanish) lion-hearted
Leo

Leolin
(Polynesian) watchful
Leoline, Llewelyn

Leoliver
(American) combo of Leo and Oliver; audacious
Leo

Leon
(Greek) tenacious
Lee, Leo, Leone, Leonn

Leonard
(German) courageous
Lee, Leo, Leonar, Leonerd, Leonord, Lynar, Lynard, Lynerd

Leonardo
(Italian) lion-hearted
Leo

Leoncio
(Spanish) lion-hearted
Leon, Leonce, Leonse

Leondras
(African American) lionine
Leon, Leondre, Leondrus, Leonid

Leonidus
(Latin) strong
Leon, Leone, Leonidas, Leonydus

Leopaul
(American) combo of Leo and Paul; brave; calm
Leo-Paul

Leopold
(German) brave
Lee, Leo

Leor
(Latin) listens

Leoti
(American) outdoorsy
Lee, Leo

Leovardo
(Spanish) form of Leonardo; brave
Leo, Leovard

Lepoldo
(Spanish) form of Leopold; brave
Lee, Lepold, Poldo

Lepolo
(Polynesian) handsome

Lerey
(American) form of Larry
Lerrie, Lery

Leron
(American) combo of Lee and Ron; courageous
LeRon, Lerone, Liron, Lirone, Lyron

Leroy
(French) king; royal
Leeroy, Leroi, Le-Roy, Roy, Roye

Les
(English) short for Leslie
Lez, Lezli

Leshawn
(African American) cheery
Lashawn, Leshaun, Le-Shawn

Leslie
(Scottish) fortified
Lee, Les, Lesley, Lesli, Lezlie, Lezly

Lesner
(Last name as first name) serious
Les, Lez, Lezner

Lester
(American) large persona
Les, Lestor

Lev
(Russian) lionine

Levar
(American) softspoken
Levarr

Leverett
(Last name as first name) planner
Lev, Leveret, Leverit, Leveritt

Leverton
(Last name as first name) town of Lever; organized

Levi
(Hebrew) harmonious
Lev, Levey, Levie, Levy

Levonne
(African American) forward-thinking
Lavonne, Leevon, Levon

Lew
(Polish) lion-like
Leu

Leward
(French) contentious
Lewar, Lewerd

Lew-Gene
(American) combo of Lew and Gene; renowned fighter
Lou-Gene

Lewie
(French) form of Louie
Lew, Lewee, Lewey, Lewy

Lewin
(Last name as first name) lion-like

Lewis
(German, French) powerful ruler
Lew, Lewey, Lewie, Lewus, Lewy

Lewy
(Irish) giving

Lex
(English) short for Alexander; mysterious
Lexa, Lexe, Lexi, Lexie, Lexy

Leyland
(Last name as first name) protective

Li
(Chinese) strong man

Liam
(Irish) protective; handsome
Leam, Leeam, Leeum

Liang
(Chinese) good man

Liberio
(Spanish) liberated
Libere, Lyberio

Liberty
(American) freedom-loving
Lib

Libor
(Czech) free

Librada
(Italian, Spanish) free

Lictor
(Invented) form of Lecter; disturbed
Lec, Lek

Lidio
(Greek) pleasant man

Lidon
(Hebrew) judge

Liem
(Vietnamese) truthful

Lif
(Scandinavian) full of life

Lihau
(Hawaiian) cool; fresh

Like
(Asian) soft-spoken

Liko
(Hawaiian) budding; flourishing

Lillo
(American) triple-threat talent
Lilo

Limo
(Invented) from the word limousine; sporty
Lim

Limu
(Polynesian) seaweed; natural

Linc
(English) short for Lincoln; leader
Link, Links

Lincoln
(English, American) quiet
Linc, Link

Lindberg
(German) blond good looks
Lin, Lind, Lindburg, Lindie, Lindy, Lyndberg, Lyndburg

Lindell
(Last name as first name) in harmony with nature
Lindall, Lindel, Lyndall, Lyndell

Linden
(Botanical) tree
Lindun

Lindoh
(American) sturdy
Lindo, Lindy

Lindsay
(English) natural
Lind, Lindsee, Lindsey, Linz, Linzee, Lyndsey, Lyndzie, Lynz, Lynzie

Lindy
(German) form of Lindberg; daring
Lind

Linford
(Last name as first name) bold man
Lynford

Linfred
(Last name as first name) proactive

Linley
(English) open-minded
Lin, Linlee, Linleigh, Lynlie

Linnard
(German) form of Leonard; bold
Linard, Lynard

Lino
(American) form of Linus
Linus

Linus
(Greek) blond
Linas, Line, Lines

Linton
(English) lives near lime trees
Lintonn, Lynton, Lyntonn

Linwood
(American) open

Lionel
(French) fierce
Li, Lion, Lionell, Lye, Lyon, Lyonel, Lyonell

Liron
(Hebrew) my song
Lyron

Lisiate
(Polynesian) courageous

Lisimba
(African) attacked by lion; victim

Lister
(Origin unknown) intelligent

Litton
(English) centered
Lyten, Lyton, Lytton

Liu
(Asian) quiet

Liuz
(Polish) light

Livingston
(English) comforting
Liv, Livey, Livingstone

Liwanu
(Asian) released

Llano
(Place name) river in Texas; flowing
Lano

Llewellyn
(English) fiery; fast
Lew, Lewellen, Lewellyn

Lloyd
(English) spiritual; joyful
Loy, Loyd, Loydde, Loye

Lobo
(Spanish) wolf
Loboe, Lobow

Lochan
(Irish) lively; (Hindu) eyes

Lochlain
(Irish) assertive
Lochlaine, Lochlane, Locklain

Lock
(English) natural
Locke

Lodewuk
(Scandinavian) warrior
Ladewijk, Ludovic

Lodge
(English) safe haven

Lodur
(Scandinavian) vivid

Loey
(American) daring
Loie, Lowee, Lowi

Lofton
(Last name as first name)
lofty
Loften

Logan
(Irish) eloquent
Logen, Loggy, Logun

Lohan
(Last name as first name)
capable

Lokela
(Hawaiian) famed
spearthrower

Lokene
(Hawaiian) form of Rodney;
open-minded

Lokni
(Hawaiian) red rose

Loman
(Irish) bare

Lomas
(Spanish) good man

Lombard
(Italian) winning

Lombardi
(Italian) winner
*Bardi, Bardy, Lom,
Lombard, Lombardy*

Lon
(Irish) intense

Lonato
(Native American)
flintstone; calm

London
(English) ethereal; capital
of Great Britain
Londen

Long
(Last name as first name)
Chinese dragon; methodical

Lonnie
(Spanish) short for Alonzo
Lonney, Lonni, Lonny

Lono
(Slavic) form of Lonna; light

Loocho
(Invented) form of Lucho

Lorance
(Latin) form of Lawrence;
long-suffering; patient
Lorans, Lorence

Lorca
(Last name as first) poet,
playwright; tragic

Lorcan
(Irish) fiery

Lord
(English) regal
Lorde

Lordlee
(English) regal
Lordly, Lords

Loredo
(Spanish) smart; cowboy
*Lorado, Loredoh, Lorre,
Lorrey*

Loren
(Latin) hopeful; winning
Lorin, Lorrin

Lorens
(Scandinavian) form of
Laurence

Lorenzo
(Spanish, Italian) bold and
spirited
*Larenzo, Loranzo, Lore,
Lorence, Lorenso, Lorentz,
Lorenz, Lorrie, Lorry*

Lorimer
(Last name as first name)
brash
Lorrimer

Loring
(German) brash
Looring, Lorrie, Louring

Lorne
(Latin) grounded
Lorn, Lorny

Lorry
(English) form of Laurie
Lore, Lorri, Lorrie, Lorry, Lory

Lot
(Hebrew) furtive
Lott

Lothario
(German) lover
*Lotario, Lothaire, Lotherio,
Lothurio*

Lou
(German) short for Louis
Lew

Loudon
(American) enthusiastic
Louden, Lowden, Lowdon

Louie
(German) short for Louis
Louey

Louis
(German, French) powerful ruler
Lew, Lewis, Lou, Louie, Lue, Luie, Luis

Loundis
(American) visionary
Lound, Loundas, Loundes, Lowndis

Louvain
(English) city in Belgium; wanderer

LouVon
(American) combo of Lou and Von; searching
Lou Von, Louvaughan, Louvawn, Lou-Von

Lovell
(English) brilliant
Lovall, Love, Lovelle, Lovie

Lovett
(Last name as first name) loving
Lovat, Lovet

Low
(American) word as a name; low-key
Lowey

Lowell
(English) loved
Lowall, Lowel

Lowry
(Last name as first name) leader
Lowree, Lowrey

Loyal
(English) true to the word
Loy

Loys
(American) loyal
Loyce, Loyse

Lubomil
(Polish) loves grace

Luboslaw
(Polish) loves glory

Luc
(French) light; laidback
Lucca, Luke

Luca
(Italian) light-hearted
Louca, Louka, Luka

Lucan
(Irish) light

Lucas
(Greek) patron saint of doctors/artists; creative
Lucca, Luces, Luka, Lukas, Luke, Lukes, Lukus

Lucho
(Spanish) lucky; light

Lucian
(Latin) soothing
Lew, Luciyan, Lushun

Luciano
(Italian) light-hearted
Luca, Lucas, Luke

Lucious
(African American) light; delicious
Luceous, Lushus

Lucius
(Latin) sunny
Lucca, Luchious, Lushus

Lucky
(American) lucky
Luckee, Luckey, Luckie

Ludger
(Scandinavian) wielding spears

Ludie
(English) glorious
Ludd

Ludlow
(German) respected
Ludlo, Ludloe

Ludolf
(English) form of Rudolf; glorious

Ludomir
(Polish) of well-known ancestry

Ludoslav
(Polish) of glorified people

Ludovic
(Slavic) smart; spiritual
Luddovik, Lude, Ludovik, Ludvic, Vick

Ludwig
(German) talented
Ludvig, Ludweg, Ludwige

Luigi
(Italian) famed warrior
Lui, Louie

Luis
(Spanish) outspoken
Luez, Luise, Luiz

Luister
(Irish) form of Louis; strong

Lujo
(Spanish) luxurious
Luj

Luka
(Italian, Croatian) easygoing
Luca, Luke

Lukah
(Invented) form of Luca

Lukas
(Greek) light-hearted;
creative
Lucus

Luke
(Latin) worshipful
Luc, Lucc, Luk, Lukus

Lukman
(Last name as first name)
vivacious

Lulani
(Hawaiian) light sky

Lumer
(American) light
Lumar, Lume, Lumur

Luna
(Spanish) moon

Lundy
(Scandinavian) island-lover

Lunn
(Irish) smart and brave
Lun, Lunne

Lunt
(Scandinavian) grove-
dweller

Luong
(Vietnamese) from the land
of bamboo

Lusk
(Last name as first name)
hearty
*Lus, Luske, Luskee, Luskey,
Luski, Lusky*

Lutalo
(African) bold fighter

Lute
(Polynesian) pigeon;
inconspicuous

Luther
(German) reformer
Luthar, Luth, Luthur

Luthus
(American) form of Luther;
prepared and armed
Luth, Luthas

Lux
(English) light

Lyal
(English) form of Lyle;
islander
Lye

Lyle
(French) unique
Lile, Ly, Lyle

Lyman
(English) meadow-man;
sportsman
Leaman, Leyman

Lyndall
(English) nature-lover
Lynd, Lyndal, Lyndell

Lyndon
(English) verbose
Lindon, Lyn, Lynd, Lyndonn

Lynge
(Scandinavian) sylvan nature

Lynn
(English) water-loving
Lin, Linn, Lyn, Lynne

Lynshawn
(African American) combo
of Lyn and Shawn; helpful
*Linshawn, Lynnshaw,
Lynshaun*

Lynton
(Engilsh) town of nature
lovers
Linton

Lyon
(Place name) city in France
Lyone

Lyron
(Hebrew) my song

Lysande
(Greek) freewheeling
Lyse

Lysander
(Greek) lover
Lysand

Lyulf
(German) haughty;
combative
Lyulfe, Lyulff

Mablevi
(African) do not deceive

Mac
(Irish, Scottish) short for
"Mc" or "Mac" surname;
friendly
*Mack, Mackee, Macki,
Mackie, Macky*

MacAdam
(Scottish) son of Adam; first

Macaffie
(Scottish) charming
*Mac, Mack, Mackey,
McAfee, McAffee, McAffie*

Macario
(Spanish) blessed
Macareo, Makario

Macarlos
(Spanish) manly
Carlos

Macauley
(Scottish) righteous;
dramatic
Mac, Macaulay, McCauley

Macauliffe
(Last name as first name)
bookish
Macaulif, Macauliff

Macbey
(American) form of Mackey
Mackbey, Makbee, Makbi

Macdowell
(Last name as first name)
giving
Macdowl

Macedonio
(Spanish) from Macedonia;
travels

MacEgan
(Last name as first name)
son of Egan; capable

Macgowan
(Irish) able; gallant
Macgowen, Macgowyn

Mackeane
(Last name as first name)
attractive
Mackeene

Mackenna
(Irish) giving; leader
Mackena

Mackenzie
(Irish) giving
*Mack, Mackenzy,
Mackinsey, Makinzie,
McKenzie*

Mackeon
(Last name as first name)
smiling

Mackie
(Irish) friendly
Mackey

MacKinley
(Irish) son of Kinley;
educated

Mackinney
(Last name as first name)
good-looking
Mackinny

Macklin
(Irish) also McClain; good-
humored

Maclain
(Irish) natural wonder
McLain, McLaine, McLean

Maclean
(Irish) dependable
Macleen

MacMurray
(Irish) loves the sea

Macnair
(Scottish) practical

Macon
(Place name) creative;
southern
Makon

Macy
(French) lasting; wealthy
Mace, Macee, Macey, Macye

Madan
(Hindi) god of love; loving

Madden
(Pakistani) planner
*Maddin, Maddyn, Maden,
Madin, Madyn*

Maddock
(Welsh) generous
*Maddoc, Madocock,
Maddox, Madox*

Maddox
(English) giving
Maddocks, Maddy, Madox

Madhav
(Hindi) sweet
Madhu

Madison
(English) good
*Maddison, Maddy,
Madisan, Madisen, Son*

Madock
(American) giving
Maddock, Maddy, Madoc

Madras
(Place name) city in India

Madu
(African) manly

Madzimoyo
(African) nourished by
water; simple

Magaidi
(African) last

Magdaleno
(Spanish) from Magdelene
(Biblical); spiritual

Magee
(Irish) practical; lively
Mackie, Maggy, McGee

Magglio
(Hispanic) athletic

Magic
(American) magical
Majic

Magne
(Latin) great

Magnus
(Latin) outstanding
Maggy, Magnes

Maguire
(Irish) subtle
Macky, Maggy, McGuire

Mahan
(American) cowboy
Mahahn, Mahand, Mahen, Mayhan

Mahatma
(Sanskrit) spiritually elevated

Mahir
(Arabic) skilled

Mahler
(Last name as first) famous composer; sweeping, free

Mahluli
(African) conqueror

Mahmud
(Arabic) remarkable

Maimon
(Arabic) of good fortune

Main
(Place name) river in Gemany; leader
Mainess, Mane, Maness

Maisel
(Persian) warrior
Meisel

Maitland
(English) of the meadow; fresh ideas

Majeed
(Arabic) majestic
Majid

Majid
(Arabic) glorious

Major
(Latin) leading
Mage, Magy, Majar, Maje, Majer

Makale
(Invented) form of Mikhail

Makio
(Hawaiian) from Makimo; great

Makoto
(Japanese) true

Maks
(Russian) short for Maksimilian

Maksimilian
(Russian) competitor
Maksim

Makya
(Native American) hunter

Mal
(Hindi) gardens; flourishes

Malachi
(Hebrew) angelic; magnanimous
Malachy, Malakai, Malaki, Maleki

Malawa
(African) flowering

Malcolm
(Scottish) peaceful
Mal, Malkalm, Malkelm, Malkolm

Maldon
(French) strong and combative
Maldan, Malden

Malfred
(German) feisty
Malfrid, Mann

Malik
(Arabic) angelic
Malic

Malise
(French) masterful

Malla-Ki
(Invented) form of Malachi

Mallin
(English) rowdy; warrior
Malen, Malin, Mallan, Mallen, Mallie, Mally

Mallory
(French) wild spirit
Mal, Mallie, Malloree, Mallorie, Mally, Malory

Maloney
(Irish) religious
Mal, Malone, Malonie, Malony

Malvin
(English) open-minded
Mal, Malv, Malven, Malvyne

Mamun
(Arabic) trustworthy

Manasseh
(Hebrew) cannot remember
Manases

Manchester
(English) dignity; (place name) city in England

Manchu
(Chinese) unflawed

Mandell
(German) tough; almond
Mandee, Mandel, Mandela, Mandie, Mandy

Mandy
(Latin) lovable
Mandey

Manfred
(English) peaceful
Manferd, Manford, Mannfred, Mannie, Manny, Mannye

Manfredo
(Italian) strong peacefulness

Manila
(Place name) capital of Philippines
Manilla

Maninder
(Hindi) masculine; potent

Manley
(English) virile; haven
Man, Manlee, Manlie, Manly

Mann
(German) masculine
Mannes, Manning

Manning
(English) heroic
Man, Maning, Mann

Mannis
(Irish) great
Manish, Manus

Mannix
(Irish) spiritual
Manix, Mann, Mannicks

Manny
(Spanish) short for Manuel
Manney, Manni, Mannie

Manolo
(Spanish) from Spanish shoe designer Manolo Blahnik; cutting-edge

Mansfield
(English) outdoorsman
Manesfeld, Mans, Mansfeld, Mansfielde

Manse
(English) winning

Manshel
(English) or Mansel (of the house); domestic

Mantel
(English) formidable
Mantell, Mantle

Manton
(English) man's town; special

Manu
(Hindi) father of people; masculine

Manuel
(Hebrew, Spanish) gift from God
Mann, Mannuel, Manny, Manual, Manuelle

Manus
(American) strong-willed
Manes, Mann, Mannas, Mannes, Mannis, Mannus

Manvel
(French) great town; hardworking
Mann, Manny, Manvil, Manville

Mao
(Chinese) hair

Marc
(French) combative
Markee, Markey, Markeye, Mark, Markie, Marko, Marky

Marc-Anthony
(French) combo of Marc and Anthony
Marcantony, Mark-Anthony, Markantony

Marcel
(French) singing God's praises
Marcell, Mars, Marsel

Marcellus
(Latin) romantic; persevering
Marcel, Marcelis, Marcey, Marsellus, Marsey

March
(Calendar month) fruitful
Marche

Marcial
(Spanish) martial; combative
Mars

Marciano
(Italian) manly; macho
Marcyano

Marcin
(Polish) form of Martin; warlike

Marco
(Italian) tender
Marc, Mark, Markie, Marko, Marky

Marconi
(Italian) inventive; tough

Marcos
(Spanish) outgoing
Marco, Marko, Markos, Marky

Marco-Tulio
(Spanish) fighter; substantial
Marco Tulio, Marcotulio

Marcoux
(French) aggressive; manly
Marce, Mars

Marcus
(Latin) combative
Marc, Mark, Markus, Marky

Marcus-Anthony
(Spanish) valuable; aggressive
Marc Anthony, Marc-Antonito, Marcus-Antoneo, Marcusantonio, Markanthony, Taco, Tonio, Tono

Marek
(Polish) masculine

Margarito
(Spanish) from Margarite; sunny

Marguez
(Spanish) noble
Marguiz

Mariano
(Italian) combative; manly
Mario

Marin
(French) ocean-loving
Maren, Marino, Maryn

Mariner
(Greek) from Marinos; seafarer

Mario
(Italian) masculine
Marioh, Marius, Marrio, Morio

Marion
(Latin) suspicious
Mareon, Marionn

Marius
(German) masculine; virile
Marrius

Marjuan
(Spanish) contentious
Marhwon, Marwon, Marwond

Markell
(African American) personable
Markelle

Markham
(English) homebody
Marcum, Markhum, Markum

Markos
(Greek) warring; masculine
Marc, Mark

Marl
(English) rebel
Marley, Marli

Marley
(English) secretive
Marlee, Marleigh, Marly

Marlin
(English) opportunistic; fish
Marllin

Marlo
(English) hill by a lake; optimistic
Mar, Marl, Marlow, Marlowe

Marlon
(French) wizard; strange
Marlan, Marlen, Marlin, Marly

Marmaduke
(English) haughty
Duke, Marmadook, Marmahduke

Marmion
(French) famed
Marmeonne, Marmyon

Marnin
(Hebrew) ebullient

Marq
(French) noble
Mark, Marque, Marquie

Marque
(French) noble; smart
Marcqe, Marcque, Marqe

Marquel
(French) nobleman

Marques
(African American) noble
Marqes, Marqis, Marquez, Marquis

Marquise
(French) noble
Mark, Markese, Marky, Marq, Marquese, Marquie, Marquis

Mars
(Latin) warlike; god of war
Marrs, Marz

Marsdon

(English) comforting
*Marr, Mars, Marsden,
Marsdyn*

Marsh

(English) handsome
*Marr, Mars, Marsch, Marsey,
Marsy*

Marshall

(French) giving care
*Marsh, Marshal, Marshel,
Marshell, Marsy*

Marshawn

(American) combo of Mark
and Shawn; outgoing

Marston

(English) personable
*Mars, Marst, Marstan,
Marsten*

Martial

(French) form of Mark;
combative

Martin

(Latin) combative; from Mars
*Mart, Marten, Marti, Martie,
Marton, Marty*

Marty

(Latin) short for Martin
*Mart, Martee, Martey,
Marti, Martie, Martye*

Marv

(English) short for Marvin;
good friend
Marve, Marvy

Marvell

(French) marvelous man
*Marvel, Marvil, Marvill,
Marvyl, Marvyll*

Marvin

(English) steadfast friend
Marv, Marven, Marvy

Marwood

(English) forest man

Masa

(African) centered

Masaaki

(African) from Maskini;
unfortunate

Masajiro

(Japanese) integrity
Masahiro, Masaji

Masamba

(African) departs

Masamitsu

(Japanese) feeling

Masanao

(Japanese) good

Masayuki

(Japanese) problematic

Mashael

(Invented) form of Michael

Mashawn

(African American) vivacious
*Masean, Mashaun,
Mayshawn*

Maslen

(American) promising
Mas, Masline, Maslyn

Mason

(French) ingenious; reliable;
stone mason
Mace, Mase

Masood

(Iranian) helpful

Massey

(English) doubly excellent
Maccey, Masey, Massi

Massimo

(Italian) great
*Masimo, Massey,
Massimmo*

Masura

(Japanese) fated for good
life

Mateo

(Italian) gift

Mateus

(Italian) God's gift

Mathau

(American) spunky
Mathou, Mathow, Mathoy

Mather

(English) leader; army;
strong
Mathar

Matheson

(English) son of God's gift
*Mathesen, Mathisen,
Mathison, Mathysen,
Mathyson*

Matheu

(French) form of Matthew;
God's gift
Matt, Matty

Mathias

(German) form of Matthew;
dignified
*Mathies, Mathyes, Matt,
Matthias, Matty*

Mathieu

(French) from Matthew

Matias

(Spanish) gift from God
Mathias, Matios, Mattias

Matin

(Hebrew) gift; also Matan

Matisse
(French) gifted

Matland
(English) Mat's land; homesteader

Matlock
(American) rancher
Lock, Mat, Matt

Mato
(Native American) bear; brawler

Matson
(Hebrew) son of Matthew
Matsan, Matsen, Matt, Matty

Matt
(Hebrew) short for Matthew
Mat, Matte

Matteson
(English) son of Matt; God's gift

Matthew
(Hebrew) God's gift
Math, Matheu, Mathieu, Matt, Mattie, Mattsy, Matty

Matthewson
(Last name as first name) son of Matthew; devout
Mathewsen, Mathewson, Matthewsen

Matti
(Scandinavian) form of Matthias; God's gift
Mat, Mats

Mattison
(Last name as first name) son of Matti; worldly
Matisen, Matison, Matisen, Mattysen, Mattyson, Matysen, Matyson

Matts
(Swedish) gift from God

Matty
(Hebrew) short for Matthew
Mattey, Matti

Matunde
(African) from Matthew; God's gift

Mauri
(Latin) short for Maurice; dark

Maurice
(Latin) dark
Maur, Maurie, Maurise, Maury, Moorice, Morice, Morrie, Morry

Mauricio
(Italian) dark
Mari, Mauri, Maurizio

Maurizio
(Italian) dark
Marits, Miritza, Moritz, Moritza, Moritzio

Maury
(Latin) short for Maurice; dark
Mauree, Maurey

Maverick
(American) unconventional
Mav, Mavarick, Mavereck, Mavreck, Mavvy

Mavis
(French) bird; thrush; free
Mavas, Mavus

Mawali
(African) vibrant

Mawulol
(African) thanks God; also Mawuli

Max
(Latin) best
Mac, Mack, Macks, Maxey, Maxie, Maxx, Maxy

Maxfield
(English) of the great field; lives large

Maxime
(French) greatest
Max, Maxeem, Maxim

Maximilian
(Latin) most wonderful
Max, Maxemillion, Maxie, Maxima, Maximillion, Maxmyllyun, Maxy

Maximino
(Spanish) maximum; tops
Max, Maxem, Maxey, Maxi, Maxim, Maxy

Maxinen
(Spanish) maximum
Max, Maxanen, Maxi

Maxwell
(English) full of excellence
Maxe, Maxie, Maxwel, Maxwill, Maxy

Mayer
(Hebrew) smart
Mayar, Maye, Mayor, Mayur

Mayfield
(English) grace

Maynard
(English) reliable
Mayne, Maynerd

Mayo
(Irish) nature-loving
Maio, Maioh, May, Mayes, Mayoh, Mays

Mayon
(Place name) volcano in the Philippines
May, Mayan, Mays, Mayun

Mays
(English) of the field; athlete

Maz
(Hebrew) aid
Maise, Maiz, Mazey, Mazi, Mazie, Mazy

Mazal
(Arabic) sedate

McCoy
(Irish) jaunty; coy
Coye, MacCoy

McDonald
(Scottish) open-minded
Mac-D, Macdonald

McFarlin
(Last name as first name) son of Farlin; confident
Far, Farr

McGill
(Irish) tricky

McGowan
(Irish) feisty
Mac-G, Mcgowan

McGregor
(Irish) philanthropic
Macgregor

McKay
(Scottish) connives

McKinley
(Last name as first name) son of Kinley; holding his own
Kin, Kinley, McKinlee

McLean
(Scottish) stays lithe

McLin
(Irish) careful
Mac, Mack

Mead
(English) outdoorsman
Meade, Meede

Meallan
(Irish) sweet
Maylan, Meall

Medford
(French) natural; comical
Med, Medfor

Medgar
(German) strong

Medwin
(German) friendly

Mehmet
(Sanskrit) royal

Meindert
(German) hearty boy
Meinhard, Meinrad

Meir
(Hebrew) teacher
Mayer, Myer

Mel
(Irish) short for Melvin
Mell

Melanio
(Spanish) royal

Melar
(English) mill man; pleases

Melbourne
(Place name) city in Australia; serene
Mel, Melborn, Melbourn, Melburn, Melburne

Melburn
(English) sylvan; outdoorsy
Mel, Melbourn, Melburne, Milbourn, Milburn

Melchor
(Polish) city's king

Meldon
(English) destined for fame
Melden, Meldin, Meldyn

Meldric
(English) leader
Mel, Meldrik

Melecio
(Spanish) cautious
Melesio, Melezio, Mesio

Meletius
(Greek) ultra-cautious
Meletios, Meletus

Melito
(Spanish) small and calm

Melos
(Greek) favorite
Milos

Melquiades
(Literature) gypsy

Melroy
(American) form of Elroy
Mel

Melton
(English) nature; natural
Mel, Meltan

Melville
(French) mill town
Mel, Mell, Melvil, Melvill

Melvin
(English) friendly
Mel, Melvine, Melvon, Melvyn, Milvin

Melvis
(American) form of Elvis; songbird
Mel, Melv

Memphis
(Place name) city in Tennessee
Memphus

Menas
(Hebrew) forgets

Mendel
(English) methodical
Mendl, Menka, Menke, Mela, Menlin

Mensa
(African) third son; genius
Mensah

Mercer
(English) affluent
Merce, Mercur, Murcer

Mercutio
(Literature) mercurial; comical

Meredith
(Welsh) protector
Merdith, Mere, Meredyth, Meridith, Merrey

Merlin
(English) clever
Merl, Merlan, Merle, Merlinn, Merlun, Murlin

Merrick
(English) bountiful seaman
Mere, Meric, Merik, Merrack, Merrik

Merrie
(English) giving
Merey, Meri, Merri

Merrill
(French) renowned
Mere, Merell, Merill, Merrell, Merril, Meryll

Merritt
(Latin) worthy
Merid, Merit, Merret, Merrid

Merv
(Irish) short for Mervin; bold
Murv

Mervin
(Irish) bold
Merv, Merven, Mervun, Mervy, Mervyn, Murv, Murvin

Meshach
(Hebrew) fortunate
Meeshak, Meshack, Meshak

Mesquite
(American) rancher; spiny shrub
Meskeet

Meyer
(Hebrew) brilliant
Maye, Meier, Mye, Myer

Meyshaun
(African American) searching
Maysh, Mayshaun, Mayshawn, Meyshawn

Micha
(Hebrew) prophet; sees all
Mica, Micah, Michah

Michael
(Hebrew) spiritual patron of soldiers
Mical, Michaelle, Mickey, Mikael, Mike, Mikey, Mikiee, Miko

Michel
(French) fond
Mich, Michelle, Mike, Mikey

Michelangelo
(Italian) God's angel/messenger; artistic
Michel, Michelanjelo, Mikalangelo, Mike, Mikel, Mikelangelo

Michon
(French) form of Michel; godlike
Mich, Michonn, Mish, Mishon

Mick
(Hebrew) closest to God
Mic, Mik

Mickel
(American) form of Michael; friend
Mick, Mikel

Mickey
(American) enthusiastic
Mick, Micki, Mickie, Micky, Miki, Myck

Mickey-Lee
(American) friendly
Mickey Lee, Mickeylee, Mickie-Lee

Miga
(Spanish) persona; essence

Miguel
(Spanish) form of Michael
Megel, Migel, Migelle

Miguelangel
(Spanish) angelic
Miguelanjel

Mihir
(Hindi) sunny

Mika
(Hebrew) form of Micah
Mikah, Mikie, Myka, Mykie, Myky

Mikael
(Scandinavian) warrior
Michael, Mikel, Mikkel

Mike
(Hebrew) short for Michael
Meik, Miik, Myke

Mikhail
(Russian) god-like; graceful
Mika, Mikey, Mikkail, Mykhey

Mikolas
(Greek) form of Nicholas; bright
Mick, Mickey, Mickolas, Mik, Miko, Mikolus, Miky

Milagros
(Spanish) miracle
Milagro

Milam
(Last name as first name) uncomplicated
Mylam

Milan
(Place name) city in Italy; smooth
Milano

Milburn
(Scottish) volatile
Milbyrn, Milbyrne, Millburn

Miles
(German) forgiving
Mile, Miley, Myles, Myyles

Miley
(American) reliable; forgiving
Mile, Miles, Mili, Mily, Myles, Myley

Milford
(English) from a calm (mill) setting; country
Milferd, Milfor

Millard
(Latin) old-fashioned
Milard, Mill, Millerd, Millurd, Milly

Miller
(English) practical
Mille, Myller

Mills
(English) safe
Mill, Milly, Mylls

Milo
(German) soft-hearted
Miles, Milos, Mye, Mylo

Milos
(Slavic) kind
Mile, Miles, Myle, Mylos

Milton
(English) innovative
Melton, Milt, Miltey, Milti, Miltie, Milty, Mylt, Mylton

Mimi
(Greek) outspoken
Mims

Miner
(Last name as first name) hard-working; miner
Mine, Miney

Mingo
(American) flirtatious
Ming-O, Myngo

Minnow
(American) beachcomber

Minter
(Last name as first name) dull

Mirlam
(American) great
Mir, Mirsam, Mirtam

Mirsab
(Arabic) judicious

Misael
(Hebrew) godlike

Misha
(Russian) short for Mikhail

Mitch
(English) short for Mitchell; optimist

Mitchell
(English) optimistic
Mitch, Mitchel, Mitchelle, Mitchie, Mitchill, Mitchy, Mitshell, Mytchil

Mitchum
(Last name as first name) dramatic; known
Mitchem

Modesto
(Spanish) modest
Modysto

Modred
(Greek) unafraid
Modrede, Modrid

Moe
(American) short for names beginning with Mo or Moe; easygoing
Mo

Moey
(Hebrew) easygoing
Moe, Moeye

Mohammad
(Arabic) praiseworthy
*Mohamad, Mohamid,
Mohamud, Muhammad*

Mohan
(Hindi) compelling

Mohana
(Sanskrit) handsome
Mohann

Mohawk
(Place name) river in New
York

Mohsen
(Persian) one who does good
Mosen

Moises
(Hebrew) drawn from the
water
Moe

Mojave
(Place name) desert in
California; towering man
Mohave, Mohavey

Moline
(American) narrow
Moleen, Molene

Momo
(American) rascal

Monahan
(Irish) believer
*Mon, Monaghan, Monehan,
Monnahan*

Money
(American) word as name;
popular
Muney

Monico
(Spanish) form of Monaco;
player
Mon

Monroe
(Irish) delightful;
presidential
*Mon, Monro, Munro,
Munroe*

Montague
(French) forward-thinking
*Mont, Montagew, Montagu,
Montegue, Monty*

Montana
(Spanish) mountain;
(Place name) U.S. state;
(American) sports icon
*Mont, Montane, Montayna,
Monty*

Monte
(Spanish) short for
Montgomery and
Montague; handsome
*Mont, Montee, Monti,
Monts, Monty*

Monteague
(African American) combo of
Monty and Teague; creative
*Mont, Montegue, Monti,
Monty*

Montgomery
(English) wealthy
*Mongomerey, Monte,
Montgomry, Monty*

Montraie
(African American) fussy
*Mont, Montray, Montraye,
Monty*

Montrel
(African American) popular
Montrell, Montrelle, Monty

Montrose
(French) high and mighty
*Mont, Montroce, Montros,
Monty*

Monty
(English) short for
Montgomery and Montague
*Monte, Montee, Montey,
Monti*

Moody
(American) expansive
Moodee, Moodey, Moodie

Moon
(African) dreamer

Mooney
(American) dreamer
Moon, Moonee, Moonie

Moore
(French) dark-haired
Mohr, Moores, More

Mooring
(Last name as first name)
centered
Moring

Moose
(American) large guy
Moos, Mooz, Mooze

Mordecai
(Hebrew) combative
*Mord, Morde, Mordekai,
Morducai, Mordy*

Moreland
(Last name as first name) of
wealth
*Mooreland, Moorland,
Moorlande, Morland,
Morlande*

Morell
(French) secretive
*More, Morelle, Morey,
Morrell, Mourell, Murell*

Morey
(Latin) dark
Morrie, Morry

Morgan
(Celtic) confident; seaman
Morg, Morgen, Morghan

Morlen
(English) outdoorsy
Morlan, Morlie, Morly

Moroni
(Place name) city in
Comoros; joyful
*Maroney, Maroni, Marony,
Moroney, Morony*

Morpheus
(Greek) god of dreams;
shapes

Morris
(Latin) dark
*Maurice, Moris, Morse,
Mouris*

Morrison
(Last name as first name)
son of Morris; dark
*Morrisen, Morrysen,
Morryson*

Morrley
(English) outdoors-loving
*More, Morlee, Morley,
Morly, Morrs*

Morrow
(Last name as first name)
follower
Morrowe

Morry
(Hebrew) taught by God;
old friend
Morey, Morrey, Mory

Morse
(English) bright; code-
maker
*Morce, Morcey, Morry,
Morsey*

Mortimer
(French) deep
*Mort, Mortemer, Mortie,
Morty, Mortymer*

Morton
(English) sophisticated
Mort, Mortan, Mortun, Morty

Moses
(Hebrew) appointed for
special things
*Mosa, Mose, Mosesh,
Mosie, Mozes, Mozie*

Moshe
(Hebrew) special
Mosh, Moshie

Moss
(Irish) giving
Mossy

Mostyn
(Welsh) mossy

Motor
(American) word as name;
speedy; active
Mote

Mottel
(Hebrew) from Max; fighter

Mozam
(Place name) from
Mozambique
Moze

Mudge
(Last name as first name)
friendly
Mud, Mudj

Muhammad
(Arabic) form of
Mohammed; praised
Muhamed, Muhammed

Mukul
(Hindi) bird; beginnings

Mulder
(American) of the dark

Muldoon
(Last name as first name)
different
Muldoone, Muldune

Mundo
(Spanish) short for
Edmundo; prosperous
Mun, Mund

Mungo
(Scottish) loved; congenial
*Mongo, Mongoh, Munge,
Mungoh*

Murcia
(Place name) region in Spain
Mursea

Murdoch
(Scottish) rich
*Merdock, Merdok, Murd,
Murdock, Murdok, Murdy*

Murfain
(American) bold spirit
*Merfaine, Murf, Murfee,
Murfy, Murphy*

Murff
(Irish) short for Murphy;
feisty
Merf, Murf

Murl
(English) nature-lover; sea

Murphy
(Irish) fighter
*Merph, Merphy, Murfie,
Murph*

Murray
(Scottish) sea-loving; sailor
Mur, Muray, Murrey, Murry

Murrell
(English) nature-lover; sea

Murtough
(Irish) of the sea
Murtagh, Murrough

Muslim
(Arabic) religious

Mustafa
(Arabic) chosen one;
(Turkish) ingenious

Mutka
(African) New Year's baby

Myreon
(Greek) blessed; smell of oil
Myron

Mycheal
(African American) devoted
Mysheal

Myles
(German) form of Miles

Mylos
(Slavic) kind
Milos

Myrle
(American) able
Merl, Merle, Myrie, Myryee

Myron
(Greek) notable
Mi, Miron, My, Myrayn

Myrzon
(American) humorous
Merzon, Myrs, Myrz

Mystikal
(American) musician;
mystical

Nabil
(Arabic) of noble birth;
honored
Nabeel, Nobila

Nachman
(Last name as first name)
unique
*Menachem, Menahem,
Nacham, Nachmann, Nahum*

Nachson
(Last name as first name)
son of Nach; up-and-coming

Nachum
(Hebrew) comforts others

Nada
(Arabic) morning dew; giver
Nadah

Nadim
(Arabic) fellow celebrant
Nadeem

Nadir
(Arabic) rare man
Nadeer, Nadeir

Naeem
(Arabic) happy

Nafis
(Hebrew) struggles

Naftali
(African) runs in woods
*Naphtali, Naphtali, Neftali,
Nefthali, Nephtali,
Nephthali*

Nagel
(English) smooth
*Naegel, Nageler, Nagelle,
Nagle, Nagler*

Nagid
(Arabic) regal

Nahir
(Hebrew) light
Naheer, Nahor

Nahum
(Arabic) content
Nemo

Naim
(Arabic) content
Naeem

Nairn
(Last name as first name)
born again
Nairne

Nairobi
(Place name) city in Kenya;
starting out

Najib
(Arabic) noble
Nageeb, Nagib, Najeeb

Naldo
(Italian) from Reynoldo; smart tutor

Nalin
(Hindi) lotus; pretty boy
Naleen

Namir
(Hebrew) leopard; fast
Nameer

Nando
(Spanish) short for Fernando

Nandor
(Hungarian) short for Ferdinand

Nandy
(Hindi) from the god Nandin; destructs

Nanson
(American) spunky
Nance, Nanse, Nansen, Nansson

Napier
(French) mover
Neper

Napoleon
(German) lion of Naples; domineering
Nap, Napo, Napoleone, Napolion, Napolleon, Nappy

Narciso
(Spanish) form of Greek Narcissus, who fell in love with his reflection; vain
Narcis

Narcissus
(Greek) self-loving; vain
Narciss, Narcissah, Narcisse, Nars

Naren
(Hindi) best

Nasario
(Spanish) dedicated to God
Nasar, Nasareo, Nassario, Nazareo, Nazarlo, Nazaro, Nazor

Nash
(Last name as first name) exciting
Nashe, Nashey

Nashua
(Native American) thunderous

Nasser
(Arabic) winning
Naser, Nasir, Nasr, Nassar, Nasse, Nassee, Nassor

Nat
(Hebrew) short for Nathaniel
Natt, Natte, Nattie, Natty

Natal
(Hebrew) gift of God
Natale, Natalino, Natalio, Nataly

Nate
(Hebrew) short for Nathan and Nathaniel
Natey

Natividad
(Spanish) a child born at Christmastime

Nathan
(Hebrew) short for Nathaniel; magnanimous
Nat, Nate, Nathen, Nathin, Natthaen, Natthan, Natthen, Natty

Nathaniel
(Hebrew) God's gift to mankind
Nat, Nate, Nathan, Nathaneal, Nathanial, Nathe, Nathenial

Nation
(American) patriotic

Nato
(American) gentle
Nate, Natoe, Natoh

Navarro
(Spanish) place name; wild spirit
Navaro, Navarroh, Naverro

Nayan
(Hebrew) form of Nathan; God-given

Naylor
(English) likes order
Nailer, Nailor

Naveed
(Hindi) wishing you well
Navid

Nazaire
(Biblical) from Nazareth; religious boy
Nasareo, Nasarrio, Nazario, Nazarius, Nazaro, Nazor

Neal
(Irish) winner
Neale, Nealey, Neall, Nealy, Neel, Neelee, Neely, Nele

Neander
(Greek) from Neanderthal
Ander, Nean, Neand

Nebo
(Mythology) Babylonian god of wisdom

Nebraska
(Place name) U.S. state
Neb

Nectarios
(Greek) also Nektarios;
sweet nectar; immortal man
Nectaire, Nectarius, Nektario,
Nektarios, Nektarius

Ned
(English) short for Edward;
comforting
Neddee, Neddie, Neddy

Nedrun
(American) difficult
Ned, Nedd, Neddy, Nedran,
Nedro

Neely
(Scottish) winning
Neel, Neels

Negasi
(African) destined for royalty

Nehemiah
(Hebrew) compassionate
Nechemia, Nechemiah,
Nechemya, Nehemyah,
Nemo

Neil
(Scottish) victor
Neal, Neale, Neall, Nealle,
Nealon, Neel, Neile, Neill,
Neille, Neils, Nels, Nial,
Niall, Niel, Niles

Neirin
(Irish) light

Nellie
(English) short for Nelson;
singing
Nell, Nellee, Nelli, Nells,
Nelly

Nels
(Scandinavian) victor

Nelson
(English) broad-minded
Nell, Nels, Nelsen, Nelsun,
Nilsson

Nemesio
(Spanish) from Nemesis, a
god who avenges wrongs
Nemo

Nemo
(Literature) unknown entity

Neptune
(Latin) god of the sea
Neptoon, Neptoone,
Neptunne

Ner
(Hebrew) light, fire

Nereus
(Greek) of the sea
Nereo

Nero
(Latin) unyielding
Neroh

Nery
(Spanish) daring
Neree, Nerey, Nerrie, Nerry

Nesbit
(Last name as first name)
man who wanders
Naisbit, Naisbitt, Nesbitt,
Nisbet, Nisbett

Nesto
(Greek) adventurer
Nestoh, Nestoro

Nestor
(Greek) wanderer
Nest, Nester, Nestir, Nesto,
Nesty

Netar
(African American) bright
Netardas

Netzer
(American) form of Nestor
Net

Nevada
(Place name) U.S. state
Nev, Nevadah

Neville
(French) innovator
Nev, Nevil, Nevile, Nevvy,
Nevyle, Niville

Nevin
(Irish) small holy man
Nev, Nevan, Neven, Nevins,
Nevon, Niven

Newbie
(American) novice
New, Newb

Newbury
(Last name as first name)
renewal
Newbery, Newberry

Newcomb
(Last name as first name)
renewal
Newcombe

Newell
(English) fresh face in the
hall
New, Newall, Newel, Newy,
Nywell

Newland
(Last name as first name) of
a new land

Newlin
(Welsh) able; new pond
Newl, Newlynn, Nule

Newman
(English) attractive young man
Neuman, Neumann, New, Newmann

Newport
(Last name as first name) from a new seaport

Newt
(English) new

Newton
(English) bright; new mind
New, Newt

Neyman
(American) son of Ney; bookish
Ney, Neymann, Neysa

Nezer
(Arabic) winning boy

Niall
(Irish) winner
Nial

Niaz
(Hindi) gift

Nicah
(Greek) victorious
Nik, Nike

Nicandro
(Spanish) a man who excels
Nicandreo, Nicandrios, Nicandros, Nikander, Nikandreo, Nikandrios

Nicholas
(Greek) winner; the people's victory
Nichelas, Nicholus, Nick, Nickee, Nickie, Nicklus, Nickolas, Nicky, Nikolas, Nyck, Nykolas

Nichols
(English) kind-hearted
Nicholes, Nick, Nicky, Nikols

Nick
(English) short for Nicholas
Nic, Nik

Nicklaus
(Greek) form of Nicholas
Nicklaws, Niklus

Nickleby
(Last name as first name) betting on the odds

Nickler
(American) fleet-footed; perspicacious

Nicky
(Greek) short for Nicholas
Nick, Nickee, Nickey, Nicki, Nik, Nikee, Nikki

Nico
(Italian) victor
Nicos, Niko, Nikos

Nicodemus
(Greek) people's victory
Nicodemo, Nikodema

Nicol
(Italian) from Nicola; victor

Nicolas
(Italian) form of Nicholas; victorious
Nic, Nico, Nicolus

Nicomedes
(Greek) thinking of victory
Nicomedo, Nikomedes

Niels
(Scandinavian) victorious
Neels

Nigel
(English) champion
Nigie, Nigil, Nygelle

Night
(American) nocturnal

Nike
(Greek) winning
Nykee, Nykie, Nyke

Nikhil
(Russian) from Nicola; victor

Nikita
(Russian) not yet won
Nika

Niklas
(Scandinavian) winner
Niklaas, Nils, Klaas

Nikolai
(Russian) winning
Nika

Nikolas
(Greek) form of Nicholas
Nik, Nike, Niko, Nikos, Nyloas

Nikos
(Greek) victor
Nicos, Niko, Nikolos

Nikostratos
(Greek) the army's victory
Nicostrato, Nicostratos, Nicostratus

Niles
(English) smooth
Ni, Nile, Niley, Nyles, Nyley

Nimrod
(Hebrew) renegade
Nimrodd, Nymrod

Ninian
(Armenium) studious

Nino
(Spanish) child; young boy

Ninyun
(American) spirited
Ninian, Ninion, Ninyan, Nynyun

Nissan
(Hebrew) omen
Nisan, Nissyn

Nissim
(Hebrew) Nisan is seventh Jewish month; believer

Niven
(Last name as first name) smooth

Nix
(American) negative
Nicks, Nixy

Nixon
(English) audacious
Nickson, Nixen, Nixun

Njord
(Scandinavian) man of the north
Njorth

Noah
(Hebrew) peacemaker
Noa, Noe, Nouh

Noam
(Hebrew) sweet man
Noahm, Noe

Noble
(Latin) regal
Nobe, Nobee, Nobel, Nobie, Noby

Noe
(Spanish) quiet; (Polish) comforter
Noeh, Noey

Noel
(French) born on Christmas
Noelle, Noelly, Nole, Nollie

Noey
(Spanish) form of Noah; he who wanders
Noe, Noie

Nolan
(Irish) outstanding; noble
Nole, Nolen, Nolline, Nolun, Nolyn

Nolden
(American) noble
Nold

Noll
(Scandinavian) from Nolly (Oliver); smiling

Nolly
(Scandinavian) hopeful
Nole, Noli, Noll, Nolley, Nolleye, Nolli, Nollie

Noor
(Hindi) light
Nour, Nur

Norb
(Scandinavian) innovative
Noberto, Norbie, Norbs, Norby

Norbert
(German) bright north
Norb, Norbie, Norby

Nordin
(Nordic) handsome
Nord, Nordan, Norde, Nordee, Nordeen, Nordi, Nordun, Nordy

Norman
(English) sincere; man of the North
Norm, Normen, Normey, Normi, Normie, Normon, Normun, Normy

Norris
(English) from the north

Norshawn
(African American) combo of Nor and Shawn
Norrs, Norrshawn, Norshaun

North
(American) directional
Norf, Northe

Northcliff
(English) from the north cliff
Northcliffe, Northclyff, Northclyffe

Northrop
(English) northerner
Northrup

Norton
(English) dignified man of the North
Nort, Nortan, Norten

Norval
(English) from the North
Norvan

Norville
(French) resident of a northern village; warm-hearted
Norval, Norvel, Norvil, Norvill, Norvyl

Norshell
(African American) brash
Norshel, Norshelle

Norward
(English) going north
Norwerd

Norwell
(English) northward bound

Norwin
(English) friendly
Norvin, Norwen, Norwind, Norwinn

Norwood
(English) of the north woods

Nowell
(Last name as first name) dependable
Nowe

Nowey
(American) knowing
Nowee, Nowie

Nueces
(Place name) river in Texas

Nuell
(American) form of Newell (last name); in charge
Nuel

Nuey
(Spanish) short for Nueva
Nui, Nuie

Nuncio
(Spanish) messenger; informant
Nunzio

Nunry
(Last name as first name) giving
Nunri

Nuri
(Arabic) light
Noori, Nur, Nuriel, Nuris

Nuriel
(Hebrew) light of God
Nooriel, Nuriya, Nuriyah, Nurya

Nuys
(Place name) from Van Nuys, California
Nies, Nyes, Nys

Nye
(Welsh) focused
Ni, Nie, Nyee

Nyle
(American) form of Niles/Nile; smooth
Nyl, Nyles

Oak
(English) sturdy
Oake, Oakes, Oakie

Oakley
(English) sturdy; strong
Oak, Oakie, Oaklee, Oakleigh, Oakly, Oklie

Oba
(Hebrew) from Obadiah; God's servant

Obadiah
(Hebrew) serving God
Obadyah, Obediah, Obee, Obie, Oby

Obasi
(African) God-loving

Obataiye
(African) world leader

Obayana
(African) king by the fire

Obbie
(Biblical) from Biblical prophet Obadiah; serving God
Obey, Obi, Obie

Obedience
(American) strict
Obie

Oberon
(German) strong-bearing
Auberon, Auberron, Obaron, Oberahn, Oberone, Oburon

Obert
(German) rich man

Obey
(American) short for Obadiah
Obe, Obee, Obie, Oby

Obi
(African) big heart

Obie
(Hebrew) from Obadiah; serves the Lord
Obbie, Obe, Oby

Obike
(African) loved by his family

Ocean
(Greek) ocean; child born under a water sign
Oceane, Oceanus

Ocie
(Greek) short for Ocean
Osie

Octavio
(Latin) eight; able
Octave, Octavian, Octavien, Octavioh, Octavo, Ottavio

Odakota
(Native American) has many friends

Ode
(Greek) poetry as a name; poetic
Odee, Odie

Oded
(Hebrew) supportive

Odell
(American) musical
Dell, Odall, Ode, Odey, Odyll

Oder
(Place name) river in Europe
Ode

Odhran
(Irish) green; creative
Odran, Oran

Odin
(Scandinavian) Norse god of magic; soulful
Odan, Oden

Odinan
(Hungarian) rich; powerful

Odion
(African) the first twin

Odisoose
(Invented) form of Odysseus
Ode

Odissan
(African) wanderer

Odolf
(Japanese) from the field of deer; lithe

Odom
(African) the oak; strong

Odysseus
(Greek) wanderer
Ode, Odey, Odie

Ofer
(Hebrew) deer, fleetfooted

Og
(Aramaic) king

Ogano
(Japanese) wise

Ogdon
(English) literate
Og, Ogdan, Ogden

Oghe
(Irish) horserider
Oghie, Oho

Ogle
(American) word as name; leer; stare
Ogal, Ogel, Ogll, Ogul

Ogun
(Japanese) undaunted

Ohanko
(Japanese) invincible

Ohanzee
(Native American) shadowy figure

Ohin
(Japanese) wanted child

Oisin
(Irish) fawn; gentle

Oistin
(Latin) much revered

Ojay
(American) brash
O.J., Oojai

Ojo
(African) he came of a hard birth

Okan
(Turkish) horse
Oke

Okapi
(African) graceful

Okechuku
(African) God's blessing

Okello
(African) child after twins were born

Okemos
(African) advises

Okie
(American) man from Oklahoma
Okey, Okeydokey

Oko
(Japanese) evoker; charming

Okon
(Japanese) from the darkness

Okoth
(African) sad child; born during rainfall

Okpara
(African) first son

Oktawian
(African) eighth child

Ola
(African) child much honored

Oladele
(African) honored at home

Olaf
(Scandinavian) watchful
Olay, Ole, Olef, Olev, Oluf

Olafemi
(African) lucky child

Olajuwon
(Arabic) honorable
Olajuwan, Olujuwon

Olakeakua
(Hawaiian) living for God

Olamina
(African) rich of spirit

Olan
(Scandinavian) royal
ancestor
Olin, Ollee

Olaniyan
(African) honored all around

Olav
(Scandinavian) traditional
Ola, Olov, Oluf

Oldrich
(Czech) leader; strong
*Olda, Oldra, Oldrisek,
Olecek, Olik, Olin, Olouvsek*

Ole
(Scandinavian) watchful
Olay

Oleg
(Russian) holy; religious
Olag, Ole, Olig

Olvery
(English) draws others near

Olin
(English) holly; jubilant
Olen, Olney, Olyn

Olindo
(Latin) sweet fragrance

Oliver
(Latin) loving nature
*Olaver, Olive, Ollie, Olliver,
Olly, Oluvor*

Olivier
(French) eloquent
Oliveay

Oliwa
(Hawaiian) from an army of
elves

Ollie
(English) short for Oliver
Olie, Ollee, Olley, Olly

Olney
(English) lonely field

Olo
(Spanish) short for Orlando;
showy

Olorun
(African) blessed; counsels
others

Olubayo
(African) full of happiness

Olufemi
(African) God's loved child
Olviemi

Olugbala
(African) the people's God

Olujimi
(African) hand in hand with
God

Olumide
(African) God has come

Olumoi
(African) blessed by God

Olushegun
(African) marches with God

Olushola
(African) blessed

Oluwa
(African) believer

Oluyemi
(African) man full of God

Omaha
(Place name) city in
Nebraska

Omanand
(Hindi) joyful thinker

Omar
(Arabic) spiritual
Omahr, Omarr

Omie
(Italian) homebody
Omey, Omi, Omye

Omri
(Hebrew) Jehovah's servant;
giving

On
(African) desirable

Onacona
(Native American) white
owl; watchful

Oukounaka
(Asian) from the surf

Onan
(Turkish) rich

Onani
(Asian) sweet

Onaona
(Hawaiian) fragrant

Ondrej
(Czech) masculine
*Ondra, Ondravsek,
Ondrejek, Ondrousek*

Onesimo
(Spanish) number one
Onie

Onkar
(Hindi) purest one

Onofrio
(German) smart
Ono, Onofreeo, Onofrioh

Onslow
(Arabic) climbing passion's hill
Ounslow

Onur
(Turkish) promising boy

Onwoachi
(African) God's world

Oqwapi
(Native American) red cloud

Oral
(Latin) eloquent

Oran
(Irish) pale
Orin, Orran, Orren, Orrin

Orban
(Hungarian) city man; sophisticated

Ordell
(Latin) the start

Oren
(Hebrew) from Owen; sturdy (tree)

Orenthiel
(American) sturdy as a pine
Ore, Oren

Orenthiem
(American) sturdy as a pine
Orenth, Orenthe

Orestes
(Greek) leader
Oresta, Oreste, Restie, Resty

Orev
(Hebrew) raven; observing

Orford
(Last name as first name) noble

Ori
(Hebrew) flame of truth

Oriol
(Spanish) best
Orioll

Orion
(Greek) fiery hunter
Oreon, Ori, Orie, Ory

Orji
(African) sturdy tree

Orlando
(Spanish) famed; distinctive
Orl, Orland, Orlie, Orlondo, Orly

Orleans
(Latin) the golden boy
Orlins

Orman
(Latin) noble
Ormand, Ormond, Ormonde

Orme
(English) kind
Orm

Ormond
(English) kind-hearted
Ormand, Ormande, Orme, Ormon, Ormonde, Ormund, Ormunde

Oro
(Spanish) golden child

Oron
(Hebrew) light spirit

Orpheus
(Greek) darkness of night; mythological musician

Orran
(Irish) green-eyed
Ore, Oren, Orin

Orrick
(English) sturdy as an oak
Oric, Orick, Orreck, Orrik

Orrie
(American) short for Orson; solid
Orry

Orrin
(English) river boy

Orris
(Latin) from Horatio; inventive
Oris, Orriss

Orry
(Latin) Oriental; exotic
Oarrie, Orrey, Orrie

Orson
(Latin) strong as a bear
Orsan, Orsen, Orsey, Orsun

Orth
(English) honest
Orthe

Orton
(Last name as first name) reaching

Orval
(American) form of Orville; bold
Orvale

Orunjan
(African) god of the noon-time sun

Orville
(French) brave
Orv, Orvelle, Orvie, Orvil

Orvin
(Last name as first name) fated for success
Orwin, Orwynn

Orway
(American) kind
Orwaye

Osakwe
(Japanese) good destiny

Osanmwesr
(Japanese) leaving

Osayaba
(Japanese) wonders

Osbert
(English) smart

Osborne
(English) strong-spirited
Osborn, Osbourne, Osburn, Osburne, Ossie, Oz, Ozzie, Ozzy

Osburt
(English) smart
Osbart, Osbert, Ozbert, Ozburt

Oscar
(Scandinavian) divine
Ozkar

Oscard
(Greek) fighter
Oscar, Oskard

Osceola
(Native American) black drink

Osei
(African) gracious

Osgood
(English) good man
Osgude, Ozgood

Oshea
(Hebrew) kind spirit

Osiel
(Spanish)

Osileani
(Polynesian) talking forever

Oslo
(Place name) capital of
Norway
Os, Oz

Osman
(Spanish) verbose
Os, Osmen, Osmin, Ossie, Oz, Ozzie

Osmar
(English) amazing; divine

Osmond
(English) singing to the
world
Os, Osmonde, Osmund, Ossie, Oz, Ozzy

Osrec
(Scandinavian) leader
Os, Ossie

Osred
(Scandinavian) leads
mankind

Osric
(Scandinavian) leader
Osrick

Ossie
(Hebrew) powerful
Os, Oz, Ozzy

Osten
(Last name as first name)
religious leader
Ostin, Ostyn

Osvaldo
(German) divine power
Osvald, Oswaldo

Oswald
(English) divine power
Oswalde, Oswold, Oswuld, Oszie, Oz

Oswin
(English) God's ally
Osvin, Oswinn, Oswyn, Oswynn

Ota
(Czech) affluent

Otik
(German) lucky

Otadan
(Native Amercian)
abundance

Othell
(African American) thriving
Oth, Othey, Otho

Othello
(Spanish) bold
Otello, Othell

Othman
(Last name as first name)
man of bravery

Othniel
(Hebrew) rendered brave by
God's love

Otis
(Greek) intuitive
Oates, Odis, Otes, Ottes, Ottis

Otokar
(Czech) prudent in wealth

Otoniel
(Spanish) fashionable
Otonel

Otskai
(Native American) leaving

Ottah
(African) thin boy

Ottar
(Scandinavian) warring
Otomars, Ottomar

Otto
(German) wealthy
Oto, Ott, Ottoh

Ottokar
(German) can-do spirit; fighter
Otokars, Ottocar

Ottway
(German) fortunate
Otwae, Otway

Otu
(Native American) industrious

Ouray
(Native American) arrow man

Oved
(Hebrew) serving
Obed

Overton
(Last name as first name) leader
Ove, Overten

Ovidio
(Spanish) from Ovid (Roman poet); creative
Ovido

Owen
(Welsh) well-born; high-principled
Owan, Owin, Owwen

Owney
(Irish) old one
Oney

Ox
(American) animal; strong
Oxy

Oxford
(English) scholar; ox crossing
Fordy, Oxferd, Oxfor

Oz
(Hebrew) courageous; unusual

Ozell
(English) strong
Ozel

Oziel
(Spanish) strong

Ozni
(Hebrew) knows God

Ozuru
(Japanese) stork; lively hope

Ozzie
(English) short for Oswald
Oz, Ozzee, Ozzey, Ozzy

Pablo
(Spanish) strong; creative
Pabel, Pabo, Paublo

Pacian
(Spanish) peaceful
Pacien, Pace

Pack
(German) from Packard (Richard); outdoorsman
Pac, Pak

Packer
(Last name as first name) orderly
Pack

Packy
(German) from Packard (Richard); outdoorsman
Packey

Paco
(Spanish) energetic
Pak, Pakkoh, Pako, Paquito

Padden
(English) form of Patton; confident
Paddin, Paddyn

Paddy
(Irish) short for Patrick; noble; comfortable
Paddey, Paddi, Paddie, Padee

Padget
(French) learning; growing
Padgett, Pagas

Padraic
(Irish) form of Patrick; cocky
Padraick, Padraik, Padrayc, Padrayck, Padrayk

Padre
(Spanish) father; cajoles
Padrae, Padray

Page
(French) helpful
Pagey, Paige, Payg

Pageman
(Last name as first name) sharp

Pago
(Place name) Pago Pago
Pay

Paine
(Latin) countryman
Payne

Paki
(African) has seen the truth

Pall
(Scandinavian) form of
Paul; wise friend

Palladin
(Greek) confrontational; wise
*Palidin, Palladyn, Palleden,
Pallie, Pally*

Pallaton
(Native American) tough;
fighter
Palladin

Palma
(Latin) successful

Palmer
(English) open
*Pallmar, Pallmer, Palmar,
Palmur*

Palti
(Hebrew) getaway

Pampa
(Place name) city in Texas

Pan
(Greek mythology) god of
forest and shepherds
Pann

Panama
(Place name) canal
connecting North and South
America; rounder
Pan

Pancho
(Spanish) short for
Francisco; jaunty
Panchoh, Ponchito

Pancrazio
(Italian) all-powerful
Pankraz

Panfilo
(Spanish) loving all nature

Panos
(Greek) rock; sturdy

Pantaleon
(Spanish) pants; trousers;
manly
Pant, Pantalon

Pantias
(Greek) philosophical

Paolo
(Italian) form of Paul; small
and high energy
Paoloh, Paulo

Paquito
(Spanish) dear Paco

Paris
(English) lover; France's
capital
Pare, Paree, Parris

Parish
(French) priest's place;
lovely boy
Parrish, Parrysh, Parysh

Park
(English) calming
Parke, Parkey, Parks

Parker
(English) manager
Park, Parks

Parley
(Scottish) reluctant
Parly

Parnell
(French) ribald
*Parne, Parnel, Parnelle,
Perne, Parle*

Parnelli
(Italian) frisky
Parnell

Paros
(Place name) Greek island;
charming
Par, Paro

Parr
(English) protective
Par, Parre

Parris
(French) priest's place;
lovely boy
*Paris, Pariss, Parriss,
Parrys, Parryss*

Parrish
(French) separate and
unique; district

Parry
(Welsh) young son
Parrie, Pary

Parryth
(American) up-and-coming
Pareth, Parre, Parry, Parythe

Parson
(English) clergyman
Parsen

Parthik
(Greek) virginal

Partholon
(Irish) form of
Bartholomew; earthy
Parlan

Paryon
(Greek) form of Parion, ancient Greek city

Pascal
(French) boy born on Easter or Passover; spiritual
Pascalle, Paschal, Pasco, Pascual, Paskalle, Pasky

Pasquale
(Italian) spiritual
Pask, Paskwoll, Pasq, Pasquell, Posquel

Pass
(Russian) from Pasha (form of Paul); small; kind

Pastor
(English) clergyman
Pastar, Paster

Pat
(English) short for Patrick; noble
Pattey, Patti, Patty, Pattye, Pattee

Pate
(Latin) from Patrick; noble
Pait, Payte

Patek
(Latin) from Patrick; noble
Patec, Pateck

Pater
(French) fathers

Paterson
(Last name as first name) intelligent father

Patricio
(Spanish) form of Patrick; noble
Patricyo

Patrick
(Irish) aristocrat
Paddy, Partric, Patric, Patrik, Patriquek, Patryk, Pats, Patsy

Patriot
(American) patriotic

Patterson
(English) intellectual
Paterson, Pattersen, Pattersun, Pattersund

Pattison
(English) son of Pat; noble
Pattisen, Pattysen, Pattyson, Patysen, Patyson

Patton
(English) brash warrior
Patten, Pattun, Patun, Peyton

Paul
(Latin) small; wise
Pauley, Paulie, Pauly

Pauli
(Italian) dear Paul
Paulee, Pauley, Paulie, Pauly

Paulin
(German) form of Paul; small boy
Paulyn

Paulis
(Latin) form of Paul; small boy
Pauliss, Paulys, Paulyss

Paulo
(Spanish) form of Paul

Paulos
(Greek) small

Paulus
(Latin) small
Paul, Paulie, Paulis, Pauly

Pavel
(Russian) inspired
Pasha

Pavlof
(Last name as first name) reactive; small
Pavel

Pavun
(Indian) belonging to the middle

Pawel
(Polish) believer
Pawl

Pax
(Latin) peace-loving
Paks, Paxy

Paxon
(German) peaceful
Packston, Packton

Paxton
(English) from a town of peace; gentle boy
Paxten

Payne
(Latin) countryman
Paine, Payn

Payton
(English) soldier's town
Pate, Paton, Payten, Paytun, Peyton

Peabo
(Irish) rock

Peale
(English) bellringer in a church; religious
Peal, Peel, Peele

Peat
(English) form of Pete;
knowing

Pecos
(Place name) Texas river;
cowboy
Peck, Pekos

Pedaias
(Biblical) God loves
Pedaiah

Peader
(Scottish) rock or stone;
reliable
Peder, Peter

Pearson
(English) dark-eyed
*Pearse, Pearsen, Pearsun,
Peerson*

Pederson
(Scandinavian) form of
Peterson; son of Peter;
smart boy
Pedersen

Pedro
(Spanish) audacious
Pedra, Pedrin, Pedroh

Peer
(Scandinavian) rock

Peerson
(English) son of Peter;
smart
Peersen

Pegasus
(Mythology) horse; rider

Pelle
(Swedish) for Peter; rock
Pele, Pelee

Pelly
(English) happy
Peli, Pelley, Pelli

Pelon
(Spanish) joyful

Pelton
(Last name as first name)
town of Pel; respectful

Pembroke
(French) sophisticated
*Brookie, Pemb, Pembrooke,
Pimbroke*

Pender
(Last name as first name)
loves music

Penley
(Last name as first name)
strong

Penn
(German) strong-willed
*Pen, Pennee, Penney,
Pennie, Penny*

Penrod
(German) respected leader

Penrose
(Last name as first name)
liked

Pentecost
(Religion) pious person
Penticost, Pentycost

Pentige
(Last name as first name)
worthy

Pentz
(Last name as first name)
visionary

Penuel
(Hebrew) face of God

Pepin
(German) ardent
*Pepen, Pepi, Pepp, Peppi,
Peppy, Pepun*

Pepper
(Botanical) live wire
Pep, Pepp, Peppy

Peppino
(Spanish) energetic

Per
(Scandinavian) secretive

Percival
(French) mysterious
*Parsival, Perc, Perce,
Perceval, Percey, Percy,
Perseval, Purcival, Purcy*

Percy
(French) short for Percival
Percee, Percey, Perci, Percie

Peregrino
(Nature) bird; ordinary

Perfecto
(Spanish) perfect
Perfek

Pericles
(Greek) fair leader
Periklees, Perikles, Perry

Perine
(Latin) adventurer
Perrin, Perrine, Perry, Peryne

Perk
(American) perky
Perkey, Perki, Perky

Perkin
(English) opinionated
Parkin

Perkins
(English) political
Perk, Perkens, Perkey

Pernell
(French) from Parnell; small Peter; smart
Pernel

Peron
(Last name as first name) leader

Perrin
(Latin) traveler
Perrine, Pero, Per

Perris
(Greek) legendary kidnapper of Helen of Troy; daring
Paris, Peris, Periss, Perrys, Perys

Perry
(English) tough-minded
Parry, Perr, Perrey, Perri, Perrie

Perryman
(Last name as first name) nature-lover
Perry

Perseus
(Greek) destroyer; mythological hero

Perth
(Place name) capital of Western Australia
Purth

Perun
(Hindi) from the name Perunkulam

Pete
(English) easygoing
Petey, Petie

Peter
(Greek) dependable; rock
Per, Petar, Pete, Petee, Petey, Petie, Petur, Pyotr

Pethuel
(Aramaic) God's vision

Petra
(Place name) city in Arabia; dashing

Petter
(Scandinavian) form of Peter; dependable
Petya

Peverel
(Latin/French) of the piper
Peverell, Peveril

Peyton
(English) form of Payton
Pey, Peyt

Pharis
(Irish) heroic
Farres, Farrus, Pharris

Phelan
(Irish) the small wolf; fierce

Phelgen
(Last name as first name) stylish
Phelgon

Phelim
(Irish) wolfish; fierce
Phelym

Phelps
(English) droll
Felps, Filps

Phex
(American) kind
Fex

Phil
(Greek) short for Philip
Fill, Phill

Philander
(Greek) lover of many; infidel
Filander, Phil, Philandyr, Philender

Philemon
(Greek) showing affection
Filemon, Philamon, Philo

Philetus
(Greek) collector

Philip
(Greek) outdoorsman; horse-lover
Felipe, Filipp, Flippo, Phil, Phillie, Phillip, Phillippe, Philly

Philippe
(French) form of Philip
Felipe, Filippe, Philipe

Philo
(Greek) lover
Filo

Phineas
(English) far-sighted
Fineas, Finny, Pheneas, Phineus, Phinny

Phoenix
(Greek) bird of immortality; everlasting
Fee, Feenix, Fenix, Nix

Photius
(Greek) scholarly

Picardus
(Hispanic) adventurous

Pickford
(Last name as first name)
old-fashioned

Pico
(Spanish) the epitome; peak

Pierce
(English) insightful; piercing
Pearce, Peerce, Peers,
Peersey, Percy, Piercy, Piers

Piero
(Italian) form of Peter;
dependable
Pierro

Pierre
(French) socially adroit
Piere

Pierrepont
(French) social
Pierpont

Piers
(English) from Philip; horse
lover

Pierson
(English) son of Pier; rock
Peirsen, Pearson

Pietro
(Italian) reliable
Pete

Pilar
(Spanish) basic
Pilarr

Pilgrim
(English) a traveler
Pilgrym

Pillion
(French) excellence
Pilion, Pillyon, Pilyon

Pilot
(French) excellence

Pim
(Dutch) precise

Pin
(Vietnamese) joyful

Pincus
(American) dark
Pincas, Pinchas, Pinchus,
Pinkus

Pinechas
(Hebrew) form of Paul; dark

Piney
(American) living among
pines; comfortable
Pine, Pyney

Pinkston
(Last name as first name)
different
Pink, Pinky

Pinky
(American) familiar form of
Pinchas

Pinya
(Hebrew) loyal

Pio
(Italian) pious

Pip
(German) ingenious
Pipp, Pippin, Pippo, Pippy

Pippin
(English) shy

Pirney
(Scottish) from the island

Pitch
(American) word as name;
musical

Piton
(Spanish) form of Felix;
prideful

Pitt
(English) swerving
dramatically

Pittman
(English) blue-collar worker

Pius
(Polish) pious

Placid
(Latin) calm
Plasid

Placido
(Italian) serene songster
Placeedo, Placidoh, Placydo

Plan
(American) word as name;
organized

Plash
(American) splashy; zany

Plat
(French) from the flatlands;
landowner
Platt

Platinum
(Element) worthwhile

Plato
(Greek) broad-minded
Plata, Platoh

Playtoh
(Invented) form of Plato

Pluck
(American) audacious;
plucky

Plutarco
(Greek) nefarious

Poe
(Last name as first name)
dark spirit

Poet
(American) writer
Poe

Policarpo
(Greek) with much fruit

Polk
(Last name as first name)
political

Pollard
(German) closed-minded
Polard, Pollar, Pollerd,
Polley

Pollock
(Last name as first name)
creative

Pollux
(Last name as first name)
underdog

Polo
(Greek) adventurer
Poloe, Poloh

Polonice
(Polish) respects

Polygnotos
(Greek) lover of many

Pomeroy
(Last name as first name)
polite

Pomposo
(Spanish) pompous

Ponce
(Spanish) fifth; wanderer
Poncey, Ponciano, Ponse

Ponipake
(Hawaiian) good luck

Pons
(Spanish) fifth; explores
Ponse

Pontius
(Latin) the fifth
Pontias, Pontus

Pony
(Scottish) dashing
Poney, Ponie

Poogie
(American) snuggly
Poog, Poogee, Poogi,
Poogs, Pookie

Poole
(Place name) area in England
Pool

Pope
(Greek) father
Po

Porfirio
(Spanish) audacious

Port
(Latin) gatekeeper
Porte

Porter
(Latin) decisive
Poart, Port, Portur, Porty

Powder
(American) cowboy
Powd, Powe

Powell
(English) ready

Powers
(English) wields power

Prairie
(American) rural man or
rancher
Prair, Prairey, Prairi, Prairy

Prakash
(Indian) light

Pratt
(Last name as first name)
talkative

Praxedes
(Last name as first name)
prayerful

Preemoh
(Invented) form of Primo

Prentice
(English) learning
Prenticce, Prentis, Prentiss,
Printiss

Prescott
(Last name as first name)
sophisticated

Preston
(Last name as first name)
village of a priest; religious
home

Presley
(English) songbird; meadow
of the priest
Preslee, Preslie, Presly

Preston
(English) spiritual
Prestyn

Preto
(Latin) important

Price
(Welsh) vigorous
Pricey, Pryce

Priestley
(English) cottage of the
priest
Priestlea, Priestlee, Priestly

Primerica
(American) form of America;
patriotic
Prime

Primitivo
(Spanish) primitive
Primi, Tito, Tivo

Primo
(Italian) top-notch
Preemo, Primoh, Prymo

Prince
(Latin) regal leader
Preenz, Prins, Prinz, Prinze

Prine
(English) prime

Prisciliano
(Spanish) wise old man

Procopio
(Greek, Spanish) making
progress; prominent nose

Procter
(Last name as first name)
leads
Proctor

Prometheus
(Mythology) friend of man;
bringer of fire

Prop
(American) word as name;
fun-loving
Propp

Prosper
(Italian) having good
fortune
Pros

Proteus
(Greek) first

Pryor
(Latin) spiritual director
Pry, Prye

Publias
(Greek) thinker
Publius

Pullman
(English) train man;
motivator
*Pulman, Pulmann,
Pullmann*

Purvin
(English) helpful
Pervin

Purvis
(French) provider
Pervis, Purviss

Pushkin
(Last name as first) poet;
playful

Putnam
(English) fond of water
Puddy, Putnum, Puttie, Putty

Pynchon
(Last name as first)
brilliant; inventive

Pyre
(Latin) fire; excitable

Qabil
(Arabic) capable

Qadim
(Arabic) able

Qadir
(Arabic) talented
*Qadar, Qadeer, Quadeer,
Quadir*

Qamar
(Arabic) moon; dreamy

Qasim
(Arabic) generous

Qimat
(Hindi) valued

Quaashie
(African American)
ambitious

Quaddus
(African American) bright

Quadrees
(Latin) fourth
Kwadrees, Quadrhys

Quan
(Vietnamese) dignified

Quanah
(Native Aerican) good-
smelling
Quan

Quannell
(African American) strong-
willed
*Kwan, Kwanell, Kwanelle,
Quan, Quanelle, Quannel*

Quant
(Latin) knowing his worth
*Quanta, Quantae, Quantal,
Quantay, Quantea, Quantey,
Quantez*

Quaronne
(African American) haughty
*Kwarohn, Kwaronne,
Quaronn*

Quashawn
(African American) tenacious
*Kwashan, Kwashaun,
Kwashawn, Quasha,
Quashie, Quashy*

Qudamah
(Arabic) courage

Qued
(Native American) decorated robe

Quelatikan
(Native Amercan) blue horn

Quenby
(English) giving
Quenbee, Quenbie, Quenbey

Quennell
(French) strength of an oak
Quenell, Quennel

Quentin
(Latin) fifth
Kwent, Qeuntin, Quantin, Quent, Quenten, Quenton, Quientin, Quienton, Quint, Quintin, Quinton, Qwent, Qwentin, Qwenton

Quick
(American) fast; remarkable

Quico
(Spanish) stands by his friends
Paco

Quiessencia
(Spanish) essential; essence
Quiess, Quiessence

Quigley
(Irish) loving nature
Quiglee, Quigly, Quiggly, Quiggy

Quillan
(Irish) club; joined
Quill, Quillen, Quillon

Quimby
(Norse) woman's house

Quincy
(French) fifth; patient
Quensie, Quincee, Quincey, Quinci, Quincie, Quinnsy, Quinsey

Quinlan
(Irish) fit physique
Quindlen, Quinlen, Quinlin, Quinn, Quinnlan

Quinn
(Irish) short for Quinton; bright
Kwen, Kwene, Quenn, Quin

Quintavius
(African American) fifth child
Quint

Quintin
(Latin) planner
Quenten, Quint, Quinton

Quinto
(Spanish) fifth
Quiqui

Quintus
(Spanish) fifth child
Quin, Quinn, Quint

Quiqui
(Spanish) friend; short for Enrique
Kaka, Keke, Quinto, Quiquin

Quirin
(English) a magic spell

Quirinus
(Latin) spear; Roman god of war

Quito
(Spanish) lively
Kito

Qunnoune
(Native Amercian) tall

Quoitrel
(African American) equalizer
Kwotrel, Quoitrelle

Quon
(Chinese) bright; light

Qusay
(Arabic) rough hewn
Qussay

Raashid
(Arabic) form of Rashad; wise man

Rab
(Scottish) short for Raibeart; bright
Rabbie

Rabbaanee
(African) easygoing

Rabbi
(Hebrew) master

Rabbit
(Literature) character in *Rabbit Run*; fast
Rab

Rabul
(Hispanic) rich

Rachins
(Hebrew) merciful

Racqueab
(Arabic) homebody
Rad
(Scandinavian) helpful;
confident
Radd
Radbert
(English) intelligent
Rad
Radborne
(English) born happy
Radbourne, Radburn
Radcliff
(English) from the bright
cliff; able
Raddy
(Slavic) cheerful
Rad, Radde, Raddie, Radey
Radford
(English) helpful
Rad, Raddey, Raddie,
Raddy, Radferd
Radimir
(Polish) joyful
Radley
(English) sways with the
wind
Radlea, Radlee, Radleigh
Radnor
(English) boy of the bright
shore; natural
Radolf
(Anglo-Saxon) warrior
Radomir
(Slavic) delightful
Rady
(Filipino) happy

Raeshon
(American) form of
Raeshawn; brainy
Rayshawn, Rashone,
Reshawn
Raekwon
(African American) proud
Raykwonn
Rael
(African) from Roe; lamb
Rafael
(Hebrew, Spanish) renewed
Rafaelle, Rafayel, Rafayelle,
Rafe, Raphael, Raphaele
Rafe
(Irish) tough
Raff, Raffe, Raif
Rafeeq
(Arabic) gregarious
Rafferty
(Irish) wealthy
Rafarty, Rafe, Raff, Raferty,
Raffarty, Raffertie, Raffety
Raffin
(Hebrew) from Raphael;
healed by God
Rafi
(Arabic) musical; friend
Rafee, Raffy
Rage
(American) trendsetter
Raghib
(Arabic) rapturous
Ragnar
(Scandinavian) power
fighter
Raheem
(Arabic) having empathy
Rahim

Rahman
(Arabic) full of compassion
Raman, Rahmahn
Rahn
(American) form of Ron; kind
Rahnney, Rahnnie, Rahnny
Rai
(Japanese) next child
Rain
(English) helpful; smart
Raine, Rainey, Rainey, Raini,
Rains, Raney, Rayne
Rainer
(German) advisor
Rainor, Rayner, Raynor
Rainey
(German) generous
Rain, Raine, Raney, Raynie
Rainier
(Place name) distinguished
Raj
(Sanskrit) with stripes
Rajiv
Raja
(Sanskrit) king
Raj
Rajab
(Arabic) glorified
Rajan
(Pakistani) kingly
Rajendra
(Hindi) strong king
Rajesh
(Hindi) king rules
Rajoseph
(American) combo of Ra
and Joseph
Raejoseph

Rakesh
(Hindi) king

Raleigh
(English) jovial
Ralea, Ralee, Raleighe, Rawlee, Rawley, Rawlie

Ralf
(American) form of Ralph
Raulf

Ralik
(Hindi) purified

Ralis
(Latin) thin
Rallus

Ralph
(English) advisor to all
Ralf, Ralphie, Ralphy, Raulf, Rolf

Ralphie
(English) form of Ralph
Ralphee, Ralphi

Ralston
(English) Ralph's town; quirky boy
Ralfston, Rolfston

Ram
(Sanskrit) compelling; pleasant
Rama, Ramm

Rambert
(German) pleasant kid
Ramburt

Rambo
(Movie) daring; action-oriented
Ram

Ramel
(Hindi) godlike
Raymel

Rami
(Spanish) from Ramiro; flirtatious
Ramiah

Ramiro
(Spanish) all-knowing judge
Rameero, Ramero, Ramey, Rami

Ramone
(Spanish) wise advocate; romantic
Ramond, Raymond, Romon

Ramp
(American) word as name; hyper
Ram, Rams

Rams
(English) form of Ramsey; boisterous; strong
Ramm, Ramz

Ramsden
(English) born in ram valley; loves the outdoors

Ramsey
(English) savvy
Rams, Ramsay, Ramsy, Ramz, Ramzee, Ramzy

Ran
(Scottish) short for Ronald; powerful
Ranald

Rance
(American) renegade
Rans, Ranse

Ranceford
(English) from the ford of Laurence; rooted in reality

Rancye
(American) form of Rance
Rancel, Rancy

Rand
(Place name) ridge of gold-bearing rock in South Africa

Randal
(English) secretive
Randahl, Randel, Randey, Randull, Randy, Randall

Randolph
(English) protective
Rand, Randolf, Randolphe, Randy

Randy
(English) short for Randall or Randolph
Randee, Randey, Randi, Randie

Ranen
(Hebrew) joyful

Rangarajan
(Hindi) charming

Ranger
(French) vigilant
Rainge, Range, Rangur

Rani
(Hebrew) joyful
Ran, Ranie, Rannie

Rank
(American) word as name
Ran

Rankin
(English) shielded

Ransell
(English) short form of Laurence or Ransom
Rancell

Ransford
(English) the raven's ford; watchful

Ransley
(English) the rave's field; watchful

Ransom
(Latin) wealthy
Rance, Ranse, Ransome, Ransum, Ransym

Rante
(American) from Randy; amorous

Ranulf
(English) a lord chancellor from 1107–1123; regal

Raoul
(Spanish) confidant
Raul, Raulio

Raphael
(Hebrew) archangel in the Bible; painter
Rafael, Rafe, Rapfaele

Raqib
(Arabic) glorified

Rascheed
(Arabic) giving

Rashad
(Arabic) wise
Rachad, Rashaud, Rashid, Rashod, Roshad

Rashard
(American) good

Rasheed
(Arabic) intelligent

Rashid
(Arabic) focused

Rasmus
(Greek) from Erasmus; beloved

Rasool
(Arabic) herald

Rasputin
(Russian) a Russian mystic
Rasp

Rastus
(Greek) form of Erastus
Rastas

Raudel
(African American) rowdy
Raudell, Rowdel

Rauf
(Arabic) compassionate

Raul
(French) sensual
Rauly, Rawl

Raven
(American) bird; dark and mysterious
Rave, Ravey, Ravy, Rayven

Ravi
(Hindi) sun god
Ravee

Ravid
(Hebrew) searching

Ravindra
(Hindi) a strong sun

Rawdan
(English) hilly; adventurous
Rawden, Rawdin, Rawdon

Rawle
(French) form of Raul; sensitive

Rawleigh
(American) form of Raleigh
Rawlee, Rawli

Rawlins
(French) from Roland; famed

Ray
(French) royal; king
Rae, Raye, Rayray

Raybourne
(English) from the deer brook; sylvan
Rayburn, Raybin

Rayce
(American) form of Raymond; advisor
Rays, Rayse

Rayfield
(English) woodsy; capable
Rafe, Ray, Rayfe

Raymond
(English) strong
Rai, Ramand, Ramond, Ray, Raymie, Raymonde, Raymun, Raymund, Raymy

Raymont
(American) combo of Ray and Mont; distinguished
Raemon, Raymon, Raymonte

Raynaldo
(Spanish) form of Renaldo; innovative
Ray, Rayni, Raynie, Raynoldo

Raynard
(French) judge; sly
Ray, Raynaud, Renard, Renaud, Rey, Reynard, Reynaud

Rayner
(French) form of Raymond; counselor
Ray, Rayne

Rayshan
(African American) inventive
Ray, Raysh, Raysha, Rayshun

Rayshawn
(African American) combo
of Ray and Shawn
*Raeshaun, Rayshaun,
Rayshie, Rayshy*

Razi
(Aramaic) secretive

Reace
(Welsh) passionate
*Reece, Rees, Rees, Reese,
Rhys*

Read
(English) red-haired
Reade, Reed, Reid

Reagan
(Irish) kingly
*Ragan, Raghan, Reagen,
Reegan, Regan*

Reaner
(Last name as first name)
even-tempered
Rean, Rener

Rebel
(American) outlaw
Reb, Rebbe, Rebele

Red
(English) man with red hair
Redd, Reddy

Redford
(English) handsome man
with ruddy skin
*Readford, Red, Reddy,
Redferd, Redfor*

Redmon
(German) protective
*Redd, Reddy, Redmond,
Redmun, Redmund*

Reece
(Welsh) vivacious
Rees, Reese, Reez

Reed
(English) red-haired
Read, Reede, Reid

Reem
(Hebrew) horned animal or
unicorn

Rees
(Welsh) form of the name
Rhys; ardor
Reece, Reese, Reez, Rez

Reese
(Welsh) vivacious
Reis, Rhys

Reeves
(English) giving
Reave, Reaves, Reeve

Reg
(Scandinavian) short for
Regner; judgmental

Regal
(American) debonair
Regall

Regent
(Latin) word as name; royal;
grand

Reggie
(English) short for Reginald;
wise advisor
Reg, Reggey, Reggi, Reggye

Reginald
(English) wise advisor
*Reg, Reggie, Reginal,
Regineld*

Regine
(French) artistic
Regeen

Regis
(Latin) king; gilded talker
Reggis

Regulo
(Italian) from Reginald;
counsels

Rehoboam
(Biblical) son of Solomon

Reid
(English) red-haired
Reide

Reidar
(Scandinavian) soldier

Reilly
(Irish) daring
Rilee, Riley, Rilie

Reinald
(French) judges

Reinhart
(German) brave-hearted
*Reinhar, Reinhardt,
Rhinehard, Rhinehart*

Reith
(American) shy

Remi
(French) fun-loving
*Remee, Remey, Remmy,
Remy*

Remigio
(Italian) from Rheims,
France; sharp mind

Remington
(Last name as first name)
intellectual
Rem, Remmy

Remuda
(Spanish) herd of horses, or changing horses (a relay); rancher
Rem, Remmie, Remmy

Remus
(Latin) fast
Reemus, Remes, Remous

Renard
(French) smart
Renardt

Renato
(Italian) born again
Renata, Renate

Renaud
(English) powerful
Renny

René
(French) born again
Renee, Rennie, Renny, Re-Re

Renferd
(English) peaceloving
Renfred

Renfro
(Welsh) calm
Renfroe, Renfrow, Renphro, Rinfro

Renny
(French) able
Renney, Renni, Rennye

Reno
(Place name) a city in Nevada
Reen, Reenie, Renoh

Renshaw
(English) born in the raven wood

Renton
(English) born in the town of deer

Renwick
(English) born in the village of deer

Renzo
(Italian) adorned; from Lorenzo

ReShard
(African American) rough
Reshar, Reshard

Resugio
(Spanish) form of Refugio
Resuge

Rett
(Literature) form of Rhett, from *Gone with the Wind*

Reuben
(Hebrew) religious; (Spanish) creative
Rube, Rubey, Rubie, Rubin, Ruby, Rubyn

Rev
(Invented) ramped up
Revv

Revin
(American) distinctive
Revan, Revinn, Revun

Rex
(Latin) kingly
Rexe

Rexford
(American) form of Rex; noble
Rex, Rexferd, Rexfor, Rexy

Rey
(Spanish) short for Reynaldo
Ray, Reye, Reyes

Reynard
(French) brilliant
Raynard, Rayne, Renardo

Reynaud
(French) advisor/judge

Reynold
(English) knowledgeable tutor
Ranald, Ranold, Reinold, Renald, Renalde, Rey, Reye, Reynolds

Reza
(Iranian) content

Rhene
(American) smiley
Reen, Rheen

Rhett
(American) romantic
Rhet, Rhette

Rhodes
(Greek) lovely
Rhoades, Rodes

Rhodree
(Welsh) ruler
Rodree, Rodrey, Rodry

Rhyon
(American) form of Ryan
Rhyan, Rhyen

Rhys
(Welsh) also Rees; loving
Reece, Reese

Rian
(Irish) little king

Riao
(Spanish) form of Rio; river; flowing

Ribal
(American) form of ribald; revels

Ricardo
(Spanish) snappy
Recardo, Ric, Riccardo, Ricky

Rice
(English) rich
Ryes

Rich
(English) affluent
Richie, Ritchie

Richard
(English) wealthy leader
Rich, Richerd, Richey, Richi,
Richie, Rickie, Ricky, Ritchie

Richardean
(American) combo of
Richard and Dean; unusual
Richard Dean, Richard-
Dean, Richardene

Richey
(German) ruler
Rich, Richee, Richie, Ritch,
Ritchee, Ritchee, Ritchey

Richie
(English) short for Richard
Richey, Richi, Ritchey, Ritchie

Richman
(German) has power

Richmond
(German) rich and
protective
Rich, Richie, Richmon,
Richmun, Ricky, Ritchmun

Richshae
(English) from Richard;
reliable

Richter
(Last name as first name)
hopeful
Rick, Ricky, Rik, Rikter

Rick
(German) short for Richard;
friendly
Ric, Rickey, Ricki, Rickie,
Ricky, Rik

Rickard
(Scandinavian) from
Richard; reliable
Rick, Rickert, Rickward,
Rikkert

Rico
(Italian) spirited; ruler
Reco, Reko, Ricko, Rikko,
Riko

Ricotoro
(Spanish) combo of Rico
and Toro; brave bull
Ricky, Rico-Toro, Rikotoro,
Toro

Riddock
(Irish) man of the field

Rider
(American) horse rider
Ryder

Ridge
(English) on the ridge; risk-
taker

Ridglee
(English) man of the ridge
Ridgley, Ridglea

Ridhaa
(Arabic) delight

Ridley
(English) ingenious
Redley, Rid, Ridley, Ridlie,
Ridly, Rydley

Riemer
(English) from Rheims,
France; loving

Rigby
(English) high-energy
Rigbie, Rigbye, Rygby

Rigel
(Arabic) foot; star in
constellation Orion

Rigoberto
(Spanish) strong
Bert, Berto, Rigo

Rike
(American) form of Nike;
high-spirited
Rikee, Rykee, Rykie, Ryky

Rilee
(American) form of Riley
Rilea, Rileigh

Rileigh
(American) form of Riley
Ryleigh

Riley
(Irish) brave
Reilly, Rylee, Ryley, Rylie,
Ryly

Rimon
(Hebrew) pomegranate

Ringo
(English) funny
Ring, Ringgoh, Ryngo

Rio
(Spanish) water-loving
Reeo

Rione
(Spanish) flowing
Reo, Reone, Rio

Rio Grande
(Spanish) a river in Texas
Rio, Riogrande

Riordan
(Irish) lordly
Rearden

Rip
(English) serene
Ripp, Rippe

Ripley
(English) serene
Riplee

Ris
(English) outdoorsman; smart
Rislea, Rislee, Risleigh, Riz, Rizlee

Rishab
(American) from Rashad; showy

Rishi
(Arabic) first

Rishon
(Hebrew) first

Risley
(English) smart and quiet
Rislee, Risleye, Rizlee, Rizley

Ritch
(American) leader
Rich, Richee, Richey, Ritch, Ritchal, Ritchee, Ritchi

Ritchie
(English) form of Richie
Ritchee, Ritchey, Ritchy

Rito
(American) spunky
Reit

Ritt
(German) debonair
Rit, Rittie, Rittly

Ritter
(German) debonair
Riter, Rittyr

Rivan
(Literature) from the book *The Rivan Codex*; esoteric

River
(Place name) hip
Riv, Ryver

Roald
(Scandinavian) famous ruler

Roam
(American) wanderer
Roamey, Roamy, Roma, Rome

Roan
(English) form of Rowan (berry tree); red hair

Roar
(Irish) from Roark; mighty

Roarke
(Irish) ruler
Roark, Rork, Rourke

Rob
(English) short for Robert; smart
Robb

Robbie
(English) short for Robert; smart
Robbee, Robbey, Robbi, Robby

Robert
(English) brilliant; renowned
Bob, Bobbie, Bobby, Rob, Robart, Robbie, Robby, Roberto, Robs, Roburt

Roberto
(Spanish) form of Robert; bright and famous
Berto, Rob, Robert, Tito

Roberts
(Last name as first name) luminous
Rob, Robards, Robarts, Roburts

Robert-Lee
(American) patriotic
Bobbylee, Robby Lee, Robert Lee, Robert-E-Lee, Robertlee

Robeson
(English) Rob's son; bright
Roberson, Robison

Robin
(English) gregarious
Robb, Robbin, Robby, Robyn

Roble
(Last name as first name) divine
Robel, Robl, Robley

Robson
(English) sterling character
Robb, Robbson, Robsen

Rocco
(Italian) tough
Roc, Rock, Rockie, Rocko, Rocky, Rok, Rokee, Rokko, Roko

Rochester
(English) guarded
Roche

Rock
(American) hardy
Roc, Rocky, Rok

Rocket
(American) word as a name; snappy
Rokket

Rockleigh
(English) dependable; outdoorsy
Rocco, Rock, Rocklee, Rockley, Rocky, Roklee

Rockney
(American) brash

Rockwell
(American) spring of strength
Rock, Rockwelle, Rocky

Rocky
(English) hardy; tough
Rocco, Rock, Rockee, Rockey, Rocki, Rockie

Rod
(English) brash
Rodd, Roddy

Rodas
(Spanish) Spanish name for the Rhone River in France
Rod, Roda

Roddick
(Last name as first name) goes far

Roddy
(German) short for Roderick; effective
Roddee, Roddi, Roddie

Rodel
(American) generous
Rodell, Rodey, Rodie

Rodeo
(Spanish) roundup; cowboy
Rodayo, Roddy, Rodyo

Roderick
(German) effective leader
Roddy, Roddyrke, Roderic, Roderik, Rodreck, Rodrick, Rodrik

Rodger
(German) form of Roger
Rodge, Roge

Rodman
(German) hero
Rodmin, Rodmun

Rodney
(English) open-minded
Rod, Roddy, Rodnee, Rodni, Rodnie

Rodolfo
(Spanish) spark
Rod, Rudolfo, Rudolpho

Rodree
(American) leader
Rodrey, Rodri, Rodry

Rodrigo
(Spanish) feisty leader
Rod, Roddy, Rodrego, Rodriko

Rodriguez
(Spanish) hot-blooded
Rod, Roddy, Rodreguez, Rodrigues

Rodwell
(German) renowned

Roe
(English) deer

Roemello
(Italian) form of Romulus; Roman man; ingenious

Rogan
(Irish) spirited redhead

Rogelio
(Spanish) aggressive
Rojel, Rojelio

Roger
(German) famed warrior
Rodge, Rodger, Roge, Rogie, Rogyer, Rogers

Rohan
(Hindi) going higher

Roi
(French) form of Roy

Roland
(German) renowned
Rolend, Rollan, Rolland, Rollie, Rollo, Rolund

Rolando
(Spanish) famous
Rolan

Role
(American) word as name; brash
Roel, Roll

Rolf
(German) kind advisor
Rolfee, Rolfie, Rolfy, Rolph

Rollie
(English) short for Roland
Rollee, Rolley, Rolli, Rolly

Rollins
(German) form of Roland; dignified
Rolin, Rolins, Rollin, Rolyn

Rollo
(German) famous

Rolshawn
(American) combo of Roland and Shawn; notorious

Rolt
(Latin) wolfish

Roly
(English) short for Roland; famed

Roman
(Latin) fun-loving
Romen, Romey, Romi, Romun, Romy, Romain

Rombert
(Latin) from Rome; admired

Rome
(Place name) city in Italy
Romeo

Romeo
(Italian) romantic lover
Romah, Rome, Romeoh, Romero, Romey, Romi, Romy

Romer
(American) form of Rome
Roamar, Roamer

Romney
(Welsh) roamer
Rom, Romnie

Romulo
(Spanish) man from Rome
Romo

Romulus
(Latin) presumptuous
Rom, Romules, Romulo

Ron
(English) short for Ronald; kind
Ronn

Ronak
(Scandinavian) powerful

Ronald
(English) helpful
Ron, Ronal, Ronel, Ronney, Ronni, Ronnie, Ronuld

Ronan
(Irish) seal; playful

Rondel
(French) poetic
Ron, Rondal, Rondell, Rondie, Rondy

Ronford
(English) distinguished
Ronferd, Ronnforde

Roni
(Hebrew) joyful
Rone, Ronee

Ronnie
(English) short for Ronald
Ronnee, Ronney, Ronni, Ronny

Ronson
(Scottish) Ron's son; likable

Roone
(Irish) distinctive; bright face
Rooney, Roune

Rooney
(Irish) man with red hair
Rooni, Roony

Roose
(Last name as first name) high-energy
Rooce, Roos, Rooz, Ruz

Roosevelt
(Dutch) strong leader
Rooseveldt, Rosevelt, Rosy, Velte

Rooster
(American) animal as name; loud
Roos, Rooz

Roper
(American) roper
Rope

Roque
(Spanish, Portugese) form of Rocco

Rory
(German) strong
Roree, Rorey, Roreye, Rorie

Rosalio
(Spanish) rose; charmer

Rosano
(Italian) rosy prospects; romantic

Roscoe
(English) woods; nature-loving
Rosco, Roskie, Rosko, Rosky

Roser
(American) redhead; outgoing
Rozer

Roshaun
(African American) loyal
Roshawn

Rosk
(American) swift
Roske

Rosling
(Scottish) redhead; explosive
Roslin, Rosy, Rozling

Ross
(Latin) attractive
Rossey, Rossie, Rossy

Rossa
(American) exuberant
Ross, Rosz

Rossain
(American) hopeful
Rossane

Rossano
(Italian) handsome

Roswell
(English) fascinating
*Roswel, Roswelle, Rosy,
Rozwell, Well*

Roth
(German) man with red hair
Rothe, Rauth

Roupen
(American) quiet
Ropan, Ropen, Ropun

Rover
(English) wanderer
Rovar, Rovey, Rovur, Rovy

Rovonte
(French) roving

Rowan
(English) red-haired;
adorned
Rowe, Rowen

Rowand
(Last name as first) reliable

Rowdy
(English) athletic; loud
*Roudy, Rowdee, Rowdi,
Rowdie*

Rowe
(English) outgoing
Roe, Row, Rowie

Rowell
(English) rocker
Roll, Rowl

Rowland
(Scandinavian) famous;
form of Roland

Rowley
(English) from the rough
meadow; spirited

Roy
(French) king
Roi

Royal
(French) king
Roy, Royall, Royalle, Roye

Royalton
(French) king
Royal, Royallton

Royce
(English) affluent
Roy, Royse

Roycie
(American) form of Royce;
kind
*Rory, Roy, Royce, Royse,
Roysie*

Royd
(English) good humor

Royden
(English) outdoors; regal
Roy, Roydin

Royle
(English) kingly

Ruadhan
(Hindi) brash

Ruari
(Irish) red-haired
Ruairi, Ruaridh

Rube
(Spanish) short for Ruben
Rubino

Ruben
(Spanish) form of Reuben
Rube, Ruby

Rudeger
(German) friendly
*Rudger, Rudgyr, Rudigar,
Rudiger, Rudy*

Rudo
(African) loving

Rudolf
(German) wolf
Rodolf, Rudy

Rudolph
(German) wolf
*Rodolf, Rodolph, Rud, Rudee,
Rudey, Rudi, Rudolpho, Rudy*

Rudow
(German) lovable

Rudy
(German) short for Rudolph
Rude, Rudee, Rudey, Rudi

Rudyard
(English) closed off
Rud, Rudd, Ruddy

Rueban
(American) form of Ruben;
talented
Ruban

Rufino
(Spanish) redhead

Rufus
(Latin) redhead
*Fue, Rufas, Rufes, Ruffie,
Ruffis, Ruffy, Rufous*

Rugby
(English) braced for contact
Rug, Rugbee, Rugbie, Ruggy

Ruiz
(Spanish) chummy

Rulon
(Native American) spirited
Rulonn

Rumford
(English) lives at river
crossing; grounded

Runako
(African) attractive

Rune
(German) secretive
Roone, Runes

Rupad
(Hindi) secretive
Rupesh

Rupchand
(Sanskrit) as beautiful as the moon

Rupert
(English) prince
Rupe

Rurik
(Russian) famous

Rush
(English) loquacious
Rusch

Rushford
(English) from the ford of rushes; found

Rusk
(Spanish) innovator
Rusck, Ruske, Ruskk

Ruskin
(French) red-haired

Ruslan
(English) rusty hair

Russ
(French) short for Russell; dear

Russell
(French) man with red hair; charmer
Russ, Russel, Russy, Rusty

Rustice
(French) rusty hair

Rustin
(English) redhead
Rustan, Ruston, Rusty

Rusty
(French) short for Russell
Rustee, Rustey, Rusti

Rutherford
(English) dignified
Ruthe, Rutherfurd, Rutherfyrd

Rutland
(Norse) red land

Rutledge
(English) substantial
Rutlidge

Rutley
(English) from red country; fertile

Ruvim
(Hebrew) meaningful

Ryan
(Irish) royal; good-looking
Rhine, Rhyan, Rhyne, Ry, Ryane, Ryann, Ryanne, Ryen, Ryun

Ryander
(American) competitive; obstinate

Ryder
(English) outdoorsy (man who rides horses)
Rider, Rye

Rye
(Botanical) grain; basic

Ryerson
(English) fit outdoorsman
Rye

Ryker
(English) of the rye land; farms

Ryland
(English) excellent
Rilan, Riland, Rye, Rylan

Rylandar
(English) farmer
Rye, Rylan, Ryland

Ryle
(American) form of Kyle

Ryman
(English) man of rye; fundamental

Ryne
(Irish) form of Ryan; royal
Rine, Ryn, Rynn

Ryszard
(Polish) courageous leader
Reshard

Ryton
(English) from town of rye; fundamental

Saad
(Aramaic) helping others

Saahdia
(Aramaic) helped by the Lord
Saadya, Seadya

Saarik
(Hindi) sings like a bird
Saariq, Sareek, Sareeq,
Sariq

Sabene
(Latin) optimist
Sabe, Sabeen, Sabin,
Sabyn, Sabyne

Saber
(French) armed; sword
Sabar, Sabe, Sabre

Sabin
(Latin) Sabine, tribe of Italy;
daring
Sabeeno, Sabino, Savin,
Savino

Sable
(French) animal; brown-
haired child

Sacha
(Russian) defends; charms
Sascha, Sasha

Sachar
(Hebrew) well-rewarded
Sacar

Saddam
(Arabic) powerful ruler
Saddum

Sadiki
(African) loyal
Sadeeki

Sadler
(English) practical
Sadd, Saddle, Sadlar, Sadlur

Sae
(American) talkative
Saye

Saeed
(African) lucky

Safar
(Religion) from Saphar,
second month of Islamic
calendar; devout
Safer, Safyr

Safford
(English) boy from river of
willows

Saffron
(Botanical) spice/plant;
orange-haired
Saffran, Saffren, Saphron

Sagaz
(Spanish) clever
Saga, Sago

Sage
(Botanical) wise
Saje

Sager
(American) rewarded; short
Sayger

Saginaw
(Place name) city in
Michigan; (Native
American) bold
Sag, Saggy

Sagiv
(Hebrew) the best
Segev

Saguaro
(Botanical) cactus; prickly
Seguaro

Sahil
(Hindi) leader
Sahel

Saied
(Arabic) fortunate

Saith
(English) to speak
Saithe, Saythe

Sail
(American) water; natural

Sainsbury
(English) from the home of
saints; religious
Sainsberry

Saint
(Latin) holy man

Sajan
(Hindi) beloved

Sal
(Italian) short for Salvador
and Salvatore
Sall, Sallie, Sally

Saladin
(Arabic) devout
Saladdin

Salado
(Spanish) funny
Sal

Salehe
(African) good

Salem
(Hebrew) peaceful

Salford
(Place name) city in
England

Salim
(Arabic) safe; peaceful
Saleem

Salisbury
(English) born in the
willows
Salisbery, Salisberry,
Saulsberry, Saulsbery,
Saulsbury, Saulisbury

Salman
(Arabic) protected

Salt
(American) word as name;
salt-of-the-earth
Salty

Salute
(American) patriotic

Salvador
(Spanish) savior; spirited
Sal, Sally, Salvadore

Salvatore
(Italian) rescuer; spirited
*Sal, Sallie, Sally, Salvatori,
Salvatorre*

Salvio
(Latin) saved
Salvian, Salviano, Salviatus

Sam
(Hebrew) short for Samuel;
wise
*Samm, Sammey, Sammi,
Sammy*

Sami
(Lebanese) high

Samir
(Arabic) special
Sameer, Samere, Samyr

Sammon
(Arabic) grocer
Sammen

Sammy
(Hebrew) wise
*Samie, Sammee, Sammey,
Sammi, Sammie, Samy*

Samos
(Place name) casual

Samson
(Hebrew) strong man
Sam, Sampson

Samuel
(Hebrew) man who heard
God; prophet
*Sam, Samael, Sammeul,
Sammie, Sammo, Sammuel,
Sammy, Samual*

Samvel
(Hebrew) know the name of
God
Samvell, Samvelle

Sanborn
(English) one with nature
Sanborne, Sanbourn, Sandy

Sancho
(Latin) genuine
Sanch, Sanchoh

Sandberg
(Last name as first name)
writer
Sandburg

Sander
(Greek) savior of mankind;
nice
Sandor

Sanders
(English) kind
*Sandars, Sandors,
Saunders*

Sanderson
(Last name as first name)
defender
Sandersen

Sandhurst
(English) from the sandy
thicket; undaunted
Sandhirst

Sanditon
(English) from the sandy
town; perseveres

Sandy
(English) personable
Sandee, Sandey, Sandi

Sanford
(English) negotiator
*Sandford, Sandy, Sanferd,
Sanfor*

Sanjay
(Sanskrit) wins every time

Sanorelle
(African American) honest
*Sanny, Sano, Sanorel,
Sanorell*

Sansone
(Italian) strong

Santana
(Spanish) saintly
*Santa, Santanah, Santanna,
Santee*

Santiago
(Spanish) sainted; valuable
*Sandiago, Santego,
Santiagoh, Santy, Tago*

Santino
(Italian) sacred
Santeeno, Santyno

Santos
(Italian) holy; blessed
Sant, Santo

Sapir
(Hebrew) sapphire; jewel
Safir, Saphir, Saphiros

Sarday
(American) extrovert
Sardae, Sardaye

Sargent
(French) officer/leader
Sarge, Sergeant

Sasha
(Russian) helpful
Sacha, Sash, Sasha

Sassacus
(Native American) wild soul

Sasson
(Hebrew) happy

Satchel
(American) unique
Satch, Satchell

Saturnin
(Spanish) from planet
Saturn; melancholy
Saturnino

Saunder
(English) defensive;
focused
Saunders

Saul
(Hebrew) gift
Sawl, Saulie, Sol, Solly

Savage
(Last name as first name)
wild
Sav

Saviero
(Spanish) from Xavier;
renewal

Saville
(French) stylish
Savelle, Savile, Savill

Savion
(American) from Savion
Glover, actor/dancer
Xavion, Savionn

Savoy
(Place name) region in France
Savoe

Savyon
(Spanish) great attitude

Sawyer
(English) hardworking
Saw, Sawyrr

Saxe
(English) short for Saxon
Sax, Saxee, Saxey, Saxie

Saxon
(English) sword-fighter;
feisty
*Sackson, Sax, Saxan, Saxe,
Saxen*

Saxton
(Place name) stern
Saxten

Sayre
(Welsh) skilled
Saye, Sayer, Sayers

Scafell
(Place name) mountain in
England

Scanlon
(Irish) devious
*Scan, Scanlin, Scanlun,
Scanne*

Scant
(American) word as name;
too little
Scanty

Schae
(American) safe; careful
Schay

Schaffer
(German) watchful
Schaffur, Shaffer

Schelde
(Place name) river in
Europe; calm
Shelde

Schmidt
(German) hardworking;
blacksmith
Schmit

Schneider
(German) stylish; tailor
Sneider, Snider

Schubert
(German) cobbler
Shubert

Schumann
(Last name as first) famous
composer; romantic

Schuyler
(Dutch) protective
Skylar, Skyler

Scipio
(Greek) leader

Scirocco
(Italian) warmth of the wind
Cirocco, Sirocco

Scorpio
(Latin) lethal
Scorp, Scorpioh

Scott
(English) from Scotland;
happy
Scot, Scotty

Scotty
(English) happy
Scottee, Scottey, Scotti

Scout
(French) hears all; scouts
for information

Scribner
(English) the one who writes

Scully
(Irish) vocal
Scullee, Sculley, Scullie

Seabert
(English) shines like the sea
Seabright, Sebert, Seibert

Seabrook
(English) outdoorsy
Seabrooke

Seabury
(English) lives by the sea
Seaberry, Seabry

Seal
(American) singer; water; natural

Seaman
(English) seafarer

Seamus
(Gaelic) replacement; bonus
Seemus, Semus

Sean
(Hebrew, Irish) grace in God
Seann, Shaun, Shaune, Shawn

Searcy
(English) fortified
Searcee, Searcey

Searles
(English) fortified
Searl, Searle, Serles, Serls

Seaton
(Place name) Seaton, Illinois; calm
Seaten, Seeten, Seeton

Seaver
(Last name as first name) safe
Seever

Sebastian
(Latin) dramatic; honorable
Bastian, Seb, Sebashun, Sebastien, Sebastion, Sebastuan, Sebo

Sebe
(Latin) short for Sebastian
Seb, Sebo, Seborn, Sebron, Sebrun

Secondo
(Italian) second-born boy
Segundo

Sedgley
(American) classy
Sedg, Sedge, Sedgeley, Sedgely

Sedgwick
(English) from place of swords; defensive
Sedgewick, Sedgewyck, Sedgwyck

Seely
(Last name as first name) fun-loving
Sealy, Sealey, Seeley

Seerath
(Indian) great

Seferino
(Spanish) flying in the wind
Cefirino, Sebarino, Sephirio, Zefarin, Zefirino, Zephir, Zephyr

Sefton
(English) from the town in the rushes; safe

Seger
(Last name as first name) singer
Seager, Seeger, Sega, Segur

Segundo
(Spanish) second child

Sekani
(African) laughing

Sela
(Hebrew) from the cliff; dares
Selah

Selby
(English) from a village of mansions; rich
Selbey, Shelbey, Shelbie, Shelby

Seldon
(English) from the willow valley; swaying
Selden, Sellden, Shelden

Selestino
(Spanish) heavenly
Celeste, Celestino, Celey, Sele, Selestyno

Selig
(German) blessed boy
Seligman, Seligmann, Zelig

Selkirk
(Scottish) church home boy; conflicted

Sellers
(English) dweller of marshland; sturdy
Sellars

Selvon
(American) gregarious
Sel, Selman, Selv, Selvaughn, Selvawn

Selwyn
(English) friend from the mansion; wealthy
Selwin, Selwinn, Selwynn, Selwynne

Seminole
(Native American) tribe name; unyielding

Sender
(Hebrew) form of Alexander; protective

Seneca
(Native American) tribe name; revered

Senior
(French) older
Sennyur, Senyur, Sinior

Sennen
(English) aged

Sennett
(French) old spirit
Sennet

Septimus
(Latin) seventh child; neglected

Sequoia
(Native American) tree; sturdy

Serafín
(Spanish) from the Hebrew Seraphim, full of fire

Seraphim
(Hebrew) full of fire
Sarafim, Saraphim, Serafim, Serephim

Sereno
(Latin) serene
Cereno

Serge
(French) gentle man
Serg

Sergeant
(French) officer; leader
Sarge, Sargent

Sergei
(Russian) good looking
Serg, Serge, Sergie, Sergy, Surge

Sergio
(Italian) handsome
Serge, Sergeeo, Sergeoh, Sergyo

Servacio
(Spanish) saved

Servas
(Latin) saved
Servaas, Servacio, Servatus

Sesame
(Botanical) seed; flavors
Sesamey, Sessame, Sessamee

Seth
(Hebrew) chosen
Sethe

Seton
(English) from sea town; loves the water

Seven
(American) dramatic; seventh child
Sevene, Sevin

Several
(American) word as name; multiplies
Sevral, Sevrull

Severin
(Latin) severe
Saverino, Sverinus, Seweryn

Severence
(French) strict
Severince, Severynce

Severn
(English) having boundaries

Severo
(Italian) unbending; harsh

Sevester
(American) form of Sylvester
Seveste, Sevy

Seward
(English) guarding the sea
Sew, Sewerd, Sward

Sewell
(Last name as first name) seaward
Seawell, Seawel, Sewel

Sexton
(English) church-loving
Sextan, Sextin, Sextown

Sextus
(Latin) sixth child; mischievous
Sesto, Sixto, Sixtus

Seymour
(French) prayerful
Seamore, See, Seye, Seymore

Shabat
(Hebrew) the end
Shabbat

Shachar
(Hebrew) the dawn

Shade
(English) secretive
Shadee, Shadey, Shady

Shadow
(English) mystique
Shade, Shadoe

Shad
(African) joyful

Shadman
(Hebrew) farm

Shadrach
(Biblical) godlike; brave
Shad, Shadd, Shadrack, Shadreck, Shadryack

Shafiq
(Arabic) forgiving
Shafeek, Shafik

Shafir
(Hebrew) handsome
Shafeer, Shafer, Shefer

Shahzad
(Persian) royalty; king

Shai
(Hebrew) the gift

Shakil
(Arabic) attractive
Shakeel, Shakill, Shakille, Shaqueel, Shaquil, Shaquille

Shakir
(Arabic) appreciative
Shakee, Shakeer

Shakur
(Arabic) thankful
Shakurr

Shale
(Hebrew) short for Shalev; calm
Shaile, Shayle

Shalom
(Hebrew) peaceful
Sholem, Sholom

Shaman
(Russian) mystical
Shamain, Shamon, Shayman

Shamir
(Hebrew) thorn
Shameer

Shamus
(Irish) seizing
Schaemus, Schamus, Shamuss

Shanahan
(Irish) giving
Shanihan, Shanyhan

Shance
(American) form of Chance; open
Shan, Shanse

Shand
(English) loud
Shandy

Shandee
(English) noisy
Shandi, Shandy

Shane
(Irish) easygoing
Shain, Shay, Shayne

Shani
(African) a wonder;
(Hebrew) red

Shanley
(Irish) old soul
Shannley

Shannon
(Irish) wise
Shana, Shanan, Shane, Shanen, Shann, Shannen, Shanon

Shante
(American) poised
Shantae, Shantay

Shaq
(Arabic) short for Shaquille
Shack, Shak

Shaquille
(Arabic) handsome
Shak, Shakeel, Shaq, Shaquil, Shaquill

Sharif
(Arabic) truthful
Shareef, Sheref

Shashhi
(Hindi) moon

Shasta
(Place name) Oregon mountain; high hopes

Shaun
(Irish) form of Sean
Seanne, Shaune, Shaunn

Shavon
(American) combo of Sha and Von; open mind
Shavonne, Shivaun, Shovon

Shaw
(English) safe; in a tree grove
Shawe

Shawn
(Irish) form of Sean
Shawnay, Shawne, Shawnee, Shawney

Shawnell
(African American) talkative
Shaunell

Shawner
(American) form of Shawn

Shawon
(African American) optimistic
Shawan, Shawaughn,
Shawaun

Shay
(Irish) short for Shamus;
bolstering
Shai

Shayan
(Native American) from
Cheyenne; tribe; erratic

Shayde
(Irish) confident
Shaedy, Sheade

Shaykeen
(African American)
successful
Shay, Shaykine

Shayshawn
(American) combo of Shay
and Shawn; able
Shaeshaun, Shaeshawn,
Shayshaun

Shea
(Irish) vital
Shay

Sheehan
(Irish) clever
Shehan, Shihan

Sheen
(English) bright and
shining; talented
Shean, Sheene

Shel
(Hebrew) mine

Shelby
(English) established
Shel, Shelbee, Shelbey,
Shelbie, Shell, Shelly

Sheldon
(English) quiet
Shel, Sheld, Shelden,
Sheldin, Shell, Shelly

Shelley
(English) form of Shelby;
meadow ledge boy
Shelly

Shelton
(English) from the village of
ledges

Shem
(Hebrew) famous

Shen
(Chinese) introspective

Shenandoah
(Place name) valley;
nostalgic

Sheng
(Chinese) winning

Shep
(English) watchful
Shepp, Sheppy

Shepherd
(Last name as first name)
vigilant
Shepard, Sheperd,
Shephard

Shepley
(English) from the sheep
meadow; tender
Sheplea, Shepleigh,
Shepply, Shipley

Sherborn
(English) from the bright
shiny stream; careful
Sherborne, Sherbourn,
Sherburn, Sherburne

Sheridan
(Irish) wild-spirited
Sharidan, Sheridon, Sherr,
Sherrey, Shuridun

Sherill
(English) from the shining
hill; special
Sherrill

Sherlock
(English) fair-haired; smart
Sherlocke, Shurlock

Sherm
(English) worker; shears
Shermy

\Sherman
(English) tough-willed
Cherman, Shermann,
Shermy, Shurman

Sherrerd
(English) from open land;
rancher
Sherard, Sherrard, Sherrod

Sherrick
(Last name as first name)
already gone
Sherric, Sherrik, Sherryc,
Sherryck, Sherryk

Sherwin
(English) fleet of foot
Sherwind, Sherwinn,
Sherwyn, Sherwynne

Sherwood
(English) bright options
Sherwoode, Shurwood,
Woodie, Woody

Shevon
(African American) zany
Shavonne, Shevaughan,
Shevaughn

Shiloh
(Hebrew) gift from God; charmer
Shile, Shilo, Shy, Shye

Shingo
(Japanese) clutch

Shipley
(English) meadow of sheep
Ship

Shipton
(English) from the ship village; sailor

Shire
(Place name) English county; humorous
Shyre

Shiva
(Hindi) of great depth and range; life/death
Shiv

Shlomo
(Hebrew) form of Solomon; peace-loving
Shelomi, Shelomo, Shlomi

Shomer
(Hebrew) watches

Shon
(American) form of Shawn
Sean, Shaun, Shonn

Shontae
(African American) hopeful
Shauntae, Shauntay, Shawntae, Shontay, Shontee, Shonti, Shontie, Shonty

Shorty
(American) small in stature
Shortey, Shorti

Shoshone
(Native American) tribe; wanderer
Shoshoni

Shoval
(Hebrew) on the right path

Shura
(Russian) protective
Schura, Shoura

Shuu
(Japanese) responsible

Si
(Hebrew) short for Simon
Sy

Sicily
(Place name) traveler
Sicilly

Sid
(French) short for Sidney
Cyd, Sidd, Siddie, Siddy, Syd, Sydd

Sidney
(French) attractive
Ciddie, Cidnie, Cyd, Cydnee, Sidnee, Sidnie, Syd, Sydney

Sidonio
(Spanish) from Sidney; sly

Sidor
(Russian) gifted
Isidor, Sydor

Sidus
(Latin) star
Sydus

Siegfried
(German) victor
Siegfred, Sig, Sigfred, Sigfrid, Siggee, Siggie, Siggy

Sierra
(Spanish) dangerous
See-see, Serra, Siera, Sierrah

Sig
(German) short for Sigmund and Siegfried
Siggey, Siggi, Sigi, Syg

Sigga
(Scandinavian) from Siegfried; peaceful; winning
Sig

Sigmund
(German) winner
Siegmund, Sig, Siggi, Siggy, Sigi, Sigmon, Sigmond

Signe
(Scandinavian) victor
Signy

Sigwald
(German) leader
Siegwald

Sigurd
(Scandinavian) winning personality

Silas
(Latin) saver
Si, Siles, Silus

Sill
(English) beam of light
Sills

Silous
(American) form of Silas; brooding
Si, Silouz

Silvano
(Latin) of the woods; unique
Silvan, Silvani, Silvio, Sylvan

Silver
(Spanish) form of Silva; outgoing
Sylver

Silverman
(German) works with silver; craftsman

Silverton
(English) from town of silversmiths
Silvertown

Silvester
(Latin) from the woods
Silvestre, Silvestro, Sylvester

Simba
(African) lionlike

Simcha
(Hebrew) joyful

Simeon
(French) listener
Si, Simion, Simone, Simyon, Sy

Simms
(Hebrew) good listener
Sims

Simon
(Hebrew) good listener; thoughtful
Si, Siman, Simen, Simeon, Simmy, Sye, Symon, Syms

Simpson
(Hebrew) simplistic
Simpsen, Simpsun, Simson

Sinclair
(French) prayerful
Clair, Sinc, Sinclare, Synclaire

Sindbad
(Literature) daring
Sinbad

Singer
(Last name as first name) vocalist
Synger

Sinjin
(English) form of St. John; religious

Sion
(Hebrew) heavenly peak
Zion

Siraj
(Arabic) shines

Sirius
(Star) shining

Sisto
(American) cowboy

Sisyphus
(Greek) in mythology, a cruel king

Six
(American) number as name
Syx

Sixtus
(Latin) sixth child

Sivney
(Irish) satisfied
Sivneigh, Sivnie

Skeeter
(English) fast
Skeater, Skeet, Skeets

Skeetz
(American) zany
Skeet, Skeeter, Skeets

Skelly
(Irish) bard
Scully

Skerry
(Scandinavian) from the island of stone; pragmatist

Skilling
(English) masterful
Skillings

Skinner
(English) skins for a living

Skip
(American) short for Skipper
Skipp, Skyp, Skyppe

Skippy
(American) fast
Skippee, Skippie, Skyppey

Skye
(Dutch) goal-oriented
Sky

Skylar
(Dutch) protective
Skilar, Skye, Skyeler, Skylir

Slade
(English) quiet child
Slaid, Slaide, Slayd, Slayde

Sladkey
(Slavic) glorious
Sladkie

Slam
(American) friendly
Slams, Slamz

Slater
(Last name as first name) precocious
Slaiter, Slayter

Slavek
(Polish) smart; glorious
Slavec, Slavik

Slavin
(Irish) mountain man; hermit
Slawin, Slaven

Slawomir
(Slavic) great glory; famed
Slavek, Slavomir

Slim
(English) nickname for slim guy

Sloan
(Irish) sleek
Sloane, Slonne

Slocum
(Last name as first name) happy
Slo, Slocom, Slocumb

Slover
(Last name as first name)
Slove

Sly
(Latin) from Sylvester; of the forest

Smedley
(English) of the flat meadow
Smedleigh, Smedly

Smerdyakov
(Literature) sinister

Smith
(English) crafty; blacksmith
Smid, Smidt, Smit, Smitt, Smitti, Smitty

Smithson
(Last name as first name) son of Smith; craftsman

Smitty
(English) craftsman
Smittey

Smokey
(American) smokin'
Smoke, Smokee, Smoky

Snake
(Place name) U.S. river

Snowden
(English) from a snowy hill; fresh
Snowdon

Snyder
(German) tailor's clothing; stylish
Schneiger, Snider

So
(Vietnamese) smart

Socorro
(Spanish) helpful
Sokorro

Socrates
(Greek) philosophical; brilliant
Socratez, Socratis, Sokrates

Sofian
(Arabic) devoted

Sofus
(Greek) wise
Sophus

Sohan
(Hindi) charmer

Sohil
(Hindi) handsome

Sol
(Hebrew) short for Solomon
Solly

Solly
(Hebrew) short for Solomon
Sollee, Solley, Solli, Sollie

Solomon
(Hebrew) peaceful and wise
Salamon, Sol, Sollie, Solly, Soloman

Somerby
(English) from the summer village; lighthearted
Somerbie, Somersby, Sommersby

Somerley
(Irish) summer sailor
Somerled, Sorley

Somers
(English) loving summer
Sommers

Somerset
(English) talented
Somer, Somers, Sommerset, Summerset

Somerton
(English) from summer town
Somervile, Somerville

Sommar
(English) summer
Somer, Somers, Somm, Sommars, Sommer

Son
(English) boy
Sonni, Sonnie, Sonny

Sonny
(English) boy
Son, Sonney, Sonni, Sonnie

Sonteeahgo
(Invented) form of Santiago

Sophocles
(Greek) playwright

Soren
(Scandinavian) good communicator
Soryn

Sorrel
(French) reddish-brown
horse; horse lover
Sorre, Sorrell, Sorrey

Sothern
(English) from the south;
warm-hearted
Southern

Sound
(American) word as a name;
dynamic

Southwell
(English) living by the
southern well

Spanky
(American) outspoken;
stubborn
Spank, Spankee, Spankie

Sparky
(Latin) ball of fire; joyful
*Spark, Sparkee, Sparkey,
Sparki, Sparkie*

Spaulding
(Last name as first name)
comic
*Spalding, Spaldying,
Spauldyng*

Speed
(English) plucky

Speers
(English) good with spears;
swift-moving
Speares, Spears, Spiers

Spence
(English) short for Spencer
Spens, Spense

Spencer
(English) giver; provides
well
*Spence, Spencey, Spenser,
Spensor, Spensy*

Sperry
(Last name as first name)
inventive
Sperrey

Spider
(American) scary
Spyder

Spidey
(American) variant of
Spiderman; zany

Spike
(American) word as name
Spiker

Spiker
(English) go-getter
Spike, Spikey, Spyk

Spiridon
(Greek) like a breath of
fresh air
*Speero, Spero, Spiridon,
Spiro, Spiros, Spyridon,
Spyros*

Spiro
(Greek) coil; spiral
*Spi, Spiroh, Spiros, Spy,
Spyro*

Springer
(English) fresh
Spring

Sprague
(French) high-energy

Spud
(English) energetic

Spurgeon
(Botanical) from the shrub
spurge; natural
Spurge

Spunk
(American) spunky; lively
Spunki, Spunky

Spurs
(American) boot devices
used to spur horses; cowboy
Spur

Squire
(English) land-loving
Squirre, Skwyre

Stace
(English) optimist
Stayce

Stacey
(English) hopeful
*Stace, Stacee, Stacy, Stase,
Stasi*

Stadler
(Last name as first name)
staid
Stadtler

Stafford
(English) dignified
*Staff, Staffard, Stafferd,
Staffi, Staffie, Staffor, Staffy*

Stamos
(Greek) reasonable
Stammos, Stamohs

Stan
(Latin) short for Stanley

Stanbury
(English) fortified
*Stanberry, Stanbery,
Stanburghe, Stansberry,
Stansburghe, Stansbury*

Stancliff
(English) from the stone cliff; prepared
Stancliffe, Stanclyffe, Stanscliff, Stanscliffe

Standish
(English) farsighted
Standysh

Stanfield
(English) from the stone field; able
Stansfield

Stanford
(English) dignified
Stan, Stanferd, Stann

Stanislaus
(Latin) glorious
Staneslaus, Stanis, Stanislus, Stann, Stanus

Stanislav
(Russian) glory in leading
Slava, Stasi

Stanley
(English) traveler
Stan, Stanlea, Stanlee, Stanli, Stanly

Stanmore
(English) lake of stones; ill-fated

Stanton
(English) stone-hard
Stan

Stanway
(English) came from the stone road
Stanaway, Stannaway, Stannway

Stanwick
(English) born in village of stone; hard
Stanwicke, Stanwyck

Stanwood
(English) stone woods man; tough

Stark
(German) high-energy
Starke, Starkey

Starling
(English) singer; bird
Starlling

Starr
(English) bright star
Star, Starri, Starrie, Starry

Stavros
(Greek) winner
Stavrohs, Stavrows

Steadman
(English) landowner; wealthy
Steadmann, Sted, Stedmann

Steed
(English) horse of high spirits

Steele
(English) hardworking
Steel, Stille

Stefan
(Scandinavian) crowned; (German) chosen one
Stefawn, Steff, Steffan, Steffie, Steffon, Steffy, Stefin, Stephan

Stefano
(Italian) supreme ruler
Stef, Steffie, Steffy, Stephano, Stephanos

Stehlin
(Last name as first name) genius
Staylin, Stealan, Stehlan

Stein
(German) stonelike
Steen, Sten, Steno

Steinar
(Scandinavian) muse; rock
Steinard, Steinart, Steinhardt

Steinbeck
(Last name as first) writer John

Stellan
(Swedish) star

Sten
(Scandinavian) star stone
Stene, Stine

Stennis
(Scottish) prehistoric standing stones; eternal

Stepan
(English) from Stephen; crowned
Stepen, Stepyn

Steph
(English) short for Stephen; triumphant
Stef, Steff, Steffy

Stephan
(Greek) form of Stephen; successful

Stephanos
(Greek) crowned; martyr
Stef, Stefanos, Steph, Stephanas

Stephen
(Greek) victorious
Stephan, Stephon, Stevee, Steven, Stevey, Stevi, Stevie, Stevy

Stephene
(French) form of Stephen; wearing a crown
Stef, Steff, Steph

Sterling
(English) worthwhile

Stern
(German) bright; serious
Stearn, Sterns

Stetson
(American) cowboy
Stetsen, Stetsun, Stettson

Steubing
(Last name as first name) stepping
Steuben, Stu, Stuben, Stubing

Steve
(Greek) short for Steven and Stephen; prosperous
Stevie

Steven
(Greek) victorious
Stevan, Steve, Stevey, Stevie

Steveo
(American) form of Steve

Stevie
(English) short for Steven, Stephen
Stevee, Stevey, Stevi, Stevy

Stewart
(English) form of Stuart; steward or keeper
Stewert, Stu, Stuie

Stian
(Scandinavian) traveler

Stieran
(Scandinavian) wandering
Steeran, Steeren, Steeryn, Stieren, Stieryn

Stig
(Scandinavian) upwardly mobile
Stigg, Styg, Stygg

Stiles
(English) practical
Stile, Stiley, Styles

Stillman
(English) quiet boy

Sting
(English) spike of grain

Stoat
(Animal) small mammal also called ermine; white
Stoate, Stote

Stobart
(German) harsh
Stobe, Stobey, Stoby

Stock
(American) macho
Stok

Stockard
(English) dramatic
Stock, Stockerd, Stockord

Stocker
(English) foundation
Stock

Stockley
(English) in a field of tree stumps (stock); rooted in reality

Stockton
(English) strong foundation
Stockten

Stockwell
(English) from the well by tree stumps; grounded

Stoddard
(English) caretaker of horses
Stoddart

Stoli
(Russian) celebrant

Stone
(English) athletic
Stonee, Stoney, Stonie, Stony

Stonewall
(English) fortified
Stone, Stoney, Wall

Stoney
(American) form of Stone; friendly
Stonee, Stoni, Stonie

Storey
(English) one story of a house; storyteller
Story

Storm
(English) impetuous; volatile
Storme, Stormy

Stowe
(English) secretive
Stow, Stowey

Strahan
(Irish) sings stories
Strachan

Stratford
(English) river-crossing boy; happy
Strafford

Strato
(Invented) strategic
Strat, Stratt

Stratton
(Scottish) home-loving
Straton, Strattawn

Straus
(German) ostrich; in disbelief
Strauss

Stretch
(American) easygoing
Stretcher

Strickland
(English) field of flax; outdoorsy

Strider
(Literature) great warrior

Strike
(American) word as name; aggressive
Striker

Stroheim
(Last name as first) great director

Strom
(German) water-lover
Strome, Stromm

Strong
(English) strength of character

Strother
(Irish) strict
Strothers, Struther, Struthers

Struther
(Last name as first name) flowing
Strother, Strothers, Struthers

Stu
(English) short for Stuart
Stew, Stue, Stuey

Stuart
(English) careful; watchful
Stewart, Stu, Stuey

Studs
(American) cocky
Studd, Studds

Sture
(Scandinavian) difficult
Sturah

Styles
(English) practical
Stile, Stiles, Style

Stylianos
(Greek) stylish
Styli

Sudbury
(English) southern town boy; lackadaisical
Sudbery, Sudberry, Sudborough

Suffield
(English) man from south field; farms

Suffolk
(English) from southern folks

Sugar-Ray
(American) strong; singer
Sugar Ray

Sujay
(Hindi) good
Sujit

Sulaiman
(Arabic) loves peace
Suleiman, Suleyman

Sullivan
(Irish) dark-eyed; quiet
Sullavan, Sullie, Sullivahn, Sully

Sully
(Irish) melancholy; hushed
Sull, Sullee, Sulley, Sullie

Sultan
(American) bold
Sultane, Sulten, Sultin

Suman
(Hindi) ingenious

Sumner
(Last name as first name) honorable; fortified

Sumney
(American) ethereal
Summ, Summy, Sumnee, Sumnie

Sunil
(Hindi) blue; sad

Sunny
(American) happy baby boy
Sunney, Sunnie

Sutcliff
(English) from the south cliff; edgy
Sutcliffe

Sutherland
(Scandinavian) sunny; southerner
Southerland

Sutter
(English) southern
Sutt, Suttee, Sutty

Sutton
(English) sunny; southerner

Svatomir
(Slavic) known for being spiritual

Svatoslav
(Slavic) having the glory of being devout

Sven
(Scandinavian) young boy
Svein, Svend, Swen

Swahili
(Arabic) language of East Africa; verbal

Swain
(English) rigid; leading the herd
Swaine, Swayne

Swanton
(English) where swans live; sylvan boy

Sweeney
(Irish) hero
Schwennie, Sweeny

Swift
(English) fast
Swifty

Swinburne
(English) seeing pigs in the stream
Swinborn, Swinbourne, Swinburn, Swinbyrn, Swynborne

Swindell
(English) polished
Schwindell, Swin, Swindel

Swinford
(English) seeing pigs in the ford
Swynford

Swinton
(English) from the town of swine

Swithin
(English) swift
Swithinn, Swithun

Sy
(Latin) short for Silas,
Sylas, Si

Sydney
(French) form of Sidney
Cyd, Syd, Sydie

Sylvain
(Latin) reclusive
Syl

Sylvan
(Spanish) nature-loving
Silvan, Syl, Sylvany, Sylvin

Sylvester
(Latin) forest dweller; heavy-duty
Sil, Silvester, Sly, Syl

Symms
(Last name as first name) landowner

Symotris
(African American) fortunate
Sym, Symetris, Symotrice, Syms

Syon
(Sanskrit) lucky boy

Tab
(German) intelligent
Tabby, Tabbey, Tabby

Tabbai
(Hebrew) good boy

Tabbebo
(Native American) boy of the sun

Tabib
(Turkish) physician
Tabeeb

Tabor
(Aramaic) unfortunate
Taber, Taibor, Tayber, Taybor

Tad
(Greek) short for Thaddeus
Tadd, Taddee, Taddey, Taddie, Taddy

Tadeusz
(Polish) praise-worthy
Tad, Taduce

Tadhg
(Irish) poetic
Taidghin, Teague, Teige

Tadi
(Native American) wind child

Tadzi
(Polish) praised

Taff
(American) sweet
Taf, Taffee, Taffey, Taffi, Taffy

Taft
(English) flowing
Tafte, Taftie, Taffy

Taggart
(Last name as first name)
keeps track; singer

Taghee
(Native American) chief
Taighe, Taihee, Tyee, Tyhee

Taha
(Polynesian) first
Tahatan

Taheton
(Native American) like a
hawk

Tahi
(Polynesian) by the sea

Tahir
(African) pure

Tahoe
(Place name) Lake Tahoe,
Nevada
Taho

Tahoma
(Native American) mountain
peak; high hopes
Tohoma

Tai
(Vietnamese) talented

Taimah
(Native American) thunder

Taiwo
(African) first of twins

Taizo
(Japanese) third son

Taj
(Sanskrit) royal; crowned

Takeshi
(Japanese) unbending

Taklishim
(Native American) gray-
haired

Takoda
(Native American) friend

Tal
(Hebrew) worrier
Tallee, Talley, Talli, Tally

Talbot
(French) skillful
*Tal, Talbert, Talbott, Tallbot,
Tallbott, Tally*

Talcot
(English) lake-cottage
dweller; laidback

Tale
(African) green; open

Talfryn
(Welsh) on the high hill

Talib
(African) looking for
enlightenment

Taliesin
(Welsh) head that shines
Taltesin

Talli
(Hebrew) dew; fresh

Talmai
(Aramaic) born on a hill

Talmadge
(English) natural; living by
lakes
Tal, Tally, Tamidge

Talman
(Hebrew) from my hill
Tallie, Tally, Talmon

Talon
(French) wily
Tallie, Tallon, Tally, Tawlon

Talor
(French) cutter; tailor

Tam
(Hebrew) truthful
Tammy

Taman
(Hindi) needed

Tamarius
(African American) stubborn
*Tam, Tamerius, Tammy,
T'Marius*

Tamir
(Arabic) owner

Tammany
(Native American) friendly
boy
Tamanend

Tammy
(English) short for Thomas
and Tamarius
Tammee, Tammie, Tammey

Tan
(Japanese) high achiever

Tanafa
(Polynesian) drumbeat

Tanaki
(Polynesian) boy who
counts

Tanay
(Hindi) son

Tandie
(African American) virile

Tane
(Polynesian) sky god; fertile
Tain

Tangaloa
(Polynesian) gutsy

Tanh
(Vietnamese) having his way

Tani
(African American) short for Tanier; hide tanner

Tank
(American) big; bullish

Tankie
(American) large
Tank, Tankee, Tanky

Tanner
(English) tanner of skins
Tan, Tanier, Tann, Tannar, Tanne, Tanney, Tannie, Tannor, Tanny

Tano
(Mythology) from Tane, fertility god

Tanton
(English) town of tanners

Taos
(Place name) town in New Mexico
Tao, Tayo

Tap
(American) word as name
Tapp, Tappi, Tappy

Tarhe
(Native American) strength of a tree

Tarik
(Arabic) knocks
Taril, Tarin, Tariq

Tariq
(African American) conquerer
Tarik

Tarlach
(Hebrew) wild

Tarleton
(English) stormy
Tally, Tarlton

Taro
(Japanese) first-born son

Tarquin
(Roman clan) impulsive

Tarrance
(Latin) smooth
Terance, Terrance, Terry

Tarrant
(Place name) county in Texas; lawful

Tarri
(American) form of Terry
Tari, Tarree, Tarrey, Tarry

Tarso
(Italian) dashing

Tarun
(Arabic) knocks

Taryll
(American) form of Terrell
Tarell

Tas
(TV) Tasmanian devil cartoon character
Taz

Tashunka
(Native American) horse lover
Tasunke

Tassilo
(Scandinavian) fearless protector

Tassos
(Italian) dark

Tatankamimi
(Native American) the buffalo walks

Tate
(English) happy
Tait, Taitt, Tatey, Tayt, Tayte

Tatonga
(Native American) deer; swift

Tatry
(Place name) mountains in Poland
Tate, Tatree, Tatri

Tau
(African) lionine

Taurean
(African American) reclusive; quiet
Taureen

Taurus
(Astrological sign) macho
Tar, Taur, Tauras, Taures

Tava
(Polynesian) fruit; fertile

Tavares
(African American) hopeful
Tavarus

Tavarius
(African American) fun-loving
Tav, Taverius, Tavurius, Tavvy

Tavas
(Hebrew) peacock; handsome

Tavi
(Aramaic) good

Tavish
(Scottish) upbeat
Tav, Taven, Tavis, Tevis

Tavor
(Aramaic) unfortunate
Tabor

Tawa
(Native American) sun boy

Tawagahe
(Native American) builder

Tawanima
(Native American) measures
the sun
Tewanima

Tawfiq
(Arabic) fortunate
Tawfi

Tawl
(Arabic) tall
Taweel

Tawno
(American) small

Tay
(Scottish) river in Scotland;
jaunty
Tae, Taye

Tayib
(Arabic) also Tayibe; city in
Israel; spiritual

Taylor
(English) tailor
Tailor, Talor, Tayler, Tayley

Tayton
(American) form of Payton
*Tate, Taye, Tayte, Tayten,
Taytin*

Taz
(Arabic) cup; vibrant

Teague
(Irish) bard; poet
Teaguey, Tege

Tearlach
(Scottish) adult man; bold

Techomir
(Czech) famed comfort

Techoslav
(Native American) glorious
comfort

Tecumseh
(Native American) shooting
star; bright

Ted
(English) short for Theodore
*Teddee, Teddey, Teddi,
Teddy*

Teddy-Blue
(American) smiley
*Blu, Blue, Teddie-Blue,
Teddy, Teddyblu, Teddy-Blu,
Teddyblue*

Tedmund
(American) shy
Tedmond

Tedrick
(African American) form of
Cedrick
Ted, Tedrik

Tedshawn
(American) combo of Ted
and Shawn
Teddshawn, Tedshaun

Tedwayne
(American) combo of Ted
and Wayne; friendly
Ted Wayne, Ted-Wayne

Tegan
(Irish) form of Teague;
literary figure
Tege, Tegen, Tegun, Teige

Tejomay
(Hindi) glorious
Tej

Tekonsha
(Native American) caribou

Telamon
(Greek) mythological hero

Telek
(Polish) ironworker

Telem
(English) from Teleson;
amulet

Telemachus
(Mythological) son of
Ulysses

Telesphoros
(Greek) leading to an end;
centered

Telford
(English) cutting iron;
targeted
Telfer, Telfor, Telfour

Teller
(English) relates stories;
storytelling
Tellie, Telly

Telvis
(American) form of Elvis
Telly

Tem
(African) short form of
Temani; spiritual

Teman
(Hebrew) Temani are Jews
from Yeman; spiritual

Tempest
(French) stormy; volatile
Tempie, Tempy, Tempyst

Temple
(Latin) spiritual
Tempie, Templle, Tempy

Templeton
(English) from religious place
Temp, Tempie, Temple, Temps

Ten
(American) word as name; tenth

Tendoy
(Native American) he who climbs higher
Tendoi

Teneangopte
(Native American) bird; flies high

Tennant
(American) capable
Tenn

Tennessee
(Native American) able fighter; U.S. state
Tenns, Tenny

Tennyson
(English) storyteller
Tenie, Tenn, Tenney, Tenneyson, Tennie, Tenny, Tennysen

Teo
(Greek) gift of God

Teodoro
(Spanish) God's gift
Tedoro, Teo, Teodore, Theo

TeQuarius
(African American) secretive
Teq, Tequarius, Tequie

Terach
(Hebrew) wild goat; contentious
Tera, Terah

Terard
(Invented) form of Gerard
Terar, Tererd, Terry

Terence
(Irish) tender
Tarrance, Terencio, Terrance, Terrence, Terrey, Terri, Terry

TeRez
(African American) creative

Termell
(Invented) form of Terrell; militant
Termel

Terrance
(Latin) calm
Terance, Terence, Terre, Terree, Terrence, Terrie, Terry

Terrelle
(German) thunderous; outspoken
Terel, Terele, Terell, Teril, Terille, Terral, Terrale, Terre, Terrel, Terril, Terrill, Terrille, Terry, Tirill, Tirrill, Tyrel, Tyril

Terrill
(African American) combo of Terry and Derrell
Terrall, Terrel, Terrell, Terryl, Terryll, Tirrell, Tyrrell

Terry
(English) short for Terrence
Terree, Terrey, Terri, Terrie

Tesher
(Hebrew) gift

Teshombe
(African American) able

Tet
(Vietnamese) Vietnamese New Year

Teva
(Hebrew) natural
Tevah

Tevaughn
(African American) tiger
Tev, Tevan, Tevaughan, Tivan, Tivaughan

Tevey
(Hebrew) good
Tev, Tevi, Tevie

Tevin
(African American) outgoing
Tev, Tevan, Tivan

Tevis
(American) flamboyant
Tev, Tevas, Teves, Teviss, Tevy

Tevita
(Spanish) variant of Evita; strong

Tex
(American) from Texas; cowboy
Texas, Texx

Texas
(Place name) U.S. state; cowboy
Tex

Thabiti
(African) real man

Thad
(Greek) short for Thaddeus; brave
Thadd, Thaddy

Thaddeus
(Greek) courageous
Taddeo, Tadeo, Tadio, Thad, Thaddaus, Thaddius, Thaddy, Thadeus, Thadius

Thady
(Irish) thankful
Thad, Thaddee, Thaddie, Thaddy, Thads

Thai
(Vietnamese) winner

Thandiwe
(African) loved

Thane
(English) protective
Thain, Thaine, Thayn, Thayne

Thang
(Vietnamese) victorious

Thanh
(Vietnamese) tops

Thanos
(Greek) praiseworthy
Thanasis

Thanus
(American) landowner; wealthy
Thainas, Thaines

Thatcher
(English) practical
Thacher, Thatch, Thatchar, Thaxter

Thaw
(Place name) from Thawville, Illinois; warm spirit

Thayer
(English) protected; sheltered
Thay, Thayar

Themba
(African) hopeful

Theo
(Greek) godlike

Theobald
(German) brave man
Thebaud, Thebault, Thibault, Thibaut, Tibold, Tiebold

Theodore
(Greek) God's gift; a blessing
Teador, Ted, Tedd, Teddey, Teddie, Teddy, Tedor, Teodor, Teodoro, Theeo, Theo, Theodor, Theos

Theodoric
(African American) God's gift
Thierry

Theodoros
(Greek) God's gift
Theo, Theodor

Theophilos
(Greek) loved by God
Teofil, Theo, Theophile

Therman
(Scandinavian) thunderous
Thur, Thurman, Thurmen

Theron
(Greek) industrious
Therron, Theryon

Theseus
(Mythology) brave

Thiassi
(Scandinavian) wily
Thiazi, Thjazi

Thierno
(American) humble
Therno, Their

Tho
(Vietnamese) long-living

Thomas
(Greek) twin; lookalike
Thom, Thomes, Thommy, Thomus, Tom, Tomas, Tommi, Tomus

Thompson
(English) prepared
Thom, Thompsen, Thompsun, Thomson, Tom, Tommy

Thor
(Scandinavian) protective; god of thunder
Thorr, Tor, Torr

Thorald
(Scandinavian) thundering
Thorold, Torald

Thorbert
(Last name as first name) warring

Thorburn
(Last name as first name) warlike

Thorer
(Scandinavian) warrior
Thorvald

Thorin
(Scandinavian) form of Thor; god of thunder
Thorrin, Thors

Thorley
(Last name as first name)
warrior
*Thorlea, Thorlee, Thorleigh,
Thorly, Torley*

Thormond
(Last name as first name)
world of thunder
Thurmond, Thurmund

Thorn
(English) thorny; bothersome

Thorndike
(Last name as first name)
powerful
Thorndyck, Thorndyke

Thorne
(English) complex
*Thorn, Thornee, Thorney,
Thornie, Thorny*

Thornley
(Last name as first name)
empowered
*Thornlea, Thornleigh,
Thornly*

Thornston
(Scandinavian) protected
Thornse, Thors

Thornton
(English) difficult
Thorn, Thornten

Thorpe
(English) homebody
Thor, Thorp

Thrace
(Place name) region in
southeast Europe
Thrase

Thu
(Vietnamese) born in the fall

Thuc
(Vietnamese) alert

Thuong
(Vietnamese) in pursuit

Thurlow
(Last name as first name)
helping

Thurman
(Last name as first name)
popular
*Thurmahn, Thurmen,
Thurmie, Thurmy*

Thurmond
(Norse) sheltered
Thurman, Thurmon

Thurston
(Scandinavian) thundering
*Thor, Thors, Thorst,
Thorstan, Thorstein,
Thorsteinn, Thorsten, Thur,
Thurs, Thurstain, Thurstan,
Thursten, Torstein, Torsten,
Torston*

Thurstron
(Scandinavian) volatile
*Thorst, Thorsten, Thorstin,
Thurs, Thurstran*

Thuy
(Vietnamese) kind

Tiago
(Hispanic) brave
Ti, Tia

Tiarnach
(Irish) lordlike
Tighearnach

Tibor
(Czech) artist
Tybald, Tybalt, Tybault

Tien
(Vietnamese) first and
foremost

Tiernan
(Irish) regal
Tierney

Tige
(American) easygoing
Tig, Tigg

Tiger
(American) ambitious;
strong
*Tig, Tige, Tigur, Tyg, Tyge,
Tyger, Tygur*

Tiki
(Mythology) first man

Tilak
(Hindi) leader; troubled

Tilden
(Place name) Tilden,
Nebraska; conservative

Tilford
(Last name as first name)
tilling the soil

Till
(German) short for Tillman;
tiller of soil

Tillery
(German) ruler
Till, Tiller

Tillman
(German) leader
Tilman

Tilon
(Hebrew) mound; giver

Tilton
(English) prospering
Till, Tillie, Tylton

Tim
(Greek) short for Timothy
Timmy, Tym

Timber
(American) word as name
*Timb, Timby, Timmey,
Timmi, Timmy*

Timin
(Irish) honors God

Timmy
(Greek) truthful
*Timi, Timmee, Timmey,
Timmie*

Timo
(Finnish) form of Timothy or
Timon

Timon
(Literature) from
Shakespeare's *Timon of
Athens*; wealthy man
Tim

Timothy
(Greek) reveres God
*Tim, Timathy, Timmie,
Timmothy, Timmy, Timo,
Timon, Timoteo, Timothe,
Timothey, Timothie, Timuthy,
Tymmothy, Tymothy*

Timur
(African) timid

Tin
(Vietnamese) proud;
pondering

Tinks
(American) coy
*Tink, Tinkee, Tinki, Tinky,
Tynks, Tynky*

Tino
(Spanish) respected
Tyno

Tinsley
(English) personable
*Tensley, Tins, Tinslee,
Tinslie, Tinsly*

Tip
(American) small boy
*Tipp, Tippee, Tippey, Tippi,
Tippy, Typp*

Tipu
(Hindi) tiger

Tiru
(Hindi) pious

Tisa
(African) ninth child

Titan
(Greek) powerful giant
Titun, Tityn

Tito
(Latin) honored
Teto, Titoh

Titus
(Latin) heroic
Titas, Tite, Tites

Tivon
(African American) popular

Toa
(Polynesian) brave-hearted

Toafo
(Polynesian) in the wild;
spontaneous

Toal
(Irish) from strong roots

Tobes
(Hebrew) form of Tobias;
believing the Lord is good
Tobee, Tobi, Tobs

Tobias
(Hebrew) believing the Lord
is good
*Tobe, Tobey, Tobi, Tobiah,
Tobie, Tobin, Toby, Tobyas,
Tovi*

Tobbar
(African American) physical

Tobikuma
(Japanese) cloud; misty

Tobin
(Hebrew) form of Tobias;
believing the Lord is good
Toban, Toben, Tobun, Tobyn

Toby
(Hebrew) short for Tobias;
having faith in the Lord
*Tobe, Tobee, Tobey, Tobie,
Toto*

Todd
(English) sly; fox
Tod, Toddy

Todros
(Hebrew) gifted; treasure
Todos

Togo
(Place name) country in
West Africa; jaunty

Tohon
(Native American) loves the
water

Tokala
(Native American) fox; sly

Toks
(American) carefree

Tokutaro
(Japanese) virtuous son

Tolan
(American) studious
Tolen, Toll

Tolbert
(English) bright prospects
Talbart, Talbert, Tolbart, Tolburt, Tollee, Tolley, Tollie, Tolly

Toledo
(Place name) city in Ohio; casual
Tol, Tolly

Tolfe
(American) outgoing

Tolomey
(French) planner

Tom
(English) short for Thomas; twin
Thom, Tommy

Tomas
(Spanish) form of Thomas

Tomasso
(Italian) doubter
Maso, Tom

Tomer
(Hebrew) tall

Tomi
(Spanish) short for Tomas; twin

Tomlin
(Last name as first name) ambitious

Tommie
(Hebrew, English) short for Thomas
Tomee, Tommee, Tommey, Tommi, Tomy

Tomochichi
(Hawaiian) seeking truth and beauty
Tomocheechee

Tong
(Chinese) name of a secret society; keeps a secret

Toni
(Greek, Italian, American, English) soaring
Tonee, Toney, Tonie, Tony

Tonion
(American) from Tony/Anthony; priceless

Toopweets
(Native American) strong man

Topwe
(American) jovial

Tor
(Scandinavian) thunder; brash
Thor, Torr, Torri, Torrie, Torry

Torao
(Japanese) tiger male; wild

Torcall
(Scandinavian) summoned by thunder

Tord
(Dutch) peaceful

Torger
(Scandinavian) Thor's spear
Terje, Torgeir

Toribio
(Spanish) strong; bullish

Toril
(Hindi) having attitude

Torin
(African American) like thunder

Torio
(Spanish) fierce

Torkel
(Scandinavian) protective
Thorkel, Torkil, Torkild, Torkjell, Torquil

Torless
(Literature) from *The Confusions of Young Torless* by Musil

Tormod
(Scottish) man of the north

Torn
(Last name as first name) whirlwind
Torne, Tornn

Toro
(Spanish) bull

Torolf
(Scandinavian) wolf of Thor
Thorolf, Tolv, Torolv, Torulf

Toronto
(Place name) jaded
Torontoe

Torq
(Scandinavian) form of Thor, god of thunder
Tork

Torquil
(Scandinavian) a kettle of thunder; trouble

Torr
(English) tower; tall
Torre

Torrence
(Latin) smooth
Torrance, Torence, Torey, Tori, Torr, Torrance, Torrie, Tory

Torri
(English) calming
Toree, Tori, Torre, Torree, Torrey, Torry

Toru
(Scandinavian) thundering

Toshiro
(Japanese) smart

Tov
(Hebrew) good
Tovi, Toviel, Tovya, Tuvia, Tuviah, Tuviya

Tova
(Hebrew) good
Tov

Tove
(Scandinavian) ruling; leads
Tuve

Townie
(American) jovial
Townee, Towney, Towny

Townley
(Last name as first name) citified
Townlea, Townlee, Townleigh, Townlie, Townly

Townsend
(Last name as first name) went to town

Toyah
(Place name) town in Texas; saucy
Toy, Toya, Toye

Trace
(French) careful
Trayse

Tracy
(French) spunky
Trace, Tracee, Tracey, Traci

Trae
(American) form of Trey; third

Trahan
(English) handsome
Trace, Trahahn, Trahain, Trahane, Trahen

Trahaearn
(Welsh) strong man
Trahern, Traherne

Trai
(Vietnamese) pearl in the oyster

Trampus
(American) talkative
Amp, Tramp, Trampy

Trap
(American) word as name; masculine
Trapp, Trappy

Traves
(American) traversing different roads
Trav, Travus, Travys

Travers
(English) helpful

Travis
(English) conflicted
Tavers, Traver, Travers, Traves, Travess, Travey, Travus, Travuss, Travys

Travon
(African American) brash
Travaughn

Trayton
(English) third
Tray, Trey

Treebeard
(Literature) noble; strong

Trefor
(Welsh) form of Trevor; large home

Tremayne
(French) protector
Tramaine, Treemayne, Trem, Tremain, Tremaine, Tremane, Tremen

Trent
(Latin) quick-minded
Trente, Trenten, Trentin, Trenton, Trenty, Trint, Trynt

Trenton
(Latin) fast-moving
Trent, Trentan, Trenten, Trentin

Treva
(Irish) wise
Trevan

Trevan
(African American) outgoing
Trevahn, Trevann

Trevelyan
(English) from Elyan's home; comforted

Trevon
(African American) studious
Trevaughan

Trevor
(Irish) wise
Trefor, Trev, Trevar, Trever, Trevis, Trevur, Treve

Trey
(English) third-born; creatively brilliant
Trae, Tray, Tre, Treye

Trigg
(American) short for Trigger; horse or trigger finger
Trig, Trygg

Trinee
(Spanish) musical
Triney, Trini

Trinity
(Latin) triad
Trinitie

Trip
(English) wanderer
Tripe, Tripp

Tripsy
(English) dancing
Trippsie, Tryppsi

Tristan
(English) impulsive
Trestan, Trestyn, Trist, Tristen, Tristie, Triston, Tristy, Tristyn

Triste
(French) sad; wistful
Tristan

Tristram
(Welsh) sorrowful

Trivett
(Last name as first name) trinity
Trevett, Triv

Trivin
(American) form of Devin; clever
Trevin

Trocky
(American) manly
Trockey, Trockie

Trond
(Scandinavian) from Trondheim, Norway; blond

Trowbridge
(Place name) Trowbridge Park, Michigan; staunch

Troy
(French) good-looking
Troi, Troye, Troyie

Troylane
(American) combo of Troy and Lane
Troy Lane, Troy-Lane

Trudell
(English) remarkable for honesty
Trude, True

True
(English) truthful
Tru

Truitt
(English) honest
Tru, True, Truett, Truitte

Truk
(Place name) islands in the West Pacific; tough
Truck

Truman
(English) honest man
Tru, True, Trueman, Trumaine, Trumann

Trumble
(Last name as first name) sincere
Trumball, Trumbell, Trumbull

Trusdale
(English) truthful
Dale, Tru, True

Tsalani
(African) says good-bye; leaving

Tsatoke
(Native American) hunter on a horse

Tsela
(Native American) star

Tsin
(Native American) Tsen; riding a horse

Tsoai
(Native American) tree; big

Tu
(Vietnamese) fourth

Tuan
(Vietnamese) simple

Tucker
(English) stylish
Tuck, Tucky, Tuckyr

Tucks
(English) short for Tucker; fanciful
Tuk

Tudor
(Welsh) leader; special

Tukuli
(African) moon child

Tullis
(Latin) important
Tull, Tullice, Tullise, Tully

Tully
(Irish) short for Tullis;
interesting
Tull, Tulley, Tulli, Tullie

Tulsa
(Place name) city in
Oklahoma; cowboy; rancher

Tulsi
(Hindi) holy

Tumaini
(African) optimist

Tune
(American) dancer; musical
Toone, Tuney

Tung
(Chinese, Vietnamese)
dignified; wise

Tunu
(Place name) from Tununak,
Alaska; natural

Tuong
(Vietnamese) everything

Tupi
(Spanish) a language family
with Brazilian roots

Turk
(English) tough
Terk, Turke

Turlough
(Hebrew) form of Tuvyeh;
good

Turner
(Latin) skilled

Turone
(African American) form of
Tyrone
Ture, Turrey, Turry

Turner
(Latin) skilled
Turn

Tut
(Arabic) brave
Tuttie, Tutty

Tuvia
(Hebrew) good
Tuvyah

Tuwa
(Native American) earth-
loving

Tuyen
(Vietnamese) angelic

Twain
(English) dual-faceted
Twaine, Tway, Twayn

Twyford
(English) debonair

Ty
(English) short for Tyler
Ti, Tie, Tye

Tybalt
(Greek) always right

Tyce
(American) lively
Tice

Tycho
(Scandinavian) focused
Tyge, Tyko

Tydeus
(Mythology) determined

Tyee
(African American) goal-
oriented

Tygie
(American) energetic
Tygee, Tygey, Tygi

Tyke
(Scandinavian) determined

Tyler
(English) industrious
*Tile, Tiler, Ty, Tye, Tylar, Tyle,
Tylir, Tylor*

Tymon
(Polish) honored by God

Tynan
(Place name) a town in,
Texas; rancher

Tyonne
(African American) feisty
Tye, Tyon

Typhoon
(Weather name) volatile
Tifoon, Ty, Tyfoon, Tyfoonn

Tyr
(Scandinavian) Norse god;
daring warrior

Tyre
(English) thunders
Tyr

Tyree
(African American) courteous
Ty, Tyrae, Tyrie, Tyry

Tyreece
(African American) combative
Tyreese

Tyrell
(African American)
personable
*Trelle, Tyrel, Tyrelle, Tyril,
Tyrrel*

Tyron
(African American) self-reliant
Tiron, Tyronn

Tyrone
(Greek) self-starter; autonomous
Terone, Tiron, Tirone, Tirus, Ty, Tyronne, Tyron, Tyroon, Tyroun

Tyroneece
(African American) ball of fire
Tironeese, Tyronnee

Tys
(American) fighter
Thysen, Tyes, Tys, Tyse, Tysen

Tyson
(French) son of Ty
Tieson, Tison, Tyse, Tysen, Tysson, Tysy

Tzach
(Hebrew) unblemished
Tzachai, Tzachar

Tzadik
(Hebrew) fair
Tzadok, Zadik, Zadoc, Zadok, Zaydak

Tzadkiel
(Hebrew) righteous
Zadkiel

Tzalmon
(Hebrew) dark
Zalmon

Tzephaniah
(Hebrew) man protected by God
Tzefanya, Zefania, Zefaniah, Zephania, Zephaniah

Tzevi
(Hebrew) graceful; deer
Tzeviel, Zevi, Zeviel

Tzuriel
(Hebrew) depends on God
Zuriel

Ualtar
(Irish) strong
Ualtarr

Uba
(African) rich

Ubald
(French) brave one
Ubaldo, Ube

Ubanwa
(African) wealth in children

Uben
(German) practice
Ubin, Ubyn

Ubrig
(German) big
Ubrigg, Ubryg, Ubrygg

Ubrigens
(German) bothered
Ubrigins, Ubrigyns

Uchtred
(English) cries
Uchtrid, Uchtryd, Uctred, Uctrid, Uctryd, Uktred, Uktrid

Udall
(English) certain; valley of trees
Eudall, Udahl, Udawl, Yudall

Udeh
(Hindi) praised

Udel
(English) growing

Udell
(English) from a tree grove
Del, Dell, Udale, Udall

Udenwa
(African) thriving

Udo
(German) shows promise

Udolf
(German) stodgy

Ufer
(German) dark mind

Ugo
(Italian) bright mind

Uhr
(German) disturbed

Uilleac
(Irish) ready
Uilleack, Uilleak, Uilliac, Uilliack, Uilliak, Uillyac, Uillyack, Uillyak

Uilleog
(Irish) prepared
Uilliog, Uillyog

Ukel
(American) player
Ukal, Uke, Ukil

Ukraine
(Place name) republic

Ulan
(Place name) city in Russia, Ulan Ude
Ulane

Uland
(African) first-born twin
Ulande

Ulas
(German) noble

Ulbrich
(German) aristocratic

Ulfat
(Norse) wolf

Ulff
(Scandinavian) wolf; wild
Ulf, Ulv

Ulfred
(Norse) noble

Ulgar
(German) high-born

Ulices
(Latin) form of Ulysses;
wanderer
Uly

Ulick
(Irish) for William; up-and-
coming

Ulissus
(Invented) form of Ulysses

Ulland
(English) noble lord
Uland, Ullund

Ullock
(Irish) nobleman

Ulman
(German) the wolf's infamy
Ulmann, Ullman, Ullmann

Ulmer
(German) wolf; cagy

Ulriah
(German) from Ulric;
powerful wolf
Ulria, Ulrya, Ulryah

Ulrich
(German) ruling; powerful
*Ric, Rick, Rickie, Ricky,
Ulrek, Ulric, Ulriche, Ulrick,
Ulrico*

Ulster
(Scandinavian) wolf

Ultan
(Irish) noble
Ultann

Ultar
(Scandinavian) wolf
Ultarr

Ultman
(Hindi) godlike

Ulysses
(Latin) forceful
Ule, Ulesses, Ulises, Ulisses

Umar
(Hindi) doing well

Umbard
(German) from Humbert;
renowned
Umbarde

Umber
(French) brown; plain

Umberto
(Italian) earthy

Umed
(Hindi) has an aim

Umher
(Arabic) controlling

Umi
(African) life

Unique
(American) word as name
Uneek, Unik

Unitas
(American) united

Unser
(Last name as first name)
drives hard and fast

Unten
(English) not a friend
Untenn

Unus
(Latin) one
Unuss

Unwin
(Last name as first name)
modest

Updike
(Last name as first name)
from up above

Upjohn
(English) creative
Upjon

Upton
(English) highbrow writer
*Uppton, Uptawn, Upten,
Uptown*

Upwood
(Last name as first name)
upper woods is home

Uranus
(Greek) the heavens

Urban
(Latin) city dweller
*Urb, Urbain, Urbaine, Urbane,
Urben, Urbin, Urbun, Urby*

Uri
(Hebrew) short for Uriel;
light

Ury
(Hebrew) shining, lit by God

Uriah
(Hebrew) bright; led by God
Uri, Urie, Uryah

Urian
(Irish) from heaven
Urion

Urias
(Hebrew) Lord as my light;
old-fashioned
Uraeus, Uri, Uria, Urius

Uriel
(Hebrew) light; God-
inspired

Urien
(Mythology) lights life

Urs
(Scandinavian) bear; growly
Urso

Ursan
(French) from Orson;
softspoken
Ursen, Ursyn

Urteil
(German) judgment
Urteel, Urtiel

Urvano
(Spanish) city boy
Urbano

Urvine
(Place name) form of Irvine,
California
Urveen, Urvene, Urvi

Ury
(Hispanic) God-loving

Usaid
(Arabic) laughs

Usaku
(Japanese) moonlit

Usher
(Latin) decisive

Utah
(Place name) U.S. state

Uthman
(Arabic) bird
Uthmann

Utz
(American) befriends all

Uwe
(Welsh) gentle

Uziah
(Hebrew) believes

Uziel
(Hebrew) soothed by God's
strength

Uzondu
(African) attracts others

Vachel
(French) keeps cows
Vachell

Vadim
(French) creative
Vadeem

Vadin
(Hindi) speaks well

Vaduz
(Place name) city in Germany

Vail
(English) serene
*Bail, Bale, Vaile, Vaill, Vale,
Valle*

Vaino
(Welsh) from Vanora; white

Val
(Latin) short for Valery and
Valentine; strong
Vall

Vala
(Latin) from Valentine;
powerful

Valdemar
(Scandinavian) famous
leader
Waldemar

Valenti
(Italian) mighty; romantic
*Val, Valence, Valentin,
Valentyn*

Valentin
(Russian) healthy; robust
Val, Valeri

Valentine
(Latin) robust
*Val, Valentijn, Valentin,
Valentinian, Valentino,
Valentinus,, Valentyn,
Valentyne, Valyntine*

Valentino
(Italian) strong; healthy
Val

Valeri
(Russian) athletic; mighty
Val, Valerian, Valerio, Valry

Valerian
(Russian) strong leader
*Valerien, Valerio, Valerius,
Valery, Valeryan*

Vali
(Scandinavian) brave man

Valin
(Latin) from Valentin; tenacious
Valen, Valyn

Valu
(Polynesian) eight

Van
(Dutch) from the family of...
Vann, Von, Vonn

Vance
(English) brash
Vans, Vanse

Vanda
(Russian) form of Walter; wars

Vandan
(Hindi) saved

Vander
(Greek) short for Evander
Vand

Vandiver
(American) quiet
Van, Vand, Vandaver, Vandever

Vandwon
(African American) covert
Vandawon, Vandjuan

Vandyke
(Last name as first name) educated

Vane
(Last name as first name) gifted

Vannevar
(Scandinavian) from Evander; good

Vanslow
(Scandinavian) sophisticated
Vansalo, Vanselow, Vanslaw

Vanya
(Russian) right
Van, Yard, Yardy

Vardon
(French) also Varden; green hill is home
Varden, Verdon, Verdun

Varen
(Hindi) rain god Varun

Varesh
(Hindu) God is superior

Varick
(German) defender
Varrick, Warick, Warrick

Varil
(French) faithful

Varkey
(American) boisterous

Varlan
(American) tough
Varland, Varlen, Varlin

Varma
(Hindi) fruitful

Varner
(Last name as first name) formidable
Varn

Vartan
(Russian) gives roses

Varun
(Hindi) water lord; excellent
Varoun

Vas
(Slavic) protective
Vaston, Vastun, Vasya

Vasant
(Sanskrit) brings spring

Vashon
(American) delightful
Vashaun, Vashonne

Vasil
(Slavic) form of William; quiet
Vasile, Vasilek, Vasili, Vasilis, Vasilos, Vasily, Vassily

Vasilis
(Russian) also Vasili; king
Vasileios, Vasilij, Vasily, Vaso, Vasos, Vassilij, Vassily, Vasya, Wassily

Vasin
(Hindi) rules all

Vassil
(Bulgarian) king
Vass

Vasu
(Sanskrit) rich boy

Vaughn
(Welsh) compact
Vaughan, Vaunie, Von

Vea
(Vietnamese) short for Veasna; lucky

Veasna
(Vietnamese) fortunate

Veejay
(American) talkative
V.J., Vee-Jay, Vejay

Vegas
(Place name) from Las Vegas, Nevada
Vega

Vejis
(Invented) form of Regis; outgoing
Veejas, Veejaz, Vejas, Vejes

Velle
(American) tough
Vell, Velley, Velly, Veltree

Veltry
(African American) hopeful

Velvet
(American) smooth
Vel, Velvat, Velvit

Venancio
(Spanish) glorious

Vencel
(Hungarian) king

Venedict
(Greek) from Benedict;
blessed
Venedikt, Venka, Venya

Venezio
(Italian) glorious
Venetziano, Veneziano

Ventura
(Spanish) good fortune

Venturo
(Italian) lucky
Venturio

Verdun
(French) from verdant;
growing

Vere
(Latin) springlike

Vered
(Hebrew) rose-loving

Vergel
(Spanish) writer
Vergele, Virgil

Verile
(German) macho
Verill, Verille, Verol, Verrill

Verlie
(American) from Verle;
countrified
Verley

Verlyn
(African American) growing
*Verle, Verlin, Verllin, Verlon,
Verlyn, Virle, Vyrle*

Vermont
(Place name) U.S. state

Vern
(Latin) short for Vernon
Verne, Vernie, Verny

Vernados
(Greek) hearty

Verner
(German) resourceful
Vern, Verne, Vernir, Virner

Verniamin
(Greek) form of Benjamin;
son of the right hand

Vernon
(Latin) fresh and bright
*Lavern, Vern, Vernal, Verne,
Vernen, Vernin, Verney*

Verona
(Italian) man of Venice or
Verona, both Italian cities
Verone

Verrier
(French) faithful

Verrill
(German) manly
*Verill, Verrall, Verrell,
Verroll, Veryl*

Vester
(Latin) from Vesta; he who
guards the fire

Vesuvio
(Place name) Mount
Vesuvius; spontaneous

Vic
(Latin) short for Victor
Vick, Vickey, Vik

Vicente
(Spanish) winner
Vic, Vicentay, Visente

Victor
(Latin) victorious
*Vic, Vick, Vickter, Victer,
Victorien, Victorin, Vidor,
Vikki, Viktor, Vitorio,
Vittorio*

Vittorios
(Italian) victor

Vida
(Hebrew) beloved; vibrant

Vidal
(Spanish) full of vitality
Bidal, Videl, Videlio

Vidalo
(Spanish) energetic
Vidal

Vidar
(Scandinavian) soldier

Vidkun
(Scandinavian) gives

Vidor
(Hungarian) delightful

Viggo
(Scandinavian) exuberant
Viggoa, Vigo

Vigile
(American) vigilant
Vegil, Vigil

Vihs
(Hindu) increase

Vijay
(Hindi) winning
Bijay, Vijun

Vila
(Czech) from William
Vili, Ville

Viliami
(Slavic) from William; high goals

Villard
(French) village man

Villiers
(French) kind-hearted

Vilmos
(Italian) happy
Villmos

Vilok
(Hindu) to see

Vimal
(Hindi) unblemished

Vin
(Italian) short for Vincent
Vinn, Vinney, Vinni, Vinnie

Vinay
(Hindi) good manners

Vince
(English) short for Vincent
Vee, Vence, Vins, Vinse

Vincent
(Latin) victorious
Vencent, Vicenzio, Vin, Vince, Vincens, Vincente, Vincentius, Vincents, Vincenty, Vincenz, Vincenzio, Vincenzo, Vincien, Vinicent, Vinnie, Vinny, Vinzenze, Wincenty, Vinciente, Vinn, Vinny

Vincenzo
(Italian) conquerer
Vincenze, Vinnie, Vinny

Vine
(Latin) from Vin; wins

Vinod
(Hindi) effervescent

Vinson
(English) winning attitude
Venson, Vince, Vinny, Vins

Vinton
(English) town of wine; reveler

Vireo
(Latin) brave

Virgil
(Latin) holding his own; writer
Verge, Vergil, Vergilio, Virge, Virgie, Virgilio, Virgy

Virginius
(Latin) virginal
Virginio

Vischer
(Last name as first name) longing
Visscher

Vitale
(Italian) important

Vitalis
(Latin) bubbly; vital

Vitas
(Latin) animated
Vidas, Vite

Vito
(Italian) short for Vittorio; lively; victor
Veto, Vital, Vitale, Vitalis, Vitaly, Vitas, Vite, Vitus, Witold

Vittorio
(Italian) victorious
Vite, Vito, Vitor, Vitorio, Vittore

Vitus
(Latin) winning

Vivar
(Greek) alive
Viv

Vivek
(Hindi) wise

Vivian
(Latin) lively
Viviani, Vivien, Vivyan, Vyvian, Vyvyan

Vlad
(Russian) short for Vladimir

Vladimir
(Russian) glorious leader
Vlada, Vladameer, Vladamir, Vlademar, Vladimeer, Vlakimar, Wladimir, Wladimyr

Vladislav
(Czech) glorious leader

Vladja
(Russian) short for Vladislav

Volf
(Hebrew) form of Will; bold

Volker
(German) prepared to defend
Volk

Volney
(Greek) hidden

Volya
(Slavic) hopes

Von
(German) bright
Vaughn, Vonn, Vonne

Vonzie
(American) form of Fonzie;
personable
*Vons, Vonze, Vonzee,
Vonzey, Vonzi*

Voshon
(Slavic) generous

Vui
(African) saves

Waclaw
(Polish) glorified

Wade
(English) mover; crossing a
river
Wadie, Waide, Wayde

Wadell
(English) southerner
Waddell, Wade

Waden
(American) form of Jaden; fun
Wade, Wedan

Wadley
(Last name as first name)
by the water
Wadleigh, Wadly

Wadsworth
(English) homebody
Waddsworth, Wadswurth

Wagner
(German) musical; practical
*Wagg, Waggner, Waggoner,
Wagnar, Wagnur*

Wagon
(American) conveyance
Wag, Wagg, Waggoner

Wain
(English) industrious

Wainwright
(Last name as first name)
works hard
*Wain, Wainright, Wayne,
Wayneright, Waynewright,
Waynright, Wright*

Wait
(American) word as name;
patient
Waite

Wake
(Place name) island in the
Marshall Islands

Wakefield
(English) the field worker
Field, Wake

Wakely
(Last name as first name)
wet

Wakeman
(Last name as first name)
wet
Wake

Wal
(Arabic) short for Waleed;
baby

Walbert
(German) protective; stodgy

Walcott
(Last name as first name)
steadfast
Wallcot, Wallcott, Wolcott

Waldemar
(German) famous leader
Valdemar, Waldermar, Waldo

Walden
(English) calming
*Wald, Waldan, Waldi, Waldin,
Waldo, Waldon, Waldy, Welti*

Waldo
(German) short for Oswald;
zany
Wald, Waldoh, Waldy

Waleed
(Arabic) newborn
Waled, Walid

Walenty
(Polish) strong

Walerian
(Polish) powerful

Wales
(English) from Wales in the
United Kingdom
*Wael, Wail, Wails, Wale,
Waley, Wali, Waly*

Walford
(English) wealthy; from
Wales

Walfred
(English) from Wales; loyal

Wali
(Arabic) newborn

Walker
(English) distinctive
Walk, Wally

Wallace
(English) from Wales; charming
Wallas, Walley, Walli, Wallice, Wallie, Wallis, Wally, Walsh, Welsh

Waller
(English) man from Wales; confident

Wallis
(English) man from Wales; smooth

Walls
(American) walled
Walen, Wally, Waltz, Walz

Wally
(English) short for Walter
Wall, Walley, Walli, Wallie

Walmond
(Last name as first name) laidback

Walsh
(English) inquisitive
Walls, Welce, Welch, Wells, Welsh

Walt
(German) army leader
Waltey, Waltli, Walty

Walter
(German) army leader
Walder, Wallie, Wally, Walt, Walther, Waltur, Walty, Wat

Walther
(German) army leader; powerful

Walton
(English) shut off; protected
Walt, Walten, Waltin

Walworth
(English) introvert

Walwyn
(English) reticent
Walwin, Walwinn, Walwynn, Walwynne, Welwyn

Wang
(Chinese) hope; wish

Waqar
(Arabic) talkative

Warburton
(Last name as first name) still

Ward
(English) vigilant; alert
Warde, Warden, Worden

Wardell
(English) guarded

Warden
(English) watchful
Warde, Wardie, Wardin, Wardon

Wardley
(English) careful
Wardlea, Wardleigh

Ware
(English) aware; cautious
Warey, Wary

Warfield
(Last name as first name) cautious

Warford
(Last name as first name) defensive

Waring
(English) dashing
Wareng, Warin, Warring

Wark
(American) watchful

Warley
(Last name as first name) worthy people

Warner
(German) protective
Warne

Warren
(German) safe haven
Ware, Waren, Waring, Warrenson, Warrin, Warriner, Warron, Warry, Worrin

Warton
(English) defended town

Warwen
(American) defensive
Warn, Warwun, Warwun

Warwick
(English) lavish
War, Warick, Warrick, Warweck, Warwyc, Warwyck, Wick

Washburn
(English) bountiful
Washbern, Washbie, Washby

Washington
(English) leader
Wash, Washe, Washing

Wasim
(Arabic) pretty baby

Wat
(English) short for Watkins; jolly

Watford
(Last name as first name) softspoken

Watkins
(English) able
Watkens, Wattie, Wattkins, Watty

Watson
(English) helpful
Watsen, Watsie, Watsun, Watsy, Wattsson

Wave
(American) word as a name
Waive, Wave, Wayve

Waverley
(Place name) city in New South Wales
Waverlee, Waverli, Waverly

Way
(English) landed; smart
Waye

Wayland
(English) form of Waylon; country boy

Wayling
(English) the right way
Waylan, Wayland, Waylen, Waylin

Waylon
(English) country boy
Wallen, Walon, Way, Waylan, Wayland, Waylen, Waylie, Waylin, Waylond, Waylun, Wayly, Weylin

Wayman
(English) traveling man
Way, Waym, Waymon, Waymun

Waymon
(American) knowing the way
Waymond

Wayne
(English) wheeler and dealer
Wain, Wanye, Way, Wayn, Waynell, Waynne

Wazir
(Arabic) minister, advisor

Webb
(English) intricate mind
Web, Webbe, Weeb

Weber
(German) intuitive
Webb, Webber, Webner

Webley
(English) weaves; intuitive
Webbley, Webbly, Webly

Webster
(English) creative
Web, Webstar, Webstur

Weddel
(Last name as first name) has an angle

Weebie
(American) wily
Weebbi

Weido
(Italian) bright; personable
Wedo

Wel-Quo
(Asian) bothered
Wel

Welborne
(Last name as first name) where the well is
Welborn, Welbourne, Welburn, Wellborn, Wellborne, Wellbourn, Wellburn

Welby
(German) astute
Welbey, Welbi, Welbie, Wellby

Weldon
(Last name as first name) where the well is

Welford
(English) unusual
Walferd, Wallie, Wally

Wellington
(English) nobility
Welling

Wells
(English) place name; unique
Well, Wellie, Welly

Welsh
(English) form of Walsh
Welch, Wellsh

Welton
(English) spring town

Wenceslaus
(Polish) glorified king
Wenceslas, Wenczeslaw, Wenzel, Wiencyslaw

Wendell
(German) full of wanderlust
Wandale, Wend, Wendall, Wendel, Wendey, Wendie, Wendill, Wendle, Wendull, Wendy

Wenford
(English) confessing
Wynford

Went
(American) ambitious
Wente, Wentt

Wenworth
(English) adventures

Werner

Werner
(German) warrior

Wes
(English) short for Wesley
Wess, Wessie, Wessy

Wesh
(German) from the west

Wesley
(English) bland
Wes, Weslee, Wesleyan,
Weslie, Wesly, Wessley,
West, Westleigh, Westley,
Westly, Wezlee, Wezley

Wesson
(American) from the west
Wess, Wessie

West
(English) westerner
Weste, Westt

Westbrook
(Last name as first name)
from the west brook;
nature-loving
Brook, West, Westbrooke

Westby
(English) near the west

Westcott
(English) from a western
cottage
Wescot, Wescott, Westcot

Westie
(American) capricious
West, Westee, Westey,
Westt, Westy

Westleigh
(English) western
Westlea, Westlie, Wezlee

Westley
(English) from the west fields

Westoll
(American) open
West, Westall

Weston
(English) good neighbor
West, Westen, Westey,
Westie, Westy, Westin

Wether
(English) light-hearted
Weather, Weth, Wethar,
Wethur

Wetherby
(English) light-hearted
Weatherbey, Weatherbie,
Weatherby, Wetherbey,
Wetherbie

Wetherell
(English) light-hearted

Wetherly
(English) light-hearted

Whalley
(Last name as first name)
predicts

Wharton
(Last name as first name)
provincial
Warton

Wheat
(Invented) fair-haired
Wheatie, Wheats, Wheaty,
Whete

Wheatley
(Last name as first name)
fair-haired; fields of wheat
Whatley, Wheatlea,
Wheatleigh, Wheatly

Wheaton
(Last name as first name)
blond; wheat town

Wheel
(American) important player
Wheele

Wheeler
(English) likes cars; wheel
maker
Weeler, Wheel, Wheelie,
Wheely

Wheeless
(English) off track
Whelus

Wheelie
(American) big-wig
Wheeley, Wheels, Wheely

Whip
(American) friendly

Whistler
(English) melodic
Whis, Whistlar, Whistle,
Whistlerr

Whit
(English) short for Whitman
Whitt, Whyt, Whyte, Wit,
Witt

Whitby
(English) white-haired;
white-walled town

Whitcomb
(English) light in the valley;
shining
Whitcombe, Whitcumb

Whitelaw
(English) white
Whitlaw

Whitey
(English) fair-skinned
White

Whitfield
(English) from a white field

Whitford
(English) the light source

Whitley
(English) white area is home
Whitlea, Whitlee, Whitleigh

Whitman
(English) man with white hair
Whit, Whitty, Witman

Whitmore
(English) white
Whitmoor, Whittemore, Witmore, Wittemore

Whitney
(English) likes white spaces
Whit, Whitnee, Whitnie, Whitt, Whittney, Widney, Widny, Witt

Whitson
(English) son of Whit
Whitt, Witt

Whittaker
(English) outdoorsy
Whitaker, Whitt, Witaker, Wittaker

Wick
(American) burning
Wic, Wik, Wyck

Wickham
(Last name as first name) living in a hamlet
Wick

Wickley
(Last name as first name) coming from a small home
Wicley

Wilberforce
(German) wild and strong

Wilbert
(German) smart
Wilberto, Wilburt

Wilbur
(English) fortified
Wilbar, Wilber, Willbur, Wilburt, Willbur, Wilver

Wilburn
(German) brilliant
Bernie, Wil, Wilbern, Will

Wilder
(English) wild man
Wildar, Wilde, Wildey

Wildon
(Last name as first name) willing support
Wilden, Willdon

Wiles
(American) tricky
Wyles

Wiley
(English) cowboy
Wile, Willey, Wylie

Wilford
(English) willowy; peaceful wishes

Wilfred
(German) peacemaker
Wilferd, Wilfrid, Wilfride, Wilford, Wilfried, Wilfryd, Will, Willfred, Willfried, Willie, Willy

Wilfredo
(Italian) peaceful
Fredo, Wifredo, Willfredo

Wilhelm
(German) resolute; determined
Wilhelmus, Wilhem, Willem

Wilkie
(English) willful

Wilkins
(English) affectionate
Welkie, Welkins, Wilk, Wilkens, Wilkes, Wilkie, Wilkin, Willkes, Willkins

Wilkinson
(English) son of Wilkin; capable
Willkinson

Will
(English) short for William; likable
Wil, Wilm, Wim, Wyll

Willard
(German) courageous
Wilard, Willerd

William
(English) staunch protector
Bill, Will, Willeam, Willie, Wills, Willy, Willyum, Wilyam

Williams
(German) brave
Williamson

Willie
(German) short for William; protective
Will, Wille, Willey, Willeye, Willi, Willy, Wily

Willis
(German) youthful
Willace, Willece, Willice, Wills, Willus

Willoughby
(Last name as first name) lives with grace
Willoughbey, Willoughbie

Wills
(English) willful

Wilmer
(German) resolute; ambitious
Willmar, Willmer, Wilm, Wilmar, Wilmyr, Wylmar, Wylmer

Wilmot
(German) tough-minded

Wilson
(English) extraordinary
Willson, Wilsen, Wilsun, Willson

Wilt
(English) talented
Wiltie

Wilton
(English) practical and open
Will, Wilt, Wiltie, Wylten, Wylton

Win
(German) flirtatious
Winn, Winnie, Winny

Winchell
(English) meandering
Winchie, Winshell

Wind
(American) word as name; breezy
Windy

Windell
(German) wanderer
Windelle, Windyll

Windsor
(English) royal
Win, Wincer, Winnie, Winny, Winsor, Wyndsor, Wynser

Winfield
(English) peace in the country
Field, Winifield, Winnfield, Wynfield, Wynnfield

Winfried
(English) peaceful

Wing
(Chinese) in glory
Wing-Chiu, Wing-Kit

Wingate
(Last name as first name) glorified

Wingi
(American) spunky

Wings
(American) soaring; free
Wing

Winkel
(American) bright; conniving
Wink, Winky

Winlove
(Filipino) winning favor

Winslow
(English) friendly
Winslo, Wynslo, Wynslow

Winsome
(English) gorgeous; charming
Wins, Winsom, Winz

Winston
(English) dignified
Win, Winn, Winnie, Winny, Winstan, Winsten, Winstonn, Winton, Wynstan, Wynsten, Wynston

Winter
(English) born in winter
Win, Winnie, Winny, Wintar, Winterford, Wintur, Wynter, Wyntur

Winthrop
(English) winning; stuffy
Win, Winn, Winnie, Winny, Wintrop

Winton
(English) winning
Wynten, Wynton

Winward
(English) friendly

Wiss
(American) carefree
Wissie, Wissy

Wit
(Polish) life
Witt, Wittie, Witty

Witek
(Polish) from Victor; conqueror

Witha
(Arabic) vibrant, handsome

Witold
(Polish) lively

Witt
(Slavic) lively
Witte

Witter
(Last name as first name) alive

Witton
(Last name as first name) lively

Witty
(American) humorous
Wit, Witt, Witte, Wittey, Wittie

Wize
(American) smart
Wise, Wizey, Wizi, Wizie

Wladymir
(Polish) famous ruler
Vladimir

Wladyslaw
(Polish) good leader
Slaw

Wohn
(African American) form of
John

Wojtek
(Polish) comforter; warrior

Wolcott
(English) home of wool

Wolf
(German) short for
Wolfgang
Wolff, Wolfie, Wolfy

Wolfe
(German) wolf; ominous
Wolf, Wolff, Wulf, Wulfe

Wolfgang
(German) talented; a wolf
walks
*Wolf, Wolff, Wolfgans,
Wolfy, Wulfgang*

Wolley
(American) form of Wally
Wolly

Wood
(English) short for Woodrow
Woode, Woody

Woodery
(English) woodsman
*Wood, Wooderree,
Woodree, Woodri, Woodry,
Woods, Woodsry, Woody*

Woodfield
(Last name as first name)
enjoys the woods

Woodfin
(English) attractive
*Wood, Woodfen, Woodfien,
Woodfyn, Woodie, Woody*

Woodford
(Last name as first name)
forester

Woodrow
(English) special
Wood, Woodrowe, Woody

Woodruff
(Last name as first name)
smooth; natural

Woodson
(Last name as first name)
son of Wood; suave

Woodward
(English) watchful
*Wood, Woodie, Woodard,
Woodwerd, Woody*

Woodville
(Last name as first name)
from town of trees

Woody
(American) jaunty
*Wooddy, Woodey, Woodi,
Woodie*

Woolsey
(English) leader
*Wools, Woolsi, Woolsie,
Woolsy*

Worcester
(English) secure

Word
(American) word as name;
talkative
Words, Wordy, Wurd

Worden
(American) careful
Word, Wordan, Wordun

Wordsworth
(English) poetic
Words, Worth

Worie
(English) cautious

Worsh
(American) from the word
worship; religious
Wor

Worth
(English) deserving; special
*Werth, Worthey, Worthie,
Worthington, Worthy, Wurth*

Worthington
(English) fun; worthwhile
*Worth, Worthey, Worthing,
Worthingtun, Wurthington*

Wrangle
(American) cowboy
Wrang, Wrangler, Wrangy

Wray
(American) cornered

Wren
(American) leader of men
Ren, Rin, Rinn, Wrenn

Wright
(English) clear-minded;
correct
Right, Rite, Wrighte, Write

Wrisley
(American) smart
Wrisee, Wrislie, Wrisly

Wriston
(American) good proportions
Wryston

Wulf
(Hebrew) wolf
Wolf

Wyatt
(French) ready for combat
Wiatt, Wy, Wyat, Wyatte, Wye, Wyeth

Wybert
(Last name as first name) good profile

Wyborn
(Last name as first name) well-born

Wyck
(English) light

Wyclef
(American) trendy
Wycleff

Wycliff
(English) edgy
Cliffie, Cliffy, Wicliff, Wyclif, Wycliffe

Wydee
(American) form of Wyatt; fighter
Wy, Wydey, Wydie

Wylie
(English) charmer
Wiley, Wye, Wylee

Wymann
(English) contentious
Wimann, Wye, Wyman

Wymer
(English) rambunctious; fighter

Wyn
(Welsh) gregarious

Wyndham
(English) from a hamlet
Windham, Wynndham

Wynne
(English) dear friend
Winn, Wyn, Wynn

Wyshawn
(African American) friendly
Shawn, Shawny, Why, Whysean, Wieshawn, Wye, Wyshawne, Wyshie, Wyshy

Wystan
(English) struggles

Wythe
(English) fair

Wyton
(English) fair-haired; crowd-pleaser
Wye, Wytan, Wyten, Wytin

Wyze
(American) sizzle; capable
Wise, Wye, Wyse

Xan
(Greek) short for Alexander; defends mankind

Xander
(Greek) short for Alexander
Xan, Xande, Xandere, Xandre

Xanthin
(Greek) from Xanthe; gold hair

Xanthus
(Greek) golden-haired child

Xanthos
(Greek) attractive

Xat
(American) saved
Xatt

Xaver
(Spanish) from Xavier; home

Xaverius
(Spanish) from Xavier; home
Xaverious, Xaveryus

Xavier
(Arabic) shining
Saverio, Xaver, Zavey, Zavier

Xavion
(Spanish) from Xavier; home

Xaxon
(American) happy
Zaxon

Xayvion
(African American) dwells in new house
Savion, Sayveon, Sayvion, Xavion, Xayveon, Zayvion

Xebec
(French) from Quebec; cold
Xebeck, Xebek

Xen
(African American) original
Zen

Xenik
(Russian) sly
Xenic, Xenick, Xenyc,
Xenyck, Xenyk

Xeno
(Greek) gracious
Xenoes, Zene, Zenno,
Zenny, Zeno, Zenos

Xenon
(Greek) gracious

Xenophon
(Greek) gracious

Xenos
(Greek) with grace
Xeno, Zenos

Xerarch
(Greek) dancing
Xerarche

Xeres
(Persian) from Xerxes; leads
Xeries

Xerxes
(Persian) leader
Xerk, Xerky, Zerk, Zerkes,
Zerkez

Xhosas
(African) South African tribe
Xhoses, Xhosys

Xiaoping
(Chinese) brightest star

Ximen
(Spanish) obeys
Ximenes, Ximon, Ximun

Ximena
(Spanish) good listener

Xing-Fu
(Chinese) happy

Xi-Wang
(Chinese) optimistic

Xuthus
(Last name as first name)
long-suffering

Xyle
(American) helpful
Zye, Zyle

Xylo
(Greek) from Xylon; noisy

Xylon
(Greek) forester

Xyshaun
(African American) zany
Xye, Zye, Zyshaun, Zyshawn

Xyst
(Archaelogy) a portico;
systematic
Xist

Xystum
(Greek) promenade
Xistoum, Xistum, Xysoum

Xystus
(Greek) promenade
Xistus

Yaameen
(Hebrew) right hand

Yachna
(Hebrew) gracious

Yadon
(Last name as first name)
different
Yado, Yadun

Yadua
(Hindi) judged

Yael
(Hebrew) teacher
Yail, Yaley, Yalie

Yagil
(Hebrew) celebrant

Yahya
(Arabic) vital
Yahiya

Yakar
(Hebrew) adored

Yakez
(Scandinavian) celestial

Yale
(German) producer

Yamato
(Japanese) mountain;
scaling heights

Yana
(Native American) bearlike

Yancy
(American) vivacious
Yanci, Yancie, Yancy, Yanzie

Yanis
(Hebrew) God's gift
Yannis, Yantsha

Yank
(American) Yankee
Yanke

Yankel
(Hebrew) supportive
Yaki, Yakov, Yekel

Yannis
(Greek) believer in God
Yannie

Yanton
(Hebrew) from Jonathon; overwhelming

Yao
(Chinese) athletic; Thursday's child

Yaphet
(Hebrew) from Japheth; gorgeous
Yapheth, Yefat, Yephat

Yarb
(Gypsy) spicy

Yarden
(Hebrew) flowing
Yard, Yardan, Yarde, Yardene, Yardun

Yardley
(English) adorned; separate
Yard, Yarde, Yardie, Yardlea, Yardlee, Yardly, Yardy

Yarkon
(Hebrew) green

Yarom
(Hebrew) sings
or Yaron

Yash
(Hindi) famous

Yasin
(Arabic) seer

Yasir
(Arabic) rich

Yasmuji
(Asian) flowering

Yasuo
(Japanese) calm

Yasutaro
(Japanese) peaceful

Yates
(English) smart; closed
Yate, Yattes, Yeats

Yave
(Hindi) from Yavar; giving

Yavin
(Hebrew) believes

Yawo
(African) Thursday's child

Yazeed
(Arabic) growing in spirit

Yeats
(English) gates
Yates

Yediel
(Hebrew) loved by Jehovah

Yehoshua
(Hebrew) alive by God's salvation

Yehuda
(Hebrew) praised
Yehudi

Yemin
(Hebrew) guarded

Yemyo
(Asian) serene

Yen
(Chinese) calming; capable

Yens
(Vietnamese) Yen; calm

Yeoman
(English) helping
Yeomann, Yo, Yoeman, Yoman, Yoyo

Yero
(African) studious

Yesel
(Hebrew) won by God

Yeshaya
(Hebrew) treasured

Yesher
(Hebrew) God's salvation

Yeshurun
(Hebrew) focuses on God

Yevgeny
(Russian) life-giving

Yianni
(Greek) creative

Yigal
(Turkish) lively

Yimer
(Scandinavian) giant

Yishai
(Hebrew) from Jessie; proud

Yisrael
(Hebrew) struggles with God

Yitro
(Hebrew) from Jethro; jolly

Yitzhak
(Hebrew) laughing
Yitz, Yitzchak

Yngvar
(Scandinavian) god of fertility
Ingvar;

Yo
(Vietnamese) truthful

Yoav
(Hebrew) form of Joab

Yobachi
(African) prayerful

Yochanan
(Hebrew) from John; believes in a gracious Lord
Yohanan

Yoel
(Hebrew) form of Joel

Yogi
(Japanese) yoga practicer

Yohann
(German) form of Johann
Yohan, Yohn

Yojiro
(Japanese) hopes

Yonah
(Hebrew) form of Jonah

Yonatan
(Hebrew) from Jonathon;
straightforward
Yonathan, Yonathon

Yong
(Chinese) brave

Yoosef
(Hebrew) favorite
Yosef

Yoran
(Hebrew) to sing

Yorick
(Literature) Hamlet's jester

York
(English) affluent
*Yorke, Yorkee, Yorkey, Yorki,
Yorky*

Yorker
(English) rich
York, Yorke, Yorkur

Yosef
(Hebrew) form of Joseph
Yose, Yoseff, Yosif

Yosemite
(Place name) natural
wonder

Yoshe
(Hebrew) wise

Yoshiaki
(Japanese) attractive

Yoshikatsu
(Japanese) good

Yoshinobu
(Japanese) goodness

Yoshio
(Japanese) giving

Yossel
(Hebrew) favored
Yoska, Yossi

Yosuke
(Japanese) helps

Young
(English) fledgling
Jung, Younge

Yov
(Russian) reliable

Yovan
(Slavic) form of Jovan

Yu
(Chinese) shiny; smart

Yuan
(Chinese) circle

Yudel
(Hebrew) jubilant
Yudi

Yui
(Chinese) yue (moon);
universal

Yuji
(Japanese) snow

Yuke
(American) short for Yukon

Yuki
(Japanese) loves snow

Yukichi
(Japanese) lucky snow

Yukio
(Japanese) man of snow

Yukon
(Place name) individualist

Yul
(Chinese) infinity

Yule
(English) Christmas-born
Yuel, Yul, Yuley, Yulie

Yuli
(Basque) childlike

Yuma
(Place name) city in
Arizona; cowboy
Yumah

Yurcel
(Turkish) the best

Yuri
(Russian) dashing
*Yurah, Yure, Yurey, Yurie,
Yurri, Yury*

Yurik
(Japanese) Yuri's child

Yuris
(Latin) farmer
Yures, Yurus

Yursa
(Japanese) lily; delicate

Yutu
(African) hunter

Yuval
(Hebrew) celebrant

Yves
(French) honest; handsome
Eve, Ives

Yvonn
(French) attractive
Von, Vonn, Yvon

Zab
(American) slick
Zabbey, Zabbi, Zabbie, Zabby

Zac
(Hebrew) short for Zachariah; Lord remembers
Zacary, Zach, Zachary, Zachry

Zacary
(Hebrew) form of Zachary
Zac, Zacc, Zaccary, Zaccry, Zaccury

Zaccheus
(Hebrew) unblemished
Zac, Zacceus, Zack

Zace
(American) pleasure-seeking
Zacey, Zacie, Zase

Zach
(Hebrew) short for Zachary
Zac, Zachy

Zachariah
(Hebrew) Lord remembers
Zac, Zacaria, Zacarias, Zacary, Zacaryah, Zaccaria, Zaccariah, Zaccheus, Zach, Zachaios, Zacharia, Zacharias, Zacharie, Zachary, Zacheriah, Zachery, Zacheus, Zachey, Zachi, Zachie, Zachy, Zack, Zackariah, Zackerias, Zackery, Zak, Zakarias, Zakarie, Zakariyyah, Zakery, Zechariah, Zekariah, Zekeriah, Zeke, Zhack

Zacharias
(Hebrew) devout
Zacharyas

Zachary
(Hebrew) spiritual
Zacary, Zacchary, Zach, Zackar, Zackarie, Zak, Zakari, Zakri, Zakrie, Zakry

Zack
(Hebrew) short for Zachary
Zacky, Zak

Zade
(Arabic) flourishing; trendy
Zaid

Zadok
(Hebrew) unyielding
Zadek, Zaydie, Zadik, Zayd, Zaydok

Zafar
(Hindi) victor
Zaphar

Zafir
(Arabic) wins
Zafeer, Zafyr

Zahavi
(Hebrew) golden child

Zahir
(Hebrew) bright
Zaheer, Zahur

Zahur
(Arabic) flourishes

Zain
(American) zany
Zane, Zayne

Zaire
(Place name) country in Africa; brash

Zakary
(Hebrew) form of Zachary

Zaki
(Arabic) virtuous
Zak

Zale
(Greek) strong
Zail, Zaley, Zalie, Zayle

Zalman
(Hebrew) peaceful (comes from Solomon)
Salman, Zaloman

Zamil
(German) from Samuel; jovial
Zameel, Zamyl

Zamir
(Hebrew) lyrical
Zameer, Zamyr

Zan
(Hebrew) well-nourished
Xan, Zander, Zandro, Zandros, Zann

Zander
(Greek) short for Alexander
Zande, Zandee, Zandey, Zandie, Zandy

Zandy
(American) high-energy
Zandee, Zandi

Zane
(English) debonair
Zain, Zay, Zayne, Zaynne

Zano
(American) unique
Zan

Zappa
(American) zany
Zapah, Zapp

Zaquan
(American) combo of Za and Quan; duplicitous
Zaquon, Zequan, Zequon

Zared
(Arabic) gold

Zarek
(Aramaic) light

Zartavious
(African American) unusual
Zar, Zarta

Zashawn
(African American) fiery
Zasean, Zash, Zashaun, Zashe, Zashon, Zashone

Zavier
(Arabic) form of Xavier

Zavion
(American) smiling
Zavien

Zawon
(American) combo of Za and Won; doubter
Zawan, Zewan, Zewon

Zbigniew
(Polish) free of malice; calming

Zeandre
(American) combo of Zee and Andre; confident
Zeandrae, Zeandray

Zeb
(Hebrew) short for Zebediah
Zebe

Zebby
(Hebrew) believer; rambunctious
Zabbie, Zeb, Zebb, Zebbie

Zebediah
(Hebrew) gift from God
Zeb, Zebadia, Zebb, Zebbie, Zebby, Zebedee, Zebediah, Zebi, Zebidiah

Zebulon
(Hebrew) uplifted
Zebulen, Zebulun, Zevulon, Zevulun

Zechariah
(Hebrew) form of Zachariah
Zeke

Zed
(Hebrew) energetic
Zedd, Zede

Zedediah
(Hebrew) gift from God
Zededia, Zedidia, Zedidiah

Zedekiah
(Hebrew) believing in a just God
Zed, Zeddy, Zedechia, Zedechiah, Zedekias

Zeeman
(Dutch) seafaring
Zeaman

Zeevy
(American) sly
Zeeve, Zeevi, Zeevie

Zeffy
(American) explosive
Zeff, Zeffe, Zeffi, Zeffie

Zeke
(Hebrew) friendly; outgoing
Zeek, Zekey, Zeki

Zel
(American) hearty

Zelig
(Hebrew) holy; happy
Selig, Zel, Zeligman, Zelik

Zen
(Japanese) spiritual

Zenas
(Greek) from Zeus; powerful
Zenios, Zenon

Zeno
(Greek) philosophical; stoic
Zeney, Zenie, Zenno, Zeny

Zenobios
(Greek) living Zeus; lively
Zenobius, Zinov, Zinovi

Zenon
(Greek, Polish) godlike

Zent
(American) zany
Zynt

Zephaniah
(Hebrew) protected by God
Zeph, Zephan

Zephariah
(Hebrew) Jehovah's light

Zephyr
(Greek) breezy
Zayfeer, Zayfir, Zayphir, Zefar, Zefer, Zefir, Zeffer, Zefur, Zephir, Zephiros, Zephirus, Zephyrus

Zero
(Arabic) nothing
Zeroh

Zerond
(American) helpful
Zerre, Zerrie, Zerry, Zerund

Zeshon
(African American) zany
Zeshaune, Zeshawn

Zeth
(American) form of Seth; unpredictable
Zethe

Zeus
(Greek) vibrant
Zues

Zev
(Hebrew) form of Zebulon; respected
Zevv

Zevediah
(Hebrew) form of Zebediah; broken dreams
Zevedia, Zevidia, Zevidiah

Zevi
(Hebrew) brisk
Zevie

Zevulon
(Hebrew) form of Zebulon; honorable
Zevulonn

Zhivago
(Russian) dashing; romantic
Vago

Zhong
(Chinese) middle brother; loyal

Zia
(Hebrew) in motion
Zeah, Ziah

Zie
(American) compelling
Zye, Zyey

Ziggy
(American) zany

Zigmand
(American) form of Sigmund
Zig, Ziggy

Zikomo
(African) grateful

Zimran
(Hebrew) sacred

Zindel
(Yiddish) form of Alexander
Zindil

Zino
(Greek) philosopher
Zeno

Zion
(Hebrew) sign
Sion, Zeione, Zi, Zione, Zye

Zipkiyah
(Native American) archer

Ziv
(Hebrew) energetic
Zeven, Zevy, Ziven, Zivon

Ziven
(Polish) lively
Ziv, Zivan, Zyvan

Ziya
(Turkish) light

Zoilo
(Greek) life

Zol
(American) jaunty
Zoll

Zoltan
(Hungarian) lively

Zoma
(American) loquacious
Zome

Zorba
(Greek) pleasure seeker
Zorbah, Zorbe

Zorby
(Greek) tireless
Sorby, Zorb, Zorbie

Zorshawn
(African American) jaded
Zahrshy, Zorsh, Zorshie, Zorshon, Zorshy

Zowie
(Greek) life
Zowey, Zowy

Zuberi
(African) powerful
Zooberi, Zubery

Zuhayr
(Arabic) flowers
Zuhair

Zuni
(Native American) creative

Zuriel
(Hebrew) believer

Zvon
(Croatian) short for Zvonimir
Zevon, Zevonn

Zyke
(American) high-energy
Zykee, Zyki, Zykie, Zyky

A

Aaliyah
(Hebrew) moving up
Aliya

Aamori
(African) good

Abay
(Native American) growing
Abai, Abbay, Abey, Abeye

Abayomi
(African) giving joy

Abby
(English) happy
Abbee, Abbey, Abbi, Abbie, Abbye

Abella
(French) vulnerable; capable
Abela, Abele, Abell, Bela, Bella

Abery
(Last name as first name) supportive
Abby, Aberee, Abrie, Abry

Abia, Abiah
(Arabic) excellent
Ab, Aba, Abbie

Abigail
(Hebrew, English, Irish) joyful
Abagail, Abbegayle, Abbey, Abbie, Abby, Abegail, Abey, Abigal, Abigale, Abigayle, Abygail, Abygale, Abygayle, Gail, Gayle

Abilene
(Place name) Texas town; southern girl
Abalene, Abi, Abiline, Aby

Abiola
(Spanish) God-loving
Abby, Abi, Biola

Abira
(Hebrew) strong
Adira, Amiza

Abra
(Hebrew) form of Abraham; strong and exemplary
Aba, Abbee, Abbey, Abbie, Abby

Abrianna
(American) insightful
Abriana, Abryana, Abryanna, Abryannah

Abrielle
(American) form of Abigail; rejoices
Abby, Abree, Abrey, Abrie, Abriella, Abryelle

Acacia
(Greek) everlasting; tree
Akaysha, Cacia, Cacie, Case, Casey, Casha, Casia, Caysha, Kassy, Kaykay

Acantha
(Greek) thorny; difficult

Accalia
(Latin) stand-in
Accal, Accalya, Ace, Ackie

Achantay
(African American) reliable
Achantae, Achanté

Ada
(German) noble; joyful
Adah, Addah, Adeia, Aida

Adaani
(French) pretty; noble
Adan, Adane, Adani, Daani, Dani

Adabelle
(American) combo of Ada and Belle; noble beauty
Ada, Adabel, Addabel, Belle

Adaeze
(African) prepared
Adaese

Adah
(Biblical) decorated
Ada, Adie, Adina, Dina

Adair
(Scottish) innovative
Ada, Adare, Adayr, Adayre, Adda

Adalia
(Spanish) spunky
Adahlia, Adailya, Adallyuh, Adaylia

Adalind
(American) from Adaline; noble

Adalinda
(French) from Adele; nobility

Adamina
(Hebrew) earth child

Adanna
(Spanish) beautiful baby
Adana

Adar
(Hebrew) respected

Adara
(Greek) lovely
Adarah, Adrah

Addison
(English) awesome
Addeson, Addie, Addisen, Addison, Addy, Addyson, Adeson, Adisen, Adison

Addy
(English) nickname for Addison; distinctive; smiling
Addee, Addie, Addy, Addye, Adie, Ady

Adeen
(American) decorated
Addy, Adeene, Aden, Adene, Adin

Adela
(Polish) peacemaker

Adelaide
(German) calming; distinguished
Ada, Adalaid, Adalaide, Adelade, Adelaid, Laidey Adelinda

Adeline
(English) sweet
Adaline, Adealline, Adelenne, Adelina, Adelind, Adlin, Adline

Adelita
(Spanish) form of Adela; noble
Adalina, Adalita, Adelaina, Adelaine, Adeleta, Adey, Audilita, Lita, Lite

Adelka
(German) form of Adelaide; noble
Addie, Addy, Adel, Adelkah, Adie

Adelle
(German) giving
Adel, Adell, Addy

Adelpha
(Greek) beloved sister
Adelfa, Adelphe

Adena
(Hebrew) precious
Ada, Adenna, Adina, Adynna, Deena, Dena

Aderyn
(Hebrew) from Adira; powerful

Adesina
(African) threshold child

Adia
(African) God's gift

Adiel
(Africa) goat; tough-willed
Adie, Adiell, Adiella

Adina
(Hebrew) high hopes
Addy, Adeen, Adeena, Adine, Deena, Dena, Dina

Adisa
(Hispanic) friendly
Adesa, Adissa

Aditi
(Hindi) free

Adiva
(Arabic) gracious

Adjanys
(Hispanic) lively
Adjanice, Adjanis

Adline
(German) reliable
Addee, Addie, Addy, Adleen, Adlene, Adlyne

Adolpha
(German) noble wolf; strong girl
Adolpham

Adonia
(Greek) beauty
Adona, Adonea, Adoniah, Adonis

Adora
(Latin) adored child
Adorae, Adoray, Dora, Dore, Dorey, Dori, Dorree, Dorrie, Dorry

Adorna
(Latin) adorned

Adra
(Greek) beauty

Adria
(Latin) place name
Adrea

Adrian
(English) rich
Adrien, Adryan, Adryen

Adrianna
(Greek, Latin) rich; exotic
Addy, Adree, Adriana, Adrie, Adrin, Anna

Adrienne
(Latin) wealthy
Adreah, Adreanne, Adrenne, Adriah, Adrian, Adrien, Adrienn, Adrin, Adrina

Aereale
(Hebrew) form of Ariel; light and sprite
Aereal, Aeriel, Areale

Aeronwenn
(Welsh) white; aggressor
Awynn

Affrica
(Irish) nice

Afra
(Arabic) deer; lithe
Aphra, Aphrah, Ayfara

Afton
(English) confident
Aft, Aftan, Aften, Aftie

Africa
(Place name) continent
Afrika

Afua
(African) baby born on Friday
Afuah

Agafi
(Greek) form of Agnes; pure
Ag, Aga, Agafee, Agaffi, Aggie

Agapi
(Greek) love
Agapay, Agappe, Agape

Agasha
(Greek) form of Agatha; long-suffering
Agashah, Agashe

Agata
(Italian) good girl

Agate
(English) gemstone; precious girl
Agatte, Aget, Aggey, Aggie

Agatha
(Greek) kind-hearted
Agath, Agathah, Agathe, Aggey, Aggie, Aggy

Agatta
(Greek) form of Agatha; honorable and patient
Ag, Agata, Agathi, Aggie, Agi, Agoti, Agotti

Agave
(Botanical) strong-spined; genus of plants
Ag, Agavay, Aggie, Agovay

Agentina
(Spanish) form of Argentina; colorful
Agen, Agente, Tina

Aggie
(Greek) kind-hearted
Aggee, Aggy

Aglaia
(Greek) goddess of beauty; splendid

Agnes
(Greek) pure
Ag, Aggie, Aggnes, Aggy, Agnas, Agnes, Agness, Agnie, Agnus, Nessie

Aharona
(Hebrew) beloved
Arni, Arnina, Arona

Ahimsa
(Hindu) virtuous

Ahulani
(Hawaiian) heavenly place

Ahvanti
(African) focused
Avanti

Aida
(Arabic) gift
Aeeda, Ayda, Ayeeda, Ieeda

Aidan
(Irish) from the male name Aidan; fiery
Aden, Aiden, Aidyn

Aileen
(Irish, Scottish) fair-haired beauty
Aleen, Alene, Alenee, Aline, Allee, Alleen, Allene, Allie, Ally

Ailey
(Irish) form of Aileen; light and friendly
Aila, Ailee, Ailie, Ailli, Allie

Ailsa
(Irish) noble

Aimee
(French) beloved
Aime, Aimey, Aimi, Aimme, Amee, Amy

Aimee-Lynn
(American) combo of Aimee and Lynn; lovable
Aimee Lynn, Aimeelin, Aimeelynn

Aimer
(German) leader; loved
Aimery, Ame, Amie

Aine
(Irish) blissful
Ayne

Ainsley
(Scottish) meadow;
outdoorsy
*Ainslea, Ainslee, Ainsleigh,
Ainslie, Anes, Anslie,
Aynslee, Aynsley*

Aintre
(Irish) joyous estate
*Aintree, Aintrey, Antre,
Antry*

Aisha
(Arabic, African) life; lively
*Aaisha, Aaysha, Aeesha,
Aiesha, Aieshah, Ayeesha,
Ayisha, Aysha, Ieashia,
Ieeshah, Iesha*

Aisling
(Irish) dreamy
Aislinn, Ashling, Isleen

Aislinn
(Irish) dreamy
Aisling, Aislyn, Aislynn

Aithne
(Irish) fiery
Aine, Eithne, Ena, Ethne

Akako
(Japanese) red; blushes

Akala
(Hawaiian) also Akela;
respected

Akasha
(American) combo of A and
Kasha; happy; swimmer

Ala
(Arabic) excellent
Alla

Alabama
(Place name) western
Bama

Alaine
(Gaelic) lovely
*Alaina, Alaiyne, Alenne,
Aleyna, Aleyne, Allaine,
Allayne*

Alala
(Roman mythology) sister
of Mars; protected
Alalah

Alameda
(Spanish) poplar tree; growth

Alana
(Scottish) pretty girl
*Alahna, Alahnah, Alaina,
Alainah, Alanah, Alanna,
Alannah, Allana, Allie, Ally*

Alanis
(French) shining star
*Alaniss, Alannis, Alannys,
Alanys*

Alason
(German) form of Alison;
noble; bright
Ala, Alas

Alathea
(English) heals and helps
Aleta, Letitia, Letty

Alaula
(English) heals and helps

Alaygrah
(Invented) form of Allegra;
frisky
Alay, Allay

Alaytheea
(Invented) form of Aleithea;
honest
Alay, Thea, Theea

Alba
(Italian) white

Alberta
(French) bright-eyed
*Alb, Albertah, Albie, Albirta,
Alburta, Bertie, Berty*

Albertina
(Portuguese) bright

Albertine
(English) form of Albert;
bright
*Albertyne, Albie, Albyrtine,
Teeny*

Albie
(American) casual
Albee, Albey, Alby, Albye

Albina
(Italian) white
Albyna

Alcina
(Greek) magical; strong-
willed
*Alcee, Alcie, Als, Alsena,
Alsie. Cina, Seena, Sina*

Alda
(German) the older child

Aldona
(American) sweet
Aldone

Alea
(Arabic) excellent
*Alaya, Aleah, Aleeah, Alia,
Ally*

Aleah
(American) combo of Allie
and Leah
Alayah, Alayja

Aleeza
(Hebrew) joy
Aliza

Alegria
(Spanish) beautiful movement
Allegria

Aleksandra
(Polish, Russian) helpful

Aleshia
(Greek) honest
Aleeshia, Aleeshya, Aleshya, Alyshia, Alyshya

Alejandra
(Spanish) defender
Alijandra, Alyjandra

Alessa
(Italian) helper
Alesa

Alessandra
(Italian) defender of mankind
Aless, Alessa

Alessia
(Italian) nice
Alesha, Alyshia, Allyshia

Alethea
(Greek) truthful
Alathea, Aleethia, Aletha, Aletie, Altheia, Lathea, Lathey

Aletta
(Greek) carefree
Aleta, Aletta, Eletta, Letti, Lettie, Letty

Alex
(English) protector

Alexa
(Greek) short for Alexandra
Alecksa, Aleksah, Alex, Alexia, Alixa, Alyxa

Alexakai
(American) combo of Alexa and Kai; merry
Alexikai, Lexi, Kai

Alexandra
(Greek, English, Scottish, Spanish) regal protector
Alejandra, Alejaundro, Alex, Alexandrah, Alexandria, Alexis, Alezandra, Allesandro, Ally, Lex, Lexi, Lexie

Alexandrine
(French) helpful
Alexandrie, Alex, Ally, Lexi, Lexie

Alexi
(Greek) short for Alexis; defends; sweet
Alexie, Alexy, Alixi, Alixie, Alixy, Alyxi, Alyxie

Alexia
(Greek) helpful, bright
Alexea, Alexiah, Alixea, Lex, Lexey, Lexie, Lexy

Alexis
(Greek) short for Alexandra; helpful; pretty
Aleksus, Alexius, Alexus, Alexys, Lex, Lexey, Lexi, Lexie, Lexis, Lexus

Alfonsith
(German) aggressive
Alf, Alfee, Alfey, Alfey, Alfie, Alfonsine, Allfrie, Alphonsine, Alphonsith

Alfre
(English) short for Alfreda; seer
Alfree, Alfrey, Alfri, Alfrie, Alfry

Alfreda
(English) wise advisor
Alfi, Alfie, Alfred, Alfredah, Alfrede, Alfredeh, Freda, Freddy

Ali
(Greek) short for Alexandra; defending
Aley, Allee, Alley, Ally, Aly

Alianet
(Spanish) honest; noble
Alia, Aliane

Alice
(Greek) honest
Alece, Alicea, Alise, Alliss, Ally, Allys, Alyse, Alysse, Lisie, Lisy, Lysse

Aliceann
(American) combo of Alice and Ann; well-born; southern feel
Alice Ann, Alicean, Alice-Ann

Alicia
(Greek) delicate; lovely
Alisha

Alida
(Greek) stylish
Aleda, Aleta, Aletta, Alidah, Alita, Lee, Lida, Lita, Lyda

Alima
(Hebrew) strong

Alina
(Scottish, Slavic) fair-haired
Aleena, Alene, Aline, Allene, Allie, Ally, Allyne, Alyna, Lena, Lina

Aline
(Polish) variant of Alina; noble family

Alisa
(Hebrew) happy
Alissa, Allisa, Allissah, Alyssa

Alisha
(Greek) happy; truthful
Aleesha, Alesha, Alicia, Ally, Allyshah, Alysha, Lesha, Lisha

Alison
(Scottish) noble
Alisen

Alissa
(Greek) pretty
Alesa, Alessa, Alise, Alissah, Allee, Allie, Ally, Allyssa, Alyssea

Alita
(Native American) sparkling

Aliya
(Hebrew) rises; sweetheart
Aleeya, Alya

Alka
(Polish) distinctive
Alk, Alkae

Allegra
(Italian) snappy
Aligra, All, Allagrah, Allie, Alligra, Ally

Allena
(Greek) outstanding
Alena, Alenah, Allana, Allie, Ally

Allene
(Greek) wonderful
Alene, Alyne

Allessandra
(Italian) kind-hearted
Allesandra

Allie
(Greek) smiling
Ali, Allee, Alli, Ally, Allye

Allison
(English) kind-hearted
Alisen, Alison, Allie, Allisan, Allisen, Allisun, Ally, Allysen, Allyson, Alysen, Alyson, Sonny

Allura
(Hispanic) alluring
Alura

Ally
(Greek) pure heart
Allee, Alleigh, Alley, Alli, Allie

Allyson
(English) another form of Allison
Alisaune, Allysen, Allysun, Alyson

Allysse
(Greek) smooth
Allice, Allyce, Allyss

Alma
(Latin) good; soulful
Almah, Almie, Almy

Almeria
(Arabic) princess
Alma, Almara, Almaria, Almer, Almurea, Als

Almirah
(Spanish, Arabic) princess
Allmeerah, Almira, Elmira, Mira

Alodie
(Origin unknown) thriving
Alodee

Aloha
(Hawaiian) love

Alona
(Jewish) sturdy oak
Allona

Alondra
(Spanish) bright
Alond, Alondre, Alonn

Alouette
(French) birdlike
Allie, Allo, Allou, Allouetta, Alou, Alowette

Aloyse
(German) renowned
Aloice, Aloise, Aloyce

Alpha
(Greek) first; superior
Alf, Alfa, Alfie, Alph, Alphah, Alphie

Alston
(English) a place for a noble
Allie, Ally, Alstan, Alsten, Alstun

Alta
(Latin) high place; fresh

Altea
(Polish) healer

Althaea
(Latin, Italian) healing

Althea
(Greek, English) demure; healer
Althe, Althey, Althia, Althie, Althy, Thea, They

Alva
(Spanish) fair; bright
Alvah

Alvada
(American) evasive
Alvadah, Alvayda

Alverna
(English) truthful friend (elf friend)
Alver, Alverne, Alvernette

Alvernise
(English) form of Alverne; honest (elf friend)
Alvenice

Alvina
(English) beloved; friendly
Alvee, Alveena, Alvie, Alvine, Alvy

Alvita
(Latin) charismatic

Alyda
(French) soaring
Aleda, Alida, Alita, Lida, Lyda

Alys
(English) noble

Alysia
(Greek) compelling
Aleecia, Alesha, Alicia, Alish, Alycia

Alyssa
(Greek) flourishing
Alissa, Allissa, Allissae, Ilyssah, Lissa, Lyssa, Lyssy

Alyx
(English) variant of Alex; protects

Amabe
(Latin) loved
Ama

Amabelle
(American) loved
Amabel, Amahbel

Amada
(Latin, Spanish) loved one
Ama, Amadah

Amal
(Arabic) optimistic
Amahl

Amalia
(Hungarian) industrious

Amalina
(German) worker
Am, Ama, Amaleen, Amaline, Amalyne

Amalita
(Spanish) hopeful

Amanda
(Latin, English, Irish) lovable
Amand, Amandah, Amandy, Manda, Mandee, Mandi, Mandy

Amandra
(American) variant of Amanda; lovely
Amand, Mandee, Mandi, Mandra, Mandree, Mandry, Mandy

Amara
(Greek, Italian) unfading beauty
Am, Amarah, Amareh, Amera, Amura, Mara

Amarillo
(Place name) a city in Texas; cowgirl
Ama, Amari, Amarilla, Amy, Rillo

Amaris
(Hebrew) beloved; dedicated
Amares

Amaryllis
(Greek) fresh flower
Ama, Amarillis

Amber
(French) gorgeous and golden; semiprecious stone
Ambar, Amberre, Ambur, Amburr

Amber-Dee
(American) combination of Amber and Dee; golden jewel; spontaneous
Amber D, Amber Dee

Amberkalay
(American) combo of Amber and Kalay; beautiful energy
Amber-Kalé, Amber-Kalet

Amberlee
(American) combo of Amber and Lee
Amberlea, Amberleigh, Amberley, Amberli, Amberly, Amburlee

Amberlyn
(American) combo of Amber and Lyn
Amberl, Amberlin, Amberlynn, Amlynn

Amboree
(Last name as first name) precocious
Ambor, Ambree

Ambrin
(Greek) long life

Ambrosette
(Greek) eternal
Amber, Ambie, Ambro, Ambrosa, Ambrose

Ambrosia
(Greek) eternal
Ambroze, Ambrozeah, Ambrozia

Ambrosina
(Greek) everlasting
Ambrosine

Amelia
(German) industrious
*Amalee, Amaylyuh, Amele,
Ameleah, Ameli, Amelie,
Amelya, Amilia*

Amera
(Arabic) of regal birth
Ameera, Amira

America
(American) patriotic
*Amer, Amerca, Americah,
Amerika, Amur*

Amethyst
(Greek) precious gem
Amathist, Ameth

Amica
(Latin) good friend
Ameca, Ami, Amika

Amici
(Italian) friend
Amicie, Amie, Amisie

Amie
(French) loved one

Amiga
(Spanish) friend
Amigah

Amina
(Arabic) trustworthy
Amena, Amine

Aminta
(Latin) protects

Amira
(Arabic) rules/nurtures

Amity
(Latin) a good friend
Amitee, Amitey, Amiti

Amor
(Spanish) love
Amora, Amore

Amora
(Spanish) love

Amorelle
(French) lover
*Amoray, Amore, Amorel,
Amorell*

Amoretta
(French) little love
*Amoreta, Amorreta,
Amorretta*

Amorette
(French) tiny love
Amorrette

Amorita
(Spanish) loved

Amy
(Latin) loved one
*Aimee, Amee, Amey, Ameyye,
Ami, Amie, Amye, Amye*

Amykay
(American) combo of Amy
and Kay
Amikae

Amylynn
(American) combo of Amy
and Lynn
Ameelyn, Amilynn, Amylyn

Amyrka
(Spanish) lively
*Amerka, Amurka, Amyrk,
Amyrrka*

Anabelle
(American) combo of Ana
and Belle; lovely
*Anabel, Anabell, Annabelle,
Anabella*

Anabril
(Spanish) merciful; pretty
Anabrelle, Anna, Annabril

Anais
(French) variant of Anne;
graceful

Anala
(Hindi) fiery

Analia
(Hebrew) gracious; hopeful
*Ana, Analea, Analeah,
Analiah, Analya*

Analeese
(Scandinavian) gracious
*Analece, Analeece,
Annaleese*

Analicia
(Spanish) combo of Ana
and Licia; gracious
sweetheart
*Analice, Analicea, Analisha,
Licia*

Analisa
(American) combo of Ana
and Lisa; lovely
Analise, Annalisa, Anna-Lisa

Analy
(American) graceful;
gracious
Analee, Anali

Analynne
(American) combo of Ana
and Lynne
*Analinn, Analynn,
Annalinne, Annalynn*

Anand
(Hindi) joyful; profound
Anan, Ananda

Anastace
(Spanish) from Anastasia;
reborn
*Anastayce, Anestace,
Anestayce, Anystace,
Anystayce*

Anastasiya
(Greek, Russian) reborn;
royal
Anastasia, Anastasya

Anastay
(Greek) born again;
renewed
Ana, Anastae, Anastie

Anastice
(Latin) from Anatasia;
reborn
*Anasteece, Anesteece,
Anestice, Anysteece,
Anystice*

Anatola
(Greek, French) dawn
Anatol, Anatole

Anayancy
(Spanish) combo of Ana
and Yancy; buoyant
*Ana Yancy, Anayanci,
Anayancie, Ana-Yancy*

Anaysis
(Latin) from Anatasia;
reborn
Anaysys

Anchoret
(Welsh) beloved girl

Ancret
(Welsh) short for Anchoret;
beloved

Ander
(Greek) feminine

Anders
(Scandinavian) stunning
*Andars, Andie, Andurs,
Andy*

Andes
(Greek) feminine
Andee

Andi
(English) casual
Andee, Andey, Andie, Andy

Andraa
(Greek, French) feminine
Andrah

Andrea
(Greek) feminine
*Andee, Andi, Andie, Andra,
Andrae, Andre, Andreah,
Andreena*

Andreana
(Greek) bold heart
*Andreanna, Andriana,
Andrianna, Andryana,
Andryanna*

Andreanne
(American) combo of
Andrea and Anne
Andreane, Andrie, Andry

Andree
(Greek) strong woman
Andrey, Andrie, Andry

Andrenna
(Scottish) pretty; gracious
Andreene, Adrena

Andrianna
(Greek) feminine
Andree, Andy

Andromeda
(Greek) beautiful star
Andromedah

Aneka
(Polish) forgiving

Anemone
(Greek) breath of fresh air

Anewk
(Invented) form of Anouk

Ange
(Greek) from Angela;
angelic

Angel
(Latin) sweet; angelic
*Angelle, Angie, Anjel,
Annjell*

Angela
(Greek) divine; angelic
*Angelena, Angelica,
Angelina, Angelle, Angie,
Gela, Nini*

Angelia
(American) angelic
messenger
Angelea, Angeliah

Angelica
(Latin) angelic messenger
*Angie, Anjeleka, Anjelica,
Anjelika, Anjie*

Angelika
(Greek) angel
*Angelyka, Angilika,
Angilyka, Angylika*

Angelina
(Latin) angelic
*Ange, Angelyna, Angie,
Anje, Anjelina, Anjie*

Angeline
(American) angelic
Angelene, Angelline

Angelique
(Latin, French) angelic
Angel, Angeleek, Angelik, Angie, Anjee, Anjel, Anjelique

Angelle
(Latin) angelic
Ange, Angell, Anje, Anjell, Anjelle

Angharad
(Welsh) graceful
Ancrett, Angahard

Angie
(Latin) angelic
Angey, Angi, Angye, Anjie

Aniece
(Hebrew) gracious
Ana, Anesse, Ani, Anice, Annis, Annissa

Aniela
(Polish) sent by God
Ahneela

Anika
(Hebrew) hospitable
Anec, Anecca, Aneek, Aneeka, Anic, Anica, Anik, Annika

Anila
(Hindi) wind girl

Anisha
(English) purest one
Aneesha, Anysha

Anissa
(Greek) a completed spirit
Anisa, Anise, Anysa, Anyssa, Anysse

Anita
(Spanish) gracious
Aneda, Aneeta, Anitta, Anyta

Anitra
(Invented) combo of Anita and Debra
Anetra, Anitrah, Annitra

Anjali
(Hindi) pretty; honored
Anjaly

Anjana
(Hindi) merciful; pretty
Anjann

Anjelica
(Latin) angelic
Anjelika

Anjeliett
(Spanish) little angel
Anjel, Anjeli, Jelette, Jeliett, Jeliette, Jell, Jelly

Anjul
(French) jovial
Angie, Anjewel, Anji, Anjie, Anjool

Ann
(Hebrew) loving; hospitable
Aine, An, Ana, Anna, Anne, Annie, Ayn

Ann-Dee
(American) variant of Andy; graceful
Andee, Andey, Andi, Andy, Ann Dee, Anndi

Anna
(English, Italian, German, Russian, Polish) gracious
Ana, Anae, Anah, Annah, Anne, Anuh

Annabella
(Italian) lovely girl
Anabela, Anabella, Annabela

Annabelle
(English) lovely girl
Anabell, Anabelle, Annabell

Annairis
(American) combo of Anna and Iris; sweet
Anairis, Ana-Iris, Anna Iris

Annamaria
(Italian) combo of Anna and Maria; merciful and holy
Anamaria, Anna-Maria, Annamarie

Anna-Pearl
(American) Anna and Pearl; dated
Anapearl, Anna Pearl, Annapearl

Anne
(English) generous

Anneka
(Scandinavian) from Ann; gracious girl
Anneke

Anneliese
(Scandinavian) gracious; (German) religious
Aneliece, Aneliese

Annella
(Scottish) graceful
Anell, Anella, Anelle

Annemarie
(German) combo of Anne and Marie
Anmarie, Ann Marie, Anne-Marie, Annmarie

Annes
(Hebrew) hospitable

Annette
(American) vivacious; giving
Anette, Ann, Anne, Annett, Annetta, Annie, Anny

Anne-Louise
(American) combo of Anne and Louise; sweet
Anlouise, Ann Louise, Annelouise, Annlouise, Ann-Loweez

Annice
(English) pure of heart

Annie
(Hebrew, Irish) gracious; hip
Ann, Annee, Anney, Anni, Anny

Annika
(Scandinavian) gracious
Anika

Anninka
(Russian) gracious; graceful

Annis
(English) pure

Annissa
(Greek) gracious; complete
Anissa, Anni, Annie, Annisa

Annunciata
(Italian) noticed

Anona
(Botanical) pineapple; fresh

Anora
(Latin) honored

Anouk
(French) form of Ann

Anshaunee
(African American) combo of Ann and Shaunee; happy
Annshaunee, Anshawnee

Ansley
(English) happy in the meadow
Annesleigh, Ans, Anslea, Anslee, Ansleigh, Ansli, Anslie

Anstass
(Greek) resurrected; eternal
Ans, Anstase, Stace, Stacey, Stass, Stassee

Anstice
(Greek) everlasting
Anst, Steece, Steese, Stice

Anthea
(Greek) flowering
Anthia

Antigone
(Greek) impulsive; defiant

Antique
(Word as name) old soul
Anteek, Antik

Antoinette
(Latin) quintessential; (French) feminine form of Antoine
Antoine, Antoinet, Antwanett, Antwonette, Antwonette, Toinette, Tonette

Antonetta
(Greek) praised
Antoneta

Antonia
(Latin) perfect
Antone, Antonea, Antoneah,

Antonian
(Latin) valuable
Antoinette, Antonetta, Toni, Tonia, Tonya

Antonine
(Greek) praised
Antonyne

Antwanette
(African American) form; prized
Antwan, Antwanett

Anusha
(Armenian) sweet

Anya
(Russian) grace

Aoife
(Irish) beauty

Aphra
(Hebrew) earthy; sentimental
Af, Affee, Affey, Affy, Afra, Aphree, Aphrie

Aphrodite
(Greek) goddess of love and beauty
Afrodite, Aphrodytee

Apolinaria
(Spanish) form of Greek god Apollonia; martyr
Apolinara

Apollonia
(Greek) sun goddess
Apolinia, Apolyne, Appollonia

Apple
(Botanical) fruit; quirky
Apel, Appell

April
(Latin) month of the year; springlike
Aprel, Aprile, Aprille, Apryl

Aqua
(Spanish) colorful
Akwa

Arabella
(Latin) answer to a prayer; beauty
Arabel, Arabela, Arabelle, Arbel, Arbella, Bella, Belle, Orabele, Orabella

Arabelle
(Latin) divine
Arabell

Araceli
(Latin) heavenly
Ara, Aracelli, Ari

Aracelle
(Spanish) flamboyant; heavenly
Ara, Aracel, Aracell, Araseli, Celi

Arachne
(Greek) weaver; spider

Araminta
(English) unique; precious dawn
Ara, Arama, Aramynta, Minta

Araylia
(Latin) golden
Araelea, Aray, Rae, Ray

Arbra
(American) form of Abra; sensitive
Arbrae

Arcelia
(Spanish) treasured
Arcey, Arci, Arcilia, Arla, Arlia

Arcelious
(African American) treasured
Arce, Arcel, Arcelus, Arcy, Arselious

Archon
(American) capable
Arch, Archee, Archi, Arshon

Ardath
(Hebrew) ardent
Ardee, Ardie, Ardith, Ardon

Ardele
(Latin) enthusiastic; dedicated
Ardell, Ardella, Ardelle, Ardine

Arden
(Latin) ardent; sincere
Ardan, Ardena, Ardin, Ardon, Ardyn

Ardiana
(Spanish) ardent
Ardi, Ardie, Diana

Ardie
(American) enthusiastic; special
Ardee, Ardi

Areika
(Spanish) pure
Areka, Areke, Arika, Arike

Arekah
(Greek) virtuous; loving

Arelie
(Latin) golden girl
Arelee, Arely, Arlea

Aretha
(Greek) virtuous; vocalist
Areetha

Aretta
(Greek) virtuous
Arette, Arie

Argenta
(Latin) silver

Argentina
(Place name) confident; land of silver
Arge, Argen, Argent, Argenta, Argie, Tina, Tinee

Argosy
(French) bright
Argosee, Argosie

Argus
(Greek) bright
Arguss

Argyle
(French, American) complicated
Argie, Argile, Argy, Argylle

Ari
(Hebrew) short for Ariel; lioness
Aree, Arey, Arie, Ary

Aria
(Hebrew) from Ariel; lioness
Arya

Ariadne
(Greek) holiness
Aryadne

Ariana
(Greek) righteous

Arianda
(Greek) helper
Ariand

Ariane
(Greek) very gracious
Arianne, Aryahn

Arianne
(French) kind
Ana, Ari, Ariann

Arianwen
(Welsh) from Aeronwen; blessed

Aridatha
(Hebrew) flourishing
Ar, Arid, Datha

Arisca
(Greek) form of Arista; best; delight
Ariska, Ariske, Arista

Ariel
(French, Hebrew) heavenly singer
Aeriel, Airey, Arielle

Ariella
(French) lioness
Ariela, Aryela, Aryella

Aries
(Latin) zodiac sign of the ram; contentious
Arees

Arin
(Arabic) spreads truth
Aryn

Arista
(Greek) wonderful

Aristelle
(Greek) wonder
Aristela, Aristella

Aritha
(Greek) virtuous
Arete, Aretha

Arizona
(Place name) cowgirl
Zona

Arketta
(Invented) outspoken
Arkett, Arkette, Arky

Arlea
(Greek) heavenly
Airlea, Arlee, Arleigh, Arlie, Arly

Arleana
(American) form of Arlene; dedicated
Arlena, Arlina

Arlen
(Irish) devoted
Arlin, Arlyn

Arlena
(Irish) dedicated
Arlana, Arlen, Arlenna, Arlie, Arlina, Arlyna, Arrlina, Lena, Lina, Linney

Arlene
(Irish) dedicated
Arlee, Arleen, Arlie, Arline, Arlyne, Arlynn, Lena, Lina

Arlette
(French) loyal
Arlet

Armanda
(French) disciplined

Armani
(French) fashionable
Armanee, Armanie, Armond, Armonee, Armoni, Armonie

Armida
(Latin) armed; prepared
Armi, Armid, Army

Arminell
(Latin) nobility
Arminel

Arnette
(English) little eagle; observant
Arn, Arnee, Arnet, Arnett, Ornette

Arosell
(Last name as first name) loyal
Arosel

Arpine
(Romanian) dedicated
Arpyne

Artemisia
(Mythology) from Artemis, goddess of moon/hunting
Arta, Arte, Artema

Arthlese
(Irish) rich
Arth, Arthlice, Artis

Artriece
(Irish) stable
Artee, Artreese, Arty

Aruna
(Hindi) baby of dawn

Arvis
(American) special
Arvee, Arvess, Arvie, Arviss, Arvy

Asabi
(African) outstanding

Ash
(Hebrew) short for Ashra; lucky
Ashe

Asha
(Hebrew) lucky
Aasha, Ashah, Ashra

Ashandra
(African American) dreamer
Ashan, Ashandre

Ashanti
(African) place name; graceful
Ashantay, Anshante

Ashantia
(American) outgoing
Ashantea, Ashantiah

Asharaf
(Hindi) wishful
Asha, Ashara

Ashby
(English) farm of ash trees
Ashbee

Asher
(Hebrew) blessed
Ash

Ashla
(English) form of Ashley;
gentle

Ashland
(Irish) dreamlike
*Ashelyn, Ashlan, Ashleen,
Ashlin, Ashlind, Ashline,
Ashlinn*

Ashlei
(English) variant of Ashley;
pretty
Ashee, Ashie, Ashly, Ashy

Ashleigh
(English) outdoorsy (ash
tree meadow)
Ashlynn, Ashton

Ashley
(English) woodland sprite;
meadow of ash trees
*Ash, Ashie, Ashlay, Ashlea,
Ashlee, Ashleigh, Ashli,
Ashlie, Ashly*

Ashlyn
(English) natural
Ashlin, Ashlinn, Ashlynn

Ashonika
(African American) pretty
Ashon, Ashoneka, Shon

Ashton
(English) place name; from
an eastern town; sassy
*Ashe, Ashten, Ashtun,
Ashtyn*

Asia
(Greek) reborn; continent
*Ashah, Asiah, Asya, Aysia,
Azhuh*

Asma
(Arabic) exalted; loyal

Asmay
(Origin unknown) special
Asmae, Asmaye

Asoka
(Japanese) from Asako;
morning baby

Asp
(Greek) short for Aspasia;
witty

Aspasia
(Greek) witty
Aspashia, Aspasya

Aspen
(Place name) earth mother
Aspin, Aspyn, Azpen

Asphodel
(Greek) lily beauty

Asra
(Hindi) pure
Azra

Asta
(Greek) star

Astera
(Greek) star-like
Asteria, Astra, Astree, Astrie

Astra
(Greek) star
Astrah, Astrey

Astrid
(Scandinavian, German)
beautiful goddess
*Aster, Asti, Astred, Astri,
Astridd, Astryd, Astrydd,
Atty, Estrid*

Asysa
(Arabic) lively
Aesha, Asha, Aysah

Atalanta
(Greek) athletic; fleet-footed
Addi, Atlante, Attie

Athalia
(Hebrew) ambitious

AthaSue
(American) combo of Atha
and Sue; sweet and
discriminating
Atha, Athasue, Atha-Sue

Athelean
(Greek) eternal; precocious
Athey, Athi

Athene
(Chinese) wise

Athena
(Greek) wise woman;
goddess of wisdom in
mythology
*Athene, Athenea, Athina,
Xena, Zena*

Athie
(Hebrew) wise
Athee, Athey, Athy

Atifa
(Arabic) compassionate
Ateefah

Atropos
(Mythology) one of the Greek Fates; cuts

Aube
(French) from Aubrey; experiments

Aubrey
(German) noble being; (French) blonde leader
Aubery, Aubey, Aubrea, Aubree, Aubreye, Aubri, Aubrie, Aubry

Auburne
(American) tough-minded
Aubee, Aubern, Auberne, Aubey, Aubi, Aubie, Auburn, Auby

Audie
(French) rich; (American) daring
Audee, Audey, Audi, Audy, Audye

Audra
(English) exciting
Audrah, Audray

Audrey
(Old English) strong and regal
Audi, Audie, Audra, Audree, Audreen, Audreye, Audri, Audrianna, Audrianne, Audrie, Audrina, Audry

Augustina
(Latin) great
Agustico, Agustin, Augusine, Augustine, Gusty, Tina, Tino

Augusta
(Latin) revered
Augustah, Auguste, Augustia, Augustyna, Austina

Augustine
(Latin) dignified; worthwhile
Augestinn, Augusta, Augustina, Augustyna, Augustyne, Austie, Austina, Austine, Tina

Aunjanue
(French) sparkling

Aunshaunte
(African American) believer
Anshauntay, Aunshauntay, Aunshawntay, Aunshawnte, Shauntae, Shauntay, Shaunte

Aura
(Greek) breeze
Arra

Aurease
(Latin) excellent, golden
Auree, Aureese, Aurey, Auriece, Aury

Aurelia
(Latin) dawn goddess
Arelia, Aura, Auralea, Aurel, Aurelie, Auria, Auriel, Aurielle

Auriel
(Latin) gold
Auriol

Aurora
(Latin) morning glow
Aurorah, Aurore, Rory

Aurysia
(Latin) gold
Arys, Arysia, Aurys

Austen
(Literature) austere
Austyn

Austeena
(American) statuesque
Austeenah, Austie, Austina

Austine
(Latin) respected
Austen, Austene, Austine, Austin

Autra
(Latin) gold
Aut

Autumn
(Latin) joy of changing seasons
Autum, Autumm

Ava
(Latin) pretty; delicate bird
Avah, Eva

Avalon
(Celtic) paradise

Avalynne
(American) combo of Ava and Lynne
Avaline, Avalinn, Avalynn, Avelinn

Avena
(Latin) basic; oat field

Avengelica
(Spanish) avenging
Angelica, Avenga, Avengele, Gelica

Averil
(French) flighty
Ava, Averile, Averill, Averyl, Averyll, Aviril

Avery
(French) flirtatious
Avary, Averee, Averi, Averie

Aves
(Greek) breath of fresh air

Avis
(Latin) little bird

Aviana
(Latin) fresh

Avianca
(Latin) fresh

Avisae
(American) springlike
Ava, Avas, Aves, Avi

Aviva
(Hebrew) springlike
Avivah

Avolonne
(African American) happy
*Avalonn, Ave, Avelon, Avlon,
Avo, Avolon, Avolunne*

Avon
(English) graceful
*Avaughn, Avaugn, Avonn,
Avonne*

Avril
(Irish) April; springlike

Avrit
(Hebrew) fresh
Avie, Avree, Avret, Avrie

Axelle
(French) serene
Axel, Axell

Aya
(Hebrew) bird in flight

Ayan
(Hindi) pure
Ayun

Ayanna
(Hindi) innocent
Ayunna

Ayeisha
(Arabic) feminine
*Aeesha, Aieshah, Asha,
Ayeeshea, Ayisa, Iasha,
Yeisha, Yeishee, Yisha, Yishie*

Ayla
(Hebrew) strong as an oak

Aylee
(Hebrew) light

Ayleen
(Hebrew) light-hearted
Aylene

Aylin
(Spanish) strong
Aylen

Aylwin
(Welsh) beloved
Ayle, Aylwie

Aynona
(Hebrew) form of Anne;
graceful
*Ayn, Aynon, Aynonna,
Aynonne*

Azalea
(Latin) earthy; flowering
Azalee, Azelea

Azenet
(Spanish) sun god's gift
Aza, Azey

Azriella
(Hebrew) variant of Ariella;
lioness
Azriela, Azryela, Azryella

Azimah
(Japanese) from Azami;
flower

Aziza
(African) beloved; vibrant
Asisa

Azucena
(Spanish) lily pure
Azu, Azuce, Azucina

Azura,
(French) blue-eyed
*Azuhre, Azur, Azure, Azurre,
Azzura*

Baako
(Japanese) promising; happy

Baba
(American) fun-loving

Bachiko
(Japanese) happy

Babe
(Latin) little darling; baby

Babette
(French) little Barbara

Babianne
(American) combo of Babi
and Anne; fun-loving
*Babi, Babiane, Babyann,
Biann, Bianne*

Babs
(American) short for
Barbara; lively

Bachi
(Japanese) happy
*Bachee, Bachey, Bachie,
Bochee*

Baden
(German) friendly
Boden, Bodey

Baderinwa
(African) worthy

Badger
(Irish) badger
Badge

Badriyyah
(Arabic) surprise

Baek
(Origin unknown) mysterious

Bagent
(Last name as first name) baggage
Bage

Bagula
(German) enthused
Baggy

Bahaar
(Hindi) spring

Bahama
(Place name) islands; sun-loving
Baham

Bahati
(African) lucky girl
Baha, Bahah

Bahija
(Arabic) excelling
Bahiga

Bahir
(Arabic) striking
Bah, Baheer, Bahi

Bahira
(Arabic) bright mind

Bai
(Chinese) outgoing

Baiben
(Irish) sweet; exotic
Babe, Babe, Bai, Baib, Baibe, Baibie, Baibin

Bailey
(English) bailiff
Bailee, Baylee, Bayley, Baylie

Bailon
(American) variant of Bailey; dancing; happy
Bai, Baye, Baylon

Bain
(American) thorn; pale
Baine, Bane, Bayne

Baird
(Irish) ballad singer
Bayrde

Bairn
(Scottish) child
Bairne

Baize
(Polish) from Bazyli; royalty
Bayze, Baze

Baka
(Hindi) crane; long-legged
Baca

Bakara
(African) noble

Bakul
(Hindi) flowering
Bakula

Bakura
(Hebrew) ripe; prime
Bikura

Balala
(Hindi) hopes

Balaniki
(Hawaiian) angelic

Balbina
(Latin) stammers
Balbine

Baldree
(German) brave; loquacious
Baldry

Bali
(Place name) island near Indonesia; exotic

Ballou
(American) outspoken
Bailou, Balou

Balvino
(Spanish) powerful
Balvene, Balveno

Bambi
(Italian) childlike; baby girl
Bambee, Bambie, Bambina, Bamby

Bamp
(American) vivid
Bam, Bampy

Banan
(Punjabi) held close

Banessa
(American) combo of B and Vanessa; hopeful
B'Nessa, Banesa, Benessa

Banht
(Hindi) fire

Banita
(Hindi) girl; thoughtful

Banjoko
(Asian) joy

Bano
(Persian) bride
Bannie, Banny, Banoah, Banoh

Bao
(Chinese) adorable; creative

Bao-Jin
(Chinese) precious gold

Bao-Yo
(Chinese) jade; pretty

Baptista
(Latin) one who baptizes
Baptiste, Batista, Battista, Bautista

Bara
(Hebrew) chosen
Bari, Barra

Barb
(Latin) short for Barbara

Barbara
(Greek, Latin) unusual stranger
Babb, Babbett, Babbette, Babe, Babett, Babette, Babina, Babita, Babs, Barb, Barbary, Barbe, Barbette, Barbey, Barbi, Barbie, Barbra, Barby, Basha, Basia, Bobbie, Bobi

Barbro
(Swedish) extraordinary
Bar, Barb, Barbar

Barcelona
(Place name) exotic
Barce, Lona

Barcie
(American) sassy
Barsey, Barsi

Bariah
(Arabic) does well

Barika
(Hebrew) chosen one

Barkait
(Arabic) shines
Barkat

Barran
(Arabic) song

Barrett
(Last name as first name) happy girl
Bari, Barret, Barrette, Barry, Berrett

Barrie
(Irish) markswoman
Barry, Bari, Barri, Barry

Barron
(Last name as first name) bright
Bare, Baron, Barrie, Beren, Beron

Barrow
(Last name as first name) sharp; sly
Barow

Basey
(Last name as first name) beauty
Bacie, Basi

Baseylea
(American) combo of Basey and Lee; pretty
Basey, Basilea, Basilee, Leelee

Bashiyra
(Arabic) joyful

Basia
(Greek) regal
Basha, Basya

Basilia
(Greek) regal
Basila, Basilea, Basilie

Basimah
(Arabic) smiling
Basima, Basma

Bastienna
(French) from male name Bastien; clever
Bastee, Bastienne

Bat
(German) female warrior
Bet

Bathia
(German) woman who wars
Basha, Baspa, Batia, Batya, Bitya

Bathilda
(German) woman in war
Bathild, Bathilde, Berthilda, Berthilde

Bathsheba
(Hebrew) beautiful; daughter of Sheba
Bathseva, Batsheba, Batsheva, Batshua, Sheba

Bathshira
(Arabic) happy; seventh

Batia, Batya
(Hebrew) daughter of God
Batea

Batice
(American) warrior; attractive
Bateese, Batese, Batiece, Batty

Batini
(African) ponders much

Batzra
(Hebrew) daughter of God

Bay
(Vietnamese) Saturday's child; patient; unique
Bae, Baye

Baylor
(French) of the bay; water-loving
Bayler

Bayo
(African) bringing joy

Baynes
(American) from male name Baines; confident
Bain, Baines, Bayne

Bayonne
(Greek) joyful victor
Bay, Baye, Bayonn, Bayonna, Bayunn

Bea
(American) short for Beatrice

Beata
(German) blessed
Bayahta, Beate

Beatha
(Latin) blessed
Betha

Beatrice
(Latin) blessed woman, joyful
Beat, Beatrisa, Beatrise, Beattie, Bebe, Bee, Beitris, Beitriss, Bibi, Treece, Trice

Beatrix
(Latin) happy

Beatriz
(American) joy

Bebe
(French) baby
Babee, Baby, Bebee

Bebhinn
(Irish) sweet girl

Becca
(Hebrew) short for Rebecca; lively
Bekka

Bechet
(French)

Bechira
(Hebrew) chosen child

Becky
(English) short for Rebecca; spunky
Becki, Beki

Bedelia
(Irish) form of Bridget; powerful

Bedriska
(Irish) from Bedelia; active

Beegee
(American) laidback; calm
B.G., Begee, Be-Gee

Beeja
(Hindi) the beginning; happy
Beej

Bee-Sun
(Filipino) nature-loving; glad
Bee Sun

Bego
(Hispanic) spunky
Beago

Begonia
(Botanical) flower

Behira
(Hebrew) shines

Behorah
(Invented) friend
Be, Behi, Behie, Behora

Beige
(American) simple; calm
Bayge

Beige-Dawn
(American) clear morning
Bayge-Dawn, Beige Dawn

Beila
(Spanish) beautiful

Beilarosa
(Spanish) combo of Beila and Rosa; beautiful rose
Beila, Beila-Rosa, Beila-Rose, Beiliarose, Rose

Bel
(Latin) beauty

Bela
(Czech) white
Belah

Belanie
(Invented) combo of B and Melanie; lovely
Bela, Belan, Belanee, Belaney, Belani, Belle

Belann
(Spanish) pretty
Bela, Belan, Belana, Belane, Belanna

Belem
(Spanish) pretty
Bel, Beleme, Bella

Belen
(Latin) beauty

Belgica
(American) white
Belgika, Belgike, Belgyke, Bellgica

Belia
(Spanish) beauty
Belea, Beliano, Belica, Belicia, Belya, Belyah

Belicia
(Spanish) believer
Belia

Belinda
(Latin, Spanish) beautiful serpent
Belynda

Belita
(Spanish) pretty little one; (French) beauty

Bella
(Italian) beautiful

Bellace
(Invented) pretty
Bellase, Bellece, Bellice

Belle
(French) beautiful
Bela, Bele, Bell, Bella

Bellina
(French) beautiful

Belva
(Latin) beautiful view

Belvia
(Invented) practical
Bell, Belva, Belve, Belveah

Bemedikta
(Scandinavian) from Benedicta; blessed
Benedikte

Bena
(Native American) pheasant; highbrow

Bendite
(Latin) well blessed
Ben, Bendee, Bendi, Bennie, Benny, Binni

Bene
(Latin) blessed

Benecia
(Latin) short for Benedicta

Benedetta
(Latin) blessed
Benedicta, Benedicte, Benedikta, Benetta, Benita, Benni, Benoite

Benedicta
(Latin) woman blessed
Benna, Benni

Beneva
(American) combo of Ben and Eva; kind
Benevah, Benna, Benni, Bennie, Benny, Bineva

Bening
(Filipino) blessing

Benita
(Latin, Spanish) lovely
Bena, Benetta, Benitri, Bennie, Binnie

Benni
(Latin) short for Benedicta; blessed
Bennie, Binny

Bente
(Latin) blessed

Bentley
(English) meadow; luxury life
Bentlea, Bentlee, Bentleigh, Bently

Bera
(German) bearish

Berachan
(Hebrew) blessing
Beracha, Berucha, Beruchiya, Beruchya

Berdina
(German) bright; robust
Berd, Berdie, Berdine, Berdyne, Burdine, Burdynne, Dina, Dine

Berdine
(German) glows

Berecyntia
(Mythology) earth goddess

Bergen
(American) pretty
Berg, Bergin

Berget
(Irish) form of Bridget
Bergette

Berit
(Scandinavian) glorious
Beret, Berette

Berkley
(American) smart
Berkeley, Berkie, Berklie, Berkly

Berlynn
(English) combo of Bertha and Lynn
Berla, Berlinda, Berlyn

Bermuda
(Place name) island; personable
Bermudoh

Bernadette

(French) form of Bernadine
Berna, Bernadene, Bernadett, Bernadina, Bernadine, Bernarda, Bernardina, Bernardine, Berneta, Bernetta, Bernette, Berni, Bernie, Bernita, Berny

Bernadine

(German) brave; (English) feminine form of Bernard
Bernadene, Berni, Bernie

Berneen

(Irish) hearty

Bernice

(Greek) victorious
Beranice, Berenice, Bernelle, Berneta, Bernetta, Bernette, Berni, Bernicia, Bernie, Bernyce

Bernie

(American) winning
Bernee, Berney, Berni, Berny

Bernita

(Greek) from Bernice; winning

Berry

(Botanical) tiny; succulent
Berree, Berri, Berrie

Bersaida

(American) sensitive
Bersaid, Bersaide, Bersey, Bersy, Sada, Saida

Bertha

(German) bright
Barta, Berta, Berte, Berthe, Berti, Bertie, Bertilda, Bertilde, Bertina, Bertine, Bertita, Bertuska, Berty, Bird, Birdie, Birdy, Birtha

Bertie

(German) bright
Bert, Bertee, Bertey, Berty

Bertille

(German) from Bertilde; bright maiden

Bertina

(German) shining bright; feminine form of Bert

Berule

(Greek) bright; pure
Berue, Berulle

Berura

(Hebrew) chaste
Beruria

Beryl

(Greek) bright and shining gem
Beril, Berlie, Berri, Berrill, Berry, Beryla, Beryle, Beryn

Bess

(Hebrew) form of Elizabeth
Bessie

Bet

(Hebrew) daughter

Beta

(Greek) from Greek alphabet; beginning
Betka, Betuska

Beth

(Hebrew) form of Elizabeth

Betha

(Welsh) devoted to God
Bethah, Bethanne

Bethann

(English); combo of Beth and Ann; devout
B-Anne, Bethan, Beth-ann, Bethanne

Bethany

(Hebrew) God's disciple
Beth, Bethanee, Bethani, Bethania, Bethanie, Bethann, Bethanne, Bethannie, Bethanny, Betheny, Bethina

Bethel

(Hebrew) in God's house; holy child

Bethesda

(Hebrew) child of a merry home

Bethia

(Hebrew) Jehovah's daughter
Betia, Bithia

Beti

(English) small woman

Betriss

(Welsh) blessed
Betrys

Betsy

(Hebrew) form of Elizabeth
Bet, Betsey, Betsi, Betsie, Betts

Bette

(French) lively; God-loving

Bettina

(Spanish) combo of Beth and Tina
Betina, Betti, Bettine

Betty

(Hebrew) God-loving; form of Elizabeth
Bett, Betti, Bettye

Betuel

(Hebrew) in God's house
Bethuel

Betula
(Hebrew) dedicated;
religious
*Bee, Bet, Bethula, Bethulah,
Bett, Betulah*

Beulah
(Hebrew) married
Bealah, Beula, Bew, Bewla

Bev
(English) short for Beverly;
friendly

Beverly
(English) beaver stream;
friendly
*Bev, Beverelle, Beverle,
Beverlee, Beverley, Beverlie,
Beverlye, Bevvy, Verly*

Bevina
(Irish) vocalist
*Beavena, Bev, Beve, Beven,
Bevena, Bevin, Bevy,
Bovana*

Bevinn
(Irish) royal
Bevan

Bhamini
(Hindi) beautiful girl

Bhanumati
(Hindi) bright

Bharaati
(Hindi) careful

Bhavika
(Hindi) devoted girl

Bhuma
(Hindi) of the earth

Bian
(Vietnamese) hides from
life

Bianca
(Italian) white
*Beanka, Beonca, Beyonca,
Biancha, Biancia, Bionca,
Bionka, Blanca, Blancha*

Bibi
(Arabic, Latin, French) girl;
lively
*Bebe, Bibiana, Bibianna,
Bibianne, Bibyana*

Bibiane
(Latin) vibrant

Bidelia
(Irish) from Bridget; lively
Bedilia, Biddy, Bidina

Bienvenida
(Spanish) welcomed baby

Bijou
(French) saucy
*Bejeaux, Bejou, Bejue,
Bidge, Bija, Bijie, Bijy*

Bik
(Chinese) jade

Bikini
(Place name) fun-loving
Bikinee

Billie
(German) form of
Wilhelmina;
(English) strong-willed
*Billa, Billee, Billey, Billi,
Billy, Billye*

Billie-Jean
(American) combo of Billie
and Jean
Billie Jean, Billijean

Billie-Jo
(American) combo of Billie
and Jo
Billie Jo, Billyjo

Billie-Sue
(American) combo of Billie
and Sue
Billie Sue, Billysue

Billina
(English) from male name
Bill; kind
Belli, Bill, Billee, Billie, Billy

Billings
(American) bright
*Billey, Billie, Billing, Billy,
Billye, Billyngs, Byllings*

Bina
(Hebrew) perceptive woman
Bena, Binah, Byna

Binali
(Hindi) music girl

Binase
(Hebrew) bright
*Beanase, Benace, Bina,
Binah, Binahse*

Binti
(African) dancer

Binyamina
(Hebrew) from Benjamin;
loyal

Bionda
(Italian) black
Beonda, Biondah

Bira
(Hebrew) fortified; strong
Biria, Biriya

Bircit
(Scandinavian) from
Bridget; best

Bird
(English)
Birdy

Birdie
(English) bird
Birdee, Birdey, Birdi, Byrdie

Birgit
(Scandinavian) spectacular
Bergette, Berit, Birgetta, Birgite, Britta, Byrget, Byrgitt

Birgitta
(Scandinavian) strong; (Swedish) excellent splendor
Birgette, Brita, Byrgetta, Byrgitta

Birgitte
(Scandinavian) strong

Birte
(Scandinavian) form of Bridget; powerful
Berty, Birt, Birtey, Byrt, Byrtee

Bishop
(Last name as first name) loyal
Byshop

Bithia
(Hebrew) Jehovah's daughter

Bithron
(Biblical) resounding

Bitki
(Spanish) variant of Beatrix; happy

Bitsie
(American) small
Bitsee, Bitzee, Bitzi, Bytsey

Bitta
(Scandinavian) variant of Bridget; excellent
Bit, Bitt, Bittey

Bittan
(Origin unknown) gives joy

Bivona
(African American) feisty
BeBe, Biv, Bivon, Bivonne

Bjork
(Icelandic) unique
Byork

Blade
(English) glorified
Blaide, Blayde

Blaine
(Irish) thin
Blane, Blayne

Blair
(Scottish) plains-dweller
Blaire, Blayre

Blaise
(Latin, French) stammerer
Blaize, Blase, Blaze

Blake
(English) dark

Blakely
(English) dark
Blakelee, Blakeley, Blakeli

Blanca
(Spanish) white
Blancah, Blonka, Blonkah

Blanche
(French) white
Blanca, Blanch, Blancha, Blanchette, Blanka, Blanshe, Blenda

Blanchefleur
(French) white flower; pretty

Blanda
(Latin) seductive
Blandina, Blandine

Blasia
(Spanish) from Blaise; stutters
Blaise

Blath
(Irish) flower

Blaze
(French) stammers; blazing
Blaize, Blayze

Bless
(American) blessed
Blessie

Blessing
(English) dedicated

Bleu
(French) blue
Blue

Blima
(Hebrew) blossoming girl
Blimah, Blime

Bliss
(English) blissful girl

Blodwen
(Welsh) white flower
Blodwyn, Blodyn

Blom
(Hebrew) from Blum; flower

Blondelle
(French) blonde girl
Blondell, Blondie, Blondy

Blondie
(American) blonde
Blondee

Blondelle
(French) fair of hair
Blondie

Blossom
(English) flower

Bluebell
(Flower name) pretty
*Belle, Blu, Blubel, Blubell,
Blue, Bluebelle*

Blum
(Hebrew) flower
Bluma

Blush
(American) pink-cheeked
Blushe

Bly
(American) soft; sensual
Blye

Blythe
(English) carefree
Blithe, Blyth

Bo
(Chinese) precious girl

Boanah
(American) good
*Boana, Bonaa, Bonah,
Bonita*

Bobbi
(American) form of Barbara
*Bobbee, Bobbette, Bobbie,
Bobby, Bobbye, Bobi, Bobina*

Bobbiechristine
(American) combo of
Bobbie and Christine
*BobbiChris, Bobbichristine,
Bobbie-Christine*

Bobbi-Ann
(American) combo of Bobbi
and Ann
*Bobbiann, Bobbyann,
Bobbyanne*

Bobbi-Jo
(American) combo of Bobbi
and Jo
Bobbiejo, Bobbijo, Bobijo

Bobbi-Lee
(American) combo of Bobbi
and Lee
Bobbilee, Bobbylee

Bobby-Kay
(American) combo of Bobby
and Kay
Bobbikay

Bobby-Sue
(American) combo of Bobby
and Sue
Bobbisue, Boby-Sue

Bodil
(Polish) heroic
Bothild, Botilda

Bogdana
(Polish) gift from God
*Boana, Bocdana, Bogda,
Bogna, Bohdana, Bohdana,
Bohna*

Bogumila
(Polish) loved by God

Boguslawa
(Polish) in God's glory

Boinaiv
(Native American) girl in the
grass

Bola
(Origin unknown) clever
Bolo

Bolade
(African) honored girl

Bolanile
(African) rich in spirit

Boleslawa
(Polish) strong

Bona
(Latin, Italian, Polish,
Spanish) good
Bonah, Bonna

Bonda
(Spanish) good
Bona

Bonfilia
(Italian) good daughter

Bong-Cha
(Korean) excellent daughter

Bonita
(Spanish) good; pretty
*Bo, Bona, Boni, Bonie,
Bonitah, Nita*

Bonn
(French) satisfied; good
Bon, Bonne

Bonnevie
(Scandinavian) good life

Bonnie
(English, Scottish) pretty
face
*Boni, Bonie, Bonne,
Bonnebell, Bonnee, Bonni,
Bonnibel, Bonnibell,
Bonnibelle, Bonny*

Bonnie-Bell
(American) combo of Bonnie and Belle; lovely
Bonnebell, Bonnebelle, Bonnibelle

Booth
(German) from the dwelling; home-loving
Boothe

Bootsey
(American) cowgirl
Boots, Bootsie

Borghild
(Scandinavian) prepared

Borgny
(Scandinavian) fortified; strong

Bors
(Latin) foreign
Borse

Boske
(Hungarian) strays

Boston
(American) courteous
Boste, Bosten, Bostin

Boswell
(Last name as first name) intellectual
Boz, Bozwell

Boupha
(Vietnamese) flower girl

Bowdy
(American) outgoing
Bow, Bowdee, Bowdey, Bowdie

Boxidara
(Slavic) divine
Boza, Bozena, Bozka

Bracha
(Hebrew) blessed; sways in wind
Brocha

Bradley
(English) girl of the broad meadow; carefree
Bradlee, Bradleigh, Bradlie, Bradly

Brady
(Irish) spirited child
Bradee, Bradey, Bradi, Bradie

Braisly
(American) cautious
Braise, Braislee, Braize, Braze

Branca
(American) from Blanca; white

Brandy
(Dutch) after-dinner drink; fun-loving
Bran, Brandais, Brande, Brandea, Brandee, Brandeli, Brandi, Brandye, Brandyn, Brani, Branndea

Brandy-Lynn
(American) combo of Brandy and Lynn
Brandelyn, Brandilynn, Brandlin, Brandy-Lyn

Branka
(Czech) glory
Bran, Branca, Bronca, Bronka

Brayden
(American) humorous
Braden, Brae, Braeden, Bray, Brayd, Braydan, Braydon

Braxton
(English) from town of Brock; safe
Braxten

Breana
(Irish) form of Briana
Bre-Anna, Breanne, Breeana, Briana, Briane, Briann, Brianna, Brianne, Briona, Bryanna, Bryanne

Breann
(Irish) form of Briana
Bre-Ann, Bree, Breean, Breeann

Breck
(Irish) freckled

Bree
(Irish) upbeat
Brea, Bria, Brie, Brielle

Breena
(Irish) glowing
Brena

Breeshonna
(African American) happy-go-lucky
Bree, Brie, Brieshona

Breezy
(American) easygoing
Breezee, Breezie

Brehea
(American) self-sufficient
Breahay, Brehae, Brehay

Bren
(American) short for Brenda
Breyn

Brena
(Irish) strong-willed
Brenna

Brenda
(Irish) royal; glowing
Bren, Brendalynn, Brenn, Brenna, Brennda, Brenndah, Brinda, Brindah, Brinna

Brenda-Lee
(American) combo of Brenda and Lee
Brandalee, Brindlee, Brinlee

Brendette
(French) small and royal

Brendie
(American) form of Brenda
Brendee, Brendi

Brendelle
(American) distinctive

Brendolyn
(Invented) combo of Brenda and Madolyn; intelligent
Brend, Brendo, Brendolynn, Brendy

Brenna
(Irish) form of Brenda; dark-haired
Bren, Brenn, Brenie

Bretislava
(Polish) glorious
Breeka, Breticka

Brett
(Latin) jolly
Bret, Bretta, Brette

Breyawna
(African American) variant of Brianna
Bryawn, Bryawna, Bryawne

Bria
(Irish) short for Briana; pure; spirited

Briana
(Irish) virtuous; strong
Breana, Breann, Bria, Brianna, Briannah, Brie-Ann, Bryanna

Brianne
(Irish) strong
Briane, Brienne, Bryn

Briar
(French) heather
Brear, Brier

Briar-Rose
(Literature) from "Sleeping Beauty"; princess
Briar, Rose

Brice
(English) quick

Bryce
(Welsh) aware

Briceidy
(English) precocious
Brice, Bricedi, Briceidee, Briceidey

Bride
(Scottish) from Bridget; wise

Bridey
(Irish) wise
Bredee, Breedee, Bride, Bryde

Bridged
(Scottish) has the strength of fire
Bridgid, Briged, Brigid

Bridget
(Irish) powerful
Birgit, Birgitt, Birgitte, Breeda, Brid, Bride, Bridge, Bridgett, Bridgette, Bridgitte, Bridgey, Brigantia, Briget, Brigette, Brighid, Brigid, Brigida, Brigit, Brigitt, Brigitta, Brigitte, Brijette, Brygett, Brygida, Brygitka

Brie
(French) from Rozay-en-Brie, a town in France known for its cheese
Bree, Brielle

Brielle
(Invented) combo of Bri and Elle
Briell, Bryelle

Brier
(French) heather; nature
Briar

Briesha
(African American) giving
Bri, Brieshe

Brigida
(Italian) strong
Brigeeda

Brigidine
(Invented) combo of Brigit and Dine (from Geraldine)
Brige, Brigid

Brigitta
(Romanian) strong
Brigeeta, Brigeetta, Brigita

Bril
(American) strong
Brill

Briley
(Last name as first name)
popular
BeBe, Bri, Brile

Brina
(Latin) short for Sabrina
*Breena, Brena, Brinna,
Bryn, Bryna, Brynn, Brynna,
Brynne*

Brindle
(Irish) versatile
Bryndle

Brine
(Irish) strong
Bryne

Brinlee
(American) sweetheart
Brendlie, Brenlee, Brenly

Brionna
(Irish) happy
Breona, Briona

Brinkelle
(American) independent
nature
*Binkee, Binky, Brinkee,
Brinkel, Brinkell, Brinkie*

Brisa
(Spanish) beloved; in
mythology, the loved one of
Achilles
*Breezy, Breza, Brisha,
Brisia, Brissa, Briza, Bryssa*

Brisco
(American) high-energy
woman
*Briscoe, Briss, Brissie,
Brissy*

Briseis
(Mythology) prized; loved

Brissellies
(Spanish) happy
*Briselle, Briss, Brisse,
Brissel, Brissell, Brissey,
Brissi, Brissies*

Brit
(Latin) British

Britaney
(English) place name
*Britanee, Britani, Briteny,
Brittaney, Brittenie, Britnee,
Britney, Britni*

Brites
(Spanish) strong

Britt
(Latin) from Britain
Brit

Britta
(Swedish) strong woman
Brita

Brittany
(English) place name; trendy
*Brinnee, Britany, Briteney,
Britney, Britni, Brittan,
Brittaney, Brittani, Brittania,
Brittanie, Brittannia, Britteny,
Brittni, Brittnie, Brittny*

Britty
(Irish) short for Brittney; girl
from Britain
*Britee, Britey, Briti, Britie,
Brittee, Brittey, Britti,
Brittie, Brity*

Brody
(Irish) girl from the canal
*Brodee, Brodey, Brodi,
Brodie*

Brona
(Italian) Bruna; brown-
haired girl

Bronislava
(Polish) protective
*Brana, Branislava, Branka,
Brona, Bronicka, Bronka*

Bronislawa
(Polish) protective
Bronya

Bronte
(Literature) romantic
Brontae, Brontay

Bronwyn
(Welsh) white-breasted
*Bron, Bronwen, Bronwhen,
Bronwynn*

Brook
(English) sophisticated
Brooke, Brooky

Brooklyn
(Place name) combo of
Brook and Lynn
*Brookelyn, Brookelynn,
Brooklynn, Brooklynne*

Browning
(Literature) romantic

Brucie
(French) from Bruce; royal
Brucina, Brucine

Bruenetta
(French) brown-haired
Bru, Brunetta

Bruna
(Italian) brown-haired girl

Bruneita
(German) brown-haired
*Broon, Brune, Bruneite,
Brunny*

Brunella
(German) intelligent
Brun, Brunela, Brunella, Brunelle, Brunetta, Brunette, Brunilla, Brunne

Brunhilda
(German) warrior
Brunhild, Brunhilde, Brunnhilda, Brunnhilde, Brynhild, BrynhildaHilda

Bryanna
(Gaelic) powerful female
Breanna, Brianna, Bryana

Bryanta
(American) form of male name Bryan; strong
Brianta, Bryan, Bryianta

Bryce
(American) happy
Brice

Bryleigh
(English) spinoff of Brittany; jovial
Brilee, Briley, Brily, Brilye, Brylee, Brylie

Bryn
(Welsh) hopeful; climbing a hill
Brenne, Brinn, Brynn, Brynne, Brynnie

Brynn
(Welsh) hopeful
Brenn, Brinn, Brynne

Brynna
(Welsh) optimistic
Brinn, Brinna

Bryonie
(Latin) clinging vine
Breeonee, Brioni, Bryony

Bryony
(Latin) vine; clingy
Briony, Bronie, Bryonie

Bua
(Vietnamese) fortunate
Boo, Bu

Bubbles
(American) saucy
Bubb

Buena
(Spanish) goodness

Buffy
(American) plains-dweller
Buffee, Buffey, Buffie

Bukola
(African) wealthy
Bucola

Bunard
(American) good
Bunerd, Bunn, Bunny

Bunmi
(Hindi) earth

Bunny
(English) little rabbit; bouncy
Bunnee, Bunni, Bunnie

Burgundy
(French) red wine; unique
Burgandi, Burgandy

Burke
(American) loud
Berk, Burk, Burkie

Burkeley
(English) birches; outdoorsy
Burkelee, Burkeleigh, Burkeli, Burkelie, Berkeley, Burkely, Burklee, Burkleigh, Burkley, Burkli, Burklie, Burkly

Burns
(Last name as first name) presumptuous
Bernes, Berns, Burn, Burnee, Burnes, Burney, Burni, Burny

Buseje
(African) interesting

Buthaayna
(Arabic) lovely body
Busayna, Buthaynah

Butte
(Place name) landscape

Butter
(American) sweet
Budter

Buzzie
(American) spirited
Buzz, Buzzi

Bwyana
(African American) smart
Bwya, Bwyanne

Byhalia
(Native American) strong oak

Byronae
(American) form of Byron; smart
Byrona, Byronay

C

Cabot
(French) fresh-faced

Cabrina
(American) combo of C and Sabrina; innovator

Cabriole
(French) adorable
Cabb, Cabby, Cabriolle, Kabriole

Cacalia
(Botanical) accomodating

Cachay
(African American) distinctive

Cachet
(French) fetching
Cache, Cachee

Caddy
(American) elusive; alluring

Cade
(American) precocious
Kade, Kaid

Cadena
(Latin) rhythmic

Cadence
(American) hip
Kadence

Cady
(English) fun-loving
Cadee, Cadey, Cadye, Caidee, Caidy, Kadee, Kady

Caesaria
(Greek) from Caesar; leader

Cai
(Chinese) wealthy; girlish

Cailida
(Spanish) passionate

Cailidora
(Greek) gifted with a beautiful face

Cailin
(American) happy
Cailyn, Cailynn, Calyn, Cayleen, Caylin, Caylyn, Caylynne

Caimile
(Spanish) helps

Cainwen
(Welsh) lovely treasure
Ceinwen, Kayne, Keyne

Cairo
(Place name) Egypt's capital; confident
Kairo, Kiero

Cait
(Greek) purest
Cate, Kate

Caitlin
(Irish) virginal
Cailin, Caitleen, Caitlen, Caitlinn, Caitlyn, Catlin, Catlyn, Catlynne Caitrianne

Caitrin
(Irish) pure of heart

Cakusola
(African) lionhearted

Cala, Calla
(Arabic) strong
Callah

Calandra
(Greek) lark
Calendra, Calondra, Kalandra

Calantha
(Greek) gorgeous flower
Calanth, Calanthe, Callantha, Calli

Calatea
(Greek) flowering
Calatee

Cale
(Latin) respected
Kale

Caledonia
(Latin) from Scotland; worthy
Kaledonia

Caleigh
(American) beauty
Calleigh

Caley
(American) warm
Caleigh, Kaylee

Calhoun
(Last name as first name) surprising

Calia
(American) beauty

Calida
(Spanish) warmth

California
(Place name) hip; cool
Callie, Kalifornia, Kallie

Calinda
(American) combo of Cal and Linda
Cal, Calenda, Calli, Callie, Cally, Kalenda, Kalinda

Caliopa
(Greek, Spanish) singing beautifully
Kaliopa

Calise
(Greek) gorgeous

Calista
(Greek) most beautiful
Calysta, Kali, Kalista, Kalli, Kallista, Callista

Calla
(Greek) beautiful
Cala, Callie, Cally

Callidora
(Greek) gift of beauty

Callie
(Greek) beautiful
Caleigh, Callee, Calley, Calli, Cally, Kali, Kallee, Kallie

Calligenia
(Italian) beauty's child

Calliope
(Greek) poetry muse
Kalliope, Kallyope

Callison
(American) combo of Calli and Allison; pretty offspring
Cal, Calli, Callice, Callis, Callisen, Callisun

Callista
(Greek) most beautiful
Calesta, Calista, Callista, Calysta, Kallista

Callula
(Latin) beautiful

Caltha
(Latin) gold flower

Calumina
(Scottish) calm

Calvina
(Latin) has no hair
Calvine

Calypso
(Greek) sea nymph who held Odysseus captive

Cam
(American) short for Cameron
Cami, Camie, Cammie

Camaren
(American) from Cameron; crooked nose; actor

Camassia
(American) combo of Camey and Massia; aloof

Cambay
(Place name) saucy
Cambaye, Kambay

Camber
(American) from Amber; has potential
Cambie, Cambre, Cammy, Kamber

Cambree
(Place name) from Cambria, Wales; ingenious
Cambre, Cambrie, Cambry, Cambry, Kambree, Kambrie

Cambria
(English) the people

Camden
(American) glorious face
Cam, Camdon, Cammi, Cammie, Cammy

Cameka
(African American) form of Tameka/Tamika
Cammey, Cammi, Cammy, Kameka, Kammy

Camellia
(Italian) flower
Camelia, Kamelia

Camelina
(American) from Camilla; shy

Camelot
(English) elegant
Cam, Cami, Camie, Camy

Cameo
(French) piece of jewelry; singular
Cameoh, Cammie, Kameo

Camera
(Word as name) stunning
Kamera

Camerino
(Spanish) unblemished
Cam, Cammy

Cameron
(Scottish) popular (crooked nose)
Cameran, Camren, Camryn, Kameron, Kamryn

Cami
(French) short for Camille, Camilla, or Cameron
Camey, Camie, Cammie, Cammy

Camilla
(Latin, Italian) wonderful
Cam, Camelia, Camellia, Camila, Camile, Camille, Camillia

Camille
(French) swift runner; great innocence
Camila, Cammille, Cammy, Camylle, Kamille

Cammy
(American) short for Camilla; helps

Camp
(American) hip
Cam, Campy

Campbell
(Last name as first name) amazing
Cam, Cambell, Camey, Cami, Camie, Camy

Camrin
(American) variant of Cameron
Camren, Camryn

Canace
(American) from Candace; white brilliance

Canada
(Place name) decisive
Cann, Kanada

Candace
(Greek) glowing girl
Caddy, Candice, Candis, Candys, Kandace

Candelara
(Spanish) spiritual
Cande, Candee, Candelaria, Candi, Candy, Lara

Candenza
(Italian) from Candace; white brilliance

Candida
(Latin) white

Candra
(Latin) she who glows
Candria, Kandra

Candy
(American) short for Candace
Candee, Candi, Candie

Caneadea
(Native American) the horizon; far-reaching goals

Canei
(Greek) pure

Cannes
(French) place name
Can, Kan

Cannon
(American) vital

Cantara
(Arabic) bridge
Canta, Kanta, Kantara

Capelta
(American) fanciful
Capeltah, Capp, Cappy

Caplice
(American) spontaneous
Capleece, Capleese, Kapleese

Capri
(Place name) island off coast of Italy
Caprie, Kapri

Caprice
(Italian) playful; capricious
Caprece, Capreese, Capricia, Caprise

Capote
(Spanish) cloak; protected

Capucine
(French) cloak
Cappy

Car
(American) zany
Carr, Kar, Karr

Cara
(Latin, Italian) dear one
Carah, Kara

Caramia
(Italian) my dear
Cara Mia, Cara-Mia

Cardia
(Spanish) giving
Candi, Kardia

Caren
(American) also Karen; dear
Carine

Carenleigh
(American) combo of Caren and Leigh
Caren-Leigh

Caresse
(Greek) well-loved

Carey
(Welsh) by a castle; fond
Caree, Cari, Carrie, Cary

Cari
(Latin) giving

Caridad
(Spanish) giving
Cari

Carie
(Latin) generous

Carina
(Greek, Italian) dearest
Careena, Carena, Carin, Carine, Kareena, Karina

Carinthia
(Place name) city in Austria; dear girl

Carissa
(Greek, Italian) beloved
Carisa, Caryssa, Karessa, Karissa

Carita
(Latin) giving; loved
Caritta, Carrita, Carritta, Karita

Caritina
(Spanish) combo of Cari and Tina; dearest
Cari, Cartine, Tina

Carla
(German) feminine of Charles, Carl, Carlo
Carlah, Carlee, Carli, Carlia, Carlie, Carly, Karla, Karlah

Carleas
(American) from Carlissa; smooth moves

Carlee
(German) darling
Carleigh, Carley, Carli, Carly, Karlee, Karley

Carlene
(American) sweet
Carleen, Carlina, Carline, Carlyn

Carlanda
(American) darling
Carlan, Carland, Carlande, Carlee, Carlie, Carly, Karlanda

Carlessa
(American) combo of Carla and Lessa; restless

Carlett
(Spanish) affectionate
Carle, Carlet, Carletta, Carlette, Carley, Carli

Carlianne
(American) combo of Carli and Anne; affectionate

Carlin
(Latin, German) winner
Caline, Carlan, Carlen

Carlisle
(Place name) city on the border of Engalnd and Scotland; sharp
Carlile, Carrie, Karlisle

Carlisa
(Italian) combo of Carla and Lisa; fond of friends
Carlie, Carlissa, Carly, Carlysa, Karlese, Karlisa

Carlissa
(American) pleasant
Carleeza, Carlisse

Carlita
(Italian) outstanding

Carlotta
(Italian, Spanish) feminine form of Carlo and Carlos; sweetheart
Karlotta

Carly
(German) darling
Carlee, Carley, Carli, Carlie, Karlee

Carma
(Hebrew) short for Carmel; special garden
Car, Carmee, Carmi, Carmie, Karma

Carmel
(Hebrew) place name; garden
Carmela, Carmella, Karmel

Carmela
(Hebrew, Italian) fruitful
Carmalla, Carmel, Carmella, Carmie, Carmilla

Carmelina
(Italian) combo of Carmelo and Lina; in the garden
Carmalina, Carmelena, Carmela, Carmelita

Carmen
(Hebrew) crimson
Carma, Carman, Carmela, Carmelinda, Carmita, Carmynne, Chita, Mela, Melita

Carmensita
(Spanish) dear girl
Carma, Carmens, Carmense, Karmence

Carmiela
(Hebrew) from Carmel; garden girl

Carmiya
(Hebrew) from Carmel; garden girl

Carmine
(Italian) sexy
Carmyne, Karmine

Carminia
(Italian) dearest
Carma, Carmine, Carmynea, Karm, Karminia, Karmynea

Carna
(Latin) horn; sound of joy
Carni

Carni
(Latin) horn; vocal
*Carna, Carney, Carnia,
Carnie, Carniela, Carniella,
Carniya, Carny, Karni,
Karnia, Karniela, Karniella,
Karniya*

Carnation
(Botanical) flower
*Carn, Carna, Carnee, Carney,
Carny*

Carnethia
(Invented) fragrant
*Carnee, Carney, Carnithia,
Karnethia*

Carnie
(American) happy
Carni, Karni, Karnie

Carody
(American) humorous
*Caridee, Caridey, Carodee,
Carodey, Carrie, Karodee,
Karody*

Carol
(English) feminine; (French)
joyful song; (German)
farming woman
*Carole, Carroll, Caryl, Karol,
Karrole*

Carolanne
(American) combo of Carol
and Anne
Carolane, Carolann

Carole
(French) a joyous song
Karol, Karole

Carolina
(Italian) feminine
Carrolena, Karolina

Caroline
(German) petite woman
*Caraline, Carilene, Cariline,
Caroleen, Carolin, Carrie,
Karalyn, Karolina, Karoline,
Karolyn, Karolynne*

Carolyn
(English) womanly
*Carilyn, Carilynn, Carolyne,
Carolynn, Karolyn*

Caron
(Welsh) giving heart
Carron, Karon

Caronsy
(American) form of Caron;
sweet
Caronnsie, Caronsi, Karonsy

Carrelle
(American) lively
Carrele

Carrie
(French, English) joyful
song
Carey, Cari, Carri, Carry, Kari

Carson
(Nordic) dramatic
*Carse, Carsen, Carsun,
Karrson, Karsen, Karson*

Carsyn
(American) variant of
Carson; confident

Carylan
(American) combo of Caryl
and An; soft
*Carolann, Caryland,
Carylanna, Karylan*

Caryn
(Danish) form of Karen;
loving
*Caren, Carrin, Caryne,
Carynn*

Carys
(Welsh) love

Casey
(Greek, Irish) attentive
female
*Casie, Cassee, Cassey, Casy,
Caysee, Caysie, Caysy,
Kasey*

Cashonya
(African American) monied;
lively
Kashonya

Casielee
(American) combo of Casie
and Lee; popular
*Caseylee, Casie Lee, Casielea,
Casie-Lee, Casieleigh*

Casilda
(Latin) from the dwelling

Casilde
(Spanish) combative
*Casilda, Casill, Cass, Cassey,
Cassie*

Cason
(Greek) seer; spirited
Case, Casey, Kason

Cassandra
(Greek) insightful
*Casandra, Casandria, Cass,
Cassie, Cassondra,
Kassandra*

Cassia
(Greek) spicy; cinnamon

Cassidy
(Irish) clever girl
Casadee, Cass, Cassidee,
Cassidi, Kassidy

Cassie
(Greek) short for
Cassandra; tricky
Cassey, Cassi

Cassiopeia
(Greek) starry-eyed
Cass, Cassi, Kass, Kassiopia

Cassis
(American) variant of
Carson; confident

Casta
(Spanish) short for
Castalina; chaste

Castalia
(Mythology) ill-fated

Castalina
(Spanish) variant of
Catalina; chaste

Castara
(Greek) from Catherine; pure
Castera, Castora

Catalina
(Spanish) pure
Catalena, Katalena, Katalina

Catarina
(Greek, Italian) pure
Caterina, Catrina, Katarina

Catava
(Greek) uncorrupted

Catharina
(Greek) from Catherine;
pure

Cather
(Literature) earthy
Kather

Catherine
(Greek, Irish, English) pure
Cartharine, Cathrine,
Cathryn, Katherine

Cathleen
(Irish) pure; immaculate
Cathelin, Cathleyn,
Cathlinne, Cathlyn, Cathy

Cathresha
(African American) pure;
outspoken
Cathrisha, Cathy, Kathresha,
Resha

Cathryn
(Greek) pure female; form
of Catherine

Cathy
(Greek) pure; innocent
Cathee, Cathey, Cathie,
Kathy

Catima
(Greek) pure
Cattima

Catline
(Irish) form of Caitlin; virtuous
Cataleen, Catalena, Catleen,
Catlen, Katline

Catrice
(Greek) form of Catherine;
wholesome
Catrece, Catreece, Catreese,
Katreece, Katrice

Catrina
(Greek) pure
Catreena, Catreene,
Catrene, Katrina

Catriona
(Greek) from Catherine;
pure
Katriona

Cavender
(American) emotional
Cav, Cavey, Kav, Kavender

Cayenne
(Word as name) peppery;
spice

Caykee
(American) combo of Cay
and Kee; lively
Caycay, Caykie, Kaykee, Kee

Cayla
(Hebrew) unblemished
Cailie, Calee, Cayley, Caylie,
Kayla

Cayley
(American) joyful
Caelee, Caeley, Cailey,
Cailie, Caylea, Caylee,
Cayleigh, Caylie

Caylisa
(American) combo of Cay
and Lisa; lighthearted
Cayelesa, Cayl, Cay-Lisa,
Caylise, Kayl, Kaylisa

Cayman
(Place name) the islands;
free spirit
Caman, Caymanne, Kayman

Cayne
(American) generous
Cain, Kaine

Ceara
(Irish) variant of Ciara;
clear-eyed

Ceaskarshenna
(African American)
ostentatious
Ceaskar, Karshenna,
Shenna

Cece
(Latin) from Cecilia; blind;
hopeful

Ceci
(Latin) short for Cecilia;
dignity

Cecile
(Latin) short for Cecilia;
genteel
Cecily

Cecilia
(Latin, Polish) blind; short-
sighted
*Cacelia, Cece, Cecelia, Ceil,
Celia, Cice, Cicilia, Cilley,
Secilia, Sissy*

Cedrica
(English) chief; leader

Cedrice
(American) form of male
name Cedric; feisty
Ced, Cedrise

Ceil
(Latin) blythe
Ceel, Ciel

Ceinwen
(Welsh) blessed baby

Ceirra
(Irish) clear-eyed
CeAirra, Cierra

Ceiteag
(Scottish) purest

Celand
(Latin) heavenward
Cel, Cela, Celanda, Celle

Celandine
(Greek) wildflower; natural
beauty

Celebration
(American) word as name;
celebrant
Cela, Sela

Celena
(Greek) heavenly; form of
Selena
Celeena, Celene

Celery
(Food name) refreshing
*Cel, Celeree, Celree, Celry,
Sel, Selery, Selry*

Celeste
(Latin) gentle and heavenly
*Celest, Celestial, Celestine,
Seleste*

Celestia
(Latin) heavenly
*Celeste, Celestea, Celestiah,
Seleste, Selestia*

Celestyna
(Polish) heavenly
*Cela, Celeste, Celesteenah,
Celestinah, Celestyne*

Celina
(Greek) loving; form of
Celena
Selina, Celena

Celine
(Greek) lovely
Celeen, Celene

Celisha
(Greek) flaming; passionate

Celka
(Latin) celestial
*Celk, Celkee, Celkie, Selk,
Selka*

Celkee
(Latin) form of Celeste; sweet
Celkea, Celkie, Cell, Selkee

Celosia
(Greek) flaming

Cena
(English) special
Cenna, Sena

Cenobia
(Spanish) power of Zeus;
strong girl
Cenobie, Zenobia, Zenobie

Cerella
(Latin) springlike

Cerelia
(Latin) spring baby

Ceporah
(Hebrew) variant of
Zipporah; bird; dainty

Cera
(French) colorful

Cerea
(Greek) thriving
Serea

Cerelia
(Latin) spring
Cerallua, Cerellia, Cerelly

Ceres
(Latin) joyful

Ceridwen
(Welsh) poetic; blessed
Ceri, Ceridwyn

Cerina
(Latin) variant of Serena;
peaceful girl

Cerise
(French) cherry red
*Cerese, Cerice, Cerrice,
Ceryce*

Cerys
(Mythology) harvest goddess
Ceri, Ceries, Cerri, Cerrie

Cesaria
(Latin) from Caesar; leader

Cesarina
(Latin) hairy; strong spirit
Cesarea, Cesarie, Cesarin

Cesary
(Polish) outspoken
Cesarie, Cezary, Ceze

Cesia
(Spanish) celestial
Cesea, Sesia

Chablis
(French) white wine
Chabli

Chacita
(Spanish) lively girl
Chaca, Chacie, Chaseeta, Chaseta

Chadee
(French) goddess
Shadee

Chaemarique
(Invented) combo of Chae and Marique; pretty
Chae, Chaemareek, Marique, Shaymarique

Chafin
(Last name as first name) sure-footed
Chaffin, Shafin

Chahna
(Hindi) she lights the world

Chai
(Hebrew) life-giving
Chae, Chaeli

Chaitali
(Hindi) light

Chaka-Khan
(Invented) singer

Chaille
(American) variant of Chelle, short for Michelle/Rochelle; feminine

Chakra
(Sanskrit) energy
Chak, Chaka, Chakara, Chakyra

Chala
(African American) exuberant
Chalah, Chalee, Chaley, Chalie

Chalese
(French) goblet; toasts life

Chalette
(American) good taste
Chalett, Challe, Challie, Shalette

Chalice
(French) a goblet; toasting
Chalace, Chalece, Chalyse, Chalyssie

Chalina
(Spanish) rose; fragrant

Chaline
(American) smiling
Chacha, Chaleen, Chalene

Chalis
(African American) sunny disposition
Chal, Chaleese, Chalise

Chalissa
(African American) optimistic
Chalisa, Chalysa, Chalyssa

Challie
(American) charismatic
Challee, Challi, Chally

Chalondra
(African American) pretty
Chacha, Chalon, Chalondrah, Cheilonndra, Chelondra

Chalsey
(American) variation of Chelsea
Chalsea, Chalsee, Chalsi, Chalsie, Chalsie

Chamania
(Hebrew) sunflower; bright
Chamaniya, Hamania, Hamaniya

Chamaran
(Hebrew) from Chamania; sunflower

Chambray
(French) fabric; hardy
Chambree

Chameli
(Hindi) jasmine; fragrant

Champagne
(French) wine; luxurious

Chan
(Vietnamese) fragrant

Chana
(Hindi) moonlike

Chanah
(Hebrew) graceful
Chanach, Channah

Chanal
(American) moonlike

Chanda
(Hindi) moon goddess
Chandi, Chandie, Shanda

Chandani
(Hindi) moonbeams
Chandni, Chandree, Chandrika

Chandelle
(French) candle-lighter
Chandal, Shandalle, Shandel

Chandi
(Sanskrit) goddess

Chandler
(English) romantic; candle-maker
Chandlee, Shandler

Chandra
(Hindi) of the moon
Chandre, Shandra, Shandre

Chanel
(French) fashionable; designer name
Chan, Chanell, Chanelle, Channel, Shanel, Shanell, Shanelle

Chanelle
(American) stylish
Shanell, Shanelle

Chaney
(English) short for Chandler; cute
Chanie, Chaynee, Chayney

Chania
(Hebrew) blessed by Lord's grace
Chaniya, Hania, Haniya

Chanicka
(African American) loved
Chaneeka, Chani, Chanika, Nicka, Nika, Shanicka

Chanina
(Hebrew) knows a gracious Lord

Chanise
(American) adored
Chanese, Shanise

Chanit
(Hebrew) spear; ready for combat
Chanita, Hanit, Hanita

Channa
(Hindi) chickpea; little thing

Channary
(Vietnamese) moon girl

Channing
(Last name as first name) clever

Chanon
(American) shining
Chanen, Chann, Channon, Chanun

Chansanique
(African American) girl singing
Chansan, Chansaneek, Chansani, Chansanike, Shansanique

Chantal
(French) singer of songs
Chandal, Chantale, Chantalle, Chante, Chantee, Chantel, Chantell, Chantelle, Chantile, Chantille, Chawntelle, Shanta, Shantel, Shawntel, Shontelle

Chantee
(American) singer
Chante, Chantey, Chanti, Chantie, Shantee, Shantey

Chanterelle
(French) singer; prized

Chanti
(American) melodious
Chantee, Chantie

Chantilly
(French) beautiful lace
Chantille, Shantilly

Chantou
(French) singer

Chantrea
(Vietnamese) moonlight

Chantrice
(French) singer of songs
Shantreece, Treece

Chanya
(Hebrew) blessed by Jehovah's love

Chanyce
(American) risk-taker
Chance, Chancie, Chaneese, Chaniece, Chanycey

Chapa
(Native American) beaver; active

Chapawee
(Native American) beaver; active

Chaquanne
(African American) sassy
Chaq, Chaquann, Shakwan

Chara
(Greek) from Charis; graceful movements
Charo

Charanne
(American) combo of Char and Anne; charitable
Charann, Cherann

Charbonnet
(French) loving and giving
Charbonay, Charbonet, Charbonnay, Sharbonet, Sharbonnet

Charde
(French) wine
Charday, Chardea, Shardae

Chardonnay
(French) white wine
Char, Chardonee, Chardonnae, Shardonnay

Charelle
(French) from Charlotte; feminine

Charian
(French) from Charlotte; feminine

Charie
(Greek) from Charis; feminine
Chari

Charille
(French) variant of Charlotte; feminine; delightful
Char, Chari, Charill, Shar, Sharille

Charis
(Greek) graceful
Charice, Charisse

Charish
(American) cherished
Chareesh

Charisma
(American) charming
Char, Karismah

Charissa
(Greek) giving
Char, Charesa, Charisse, Charissey

Charita
(Spanish) sweet
Cherita

Charity
(Latin) loving; affectionate
Carisa, Charis, Charita, Chariti, Charry, Cherry, Chirity, Sharity

Charla
(French) from Charlotte; feminine
Char

Charlaine
(English) small woman; form of Charlene
Charlane

Charlana
(American) form of Charlene; feminine
Chalanna

Charlene
(French) petite and beautiful
Charla, Charlaine, Charleen, Charline, Sharlene

Charlesetta
(German) form of Charles; royal
Charlesette, Charlsetta

Charlesia
(American) form of Charles; royal; womanly
Charlese, Charlisce, Charlise, Charlsie, Charlsy, Sharlesia

Charlesey
(American) expansive; generous
Charlesee, Charlie, Charlsie, Charlsy

Charli
(English) feminine

Charlianne
(American) combo of Charlie and Anne
Charlann, Charleyann

Charlie
(American) easygoing
Charl, Charlee, Charley, Charli

Charlize
(American) pretty

Charlotta
(French) womanly

Charlotte
(French) little woman
Carly, Charla, Charle, Charlott, Charolot

Charlottie
(French) small
Charlotty

Charlsheah
(American) happy

Charlsie
(French) womanly

Charluce
(American) form of Charles; feminine; royal
Charl, Charla, Charluse

Charm
(Greek) short for Charmian; charming
Charma, Charmay, Sharm

Charmaine
(Latin) womanly; (French) singer
Charma, Charmagne, Charmain, Charmane, Charmayne, Charmian, Charmine, Charmyn, Sharmaine, Sharmane, Sharmayne, Sharmyne

Charmian
(Greek) joy baby; charming

Charmine
(French) charming
Charmen, Charmin

Charminique
(African American) dashing
Charmineek

Charmonique
(African American) charming
Charm, Charmi, Charmon, Charmoneek, Charmoni, Charmonik, Sharmonique

Charnee
(American) effervescent
Charney, Charnie, Charny

Charneeka
(African American) obsessive
Charn, Charnika, Charny

Charnelle
(American) sparkling
Charn, Charnel, Charnell, Charney, Sharnell, Sharnelle

Charnesa
(African American) noticed
Charnessa, Charnessah

Charo
(Spanish) flower
Charro

Charra
(French) womanly

Charron
(African American) variant of Sharon; pretty
Charryn, Cheiron

Charsetta
(American) form of Charlene; emotional
Charsee, Charsette, Charsey, Charsy

Chartra
(American) classy
Chartrah

Chartres
(French) planner
Chartrys

Charu
(Hindi) gorgeous

Charumat
(Hindi) lovely and smart

Charysse
(Greek) graceful girl
Charece, Charese, Charisse

Chashmona
(Hebrew) princess

Chasia
(Hebrew) sheltered
Chasya, Hasia, Hasya

Chasida
(Hebrew) religious
Chasidah, Hasida

Chasina
(Aramaic) strength of character

Chasity
(Latin) pure
Chassity

Chassie
(Latin) form of Chastity; virtuous
Chass, Chassey, Chassi

Chastity
(Latin) pure woman
Chasta, Chastitie

Chateria
(Vietnamese) moonlight

Chau
(Aramaic) strength of character

Chaucer
(English) demure
Chauser, Chawcer, Chawser

Chava
(Hebrew) life-giving
Chavah, Chave, Hava

Chavi
(Gypsy) girlish

Chaviva
(Hebrew) beloved

Chavon
(Hebrew) life; Chava
Chavonne

Chaya
(Jewish) living

Chayan
(Native American) variant of Cheyenne; tribe
Chay, Chayanne, Chi, Shayan, Shy

Chazmin
(American) from Jasmine; exuberant
Jasmine

Chazona
(Hebrew) seer

Chea
(American) witty
Chea, Cheeah

Chedra
(Hebrew) happy

Cheer
(American) joyful

Cheifa
(Hebrew) enjoys a safe harbor

Chekia
(Invented) cheeky
Chekie, Shekia

Chela
(Spanish) exuberant
Chelan, Chelena

Cheletha
(African American) smiling
Chelethe, Cheley

Chelle
(American) short for Chelsea; secure
Shell

Chelsea
(Old English) safe harbor
Chelcy, Cheli, Chellsie, Chelse, Chelsee, Chelsei, Chelsey, Chelsie, Kelsey, Shelsee

Chemarin
(French) fertile; dark

Chemash
(Hebrew) servant of God
Chema, Chemesh, Chemosh

Chemda
(Hebrew) charismatic

Chemdiah
(Hebrew) loves God
Chemdia, Chemdiya, Hemdia, Hemdiah

Chenia
(Hebrew) lives by the grace of God
Chen, Chenya, Hen, Henia, Henya

Chenille
(American) soft
Chenelle, Chenile, Chinille

Chenoa
(American) form of Genoa; fun
Cheney, Cheno

Cher
(French) dear
Chere, Sher

Cherelle
(French) dear
Charell, Cherrelle, Sharelle

Cherie
(French) dear
Cherey, Cheri, Cherice, Cherree, Cherrie, Cherry, Cherye

Cherika
(French) form of Cherry; kind; dear
Chereka, Cherikah

Cherilynn
(American) combo of Cheryl and Lynn; kind-hearted
Cheryl-Lynn, Cherylynne, Sherilyn, Sherilynn, Sherralin

Cherinne
(American) happy
Charinn, Cherin, Cherry

Cherise
(French) cherry
Cherece, Cherice, Cherish, Cherrise

Cherish
(French) precious girl
Charish, Cherishe, Sherishe

Cherisha
(American) endearing
Cherishah, Cherishuh

Cherita
(Spanish) dearest
Cheritt, Cheritta, Cherrita

Cheritte
(American) held dear
Cher, Cherette, Cheritta

Cherly
(American) form of Shirley; natural; bright meadow
Cherlee, Sherly

Cherlyn
(American) combo of Cher and Lyn; dear one
Cherlin, Cherlinn, Cherlynn, Cherlynne

Chermona
(Hebrew) goes to the sacred mountain

Cherokee
(Native American) Indian tribe member

Cherron
(American) graceful dancer
Cher, Cheron, Cherronne

Cherry
(Latin, French) cherry red
Cheree, Cherey, Cherrye, Chery

Cherrylee
(French, American) combo of Cherry and Lee; lively
Charalee, Charralee, Cheralee, Cherilea, Cherilee, Cherileese, Cher-Lea, Cherry-Lee, Cherylee, Sharilee, Sheralea, Sherryleigh

Cherry-Sue
(American) combo of Cherry and Sue

Cheryl
(French) beloved
Charyl, Cherel, Cherelle, Cheryll

Chesley
(English) pretty; meadow
Ches, Cheslay, Cheslea, Chesleigh

Chesma
(Slavic) also Chesna; peaceloving

Chesna
(Slavic) peace
Ches, Chesnah

Chesney
(English) peacemaker
Chesnee, Chesni, Chesnie, Chessnea

Chessa
(Slavic) peace

Chesskwana
(African American) evoker
Chesskwan, Chessquana, Chessy

Chessteen
(American) needed
Ches, Chessy, Chesteen, Chestene

Chestnut
(Botanical) unique

Chet
(American) vivacious
Chett

Chevona
(Irish) loves a gracious God

Chevy
(American) funny
Chev, Chevee

Cheyann
(Native American) also Cheyenne; tribe; optimist

Cheye
(American) from Cheyenne; optimist

Cheyenne
(Native American) Indian tribe; capital of Wyoming
Chayanne, Cheyan, Cheyanna, Cheyene, Chynne, Shayan, Shayann, Sheyenne

Chhaya
(Hebrew) life; vibrant

Chi
(African) Ibo god; light

Chiante
(Italian) wine
Chianti

Chiara
(Italian) bright and clear
Cheara, Chiarra, Kiara, Kiarra

Chiba
(Hebrew) love

Chica
(Spanish) girl
Chika

Chick
(American) fun-loving
Chicki, Chickie

Chickadee
(American) cute little girl
Chicka, Chickady, Chickee, Chickey, Chicky

Chidi
(Spanish) cheerful

Chidori
(Japanese) a shorebird

Chika
(Japanese) dear girl; wise

Chikira
(Spanish) dancer
Shakira

Chiku
(African) loquacious

Chilali
(Native American) snowbird

Childe
(American) literary
Child

Childers
(Last name as first name) dignified
Chelders, Childie, Chillders, Chylders

Chimalis
(Native American) snowbird

Chimene
(French) self-starter; eager

China
(Place name) unique
Chinnah, Chyna, Chynna

Chinadoll
(Invented) fun
China Doll, China-Doll, Chynadoll

Chinasia
(Place name) China and
Asia; different

Chinenye
(Place name) from China

Chinue
(African) blessed by Chi

Chipo
(American) from Chip; alike

Chiquida
(Spanish) form of Chiquita;
small
Chiquide

Chiquita
(Spanish) small girl
Chica, Chick, Chickie, Chikita,
Chiquitia, Chiquitta, Shiquita

Chiriga
(African) triumphant;
capable

Chirline
(American) variant of
Charline; sweet
Chirl, Chirlene, Shirl, Shirline

Chislaine
(French) loyal

Chita
(Spanish) girlish; from Chica

Chitsa
(Spanish) from Carmen;
runs the orchard

Chivonne
(American) happy
Chevonne, Chivaughan,
Chivaughn, Chivon, Chivonn

Chiyena
(Hebrew) in the Lord's grace

Chiyoko
(Japanese) forever

Chizoba
(African) well-protected;
strong

Chizu
(Japanese) a thousand
storks; bountiful

Chizuko
(Japanese) abundant

Chloe
(Greek) flowering
Chloee, Clo, Cloe, Cloee,
Cloey, Khloe, Kloe

Chloris
(Greek) pale-skinned
Chloras, Cloris, Kloris

Cho
(Japanese) dawn of day
Choko, Choyo

Chofa
(Polish) able

Cholena
(Native American) birdlike;
sings

Chris
(Greek) form of Christina;
best
Chrissie, Chrissy, Kris

Chrisana
(American) boisterous
Chris, Chrisanah, Crisane

Chriselda
(German) from Griselda;
fights

Chrissa
(Greek) form of Christina
Crissa, Cryssa, Krissa

Chrissy
(English) short for Christina
Chrissie, Chrysie, Krissy

Christa
(German, Greek) loving
Crista, Krista

Christabelle
(American) combo of
Christa and Belle
Cristabel

Christal
(Latin) form of Crystal
Christall, Christalle, Christel

Christalin
(American) combo of
Christa and Lin
Christalinn, Christalynn

Christanda
(American) smart
Christandah, Christawnda

Christauna
(American) spiritual
Christaun, Christawna,
Christown, Christwan

Christen
(Greek) form of Christina;
Christian
Christan, Christin, Cristen,
Kristen

Christian
(Greek) Christian

Christiana
(Greek, German) Christ's
follower
Christa, Christianna,
Christianne, Christie,
Chystyana, Crystianne,
Crysty-Ann, Kristiana

Christie
(Greek) short for Christina
Christi, Kristi, Kristie

Christina
(Greek, Scottish, German, Irish) the anointed one
Chris, Chrissie, Christi, Christiana, Chrystina, Crista, Kristina

Christine
(French, English, Latin) faithful
Christene, Christin, Cristine, Kristine

Christmas
(English) Christmas baby

Christopher
(Greek) devout Christian
Kris, Krissie, Krissy, Krista, Kristofer, Kristopher

Christy
(Scottish) Christian
Christee, Christi, Christie

Chrysanthemum
(American) flower
Chrys, Chrysanthe, Chrysie, Mum

Chrysanthum
(Invented) from flower chrysanthemum; flowering
Chrys, Chrysan, Chrysanth

Chuki
(African) born in a sour time

Chula
(Native American) flower; colorful

Chulda
(Hebrew) fortune-teller
Hulda, Huldah

Chulisa
(Invented) clever
Chully, Ulisa

Chuma
(Hebrew) warm
Chumi, Huma, Humi

Chumana
(Native American) dew; morning fresh

Chumani
(Native American) dewdrop

Chumina
(Hebrew) warmth

Chun
(Chinese) springlike

Chyan
(American) variant of Cheyenne; able

Chynna
(Chinese) China; wise; musical
Chyna

Ciandra
(Italian) light

Ciannait
(Irish) an old soul

Ciannata
(Latin) old spirit

Ciara
(Irish) brunette
Cearra, Ciarah, Ciarra, Ciera, Keera, Keerah

Cicely
(Latin) form of Cecilia; clever
Cicelie, Cici, Sicely

Cid
(American) fun
Cyd, Syd

Cida
(American) from Cindy; light

Cidni
(American) jovial
Cidnee, Cidney, Cidnie

Cidrah
(American) unusual
Cid, Ciddie, Ciddy, Cidra

Cieara
(Spanish) dark
CiCi, Ciear, Sieara

Ciera
(Irish) dark
Cíera, Cia, Cieera, Cierra, Cierre

Cilla
(Greek) vivacious
Cika, Sica, Sika

Cille
(American) short for Lucille
Ceele

Cima
(Place name) short for Cimarron; western

Cimm
(Place name) short for Cimarron; western

Cinderella
(French) imaginative; hopeful
Cinda, Cindi, Cindie, Cindy

Cindy
(Greek, Latin) moon goddess
Cindee, Cindi, Cyndee, Cyndi, Cyndie, Sindee, Syndi, Syndie, Syndy

Cinnamon
(Spice) sweet
*Cenamon, Cinna,
Cinnammon, Cinnamond,
Cinamen, Cynamon*

Cinta
(Spanish) mountain of good

Cinzia
(Italian) mountain;
reasonable

Ciona
(American) steadfast
Cinonah, Cionna, Cyona

Ciprianna
(Italian) from Ciprus;
cautious
*Cipri, Cipriannah, Cypriana,
Cyprianna, Cyprianne,
Sipriana, Siprianna*

Circe
(Greek) sorceress deity;
mysterious
Circee, Cirsey, Cirsie

Ciri
(Latin) regal
Ceree, Ceri, Seree, Siri

Cirila
(Latin) heavenly
*Ceri, Cerila, Cerilla, Cerille,
Cerine, Ciria, Cirine*

Cissy
(American) sweet
Ciss, Cissey, Cissi, Sissi

Cita
(American) from citara
(instrument); musical

Citare
(Greek) musical; variant of
the Indian lute sitar
Citara, Sitare

Claire
(Latin, French) smart
*Clair, Clairee, Claireen,
Claireta, Clairy, Clare,
Clarette, Clarry, Klair*

Clarieca
(Latin) bright
*Claire, Clare, Clari, Clarieka,
Clary, Klarieca, Klarieka*

Clancey
(American) a devil-may-care
attitude
*Clance, Clancee, Clancie,
Clancy*

Clara
(Latin) bright one
*Clarie, Clarine, Clareta,
Clarette, Clare, Claire, Clary*

Clarabelle
(Latin) combo of Clara and
Belle; bright lovely woman
Claribel

Claresta
(Greek) from Clarissa; smart

Clareta
(Spanish) from Clarita;
bright

Clarice
(Latin, Italian) insightful
*Clairece, Claireece, Clairice,
Clarece, Clareece, Clariece,
Clarise*

Clarimond
(Latin) shining defender;
bright

Clarinda
(Latin) from Claire; bright

Clarissa
(Latin, Greek) smart and
clear-minded
*Claressa, Clarice, Clarisa,
Clarise, Clerissa*

Clarity
(American) clear-minded
Clare, Claritee, Claritie

Clasina
(Latin) bright

Claudia
(Latin, German, Italian)
persevering
*Claudelle, Claudie,
Claudina, Clodia, Klaudia*

Claudia-Rose
(American) combo of
Claudia and Rose

Claudette
(French) persistant
*Claude, Claudee, Claudet,
Claudi, Claudie, Claudy*

Clava
(Spanish) earnest; sincere

Clea
(Invented) short for Cleanthe
and Cleopatra; famed
Clia, Klea, Klee

Cleanthe
(English) famed
*Clea, Cleantha, Cliantha,
Klea, Kleanth*

Clelia
(Latin) glorious girl

Clematia
(Greek) winding vine

Clematis
(Greek) vine; clings

Clemence
(Latin) easygoing; merciful
*Clem, Clemense, Clements,
Clemmie, Clemmy*

Clementina
(Spanish) kind; forgiving
*Clementas, Clementi,
Clementis, Clementyna,
Clymentyna, Klementina*

Clementine
(Latin) gentle; (German)
merciful
*Clemencie, Klementine,
Klementynne*

Cleo
(Greek) short for Cleopatra

Cleodal
(Latin) glory
Cleodel, Cleodell

Cleopatra
(Greek) Egyptian queen
Cleo, Clee, Kleeo, Kleo

Cleva
(English) from the hill

Cliantha
(Greek) flower of glory
Cleantha, Cleanthe, Clianthe

Clio
(Greek) history muse
Kleeo, Klio

Cliodhna
(Irish) dark
Clidna, Cliona

Cliona
(Greek) from Clio (history
muse); remembers well

Cloe
(Greek) flourishing
Cloee, Cloey

Cloreen
(American) happy
*Clo, Cloreane, Cloree,
Cloreene, Corean, Klo,
Klorean, Kloreen*

Cloressa
(American) consoling
Cloresse, Kloressa

Clorinda
(Latin) happy
*Cloee, Cloey, Clorinde,
Clorynda, Klorinda*

Cloris
(Latin) pale
Chloris

Clotho
(Mythology) one of the
Greek Fates; spins web of
fate

Clory
(Spanish) smiling
Clori, Clorie, Kloree, Klory

Closetta
(Spanish) secretive
*Close, Closette, Klosetta,
Klosette*

Clotilda
(German) famed fighter
*Clotilde, Clothilde, Tilda,
Tillie, Tilly*

Clotilde
(French) combative

Cloud
(Weather name) light-
hearted
Cloudee, Cloudie, Cloudy

Clove
(Spice) distinctive
Klove

Clover
(Botanical) natural
Clovah, Clove, Kloverr

Clydette
(American) form of Clyde
*Clidette, Clydett, Clydie,
Klyde, Klydette*

Clymene
(Greek) all know her

Clytie
(Greek) excellent; in love
with love
*Cly, Clytee, Clytey, Clyty,
Klytee, Klytie*

Co
(American) jovial
Coco, Ko, Koko

Coahoma
(Native American) panther;
stealthy

Coby
(American) glad
Cobe, Cobey, Cobie

Cochava
(Hebrew) star girl

Cocheta
(Italian) from Concetta;
pure

Coco
(Spanish) coconut
Koko

Cocoa
(Spanish) chocolate;
spunky girl

Cody
(English) soft-hearted; pillow
Codi, Codie, Kodie

Coffey
(American) lovely
Cofee, Caufey

Coiya
(American) coquettish
Coyuh, Koya

Cokey
(American) intelligent
Cokie

Colanda
(African American) from Yolanda; generous

Colberdee
(American) combo of Colber (Colby) and Dee; ostentatious

Colby
(English) enduring
Cobie, Colbi, Kolbee

Cole
(Last name as first name) laughing
Coe, Colie, Kohl

Colemand
(American) adventurer
Colmyand

Colette
(French) spiritual; victorious
Coey, Collette, Kolette

Colina
(American) righteous
Colena, Colin, Colinn

Coline
(Irish) from Colin; girlish

Colinette
from Colleen; victorious

Colisa
(English) delightful
Colissa, Collisa, Collissa

Colleen
(Irish) young girl
Coleen, Colene, Coley, Colleene, Collen, Colli, Kolene, Kolleen

Colley
(English) fearful; worrier
Col, Collie, Kolley

Colmbyne
(Latin) from Columbine; dove; serene

Colola
(African American) combination of Co and Lola; victor
Co, Cola, Colo

Coloma
(Spanish) calm
Colo, Colom, Colome

Columbia
(Latin) from Columbine; dove; serene
Colombe, Columba, Columbine

Columbine
(Latin) dove; flower

Comfort
(American) comforting; easygoing
Komfort

Comfortyne
(French) comforting
Comfort, Comfortine, Comfurtine, Comfy

Comsa
(Greek) variant of Cosma; universal spirit

Concepcion
(Spanish) conceived; begins
Conception

Concetta
(Italian) pure female

Conchetta
(Spanish) wholesome
Concheta, Conchette

Conchie
(Latin) conception
Conchee, Conchi, Konchey, Konchie

Conchita
(Spanish) girl of the conception
Chita, Concha, Conchi

Conchiteen
(Spanish) pure
Conchita, Conchitee, Connie

Conchobarre
(Irish) willful

Concordia
(Latin) goddess of peace

Condoleezza
(American) smart; with sweetness
Condeleesa, Condilesa, Condolissa

Coneisha
(African American) giving
Coneisha, Conisha, Conishah, Conniesha

Conesa
(American) free-flowing nature
Conisa, Connesa, Konesa

Conlee
(American) form of Connelly; radiant
Con, Conlee, Conley, Conlie, Conly, Conly, Connie, Konlee, Konlee, Konlie

Conner
(American) brave
Con, Coner, Coni, Connie, Connor, Conny, Conor

Connie
(Latin, English) short for Constance; constant
Con, Conni, Conny, Konnie

Connie-Kim
(Vietnamese) golden girl
Conni-Kim

Conradina
(German) form of Conrad; brave
Connie, Conradine, Conradyna, Konnie, Konradina

Conroe
(Place name) small town in Texas
Conn, Connie, Konroe

Conroy
(Last name as first name) stately; literary
Conroi, Konroi, Konroy

Conseja
(Spanish) advises

Consolata
(Spanish) consoles others

Constance
(Latin) loyal
Con, Connie, Conny, Constantia, Constantina, Constantine, Constanza

Constantina
(Italian) loyal; constant
Conn, Connee, Conni, Connie, Conny, Constance, Constanteena, Constantinah

Constanza
(Hebrew) constant
Constanz, Connstanzah

Constanze
(German) unchanging
Con, Connie, Stanzi

Consuelo
(Spanish) comfort-giver
Chelo, Consolata, Consuela

Contessa
(Italian) pretty
Contesa, Contessah, Contesse

Cookie
(American) cute
Cooki

Copeland
(Last name as first name) good at coping
Copelan, Copelyn, Copelynn

Copper
(American) redhead
Coper

Coppola
(Italian) theatrical
Copla, Coppi, Coppo, Coppy, Kopla, Kopola, Koppola

Cora
(Greek) maid; giving girl
Corah, Corra, Correna, Corene, Coretta, Corette, Corrie, Corinna, Kora Corabelle

Coral
(Latin) natural; small stone
Corall, Coralle, Coraly, Core, Corel, Koral, Koraly

Coralee
(American) combo of Cora and Lee
Cora-Lee, Coralie, Koralie

Coraline
(American) country girl

Coralynn
(American) combo of Cora and Lynn
Coralene, Coralyn, Cora-Lyn, Cora-Lynn, Coralynne, Corline, Corlynn

Corazon
(Spanish) heart
Cora, Corrie, Zon, Zonn

Corby
(Latin) raven; dark

Corday
(English) prepared; heart
Cord, Cordae, Cordie, Cordy, Korday

Cordelia
(Latin) warm-hearted woman
Cordeelia, Cordalia, Cordelie, Cordi, Cordie, Cordilia, Kordelia, Kordey, Kordi

Cordelita
(Latin, Spanish) heartfelt
Cordelia, Cordelite, Cordella

Cordillera
(Latin) from Cordelia; kind heart

Cordula
(Latin) heart; (German) jewel
Cord, Cordie, Cordoola, Cordoolah, Cordy

Corette
(Greek) from Cora; sweet maiden

Corey
(Irish) perky
Cori, Corree, Corrie, Korey, Korri, Korrie

Corgie
(American) funny
Corgi, Korgee, Korgie

Cori
(Greek, Irish) caring person
Corey, Corri, Corrie, Cory

Coriander
(Botanical) seasoning; simplistic

Corinna
(Greek) young girl
Corina, Corrinna, Corryna, Corynna

Corinne
(Greek) maiden; (French) protective
Coreen, Corina, Corine, Corinna, Corrina, Coryn, Corynn, Koreene, Korinne

Corinthian
(Place name) Corinth, a town in Greece; religious

Coris
(Greek) singer
Corris, Koris, Korris

Corissa
(Greek) kind-hearted
Korissa

Corky
(American) energetic
Corkee, Corkey, Corki, Corkie, Korkee, Korky

Corlinda
(American) combo of Cora and Linda; pretty, yellow-haired girl

Corliss
(English) open-hearted
Corless, Corlise, Corly, Korlis, Korliss

Corly
(American) energetic
Corlee, Corli, Corlie, Korli, Korly

Corlyn
(American) innovative
Corlin, Corlinn, Corlynn, Corlynne, Korlin, Korlyn

Cormella
(Italian) fiery
Cormee, Cormela, Cormelah, Cormellia, Cormey, Cormie

Cornae
(Origin unknown) all seeing
Coma, Korna, Kornae

Cornecia
(Latin) yellow hair; horn

Cornelia
(Latin) practical
Carnelia, Corney, Corni

Cornelius
(Latin) realistic
Corneal, Corneelyus, Corney, Corny

Cornesha
(African American) talkative
Cornee, Corneshah, Cornesia

Corona
(Spanish) crowned
Corone, Coronna, Korona

Correne
(American) musical
Coree, Coreen, Correen, Correna, Korrene, Korene

Corrianna
(American) joyful
Coreanne, Corey, Corianna, Corri, Corriana

Corrie
(English) variant of Coral; delight

Corrinda
(French) girlish
Corri, Corrin, Korin, Korinda

Cortanie
(American) variation on Courtney
Cortanny, Cortany

Cortland
(American) distinctive
Cortlan, Courte, Courtland, Courtlin

Cortlinn
(American) happy
Cortlenn, Cortlin, Cortlyn, Cortlynn

Corvette
(Car model) speedy; dark
Corv, Corva, Corve, Korvette

Corvina
(Latin) raven; brunette

Cosetta
(French) pretty thing

Cosette
(French) warm
Cossette

Cosima
(Greek, German, Italian) the
universe in harmony
Coseema, Koseema, Kosima

Cosmee
(Greek) organized
Cos, Cosmi, Cosmie

Cossette
(French) winning
*Coss, Cossie, Cossy,
Kossee, Kossette*

Costanza
(Last name as first name)
strong-willed; funny

Costner
(American) embraced
*Cosner, Cost, Costnar,
Costnor, Costnur*

Cota
(Spanish) lively

Cotcha
(African American) stylish
*Kasha, Katcha, Katshay,
Kotsha*

Cotia
(Spanish) full of vitality

Cotrena
(American) form of Katrina;
pure
*Catreena, Catrina, Catrine,
Cotrene, Katrine, Kotrene*

Cotton
(American) comforting
Cottie

Countess
(American) blueblood
Contessa

Cournette
(American) form of coronet;
regal
Courney, Kournette

Courney
(English) from Courtney; in
the court; involved

Courtney
(English) regal; (French)
patient
*Cortney, Courtenay,
Courteney, Courtnay,
Courtnee, Courtny, Kortnee,
Kortney*

Covin
(American) unpredictable
Covan, Cove, Coven, Covyn

Coy
(American) sly
Coye, Koi, Koy

Coyah
(American) singular
Coya, Coyia

Coyote
(American) wild
Coyo, Kaiote, Kaiotee

Cozette
(French) darling

Cramer
(American) jolly
Cramar, Cramir, Kramer

Cramisa
(Invented) nice
Cramissa, Kramisa .

Cree
(American) wild spirit
Crea, Creeah

Creed
(American) boisterous
Crede, Cree, Kreed

Creirwy
(Welsh) lucky amulet

Cresa
(English) fickle

Crescente
(American) impressive
*Crescent, Cresent, Cress,
Cressie*

Crescentia
(Spanish) crescent-faced;
smiling
*Creseantia, Crescent,
Cressentt*

Cressa
(Greek) delicate; from the
name Cressida
*Cresa, Cressah, Cresse,
Cress, Kressa*

Cressida
(Greek) infidel
Cresida, Cresiduh, Cresside

Cressie
(American) growing; good
Cress, Cressy, Kress, Kressie

Creston
(American) worthy
*Crest, Crestan, Creste,
Cresten, Crestey, Cresti,
Crestie*

Cresusa
(English) fickle

Cricket
(American) energetic
Kricket

Crimson
(American) deep
Cremsen, Crims, Crimsen, Crimsonn, Crimsun

Criselda
(Spanish) wild
Crisselda

Crishonna
(American) beautiful
Crishona, Crisshone, Crissie, Crissy, Krishona, Krishonna

Crisiant
(Welsh) crystal; clear
Cris, Crissie

Crispa
(Latin) curly hair

Crispina
(Latin) curly-haired girl

Crispy
(Invented) fun-loving; zany
Crispee, Krispy

Crista
(Italian) form of Christina
Krista

Cristin
(Irish) dedicated
Cristen, Crystyn, Kristin, Krystyn

Cristina
(Greek) form of Christina; devout
Christina, Kristina

Cristos
(Greek) dedicated
Criss, Crissie, Christos

Cristy
(English) spiritual
Cristi, Crysti, Krystie, Kristi

Crystal
(Latin) clear; open-minded
Christal, Chrystal, Cristal, Cristalle, Crys, Crystelle, Krystal

Crystilis
(Spanish) focused
Chrysilis, Crys, Cryssi, Cryssie, Crystylis

Csilla
(Hungarian) defensive

Cuba
(Place name) island; fun-loving girl

Cullen
(Irish) attractive
Cullan, Cullie, Cullun, Cully

Cumale
(American) open-hearted
Cue, Cuemalie, Cue-maly, Cumahli

Cumthia
(American) open-minded
Cumthea, Cumthee, Cumthi, Cumthie, Cumthy

Cupid
(American) romantic
Cupide

Curine
(American) attractive
Curina, Curinne, Curri, Currin

Curry
(American) languid
Curree, Currey, Curri, Currie

Cursten
(American) form of Kirsten
Curst, Curstee, Curstie, Curstin

Cushaun
(American) elegant
Cooshaun, Cooshawn, Cue, Cushawn, Cushonn, Cushun

Cyan
(American) colorful
Cyanne, Cyenna, Cyun

Cyanea
(Greek) blue-eyed baby

Cyanetta
(Greek) little blue
Cyan, Cyanette, Syan, Syanette

Cybele
(Greek) conflicted

Cybill
(Latin) prophetess
Cybell, Cybelle, Cybil, Sibyl, Sibyle

Cydell
(American) country girl
Cydee, Cydel, Cydie, Cydile, Cydy

Cydney
(American) perky
Cyd, Cydni, Cydnie

Cylee
(American) darling
Cye, Cyle, Cylea, Cyli, Cylie, Cyly

Cylene
(American) melodious
Cylena, Cyline

Cyllene
(American) sweet

Cyma
(Greek) does well

Cymbeline
(Greek) Shakespearean play
Beline, Cymba, Cymbe, Cymbie, Cyme, Cymmie, Symbe

Cyn
(Greek) short for Cynthia
Cynnae, Cynnie, Syn

Cynara
(Greek) prickly; particular
Cynarra

Cynder
(English) having wanderlust
Cindee, Cinder, Cindy, Cyn, Cyndee, Cyndie, Cyndy

Cyntanah
(American) singer
Cintanna, Cyntanna

Cynthia
(Greek, English) moon goddess
Cindy, Cyn, Cyndee, Cyndy, Cynthea, Cynthee, Cynthie

Cyntia
(Greek) variant of Cynthia; smiling goddess
Cyn, Cyntea, Cynthie, Cyntie, Syntia

Cyntrille
(African American) gossipy
Cynn, Cyntrell, Cyntrelle, Cyntrie

Cypress
(Botanical) swaying
Cypres, Cyprice, Cypris, Cypriss, Cyprus

Cyra
(American) willing
Cye, Cyrah, Syra

Cyreen
(American) sensual
Cyree, Cyrene, Cyrie

Cyrena
(American) variant of Serena; siren

Cyrenian
(American) bewitching
Cyree, Cyren, Cyrenean, Cyrey, Siren, Syrenian

Cyrenna
(American) straightforward
Cyrena, Cyrennah, Cyrinna, Cyryna, Cyrynna

Cyriece
(American) artistic
Cyreece, Cyree, Cyreese, Cyrie

Cyrilla
(Latin) royal; little minx
Cirila

Cytherea
(Greek) from Cythera; celestial

Czarina
(Russian) royal

Daba
(Hebrew) kindhearted

D'Anna
(Hebrew) special

Dacey
(Irish) a southerner
Dace, Dacee, Daci, Dacia, Dacie, Dacy, Daicie, Daycee

Dacia
(Latin) old soul
Dacie, Dachia, Dachi

Dae
(English) day
Day, Daye

Daelan
(English) aware
Dael, Daelan, Daeleen, Daelena, Daelin, Daely, Daelyn, Daelynne, Dale, Daley, Daylan, Daylin, Daylind, Dee

Daeshawna
(American) combo of Dae and Shawna; daylight
Daeshan, Daeshanda, Daeshandra, Daeshandria, Daeshaun, Daeshauna, Daeshaundra, Daeshaundria, Daeshavon, Daeshawn, Daeshawnda, Daeshawndra, Daeshawndria, Daeshawntia, Daeshon, Daeshona, Daeshonda, Daeshondra, Daeshondria

Daeshonda
(African American) combo of Dae and Shonda
Daeshanda, Daeshawna, Daeshondra

Daffodil
(Botanical) flower
Daffy

Dafnee
(Greek, American) form of Daphne; pretty
Dafney, Dafnie

Dagmar
(German, Scandinavian) glorious day
Dag, Dagmara, Dagmarr

Dagny
(Scandinavian) day
Dagna, Dagnanna, Dagne, Dagney

Dahlia
(Scandinavian) flower
Dahl, Dollie

Dai
(Welsh, Japanese) beloved one of great importance

Daira
(American) outgoing
D'Aira, Daire, Dairrah, Darrah, Derrah

Daisha
(American) sparkling
D'Aisha, Daish, Daishe, Dasha, Dashah

Daisy
(English) flower and day's eye
Daisee, Daisey, Daisi, Daisia, Daisie, Daissy, Daizee, Daizi, Daizy, Dasey, Dasi, Dasie, Dasy, Daysee, Daysie, Daysy

Daisyetta
(American) combo of Daisy and Etta; spunky; the day's eye
Daiseyetta, Daizie, Daiziette, Dasie, Dazeyetta, Daziette

Daiton
(American) wondrous
Day, Dayten, Dayton

Daja
(American) intuitive
Dajah

Dajanae
(African American) persuasive
Daije, Daja, Dajainay, Dayjanah

Dajon
(American) gifted
D'Jon, Dajo, Dajohn, Dajonn, Dajonnay, Dajonne

Dakara
(American) firebrand
Dacara, Dakarah, Dakarea, Dakarra

Daking
(Asian) friendly

Dakota
(Native American) tribal name; solid friend
Dacota, Dakohta, Dakotah, Dakotha, Dakotta, Dekoda, Dekota, Dekotah, Dekotha

Dalacie
(American) brilliant
Dalaci, Dalacy, Dalasie, Dalce, Dalci, Dalse

Dalaina
(American) spirited
Dalana, Dalayna, Delaina, Delaine, Delayna

Dalaney
(American) hopeful
Dalanee, Dalaynee, Dalayni

Dale
(English) valley-life
Daile, Daleleana, Dalena, Dalina, Dayle

Daleah
(American) pretty
Dalea

Daley
(Irish) leader
Dailey, Dalea, Daleigh, Dali, Dalie, Daly

Dalia
(Spanish) flower
Daliah, Daliyah, Dayliah, Doliah, Dolliah, Dolya

Dalian
(Place name) joy
Dalean

Daliana
(American) joyful spirit
Daliane, Dalianna, Dilial, Dollianna

Dalice
(American) able
Daleese, Dalleece

Dalila
(African) gentle
Dahlila, Dahlilla, Dalia, Dalilah, Dalilia

Dalin
(American) calm
Dalen, Dalenn, Dalun

Dalita
(American) smooth
Daleta, Daletta, Dalite, Dalitee, Dalitta

Dallas
(Place name) confident
*Dalis, Dalisse, Daliz, Dallice,
Dallis, Dallsyon, Dallus,
Dallys, Dalyce, Dalys*

Dallen
(American) outspoken
Dal, Dalin, Dallin, Dalen

Dallise
(American) gentle
*Dalise, Dallece, Dalleece,
Dalleese*

Dalondra
(Invented) generous
*Dalandra, Dalon,
Dalondrah, Delondra*

Dalonna
(Invented) generous
Dalohn, Dalona, Dalonne

Dalphine
(French) form of Delphine;
delicate and svelte
*Dal, Dalf, Dalfeen, Dalfene,
Dalphene*

Dalton
(American) smart
*Dallee, Dalli, Dallie, Dallton,
Dally, Daltawyn*

Daltrey
(American) quiet
Daltree, Daltri, Daltrie

Dalyn
(American) smart
*Dalin, Dalinne, Dalynn,
Dalynne*

Dama
(Hindi) temptress
Dam

Damalla
(Greek) fledgling; young
*Damala, Damalas, Damalis,
Damall*

Damara
(Greek) gentle
Damaris, Damarra

Damaris
(Greek) calm
*Damalis, Damar, Damara,
Damares, Damaret,
Damarius, Damary, Damarys,
Dameress, Dameris, Damiris,
Dammaris, Dammeris,
Damrez, Damris, Demaras,
Demaris, Demarays*

Damecia
(Invented) sweet
*Dameisha, Damesha,
Demecia, Demisha, Demeshe*

Dami
(Greek) short for Damia;
spirited
*Damee, Damey, Damie,
Damy*

Damia
(Greek) spirited
*Damiah, Damya, Damyah,
Damyen, Damyenne,
Damyuh*

Damianne
(Greek) one who soothes
Damiana

Damica
(French) open-spirited
*Dameeka, Dameka,
Damekah, Damicah, Damie,
Damika, Damikah,
Demeeka, Demeka,
Demekah, Demica, Demicah*

Damita
(Spanish) small woman of
nobility
*Dama, Damah, Damee,
Damesha, Dameshia,
Damesia, Dametia,
Dametra, Dametrah*

Damon
(American) sprightly
Damoane, Damone

Damone
(American) mighty
Dame

Dana
(English) bright gift of God
*Daina, Dainna, Danae,
Danah, Danai, Danaia,
Danalee, Danan, Danarra,
Danayla, Dane, Danean,
Danee, Daniah, Danie,
Danna, Dayna, Daynah*

Danae
(Greek) bright and pure
*Danay, Danayla, Danays,
Danea, Danee, Dannae,
Danays, Danee, Denae,
Denee*

Danala
(English) happy, golden
*Dan, Danalla, Danee,
Danela, Danney, Danny*

Danasha
(African American) combo
of Dana and Tasha; spirited
*Anasha, Danas, Danash,
Danashah, Daneash,
Danesha*

Danasia
(American) combo of Dana
and Asia; dances

Danay
(American) happy
D'Nay, Dánay, Danaye

Dancel
(French) energetic
*Dance, Dancell, Dancelle,
Dancey, Dancie, Danse,
Dansel, Danselle*

Dancie
(American) from the word
dancer
Dancy

Daneil
(Hebrew) judged by God;
spiritual
*Daneal, Daneala, Daneale,
Daneel, Daneela, Daneila*

Danelle
(Hebrew) kind-hearted;
combo of Dan and Nelle
*Danael, Danalle, Danel,
Danele, Danell, Danella,
Dani, Dannele, Danny*

Danelly
(Spanish) form of Daniel;
judged by God
*Daneli, Danellie, Dannelley,
Dannelly*

Danessa
(American) dainty
*Danesa, Danese, Danesha,
Danesse, Daniesa, Daniesha,
Danisa, Danisha, Danissa*

Danessia
(American) delicate child
*Danesia, Danieshia,
Danisla, Danissia*

Danette
(American) form of Danielle
Danetra, Danett, Danetta

Dangela
(Latin) form of Angela;
angelic
*Angee, Angelle, Angie,
Dangelah, Dangelia,
Dangey, Dangi, Dangie*

Dani
(Hebrew) short for Danielle;
judged by God
*Danee, Danie, Danne,
Dannee, Danni, Dannie,
Danny, Dany*

Dania
(Hebrew) short for Danielle
Daniah, Danya, Danyah

Daniah
(Hebrew) judged
Dan, Dania, Danny, Danya

Danica
(Latin, Polish) star of the
morning
*Daneeka, Danika, Danneeka,
Dannica, Dannika*

Danice
(American) combo of
Danelle and Janice;
romantic

Danielle
(Hebrew, French) form of
Daniel; judged by God
alone
*Danelle, Daniell, Daniele,
Danniella, Danyel*

Daniella
(Italian) form of Danielle
Danilla

Danir
(American) fresh
Daner

Danit
(Hebrew) judged by God
*Danett, Danis, Danisha,
Daniss, Danita, Danitra,
Danitza, Daniz, Danni*

Danita
(American) combo of Dan
and Anita; gregarious
Danni, Danny, Denita, Denny

Danna
(American) cheerful
*D'Ana, D'Anna, Dannae,
Danni, Danny*

Danube
(Place name) river; flowing
spirit

Danuta
(Polish) God's gift

Daphiney
(Greek) form of Daphne;
nymph
Daff, Daph

Daphne
(Greek) pretty nymph
*Daphane, Daphaney,
Daphanie, Daphany,
Daphiney, Daphnee,
Daphney, Daphnie, Daphny,
Daphonie, Daphy*

Daquisha
(African American) talkative

Dara
(Hebrew) compassionate
*Dahra, Dahrah, Darah,
Darra, Darrah*

Daralice
(Greek) beloved
Dara, Daraleese, Daraliece

Daravia
(Hebrew) loving

Darby
(Irish) a free woman
Darb, Darbee, Darbi,
Darbie, Darbye

Darceece
(Irish) from Darci; dark

Darcelle
(American) secretive
Darce, Darcel, Darcell, Darcey

Darci
(Irish) dark
Darce, Darcee, Darcie,
Darcy, Dars, Darsey

Darda
(Hebrew) wise

Dari
(Czech) rich

Daria
(Greek, Italian) rich woman
of luxury
Dare, Darea, Dareah, Dari,
Darian, Darianne, Darria,
Darya

Darian
(Anglo-Saxon) precious
Dare, Darien, Darry, Derian,
Derian

Darice
(English) contemporary
Dareese, Darese, Dari,
Dariece, Darri, Darrie, Darry

Darielle
(French) rich
Darell, Darelle, Dariel,
Darriel, Darrielle

Darienne
(Greek) great

Darilyn
(American) darling
Darilin, Darilinn, Darilynn,
Derilyn

Darina
(Greek) rich

Darionne
(American) adventuresome
Dareon, Darion, Darionn,
Darionna

Dariya
(Russian) sweet
Dara, Darya

Darla
(English) short for Darlene
Darl, Darlee, Darley, Darli,
Darlie, Darly

Darlee
(English) darling
Darl, Darley, Darli, Darlie

Darlene
(French) darling girl
Darlean, Darleen, Darlena,
Darlenia, Darlin, Darling

Darlie-Lynn
(American) combo of Darlie
and Lynn

Darling
(American) precious
Darline, Darly, Darlyng

Darlonna
(African American) darling
Darlona

Darlye
(French) darling

Darnelle
(Irish) seamstress
Darnel, Darnell, Darnella,
Darnyell

Daroma
(American) treasured

Daron
(Irish) great woman
Daren, Darun, Daryn

Darrelle
(English) loved

Darrien
(Irish) great

Darrow
(Last name as first name)
cautious
Darro, Darroh

Darryl
(French, English) beloved
Darel, Darelle, Daril, Darrell,
Darrill, Daryl, Daryll, Derel,
Derrell

Darshelle
(African American)
confident
Darshel, Darshell

Dart
(English) tenacious
Darte, Dartee, Dartt

Daruce
(Hindi) from Daru; pine
tree; sturdy

Darva
(Invented) sensible
Darv, Darvah, Darvee,
Darvey, Darvi, Darvie

Daryn
(Greek, Irish) gift-giver
Daryan, Darynn, Darynne

Dash
(American) fast-moving
Dashee, Dasher, Dashy

Dasha
(Russian) darling
Dashah

Dashanda
(African American) loving
Dashan, Dashande

Dashawn
(African American) brash
Dashawna, Dashay

Dashawntay
(African American) careful
Dash, Dashauntay

Dashea
(Hebrew) patient

Dasheena
(African American) flashy
Dashea, Dasheana

Dashelle
(African American) striking
Dachelle, Dashel, Dashell, Dashy

Dashika
(African American) runner
Dash, Dasheka

Dashiki
(African) loose shirt; casual
Dashi, Dashika, Dashka, Desheka, Deshiki

Dashilan
(American) solemn
Dashelin, Dashelin, Dashlinne, Dashlyn, Dashlynn, Dasialyn

Dasmine
(Invented) sleek
Dasmeen, Dasmin, Dazmeen, Dazmine

Dassia
(American) pretty
Dasie, Dassea, Dasseah, Dassee, Dassi, Dassie, Deassiah

Dati
(Hebrew) believer

Dativa
(Hebrew) believer

Daureen
(American) darling
Dareen, Daurean, Daurie, Daury, Dawreen

Davalynn
(American) combo of Dava and Lynn; sparkling eyes
Davalin, Davalinda, Davalyn, Davalynda, Davalynne, Davelin, Davelyn, Davelynn, Davelynne, Davilin, Davilyn, Davilynn, Davilynne

Daveena
(Scottish) form of David; loved
Daveen, Davena, Davey, Davina, Davinna

Davelyn
(Invented) combo of Dave and Lynn; loved
Davalin, Davalynn, Davalynne, Dave, Davey, Davie, Davilynn

Davianna
(English) beloved

Davida
(Hebrew) beloved one
Daveeda, Daveisha, Davesia, Daveta, Davetta, Davette, Davika, Davisha, Davita

Davina
(Hebrew) believer; beloved
Dava, Daveena, Davene, Davida, Davita, Devina, Devinia, Devinya

Davincia
(Spanish) God-loving; winner
Davince, Davinse, Vincia

Davinique
(African American) believer; unique
Davin, Davineek, Vineek

Davis
(American) boyish
Daves

Davisnell
(Invented) vivacious
Daviesnell, DavisNell

Davonna
(Scottish) well-loved
Davon, Davona, Davonda

Davonne
(African American) splashy
Davaughan, Davaughn, Davion, Daviona, Davon, Davone, Davonn

Davrush
(Yiddish) loves others

Dawa
(Tibetan) girl born on Monday

Dawanda
(African American) righteous
Dawana, Dawand, Dawanna, Dawauna, Dawonda, Dawonna, Dwanda

Dawn
(English) dawn
Daun, Dawna, Dawne

Dawna
(English) eloquence of dawn
Dauna, Daunda, Dawn, Dawnah, Dawnna, Dawny, Dawnya

Dawnika
(African American) dawn
Dawneka, Dawneeka, Dawnica, Donika

Dawnisha
(African American) breath of dawn
Daunisha, Dawnish, Dawny, Nisa, Nisha

Dawntelle
(African American) morning bright
Dawntel, Dawntell, Dontelle

Dawona
(African American) smart
Dawonna, Dawonne

Day
(English) day; bright

Dayana
(American) variant of Diana; darling
Dayannah, Dyana

Dayanara
(Spanish) form of Deyanira; forceful; destructive
Day, Daya, Dayan, Dianara, Diannare, Nara

Daylee
(American) calm; reserved
Dailee, Day, Dayley, Dayly

Dayna
(English) variant of Dana; bright gift of God
Daynah

Daysha
(Russian) also Dasha; serene
Dayeisha

Dayshanay
(African American) saucy
Daysh, Dayshanae, Dayshannay, Dayshie

Dayshawna
(American) laughing
Dayshauna, Dayshona, Dashonah

Dayshay
(African American) lovable
Dashae, Dashay, Dashea

Dayton
(Place name) town in Ohio; fast

Daytona
(American) speedy
Dayto, Daytonna

Dayvonne
(African American) careful
Dave, Davey, Davonne, Dayvaughn

De
(Chinese) virtuous

Deacon
(Greek) joyful messenger
Deak, Deakon, Deecon, Deke

Dean
(English) practical
Deanie, Deanni

Deana
(Latin) divine girl
Deane, Danielle, Deanna

Deandra
(English) combo of Deanna and Sandra; pretty face
Andie, Andra, Dee

Deandralina
(American) combo of Deandra and Lina; divine seer
Deandra-Lina, Deandra Lina. Deanalina, Lina, Deandra, Dee, DeeDee

Deandria
(American) sweetheart
Deandreah, Deandriah

Deanie
(English) form of Dean; from the valley
Deanee, Deaney, Deani

Deanna
(Latin, English) divine girl
Deana, Deanne, Dee

Deanne
(Latin) from Diana; moon goddess
Deann, Dee, Deeann

Dearbhail
(Welsh) held close

Dearon
(American) dear one
Dear, Dearan, Dearen, Deary

Dearoven
(American) form of Dearon
Derovan, Deroven

Deasa
(Spanish) delightful

Debarath
(Hebrew) bee; busy
Deborath, Daberath

Debbie

(Hebrew) short for Deborah
*Deb, Debbee, Debbey,
Debbi, Debby, Debbye,
Debee, Debi, Debie*

Debbie-Jean

(American) combo of
Debbie and Jean

Debbielou

(American) combo of
Debbie and Lou
Debilou

Debbie-Sue

(American) combo of Debbi
and Sue
Debbisue

Deborah

(Hebrew) prophetess
*Debbie, Debbora,
Debborah, Debor, Deboreh,
Deborrah, Debra*

Debra

(Hebrew) prophetess
Debbra, Debbrah, Debrah

Debran

(American) form of Deborah

Debray

(American) form of
Deborah; prophetess
*Dabrae, Deb, Debrae,
Debraye*

Debra-Jean

(American) combo of Debra
and Jean

DeChell

(Invented) combo of De and
Chell; quiet
Dechelle, Dee

Decima

(Latin) tenth girl

Decuma

(Mythology) one of the
Roman Fates; measures

Dedra

(American) spirited
*Dee, DeeDee, Deeddra,
Deedra, Deedrea, Deedrie,
Deidra, Deirdre*

Dee

(English, Irish) lucky one
*Dedee, Dea, Deah, DeeDee,
Dee-Dee, Didee*

Deedee

(American) short for D
names; vivacious
*D.D., Dee Dee, DeeDee,
Dee-Dee*

Deena

(American) soothes

Deepa

(Hindi) light

DeErica

(African American)
audacious
Dee-Erica

Deesha

(American) dancing
*Dedee, Dee, Deesh,
Deeshah, Deisha*

Deidra

(Irish) sparkling
Deedra, Deidre, Dierdra

Deighan

(American) exciting
Daygan, Deigan

Deiondra

(Greek) partier; wine-loving
*Deandrah, Deann,
Deanndra, Dee, Deean,
Deeann, DeeDee, Deondra*

Deirdre

(Irish) passionate
*Dedra, Dee, Deedee,
Deedrah, Deerdra, Deerdre,
Didi*

Deishauna

(African American) combo
of Dei and Shauna; pious;
day of God
*Dayshauna, Deisha,
Deishaun, Deishaune,
Shauna*

Deissy

(Greek) form of Desma;
sworn; loyal
*Deisi, Deissey, Deissie,
Desma, Desmee, Desmer,
Dessi*

Deitra

(Greek) goddess-like
Deetra, Detria

Deja

(French) already seen
D'Ja, Dejah

Deja-Marie

(American) combo of Deja
and Marie
Deja, Dejamarie

Dejon

(French) she came before
Daijon, Dajan, Dajona

Deka

(African) a pleasure
Dekah, Dekka

Dela
(English) dramatic

Delace
(American) combo of De and Lace; smart

Delaine
(American) combo of D and Elaine; smart
D'Laine, Delane

Delana
(German) protective
Dalana, Dalanna, Dalayna, Daleena, Dalena, Dalenna, Dalina, Dalinna, Deedee, Delaina, Delainah, Delena

Delanah
(American) wise
Delana, Dellana, Delano

Delaney
(Irish) challenging
Dalaney, Dalania, Dalene, Daleney, Daline, Del, Delainey, Delane, Delanie, Dalayne, Delaynie, Deleani, Dell, Della, Dellaney

Delandra
(American) outgoing
Delan, Delande

Delaney
(Irish) bouncy; enthusiastic
Dalanie, Delaine, Delainey, Delane, DeLayney, Dellie, Dulaney

Delcarmen
(Spanish) combo of Del and Carmen; worldly
Del, Del Carmen, Del-Carmen, Delcee, Delcy

Delcia
(Latin) delightful

Delcine
(Latin) a delight

Delcy
(American) friendly
Del, Delcee, Delci

Dele
(American) rash; noble
Del, Dell

Delfina
(Latin, Italian) flowering
Dellfina, Delphina

Delgadina
(Spanish) derivative of Delgado; slender
Delga, Delgado

Delia
(Greek) lovely; moon goddess
Dehlia, Deilyuh, Del, Delea, Deli, Dellia, Dellya, Delya, Delyah

Delicia
(English) delights
Delesha, Delice, Delisa, Delise, Delisha, Delisiah, Delya, Delys, Delyse, Delysia

Delight
(French) wonderful

Delilah
(Hebrew) beautiful temptress
Dalia, Dalila, Delila, Lilah

Delinda
(American) form of Melinda; pretty
Delin, Delinde, Delynda

Delise
(Latin) delicious
Del, Delice, Delicia, Delisa, Delissa

Delite
(American) a pleasure
Delight

Dell
(Greek) kind
Del

Della
(Greek) kind
Dee, Del, Dela, Dell, Delle, Delli, Dells

Dellana
(Irish) form of Delaney; vibrant; delight
Delaine, Delana, Dell, Dellaina, Dellane, Dellann

Delma
(American) combo of Dell and Velma; practical

Dell-Marie
(American) combo of Dell and Marie; helpful; gracious
Dell Marie, Delmaria, Delmarie

Delma-Lee
(American) combo of Delma and Lee; uncomplicated
Delmalea, Delmalee

Delmee
(American) star
Del, Delmey, Delmi, Delmy

Delmys
(American) incredible
Del, Delmas, Delmis

Delon
(American) musical
Delonn, Delonne

Delora
(Spanish) from Delores; pensive
Dellora, Delorita

Delores
(Spanish) woman of sorrowful leaning
Del, Delora, Delore, Dolores, Deloria, Delories, Deloris, Delorise

Delos
(Greek) beautiful brunette; a small Aegean isle; stunning
Delas

Delpha
(Greek) from Delphi, or the flower delphinium; flourishing
Delfa

Delphina
(Greek) dolphin; smart

Delphine
(Latin) swimmer
Delfina, Delfine, Delpha, Delphe, Delphene, Delphi, Delphia, Delphina, Delphinia, Delvina

Delta
(Greek) door; Greek alphabet letter; (American) land-loving
Del, Dell, Dellta, Delte, Deltra

Deltrese
(African American) jubilant
Del, Delltrese, Delt, Delta, Deltreese, Deltrice

Delwyn
(English, Welsh) beautiful friend
Delwen, Delwenne, Delwin

Demery
(American) combo of D and Emery; demure

Demetress
(Greek) form of Demetria, goddess of harvest
Deme, Demetra, Demetres, Demetri, Demetria, Dimi, Tress, Tressie, Tressy

Demetria
(Greek) harvest goddess
Deitra, Demeta, Demeteria, Demetra, Demetrice, Demetris, Demetrish, Demetrius, Demi, Demita, Demitra

Demi
(French) half
Demiah, Demie

Dena
(English) laidback; valley
Deane, Deena, Deeyn, Denae, Denah, Dene, Denea, Deney, Denna

Denae
(Hebrew) from Dena; shows the truth
Danay, Denee

Deneane
(English) from Denise; lively

Denedra
(American) lively; natural
Den, Dene, Denney

Denee
(French) robust

Deneen
(American) absolved
Denean, Denene

Denes
(English) nature-lover
Denis, Denne, Denny

Denesha
(American) rowdy

Denetria
(Greek) from God
Denitria, Denny, Dentria

Denetrice
(African American) optimistic
Denetrise, Denitrise, Denny

Denise
(French) wine-lover
Danice, Daniece, Danise, Denese, Deni, Denica, Deniece, Denni, Denny

Denisha
(American) jubilant
Danisha, Deneesha, Deneesha, Denesha, Deneshea, Deniesha, Denishia

Denton
(American) Texas town
Dent, Dentun, Denty, Dentyn

Denver
(English) born in a green valley
Denv, Denvie

Denz
(Invented) lively
Dens

Deoniece
(African American) feminine
Dee, DeeDee, Deo, Deone,
Deoneece, Deoneese

Deonsha
(American) from Deone;
charismatic

Dericka
(American) dancer
D'ericka, Derica, Dericca,
Derika, Derrica, Derricka,
Derrika

Derie
(Hebrew) form of Derora;
dear; bird
Derey, Drora, Drorah

Deronique
(African American) unique
girl
Deron, Deroneek

Derrona
(American) natural
Derona, Derone, Derry

Derry
(Irish) red-haired woman
Deri, Derrie

Deryn
(Welsh) birdlike; small
Derren, Derrin, Derrine,
Deryne

Desdemona
(Greek) a name from Greek
drama and Shakespeare's
Othello; tragic figure
Des, Desde, Dez

Deshawna
(African American)
vivacious
Dashawna, Deshan,
Deshanda, Deshandra,
Deshane, Deshaun,
Deshauna, Deshaundra,
Deshaune, Deshawnna,
Deshawn, Deshawndra,
Desheania, Deshona,
Deshonda, Deshonna

Deshaye
(American) combo of Dee
and Shaye; romantic

Deshette
(African American) dishy
Deshett

Deshondra
(African American)
vivacious
Deshaundra, Deshondrah,
Deshondria

Desi
(French) short for Desiree
Dezi, Dezzie

Desiah
(French) from Desiree;
desired

Desire
(English) desired
Dezire

Desiree
(French) desired
Des'ree, Desairee, Desarae,
Desaray, Desaraye, Desaree,
Desarhea, Desary, Deseri,
Desree, Des-Ree, Dezaray,
Deziree, Dezray

Destin
(American) destiny
Destinn, Destyn

Destina
(Spanish) destiny
Desteena, Desteenah

Destiny
(French) fated
Destanee, Destanie,
Desteney, Destinay,
Destinee, Destinei, Destini,
Destinyi, Destnay, Destney,
Destonie, Destony, Destyni

Destry
(American) well-fated;
western feel
Destrey, Destri, Destrie

Deterrion
(Latin) form of Detra;
blessed
Deterr, Deterreyon, Detra,
Detrae

Detra
(Latin) form of Detta;
blessed
Detraye

Deva
(Hindi) moon goddess;
wielder of power
Devi

Devahuti
(Hindi) from Deva, moon
goddess

Devalca
(Spanish) generous
Deval

Devan
(Irish) poetic
Devana, Devn

Devashka
(Hebrew) variant of
Devasha; honey

Devi
(Hindi) beloved goddess
*Devia, Deviann, Devian,
Devie, Devri*

Devin
(Irish) poetic
*Devan, Devane, Devanie,
Devany, Deven, Devena,
Deveny, Deveyn, Devine,
Devinne, Devn, Devyn,
Devynne*

Devina
(Irish) divine; creative
*Davena, Devie, Devine,
Devy, Divine*

Devon
(English) place name; poetic
*Dev, Devaughan,
Devaughn, Devie, Devonne,
Devy*

Devonna
(English) girl from
Devonshire; happy
*Davonna, Devon, Devona,
Devonda, Devondra*

Devorah
(American) combo of Devon
and Deborah
*Devora, Devore, Devra,
Devrah*

Dew
(American) from the word
dew; fresh
Dewi, Dewie

Dewanna
(African American) clingy
D'Wana, Dewana, Dewanne

Dexhiana
(Origin Unknown) nimble

Dexter
(English) spunky; dexterous
*Dex, Dexee, Dexey, Dexie,
Dext, Dextar, Dextur, Dexy*

Dextra
(Latin) skilled

Deyanira
(Spanish) aggressor
*Deyan, Deyann, Dianira,
Nira, Nira*

Dharcia
(American) sparkler
Darch, Darsha, Dharsha

Dharika
(American) sad
Darica, Darika

Dharma
(Hindi) morality; beliefs
Darma, Darmah

Dhazalai
(African) sweet
Dhaze, Dhazie

Dhelal
(Arabic) coy

Dhessie
(American) glowing
*Dhessee, Dhessey, Dhessi,
Dhessy*

Dhumma
(Hebrew) from Dumia; quiet

Di
(Latin) short for Diane or
Diana
Didi, Dy

Dia
(Greek) shining
Di

Diaelza
(Spanish) divine; pretty
Diael, Dialza, Elza

Diah
(American) pretty
Dia

Diamantina
(Spanish) sparkling
Diama, Diamante, Mantina

Diamond
(Latin) precious gemstone
*Diamin, Diamon, Diamonda,
Diamonds, Diamonte,
Diamun, Diamyn, Diamynd,
Dyamond*

Diamondah
(African American) glowing
Diamonda, Diamonde

Diamondique
(African American)
sparkling
Diamondik

Diamony
(American) gem
*Diamonee, Diamoney,
Diamoni, Diamonie*

Diana
(Latin) divine woman;
goddess of the hunt and
fertility
*Dee, Di, Diahana, Diahna,
Dianah, Diannah, Didi,
Dihanna, Dyanna, Dyannah,
Dyhana*

Dianalynn
(American) combo of Diana
and Lynn
*Dianalin, Dianalinne,
Dianalyn*

Diandro
(American) special
Diandra, Diandrea, Diandroh

Diane
(Latin) goddess-like; divine
Deane, Deanne, Deeann, Deeanne, Deedee, Di, Diahann, Dian, Diann, Dianne, Didi

Dianette
(American) combo of Diane and Ette; high-spirited
Di, Diane, Dianett, Didi, Diette, Diyannette, Dyan, Dyanette, Dyanne, Dyenette

Diantha
(Greek) flower; heavenly
Dianth

Diarah
(American) pretty
Dearah, Di, Diara, Diarra, Dierra

Diavonne
(African American) jovial
Diavone, Diavonna, Diavonni

Dicey
(American) impulsive
Di, Dice, Dicee, Dicy, Dycee, Dycey

Dicia
(American) wild
Desha, Dicy

Diedre
(Irish) variant of Deidre; spunky
Diedra, Diedré

Diella
(Latin) worships
Dielle

Diesha
(African American) zany
Diecia, Dieshah, Dieshie, Dieshay

Diethild
(German) believer

Diggs
(American) tomboyish
Digs, Dyggs

Dihana
(American) natural
Dihanna

Dijonaise
(Invented) condiments; combo of Dijon and mayonnaise
Deejonaise, Dijon, Dijonais, Dijonaze, Naise

Dijonnay
(American) fun-loving
Dijon, Dijonae, Dijonay, Dijonnae, Dijonnaie

Dilan
(American) form of Dylan
Dillan, Dilon

Dillyana
(English) worshipful
Diliann, Dilli, Dillianna, Dilly

Dilsey
(American) dependable; one who endures

Dilynn
(American) variant of Dylan; loving the sea
Di, Dilenn, Dilinn, Dilyn, Lynn

Dima
(American) high-spirited
Deemah, Dema

Dimond
(American) from Diamond; shines

Dina
(Hebrew, Scottish) right; royal

Dinah
(Hebrew) fair judge
Dina, Dinah, Dinna, Dyna, Dynah

Dinesha
(American) happy
Dineisha, Dineshe, Diniesha

Dini
(American) joyful
Dinee, Diney, Dinie

Dinora
(Spanish) judged by God
Dina, Dino, Nora

Dioma
(Greek) from Diona; loves God

Diona
(Greek) divine woman
Dee, Di, Dion, Dionah, Dionuh

Dioneece
(American) daring
Dee, DeeDee, Deon, Deone, Deonece, Deoneece, Dioniece, Neece, Neecey

Dionicia
(Spanish) vixen
Di, Dione, Dionice, Dionise, Nicia, Nise, Nisee

Dionndra
(American) loving
Diondra, Diondrah, Diondruh

Dionne
(Greek) love goddess
Deona, Deondra, Deonia, Deonna, Deonne, Dion, Dione, Dionna

Dionshay
(African American) combo of Dion and Shay; loving
Dionsha, Dionshae, Dionshaye

Dior
(French) stylish
Diora, Diorah, Diore, Diorra, Diorre

Diotima
(Latin) in the time of God

Dira
(Arabic) soft-spoken

Direll
(American) svelte
Di, Direl, Direlle

Dirisha
(African American) outgoing
Di, Diresha, Direshe

Disa
(Scandinavian) goddess

Disha
(American) fine
Dishae, Dishuh

Dishawna
(African American) special
Dishana, Dishauna, Dishawnah, Dishona, Dishonna

Divina
(American) divine being

Divine
(Italian) divine soul
Divin, Divina

Divinity
(American) sweet; devout
Divinitee, Diviniti, Divinitie

Dix
(French) live wire

Dixann
(American) combo of Dixie and Ann
Dixan, Dixanne, Dixiana, Dixieanna

Dixie
(English, French, American) Southern girl
Dixee, Dixi, Dixy

D'Nicola
(American) combo of D and Nicola
D'nicole, Deenicola, Dnicola

Dnisha
(African American) rejoicing
D'Nisha, Dnisa, Dnish, Dnishay, Dnishe

Dobie
(American) cowgirl
Dobee, Dobey, Dobi

Docia
(Latin) from Docilla; docile
Docie

Docilla
(Latin) docile
Docila, Docile

Dodie
(Greek, Hebrew) short for Dorothy; beloved woman
Doda, Dodee, Dodi, Dody

Dodona
(Greek) ancient city in Greece

Doherty
(American) ambitious
Dhoertey, Dohertee, Dohertie

Dolcy
(American) a vision
Dolcee, Dolcie, Dolsee

Dolly
(American) effervescent
Dol, Doll, Dollee, Dolli, Dollie

Dolores
(Spanish) woman of sorrowful leaning
Delores

Domel
(Place name) steadfast; faithful
Domela, Domella

Dometria
(American) form of Greek Demetria; goddess; fruitful
Dome, Dometrea, Domi, Domini, Domitra

Domina
(Latin) ladylike

Domini
(Latin) form of Dominick
Dom, Dominee, Domineke, Dominey, Dominie, Dominika, Domino, Dominy

Dominica
(Latin) follower of God
Domenica, Domenika, Domineca, Domineka, Domini, Dominika, Domenika, Domineca, Dom, Domonica, Domonika

Dominique
(French) bright; masterful
Dom, Domanique, Domeneque, Domenique, Domino, Domonik

Dona
(Latin) always giving
Donail, Donalea, Donalisa, Donay, , Donelle, Donetta, Doni, Donia, Donice, Donie, Donise, Donisha, Donishia, Donita, Donitrae

Donalda
(Scottish) loves all
Donalda, Donaldina, Donaleen, Donelda, Donella, Donellia, Donette, Doni, Donita, Donnella, Donnelle

Donata
(Italian) celebrating
Donada, Donatah, Donatha, Donatta, Donni, Donnie, Donny

Donatella
(Latin, Italian) gift
Don, Donnie, Donny

Donava
(African) jubilant
Donavah

Donela
(Italian) leader
Donella

Donia
(American) from Donna; controls

Donika
(African American) stemming from Donna; home-loving
Donica

Donisha
(African American) laughing; cozy
Daneesha, Danisha, Doneesha

Donna
(Italian) ladylike and genteel
Dom, Don, Dona, Dondi, Donnie, Donya

Donnata
(Latin) giving
Dona, Donata, Donni

Donnelly
(Italian) lush
Donally, Donelly, Donnell, Donnelli, Donnellie, Donni, Donnie, Donny

Donnis
(American) pleasant; giving
Donnice

Donserena
(American) dancer; giving
Donce, Doncie, Dons, Donse, Donsee, Donser, Donsey

Donyale
(African American) form of Danielle; kind
Donyelle

Dora
(Greek) gift from God
Dorah, Dori, Dorie, Dorra, Dorrah

Dorat
(French) a gift
Doratt, Dorey, Dorie

Dorcea
(Greek) sea girl
Dorcia

Dore
(Irish) from Dora; comtemplative

Doreen
(Greek, Irish) capricious
Dorene, Dorine, Dory

Dori
(French) adorned
Dore, Dorey, Dorie, Dory, Dorree, Dorri, Dorrie, Dorry

Doria
(Greek) from Dorian; secrets
Dori, Doriana, Doriann, Dorianna, Dorianne

Dorian
(Greek) happy
Dorean, Doreane, Doree, Doriane, Dorri, Dorry

Dorianne
(American) combo of Doris and Ann; sparkly

Dorika
(Greek) God's gift
Doreek, Dorike, Dory

Dorin
(Greek) from Dorian; sea-loving

Dorina
(Hawaiian) loved

Dorinda
(Spanish) loved

Doris
(Greek) place name; sea-loving; sea nymph
Dor, Dori, Dorice, Dorise, Doriss, Dorris, Dorrise, Dorrys, Dory

Dorit
(Greek) God's gift; shy
Dooritt

Dornay
(American) involved
Dorn, Dornae, Dornee,
Dorny

Dorothea
(Greek) gift from God
Dorethea, Dorotha,
Dorothia, Dorotthea,
Dorthea, Dorthia

Dorothy
(Greek) gift of God
Dorathy, Dorthy

Dorren
(Irish) sad-faced
Doren

Dorte
(Scandinavian) God's gift

Dortha
(Greek) God's gift; studious
Dorth, Dorthee, Dorthey,
Dorthy

Dory
(French) gilded; gold hair
Dora, Dore, Dorie

Dorthe
(Scandinavian) God's gift

Dosia
(Russian) happy

Dossey
(Last name as first)
rambunctious
Dosse, Dossi, Dossie,
Dossy, Dozze

Dot
(Greek) spunky
Dottee, Dottie, Dotty

Dottie
(Greek) from Dorothy; God's
gift; spunky

Douce
(French) sweet
Doucia, Dulce, Dulci, Dulcie

Dougiana
(American) combo of Dougi
and Ana
Dougi

Dove
(Greek) dreamy

Doxie
(Greek) fine
Doxy

Drahomira
(Czech) dearest

Draven
(American) loyal
Dravan, Dravin, Dravine

Draxy
(American) faithful
Drax, Draxee, Draxey, Draxi

Drea
(American) adorable

Dream
(American) dream girl; misty
Dreama, Dreamee, Dreamey,
Dreami, Dreamie, Dreamy

Dreda
(Anglo-Saxon) thoughtful
Drida

Dree
(American) soft-spoken

Dreena
(American) cautious
Dreenah, Drina

Drelan
(Origin Unknown) watches

Drew
(Greek) woman of valor
Dru, Drue

Drover
(American) surprising
Drovah, Drovar

Dru
(American) bright
Drew, Drue

Druanna
(American) bold
Drewann, Drewanne,
Druanah, Druannah

Drucelle
(American) smart
Druce, Drucee, Drucel,
Drucell, Drucey, Druci, Drucy

Druella
(Latin) from Drusilla; strong

Drusa
(Latin) from Drusilla; forceful
Drusie, Drucie

Drusi
(Latin) strong girl
Drucey, Drucie, Drucy,
Drusey, Drusie, Drusy

Drusilla
(Latin) strong
Dru, Drucilla

Dryden
(Last name as first name)
special
Dydie

Duana
(Irish) dark
Dwana

Dubethza
(Invented) sad
Dubeth

Duchess
(American) fancy
Duc, Duchesse, Ducy, Dutch, Dutchey, Dutchie, Dutchy

Duena
(Spanish) chaperones; guards

Duffy
(Irish) spunky

Dufvenius
(Swedish) lovely
Duf, Duff

Duhnell
(Hebrew) kind-hearted
Danee, Danny, Nell

Dulce-Maria
(Spanish) sweet Mary
Dulce, Dulcey

Dulcie
(Latin, Spanish) sweet one
Dulce, Dulcey, Dulcy

Dulcinea
(Latin) sweet nature

Duma
(African) quiet help
Dumah

Duna
(Spanish) protects

Dune
(American) summery
Doone, Dunah, Dunie

Dumia
(Hebrew) quiet
Dumi

Dunesha
(African American) warm
Dunisha

Dupre
(American) soft-spoken
Dupray, Duprey

Durene
(American) combo of Dura and Renne; planner

Durrah
(Hindi) heroine

Dusanka
(Slavic) soulful
Dusan, Dusana, Dusank, Sanka

Duscha
(Russian) happy
Dusa, Duschah, Dusha, Dushenka

Dusky
(Invented) dreamy

Dusky-Dream
(Invented) dreamy
Duskee-Dream

Dustine
(German) go-getter
Dustee, Dusteen, Dustene, Dusti, Dustie, Dustina, Dusty

Dusty
(American) southern
Dustee, Dusti, Dustie, Dustey

Dwanda
(American) athletic
Dwana, Dwayna, Dwunda

Dyan
(Latin) form of Diane; divine
Dian, Dyana, Dyane, Dyani, Dyann, Dyanna, Dyanne

Dyandra
(Latin) sleek
Diandra, Dianndrah, Dyan, Dyandruh

Dylan
(Welsh) creative; from the sea
Dilann, Dyl, Dylane, Dylann, Dylanne, Dylen, Dylin, Dyllan, Dylynn

Dylana
(Welsh) sea-loving

Dymond
(American) variant of diamond
Dymahn, Dymon, Dymonn, Dymund

Dymphia
(Irish) poetic
Dimphia

Dynasty
(Word) substantial; rich

Dyney
(American) consoling others
Diney, DiNey, Dy

Dyonne
(American) marvelous
Dyonn, Dyonna, Dyonnae

Dyronisha
(African American) fine
Dyron

Dyshaunna
(African American) dedicated
Dyshaune, Dyshawn, Dyshawna

Dyshawna
(American) combo of Dy and Shawna; outrageous; smiles
Dyshanta, Dyshawn, Dyshonda, Dyshonna

Dywon
(American) bubbly
Diwon, Dywan, Dywann, Dywaughn, Dywonne

Dzidzo
(African) universal child

Eadrianne
(American) standout
Eddey, Eddi, Eddy, Edreiann, Edrian, Edrie

Earla
(English) leader
Earlah, Erla, Erlene, Erletta, Erlette

Earlean
(Irish) dedicated
Earla, Earlecia, Earleen, Earlena, Earlene, Earlina, Earlinda, Earline, Erla, Erlana, Erlene, Erlenne, Erlina, Erlinda, Erline, Erlisha

Early
(American) bright
Earlee, Earlie, Earlye, Erly

Eartha
(English) earth mother

Easter
(American) born on Easter; springlike
Eastan, Eastlyn, Easton

Easton
(American) wholesome
Eastan, Easten, Eeston, Eastun, Estynn

Eavan
(Irish) beautiful
Evaughn, Eevonne

Ebba
(English, Scandinavian) strong
Eb, Eba, Ebbah

Ebban
(American) pretty; affluent
Ebann, Ebbayn

Ebony
(Greek) hard and dark
Eb, Ebanie, Ebbeny, Ebbie, Ebonea, Ebonee, Eboney, Eboni, Ebonie, Ebonni

Ebrel
(Cornish) from the month April
Ebby, Ebrelle, Ebrie, Ebrielle

Echo
(Greek) smitten
Eko

Ecstasy
(American) joyful
Ecstasey, Ecstasie, Stase

Eda
(Irish) from Edith; treasured

Edaena
(Irish) fiery; energetic
Ed, Eda, Edae, Edana, Edanah, Edaneah, Eddi

Edalene
(German) refined
Eda, Edalyne, Edeline, Ediline, Lena, Lene

Edana
(Irish) flaming energy
Eda, Edan, Edanna

Eddi
(English) form of Edwina; spirited brunette
Eddie, Eddy, Edy

Edel
(German) clever; noble
Edell, Eddi

Eden
(Hebrew) paradise of delights
Ede, Edena, Edene, Edin, Edyn

Edenathene
(American) combo of Eden and Athene

Edie
(English) short for Edith; blessed
Eadie, Edee, Edi, Edy, Edye, Eydie

Edith
(English) a blessed girl who is a gift to mankind
Eadith, Ede, Edetta, Edette, Edie, Edithe, Editta, Ediva, Edy, Edyth, Edythe, Eydie

Edju
(Origin unknown) giving
Eddju

Edlin
(German) noble;
sophisticated
*Eddi, Eddy, Edlan, Edland,
Edlen*

Edmee
(American) spontaneous
Edmey, Edmi, Edmy, Edmye

Edmonda
(English) form of Edmond;
rich
*Edmon, Edmond, Edmund,
Edmunda, Monda*

Edna
(Hebrew) youthful
*Eddie, Ednah, Edneisha,
Ednita, Eydie*

Edreanna
(American) merry
*Edrean, Edreana, Edreanne,
Edrianna*

Edrina
(American) old-fashioned
*Ed, Eddi, Eddrina, Edrena,
Edrinah*

Edsel
(American) plain
Eds, Edsell, Edzel

Edshone
(American) wealthy
Ed, Eds, Edshun

Edwina
(English) prospering female
*Eddi, Eddy, Edina,
Edweena, Edwena,
Edwenna, Edwine, Edwyna,
Edwynna*

Effemy
(Greek and German) good
singer
*Efemie, Efemy, Effee,
Effemie, Effey, Effie, Effy*

Effie
(Greek) of high morals;
(German) good singer
Effi, Effia, Effy, Ephie

Efrat
(Hebrew) bountiful
Efrata

Egan
(American) wholesome
Egen, Egun

Egypt
(Place name) exotic
Egyppt

Egzanth
(Invented) form of Xanthe;
beautiful blonde

Eileen
(Irish) bright and spirited
*Eilean, Eilee, Eileena,
Eileene, Eilena, Eilene,
Eiley, Eilleen, Eillen, Eilyn,
Elene, Ellie*

Eireen
(Scandinavian) peacemaker
Eirena, Erene, Ireen, Irene

Eires
(Greek) peaceful
Eiress, Eres, Heris

Eirianne
(English) peaceful
Eirian, Eriann

Elaine
(French) dependable girl
*Elain, Elaina, Elainia,
Elainna, Elan, Elana, Elane,
Elania, Elanie, Elanna, Elayn,
Elayna, Elayne, Ellaine*

Elana
(Greek) pretty
*Ela, Elan, Elani, Elanie,
Lainie*

Elata
(Latin) bright; well-
positioned
Ela, Elate, Elatt, Elle, Elota

Elda
(Italian) protective

Eldora
(Spanish) golden girl
*Eldoree, Eldorey, Eldori,
Eldoria, Eldorie, Eldory*

Eleacie
(American) forthright
Acey, Elea, Eleasie

Eleanora
(Greek) light

Eldee
(American) light
El, Eldah, Elde

Eldora
(Spanish) golden spirit

Eleanor
(Greek) light-hearted
*Elana, Elanor, Elanore,
Eleanora, Elenor, Elenorah,
Eleonor, Eleonore, Elinor,
Elinore, Ellie, Ellinor, Ellinore,
Elynor, Elynore, Lenore*

Eleanora
(Greek) light
Elenora, Eleonora, Eleora, Ella nora, Ellora, Ellenora, Ellenorah, Elnora, Elora, Elynora

Electra
(Greek) resilient and bright
Elec, Elek, Elektra

Elegy
(American) lasting
Elegee, Eleggee, Elegie, Eligey

Elek
(American) star-like
Elec, Ellie, Elly

Elena
(Greek, Russian, Italian, Spanish) light and bright; beautiful
Elana, Eleana, Eleen, Eleena, Elen, Elene, Eleni, Ilena, Ilene, Lena, Leni, Lennie, Lina, Nina

Eleni
(Greek) sweet
Elenee

Eleonore
(Greek, German) light and bright
Elenore, Elle, Elnore

Eleri
(Welsh) smooth
Elere, Eleree

Elettra
(Latin, Italian) shining

Elfin
(American) small girl
El, Elf, Elfan, Elfee, Elfey, Elfie, Elfun, Els

Elfrida
(German) peaceful spirit
Elfie, Elfrea, Elfredda, Elfreeda, Elfreyda, Elfryda

Eliana
(Latin, Greek, Italian) sunny
Eliane, Elianna, Elianne, Elliana, Ellianne, Ellie, Liana, Liane

Eliane
(French) cheerful; sunny

Elicia
(Hebrew) dedicated
Ellicia

Elisa
(English, Italian) God-loving; grace
Elecea, Eleesa, Elesa, Elesia, Elisia, Elissa, Elisse, Elisya, Ellisa, Ellisia, Ellissa, Ellissia, Ellissya, Ellisya, Elysa, Elysia, Elyssia, Elyssya, Elysya, Leese, Leesie, Lisa

Elisabet
(Hebrew, Scandinavian) God as her oath
Bet, Elsa, Else, Elisa

Elisabeth
(Hebrew, French, German) sworn to God
Bett, Bettina, Elisa, Elise, Els, Elsa, Elsie, Ilsa, Ilyse, Liesa, Liese, Lisbeth, Lise

Elise
(French, English) soft-mannered
Elice, Elisse, Elle, Ellyse, Lisie

Elisha
(Greek) God-loving
Eleacia, Eleasha, Elecia, Eleesha, Eleisha, Elesha, Eleshia, Elicia, Eliesha, Ellie, Lisha

Elissa
(Greek) God-loving
Ellissa, Ellyssa, Elyssa, Ilissa, Ilyssa

Elita
(French) selected one
Elida, Elitia, Elitie, Ellita, Ellitia, Ellitie, Ilida, Ilita, Litia

Elite
(Latin) best
Elita

Eliza
(Irish) sworn to God
Aliza, Elieza, Elize, Elyza

Elizabeth
(Hebrew) God-directed; beauty
Beth, Betsy, Elisabeth, Elizebeth, Lissie, Liza

Elke
(Dutch) distinguished
Elki, Ilki

Elkie
(Dutch) variant of Elke; distinguished
Elk, Elka

Ella
(Greek) beautiful and fanciful
Ellamae, Elle, Ellia, Ellie, Elly

Ella Bleu
(Invented) combo of Ella and Bleu; gorgeous daughter of fame
Ella-Bleu

Ellaina
(American) sincere
Elaina, Ellana, Ellanuh

Ellan
(American) coy
Elan, Ellane, Ellyn

Elle
(Scandinavian) woman
Ele

Ellen
(English) open-minded
El, Elen, Elenee, Eleny, Elin, Ellene, Ellie, Ellyn, Ellynn, Elyn

Ellender
(American) decisive
Elender, Ellander, Elle, Ellie

Elletra
(Greek, Italian) shining
Elletrah, Illetrah

Elli
(Scandinavian) aged
Ell, Elle, Ellie

Ellice
(English) also Elyse; loves God
Ellecia, Ellyce, Elyce

Ellie
(English) candid
Ele, Elie, Elly

Ellyanne
(American) combo of Elly and Anne
Elian, Elianne, Ellyann, Elyann

Elma
(Turkish) sweet
El

Elmas
(Armenian) diamondlike
Elmaz, Elmes, Elmis

Elnora
(American) sturdy
Ellie, Elnor, Elnorah

Elodia
(Spanish) flowering
Elodi

Eloise
(German) high-spirited
Eluise, Luise

Elora
(American) fresh-faced
Elorah, Flory, Floree

Elpidia
(Spanish) shining
El, Elpey, Elpi, Elpie

Elrica
(German) leader
Elrick, Elrika, Elrike, Rica, Rika

Elsa
(Hebrew, Scandinavian, German) patient; regal
Ellsa, Ellse, Ellsey, Els, Elsah, Elseh, Elsie, Ellsee

Elsie
(German) hard-working
Elsee, Elsi, Elsy

Elsiy
(Spanish) God-loving
El, Els, Elsa, Elsee, Elsi, Elsy

Elspeth
(Scottish)
El, Elle, Els

Elton
(American) spontaneous
Elt, Elten, Eltone, Eltun

Elva
(English) tiny
Elvenea, Elvia, Elvie, Elvina, Elvinea, Elvineah, Elvah

Elvia
(Latin) sunny
Elvea, Elviah, Elvie

Elvira
(Latin, German) light-haired and quiet
Elva, Elvie, Elvina, Elwire, Vira

Elyanna
(American) good friend
Elyana, Elyannah, Elyunna

Elyse
(English) soft-mannered
Elice, Elle, Elysee, Elysia, Ilysha, Ilysia

Elyssa
(Greek) loving the ocean; (English) lovely and happy
Elisa, Elissa, Elysa, Illysa, Lyssa

Elysia
(Latin) joyful
Elyse, Elysee, Elysha, Elyshia

Emalee
(German) thoughtful
Emalea, Emaleigh, Emaley, Emaline, Emally, Emaly, Emmalynn, Emmeline, Emmelyne

Emann
(American) soft-spoken
Eman

Ember
(American) temperamental
Embere, Embre

Emberatriz
(Spanish) respected
Emb, Ember, Embera, Emberatrice, Emberatryce, Embertrice, Embertrise

Emberli
(American) pretty
Em, Emb, Ember, Emberlee, Emberley, Emberly

Eme
(German) short for Emma; strong
Emee, Emme, Emmee

Eme
(Hawaiian) loved
Em, Emee, Emm, Emmee, Emmie, Emmy

Emelle
(American) kind
Emell

Emely
(German) go-getter
Emel, Emelee, Emelie

Emena
(Latin) of fortunate birth
Em, Emen, Emene, Emina, Emine

Emerald
(French) bright as a gemstone
Em, Emmie

Emestina
(American) form of Ernestina; competitive
Emee, Emes, Emest, Tina

Emilee
(American) combo of Emma and Lee

Emilie
(French) charmer

Emilia
(Italian) soft-spirited
Emalia, Emelia, Emila

Emily
(German) poised; (English) competitor
Em, Emalie, Emilee, Emili, Emilie, Emmi, Emmie

Emilyann
(American) combo of Emily and Ann; traditional girl

Emma
(German, Irish) strong
Em, Emmah, Emme, Emmie, Emmi, Emmot, Emmy, Emmye, Emott

Emmalee
(American) combo of Emma and Lee
Em, Emalea, Emalee, Emilee, Emliee, Emma-Lee, Emmali, Emmie

Emmaline
(French, German) form of Emily
Em, Emaline, Emalyne, Emiline, Emmie

Emmalynn
(American) combo of Emma and Lynn; today's child
Emelyn, Emelyne, Emelynne, Emilyn, Emilynn, Emilynne, Emlyn, Emlynn, Emlynne, Emmalyn, Emmalynne

Emmanuelle
(Hebrew, French) believer
Em, Emmi, Emmie, Emmy

Emmalise
(American) combo of Emma and Lise; lovely
Emalise, Emmalisa, Emmelise

Emmanuelle
(Hebrew) knows God
Emmanuela, Emmanuella

Emme
(German) feminine
Em

Emmi
(German) pretty
Emmee, Emmey, Emmy

Emmylou
(American) combo of Emmy and Lou
Emmilou, Emmi-Lou, Emylou

Emylinda
(American) combo of Emy and Linda; happy and pretty
Emi, Emilind, Emilynd, Emy, Emylin, Emylynda

Ena
(Hawaiian) intense
Eana, En, Enna, Ina

Enchantay
(American) enchanting
Enchantee

Endah
(Irish) flighty
Ena, End, Enda

Endia
(American) variant of India;
magical
*Endee, Endey, Endie, Endy,
India, Ndia*

Enedina
(Spanish) praised, spirited
Dina, Ened

Enid
(Welsh) lively
Eneid

Enore
(English) careful
Enoor, Enora

Enslie
(American) emotional
*Ens, Enslee, Ensley, Ensly,
Enz*

Enya
(Irish) fiery; musician
Enyah, Nya

Epifania
(Spanish) proof
*Epi, Epifaina, Epifanea,
Eppie, Pifanie, Piffy*

Eppy
(Greek) lively, always "on"
Ep, Eppee, Eppey, Eppi, Eps

Equoia
(African American) great
equalizer
Ekowya

Eranth
(Greek) spring bloomer
Erantha, Eranthae, Eranthe

Erasema
(Spanish) happy
Eraseme

Ercilia
(American) frank
Erci, Ercilya

Eres
(Greek) goddess of chaos
Era, Ere, Eris

Erika
(Scandinavian) honorable;
leading others
*Erica, Ericah, Ericca, Ericha,
Ericka, Erikka, Errica, Errika,
Eryka, Erykka, Eryka*

Erin
(Irish) peace-making
*Eran, Eren, Erena, Erene,
Ereni, Eri, Erian, Erine,
Erinn, Erinne, Eryn, Erynn,
Erynne*

Erina
(American) peaceful
*Era, Erinna, Erinne, Eryna,
Erynne*

Erla
(Irish) playful

Erlind
(Hebrew) from Erlinda;
angelic
Erlinda, Erlinde

Erma
(Latin) wealthy
Erm, Irma

Ermelinda
(Spanish) fresh-faced
*Ermalinda, Ermelind,
Ermelynda*

Ermine
(Latin) rich
*Erma, Ermeen, Ermie,
Ermin, Ermina, Erminda,
Erminia, Erminie*

Erna
(English) short for
Ernestine; knowing; earnest
Emae, Ernea, Ernie

Ernestine
(English) having a sincere
spirit
*Erna, Ernaline, Ernesia,
Ernesta, Ernestina,
Ernestyne*

Ertha
(English) variant of Eartha;
also from Bertha; earth
woman

Eryn
(Irish) also Erin; calm

Es
(American) short for Estella
Esa, Essie

Esbelda
(Spanish) black-haired
beauty
Es, Esbilda, Ezbelda

Esdey
(American) warm-hearted
Esdee, Esdy, Essdey

Eshah
(African) exuberant
Esha

Eshe
(African) life
Eshay

Eshey
(American) life
Es, Esh, Eshae, Eshay

Esmee
(French) much loved
Esma, Esme, Esmie

Esmeralda
(Spanish) emerald; shiny
and bright
*Emelda, Es, Esmerelda,
Esmerilda, Esmie,
Esmiralda, Esmirilda,
Ezmerelda, Ezmirilda*

Esne
(English) happy
*Es, Esnee, Esney, Esny,
Essie*

Esperanza
(Spanish) hopeful
*Es, Espe, Esperance,
Esperans, Esperanta,
Esperanz, Esperanza*

Essence
(American) ingenious
Esence, Essens, Essense

Essie
(English) shining
Es, Essa, Essey, Essie, Essy

Esta
(Hebrew) bright star
Es, Estah

Estee
(English) brightest
Esti

Estella
(French) radiant star
*Es, Estel, Estell, Estelle,
Estie, Stell, Stella*

Estelle
(French) glowing star
*Es, Essie, Estee, Estel,
Estele, Estell, Estie*

Estevina
(Spanish) adorned;
wreathed
*Estafania, Este, Estebana,
Estefania, Estevan,
Estevana*

Esthelia
(Spanish) shining
*Esthe, Esthel, Esthele,
Esthelya*

Esther
(Persian, English) shining
star
*Es, Essie, Estee, Ester,
Esthur*

Estherita
(Spanish) bright
Estereta

Estime
(French) esteemed
Es

Estrella
(Latin) shining star
Estrell, Estrelle, Estrilla

Eta
(German) short for
Henrietta
Etah

Etaney
(Hebrew) focused
Eta, Etana, Etanah, Etanee

Ethel
(English) class
*Ethelda, Ethelin, Etheline,
Ethelle, Ethelyn, Ethelynn,
Ethelynne, Ethyl*

Ethelene
(American) form of Ethel;
noble
Ethe, Etheline

Ethne
(Irish) blueblood
Eth, Ethnee, Ethnie, Ethny

Ethnea
(Irish) kernel; piece of the
puzzle
Ethna, Ethnia

Etta
(German, English) short for
Henrietta; energetic
Etti, Ettie, Etty

Eudlina
(Slavic) generous; affluent
Eudie, Eudlyna, Udie, Udlina

Eudocia
(Greek) fine
Eude, Eudocea, Eudosia

Eudora
(Greek) cherished

Eudore
(Greek) treasured

Eugenia
(Greek) regal and polished
*Eugeneia, Eugenie,
Eugenina, Eugina, Gee, Gina*

Eula
(Greek) specific
Eulia

Eulala
(Greek) spoken sweetly
Eulalah

Eulalia
(Greek, Italian) spoken
sweetly
Eula, Eulia, Eulie

Eulanda
(American) fair
Eudlande, Eulee, Eulie

Eulee
(Greek) musical
Eulie, Ulee, Uley

Eunice
(Greek) joyful; winning
Euna, Euniece, Eunique, Eunise, Euniss

Eupheme
(Greek) well-spoken
Eu, Euphemee, Euphemi, Euphemie

Euphemia
(Greek) respected
Effam, Eufemia, Euphan, Euphie, Uphie

Euphrosyne
(Greek) mirth, merriment

Eurydice
(Greek) adventurous
Euridice, Euridyce, Eurydyce

Eustacia
(Greek) industrious
Eustace, Stacey, Stacy

Euvenia
(American) hardworking
Euvene, Euvenea

Eva
(Hebrew, Scandinavian) life
Evah, Evalea, Evalee

Evadne
(Greek) pleasing; lucky
Eva, Evad, Evadnee, Evadny

Evaline
(French) form of Evelyn; matter-of-fact
Evalyn, Eveleen

Evalouise
(American) combo of Eva and Louise; witty
Eva-Louise, Evaluise

Eva-Marie
(American) combo of Eva and Marie; generous

Evan
(American) bright; precocious
Evann, Evin

Evana
(Greek) lovely woman
Eve, Ivana, Ivanna, Evania

Evangelina
(Greek) bringing joy
Eva, Evangelia, Evangelica, Evangeline, Evania, Eve, Lina

Evania
(Irish) spirited
Ev, Evana, Evanea, Evann, Evanna, Evanne, Evany, Eve, Eveania, Evvanne, Evyan

Evanthie
(Greek) flowering well
Evanthe, Evanthee, Evanthi

Eve
(French, Hebrew) first woman
Eva, Evie, Evvy

Evelina
(Russian) lively
Evalina, Evalinna

Evelyn
(English) optimistic
Aveline, Ev, Evaleen, Evalene, Evaline, Evalenne, Evalyn, Evalynn, Evalynne, Eveleen, Eveline, Evelyne, Evelynn, Evelynne, Evline

Ever
(American) cool; vibrant
Ev

Everilde
(Origin unknown) hunter

Evette
(French) dainty
Evett, Ivette

Evline
(French) nature girl
Evleen, Evlene, Evlin, Evlina, Evlyn, Evlynn, Evlynne

Evonne
(French) form of Yvonne; sensual
Evanne, Eve, Evie, Yvonne

Ewelina
(Polish) life
Eva, Lina

Eydie
(American) endearing
Eidey, Eydee

Eyote
(Native American) great
Eyotee

Ezra
(Hebrew) happy; helpful
Ezrah, Ezruh

Ezza
(American) healthy
Eza

F

Faba
(Latin) bean; thin
Fabah, Fava

Fabia
(Latin) fabulous; special
Fabiann, Fabianna, Fabianne

Fabienne
(French) farming beans
Fabiola, Fabiole

Fabio
(Latin) fabulous
Fabeeo, Fabeo, Fabeoh

Fabiola
(Spanish) royalty

Fabrizia
(Italian) manual worker
Fabrice, Fabricia, Fabrienne, Fabriqua, Fabritzia

Fae
(English) variant of Faye; fairy girl

Fahimah
(Arabic) from Fatima; renowned

Faida
(Arabic) bountiful
Fayda

Faillace
(French) delicate beauty
Faill, Faillaise, Faillase, Falace

Faine
(English) happy
Fai, Fainne, Fay, Fayne

Fairlee
(English) lovely
Fair, Fairlea, Fairley, Fairly

Faith
(English) loyal woman
Fay, Fayth

Falesyia
(Hispanic) exotic
Falesyiah, Falisyia

Faline
(Latin, French) lively
Faleen, Falene

Fall
(Season name) changeable
Falle

Fallon
(Irish) fetching; from the ruling class
Falan, Fallen, Fallyn, Falyn

Falsette
(American) fanciful
Falcette

Fanchon
(French) from France
Fan, Fanchee, Fanchie, Fanny, Fran, Frannie, Franny

Fancy
(English) fanciful
Fanci, Fancie

Fane
(American) strict
Fain, Faine

Fanfara
(Last name as first name) fanfare; excitement
Fann, Fanny

Fang
(Chinese) pleasantly scented

Fanny
(Latin) from France; bold
Fan, Fani, Fannie

Fantasia
(American) inventive
Fantasha, Fantasiah, Fantasya, Fantazia

Fanteen
(English) clever
Fan, Fannee, Fanney, Fanny, Fantene, Fantine

Farah
(English) lovely
Farrah

Faredah
(Arabic) special
Farida

Farhanah
(Arabic) lovely

Farica
(German) leader
Faricka, Fericka, Flicka

Farida
(Arabic) wanders far

Farina
(Latin) flour
Fareena

Faris
(American) forgiving
Fair, Farris, Pharis, Pharris

Farrah
(Arabic) beautiful; (English) joyful
Fara, Farah

Farren
(American) fair
Faren, Farin

Farrow
(American) narrow-minded
Farow, Farro

Faryl
(American) inspiring
Farel, Farelle

Fashion
(American) stylish
Fashon, Fashy, Fashyun

Fatima
(Arabic) wise woman; (African) dedicated
Fatema, Fatimah, Fatime

Faulk
(American) respected
Falk

Fauna
(Roman mythology) goddess of nature
Faunah, Fawna, Fawnah

Faunee
(Latin) nature-loving
Fauney, Fauneye, Fawnae, Fawni, Fawny

Faustene
(French, American) envied
Fausteen, Faustine, Fausty, Fawsteen

Faustiana
(Spanish) good fortune
Faust, Fausti, Faustia, Faustina

Faustina
(Italian) lucky
Fausta, Faustine, Fawsteena, Fostina, Fostynna

Favianna
(Italian) confident
Faviana

Fawn
(French) gentle
Faun, Fawne

Fawna
(French) soft-spoken
Fawnna, Fawnah, Fawnuh

Faye
(English, French) light-spirited
Fae, Fay, Fey

Fayette
(American) southern
Fayet, Fayett, Fayetta, Fayitte

Fayleen
(American) quiet
Faylene, Fayline, Falyn, Falynn, Faye, Fayla

Fayth
(American) form of Faith; faithful
Faithe, Faythe

Feather
(Native American) svelte
Feathyr

Febe
(Polish, Greek) bright
Febee

February
(Latin) icy
Feb

Fedora
(Greek) God's gift

Felda
(German) field girl

Felder
(Last name as first name) bright
Felde, Feldy

Felice
(Latin) happy
Felece, Felise

Felicia
(Latin) joyful
Faleshia, Falesia, Felecia, Felisha

Felicie
(Latin) happy; (German) fortunate
Feliccie, Felicee, Felicy, Felisie

Felicita
(Spanish) gracious
Felice, Felicitas, Felicitee, Felisita

Felicity
(Latin) happy girl
Felice, Felicite, Felicitee, Felisitee

Felise
(German) joyful
Felis

Femay
(American) classy
Femae

Femi
(African) love-seeking
Femmi

Femise
(African American) asking for love
Femeese, Femmis

Fenella
(Irish) white
Fionola, Fionnuala

Fenia
(Scandinavian) gold worker
Fenja, Fenya

Fenn
(American) bright
Fen, Fynn

Feo
(Greek) given by God
Fee, Feeo

Feodora
(Greek) God-given girl
Fedora

Fern
(German, English) natural
Ferne

Fernanda
(German) bold
Ferdie, Fernnande

Fernilia
(American) successful
Fern, Fernelia, Ferny, Fyrnilia

Fernley
(English) from the fern
meadow; nature girl

Feven
(American) shy
Fevan, Fevun

Ffion
(Irish) pale face
Fi

Fia
(Scandinavian) perky

Fiamma
(Italian) fiery spirit
*Feamma, Fee, Fia, Fiama,
Fiammette, Fifi*

Fiby
(Spanish) bright

Fidela
(Spanish) loyal
Fidele, Fidella, Fidelle

Fidelia
(Italian) faithful
Fidele

Fidelity
(Latin) loyal
Fidele, Fidelia

Fidelma
(Irish) loyal

Fife
(American) dancing eyes;
musical
Fifer, Fifey, Fyfe

Fifi
(French) jazzy
Fifee

Fifia
(African) Friday's child
FeeFee, Fifeea

Filia
(Greek) devoted
Filea, Feleah, Filiah

Filipa
(Italian) horse-lover

Fillis
(Greek) form of Phyllis;
devoted
*Filis, Fill, Fillees, Filly, Fillys,
Fylis*

Filma
(Greek) loved

Filomena
(Polish) beloved

Fina
(Spanish) blessed by God

Finch
(English) bird; sings

Finelle
(Irish) fair-faced
*Fee, Finell, Finn, Finny,
Fynelle*

Finesse
(American) smooth
Fin, Finese, Finess

Finn
(Irish) cool

Finola
(Italian) white

Fion
(Irish) blonde

Fiona
(Irish) fair-haired
Fi, Fionna

Fionnuala
(Irish) white
Nuala

Fiorella
(Irish) spirited
Fee, Feorella, Rella

Fire
(American) feisty
Firey, Fyre

Flair
(English) stylish
Flaire, Flairey, Flare

Flame
(Invented) sensual

Flaminia
(Latin) associated with
priesthood; flaming spirit

Flana
(Irish) red-haired
*Flanagh, Flanna, Flannerey,
Flannery*

Flanders
(Place name) creative
Fland, Flann

Flannery
(Irish) warm; red-haired
Flann

Flavia
(Latin) light-haired
Flavie

Flax
(Botanical) plant with blue flowers
Flacks, Flaxx

Fleming
(Last name as first name) adorable
Flemma, Flemmie, Flemming, Flyming

Flemmi
(Italian) pretty
Flemmy

Fleur
(French) flower
Fleura, Fleuretta, Fleurette, Fleuronne

Flicky
(American) vivacious

Flirt
(Invented) flirtatious
Flyrtt

Flis
(Polish) from Felicyta; good girl

Flo
(American) short for Florence

Flor
(Spanish) blooming
Flo, Flora, Floralia, Florencia, Florencita, Florens, Florensia, Flores, Floria, Floriole, Florita, Florite

Flora
(Latin, Spanish) flowering
Floria, Florie

Floramaria
(American) combo of Flora and Maria; spring; Mary's flower
Flora Maria, Flora-Maria

Flordeperla
(Spanish) blooms pearls

Florella
(Latin) girl from Florence; blooming

Florence
(Latin, Italian) place name; flourishing and giving
Flo, Flora, Florencia, Florense, Florenze, Florie, Florina, Florrie, Flos, Flossie, Floy

Florens
(Polish) blooming
Floren

Florent
(French) flowering
Flor, Floren, Florentine, Florin

Florida
(Place name) U.S. state; flowered
Flora, Flory

Florine
(American) blooming
Flo, Flora, Floren, Floryne, Florynne

Florizel
(Literature) Shakespearean name; in bloom
Flora, Flori, Florisel

Florrie
(English) blooms

Flossie
(English) grows beautifully

Flower
(American) blossoming beauty
Flo

Floy
(English) blooms

Fluffy
(American) fun-loving
Fluff, Fluffi, Fluffie

Flynn
(Irish) red-haired
Flenn, Flinn, Flyn

Fog
(American) dreamy
Fogg, Foggee, Foggy

Fola
(African) honored
Folah

Fonda
(American) risk-taker
Fond

Fondice
(American) fond of friends
Fondeese, Fondie

Fontaine
(French) fountaining bounty
Fontane, Fontanna, Fontanne

Fontenot
(French) special girl;
fountain of beauty
Fonny, Fontay, Fonte,
Fonteno

Ford
(Last name as first name)
confident
Forde

Fortney
(Latin) strength
Fortnea, Fortnee, Fortneigh,
Fortnie, Fortny

Fortuna
(Latin) good fortune
Fortunata

Forsythia
(Botanical) flower girl

Fortune
(Latin) excellent fate; prized

Fotine
(Greek) light-hearted
Foty, Fotyne

Fowler
(Last name as first name)
stylish
Fowla, Fowlar, Fowlir

Fran
(Latin) from France;
freewheeling
Frann, Franni, Frannie

Franca
(Italian) free spirit

France
(Place name) French girl
Frans, Franse

Francene
(French) free
Francine

Frances
(Latin) free; of French origin
Fanny, Fran, Francey, Franci,
Francie, Franse

Francesca
(Italian) form of Frances;
open-hearted
Fran, Francessca,
Franchesca, Francie,
Frankie, Frannie

Franchelle
(French) from France
Franshell, Franchelle,
Franchey

Franchesca
(Italian) smiling
Cheka, Chekkie,
Francheska, Francheska,
Franchessca

Francine
(French) form of Frances;
beautiful
Fran, Franceen, Francene,
Francie

Françoise
(French) free

Franisbel
(Spanish) beautiful French
girl
Franisbella, Franisbelle

Frankie
(American) a form of
Frances; tomboyish
Franki, Franky

Frannie
(English) friendly
Franni, Franny

Fransabelle
(Latin) beauty from France
Fransabella, Franzabelle

Frayda
(Scandinavian) fertile
woman
Frayde, Fraydel, Freyda,
Freyde, Freydel

Frea
(Scandinavian) noble;
hearty
Fray, Freas, Freya

Freda
(German) serene

Freddie
(English) short for
Frederica; spunky
Fredi, Freddy

Fredella
(American) combo of Freda
and Della; striking
Fredelle

Frederica
(German) peacemaking
Federica, Fred, Freda,
Freddie, Freida, Frida, Fritze,
Rica

Frederique
(German) serene

Free
(American) free; open

Freesia
(Botanical) fragrant flower

Freida
(German) short for
Frederica and Alfreda;
graceful
Freda, Frida, Frieda

Frenchie
(French, American) saucy
French, Frenchee, Frenchi,
Frenchy

Freya
(Scandinavian) goddess;
beautiful
Freja, Freyja

Frida
(Scandinavian) lovely

Frieda
(German) happy
Freda

Friedelinde
(German) gentle girl
Friedalinda

Frigg
(Scandinavian) loved one
Frigga

Frigga
(Scandinavian) beloved
Fri, Friga, Frigg

Fritzi
(German) leads in peace

Frond
(Botanical) growing

Frosty
(Name from a song) crisp
and cool
Frostie

Frula
(German) hardworking

Fuchsia
(Botanical) blossoming pink
Fuesha

Fructuose
(Latin) bountiful
Fru, Fructuosa, Fruta

Fruma
(Hebrew) devout

Frythe
(English) calm
Frith, Fryth

Fudge
(American) stubborn
Fudgey

Fuensanta
(Spanish) holy fountain
Fuenta

Fulgencia
(Latin) effervescent; glowing

Fulvia
(Latin) blonde

Fulvy
(Latin) blonde
Full, Fulvee, Fulvie

Fury
(Latin) raging anger
Furee, Furey, Furie

Fushy
(American) animated; vivid
Fooshy, Fueshy, Fushee

Gable
(German) farming woman
*Gabbie, Gabby, Gabe,
Gabel, Gabell, Gabl*

Gabor
(French) conflicted
Gaber, Gabi

Gabriela
(Italian, Spanish) God is her
strength
*Caby, Gabela, Gabi,
Gabrela, Gabriela,
Gabriella, Gabryela,
Gabryella*

Gabrielle
(French, Hebrew) strong, by
faith in God
*Gabi, Gabraelle, Gabreelle,
Gabreille, Gabríelle,
Gabriele, Gabriella,
Gabrilla, Gabrille, Gabryele,
Gabryelle, Gaby, Gaebriell,
Gaebrielle, Garbreal*

Gaby
(French) from Gabrielle;
devoted
Gabey, Gabi, Gabie

Gadar
(Armenian) perfect girl
Gad, Gadahr, Gaddie, Gaddy

Gae
(Greek) short for Gaea;
earth goddess
Gay, Gaye

Gaea
(Greek) earth goddess
Gaia

Gaegae
(Greek) from Gaea; earthy;
happy
Gae, Gaege, Gaegie

Gaenor
(Welsh) beautiful

Gaia
(Greek) goddess of earth
Gaea, Gaya

Gail
(Hebrew) short for Abigail;
energetic
Gaelle, Gale, Gayle

Gaily
(American) fun-loving
Gailai, Galhy

Gaitlynn
(American) hopeful
*Gaitlin, Gaitline, Gaitlinn,
Gaitlyn, Gaytlyn*

Gala
(French, Scandinavian)
joyful celebrant
*Gaila, Gailah, Galaa, Galuh,
Gayla*

Galatea
(Greek) sea nymph in
mythology
Gal, Gala

Galaxy
(American) universal
Gal, Galaxee, Galaxi

Galen
(American) decisive
*Galin, Galine, Galyn, Gaye,
Gaylen, Gaylin, Gaylyn*

Galena
(Latin) metal; tough
Galyna, Galynna

Galiana
(German) vaulted
Galiyana, Galli, Galliana

Galienna
(Russian) steady
Galiena, Galyena, Galyenna

Galina
(Russian) deserving
*Gailina, Gailinna, Galyna,
Galynna*

Galise
(American) joyful
*Galeece, Galeese, Galice,
Galyce*

Galya
(Hebrew) redeemed; merry
Galia

Garcelle
(French) flowered
Garcel, Garsell, Garselle

Gardenia
(Botanical) sweet flower
baby

Garland
(American) fancy
*Garlan, Garlande, Garlinn,
Garlynn*

Garlanda
(French) flowered wreath;
pretty girl
Gar, Garl, Garlynd, Garlynda

Garlin
(French) variant of Garland;
decorative; pretty
Garlinn, Garlyn, Garlynn

Garner
(American) style-setter
Garnar, Garnir

Garnet
(English) pretty; semi-
precious stone

Garnett
(English) red gemstone;
valued

Garnetta
(French) gemstone; precious
Garna, Garnet, Garnie, Garny

Garrett
(Last name as first name)
bashful
Garret, Gerrett

Garri
(American) energetic
*Garree, Garrey, Garry,
Garrye*

Garrielle
(American) competent
Gariele, Garielle, Garriella

Garrison
(American) sturdy
*Garisen, Garisun, Garrisen,
Garrisun*

Garrity
(American) smiling
*Garety, Garrety, Garity,
Garritee, Garritie*

Gartha
(American) form of male
name Garth; nature-loving

Garyn
(American) svelte
*Garen, Garin, Garinne,
Garun, Garynn, Garynne*

Gates
(Last name as first name)
careful
Gate

Gauri
(Hindi) golden goddess

Gavin
(American) smart
Gave, Gaven, Gavey, Gavun

Gavion
(American) daring
Gaveon, Gavionne

Gaviotte
(French) graceful
Gaveott, Gaviot, Gaviott

Gavit
(French) from Gabrielle;
devoted
Gavitt, Gavyt, Gavytt

Gavotte
(French) dancer
Gav, Gavott

Gavrielle
(French) from Gabrielle;
heroine
Gavriele, Gavryele, Gavryelle

Gay
(French) jolly
Gae, Gaye

Gayla
(American) planner
*Gaila, Gailah, Gala, Gaye,
Gaylah, Gayluh*

Gayle
(Hebrew) rejoicing

Gaylynn
(American) combo of Gay
and Lynn
*Gaelen, Gaylene, Gaylyn,
Gay-Lynn*

Gaynelle
(American) combo of Gay
and Nelle
*Gaye, Gaynel, Gaynell,
Gaynie*

Gaynor
(American) precocious
Ganor, Gayner, Gaynorre

Geanna
(American) ostentatious
Geannah, Gianna

Geary
(Hebrew) variant of Jerry;
able
*Gearee, Gearey, Geari,
Gearie, Geeree, Geerey,
Geeri, Geery*

Geena
(Italian) form of Gina;
statuesque
Gina, Ginah

Geeta
(Italian) pearl

Gelacia
(Spanish) treasure
Gela, Gelasha, Gelasia

Gelda
(American) gloomy
Geilda, Geldah, Gelduh

Gelsey
(American) combo of G and
Kelsey; vivacious
*Gelsee, Gelsey, Gelsi,
Gelsie, Gelsy*

Gem
(American) shining
Gemmy, Gim, Jim

Gemesha
(African American) dramatic
*Gemeisha, Gemiesha,
Gemme, Gemmy, Gimesha*

Gemini
(Greek) twin
Gem, Gemelle, Gemmy

Gemma
(Latin, Italian, French)
jewel-like
*Gem, Gema, Gemmie,
Gemmy*

Gemmy
(Italian) gem
Gemmee, Gemmi, Gimmy

Gems
(American) shining gem
Gem, Gemmie, Gemmy

Gena
(French) form of Gina; short
for Genevieve
*Geena, Gen, Genah, Geni,
Genia*

Genell
(American) form of Janelle
Genill

Genera
(Greek) highborn
Gen, Genere

Generosa
(Spanish) generous
Generosah, Generossa

Genesis
(Latin) fast starter;
beginning
*Gen, Gena, Genesys, Geney,
Genisis, Genisys, Genysis,
Genysys, Jenesis*

Geneva
(French) city in Switzerland;
flourishing like juniper
*Gena, Geneeva, Genyva,
Janeva, Jeneva*

Genevieve
(German, French) high-minded
Gen, Gena, Genna, Genavieve, Geneveeve, Geniveeve, Genivieve, Genovieve, Genyveeve, Genyvieve

Genica
(American) intelligent
Gen, Genicah, Genicuh, Genika, Gennica, Jen, Jenika, Jennika

Genie
(Greek) of high birth; tricky
Geenee, Geeney, Geeni, Geenie, Geeny, Genee, Geney, Geni, Geny

Genna
(English) womanly
Gen, Genny, Jenna

Gennelle
(American) combo of Genn and Elle; graceful
Genel, Genelle, Ginelle, Jenele, Jenelle

Gennese
(American) helpful
Gen, Geneece, Geniece, Genny, Ginece, Gineese

Gennifer
(American) form of Jennifer
Genefer, Genephur, Genifer

Genny
(Greek) of high birth; loving
Genney, Genni, Gennie

Genoa
(Italian) playful
Geenoa, Genoah, Jenoa

Genoveva
(American) form of Genevieve; white; light
Genny, Geno

Gentle
(American) kind
Gen, Gentil, Gentille, Gentlle

Gentry
(American) sweet
Gen, Gentree, Gentrie, Jentrie, Jentry

Geoma
(American) outstanding
Gee, GeeGee, Geo, Geomah, Geome, Gigi, Jeoma, Oma, Omah

Geonna
(American) sparkling
Gee, Geionna, Geone, Geonne, Geonnuh

Georgann
(English) bright-eyed
Georganne, Jorgann, Joryann

Georganna
(English) from Georgia; gracious
Georgana, Georgeana, Georgeanna

Georgene
(English) wandering
Georgeene, Georgena, Georgene, Georgyne, Jorgeen, Jorjene

Georgette
(French) lively and little
Georgett, Georgitt, Georgitte, Jorgette

Georgia
(Greek, English) southern; cordial
Georgi, Georgie, Georgina, Georgya, Giorgi, Jorga, Jorgia, Jorja

Georgianna
(English) combo of Georgia and Anna; bright-eyed
Georganna, Georgeanna, Jorjeana, Jorgianna

Georgie
(English) short for Georgia; sassy
Georgee, Georgey, Georgi, Georgy

Georgina
(Greek, English) earthy

Geraldine
(German) strong
Geraldyne, Geri, Gerri, Gerry

Geralena
(French) leader
Gera, Geraleen, Geralen, Geralene, Gerre, Gerrilyn, Gerry, Jerrileena, Lena

Germaine
(French) of German origin; important
Germain, Germane, Germayne, Jermaine

Gerry
(German) short for Geraldine; leader

Gertrude
(German) beloved
Gerdie, Gerti, Gertie

Gervaise
(French) strong
Gerva, Gervaisa

Gessalin
(American) loving
Gessilin, Gessalyn,
Gessalynn, Jessalin,
Jessalyn

Gessica
(American) form of Jessica
Gesica, Gesika, Gessika

Gethsemane
(Biblical) peaceful
Geth, Gethse,
Gethsemanee,
Gethsemaney,
Gethsemanie, Gethy

Geynille
(American) womanly
Geynel

Gezelle
(American) lithe
Gezzelle, Gizele, Gizelle

Ghada
(Arabic) graceful
Ghad, Ghadah

Ghadeah
(Arabic) graceful
Gadea, Gadeah

Ghandia
(African) able
Gandia, Ghanda, Ghandee,
Ghandy, Gondia, Gondiah

Ghea
(American) confident
Ghia, Jeah, Jeeah

Gherlan
(American) forgiving; joyful
Gerlan, Gherli

Ghislaine
(French) loyal

Ghita
(Italian) pearl
Gita, Gite

Gia
(Italian) lovely

Giacinte
(Italian) hyacinth; flowering
Gia, Giacin, Giacinta

Gianina
(Italian) believer
Gia, Giane, Giannina,
Gianyna, Janeena, Janina,
Jeanina

Gianna
(Italian) forgiving
Geonna, Giana, Gianne,
Gianne, Gianni, Giannie,
Gianny, Ginny, Gyana,
Gyanna

Gianne
(Italian) combo of Gi and
Anne; divine
Gia, Gian, Giann, Gigi

Giannelle
(American) hearty
Geanelle, Gianella, Gianelle,
Gianne

Giannesha
(African American) friendly
Geannesha, Gianesha,
Giannesh, Gianneshah,
Gianneshuh

Giara
(Italian) sensual
Gee, Geara, Gia, Giarah

Gidget
(American) cute
Gidge, Gidgett, Gidgette,
Gydget

Gift
(American) blessed
Gifte, Gyft

Gigi
(French) small, spunky
Geegee, Giggi

Gila
(Hebrew) joyful
Gilla, Gyla, Gylla

Gilberta
(German) smart
Bertie, Gill

Gilberte
(German) shining

Gilda
(English) gold-encrusted
Gildi, Gildie, Gill

Gillaine
(Latin) young

Gilleese
(American) funny
Gill, Gillee, Gilleece, Gillie,
Gilly

Gillen
(American) humorous
Gill, Gilly, Gillyn, Gyllen

Gilli
(American) joyful
Gill, Gillee, Gilly

Gillian
(Latin) youthful
Gila, Gili, Gilian, Giliana,
Gilien, Gilliana, Gilliane,
Gillie, Gillien, Gilly, Gillyan,
Gillyen, Gilyan, Gilyen,
Jillian

Gillis
(Last name as first name)
conservative
*Gillice, Gillis, Gilise, Gylis,
Gyllis*

Gilma
(American) form of Wilma;
fortified
Gee, Gilly

Gilmore
(Last name as first name)
striking
*Gilmoor, Gill, Gillmore,
Gylmore*

Gina
(Italian) well-born
*Geena, Gena, Gin, Ginah,
Ginny, Gyna, Gynah, Jenah*

Ginacarol
(American) combo of Gina
and Carol
*Gina-Carol, Gina-Carrol,
Gyna-Carole*

Ginamarie
(Italian) combo of Gina and
Marie
Gina-Marie, Ginamaria

Ginane
(French) well-born
*Gigi, Gina, Gine, Jeanan,
Jeanine*

Ginerva
(American) combo of G and
Minerva; strong spirit
Gynerva

Ginette
(Italian) flower

Ginevieve
(Irish) from Genevieva;
womanly
*Gineveeve, Giniveeve,
Ginivieve, Ginyveeve,
Ginyvieve*

Ginger
(Latin) spicy
Gin, Ginny, Jinger

Ginnifer
(American) form of Jennifer
*Gini, Ginifer, Giniferr, Ginifir,
Ginn*

Ginny
(English) from Virginia;
virginal; purest girl
*Ginnee, Ginney, Ginni,
Ginnie*

Gioconda
(Italian) pleasing
Gio, Giocona

Giono
(Last name as first name)
delight; friendly
Gio, Gionna, Gionno

Giorgio
(Italian) form of George;
earthy; vivacious
Giorgi, Giorgie, Jorgio

Giovanna
(Italian) gracious believer;
great entertainer
*Geo, Geovanna, Gio,
Giovahna, Giovana*

Giritha
(Sri Lankan) melodic
Giri, Girith

Gisbelle
(American) lovely girl
Gisbel

Gisella
(German) pledged for
service
Gisela

Giselle
(German) naïve;
(French) devoted friend
*Gis, Gisel, Gisela, Gisele,
Gisell, Gissel, Gissell,
Gissella, Gisselle, Gissie,
Jizele*

Gita
(Sanskrit) song
Geta, Gete, Git, Gitah

Gitana
(Spanish) gypsy

Gitele
(Hebrew) good
Gitel

Githa
(Slavic) good girl; from Gita
Gytha

Gitika
(Sanskrit) little singer
Getika, Gita, Giti, Gitikah

Giulia
(Italian) little girl

Giuletta
(Italian) tiny girl

Giva
(Sanskrit) from Gita; song
Givah, Gyva, Gyvah

Givonnah
(Italian) loyal; believer
*Gevonna, Gevonnuh,
Givonn, Givonna, Givonne,
Jevonah, Jevonna, Jivonnah,
Juvona*

Gizela
(Polish) dedicated
Giz, Gizele, Gizella, Gizzy

Gizelle
(German) pledged to serve
Giselle, Gizel, Gizele, Gizell

Gizmo
(American) tricky
Gis, Gismo, Giz

Glad
(Welsh) from Gladys; lame; light

Gladiola
(Botanical) blooming; flower
Glad, Gladdee, Gladdy

Gladys
(Welsh) flower; princess
Glad, Gladice, Gladis, Gladise, Gladiss, Gladdie

Glafira
(Spanish) giving
Glafee, Glafera, Glafi

Gleam
(American) bright girl
Glee, Gleem

Glenda
(Welsh) bright; good
Glinda, Glynda, Glynn, Glynnie

Glenys
(Welsh) holy
Glenice, Glenis

Glenn
(Irish) glen; from a sylvan setting
Glen

Glenna
(Irish) valley-living
Glena, Glenah, Glenuh, Glyn, Glynna

Glennesha
(African American) special
Glenesha, Gleneshuh, Gleniesha, Glenn, Glenneshah, Glenny, Glinnesha

Glennice
(American) top notch
Glenis, Glennis, Glenys, Glenysse, Glynnece, Glynnice

Glenys
(Welsh) holy
Glenis, Gleniss, Glenyss

Gloria
(Latin) glorious
Glorea, Glorey, Glori, Gloriah, Glorrie, Glory

Glorianne
(American) combo of Gloria and Anne
Gloriann, Glori-Ann, Glorianna, Gloryann, Glory-Anne

Glorielle
(American) generous
Gloriel, Gloriele, Glory, Gloree, Glori

Gloris
(American) glorious
Gloeeca, Glores, Gloresa, Glorisa, Glorus, Gloryssa

Glory
(Latin) shining
Gloree, Glorey, Glori, Glorie

Gloss
(American) showy
Glosse, Glossee, Glossie, Glossy

Glynis
(Welsh) from the glen
Glyniss, Glynys, Glynyss

Glynisha
(African American) vibrant
Glynesh, Glynn, Glynnecia, Glynnesha, Glynnie, Glynnisha

Glynn
(Welsh) from the glen
Glin, Glinn, Glyn

Glynnis
(Welsh) vivacious; glen
Glenice, Glenis, Glennis, Glinice, Glinnis, Glynn, Glynnie, Glynny

Goala
(American) goal-oriented
Go, GoGo, Gola

Gobnat
(Irish) cuddly

Goddess
(American) gorgeous
Godess, Goddesse

Godiva
(English) God's gift; brazen
Godeva, Godivah

Golda
(English) golden
Goldi, Goldie

Golden
(American) shining
Goldene, Goldon, Goldun, Goldy

Goldie
(English) bright and golden girl; form of Yiddish Golda
Goldee, Goldey, Goldi, Goldy

Goliad
(Spanish) goal-oriented
Goleade, Goliade

Goneril
(Literature) Shakespearean; name in *King Lear*
Gonarell, Gonarille, Gonereal

Govindi
(Sanskrit) devout; faithful

Grable
(American) handsome woman
Gray, Graybell

Grace
(Latin) graceful
Graci, Gracie, Gracy, Graice, Gray, Grayce

Graceann
(American) girl of grace
Gracean, Grace-Ann, Graceanna, Graceanne, Gracee, Gracy

Gracie
(Latin) graceful
Gracee, Gracey, Graci, Gracy, Graecie, Gray

Graciela
(Spanish) pleasant; full of grace
Chita, Gracee, Gracella, Gracey, Gracie, Graciella, Gracilla, Grasiela, Graziela

Gracilia
(Latin) graceful girl
Gracillia, Gracillya, Gracilya

Grady
(Irish) hardworking; diligent

Graham
(American) sweet
Graehm, Grayhm

Grainne
(Irish) loving girl
Graine, Grayne, Graynne

Grania
(Irish) love
Grainee, Graini

Granya
(Russian) breech baby

Gratia
(Scandinavian) graceful; gracious
Gart, Gert, Gertie, Grasha, Gratea, Grateah, Gratie

Gray
(Last name as first name) quiet
Graye, Grey

Grayson
(Last name as first) child of quiet one
Graison, Grasen, Greyson

Grazie
(Italian) graceful; pleasant
Grasie, Grazee, Grazy

Grazyna
(Polish) graceful; pleasant

Greer
(Scottish) aware
Greere, Grear, Greare, Grier

Gregory
(American) scholarly
Gregoree, Gregge, Greggy, Gregoria, Gregorie

Greshawn
(African American) lively
Greeshawn, Greshaun, Greshawna, Greshonn, Greshun

Gresia
(American) compelling
Grecia, Grasea, Graysea, Grayshea

Greta
(German) a pearl
Gretah, Grete, Gretie, Grette, Grytta

Gretchen
(German) a pearl
Grechen, Grechin, Grechyn, Gretch, Gretchin, Gretchun, Gretchyn, Grethyn

Gretel
(German) pearl; fanciful
Gretal, Grettel, Gretell, Gretelle

Greyland
(American) focused
Grey, Greylin, Greylyn, Greylynne

Griffie
(Welsh) royal
Griff, Griffee, Griffey, Griffi, Gryffie

Griffin
(Welsh) royal
Griff

Grindelle
(American) live wire
Dell, Delle, Grenn, Grin, Grindee, Grindell, Grindy, Renny

Griselda
(German) patient
Grezelda, Grisel, Grissy, Grizel, Grizelda, Grizzie

Grisham
(Last name as first name) ambitious
Grish

Griselia
(Spanish) gray; patient
Grise, Grisele, Grissy, Seley, Selia

Grizel
(Spanish) long-suffering
Griz, Grizelda, Grizelle, Grizzy

Grushenka
(Literature) desirable

Guadalupe
(Spanish) patron saint; easygoing
Guadelupe, Guadrylupe, Lupe, Lupeta, Lupita

Gubby
(Irish) cuddly
Gub, Gubee, Gubbie

Gudrun
(Scandinavian) close friend; (German) contentious
Gudren, Gudrenne, Gudrin, Gudrinne

Guendolen
(Welsh) fair born

Guenevere
(Welsh) soft; white

Guenna
(Welsh) soft
Guena

Guinevere
(Welsh) queen; white
Guenevere, Guenyveere, Guin, Gwen

Gulab
(Hindi) darken

Gunilla
(Scandinavian) warlike
Gun, Gunn

Gunun
(German) lively
Gunan, Gunen

Gurlene
(American) smart
Gurl, Gurleen, Gurleene, Gurline

Gurshawn
(American) talkative
Gurdie, Gurshauna, Gurshaune, Gurshawna, Gurty

Gussie
(Latin) short for Augusta; industrious
Gus, Gussy, Gustie

Gusta
(German) from Gustava; watchful
Gussy, Gusta, Gustana, Gusty

Gustava
(Scandinavian) royal

Guy
(French) guiding; assertive
Guye

Guylaine
(American) combo of Guy and Laine; haughty
Guylane, Gylane

Guylynn
(American) combo of Guy and Lynn; tough-minded
Guylinne, Guylyn, Guylyne

Gwen
(Welsh) short for Gwendolyn; happy
Gwyn, Gweni, Gwenn, Gwenna

Gwenda
(Welsh) beautiful
Guenda

Gwendolyn
(Welsh) mystery goddess; bright
Gwenda, Gwendalinne, Gwendalyn, Gwendelynn, Gwendolen, Gwendolin, Gwendoline, Gwendolynn, Gwennie, Gywnne

Gwenless
(Invented) fair
Gwen, Gwenles, Gwenny

Gwenllian
(Welsh) lovely

Gwenna
(Welsh) beautiful
Gwena

Gwenora
(American) combo of Gwen
and Nora; playful; fair-
skinned
*Guinn, Guinna, Guinnora,
Guinnoray, Guinore, Gwen,
Gwena, Gwenda, Gwendah,
Gwenee, Gwenna, Gwennie,
Gwennora, Gwenny,
Gwenorah, Gwenore, Nora,
Nore, Norra*

Gwladys
(Welsh) from Gladys; happy

Gwyn
(Welsh) short for Gwyneth;
happy
*Gwenn, Gwinn, Gwynn,
Gwynne*

Gwynedd
(Welsh) blessed

Gwyneth
(Welsh) blessed
*Gwennie, Gwinith,
Gwynethe, Gwynith,
Gwynithe, Gwynne,
Gwynneth, Win, Winnie*

Gylla
(Spanish) from Guillermo;
determined
Guilla, Gye, Gyla, Jilla

Gynette
(American) form of
Jeannette; believer
*Gyn, Gynett, Gynnee,
Gynnie*

Gypsy
(English) adventurer
Gippie, Gipsie, Gypsie

Gyselle
(German) variant of Giselle;
naïve
Gysel, Gysele

Gythae
(English) feisty
Gith, Gyth, Gythay

Ha
(Vietnamese) happy

Haafizah
(Arabic) librarian
Hafeezah

Haalah
(Arabic) librarian

Haarisah
(Hindi) sun girl

Haarithah
(Arabic) angel

Habbai
(Arabic) well-loved

Habiba
(Arabic) well-loved
Habeebah, Habibah

Habika
(Arabic) loved and
cherished

Hadassah
(Hebrew) form of Esther;
myrtle; love
*Hadasa, Hadasah, Hadaseh,
Hadassa, Haddasah,
Haddee, Haddi, Haddy*

Hadil
(Arabic) cooing

Hadlee
(English) girl in heather
Hadlea, Hadley, Hadli, Hadly

Hady
(Greek) soulful
*Haddie, Hadee, Hadie,
Haidee, Haidie*

Hadyn
(American) smart
Haden

Haelee
(English) form of Hailey

Hagai
(Hebrew) abandoned; alone
Haggai, Haggi, Hagi

Hagar
(Hebrew) stranger
Haggar, Hager, Hagur

Hagir
(Arabic) wanderer
Hajar

Haidee
(Greek) humble
Haydee

Hailey
(English) natural; hay
meadow
*Haile, Hailea, Hailee, Hailie,
Haily, Halee, Haley, Halie,
Hallie*

Halcyone
(Greek) calm
Halceonne, Halcyon

Halda
(Scandinavian) half-Danish
Haldaine, Haldana,
Haldane, Haldayne

Halden
(Scandinavian) half-Danish
girl
Haldin, Haldyn

Haldi
(Scandinavian) variant of
Halda; half-Danish
Haldie, Haldis

Halena
(Russian) from Helen;
staunch supporter
Haleena, Halyna

Halene
(Russian) staunch
Haleen, Haleen, Halyne

Haletta
(Greek) little country girl
from the meadow
Hale, Halette, Hallee,
Halletta, Halley, Hallie,
Hally, Letta, Lettie, Letty

Haleyanne
(American) combo of Haley
and Anne
Haleyana, Haleyanna,
Haley-Ann

Halfrida
(German) peaceful

Hali
(English) heroic

Halia
(Hawaiian) remembering

Halima
(Arabic) gentle

Haleemah
(Arabic) speaks quietly

Halimeda
(Greek) sealoving
Hallie, Hally, Meda

Halina
(Russian) faithful
Haleena, Halyna

Hall
(Last name as first name)
distinguished
Haul

Halle
(German) home ruler

Hallela
(Hebrew) from Halleli;
praiseworthy

Hallie
(German) high-spirited
Halle, Hallee, Haleigh, Hali,
Halie, Hally, Hallye

Halona
(Native American) lucky baby
Halonna

Halsey
(American) playful
Halcie, Halsea, Halsee,
Halsie

Halston
(American) stylish
Hall, Halls, Halsten

Halzey
(American) leader
Hals, Halsee, Halsi, Halsy,
Halze, Halzee

Hameedah
(Arabic) grateful

Hamilton
(American) wishful
Hamil, Hamilten, Hamiltun,
Hamma, Hamme

Hamony
(Latin) from Harmony;
together; in synch

Haneefah
(Arabic) true believer

Hanh
(Vietnamese) moral

Hanna
(Polish) grace

Hannabelle
(German) happy beauty;
from Hannibal
Hannabell, Hannahbell,
Hannahbelle

Hannah
(Hebrew) merciful; God-
blessed
Hanae, Hanah, Hanan,
Hannaa, Hanne, Hanni

Hannelore
(American) from Hannah;
gracious

Hannette
(American) form of
Jannette; graceful
Hann, Hanett, Hannett

Hansa
(Indian) swanlike
Hans, Hansah, Hansey, Hanz

Happy
(English) joyful
Hap, Happee, Happi

Haralda
(Scandinavian) rules the
army
Harelda, Hallie, Hally, Harilda

Harla
(English) country girl from
the fields
*Harlah, Harlea, Harlee,
Harlen, Harlie, Harlun*

Harlan
(English) athletic
Harlen, Harlon, Harlun

Harlequine
(Invented) romantic
Harlequinne, Harley

Harley
(English) wild thing
*Harlea, Harlee, Harleey,
Harli, Harlie, Harly*

Harlie
(English) in the field;
dreamy

Harlinne
(American) vivacious
*Harleen, Harleene, Harline,
Harly*

Harlow
(American) brash
Harlo, Harly

Harmon
(Last name as first name)
attuned
*Harmen, Harmone, Harmun,
Harmyn*

Harmony
(Latin) in synchrony
*Harmonee, Harmoni,
Harmonia, Harmonie*

Harper
(English) musician; writer
Harp

Harrah
(English) rejoicing;
merriment
Hara, Harah, Harra

Harrell
(American) leader
Harell, Harill, Haryl, Harryl

Harriet
(French) homebody
*Harri, Harrie, Harriett,
Harriette, Harrott, Hat,
Hattie, Hatty, Hatti, Hattie*

Harshita
(English) from Harrett;
home leader

Hart
(American) romantic
*Harte, Hartee, Hartie, Harty,
Heart*

Hartley
(Last name as first name)
having heart
*Hartlee, Hartleigh, Hartli,
Hartlie, Hartly*

Hasina
(African) beauty

Hassaanah
(African) first girl born

Hattie
(English) home-loving
Hatti, Hatty, Hettie, Hetty

Haute
(French, American) stylish
Hautie

Hava
(Hebrew) life; lively
Chaba, Chaya, Haya

Havana
(Cuban) loyal
*Havanah, Havane, Havanna,
Havvanah, Havanuh*

Haven
(American) safe place; open
Havin, Havun

Haviland
(American) lively; talented
Havilan, Havilynd

Hawkins
(American) wily
*Hawk, Hawkens, Hawkey,
Hawkuns*

Hawlee
(American) negotiator
*Hawlea, Hawleigh, Hawlie,
Hawley, Hawly*

Haydee
(American) capable
Hady, Hadye, Haydie

Haydon
(American) knowing
Hayden, Hadyn

Hayfa
(Arabic) slim

Hayley
(English) natural; hay
meadow
*Hailey, Haley, Haylee,
Hayleigh, Hayli, Haylie*

Hayleyann
(American) combo of Hayley and Ann
Haleyan, Haylee-Ann, Hayley-Ann, Hayli-Ann

Haze
(American) word as a name; spontaneous
Haise, Hay, Hays, Hazee, Hazey, Hazy

Hazel
(English) powerful
Hazell, Hazelle, Hazie, Hazyl, Hazzell

Heart
(American) romantic
Hart, Hearte

Heath
(English) open; healthy
Heathe

Heather
(Scottish) flowering
Heath, Heathar, Heathor, Heathur

Heaven
(English) happy and beautiful
Heavyn, Hevin

Heavenly
(American) spiritual
Heaven, Heavenlee, Heavenley, Heavynlie, Hevin

Heba
(Greek) child; goddess of youth
Hebe

Hecate
(Greek) goddess of withcraft

Hedda
(German) capricious; warring
Heda, Heddi, Heddie, Hedi, Hedy, Hetta

Hedley
(Greek) sweet
Hedlee, Hedleigh, Hedli, Hedlie, Hedly

Hedy
(German) mercurial
Hedi

Hedy-Marie
(German) capricious

Heidi
(German) noble; watchful; perky
Heide, Heidee, Heidie, Heidy, Hidi

Heidirae
(American) combo of Heidi and Rae
Heidi-Rae, Heidiray

Heidrun
(German) from Heidi; noble

Heija
(Korean) bright
Hia, Hya

Heirnine
(Greek) from Helen; light

Heirrierte
(English) from Harriet; home leader

Helaine
(French) ray of light; gorgeous
Helainne, Helle, Helyna, Hellyn

Helanna
(Greek) lovely
Helahna, Helana, Helani, Heley, Hella

Helbon
(Greek) from Helen; light
Helbona, Helbonia, Helbonna, Helbonnah

Held
(Welsh) light

Helen
(Greek) beautiful and light
Hela, Hele, Helena, Helyn, Lena, Lenore

Helena
(Greek) beautiful; ingenious
Helana, Helayna, Heleana, Helene, Hellena, Helyena, Lena

Helene
(French) form of Helen; pretty but contentious
Helaine, Heleen, Heline

Helenore
(American) combo of Helen and Lenore; light; darling
Hele, Helen, Helenoor, Helenor, Helia, Helie, Hellena, Lena, Lennore, Lenora, Lenore, Lenory, Lina, Nora, Norey, Norie

Helga
(Anglo-Saxon) pious
Helg

Helia
(Greek) sun
Heleah, Helya, Helyah

Helice
(Greek) from Helen; light

Helie
(Greek) sunny
Heley, Heli

Helina
(Greek) delightful
Helinah, Helinna, Helinnuh

Helki
(Native American) tender
Helkie, Helky

Hella
(Greek) from Helen; light
Helle

Helma
(German) helmet; well protected

Heloise
(German) hearty
Hale, Haley, Heley, Heloese, Heloyse

Helsa
(Scandinavian) God-loving
Helse, Helsie

Henda
(English) from Henna; loves color
Hende, Hendel, Heneh

Hender
(American) embraced
Hendere

Henia
(English) from Henrietta; home leader
Henna, Henie, Henye

Henley
(American) sociable
Hendlee, Hendly, Henli, Henlie, Hinlie, Hynlie

Henna
(Hindi, Arabic) plant that releases colorful dye
Hena, Hennah, Hennuh, Henny

Henrietta
(English, German) home-ruler
Harriet, Hattie, Henny, Hetta, Hettie

Hensley
(American) ambitious
Henslee, Henslie, Hensly

Hera
(Greek) wife of Zeus; radiant

Herdis
(Scandinavian) army woman

Herendira
(Invented) tender and dear
Heren

Herise
(Invented) warm
Heree, Hereese, Herice

Herleen
(American) quiet
Herlee, Herlene, Hurleen, Herley, Herline, Herly

Hermelinda
(Spanish) earthy

Hermilla
(Spanish) fighter
Herm, Hermila, Hermille

Hermina
(Greek) of the earth
Hermine

Hermione
(Greek) sensual
Hermina, Hermine

Hermosa
(Spanish) beautiful
Ermosa

Hernanda
(Spanish) feminine for Hernando; daring

Herra
(Greek) earth girl
Herrah, Hera

Hersala
(Spanish) lithe and lovely
Hers, Hersila, Hersilia, Hersy

Hersilia
(Spanish) delicate

Hertha
(English) earth
Erta, Ertha, Eartha, Erda, Herta

Hertnia
(English) earth
Herrntia

Hesper
(Greek) night star
Hespera, Hespira

Hest
(Greek) starlike; variant of Hester
Hessie, Hesta, Hetty

Hesta
(Greek) starlike
Hestia

Hester
(American) literary
Esther, Hestar, Hesther, Hett, Hettie, Hetty

Hester-Mae
(American) combo of Hester and Mae; star
Hester May, Hestermae

Hestia
(Greek) hearth, fireside

Heti
(English) short for Henrietta; rules

Hetta
(German)
Hedda, Heta, Hettie, Hetty

Hetty
(English) short for Henrietta; rules

Heven
(American) pretty
Hevan, Hevin, Hevon, Hevun, Hevven

Heyzell
(American) form of Hazel; tree; homebody
Hayzale, Heyzel, Heyzelle

Hiah
(Korean) form of Heija; bright
Hia, Hy, Hya, Hye

Hiatt
(English) form of Hyatt; splendid
Hi, Hye

Hibernia
(Latin) place name: Ireland

Hibiscus
(Botanical) pretty

Hicks
(Last name as first name) saucy
Hicksee, Hicksie

Hidee
(American) form of Heidi; wry-humored
Hidey, Hidie, Hidy, Hydee, Hydeey

Hideko
(Japanese) excellence

Hidie
(German) lively

Hilan
(Greek) happy

Hilaria
(Latin, Polish) merrymaker
Hilarea, Hilareeah, Hilariah

Hilary
(Latin) cheerful and outgoing
Hilaire, Hilaree, Hilari, Hilaria, Hillarree, Hillary, Hillerie, Hillery

Hilda
(German) practical; (Scandinavian) fighter
Hild, Hilde, Hildi, Hildie, Hildy

Hildar
(Scandinavian) feisty

Hildebrand
(German) strong

Hildegard
(German, Scandinavian) steadfast protector
Hilda, Hildagarde, Hildegarde, Hildred, Hillie

Hildegunde
(Last name as first name) princess

Hildemar
(German) strong

Hildreth
(German) struggles

Hilina
(Hawaiian) celestial

Hilma
(German) helmet; protects herself
Helma

Hilton
(American) wealthy
Hillie, Hilltawn, Hillton, Hilly

Himalaya
(Place name) mountain range; upwardly mobile
Hima

Hindal
(Hebrew) from Hinda; doe; slight

Hinton
(American) affluent
Hintan, Hinten, Hintun, Hynton

Hiroko
(Japanese) giving; wise

Hisa
(Japanese) forever
Hissa, Hysa, Hyssa

Hisaye
(Japanese) longlasting

Hodel
(German) stern
Hodi

Hodge
(Last name as first name) confident
Hodj

Holda
(German) secretive

Holden
(English) willing
Holdan, Holdun

Holder
(English) beautiful voice
Holdar, Holdur

Holiday
(American) jazzy
Holidae, Holidaye, Holladay,
Holliday, Holly

Holine
(American) special
Hauline, Holinn, Holli,
Holyne

Hollah
(German) hides much

Holland
(Dutch) place name;
expressive
Hollan, Hollyn, Holyn

Hollander
(Dutch) from Holland;
benevolent
Holander, Holender,
Holynder, Hollender,
Hollynder

Hollis
(English) smart; girl by the
holly
Hollice, Hollyce

Hollisha
(English) ingenious;
Christmas-born; holly
Holicha, Hollice, Hollichia,
Hollise

Holly
(Anglo-Saxon) Christmas-
born; holly tree
Hollee, Holleigh, Holley,
Holli, Hollie, Hollye

Holsey
(American) laidback
Holsee, Holsie

Holton
(American) whimsical
Holt, Holten, Holtun

Holyn
(American) fresh-faced
Holan, Holen, Holland,
Hollee, Hollen, Holley,
Hollie, Holly, Hollyn, Hollyn

Homer
(American) tomboyish
Homar, Home, Homera,
Homie, Homir, Homma

Honesty
(American) truthful
Honeste, Honestee,
Honesti, Honestie,
Honestye

Honey
(Latin) sweet-hearted
Honie, Hunnie

Honor
(Latin) ethical
Honer, Honora, Honour

Honora
(Latin) honorable
Honorah, Honoree,
Honoria, Honoura

Honorata
(Polish) respected woman

Honoria
(Spanish) of high integrity;
a saint
Honoreah

Honorina
(Spanish) honored
Honor, Honora, Honoryna

Hope
(Anglo-Saxon) optimistic

Hopkins
(American) perky
Hopkin

Horatia
(Latin) keeps time; careful
Horacia

Horiya
(Japanese) gardens

Hortencia
(Spanish) green thumb
Hartencia, Hartense,
Hartensia, Hortence,
Hortense, Hortensia

Hortense
(Latin) caretaking the garden
Hortence, Hortensia,
Hortinse

Hosanna
(Greek) time to pray;
worshipping
Hosana, Hosanah,
Hosannah

Hoshi
(Japanese) shines

Houston
(Place name) southern
Houst, Houstie, Huston

Hoyden
(Last name as first name)
having high spirits
Hoydin, Hoydyn

Huberta
(German) brilliant

Hud
(American) tomboyish
Hudd

Huda
(Arabic) the right way
Hoda

Hudel
(Scandinavian) lovable

Hudi
(Arabic) the right way

Hudson
(English) explorer;
adventuresome
Hud, Huds

Hueline
(German) smart
*Hue, Huee, Huel, Huela,
Huelene, Huelette, Huelyne,
Huey, Hughee, Hughie*

Huella
(American) joyous
Huela, Huelle

Huette
(German) intellectual
Hughette, Huetta, Hugette

Hulda
(Scandinavian) sweetheart
Huldy, Huldie, Huldah

Humairaa
(Asian) generous

Hun
(American) short for Hunny
Hon

Hunter
(English) searching; jubilant
*Hun, Huner, Hunner, Hunt,
Huntar, Huntter*

Hurley
(English) fit
Hurlee, Hurlie, Hurly

Hutton
(English) right
Hutten, Huttun

Huxlee
(American) creative
Hux, Huxleigh, Huxley, Huxly

Hyacinth
(Greek) flower
Hy, Hycinth, Hyacinthe

Hyatt
(English) high gate;
worthwhile
Hyat

Hyde
(American) tough-willed
Hide, Hydie

Hydie
(American) spirited
Hidi, Hydee, Hydey, Hydi

Hypatia
(Greek) tops

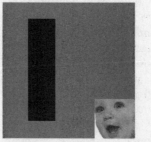

Iana
(Greek) flowering; from the
flower name Iantha
Iann

Ianeke
(Hawaiian) believer in a
gracious God
Ianete, Iani

Ianthe
(Greek) flowering
*Ianthina, Ian, Iantha,
Ianthiria*

Ida
(German) kind; (English)
industrious
Idah, Iduh

Idaa
(Hindi) earth woman

Idahlia
(Greek) sweet
*Idali, Idalia, Idalina, Idaline,
Idalis*

Idalia
(Italian) sweet

Idarah
(American) social
Idara, Idare, Idareah

Idasia
(English) joyful

Ide
(Irish) thirsty

Ideh
(German) variant of Ida;
thrives
Idit

Idelle
(Celtic) generous
Idele

Idetta
(German) serious worker
Ideta, Idettah, Idette

Idil
(Latin) pleasant
Idee, Idey, Idi, Idie, Idyll

Idola
(German) worker
Idolah, Idolia

Idolina
(American) idolizes
Idol, Idolena

Idona
(Scandinavian) fresh
Idonea, Idonia, Iduna,
Idonah, Idonia, Idonna

Idony
(Scandinavian) reborn

Idowu
(African) baby after twins

Idra
(Aramaic) rich (fig tree);
flourishes

Idriya
(Hebrew) duck; rich
Idria

Iduna
(Scandinavian) fresh
Idun

Iduvina
(Spanish) dedicated
Iduvine, Iduvynna,Vina

Ieesh
(Arabic) feminine
Ieasha, Ieesha, Iesha, Yesha

Ierne
(Irish) from Ireland

Iesha
(Arabic) feminine

Ifama
(African) well being

Ife
(African) loving

Ifigenia
(Spanish) from Effie; good
speaker

Ignacia
(Latin) passionate
Ignatia, Ignatzia, Ignacy

Ihab
(Arabic) gift

Iheoma
(Hawaiian) lifted by the Lord

Ihsan
(Arabic) good will
Ihsana, Ihsanah

Ijada
(Spanish) jade; beauty

Ikabela
(Hawaiian) from Isabella;
dedicated to God
Ikapela

Ikea
(Scandinavian) smooth
Ikee, Ikeah, Ikie

Ikeida
(Invented) spontaneous
Ikae, Ikay

Iku
(Japanese) nurturing

Ila
(Hindi) of the earth; lovely

Ilamay
(French) sweet; from an
island
Ila May, Ilamae, Ila-May,
Ilamaye

Ilana
(Hebrew) tree; gorgeous
Elana, Ilaina, Ilane, Ilani,
Illana, Lainie, Lanie

Ilaria
(Greek) girl with a good
attitude

Ilda
(German) warring; feisty

Ildiko
(Hungarian) contentious;
warrior

Ileannah
(American) soaring
Ileana, Ileanna, Ilene,
Iliana, Ilianna, Illeana,
Illiana

Ilene
(American) svelte
Ileen, Ilenia

Ilena
(Greek) regal
Ileena, Ilina

Ilesha
(Hindi) loves the Lord of the
earth

Ilia
(Greek) from ancient city
Ilion; traditional

Iliana
(Greek) woman of Troy
Ileanai, Illeana

Ilima
(Hawaiian) Oahu flower

Ilka
(Hungarian) beauty

Illana
(Greek) from Troy; Iliana;
sweet beauty

Ilma
(American) stubborn

Ilona
(Hungarian) from Helen;
beauty

Ilsa
(Scottish) glowing
Elyssa, Illisa, Illysa, Ilsah,
Ilse, Lissie

Ilse
(German) from Elizabeth;
loves God

Ilyssa
(English) variant of Alyssa; charming

Ima
(German) affluent; (Japanese) current
Imah

Imaine
(Arabic) form of Iman; exotic; believer
Imain, Iman, Imane

Imala
(Native American) strongwilled

Iman
(Arabic, African) living in the present
Imen

Imana
(Arabic) faithful; true

Imani
(Arabic) faithful

Imanuela
(Spanish) faithful

Imara
(Hungarian) ruler

Imari
(Japanese) today's girl

Imelda
(German) contentious
Imalda

Imena
(African) dreamy

Imin
(Arabic) loyal

Immaculada
(Spanish) spotless

Imogen
(Celtic, Latin) girl who resembles her mother
Emogen, Imogene

Imperia
(Latin) imperial; stately

In
(Arabic) short for Inaya; generous

Ina
(Latin) small
Inah

Inaki
(Asian) generous spirit

Inam
(Arabic) generous

Inanna
(Mythology) goddess

Inas
(Arabic) friendly

Inca
(Indian) adventurer
Incah

India
(Place name) woman of India
Indeah, Indee, Indie, Indy, Indya

Indiana
(Place name) salt-of-the-earth
Inda, India, Indianna

Indiece
(American) capable
Indeece, Indeese

Indigo
(Latin) eyes of deep blue
Indego, Indigoh

Indira
(Hindi) ethereal; god of heaven and thunderstorms
Indra

Indra
(Hindi) goddess of thunder and rain; powerful
Indee, Indi, Indira, Indre

Indranee
(Hindi) sky god's wife

Indray
(American) outspoken
Indrae, Indee, Indree

Indre
(Hindi) splendor

Ineesha
(African American) sparkling
Inesha, Ineshah, Inisha

Ineke
(Japanese) nurtures

Ines
(Spanish) chaste
Inez, Innez, Ynez

Inessa
(Russian) pure
Inesa, Nessa

Inez
(Spanish) lovely
Ines

Infinity
(American) lasting
Infinitee, Infinitey, Infiniti, Infinitie

Inga
(Scandinavian) protected by Ing, god of peace and fertility

Ingalill
(Scandinavian) fertile

Ingalls
(American) peaceful

Inge
(Scandinavian) fertile
Inga

Ingeborg
(Scandinavian) fertile

Ingegerd
(Scandinavian) from Ingrid;
fertile

Ingrad
(American) variant of Ingrid;
beauty
Inger, Ingr

Ingrid
(Scandinavian) beautiful
Inga, Inge, Inger, Ingred

Ingrida
(Scandinavian) from Ingrid;
beauty

Iniguez
(Spanish) good
Ina, Ini, Niqui

Innocence
(American) pure
*Innoce, Innocents,
Inocence, Inocencia,
Inocents*

Inoa
(Hawaiian) named

Inocencia
(Spanish) innocent
Inocenta, Inocentia

Inola
(Greek) from Iola; dawn in
clouds

Integrity
(American) truthful
Integritee, Integritie

Iola
(Greek) dawn
Iole

Iolana
(Hawaiian) violet; pretty

Iolanthe
(English) violet; delicate
Iole, Iola

Iona
(Greek, Scottish) place name
Ione, Ionia

Iosepine
(Hawaiian) from Josephine;
blessed

Ira
(Hebrew) contented;
watchful
Irah

Ireland
(Irish) place name; vibrant
*Irelan, Irelande, Irelyn,
Irelynn*

Irina
(Greek, Russian) comforting
*Ireena, Irena, Irenah, Irene,
Irenia, Irenya*

Irene
(Greek) peace-loving;
goddess of peace
Irine

Ireta
(Greek) serene
Iretta, Irette

Iris
(Greek) bright; goddess of
the rainbow

Irma
(Latin) realistic
Irmah

Irmgard
(Latin) from Irma; noble

Irodell
(Invented) peaceful
Irodel, Irodelle

Irra
(Greek) serene

Irvette
(English) friend of the sea

Isa
(Spanish) dark-eyed
Isah

Isabel
(Spanish) God-loving
*Isabela, Isabella, Isabelle,
Issie, Iza*

Isabella
(Spanish, Italian) dedicated
to God
Isabela, Izabella

Isadora
(Greek) beautiful; gift of
Isis; fertile
Dora, Dori, Dory, Isidora

Isairis
(Spanish) lively
Isa, Isaire

Isamu
(Japanese) high-energy

Isatas
(Native American) snow
Istas

Isaura
(Greek) Asian country

Isela
(American) giving
Iselah

Iseult
(Irish) lovely

Isha
(Hindi) protected

Ishana
(Hindi) sheltered

Ishi
(Japanese) rock; safe
Ishie

Ishiko
(Japanese) rock;
dependable

Isis
(Egyptian) goddess supreme
of moon and fertility

Isla
(Place name) river in
Scotland; flows

Isleana
(Latin) sun girl; jolly
Islean, Isleen, Isaeileen

Ismaela
(Hebrew) from Ishmael;
God hears
Isma, Mael, Maella

Ismat
(Arabic) protective

Ismene
(French) from the name
Esme; respected
Isme, Ismyne

Ismenia
(Place name) loyal

Ismey
(French) variant of Esme;
respected

Isoka
(African) given by God
Isoke, Soka

Isoke
(African) God's gift

Isolde
(Welsh) beautiful
*Iseult, Isolda, Isolt, Izette,
Yseult*

Isotta
(Irish) princess

Isra
(Arabic) night mover

Istvan
(Hungarian) crowned

Ita
(Irish) thirsts for knowledge

Italia
(Italian) girl from Italy

Iti
(Irish) variant of Ita; thirsts
for knowledge

Itiah
(Hebrew) God comforts her
Itia, Itiya

Itica
(Spanish) eloquent
Itaca, Iticah

Itidal
(Arabic) cautious

Itinsa
(Hawaiian) waterfall

Itka
(Irish) variant of Ita; thirsts
for knowledge

Ito
(Japanese) thread; delicate

Ituha
(Native American) sturdy
oak; white stone

Itzel
(Spanish) from Isabella;
God-loving
Itz

Itzy
(American) lively
Itsee, Itzee, Itzie

Iuana
(Welsh) believes in gracious
God

Iudita
(Hawaiian) praises;
affectionate

Iuginia
(Hawaiian) highborn
Iugina

Iulaua
(Hawaiian) eloquent

Iulia
(Irish) from Julia; young girl

Iunia
(Hawaiian) from Iune, for
June; goddess of marriage

Iusitina
(Hawaiian) justice

Iva
(Slavic) dedicated
Ivah

Ivanna
(Russian) gracious gift from
God
Iva, Ivana, Ivanka, Ivie, Ivy

Ivelisa
(American) combo of Ivy
and Lisa
*Ivalisa, Ivelise, Ivelisee,
Ivelissa, Ivelyse*

Iverem
(African) lucky girl

Iveta
(French) athletic

Ivette
(French) clever and athletic
Ivet, Ivett

Ivey
(English, American)
easygoing
Ivee, Ivie, Ivy

Iviannah
(American) adorned
Iviana, Ivianna, Ivie, Ivy

Ivisse
(American) graceful
Ivice, Iviece, Ivis, Ivise

Ivon
(Spanish) light
Ivonie, Ivonne

Ivona
(Slavic) gift
*Ivana, Ivanna, Ivannah,
Ivonah, Ivone, Ivonne*

Ivonne
(French) athlete
Ivonn

Ivory
(Latin) white
Ivoree, Ivori, Ivorie

Ivria
(Hebrew) from Abraham's
country
Ivriah, Ivrit

Ivy
(English) growing
Iv, Ivee, Ivey, Ivie

Iwa
(Japanese) strong character

Iwalani
(Hebrew) heavenly girl

Iwilla
(African American) I will rise

Iwona
(Polish) archer; athletic; gift
Iwonna

Iyabo
(African) her mother is home

Iyana
(Hebrew) sincere

Izabella
(American) variant of
Isabella
Iza, Izabela, Izabelle, Izabell

Izanne
(American) calming
Iza, Izan, Izann, Izanna, Ize

Izdihar
(Arabic) blossoming

Izebe
(African) staunch supporter

Izegbe
(African) baby who was
wanted

Izolde
(Greek) philosophical
Izo, Izolade, Izold

Izusa
(Native American) white
rock; unique

Izzy
(American) zany
Izzee, Izzie

Jaala
(Arabic) seeks clarity

Jacalyn
(American) form of
Jacqueline; discriminating
*Jacelyn, Jacelyne, Jacelynn,
Jacilyn, Jacilyne, Jacilynn,
Jacolyn, Jacolyne, Jacolynn,
Jacylyn, Jacylyne, Jacylynn*

Jacey
(Greek) sparkling
*J.C., Jace, Jacee, Jaci, Jacie,
Jacy*

Jacinda
(Greek) attractive girl
Jacenda, Jacey, Jaci, Jacinta

Jacinta
(Spanish) hyacinth; sweet
*Jace, Jacee, Jacey, Jacinda,
Jacinna, Jacintae, Jacinth,
Jacinthia, Jacy, Jacynth*

Jackalyn
(American) form of Jacqueline; cares
Jackalene, Jackalin, Jackaline, Jackalynn, Jackalynne, Jackelin, Jackeline, Jackelyn, Jackelynn, Jackelynne, Jackilin, Jackilyn, Jackilynn, Jackilynne, Jackolin, Jackoline, Jackolyn, Jackolynn, Jackolynne

Jackie
(French) short for Jacqueline
Jackee, Jacki, Jacky, Jaki, Jaky

Jacklyn
(American) careful
Jacklin, Jackline, Jackline, Jacklyne, Jacklynn, Jacklynne

Jackquel
(French) watchful
Jackquelin, Jackqueline, Jackquelyn, Jackquelynn, Jackquilin, Jackquiline, Jackquilyn, Jackquilynn, Jackquilynne

Jackson
(Last name as first name) swaggering
Jacksen, Jaksin, Jakson

Jaclyn
(French) form of Jacqueline
Jacalyn, Jackalene, Jackalin, Jackalyn, Jackeline, Jackolynne, Jacleen, Jaclin, Jacline, Jaclyne, Jaclynn

Jacoba
(Hebrew) replaces

Jacobi
(Hebrew) stand-in
Cobie, Coby

Jacomine
(Dutch) best girl, seductive

Jacoy
(French) from Jackie; standin

Jacqueline
(French) little Jacquie; small replacement
Jacki, Jackie, Jacklin, Jacklyn, Jaclyn, Jacqualin, Jacqualine, Jacqualyn, Jacqualyne, Jacquel, Jacquelyn, Jacquelynn, Jacqui, Jacquie, Jakie, Jakline, Jaklinn, Jaklynn, Jaqueline, Jaquie

Jacquelyn
(French) highbrow
Jacquelyne, Jacquelynn

Jacquet
(Invented) form of Jacquelyn
Jackett, Jackwet, Jacquee, Jacquie, Jakkett

Jacqui
(French) short for Jacquline
Jacquay, Jacque, Jacquee, Jacquie, Jakki, Jaki, Jaquay, Jaqui, Jaquie

Jacynth
(Spanish) hyacinth; flower

Jada
(Spanish) personable; precious
Jadah

Jade
(Spanish) green gemstone; courageous; adoring
Jada, Jadah, Jadda, Jadea, Jadeann, Jadee, Jaden, Jadera, Jadi, Jadie, Jadielyn, Jadienne, Jady, Jadzia, Jadziah, Jaeda, Jaedra, Jaida, Jaide, Jaiyde, Jaiden

Jaden
(African American) exotic
Jadi, Jadie, Jadin, Jadyn, Jaeden, Jaiden

Jadwiga
(Polish) religious
Jad, Jadwig, Wiga

Jae
(Latin) small; jaybird
Jaea, Jay, Jayjay

Jael
(Hebrew) high-climbing
Jaela, Jaelee, Jaeli, Jaelie, Jaelle

Jaela
(Hebrew) bright
Jael, Jaell, Jayla

Jaelyn
(African American) ambitious
Jaela, Jaelynne, Jala, Jalyn, Jaylyn

Jaenesha
(African American) spirited
Jacey, Jae, Jaeneisha, Jaeniesha, Janesha, Jaynesha, Nesha

Jaffa
(Hebrew) lovely

Jagan
(American) form of Jadan;
wholesome
Jag, Jagann, Jagen, Jagun

Jagger
(English) cutter
Jaeger, Jag, Jager

Jaguar
(American) runner
Jag, Jaggy, Jagwar, Jagwor

Jahnea
(Scandinavian) from John;
loves God

Jahnika
(Scandinavian) believes in
God

Jahnny
(American) form of Johnny
*Jahnae, Jahnay, Jahnie,
Jahnnee, Jahnney, Jahnnie,
Jahny*

Jaidan
(American) golden child
*Jaedan, Jai, Jaide, Jaidee,
Jaidi, Jaidon, Jaidun, Jaidy,
Jaidyn, Jaydan, Jaydyn*

Jaime
(French) girl who loves
*Jaeme, Jaemee, Jaima,
Jaimee, Jaimey, Jaimi,
Jaimie, Jaimy, Jamie, Jaymee*

Jaime-Day
(American) loving

Jairia
(Spanish) taught by God's
lessons

Jakira
(Arabic) warmth

Jakisha
(African American) favored
Jakishe

Jakki
(American) form of Jackie;
carefree
Jakea, Jakia, Jakkia

Jaleesa
(African American) combo
of Ja and Leesa
Gilleesa, Jalesa, Jilleesa

Jalena
(American) combo of Jay
and Lena; outgoing
*Jalayna, Jalean, Jaleen,
Jalene, Jalina, Jaline, Jalyna,
Jelayna, Jelena, Jelina, Jelyna*

Jalene
(American) combo of Jane
and Lene; pretty
*Jaleen, Jaline, Jalinn, Jalyn,
Jalyne, Jalynn, Jlayna*

Jaleshia
(American) combo of Jale
and Leshia; chatterer
Jalicia

Jalila
(Arabic) excellent
Jalile

Jalisa
(American) combo of Jay
and Lisa
Gillisa, Jalise, Jaylisa, Jelisa

Jalit
(American) sparkling
Jal, Jalitt, Jalitte, Jallit

Jamaica
(Place name) Caribbean
island
*Jama, Jamaika, Jamaka,
Jamake, Jamana, Jamea,
Jameca, Jameka, Jamica,
Jamika, Jamiqua, Jamoka,
Jemaica, Jemika, Jemyka*

Jamais
(French) ever
Jamay, Jamaye

Jamalita
(Invented) form of James;
little Jama
Jama

Jamar
(African American) strong
*Jam, Jamara, Jamareah,
Jamaree, Jamarr, Jamarra,
Jammy*

Jamashia
(African American) soulful
Jamash, Jamashea

Jameah
(African American) bold
Jamea, Jameea, Jamiah

Jamecka
(African American) studious
*Jamecca, Jameeka, Jameka,
Jameke, Jamekka, Jamie,
Jamiea, Jamieka*

Jamesetta
(American) form of James
Jamesette

Jamesha
(African American) outgoing
Jamece, Jamecia, Jameciah, Jameisha, James, Jamese, Jameshia, Jameshyia, Jamesia, Jamesica, Jamesika, Jamesina, Jamessa, Jamie, Jamisha, Jay

Jami
(Hebrew) replacement
Jamay, Jamia, Jamie, Jamy

Jamiann
(American) combo of Jami and Ann
Jami, Jamia, Jami-Ann, Jamian, Jamiane

Jamie
(Hebrew) supplants; fun-loving
Jami, Jamee, James, Jaymee

Jamielyn
(American) combo of Jamie and Lyn; pretty
Jameelyn, Jamelinn, James, Jamie, Jamie-Lynn, Jamilin, Jami-Lyn

Jamika
(African American) buoyant
Jameeka, Jamey, Jamica, Jamicka, Jamie

Jamila
(Arabic) beautiful female
Jahmela, Jahmilla, Jam, Jameela, Jami, Jamie, Jamil, Jamilah, Jamile, Jamilla, Jamille, Jamilya, Jammell, Jammie

Jamisha
(American) combo of Jami and Misha; organized

Jan
(English) short for Janet or Janice; cute
Jani, Jania, Jandy, Jannie, Janny

Jana
(Slavic, Scandinavian) gracious
Janna, Janne

Janae
(American) giving
Janea, Jannay, Jennae, Jannah, Jennay

Janaleigh
(American) combo of Jana and Leigh; friendly
Jana, Janalea, Janalee, Janalee, Jana-Lee, Jana-Leigh, Janlee, Jannalee, LeeLee, Leigh

Janalyn
(American) giving
Jan, Janalynn, Janelyn, Janilyn, Jannalyn, Jannnie, Janny

Janan
(Arabic) soulful
Jananee, Janani, Jananie, Janann, Jannani

Janara
(American) generous
Janarah, Janerah, Janira, Janirah

Janay
(American) forgiving
Janae, Janah, Janai

Janaya
(American) combo of Jana and Anaya; comical

Jancy
(American) risk-taker
Jan, Jance, Jancee, Jancey, Janci, Jancie, Janny

Jandy
(American) fun
Jandee, Jandey, Jandi

Jane
(Hebrew) believer in a gracious God
Jaine, Jan, Janelle, Janene, Janeth, Janett, Janetta, Janey, Janica, Janie, Jannie, Jayne, Jaynie

Janeana
(American) sweet
Janea, Janean, Janeanah, Janine

Janel
(French) variant of Janelle; dark eyes
Janell, Jannel, Jaynel, Jaynell

Janene
(American) form of Jane
Janeen, Jenean, Janine, Jenine

Janella
(American) combo of Jan and Ella; sporty
Jan, Janela, Janelle, Janny

Janelle
(French) exuberant
J'Nel, J'nell, Janel, Janell, Jannel, Jenelle, Nell

Janessa
(American) forgiving
Janesha, Janeska, Janessah, Janie, Janiesa, Janiesha, Janisha, Janissa, Jannesa, Jannesha, Jannessa, Jannisa, Jannisha, Jannissa, Janyssa

Janet
(English) small; forgiving
Jan, Janett, Janetta, Janette, Jannet, Jannett, Janot, Jessie, Jinett, Johnette, Jonetta, Jonette

Janeth
(American) fascinating
Janith

Janice
(Hebrew) knowing God's grace
Genese, Jan, Janece, Janecia, Janeese, Janeice, Janiece, Jannice, Janyce, Jynice

Janie
(English) form of Jane
Janey, Jani, Jany

Janiece
(American) devout; enthusiastic
Janece, Janecia, Janeese, Janese, Janesea, Janesse, Janneece, Jeneece, Jeneese

Janiecia
(African American) sporty
Janesha, Janeisha, Janeshah, Janisha, Jan, Jannes, Jannesa

Janika
(Scandinavian) believer in a gracious God
Janica, Janicah, Janik, Jannike, Janikka

Janine
(American) kind
Janean, Janeen, Janene, Janey, Janie, Jannine, Jannyne, Janyne, Jenine

Janiqua
(American) combo of Jani and Niqua; has a fortune

Janira
(American) combo of Jan and Nira; entertaining

Janis
(English) form of Jane
Janees, Janeesa, Janes, Jenice, Jenis, Janise

Janitza
(American) from Juanita; bright

Janjan
(Last name as first) sweet; believer
Jan Jan, Jange, Janja, Jan-Jan, Janje, Janni, Jannie, Janny

Janke
(Scandinavian) believer in God
Jankee, Jankey, Jankie

Jan-Marie
(American) combo of Jan and Marie; believer
Jan Marie, Janmarie, Jannemarie

Janna
(Hebrew) short for Johana; forgiving

Janneke
(Scandinavian) smart; believer

Jannette
(American) lovely
Jan, Janette, Jannett, Jannie, Janny

Jannie
(English) form of Jane and Jan
Janney, Janny, Jannye

Jansen
(Scandinavian) smooth
Jan, Jannsen, Jans, Jansie, Janson, Jansun, Jansy

Jaqualia
(American) combo of Jaquie and Alia; reserved

Jaquita
(Spanish) combo of Jaqui and Quita; temperamental

Jaqueline
(French) form of Jacquelyn
Jaqlinn, Jaqlyn, Jaqlynn, Jaqua, Jaquaeline, Jaqualine, Jaqualyn, Jaquelina, Jaquelyn, Jaquelynne, Jaquie, Jaqulene

Jaquonna
(African American) spoiled
Jakwona, Jakwonda, Jakwonna, Jaqui, Jaquie, Jaquon, Jaquona, Jaquonne

Jardana
(American) gardener
Jardana, Jarde, Jardee, Jardy

Jardena
(French) gardens
Jardan, Jardane, Jarden, Jardenia, Jardine, Jardyne

Jarene
(American) bright
Jare, Jaree, Jareen, Jaren, Jareni, Jarine, Jarry, Jaryne, Jerry

Jarita
(Arabic) carries water;
befriends
*Jara, Jari, Jaria, Jarica, Jarida,
Jarietta, Jarika, Jarina,
Jaritta, Jaritza*

Jariya
(Arabic) from Jarita; totes
water; hardworking

Jarmila
(Czech) beautiful spring

Jaranescia
(Scandinavian) magnificent

Jarone
(American) optimistic
*Jaron, Jaroyne, Jerone,
Jurone*

Jaroslava
(Czech) glorious spring

Jarren
(American) lovable
Jaren, Jarran, Jarre

Jas
(American) from Jasmine;
saucy
Jass, Jaz, Jazz, Jazze, Jazzi

Jasalin
(American) devoted
*Jasalinne, Jasalyn, Jasalynn,
Jaselyn, Jasleen, Jaslene,
Jass, Jassalyn, Jassy, Jazz,
Jazzy*

Jasira
(Polish) from Jane; religious

Jasmarie
(American) combo of
Jasmine and Marie;
attractive

Jasmine
(Persian, Spanish) fragrant;
sweet
*Jas'mine, Jasamine, Jasime,
Jasimen, Jasimin, Jasimine,
Jasmaine, Jasman, Jasme,
Jasmie, Jasmina, Jasminah,
Jasminen, Jasminne,
Jasmon, Jasmond, Jasmone,
Jasmyn, Jasmynn,
Jasmynne, Jazie, Jazmaine,
Jazman, Jazmeen, Jazmein,
Jazmen, Jazmin, Jazmine,
Jazmon, Jazmond, Jazmyn,
Jazmyne, Jazs, Jazsmen,
Jazz, Jazza, Jazzamine,
Jazzee, Jazzi, Jazzmeen,
Jazzmin, Jazz-Mine,
Jazzmun, Jazzy*

Jasna
(American) talented
Jas, Jazna, Jazz

Jaspreet
(Punjabi) pure
*Jas, Jaspar, Jasparit,
Jasparita, Jasper, Jasprit,
Jasprita, Jasprite*

Jatara
(American) combo of Jay
and Tara; popular
Jataria, Jatarra, Jatori, Jatoria

Ja-Tawn
(African American) tawny
J'Tawn, Ja Tawn, Jatawn

Jatsue
(Spanish) lively
Jat, Jatsey

Javana
(Asian) girl from Java; dancer
*Javanna, Javanne, Javon,
Javonda, Javonna, Javonne,
Javonya, Jawana, Jawanna,
Jawn*

Javiera
(Spanish) owns a home
Javeera, Viera

Jawara
(Arabic) true gem

Jaya
(Hindi) winning
Jaea, Jaia, Jay, Jayah

Jayare
(African) winner

Jayci
(American) vivacious
*Jacee, Jacey, Jaci, Jacie, Jacy,
Jaycee, Jaycey, Jayci, Jaycie*

Jaydee
(American) combo of Jay
and Dee; perky
*Jadee, Jadey, Jadi, Jadie,
Jady, Jayde, Jadey, Jayda,
Jayd, Jaydia, Jaydn, Jayia*

Jayden
(American) enthusiastic
*Jaden, Jay, Jaydeen, Jaydon,
Jaydyn, Jaye*

Jaydie
(American) lively
*Jadie, Jady, Jay-Dee,
Jaydeye, Jaydie*

Jaydra
(Spanish) treasured jewel;
jade
Jadra, Jay, Jaydrah

Jaye
(Latin) small as a jaybird
Jae, Jay

Jayla
(American) smiling
Jaila, Jaylah, Jayle, Jaylee

Jaylene
(American) combo of Jay
and Lene; conflicted
*Jayelene, Jayla, Jaylah, Jaylan,
Jayleana, Jaylee, Jayleen*

Jaylo
(American) combo of
Jennifer and Lopez;
charismatic
*J. Lo, Jalo, Jayjay, Jaylla,
Jaylon, J-Lo*

Jaylynn
(American) combo of Jay
and Lynn; conflicted
*Jaelin, Jaeline, Jaelyn,
Jaelyne, Jaelynn, Jaelynne,
Jalin, Jaline, Jalyn, Jalyne,
Jalynn, Jalynne, Jaylin,
Jayline, Jaylyn, Jaylyne,
Jaylynne*

Jayme
(English) gracious; feminine
form of James
*Jami, Jamie, Jaymee, Jaymi,
Jaymia, Jaymie*

Jayna
(Hindi) winner
Jaynae

Jayne
(Hindi, American) winning
*Jane, Janey, Jani, Jayn,
Jaynee, Jayni, Jaynie,
Jaynita, Jaynne*

Jaynell
(American) combo of Jay
and Nell; southern belle
*Janell, Janelle, Jaynel,
Jaynelle, Jeanel, Jeanell,
Jeanelle, Jeanelly*

Jazlyn
(American) combo of Jazz
and Lynn; zany
*Jazleen, Jazlene, Jazlin,
Jazline, Jazlynn, Jazlynne,
Jazzleen, Jazzlene, Jazzlin,
Jazzline, Jazzlyn, Jazzlynn,
Jazzlynne*

Jazz
(American) rhythmic
*Jas, Jassie, Jaz, Jazzi, Jazzie,
Jazzle, Jazzy*

Jazzell
(American) spontaneous
*Jazel, Jazell, Jazz, Jazzee,
Jazzie*

Jazzlyn
(American) combo of Jazz
and Lyn
*Jaz, Jazilyn, Jazlin, Jazlinn,
Jazlinne, Jazlyn, Jazlynn,
Jazlynne*

Jean
(Scottish) God-loving and
gracious
*Jeana, Jeanie, Jeanne,
Jeannie, Jeanny, Jena, Jenay,
Jenna*

Jeana
(American) variant of Gina;
audacious
Jeanna

Jeanetta
(American) impish
*Janetta, Jeannet, Jeannette,
Jeanney, Jen, Jenett, Jennita*

Jeanette
(French) lively
*Janette, Jeannete, Jeanett,
Jeanetta, Jeanita, Jeannete,
Jeannett, Jeannetta,
Jeannette, Jeannita, Jenet,
Jenett, Jenette, Jennett,
Jennetta, Jennette, Jennita,
Jinetta, Jinette*

Jeanie
(Scottish) devout;
outspoken
Jeani, Jeannie, Jeanny, Jeany

Jeanine
(Scottish) peace-loving
*Jeanene, Jeanina, Jeannina,
Jeannine, Jenine, Jennine*

Jeanisha
(African American) pretty
*Jean, Jeaneesh, Jeanise,
Jeanna, Jeannie, Jenisha*

Jearlean
(American) vibrant
*Jearlee, Jearlene, Jearley,
Jearli, Jearline, Jearly, Jerline*

Jebel
(Origin unknown) from
Jezebel; treacherous

Jecelyn
(Invented) form of Jocelyn;
innovative
Jece, Jecee, Jeselyn, Jess

Jeffrey
(German) peaceful; sparkling personality
Jef, Jeff, Jeffa, Jefferi, Jeffery, Jeffie, Jeffre, Jeffrie, Jeffy, Jefry

Jelana
(Russian) from Helen; upright

Jelane
(Russian) light heart
Jelaina, Jelaine, Jelanne, Jilane, Julane

Jelani
(American) pretty sky
Jelaney, Jelani, Jelanie, Jelainy, Jelanni

Jemima
(Hebrew) dove-like
Jamima, Jem, Jemi, Jemimah, Jemm, Jemma, Jemmi, Jemmia, Jemmiah, Jemmy, Jemora

Jemine
(American) treasured
Jem, Jemmy, Jemyne

Jemma
(Hebrew, English) nickname for Jemima; peaceful
Jem

Jems
(American) treasured
Gemas, Jemma, Jemmey, Jemmi, Jemmy

Jena
(Arabic); small
Jenaa, Janae, Jenaeh, Jenah, Jenai, Jenal, Jenay, Jenna

Jenavieve
(American) from Genevieve; generous

Jenaya
(African) hospitable

Jenci
(American) combo of Jen and Nanci; friend of all

Jencynn
(American) combo of Jen and Cynn; sweetheart
Jencin, Jen-Cynn, Jensynn

Jenell
(American) combo of Jenny and Nell
Janele, Jen, Jenaile, Jenalle, Jenel, Jenella, Jennelle, Jenny

Jenesia
(American) combo of Jen and Nesia; popular

Jeniece
(American) combo of Jen and Niece; well-liked

Jenifer
(Welsh) beautiful; fair
Gennefer, Gennifer, Ginnifur, Ginnipher, Jay, Jenefer, Jenifer, Jenjen, Jenna, Jenni, Jennifer, Jenny

Jenilee
(American) combo of Jen and Lee; fair and light
Jenalea, Jenalee, Jenaleigh, Jenaly, Jenelea, Jenelee, Jeneleigh, Jenely, Jenelly, Jenileigh, Jenily, Jennely, Jennielee, Jennilea, Jennilee, Jennilie

Jenilynn
(American) combo of Jenny and Lynn; precious
Jennalyn, Jennilin, Jennilinn, Jennilyn, Jenny-Lynn, Jennylynn

Jenisa
(American) combo of Jen and Nisa; smart
Jenisha, Jenissa, Jennisa, Jennise, Jennisha, Jennissa, Jennisse, Jennysa, Jennyssa, Jenysa, Jenyse, Jenyssa, Jenysse

Jenna
(Scottish, English) sweet
Jena, Jennah, Jennat, Jennay, Jhenna, Jynna

Jenni
(Welsh) from Jennifer; beauty
Jeni, Jenica, Jenie, Jenisa, Jenka, Jenne, Jennee, Jenney, Jennia, Jennier, Jennita, Jennora, Jensine

Jennifer
(Welsh, English) fair-haired; beautiful perfection
Gennefur, Ginnifer, Jen, Jenefer, Jenife, Jenifer, Jeniferr, Jeniffer, Jenipher, Jenn, Jenna, Jennae, Jennafer, Jennefer, Jenni, Jenniffe, Jenniffer, Jenniffier, Jennifier, Jenniphe, Jennipher, Jenniphur, Jenny, Jennyfer, Jennypher

Jennilee
(American) combo of Jeni
and Lee; dependable
*Jennalea, Jennalee,
Jennielee, Jennilea, Jennilie*

Jennilynn
(American) combo of Jenni
and Lynn; pretty
*Jennalin, Jennaline,
Jennalyn, Jennalyne,
Jennalynn, Jennalynne,
Jennilin, Jenniline, Jennilyn,
Jennilyne, Jennilynne*

Jennings
(Last name as first name)
pretty
Jen, Jenny

Jennis
(American) white; patient
*J, Jay, Jen, Jenace, Jenice,
Jenis, Jenn, Jennice*

Jennison
(American) variant of
Jennifer; darling
*Gennison, Jenison,
Jennisyn, Jenson*

Jenny
(Scottish, English) short for
Jennifer; blessed;
sweetheart
*Jen, Jenae, Jeni, Jenjen,
Jenney, Jenni, Jennie,
Jennye, Jeny, Jinny*

Jeno
(Greek) heavenly

Jensen
(Scandinavian) athletic

Jenteale
(American) combo of Jen
and Teale; blue-eyed and
pretty
*Jen, Jenny, Jenteal, Jentelle,
Jyn, Jynteale, Teal, Teale*

Jenvie
(American) lovely
Jennvey, Jenvee, Jenvy

Jenz
(Scandinavian) form of
male name Johannes;
believer in God
Jen, Jens

Jeri
(American) hopeful
*Geri, Jere, Jerhie, Jerree,
Jerri, Jerry, Jerrye*

Jerica
(American) combo of Jeri
and Erica; conniving
*Jerice, Jericka, Jerika,
Jerreka, Jerricca, Jerrice,
Jerricka, Jerrika*

Jeridean
(American) combo of Jeri
and Dean; leader; musical
*Geridean, Jerdean, Jeri
Dean, Jeri-Dean, Jerridean,
Jerrydean*

Jerilee
(American) combo of Jeri
and Lee; political

Jerilyn
(American) combo of Jeri
and Lyn; plots
*Jeralin, Jeraline, Jeralyn,
Jeralyne, Jeralynn, Jeralynne,
Jerelin, Jereline, Jerelyn,
Jerelyne, Jerelynn, Jerelynne,
Jerilin, Jeriline, Jerilyne,
Jerilynn, Jerilynne, Jerrilin,
Jerriline, Jerrilyn, Jerrilyne,
Jerrilynn, Jerrilynne*

Jerikah
(American) sparkling
*Jereca, Jerecka, Jeree, Jeri,
Jerica, Jerik, Jeriko, Jerrica,
Jerry*

Jerilyn
(American) combo of Jeri
and Lynn
*Jeralyn, Jeralynn, Jerrilin,
Jerrilyn*

Jerin
(American) daring
*Jere, Jeren, Jeron, Jerinn,
Jerun*

Jeritah
(American) combo of Jeri
and Rita; presides
Jerita

Jermaine
(French) form of Germaine
*Germaine, Jermain, Jerman,
Jermane, Jermanee, Jermani,
Jermany, Jermayne*

Jerrett
(American) spirited
*Jerett, Jeriette, Jerre, Jerret,
Jerrette, Jerrie, Jerry*

Jerrica
(American) free spirit
Jerrika

Jerusha
(Hebrew) wealthy

Jesenia
(Spanish) witty
Jesene, Jess, Jessenia, Jessie, Jessie, Jisenia, Yesenia

Jessa
(American) spontaneous
Jessah

Jessalyn
(American) combo of Jessica and Lynn; exciting
Jesalin, Jesaline, Jesalyn, Jesalyne, Jesalynn, Jesalynne, Jesilin, Jesline, Jesilyn, Jesilyne, Jesilynn, Jeslin, Jeslyn, Jessaline, Jessie, Jesslin

Jessamine
(French) form of Jasmine; sassy
Jesamyn, Jess, Jessamin, Jessamon, Jessamy, Jessamyn, Jessemin, Jessemine, Jessie, Jessmine, Jessmon, Jessmy, Jessmyn

Jesse
(Hebrew) friendly
Jesie, Jessey, Jessi, Jessy

Jessenia
(Arabic) flowering
Jescenia, Jesenia

Jessica
(Hebrew) rich
Jesica, Jess, Jessa, Jessie, Jessika, Jessy, Jezika

Jessie
(Scottish) casual
Jescie, Jesey, Jess, Jesse, Jessee, Jessi, Jessye

Jessie-Mae
(American) combo of Jessie and Mae; country girl
Jessee-May, Jessemay, Jessie Mae, Jessie May, Jessiemae, Jessmae

Jessika
(Hebrew) rich
Jesika, Jessieka, Jessika, Jessyka, Jezika

Jesusa
(Spanish) form of Jesus; worships

Jesusita
(Spanish) little Jesus

Jett
(American) high-flying
Jettie, Jetty

Jetta
(English) black gem; knowing
Jette, Jettie

Jette
(German, Scandinavian) lovely gem
Jet, Jeta, Jetia, Jetta, Jette, Jettee, Jettie

Jeudi
(French) born on Thursday

Jeune-Fille
(French) young girl

Jevae
(Spanish) desired
Jevaie, Jevay

Jevette
(American) combo of Jen and Yvette; compromises
Jetta, Jeva, Jeveta, Jevetta

Jevonne
(African American) kind
Jev, Jevaughan, Jevaughn, Jevie, Jevon, Jevona, Jevonn, Jevvy

Jewel
(French) pretty
Jeul, Jewelia, Jewelie, Jewell, Jewelle, Jewels, Juel, Jule

Jewellene
(American) combo of Jewel and Lene; treasured
Jewelene, Jeweline, Jewels, Julene

Jezebel
(Hebrew) wanton woman
Jessabel, Jessebel, Jessebelle, Jez, Jezabel, Jezabella, Jezabelle, Jeze, Jezebell, Jezel, Jezell, Jezybel, Jezzie

Jezenya
(American) flowering
Jesenya, Jeze, Jezey

Jhamesha
(African American) lovely; soft
Jamesha, Jmesha

Jianna
(Italian) trusts in God
Jiana, Jianina, Jianine

Jilan
(American) mover
Jilyn, Jillan, Jillyn, Jylan, Jylann

Jill
(English) short for Jillian; high-energy and youthful
Jil, Jilee, Jilli, Jillie, Jilly

Jillaine
(Latin) young-hearted
Jilaine, Jilane, Jilayne, Jillana, Jillane, Jillann, Jillanne, Jillayne

Jilleen
(American) energetic
Jil, Jileen, Jilene, Jiline, Jill, Jillain, Jilline, Jlynn

Jillian
(Latin) youthful
Giliana, Jill, Jillaine, Jillana, Jillena, Jilliane, Jilliann, Jillie, Jillion, Jillione, Jilly, Jilyan

Jimi
(Hebrew) replaces; reliable
Jimae

Jimmi
(American) assured
Jim, Jimi, Jimice, Jayjay

Jin
(Chinese) golden; gem
Jinn, Jinny

Jina
(Italian) variant of Gina; winning
Jena, Jinae, Jinan, Jinda, Jinna, Jinnae

Jinger
(American) form of Ginger; go-getter
Jin, Jinge

Jinkie
(American) bouncy
Jinkee, Jynki, Jinky

Jinny
(Scottish) form of Jenny
Jin, Jina, Jinae, Jinelle, Jinessa, Jinna, Jinnae, Jinnalee, Jinnee, Jinney, Jinni, Jinnie

Jinte
(Hindi) patient

Jinx
(Latin) spell
Jin, Jinks, Jinxie, Jinxy, Jynx

Jinxia
(Latin) form of Jinx; spellbinder
Jinx, Jynx, Jynxia

Jirina
(Czech) works the earth

Jnae
(American) darling
J'Nay, Jenae, Jnay, Jnaye

J'Netta
(American) form of Jeanetta; sweetness
J'netta, J'Nette, Janetta, Janny

J-Nyl
(American) flirtatious

Jo
(American) short for Josephine; spunky
Joey, Jojo

Jo-Allene
(American) combo of Jo and Allene; effervescent
Jo Allene, Joallene, Joallie, Joeallene, Joealli, Jolene

Joan
(Hebrew) heroine; God-loving
Joane, Joane, Joani, Joanie, Joanni, Joannie, Jonie

Joana
(Hebrew) kind
Joanah, Joanna, Joannah, Jonah

Joanie
(Hebrew) kind
Joanney, Joanni, Joannie, Joanny, Joany, Joni

Jo-Ann
(French) believer; gregarious
Joahnn, JoAn, JoAnn, Joann, Joanna, Joanne, Jo-Anne, Joannie

Joanna
(English) kind
Jo, Joana, Joandra, Joananna, Joananne, Joannah, Joeanna, Johannah, Josie

Joanne
(English) form of Joan; excellent friend
JoAnn, Joann, Jo-Ann, JoAnne, Joeanne

Joannie
(Hebrew) forgiving
Joani, Joany, Joanney, Joanni

Joappa
(Origin unknown) noisy

Jobelle
(American) combo of Jo and Belle; beautiful
Jobel, Jobell, Jobi, Jobie, Joebel

Jobeth
(American) combo of Jo and Beth; vivacious
Beth, Bethie, Jo, Jobee, Jobie, Joby

Jobi
(Hebrew) misunderstood; inventive
Jobee, Jobey, Jobie, Joby

Jobina
(Hebrew) hurting
Jobey, Jobie, Joby, Jobye, Jobyna

Jo-Carol
(American) combo of Jo and Carol; lively
Jo Carol, Jocarol, Jocarole

Jocasta
(Italian) light

Jocelyn
(Latin) joyful
Jocelie, Jocelin, Jocelle, Jocelyne, Jocelynn, Joci, Joclyn, Joclynn, Jocylan, Jocylen, Joycelyn

Joci
(Latin) happy
Jocee, Jocey, Jocie, Jocy, Josi

Jocklyn
(American) combo of Jock and Lyn; athletic
Jock, Joklyn

Jocosa
(Latin) laughs; jokes

Jodase
(American) brilliant
Jo, Jodace, Jodasse, Jodie, Jody

Jode
(American) from Jody; happy

Jo-Dee
(American) combo of Jo and Dee
Jo Dee, Jodee, Joedee

Jodee-Marie
(American) combo of Jodee and Marie
Jodeemarie, Jodymarie

Jodelle
(American) combo of Jo and Delle
Jodel, Jodell, Jodie, Jody

Jodie
(American) happy girl
Jo, Jodee, Jodey, Jodi, Jody

Jodiann
(American) combo of Jodi and Ann; wanted
Jodianna, Jodianne, Jodyann, Jodyanna, Jodyanne

Joedy
(American) jolly
Joedey, Joedi, Joedie

Joe-Leigh
(American) combo of Joe and Leigh; happy
Joe Leigh, Joel, Joelea, Joesey, Jolee, Joleigh, Jolie, Jollee, Jose, Joze

Joelle
(Hebrew) willing
Jo, Joel, Joela, Joele, Joelee, Joeleen, Joelene, Joeli, Joeline, Joell, Joella, Joelle, Joellen, Joelly

Joellen
(American) combo of Jo and Ellen; popular

Joely
(Hebrew) believer; lively
Jo, Joe, Joey

Joelly
(American) kindhearted
Joelee, Joeli, Joely

Joetta
(American) combo of Jo and Etta; creative
Jo, Joe, Joettah, Joette

Joey
(American) easygoing
Joe, Joeye

Joezee
(American) form of Josey; attractive
Jo, Joe, Joes, Joezey, Joezy

Johanna
(German) believer in a gracious God
Johana, Johanah, Johanna, Jonna

Johnay
(American) steadfast
Johnae, Jonay, Jonaye, Jonnay

Johnnessa
(American) combo of Johna and Nessa; restless
Jahnessa, Johnecia, Johnesha, Johnetra, Johnisha, Johnishi, Johnnise, Jonyssa

Johnette
(Hebrew) from John; believer

Johnica
(American) form of John; believer in a gracious God
Jonica

Johnna
(American) upright
Jahna, John, Johna, Johnae, Jonna, Jonnie

Johnnell
(American) happy
Johnelle, Jonell, Jonnel

Johnnetta
(American) joyful
Johneta, Johnete, Johnetta, Johnette, Jonetta, Jonette, Jonietta

Johnnisha
(African American) steady
Johnisha, Johnnita, Johnny, Jonnisha

Johnson
(Last name as first name) confident
Johns

Johntell
(African American) sweet
Johna, Johntal, Johntel, Johntelle, Jontell

Johntria
(Hebrew) believer

Johppa
(Origin unknown) different
Johppah

Joi
(Latin) joyful
Joicy, Joie, Jojo, Joy

Jo-Kiesha
(African American) vibrant
Joekiesha

Jola
(Greek) violet flower

Jolanda
(Latin, Italian) violet; pretty flower
Jola, Jolan, Jolana, Jolande, Jolander, Jolane, Jolanka, Jolantha, Jolanthe, Joli

Jolanta
(Greek) lovely girl

Jolene
(American) jolly
Jo, Joeleane, Joeleen, Joelene, Joelynn, Joleen, Joleene, Jolen, Jolena, Joley, Jolie, Joline, Jolyn, Jolynn

Joletta
(American) happy-go-lucky
Jaletta, Jolette, Joley, Joli, Jolie, Jolitta

Jolie
(French) pretty
Jo, Jole, Jolea, Jolee, Joleigh, Joley, Joli, Jollee, Jollie, Jolly, Joly

Jolienne
(American) pretty
Joliane, Jolianne, Jolien, Jolina, Joline

Joline
(English) blessed

Jolisa
(American) combo of Jo and Lisa; cheerful
Joelisa, Joleesa, Joli, Jo-Lisa, Jolise, Jolissa, Jolysa, Jolyssa, Lisa

Jolyane
(American) sweetheart
Joliane, Jollyane, Jolyan, Jolyann, Jolyanne

Jolynn
(American) combo of Jo and Lynn
Jo, Jolene, Joline, Jolinn, Jolyn, Jolynda, Jolyne

Jomaralee
(American) combo of Jo and Mara and Lee; country girl

Jonelle
(American) combo of Joan and Elle
Jahnel, Jahnell, Jahnelle, Jo, Johnel, Johnell, Johnelle, Jonel, Jonell, Jonnell, Jynel

Jones
(American) saucy

Joni
(American) short for Joan
Joanie, Jonie, Jony

Jonica
(American) sweet soul

Jonice
(American) casual
Joneece, Joneese, Jonni, Jonise

Jonina
(Hebrew) sweetheart
Jona, Jonika, Joniqua, Jonita, Jonnina

Jonita
(Hebrew) pretty little one
Janita, Jonati, Jonit, Jonite, Jonta, Jontae

Jonquill
(American) flower
Jonn, Jonque, Jonquie, Jonquil, Jonquille

Jontelle
(American) musical
Jahntelle, Jontaya, Jontel, Jontell, Jontelle, Jontia, Jontlyl

Joplin
(Last name as first name) wild girl

Jorah
(Hebrew) fresh as rain
Jora

Jo-Rain
(American) combo of Jo and Rain; zany
Jo Rain, Jorain, JoRaine

Jordan
(Hebrew) excellent descendant
Johrdon, Jordaine, Jordane, Jorden, Jordenne, Jordeyn, Jordi, Jordie, Jordin, Jordon, Jordyn, Jordynne, Joudane, Jourdan

Jordana
(Hebrew) smart; departs; lonely
Giordanna, Jordain, Jordana, Jordane, Jordann, Jordanna, Jordanne, Jordannuh, Jorden, Jordenne, Jordi, Jordin, Jordine, Jordon, Jordona, Jordonna, Jordyn, Jordyne, Jori, Jorie, Jourdana, Jourdann, Jourdanna, Jourdanne

Jordy
(American) quick
Jordee, Jordey, Jordi, Jordie, Jorey

Jorgina
(Spanish) nurturing
Jorge, Jorgine, Jorgy, Jorgie, Jorgi, Georgina, Georgeena

Jorie
(Hebrew) short for Jordan
Joree, Jorey, Jorhee, Jorhie, Jori, Jorre, Jorrey, Jorri, Jory

Joriann
(American) combo of Jori and Ann; desirable
Joriaana, Jorianne, Jorriann, Jorryann, Jorryanna, Jorryanne, Joryann, Joryanna, Joryanne

Jorja
(American) smart
Georgia, Jorge, Jorgia, Jorgie, Jorgy

Jorunn
(American) loved by God

Joscelin
(Latin) happy girl
Josceline, Joscelyn, Joscelyne, Joscelynn, Joscelynne, Joselin, Joseline, Joselyn, Joselyne, Joselynn, Joselynne, Joshlyn

Josee
(American) delights
Joesee, Joesell, Joesette, Joselle, Josette, Josey, Josi, Josiane, Josiann, Josianne, Josielina, Josina, Josy, Jozee, Jozelle, Jozette, Jozie

Josefat
(Spanish) form of Joseph; gracious
Fata, Fina, Josef, Josefa, Josefana, Josefenna, Josefita, Joseva, Josey, Josie

Josefina
(Hebrew) fertile
Jose, Josephina, Josey, Josie

Joselyn
(German) pretty
Josalene, Joselene, Joseline, Josey, Josiline, Josilyn, Joslyn, Josselen, Josseline, Josselyne, Josslyn, Josslynn, Josylynn

Josephine
(French) blessed
Fena, Fifi, Fina, Jo, Joes, Josefina, Josephene, Josie, Jozaphine

Josette
(French) little Josephine

Josetta
(French) she trusts in God

Josey
(Hebrew, American) saucy
Josee, Josi, Josie, Jozie

Joshana
(American) combo of Jo and Shana; striking beauty
Joshanna

Joshlyn
(Latin) saved by God
Joshalin, Joshalyn, Joshalynn, Joshalynne, Joshann, Joshanna, Joshanne, Joshleen, Joshlene, Joshlin, Joshline, Joshlyne, Joshlynn, Joshlynne

Joshi
(Hebrew) God loves

Josiann
(American) combo of Josey and Ann; prettiest one
Josann, Josiane, Josianne, Joseyann

Josie
(American) thrills
Josee, Josey, Josi, Josy, Josye

Josie-Mae
(American) combo of Josie
and Mae
Josee-Mae, Josiemae

Josilin
(Latin) form of Jocelyn; God
saved
*Josielina, Josiline, Josilyn,
Josilyne, Josilynn, Josilynne,
Joslin, Josline, Joslyn,
Joslyne, Joslynn, Joslynne*

Joslyn
(Latin) jocular
*Joclyn, Joslene, Joslinn,
Josslin, Josslyn, Josslynn*

Josnelle
(American) combo of Josne
and Nelle: admired

Jossalin
(Latin) form of Jocelyn; God
saved
*Jossaline, Jossalyn,
Jossalynn, Jossalynne,
Josseline, Jossellen,
Jossellin, Jossellyn, Josselyn,
Josselyne, Josselynn,
Josselynne, Jossie, Josslin,
Jossline, Josslyn, Josslyne,
Josslynn, Josslynne*

Jostin
(American) adorable
Josten, Jostun, Josty, Jostyn

Jour
(French) day

Jovannah
(Latin) regal
*Jeovana, Jeovanna, Jouvan,
Jouvanna, Jovan, Jovana,
Jovanee, Jovani, Jovanie,
Jovann, Jovanna, Jovanne,
Jovannie, Jovena, Jovon,
Jovonna, Jovonne, Jowanna*

Jovi
(Latin) jovial

Jovita
(Latin) glad
*Joveeda, Joveeta, Jovena,
Joveta, Jovetta, Jovi, Jovida,
Jovie, Jovina, Jo-Vita,
Jovitta, Jovy*

Jovonne
(American) combo of Jo and
Yvonne; queenly
*Javonne, Jovaughn, Jovon,
Jovonnie*

Jowannah
(American) happy
Jowanna, Jowanne, Jowonna

Joy
(Latin) joyful
Joi, Joie, Joya, Joye

Joyce
(Latin) joyous
*Joice, Joy, Joycey, Joyci,
Joycie, Joysel*

Joyleen
(American) combo of Joy
and Eileen; happy lady
Joyleena, Joylene, Joyline

Joylyn
(American) combo of Joy
and Lyn; joyful girl
*Joyleen, Joylene, Joylin,
Joyline, Joylyne, Joylynn,
Joylynne*

Joyous
(American) joyful
Joy, Joyus

Joyslyn
(American) form of Jocelyn;
cheery
Joycelyn, Joyslin, Joyslinn

Juanisha
(African American)
delightful
*Juanesha, Juaneshia,
Juannisha*

Juanita
(Spanish) believer in a
gracious God; forgiving
*Juan, Juana, Juaneta,
Juanika, Juanna, Juanne,
Juannie, Juanny, Wanita*

Juba
(Hebrew) ram; strongwilled

Jubelka
(African American) jubilant
Jube, Jubi, Jubie

Jubilee
(Hebrew) jubilant
Jubalie

Jubini
(American) grateful; jubilant
Jubi, Jubine

Jucinda
(American) relishing life
Jucin, Jucindah, Jucinde

Judalon
(Hebrew) merry
Judalonn, Juddalone, Judelon

Jude
(French) confident
Judea, Judee, Judde

Judit
(Hebrew) Jewish
Jude, Judi, Juditt

Judith
(Hebrew) woman worthy of praise
Judana, Jude, Judi, Judie, Judine, Juditha, Judy, Judyth, Judythe

Judy
(Hebrew) short for Judith
Judi, Judie, Joodie, Judye, Jude

Judyann
(American) combo of Judy and Ann; old-fashioned
Judiann, Judianna, Judianne, Judyanna, Judyanne

Juel
(American) dependable
Jewel, Juelle, Juels, Jule, Juile

Jueta
(Scandinavian) from Judith; praises God
Juetta, Juta

Juirl
(American) careful
Ju, Juirll

Juleen
(American) sensual
Jule, Julene, Jules

Jules
(American) brooding
Jewels, Juels

Julia
(Latin) forever young
Jula, Juliann, Julica, Julina, Juline, Julisa, Julissa, Julya, Julyssa

Julian
(Latin) effervescent
Jewelian, Julean, Juliann, Julien, Juliene, Julienn, Julyun

Juliana
(Italian, German, Spanish) youthful
Juleanna, Julianna, Juliannah, Julie-Anna, Jullyana

Julianne
(American) combo of Julie and Anne
Juleann, Jules, Julieann

Julie
(English) young and vocal
Juel, Jule, Julee, Juli, Juliene, Jullie, July, Julye

Juliet
(Italian) loving

Juliette
(French) romantic
Julie, Jules, Juliet, Julietta

Julimarie
(American) combo of Juli and Marie; young; alluring
Joolimarie, Julie Marie, Juliemarie, Julie-Marie

Julissa
(Latin) universally loved
Jula, Julessa, Julisa, Julisha

Julita
(Spanish) adorable; young
Juli, Julitte

Juliza
(Latin) from Julia; pretty

Juluette
(American) adorable; young
Jule, Jules, Julett, Julette, Julie, Julu, Julue, Juluett, Julu-Ette, LuLu

July
(Latin) month; warm

Jumoke
(African) most popular

Jun
(Chinese) honest

June
(Latin) born in June
Juneth, Junie, Junieth, Juney, Juny

Junieth
(Latin) from the month June; heavenly
Juney, Juni, Junie, Juniethe

Junko
(American) from June; warmth

Juno
(Latin) queenly
Juna, June

Juqwanza
(African American) bouncy
Jukwanza, Juqwann, Qwanza

Justice
(Latin) fair-minded
Just, Justise, Justy

Justika
(American) dancing-girl
Justeeka, Justica, Justie, Justy

Justina
(Latin) honest
Jestena, Jestina, Justeena, Justena, Justinna, Justyna

Justine
(Italian, Latin) fair-minded
Jestine, Justa, Juste, Justean, Justeen, Justena, Justene, Justi, Justie, Justina, Justinn, Justinna, Justy, Justyne, Justynn, Justynne, Juzteen

Jutta
(American) ebullient
Juta

Juvelia
(Spanish) young
Juvee, Juvelle, Juvelya, Juvie, Juvilia, Velia, Velya

Juwanne
(African American) lively
Juwan, Juwann, Juwanna, Juwon, Jwanna, Jwanne

Jynx
(American) variant of Jinx; bewitching

Kacey
(Irish) daring
Casey, Casie, K.C., K.Cee, Kace, Kacee, Kaci, Kacy, Kasey, Kasie, Kaycee, Kaycie, Kaysie

Kachina
(Native American) sacred dancer; doll-like
Cachina, Kachena, Kachine

Kacia
(Greek) variant of Acacia; has thorns; moody
Kaycia, Kaysia

Kacondra
(African American) bold
Condra, Connie, Conny, Kacon, Kacond, Kaecondra, Kakondra, Kaycondra

Kaden
(American) charismatic
Caden, Kadenn

Kadenza
(Latin) cadence; dances
Cadenza, Kadena, Kadence

Kadie
(American) virtuous
Kadee

Kady
(English) sassy
Cady, K.D., Kadee, Kadie, Kaydie, Kaydy

Kaela
(Arabic) sweet
Kaelah, Kayla, Kaylah, Keyla, Keylah

Kaelin
(Irish) pure; impetuous
Kaelan, Kaelen, Kaelinn, Kaelyn, Kaelynn, Kaelynne, Kaylin

Kaelynn
(American) combo of Kae and Lynn; beloved
Kaelin, Kailyn, Kay-Lynn

Kai
(Hawaiian, African) attractive
Kaia

Kailah
(Greek) virtuous
Kail, Kala, Kalae, Kalah

Kailey
(American) spunky
Kalee, Kaili, Kailie, Kaylee, Kaylei

Kaitlin
(Irish) pure-hearted
Caitlin, Caitlyn, Kaitlan, Kaitland, Kaitlinn, Kaitlyn, Kaitlynn, Kalyn, Katelyn, Katelynn, Katelynne, Kathlin, Kathlinne, Kathlyn

Kala
(Hindi) black; royal

Kalani
(Hawaiian) leader
Kalauni, Kaloni, Kaylanie

Kalea
(Arabic) sweet
Kahlea, Kahleah, Kailea, Kaileah, Kallea, Kalleah, Kaylea, Kayleah, Khalea, Khaleah

Kalei
(American) sweetheart
Kahlei, Kailei, Kallei, Kaylei, Khalei

Kaleigh
(Sanskrit) energetic; dark
Kalea

Kalena
(Hawaiian) chaste
Kaleena

Kalet
(French) beautiful energy
Kalay, Kalaye

Kaley
(Sanskrit) energetic
Kalee, Kaleigh, Kalleigh

Kali
(Greek) beauty
Kala, Kalli

Kalidas
(Greek) most beautiful
Kaleedus, Kali

Kalila
(Arabic) sweet; lovable
Cailey, Cailie, Caylie, Kailey, Kaililah, Kaleah, Kalela, Kalie, Kalilah, Kaly, Kay, Kaykay, Kaylee, Kayllie, Kyle, Kylila, Kylilah

Kalina
(Hawaiian) unblemished
Kalinna, Kalynna

Kalinda
(Hindi) mythical mountains; goal-oriented
Kaleenda, Kalindi, Kalynda, Kalyndi

Kalisa
(American) combo of Kay and Lisa; pretty and loving
Caylisa, Kaleesa, Kalisha, Kalyssa, Kaylisa, Kaykay

Kallan
(American) loving
Kall, Kallen, Kallun

Kallie
(Greek) beautiful
Callie, Kalley, Kali, Kalie, Kally

Kalliope
(Greek) beautiful voice
Calli, Calliope, Kalli, Kallyope

Kallista
(Greek) pretty; bright-eyed
Cala, Calesta, Calista, Callie, Callista, Cally, Kala, Kalesta, Kalista, Kalli, Kallie, Kally, Kallysta, Kalysta

Kalyn
(Arabic) loved
Calynn, Calynne, Kaelyn, Kaelynn, Kalen, Kalin, Kalinn, Kallyn

Kama
(Sanskrit) beloved

Kamala
(Arabic) perfection
Kamalah

Kamaria
(African) moonlike
Kamara, Kamaarie

Kambria
(Latin) girl from Wales
Kambra, Kambrie, Kambriea, Kambry

Kamea
(Hawaiian) adored
Kameo

Kameko
(Japanese) turtle girl; hides

Kameron
(American) variant of Cameron; crooked nose; kind
Kamren, Kamrin, Kamron

Kami
(Japanese) perfect aura
Cami

Kamilah
(Hindi) also Kaamilee; desires
Kamila, Kamilla, Kamillah

Kamilia
(Polish) pure

Kama
(Sanskrit) beloved; Hindu god of love
Kam, Kamie

Kamala
(American) interesting
Camala, Kam, Kamali, Kamilla, Kammy

Kamea
(Hawaiian) precious darling
Cammi, Kam, Kammie

Kamela
(Italian) form of Camilla; wonderful
Kam, Kamila, Kammy

Kameron
(American) spiritual
Cam, Cameron, Cami, Cammie, Kamreen, Kamrin

Kami
(Italian) spiritual little one
Cami, Cammie, Cammy, Kammie, Kammy

Kamilah
(North African) perfect

Kamilia
(Polish) perfect character
Kam, Kamila, Kammy, Milla

Kamyra
(American) light
Kamera

Kanara
(Hebrew) tiny bird; lithe
Kanarit, Kanarra

Kanda
(Native American) magical

Kandace
(Greek) charming; glowing
Candace, Candie, Candy, Dacie, Kandace, Kandi, Kandice, Kandiss, Kandy

Kandi
(American) short for Kandace
Candi, Kandie, Kandy

Kandra
(American) light
Candra

Kaneesha
(American) dark-skinned
Caneesha, Kaneesh, Kaneice, Kaneisha, Kanesha, Kaneshia, Kaney, Kanish, Nesha

Kanesha
(African American) spontaneous
Kaneesha, Kaneeshia, Kaneisha, Kanisha, Kannesha

Kanga
(Australian) short for kangaroo; jumpy

Kanisha
(American) pretty
Kaneesha, Kanicia, Kenisha, Kinicia, Kinisha, Koneesha

Kannitha
(Vietnamese) angelic

Kansas
(Place name) U.S. state
Kanny

Kanya
(Hindi) virginal
Kania

Kaprece
(American) capricious
Caprice, Kapp, Kappy, Kapreece, Kapri, Kaprise, Kapryce, Karpreese

Kapuki
(African) first girl in the family

Kara
(Danish, Greek) dearest
Cara, Carina, Carita, Kar, Karah, Kari, Karie, Karina, Karine, Karita, Karrah, Karrie, Kera

Karalee
(Invented) combo of Kara and Lee

Karalenae
(American) combo of Kara and Lenae
Kara-Lenae, Karalenay

Karalynn
(American) combo of Kara and Lynn; smiling sweetness

Karbie
(American) energetic
Karbi, Karby

Karelle
(French) joyful singer
Carel, Carelle, Karel

Karen
(Greek, Irish) pure-hearted
Caren, Carin, Caron, Caronn, Carren, Carrin, Carron, Carryn, Caryn, Carynn, Carynne, Kare, Kareen, Karenna, Kari, Karin, Karina, Karna, Karon, Karron, Karryn, Karyn, Keren, Kerran, Kerrin, Kerron, Kerrynn, Keryn, Kerynne, Taran, Taren, Taryn

Karenz
(English) from Kerenza; sweet girl
Karence, Karens, Karense

Kari
(Scandinavian) pure
Cari, Karri, Karrie, Karry

Karian
(American) daring
Kerian

Karianne
(American) combo of Kari and Anne
Kariane, Kariann, Kari-Ann, Karianna, Kerianne

Karida
(Arabic) pure
Kareeda, Karita

Karilynne
(American) combo of Kari and Lynne
Cariliynn, Kariline, Karylynn

Karima
(Arabic) giving
Kareema, Kareemah, Kareima, Kareimah, Karimah

Karin
(Scandinavian) kind-hearted
Karen, Karine, Karinne

Karina
(Russian) best of heart; (Latin) even
Kare, Karinda, Karine, Karinna, Karrie, Karrina, Karyna

Karine
(Russian) pure
Kaarrine, Karryne, Karyne

Karise
(Greek) graceful woman
Karis, Karisse, Karyce

Karissa
(Greek) longsuffering
Carissa, Karessa, Karisa

Karizma
(African) hopeful
Karisma

Karla
(German) bright-eyed; feminine form of Carl/Karl
Carla, Karlah, Karlie, Karlla, Karrla

Karla-Faye
(American) combo of Karla and Faye

Karleen
(American) combo of Karla and Arleen; witty
Karlene, Karline, Karly

Karlotta
(German) from Charlotte; pretty
Karlota, Karlotte, Lotta, Lottee, Lottey, Lottie

Karly
(Latin, American) strong-voiced
Carly, Karlee, Karlie, Karlye

Karma
(Hindi) destined for good things
Karm, Karmie, Karmy

Karmel
(Hebrew) garden
Carmel, Karmela, Karmelle

Karmen
(Hebrew) loving songs
Carmen, Karmin, Karmine

Karnesha
(American) spicy
Carnesha, Karnisha, Karny

Karolanne
(American) combo of Karol and Anne
Karol, Karolan, Karolane, Karolann, Karolen

Karolina
(Polish) form of Charles
Karaline, Karalyn, Karalynna, Karalynne, Karla, Karleen, Karlen, Karlena, Karlene, Karli, Karlie, Karlina, Karlinka, Karo, Karolina, Karolline, Karolinka, Karolyn, Karolyna, Karolyne, Karolynn, Karolynne, Leena, Lina, Lyna

Karoline
(German) form of Karl
Kare, Karola, Karolah, Karolina, Lina

Karolyn
(American) friendly
Carolyn, Kara, Karal, Karalyn, Karilynne, Karolynn

Karri
(American) from Karen; pure
Kari, Karie, Karrie, Karry

Karrington
(Last name as first name) admired
Carrington, Kare, Karring

Karyn
(American) sweet
Caren, Karen

Kasey
(American) spirited
Casey, Kacey, Kasie, Kaysie

Kasha
(Greek) variant of Katherine; pure

Kashawna
(American) combo of Kasha and Shawna; debater
Kashana, Kashawn, Kashonda, Kashonna

Kashmir
(Sanskrit) place name
Cahmere, Cashmir, Kash, Kashmere

Kashonda
(African American) dramatic
Kashanda, Kashawnda Koshonda

Kashondra
(African American) bright
Kachanne, Kachaundra, Kachee, Kashandra, Kashawndra, Kashee, Kashon, Kashondrah, Kashondre, Kashun

Kasi
(American) form of Cassie;
seer
Kass, Kassi, Kassie

Kasia
(Polish) pet form of
Katarzyna

Kasmira
(Slavic) peacemaker

Kassandra
(Greek) capricious
Cassandra, Kass, Kasandra, Kassandrah, Kassie

Kassidy
(Irish) clever
Cassidy, Cassir, Kasadee, Kass, Kassie, Kassy, Kassydi

Kassie
(American) clever
Kassee, Kassi, Kassy

Kat
(American) outrageous
Cat

Kataniya
(Hebrew) little girl

Katarina
(Greek) pure
Katareena, Katarena, Katarinna, Kataryna, Katerina, Katryna

Katarzyna
(Origin unknown) creative
Katarzina

Katchen
(Greek) virtuous
Kat, Katshen

Katchi
(American) sassy
Catshy, Cotchy, Kat, Kata, Katchie, Kati, Katshi, Katshie, Katshy, Katty, Kotchee, Kotchi, Kotchie

Kate
(Greek, Irish) pure-hearted
Cait, Caitie, Cate, Catee, Catey, Catie, Kait, Kaite, Kaitlin, Katee, Katey, Kathe, Kati, Katie, Katy, Kay-Kay

Katelyn
(Irish) pure-hearted
Caitlin, Kaitlin, Kaitlynne, Kat, Katelin, Katelynn, Kate-Lynn, Katline, Katy

Katera
(Origin unknown) celebrant
Katara, Katura

Katharine
(Greek) powerful; pure
Kat, Katharin, Katherin, Katwin, Katherine, Kathy, Kathyrn, Kaykay

Kathlaya
(American) fashionable

Kathleen
(Irish) brilliant; unflawed
Cathaleen, Cathaline, Cathleen, Kathaleen, Kathaleya, Kathaleyna, Kathaline, Kathelina, Katheline, Kathlene, Kathlin, Kathline, Kathlynn, Kathlyn, Kathie, Kathy

Kathryn
(English) powerful and pure
Kathreena, Kathren, Kathrene, Kathrin, Kathrine, Kathryne

Kathy
(English) pure;
(Irish) spunky
Cathie, Cathy, Kath, Kathe, Kathee, Kathey, Kathi, Kathie

Katia
(French) stylish
Kateeya, Kati, Katya

Katie
(English) lively
Kat, Katy, Kay, Kaykay, Kate, Kaytie

Katina
(American) form of Katrina;
virtuous
Kat, Kateen, Kateena

Katlynn
(Greek) pure
Kat, Katlinn, Katlyn

Katrice
(American) graceful
Katreese, Katrese, Katrie, Katrisse, Katry

Katrina
(German) melodious
Catreena, Catreina, Catrina, Kaitrina, Katreena, Katreina, Katryna, Kay, Ketreina, Ketrina, Ketryna

Katrine
(German, Polish) pure
Catrene, Kati, Katrene, Katrinna, Kati

Katy
(English) lively
Cady, Katie, Kattee, Kattie, Kaytee

Kaulana
(Hawaiian) well-known girl
Kaula, Kauna, Kahuna

Kavinli
(American) form of Kevin; eager
Cavin, Kaven, Kavin, Kavinlee, Kavinley, Kavinly

Kavita
(Hindi) poem
Kaveta, Kavitah

Kay
(Greek, Latin) fun-loving
Cay, Caye, Kaye, Kaykay

Kaya
(Native American) intelligent
Kaja, Kayia

Kaycie
(American) merrymaker
CayCee, K.C., Kaycee, Kayci, Kaysie

Kayla
(Hebrew, Arabic) sweet
Cala, Cayla, Caylie, Kala, Kaela, Kaila, Kaylah, Kaylyn, Keyla

Kaylee
(American) open
Cayley, Kaelie, Kaylea, Kaylie, Kayleigh

Kayleen
(Hebrew) sweet; (American) combo of Kay and Eileen
Kaileen, Kalene, Kay, Kaylean, Kayleene, Kaykay

Kayley
(Irish) combo of Kay and Lee; effervescent
Caleigh, Cayleigh, Cayley, Kaeleigh, Kailee, Kaileigh, Kailey, Kaili, Kaleigh, Kaley, Kaylea, Kaylee, Kaylie, Kaylleigh, Kaylley

Kaylin
(American) combo of Kay and Lynn
Kailyn, Kaylan, Kaylanne, Kaylen, Kaylinn, Kaylyn, Kaylynn, Kaylynne

Kaylinda
(American) combo of Kae and Linda
Kaelinda, Kaelynda, Kay-Linda

Kaylon
(American) form of Caylin; outgoing
Kay, Kaylen, Kaylun

Kaylon
(Hebrew) crowned
Kaylan, Kayln, Kaylond, Kaylon, Kalonn

Keane
(American) keen
Kanee, Keanie, Keany, Keen

Keanna
(American) curious
Keana, Keannah

Keara
(Irish) darkness
Kearia, Kearra, Keera, Keerra, Keira, Keirra, Kera, Kiara, Kiarra, Kiera, Kierra

Kearney
(Irish) winning
Kearne, Kearni, KeKe, Kerney

Keekee
(American) dancing
Keakea, Kee-Kee

Keeley
(Irish) noisy
Kealey, Kealy, Keeley, Keeli, Keelia, Keelie, Keely, Keighley, Keighly, Keili, Keilie, Keylee, Keyley, Keylie, Keylley, Keyllie

Keena
(Irish) courageous
Keenya, Kina

Keenan
(Irish) small
Keanan, Keen, Keeny

Kefira
(Hebrew) lioness
Kefeera, Kefeira, Kefirah, Kefirra

Kehohtee
(Invented) alternate spelling for Quixote

Kei
(Japanese) respectful

Keidra
(American) form of Kendra; aware
Kedra, Keydra

Keiki
(Hawaiian) child

Keiko
(Hawaiian) child of joy
Kei

Keila
(Hebrew) crowned
Keilah

Keilani
(Hawaiian) graceful leader
Kei, Lani, Lanie

Keira
(Irish) dark-skinned
Keera, Kera

Keisha
(American) dark-eyed
Keasha, Keesha, Keeshah, Keicia, Keishah, Keshia, Keysha, Kicia

Keishla
(American) dark

Keita
(Scottish) lives in the forest
Keiti

Keitha
(Scottish) from the forest
Keithana

Kelby
(English) lives in a farmhouse
Kelbea, Kelbeigh, Kelbey, Kellbie

Kelda
(Scandinavian) spring of youth
Kellda

Kelila
(Hebrew) regal woman
Kayla, Kayle, Kaylee, Kelula, Kelulah, Kelulla, Kelylah, Kyla, Kyle

Keller
(Irish) daring
Kellers

Kelley
(Irish) brave
Keli, Kellie, Kelly, Kellye

Kellyn
(Irish) brave heart
Kelleen, Kellen, Kellene, Kellina, Kelline, Kellynn, Kellynne

Kelsey
(Scottish) opinionated
Kelcey, Kelcie, Kelcy, Kellsey, Kellsie, Kelsea, Kelsee, Kelseigh, Kelsi, Kelsie, Kelsy

Kember
(American) zany
Kem, Kemmie, Kimber

Kemella
(American) self-assured
Kemele, Kemellah, Kemelle

Kempley
(English) from a meadowland; rascal
Kemplea, Kempleigh, Kemplie, Kemply

Kenda
(English) aware
Kendi, Kendie, Kendy, Kennda, Kenndi, Kenndie, Kenndy

Kendall
(English) quiet
Kendahl, Kendal, Kendell, Kendelle, Kendie, Kendylle

Kendra
(American) ingenious
Ken, Kendrah, Kenna, Kennie, Kindra, Kinna, Kyndra

Keneisha
(American) combo of Ken and Aisha
Kaneesha, Kenesha, Kenisha, Kennie, Kaykay

Kenia
(African) giving (from the place name Kenya)
Ken, Keneah

Kenna
(English) brilliant
Kenina, Kennah, Kennina, Kennette, Kynna

Kennae
(Irish) form of Ken; attractive
Kenae, Kenah

Kennedy
(Irish) formidable
Kennedie, Kenny

Kennice
(English) beauty
Kanice, Keneese, Kenese, Kennise

Kensington
(English) brash
Kensingtyn

Kentucky
(Place name) U.S. state
Kentuckie

Kenya
(Place name) country in
Africa
Kenia, Kennya

Kenyatta
(African) from Kenya

Kenzie
(Scottish) pretty
Kensey, Kinsey

Keoshawn
(African American) clever
Keosh, Keoshaun

Kerdonna
(African American)
loquacious
*Donna, Kerdy, Kirdonna,
Kyrdonna*

Kerensa
(English) lovable
Karensa, Karenza, Kerenza

Kerra
(American) bright
Cara, Carrah, Kara, Kerrah

Kerry
(Irish) dark-haired
*Carrie, Kari, Kera, Keree,
Keri, Kerrey, Kerri, Kerria,
Kerridana, Kerrie*

Kerstin
(Scandinavian) a Christian
Kersten, Kerston, Kerstyn

Kerthia
(American) giving
*Kerth, Kerthea, Kerthi,
Kerthy*

Kesha
(American) laughing
Kecia, Kesa, Keshah

Keshia
(American) bouncy
*Kecia, Keishia, Keschia,
Kesia, Kesiah, Kessiah*

Keshon
(African American) happy
*Keshann, Keshaun,
Keshonn, Keshun, Keshawn*

Keshondra
(African American) joy-filled
*Keshaundra, Keshondrah,
Keshundra, Keshundrea,
Keshundria, Keshy*

Keshonna
(African American) happy
*Keshanna, Keshauna,
Keshaunna, Keshawna,
Keshona, Keshonna*

Kesi
(African) hard-times baby

Kessie
(African) fat baby cheeks
*Kess, Kessa, Kesse, Kessey,
Kessi, Kessia, Kessiah*

Keturah
(African) long-suffering
Katura, Ketura

Kevine
(Irish) lively
*Kevina, Kevinne, Kevyn,
Kevynn, Kevynne*

Kevyn
(Irish) variant of Kevin;
lovely face
*Keva, Kevan, Kevina,
Kevone, Kevonna, Kevynn*

Keydy
(American) knowing
Keydee, Keydi, Keydie

Keyonna
(African American) energetic

Keyshawn
(American) lively
*Keyshan, Keyshann,
Keyshaun, Keyshaunna,
Keyshon, Keyshona,
Keshonna, Keykey, Kiki*

Kezia
(Hebrew) from Cassis;
cinnamon; spicy
*Kazia, Kessie, Kessy, Ketzia,
Ketziah, Keziah, Kezzie,
Kissie, Kizzie, Kizzy*

Khadijah
(Arabic) sweetheart
*Kadija, Kadiya, Khadiya,
Khadyja*

Khai
(American) unusual
Ki, Kie

Khaki
(American) personality-plus
*Kakee, Kaki, Kakie, Khakee,
Khakie*

Khali
(Origin unknown) lively
Khalee, Khalie, Koli, Kollie

Khalida
(Hindi) eternal
Khali, Khalia, Khalita

Khiana
(American) different
*Kheana, Khianah, Khianna,
Ki, Kianah, Kianna, Kiannah*

Ki
(Korean) born again

Kia
(American) short for Kiana
Keeah, Kiah

Kiana
(American) graceful
*Kia, Kiah, Kianna, Kiannah,
Quiana, Quianna*

Kiara
(Irish) dark-skinned
*Chiara, Chiarra, Keearah,
Keearra, Kiarra*

Kibibi
(African) small girl

Kidre
(American) loyal
Kidrea, Kidrey, Kidri

Kiele
(Hawaiian) aromatic flower;
gardenia
*Kiela, Kieley, Kieli, Kielli,
Kielly*

Kienalle
(American) light
Kieana, Kienall, Kieny

Kienna
(Origin unknown) brash
Kiennah, Kienne

Kiera
(Irish) dark-skinned
Keara, Keera, Kierra

Kiersten
(Greek) blessed
*Kerston, Kierstin, Kierstn,
Kierstynn, Kirst, Kirsten,
Kirstie, Kirstin, Kirsty*

Kiki
(Spanish, American)
vivacious
Keiki, Ki, Kiekie, Kikee

Kiko
(Japanese) lively
Kiki, Kikoh

Kiku
(Japanese) flower (mum)
Kiko

Kiley
(Irish) pretty
*Kilea, Kilee, Kili, Kylee,
Kyley, Kylie*

Kim
(Vietnamese) sharp
Kimey, Kimmi, Kimmy, Kym

Kimana
(American) from Kim;
meadow girl; outdoors-loving

Kimberlin
(American) combo of
Kimberly and Lin
*Kimberlinn, Kimberlyn,
Kimberlynn*

Kimberly
(English) leader
*Kim, Kimber-Lea, Kimberlee,
Kimberleigh, Kimberley,
Kimberli, Kimberlie, Kimmy,
Kymberly, Kimmie*

Kimbrell
(African American) smiling
*Kim, Kimbree, Kimbrel,
Kimbrele, Kimby, Kimmy*

Kimeo
(American) form of Kim;
happy
Kim, Kime, Kimi

Kimetha
(American) form of Kim;
happy
Kimeth

Kimi
(Japanese) spiritual

Kimone
(Origin unknown) darling
Kimonne, Kymone

Kina
(Hawaiian) girl from China

Kineisha
(American) form of
Keneisha
*Keneesha, Keneisha,
Kineasha, Kinesha,
Kineshia, Kiness, Kinisha,
Kinnisha, Kinny*

Kineta
(Greek) energetic
Kinetta

Kinsey
(English) child
*Kensey, Kinnsee, Kinnsey,
Kinnsie, Kinsee, Kinsey,
Kinsie, Kinzee*

Kinsley
*Kingslea, Kingslee,
Kingslie, Kinslea, Kinslee,
Kinslie, Kinsly, Kinzlea,
Kinzlee, Kinzley, Kinzly*

Kintra
(American) joyous
Kentra, Kint, Kintrey

Kinza
(American) relative

Kioko
(Japanese) happy baby
Kiyo, Kiyoko

Kiona
(Native American) girl from the hill

Kipling
(Last name as first name) energetic
Kiplin

Kira
(Russian) sunny; light-hearted
Keera, Kera, Kiera, Kierra, Kiria, Kiriah, Kirya, Kirra

Kiran
(Irish) pretty
Kiara, Kiaran, Kira, Kiri

Kirby
(Anglo-Saxon) right
Kirbee, Kirbey, Kirbie

Kirima
(Eskimo) hill child; high aspirations

Kirsta
(Scandinavian) Christian

Kirsten
(Scandinavian, Greek) spiritual
Karsten, Keerstin, Keirstin, Kersten, Kerstin, Kiersten, Kierstin, Kiersynn, Kirsteen, Kirstene, Kirsti, Kirstie, Kirstin, Kirston, Kirsty, Kirstynn, Kristen, Kristin, Kristyn, Krystene, Krystin

Kirstie
(Scandinavian) irrepressable
Kerstie, Kirstee, Kirsty

Kisha
(Russian) ingenious
Keshah

Kishi
(Japanese) eternal

Kismet
(Hindi) destiny; fate
Kismat, Kismete, Kismett

Kissa
(African) a baby born after twins

Kit
(American) strong
Kitt

Kita
(Japanese) northerner

Kithos
(Greek) worthy

Kitty
(Greek, American) flirty
Kit, Kittee, Kittey, Kitti, Kittie

Kiva
(Origin unknown) bright
Keva

Kiwa
(Origin unknown) lively
Kiewah, Kiwah

Kiya
(Australian) from the name Kylie; always returning; pretty girl
Kya

Kizzie
(African) energetic
Kissee, Kissie, Kiz, Kizzee, Kizzi, Kizzie, Kizzy

Klara
(Hungarian) bright
Klari, Klarice, Klarika, Klarissa, Klarisza, Klaryssa

Klarissa
(German) bright-minded
Clarissa, Klarisa, Klarise

Klarybel
(Polish) beauty
Klaribel, Klaribelle

Klaudia
(Polish) lame

Klea
(American) bold
Clea, Kleah, Kleea, Kleeah

Klementina
(Polish) forgiving
Clemence, Clementine, Klementine, Klementyna

Kleta
(Greek) form of Cleopatra; noble-born; temptress
Cleta

Klotild
(Hungarian) famous
Klothild, Klothilda, Klothilde, Klotilda, Klotilde

Kobi
(American) California girl
Cobi, Kobe

Koffi
(African) Friday-born
Kaffe, Kaffi, Koffe, Koffie

Kogan
(Last name as first name) self-assured
Kogann, Kogen, Kogey, Kogi

Koko
(Japanese) the stork comes

Kona
(Hawaiian) feminine
Koni, Konia

Konstance
(Latin) loyal
Constance, Kon, Konnie, Konstanze, Stanze

Kora
(Greek) practical
Cora, Koko, Korey, Kori

Kori
(Greek) little girl; popular
Cori, Corrie, Koree, Korey, Kory

Korina
(Greek) strong-willed; (German) small girl
Corinna, Koreena, Korena, Korinna, Koryna

Kornelia
(Latin) straight-laced
Cornelia, Kornelya, Korney, Korni, Kornie

Kortney
(American, French) dignified
Courtney, Kortnee, Kortni, Kourtney, Kourtnie

Koshatta
(Native American) form of Coushatta; diligent
Coushatta, Kosha, Koshat, Koshatte, Koshee, Koshi, Koshie, Koushatta

Kosta
(Latin) from Constance; steady
Kostia, Kostusha, Kostya

Koto
(Japanese) harp; musical

Krenie
(American) capable
Kren, Kreni, Krenn, Krennie, Kreny

Kris
(American) short for Kristina
Kaykay, Krissie, Krissy

Krishen
(American) talkative
Crishen, Kris, Krish, Krishon

Krissy
(American) friendly
Kris, Krisie, Krissey, Krissi

Krista
(German) short for Christina
Khrista, Krysta

Kristalee
(American) combo of Krista and Lee
Kristalea, Krista-Lee, Kristaleigh

Kristen
(Greek) Christ's follower; (German) bright-eyed
Christen, Cristen, Kristin, Kristyn

Kristian
(Greek) Christian woman
Kristiana, Kristianne, Kristyanna

Kristie
(American) saucy
Christi, Christy, Kristi

Kristin
(Scandinavian) high-energy
Kristen, Kristyne

Kristina
(Greek) anointed; (Scandinavian) Christ's follower
Christina, Krista, Kristie, Krysteena, Tina

Kristine
(Swedish) Christ's follower
Christine, Kristee, Kristene, Kristi, Kristy

Kristy
(American) short for Kristine
Kristi, Kristie

Krysta
(Polish) clear
Chrsta, Krista

Krystal
(American) clear and brilliant
Cristalle, Cristel, Crysta, Crystal, Crystalle, Khristalle, Khristel, Khrystle, Khrystalle, Kristel, Kristle, Krys, Krystalle, Krystalline, Krystelle, Krystie, Krystle, Krystylle

Krystalee
(American) combo of Krystal and Lee; seeks clarity
Kristalea, Kristaleah, Kristalee, Krystalea, Krystaleah, Krystlea, Krystleah, Krystlee, Krystlea, Krystleleah, Krystlelee

Krystalynn
(American) combo of Krystal and Lynn; clear-eyed
Krystaleen, Krystalina, Kristaline, Kristalyn, Kristalynn, Kristilyn, Kristilynn, Kristlyn, Krystalin, Krystalyn

Krystyna
(Polish) Christian

Kumiko
(Japanese) long hair in braids
Kumi

Kurrsten
(Scandinavian, Greek) form of Kirsten; spiritual
Kurrst, Kurst, Kurstie

Kyla
(Irish) pretty
Kiela, Kila, Ky

Kyle
(Irish) pretty
Kyall, Kyel, Kylee, Kylie, Kyll

Kylee
(Australian, Irish) pretty
Kielie, Kiely, Kiley, Kye, Kyky, Kyleigh, Kylie

Kylene
(American) cute
Kyline

Kylie
(Irish) graceful
Keyely, Kilea, Kiley, Kylee, Kyley

Kylynne
(American) fashionable
Kilenne, Kilynn, Kyly

Kym
(American) favorite
Kim, Kymm, Kymmi, Kymmie, Kymy

Kynthia
(Greek) goddess of the moon
Cinthia, Cynthia

Kyoko
(Japanese) sees herself in a mirror

Kyra
(Greek) feminine
Kaira, Keera, Keira, Kira, Kyrah, Kyreena, Kyrene, Kyrha, Kyria, Kyrie, Kyrina, Kyrra, Kyry

Kyria
(Greek) form of Kyra; ladylike
Kyrea, Kyree, Kyrie, Kyry

Labe
(American) slow-moving
Labie

Lace
(American) delicate
Lacee, Lacey, Laci, Lacie, Lase

Lacey
(Greek) cheery
Lacee, Laci, Lacie, Lacy

Lachelle
(African American) sweetheart
Lachel, Lachell, Laschell, Lashelle

Lachesis
(Mythological) one of the Greek Fates; the measurer

Lachina
(African American) fragile

Lacole
(American) sly
Lucole

Lacreta
(Spanish) form of Lacretia; efficient
Lacrete, LaLa

Lacretia
(Latin) efficient
Lacracia, Lacrecia, Lacrisha, Lacy

LaDaune
(African American) the dawn
Ladaune, LaDawn

Ladda
(American) open
Lada

Ladonna
(American) combo of La and Donna; beautiful
Ladona, LaDonna

Lady
(American) feminine
Ladee, Ladie

Ladrenda
(African American) cagy
Ladee, Ladey, Ladren, Ladrende, Lady

Laela
(Hebrew) variation of Leila; dark

Laetitia
(Latin) joy
Leticia, Lateaciah, Lateacya, Latycia, Letisia, Letyziah

Lafonde
(American) combo of La and Fonde; fond

Laguna
(Place name) Laguna Beach, California; water-loving
Lagunah

Laila
(Scandinavian) dark beauty
Laili, Laleh, Layla, Laylah, Leila

Lainil
(American) soft-hearted
Lainie, Lanel, Lanelle

Lajean
(French) soothing; steadfast
L'Jean, LaJean, Lajeanne

LaJuana
(American) combo of La and Juana
Lajuana, Lala, Lawanna

Lake
(Astrology) graceful dancer

Lakeisha
(African American) the favorite; combo of La and Keisha

Lakela
(Hawaiian) feminine
Lakla

Lakesha
(African American) favored
Keishia, Lakaisha, Lakeesha, Lakeishah, Lakezia, Lakisha

Lakya
(Hindi) born on Thursday

Lala
(Slavic) pretty flower girl; tulip

Lalage
(Greek) talkative
Lal, Lallie, Lally

Lalaney
(American) form of Hawaiian name Leilani; celestial
Lala, Lalanee, Lalani

Laleema
(Spanish) devoted
Lalema, Lalima

Lalita
(Sanskrit) charmer
Lai, Lala, Lali, Lalitah, Lalite, Lalitte

Lally
(English) babbling
Lalli

Lalya
(Latin) eloquent
Lalia, Lall, Lalyah

Lamarian
(American) conflicted
Lamare, Lamarean

Lamia
(Egyptian) calm
Lami

Lamika
(African American) variant of Tamika; calm

L'Amour
(French) love
Amor, Amour, Lamore, Lamour, Lamoura

Lana
(Latin) pretty; peacemaker
Lan, Lanna, Lanny

Lanai
(Hawaiian) heavenly
Lenai

Land
(American) word as name; confident
Landd

Landa
(American) blonde beauty
Landah

Landry
(American) leader
Landa, Landree

Landy
(American) confident
Land, Landee, Landey, Landi

Lane
(Last name as first name) precocious
Laine, Lainey, Laney, Lanie, Layne, Laynie

Lanee
(Asian) graceful

LaNiece
(Invented) form of Lenice

Lanette
(American) healthy
La-Net, LaNett, LaNette

Langley
(American) special
Langlee, Langli, Langlie, Langly

Lani
(Hawaiian) short for Leilani
Lannie

Lansing
(Place name) hopeful
Lanseng

Lantana
(Botanical) flowering
Lantanna

Laquanna
(African American) outspoken
Kwanna, LaQuanna, LaQwana, Quanna

Laquisha
(American) combo of La and Quisha; a happy life

Laquita
(American) combo of La and Queta; fifth
Laqueta, Laquetta

Lara
(Russian) lovely

Laraine
(Latin) pretty
Lareine, Larene, Loraine

Larby
(American) form of Darby; pretty
Larbee, Larbey, Larbi, Larbie

Larch
(American) full of life

Lareina
(Greek) seagull; flies over water
Larayna, Larayne, Lareine, Larena, Larrayna, Larreina

Larhonda
(African American) combo of La and Rhonda; flashy
LaRhonda, Laronda

Larinda
(American) smart
Lare, Larin, Larine, Lorinda

Larissa
(Latin) giving cheer
Laressa, Larisse, Laryssa

Lark
(American) pretty
Larke

Larkin
(American) pretty
Larken, Larkun

Larkspur
(Botanical) tall and stately

Larrie
(American) tomboyish
Larry

LaRue
(American) combo of La and Rue
Laroo, Larue

Larsen
(Scandinavian) laurel-crowned
Larson, Larssen, Larsson

Lasha
(Spanish) forlorn
Lash, Lass

Lashanda
(American) brassy
Lala, Lasha, LaShanda, LaShounda

Lashauna
(American) happy
Lashona, Leshauna, Lashawna

LaShea
(American) sparkling
Lashay, La-Shea, Lashea

Lashonda
(American) combo of La and Shonda; the grace of God

Lashoun
(African American) content
Lashaun, Lashawn, Lashown

Lassie
(American) lass
Lass

Lata
(Hindi) lovely vine; entwines

Latanya
(African American) combo of La and Tanya; the queen

Latasha
(American) combo of La and Tasha; born on Christmas Day
Latacha, LaTasha, Latayshah, Latisha

LaTeasa
(Spanish) tease
Latea, Lateasa, LaTease, LaTeese

Lateefah
(Arabic, African, Hebrew) kind queen
Lateefa, Latifa, Latifah, Lotifah, Tifa, Tifah

Latesha
(Latin, American) joyful
Lateesha, Lateisha, Lateshah, Laticia, Latisha

Latifah
(Muslim) gentle
Lateefa, Latifa, Latiffe, Latifuh

Lathenia
(American) verbose
Lathene, Lathey

Latisehsha
(African American) happy; talkative
Lati, Latise, Latiseh, Latisha

Latona
(Latin) goddess

Latonia
(African American) rich
Latone, Latonea

Latosha
(African American) happy

Latoya
(American) combo of La and Toya
LaToya, Lata, Toy, Toya, Toyah

Latreece
(American) go-getter
Latreese, Latrice, Letrice, Lettie, Letty

Latrelle
(American) laughing
Lettie, Letrel, Letrelle, Litrelle

Latrice
(Latin) noble
Latreece, Latreese

Latricia
(American) happy
Latrecia, Latreesha, Latrisha, Latrishah

Latrisha
(African American) prissy
Latrishe

Lauda
(Latin) praised

Laudomia
(Italian) praiseworthy

Laufeia
(Scandinavian) thriving

Laura
(Latin) laurel-crowned; joyous
Lara, Lora

Laurain
(English) graceful

Laurann
(American) combo of Laura and Ann
Lauran, Laurana, Lauranna, Lauranne

Lauralee
(American) combo of Laura and Lee
Laura-Lee, Loralea, Loralee, Lorilee

Laureen
(American) old-fashioned
Laurie, Laurine, Loreen

Laurel
(American) flourishing; (Latin) graceful
Laurell, Lorel, Lorell, Laural, Laurell, Laurella, Laurelle, Lorel, Lorella, Lourelle

Lauren
(English, American) flowing
Laren, Laurene, Lauryn, Laryn, Loren

Laurencia
(Latin) crowned in laurels
Laurenciah, Laurens, Laurentana

Laurent
(French) graceful
Lorent, Laurente

Lauretta
(American) graceful
Laureta, Laurettah, Lauritta, Lauritte, Loretta

Laurette
(American) from Laura; graceful
Etta, Ette, Laure, Laurett, Lorette

Laurie
(English) careful
Lari, Lauri, Lori

Lauriann
(American) combo of Laurie and Ann
Laurian, Laurianne

Laurissaa
(Greek) pleased

Laveda
(Latin) pure
Lavella, Lavelle, Laveta, Lavetta, Lavette

Lavena
(French, Latin) purest woman
Lavi, Lavie, Lavina

Lavender
(Latin) pale purple flowers; peaceful

Laverne
(Latin) breath of spring
Lavern, Lavirne, Verna, Verne

Lavette
(Latin) pure; natural
Laveda, Lavede, Lavete, Lavett

Lavinia
(Latin) cleansed
Vin, Vina, Vinnie, Vinny

Lavina
(Latin) woman of Rome

Lavita
(American) charmer
Laveta, Lavitta, Lavitte

Lavinia
(Greek) ladylike
Lavenia

Lavonne
(American) combo of La and Yvonne
Lavaughan, Lavaughn, Lavon, Lavone, Lavonn, Lavonna, Lavonnah

Lawanda
(American) sassy
LaWanda, Lawonda

Layce
(American) spunky

Layla
(Arabic) dark
Laela, Laila, Lala, Laya, Laylah, Laylie, Leila

Layne
(French) from the meadow
Laine, Lainee, Lainey

Lea
(Hawaiian) goddess-like

Leaf
(Botanical) hip

Leah
(Hebrew) tired and burdened
Lea, Lee, Leeah, Leia, Lia

Leala
(French) steadfast

Leandra
(Greek) commanding as a lioness
Leandrea, Leanndra, Leeandra, Leedie

Leanna
(English) leaning
Leana, Leelee, Liana

Leanne
(English) sweet
Lean, Leann, Lee, Leelee, Lianne

Leanora
(Greek) light
Lenora, Lanora, Lanoriah

Leanore
(English, Greek) stately
Lanore

Leatrice
(American) charming
Leatrise

Lecia
(Latin) short for Leticia; jubliation
Leecia, Leesha, Lesha, Lesia

Leda
(Greek) feminine
Ledah, Lida, Lita

Lee
(English, American, Chinese) light-footed
Lea, Leelee, Leigh

Leeanne
(English) combo of Lee and Anne
Lean, Leann, Lee Ann, Lee-Ann, Leianne

Leeannette
(Greek) form of Leandra; lionine
Leann, Lee Annette, Leeanett, Lee-Annette, Leiandra

Leelee
(American, Slavic) short for Leanne, Lena, Lisa, Leona
Lee-Lee, Lele, Lelee

Leeline
(American) combo of Lee and Line; pastural; loyal
Lee, Leela, LeeLee, Leelene

Leena
(Latin) temptress
Lina, Lena

Leeo
(American) sunny
Leo

Leeza
(American) gorgeous
Leesa, Leeze, Liza, Lize

Legend
(American) memorable
Legen, Legende, Legund

Legia
(Spanish) bright
Legea

Lehava
(Hebrew) flaming

Lei
(Hawaiian) short for Leilani
Leilei

Léi
(Chinese) open; truthful

Leigh
(English) light-footed
Lee, Leelee

Leila
(Arabic) beauty of the night
Layla, Leela, Leilah, Lelah, Leyla, Lila

Leilani
(Hawaiian) heavenly girl
Lanie

Leith
(Scottish) from the river; nature-loving
Leithe, Lethe

Lejoi
(French) joy
Joy, Lejoy

Leland
(American) special
Lelan, Lelande

Lelia
(Greek) articulate
Lee, Leelee

Lemuela
(Hebrew) loyal
Lemuelah, Lemuella, Lemuellah

Lena
(Latin) siren
Leena, Lenette, Lina

Lenesha
(African American) smiling
Leneisha, Lenisha, Lenni, Lennie, Neshie

Lenice
(American) delightful
Lenisa, Lenise

Lenita
(Latin) gentle spirit
Leneeta, Leneta, Lineta

Lenna
(Hebrew) shy

Lenoa
(Greek) form of Lenore; light
Len, Lenor, Lenora

Lenore
(Greek) a form of Eleanor; radiant

Leoda
(German) popular.
Leota

Leola
(Latin) fierce; lionine
Lee, Leo, Leole

Leona
(Greek, American) brave-hearted
Liona

Leonarda
(German) lionhearted
Lenarda, Lenda, Lennarda, Leonarde

Leondrea
(Greek) strong
Leondreah, Leondria

Leonie
(Latin) lionlike; fierce
Leola, Leonee, Leoni, Leoney, Leontine, Leony

Leonora
(English) bright light
Leanor, Leanora, Leanore, Lenora, Lenore, Leonore

Leonore
(Greek) glowing light
Lenore, Leonor, Leonora

Leonsio
(Spanish) form of male name Leon; fierce
Leo, Leonsee, Leonsi

Leopoldina
(Invented) form of Leopold; brave
Dina, Leo, Leopolde, Leopoldyna

Leora
(Greek) light-hearted
Liora, Leorah

Lera
(Russian) strong
Lerae, Lerie, Lira

Leretta
(American) form of Loretta
Lere, Lerie, Loretta

Lesley
(Scottish) strong-willed
Les, Lesle, Lesli, Leslie, Lesly, Leslye, Lezlie

Leslie
(Scottish) fiesty; beautiful and smart
Les, Lesli

Leta
(Latin) happy
Leeta, Lita

Letha
(Greek) ladylike
Litha

Leticia
(Latin, Spanish) joyful
woman
*Letecia, Leticia, Letisha,
Letitia, Lettice, Lettie, Letty,
Tiesha*

Letichel
(American) happy; important
*Chel, Chelle, Leti, Letichell,
Letishell, Lettichelle,
Lettychel*

Leto
(Greek) mother of Apollo

Letsey
(American) form of Letty;
glad
Letsee, Letsy

Lettice
(American) sweet
Letty

Lettie
(Latin, Spanish) happy
Lettee, Letti, Letty, Lettye

Levana
(Hebrew) fair
Lev, Liv, Livana

Leverne
(French) grove of trees

Levina
(Latin) lightning

Levitt
(American) straightforward
Levit

Levity
(American) humorous

Levora
(American) home-loving
*Levorah, Levore, Livee,
Livie, Livora, Livore*

Lewana
(Hebrew) moon bright

Lexa
(American) cheerful
Lex, Lexah

Lexi
(Greek) helpful; sparkling
*Lex, Lexie, Lexsey, Lexsie,
Lexy*

Lexine
(Scottish) helper

Lexus
(American) rich
*Lexi, Lexorus, Lexsis,
Lexuss, Lexxus*

Lexy
(Scottish) helper

Leya
(Spanish) true blue

Lezena
(American) smiling
Lezene, Lezina, Lyzena

Li
(Chinese) plum

Lia
(Greek, Russian, Italian)
singular
Li, Liah

Lian
(Latin, Chinese) graceful
Leane, Leanne, Liane

Liana
(Greek) flowering;
complicated
Leanna, Lee, Liane

Lianne
(English) light
Leann, Leanne, Leeann

Libby
(Hebrew) short for
Elizabeth; bubbly
Lib, Libbi, Libbie

Liber
(American) from the word
liberty; free
Lib, Libby, Lyber

Liberty
(Latin) free and open
Lib, Libbie

Librada
(Spanish) free
Libra, Libradah

Lichelle
(American) combo of Li and
Chelle
Leshel, Leshelle, Licha, Lili

Licia
(Greek) outdoorsy
Lisha

Lida
(Greek) beloved girl
Leedah, Lyda

Lidia
(Greek) pleasant spirit
Lydia

Liese
(German) given to God

Liesel
(German) pretty
Leesel, Leezel

Lieselotte
(Hebrew, French) charming woman; combo of Elizabeth and Charlotte

Light
(American) light-hearted
Li, Lite

Ligia
(Greek) talented musician
Ligea, Lygia, Lygy

Liguria
(Greek) music lover

Likiana
(Invented) likeable
Like, Likia

Lila
(American) short for Delilah, form of Leila; (Arabic) playful
Lilah, Lyla, Lylah

Lila-Lynn
(American) combo of Lila and Lynn; night-loving; delight
Lilalinn, Lilalyn, Lilalynn, Lilalynne

Lilac
(Botanical) tiny blossom
Lila

Lilakay
(American) combo of Lila and Kay
Lilaka, Lilakae, Lila-Kay, Lilakaye, Lylakay

Lileah
(Latin) lily-like
Lili, Liliah, Lill, Lily, Lilya

Lilette
(Latin) little lily; delicate
Lill, Lillette, Lillith, Lilly, Lilly

Lilia
(American) flowing
Lileah, Lyleah, Lylia

Lilian
(Latin) pure beauty

Liliana
(Italian) pretty
Lilianah, Lylianah

Lilias
(Hebrew) night
Lilas, Lillas, Lillias

Liliash
(Spanish) lily; innocent
Lil, Lileah, Liliosa, Lilya, Lyliase, Lylish

Lilibert
(English) combo of Lili and Bert; bubbly
Lilibeth, Lillibet, Lilybet

Lilith
(Arabic) nocturnal
Lilis, Lilita, Lill, Lilli, Lillie, Lillith, Lilly, Lilyth, Lilythe

Lillian
(Latin) pretty as a lily
Lila, Lileane, Lilian, Liliane, Lill, Lilla, Lillah, Lillie, Lillyan, Lillyann, Lilyanne, Liyan

Lillias
(Hebrew) night

Lillibeth
(American) combo of Lilli and Beth; flower; lovely girl
Lilibeth, Lillibethe, Lilybeth

Lily
(Latin, Chinese) elegant
Lil, Lili, Lilie

Limor
(Hebrew) myrrh; treasured
Leemor

Lin
(English, Chinese) beautiful
Linn, Lynn

Lina
(Greek, Latin, Scottish) light of spirit; lake calm
Lena, Lin, Linah, Lynn

Linda
(Spanish) pretty girl
Lind, Lindy, Lynda

Linden
(American) harmonious
Lindan, Lindun, Lynden, Lynnden

Lindsay
(English, Scottish) calming; bright and shining
Lindsee, Lindsey, Lindsi, Lindz, Lyndsie, Lyndzee, Lynz

Lindse
(Spanish) form of Lindsey; enthusiastic
Linds, Lindz, Lindze, Lyndzy

Lindy
(American) music-lover
Lind, Lindee, Lindi, Lindie, Linney, Linnie, Linse, Linz, Linze

Linette
(French, English, American) graceful and airy
Lanette, Linet, Linnet, Lynette

Lin-Lin
(Chinese) beauty of a tinkling bell
Lin, Lin Lin

Ling
(Chinese) delicate

Linnea
(Swedish) statuesque
Lin, Linayah, Linea, Linnay, Linny, Lynnea

Linsey
(English) bright spirit
Linsie, Linsy, Linzi, Linzie

Linzetta
(American) form of Linzey; pretty
Linze, Linzette, Linzey

Liora
(Hebrew) light
Leeor, Leeora, Lior, Liorit

Lisa
(Hebrew, American) dedicated and spiritual
Lee, Leelee, Leesa, Leesah, Leeza, Leisa, Lesa, Lysa

Lisamarie
(American) combo of Lisa and Marie
Lisamaree, Lisa-Marie, Lise-Marie, Lis-Maree

Lisarae
(American) combo of Lisa and Rae
Lisa-Rae, Lisa-Ray, Lisaray

Lisbeth
(Hebrew) short for Elizabeth

Lise
(German) form of Lisa; solemn
Lesa

Lisette
(French) little Elizabeth
Lise, Lisete, Lissette, Liz

Lisha
(Hebrew) short for Elisha; dark
Lish, Lishie

Lissa
(Greek) sweet
Lyssa

Lissandra
(Greek) defends others

Lisseth
(Hebrew) form of Elizabeth; devout
Liseta, Liseth, Lisette, Lisith, Liss, Lisse, Lissi

Lissie
(American) short for Elise; flowery
Lis, Lissi, Lissey, Lissy

Lita
(Latin) short for Carmelita; life-giving
Leta

Liv
(Latin, Scandinavian) lively
Leev

Livia
(Hebrew) lively
Levia, Livya

Livona
(Hebrew) vibrant
Levona, Liv, Livvie, Livvy

Liya
(Russian) lily; lovely
Leeya

Liz
(English) short for Elizabeth; excitable
Lis, Lissy, Lizy, Lizzi, Lizzie

Liza
(American) smiling
Leeza, Liz, Lizah, Lizzie, Lizzy, Lyza

Lizbeth
(American) combo of Liz and Beth; devout
Liz Beth, Liz-Beth, Lizeth

Lizeth
(Hebrew) ebullient
Liseth, Lizethe

Lizette
(Hebrew) lively
Lizet, Lizett

Lizibeth
(American) combo of Lizi and Beth
Lizabeth, Liza-Beth, Lizzie, Lizziebeth

Lizzie
(American) devout
Liz, Liza, Lizae, Lizette, Lizzee, Lizzey, Lizzi, Lizzy

Lo
(American) spunky
Loe

Loanna
(American) combo of Lo and Anna; loving
Lo, Loann, Loanne, LoLo

Loelia
(Arabic) nocturnal
Leila

Logan
(English) climbing
Lo, Logun

Loibeth
(American) combo of Loy and Beth; popular
Beth, Loi, Loy Beth, Loy, Loybeth, Loy-Beth

Loicy
(American) delightful
Loice, Loisee, Loisey, Loisi, Loy, Loyce, Loycy, Loyse, Loysie

Loire
(Place name) river in France; lovely wonder
Loir, Loirane

Lois
(Greek) good
Lo, Loes

Lojean
(American) combo of Lo and Jean; bravehearted
Lojeanne

Lola
(Spanish) pensive
Lo, Lolah, Lolita

Loleen
(American) jubilant
Lolene

Lolita
(Spanish) sad
Lo, Lola, Loleta, Lita

Lolly
(English) candy; sweet

Lomita
(Spanish) good

Lona
(Latin) lionlike
Lonee, Lonie, Lonna, Lonnie

Londa
(American) shy
Londah, Londe, Londy

London
(Place name) calming
Londen, Londun, Londy, Loney, Lony

Loni
(American) beauty
Loney, Lonie, Lonnie, Loney

Lonnette
(American) pretty
Lonett, Lonette, Lonnie, Lonn

Lora
(Latin) regal
Laura, Lorah, Lorea, Loria

Loranden
(American) ingenious
Lorandyn, Lorannden, Luranden

Loreen
(American) variation on Lauren
Lorene

Lorel
(German) tempting
Loreal

Lorelei
(German) siren
Loralee, Lorilie, LoraLee, Lurleen, Lurlene

Lorelle
(American) lovely
Lore, Loreee, Lorel, Lorey, Lori, Lorie, Lorille, Lorel, Lorille

Loren
(American) form of Lauren; picture-perfect
Lorren, Lorri, Lorrie, Lorron, Lorryn, Lory, Loryn, Lourie

Lorena
(English) photogenic
Loreen, Lorene, Lorrie, Lorrine

Lorenza
(Latin) variant of Laura; wears laurel wreath
Laurenza

Loretta
(English) large-eyed beauty
Lauretta

Lori
(Latin) laurel-crowned and nature-loving
Laurie, Loree, Lorie, Lory

Lorinda
(American) combo of Lori and Linda; gregarious
Larinda, Lorenda, Lori, Lorie

Loris
(Greek, Latin) fun-loving
Lorice, Lauris

Lorna
(Latin) laurel-crowned; natural
Lorenah

Lorola
(Origin unknown) family

Lorraine
(Latin, French) sad-eyed
Laraine, Lauraine, Lorain, Loraine, Lorrie, Lors

Lotta
(Swedish) sweet

Lottie
(American) old-fashioned
Lottee, Lotti, Lotty

Lotus
(Greek) flowery
Lolo, Lotie

Lou
(American) short for Louise
Loulou, Lu

Louella
(English) elf
*Loella, Loellah, Loelle,
Luella, Luela*

Louie
(American) strong

Louisa
(English) patient
Lou, Loulou, Luisa, Luizza, Lu

Louise
(German) hardworking and
brave
Lolah, Lou, Loulou, Luise

Lourdes
(French) girl from Lourdes,
France; hallowed
Lourd, Lordes, Lordez

Lordyn
(American) enchanting
*Lorden, Lordin, Lordine,
Lordun, Lordynn*

Love
(English, American) loving
Lovey, Lovi, Luv

Loveada
(Spanish) loving
Lova, Lovada

Loveanna
(American) combo of Love
and Anna; loving
*Lovanna, Love-Anna,
Loveanne, Luvana, Luvanna*

Lovejoy
(Invented) combo of Love
and Joy; jubliant

Lovella
(Native American) soft spirit
Lovela

Lovely
(American) loving
*Lovelee, Loveley, Loveli,
Lovey*

Lovie
(American) warm
Lovee, Lovey, Lovi, Lovy

Lovina
(American) warm
*Lovena, Lovey, Lovinah,
Lovinnah*

Lowell
(American) lovely
Lowel

Lowena
(American) from Louise;
warrior
Lowenek, Lowenna

Loyalty
(American) loyal
Loyaltie

Luann
(Hebrew) combo of Lou and
Ann; happy girl
*Lou, Louann, Louanne,
Loulou, Luan, Luanne*

Luba
(Yiddish) dear
Liba, Lubah, Lyuba

Luberda
(Spanish) light; dear
Luberdia

Luca
(Italian) light
Luka

Lucasta
(Spanish) bringer of light

Luceil
(French) light; lucky
Luce, Lucee, Lucy

Lucerne
(Latin) born into the light
Lucerna

Lucero
(Italian) light-hearted
Lucee, Lucey, Lucy

Lucetta
(English) radiating joy

Lucette
(French) pale light

Lucia
(Italian, Greek, Spanish)
light; lucky in love
*Chia, Luceah, Lucey, Lucey,
Luci*

Luciana
(Italian) fortunate
Louciana, Luceana, Lucianah

Lucie
(French, American) lucky girl
Lucy

Lucienne
(French) lucky
*Lucien, Lucianne, Lucienn,
Lucy-Ann*

Lucilla
(English) from Lucille; bright
Loucilla, Loucilah, Loucilla, Lucilah, Lucylla, Lusyla, Luzela

Lucille
(English) bright-eyed
Loucil, Loucile, Loucille, Lucyl, Lucie, Lucile, Lucy

Lucina
(American) happy
Lucena, Lucie, Lucinah, Lucy, Lucyna

Lucinda
(Latin) prissy
Cinda, Cindie, Lu, Luceenda, Lucynda, Lulu

Lucita
(Spanish) light
Lusita, Luzita

Lucja
(Polish) light
Luscia

Luckette
(Invented) lucky
Luckett

Lucretia
(Latin) wealthy woman
Lu, Lucrecia, Lucreesha, Lucritia

Lucy
(Latin, Scottish, Spanish)
light-hearted
Lu, Luca, Luce, Luci, Lucie

Lucyann
(American) combo of Lucy and Ann; gracious light
Luce, Luciana, Luciann, Lucianne, Lucy, Lucyan, Lucy-Ann, Lucyanne

Lucylynn
(American) combo of Lucy and Lynn; light-hearted
Lucilyn, Lucylin, Lucy-Lynn

Ludivina
(Slavic) loved

Ludmilla
(Slavic) beloved one
Lu, Ludie, Ludmila, Ludmylla, Lule, Lulu

Lue-Ella
(English) combo of Lue and Ella; tough; assertive
Louel, Luella, Luelle

Luella
(German) conniving
Loella, Louella, Lu, Lula, Lulah, Lulu

Luenetter
(American) egotistical
Lou, Lu, Luene, Luenette

Luisa
(Spanish) smiling
Louisa

Luisana
(Place name) form of Louisiana; combative
Luisanna, Luisanne, Luisiana

Luke
(American) bouncy
Luc, Luka, Lukey, Lukie

Lula
(German) all-encompassing
Lulu

Lulani
(Polynesian) heavensent
Lula, Lani, Lanie

Lulu
(German, English) kind
Lou, Loulou, Lu, Lulie

Lulubell
(American) combo of Lulu and Bell; well-known
Bell, Bella, Belle, Lulu, Lulubel, Lulu-Bell, Lulubelle

Luminosa
(Spanish) luminous

Luna
(Latin) moonstruck
Loona

Lund
(German) genius
Lun, Lunde

Lundy
(Scottish) grove by an island
Lundea, Lundee, Lundi

Lundyn
(American) different
Lundan, Lunden, Lundon

Lupe
(Spanish) enthusiastic
Loopy, Loopey, Lupeta, Lupey, Lupie, Lupita

Luquitha
(African American) fond
Luquetha, Luquith

Lura
(American) loquacious
Loora, Lur, Lurah, Lurie

Lurajane
(American) combo of Lura and Jane; cuddly little one
Janie, Loorajane, Lura-Jane, Luri, Lurijane

Lurissa
(American) beguiling
Luresa, Luressa, Luris, Lurisa, Lurissah, Lurly

Lurlene
(German) tempting; (Scandinavian) bold
Lura, Lurleen, Lurlie, Lurline

Luvelle
(American) light
Luvee, Luvell, Luvey, Luvy

Luvy
(American) spontaneous
Lovey, Luv

Lux
(Latin) light
Luxe, Luxee, Luxi, Luxy

Luz
(Spanish) light-hearted
Lusa, Luzana, Luzi

Luzille
(Spanish) light
Luz, Luzell

Lyanne
(Greek) melodious
Liann, Lianne, Lyan, Lyana, Lyaneth, Lyann

Lyawonda
(African American) friend
Lyawunda, Lywanda, Lywonda

Lycoris
(Greek) twilight

Lydia
(Greek) musical; unusual
Lidia, Lidya, Lyddie, Lydie, Lydy

Lyla
(French) island girl
Lila, Lilah, Lile

Lyle
(English) strident
Lile

Lymekia
(Greek) form of Lydia; royal
Lymekea

Lynda
(Spanish) beautiful
Linda, Lindi, Lynde, Lyndie, Lynn

Lyndsay
(Scottish) bright and shining
Lindsay, Lindsey

Lynelle
(English) pretty girl; bright as sunshine
Linelle, Lynel, Lynie, Lynn

Lynette
(French) small and fresh
Lyn, Lynet, Lynnet, Lynette, Lynnie

Lynn
(English) fresh as spring water
Lin, Linn, Linnie, Lyn, Lynne

Lynsey
(American) form of Lindsay
Linzie, Lyndsey, Lynze, Lynzy

Lyra
(Greek) musical
Lyre

Lyric
(Greek) musical
Lyrec

Lyris
(Greek) plays the lyre
Liris, Lirisa, Lirise

Lysa
(Hebrew) God-loving
Leesa, Lisa

Lysandra
(Greek) liberator; she frees others
Lyse, Lysie

Lysanne
(Greek) helpful
Lysann

Lysett
(American) pretty little one
Lyse, Lysette

Lyssan
(Greek) form of Alexandra; supportive
Liss, Lissan, Lissana, Lissandra, Lyss

Lytanisha
(African American) scintillating
Litanisha, Lyta, Lytanis, Lytanish, Lytanishia, Nisa, Nisha

Mab
(Literature) Shakespearean queen of fairies

Mabel
(Latin) well-loved
Mabbel, Mabil, Mable, Mabyl, Maybel, Maybie

Macallister
(Irish) confident

Macarena
(Spanish) name of a dance; blessed
Macarene, Macaria, Macarria, Rena

Macaria
(Spanish) blessed
Maca, Macarea, Macarie, Maka

Macey
(American) upbeat; happy
Mace, Macie, Macy

Mackenzie
(Irish) leader
Mac, Mackenzee, Mackenzey, Mackenzi, Mackenzie, Mackenzy, Mackie, Mackinsey, Mckenzie, McKinsey, McKinzie

Mada
(American) helpful
Madah, Maida

Madalena
(Greek) from Madeline; jaunty
Madalayna, Madaleyna, Madelyna, Madelayna, Madelena, Madeleyna

Madalyn
(Greek) high goals
Madelyn

Madchen
(German) girl
Madchan, Madchin, Maddchen

Maddie
(English) form of Madeline
Mad, Maddee, Maddey, Maddi, Maddy, Mady

Maddox
(English) giving
Maddax, Maddee, Maddey, Maddie, Maddux, Maddy

Madelcarmen
(American) combo of Madel and Carmen; old-fashioned
Madel-Carmen, Madlecarmen

Madeleine
(French) high-minded
Madelon

Madeline
(Greek) strength-giving
Madaleine, Maddie, Maddy, Madelene, Madi

Madelyn
(Greek) strong woman
Madalyn, Madlynne, Madolyn

Madge
(Greek, American) spunky
Madgie, Madg

Madhur
(Hindi) sweet girl

Madina
(Greek) form of Madeline; happy
Mada, Maddelina, Maddi, Maddy, Madele, Madena, Madlin

Madison
(English) good-hearted
Maddie, Maddison, Maddy, Madisen, Madysin

Madonna
(Latin) my lady; spirited

Madora
(Place name) from Madeira Spain; volcanic
Madorra

Madrina
(Spanish) godmother
Madra, Madreena, Madrine

Madrona
(Spanish) mother; maternal
Madrena

Mae
(English) bright flower
May

Maegan
(Irish) a gem of a woman
Megan

MaElena
(Spanish) light
Elena, Lena

Maeli
(English) great; from Mae
Maelee, Maeley, Maelie, Maely, Maylee, Mayley, Mayli, Maylie, Mayly

Maeve
(Irish) queen
Maive, Mave, Mayve

Maezelma
(American) combo of Mae and Zelma; practical
Mae Zelma, Maez, Mae-Zelma, Maezie, Mayzelma

Magan
(Greek) heavy-hearted
Mag, Magen, Maggie

Magda
(Scandinavian) believer
Mag, Maggie

Magdala
(Greek) girl in the tower
Magdalla

Magdalene
(Greek, Scandinavian) spiritual
Mag, Magda, Magdalena, Magdaline, Magdalyn, Magdelin, Magdylena Maggie

Maggie
(Greek, English, Irish) priceless pearl
Mag, Maggee, Maggi

Magina
(Russian) hard-working
Mageena, Maginah

Magnolia
(Botanical) flower; (Latin) flowering and flourishing
Mag, Maggi, Maggie, Maggy, Magnole, Nolie

Magryta
(Slavic) desired

Mahal
(Filipino) loving woman
Mah, Maha

Mahala
(Hebrew, Native American) tender female
Mah, Mahalah, Mahalia, Mahla, Mahlie

Mahelia
(Arabic) from Mahala; tenderness
Maheelia, Maheelya, Mahelya

Mahina
(Hawaiian) moonbeam

Mahira
(Hebrew) vibrant

Mahogany
(Spanish) rich as wood
Mahagonie, Mahogony

Mahoney
(American) high energy
Mahhony, Mahonay, Mahonie, Mahony

Mai
(Scandinavian, Japanese) treasure; flower; singular
Mae, May

Maia
(Greek) fertile; earth goddess
Maya, Mya

Maida
(Greek) shy girl
Mady, Maidie, May, Mayda

Maidie
(Scottish) maiden; virgin
Maidee, Maydee, Maydie

Mair
(Irish) from Mary; religious
Maire

Maira
(Hebrew) bitter; saved
Mara, Marah

Maired
(Irish) pearl; treasured
Mairead, Mared

Mairin
(Irish) from Mary; reverent

Maisie
(Scottish) treasure
Maesee, Maesey, Maesi, Maesie, Maesy, Maisee, Maisey, Maisi, Maisy, Maizie, Mazee

Maitland
(American) variant of Maitlyn; generous
Maitlande, Mateland, Matelande, Maytland, Maytlande

Maitlin
(American) variant of Maitlyn; kind
Maitlyn, Matelin, Matelyn, Maytlin, Maytlyn

Maja
(Scandinavian) fertile

Majidah
(Arabic) slendid

Makala
(Hawaiian) natural outdoors
Makal, Makie

Makayla
(American) magical
Makaila, Makala, Michaela, Mikaela, Mikayla, Mikaylah

Makyll
(American) innovative
Makell

Makynna
(American) friendly
Makenna, Makinna

Malak
(Arabic) angelic

Malay
(Place name) softspoken
Malae

Malaya
(Filipino) free and open
Malea

Malene
(Scandinavian) in the tower
Maleen, Maleene, Malyne

Malha
(Hebrew) queenlike and regal

Mali
(Thai) flowering beauty
Malee, Maley, Mali, Malie, Malley, Mallie, Maly

Malia
(Hawaiian) thoughtful
Maylia

Maliaval
(Hawaiian) peaceful

Malika
(Hungarian) hardworking and punctual
Maleeka

Malin
(Native American) comfort-giver
Malen, Maline, Mallie

Malina
(Scandinavian) in the tower
Maleena, Maleenah, Malinah, Malyna, Malynah

Malinda
(Greek, American) honey
Melinda

Malissa
(American, Greek) combo of May and Melissa; sweet
Melissa

Mallika
(Indian) watchful; tending the garden
Malika

Mallory
(French, German, American) tough-minded; spunky
Mal, Malery, Mallari, Mallery, Mallie, Mallorey, Mallori, Mallorie, Maloree, Malorey, Malori, Malorie, Malory

Malu
(Hawaiian) peaceful
Maloo

Malvina
(Scottish) romantic
Malv, Malva, Malvie, Melvina

Mame
(American) from Margaret; pearl; treasured
Maime, Mayme

Mamie
(American) from Margaret; little pearl; treasured
Mamee, Mamey, Mami, Mamy

Mancie
(American) hopeful
Manci, Mansey, Mansie

Manda
(American) short for Amanda; beloved
Amand, Mandee, Mandi, Mandy

Mandy
(Latin) lovable
Manda, Mandee, Mandey, Mandi, Mandie

Mandymay
(American) combo of Mandy and May
Mandeemae, Mandimae, Mandimay, Mandymae

Mane
(American) top
Main, Manie

Manee
(Korean) peace giving
Mani, Manie

Manilow
(Last name as first name) musical

Manisha
(African) kind; (Hindi) intelligent

Manju
(Hindi) sweetheart

Manna
(Hawaiian) perceptive
Mana, Manah, Mannah

Manon
(French) exciting

Mantill
(American) guarded
Mant, Mantell, Mantie

Manuela
(Spanish) sophisticated girl
Manuella

Manzie
(Native American) flower
Mansi

Mara
(Greek) thoughtful believer
Marah, Marra

Marajayne
(American) combo of Mara
and Jayne; lively
*Mara Jayne, Marajane,
Mara-Jayne, Maryjayne*

Maranda
(Latin) wonderful
Marandah, Miranda

Marbella
(Spanish) pretty
Marb, Marbela, Marbelle

Marbury
(American) substantial
Mar, Marbary

Marcelina
(Latin) contentious
*Marceleena, Marcelyna,
Marcileena, Marcilina,
Marcilyna, Marcyleena*

Marceline
(Latin) argumentative
*Marceleene, Marcelyne,
Marcileene, Marcilyne,
Marcyleene*

Marcella
(Latin) combative
*Marce, Marcela, Marci,
Marcie, Marse, Marsella*

Marcelline
(French) pretty
*Marceline, Marcelyne,
Marcie, Marcy, Marcyline*

Marcellita
(Spanish) desired, feisty
*Marcel, Marcelita,
Marcelite, Marcelle,
Marcelli, Marcey, Marci*

Marcena
(Latin, American) spirited
*Marce, Marceen, Marcene,
Marcie*

Marcia
(Latin, American) combative
Marcie, Marsha

Marcie
(English) chummy
*Marcee, Marcey, Marci,
Marcy, Marsi, Marsie*

Marcilyn
(American) combo of Marci
and Lyn; physical
*Marce, Marcie-Lyn, Marci-
Lyn, Marclinne, Marclyn,
Marcy, Mars, Marse,
Marslin, Marslyn*

Marcine
(American) bright
Marceen, Marceene

Marcy
(English, American)
opinionated
Marci, Marsie, Marsy

Mardonia
(American) approving
*Mardee, Mardi, Mardone,
Mardonne, Mardy*

Mare
(American) living by the
ocean

Maren
(American) ocean-lover
Marin, Marren, Marrin

Maret
(English) from Mary;
bittersweet
*Marett, Marit, Maritt, Maryt,
Marytt*

Marg
(American) tenacious
Mar

Margaret
(Greek, Scottish, English)
treasured pearl; pure-
spirited
*Mag, Maggie, Marg,
Margerite, Margie, Margo,
Margret, Meg, Meggie*

Margaretta
(Spanish) pearl

Margarita
(Italian, Spanish) winning
*Marg, Margarit, Margarite,
Margie, Margrita,
Marguerita*

Margarite
(Greek, German) pearl
*Gretal, Marga, Margareeta,
Margaryta, Margereeta,
Margerita, Margeryta,
Margit, Margot*

Margaux
(French) variant of
Margaret; treasure

Marge
(English, American) short
for Marjorie; easygoing
Marg, Margie

Margery
(English) pearl
Marge, Margie

Marghanita
(Spanish) pearl

Margherita
(Italian, Greek) treasured pearl
Marg

Margia
(American) form of Margie; friendly
Marge, Margea, Margy

Margie
(English) friendly
Margey, Margy, Marjie

Margina
(American) centered

Margoletta
(French) little Margo; spunky

Margot
(French) lively
Margaux, Margo

Margrita
(Spanish) treasure
Margreeta, Margrytaa

Marguerite
(French) stuffy
Maggie, Marg, Margerite, Margie, Margina, Margurite

Mari
(Japanese) ball; round

Maria
(Latin, French, German, Italian, Polish, Spanish) desired child
Maja, Malita, Mareea, Marica, Marike, Marucha, Mezi, Mitzi

Mariah
(Hebrew) sorrowful singer
Marayah, Mariahe, Marriah, Meriah, Moriah

Marializa
(Spanish) combo of Maria and Liza; desired
Liza, Maria Liza, Maria, Maria-Liza, Mariliza

Marialourdes
(Spanish) combo of Maria and Lourdes; sweet
Maria Lourdes, Maria-Lourdes

Mariamne
(French) form of Miriam; sea of sadness
Mariam, Marianne

Marian
(English) thoughtful
Mariane, Marianne, Maryann, Maryanne

Mariana
(Spanish) quiet girl
Maryanna

Marianella
(French) combo of Marian and Ella; girl of the sea
Ella, Marian, Mariane

Mariangela
(American) combo of Mary and Angela; angelic
Mary Angela, Mary-Angela, Mariangelle

Maria-Teresa
(Spanish) combo of Maria and Teresa; desired
Maria Teresa, Mariateresa, Maria-Terese, Maria-Theresa

Maribel
(French, English, American) combo of Mary and Belle
EmBee, Marabel, Maribela, Merrybelle

Maribeth
(American) combo of Mari and Beth
Mary Beth Mary-Beth, Marybeth

Marie
(French) form of Mary; dignified and spiritual
Maree, Marye

Mariel
(German) spiritual
Mari, Mariele, Marielle

Marielena
(Spanish) combo of Marie and Lena; desired
Mari, Mari-Elena, Marie-Lena, Maryelenna

Mariella
(Italian) from Maria; blessed

Mariellen
(American) combo of Mari and Ellen; dancer
Mare, Marelle, Mariella, Maryellen, MaryEllen

Mariene
(Spanish) devout
Mari, Marienne

Mariet
(French) variant of Marie; bittersweet
Mariett, Mariette, Maryet, Maryett, Maryette

Marietta
(French) combo of Mary and Etta; spright spirit
Marieta, Maryeta, Maryetta

Marigold
(Botanical) sunny
*Maragold, Marigolde,
Marigole, Marrigold,
Marygold, Marygolde*

Marihelen
(American) combo of Mary
and Helen; steadfast friend
Marihelene, MaryHelen

Marika
(Slavic, American)
thoughtful and brooding
*Mareeca, Mareecka,
Mareeka, Marica, Maricka,
Maryca, Marycka, Maryka,
Merica, Merika, Merk, Merkie*

Marikaitlynn
(American) combo of Mari
and Kaitlynn; desired
*Kait, Kaiti, Mari,
Marreekaitlyn, Mary
Kaitlynn, Mary-Kaitlynn*

Marilee
(American) combo of Mary
and Lee; dancing
Marylee, Merilee, Merrilee

Marilene
(American) combo of Mari
and Ilene; talented

Marilou
(American) combo of Mary
and Lou; jubilant
*Marilu, Marrilou, Marylou,
Marylu*

Marilyn
(Hebrew) fond-spirited
*Maralynne, Mare, Marilin,
Mariline, Marilinn, Marilynn,
Marrie, Marrilyn, Marylyn,
Marylynn, Merilyn, Merrilyn*

Marin
(Latin) sea-loving
Mare, Maren

Marina
(Latin) lover of the ocean
*Mareena, Marena, Marina,
Maryna*

Marinella
(French) combo of Marin
and Ella; soft
*Ella, Marin, Mari-Nella,
Marin-Ella, Nella*

Marion
(French) form of Mary;
delicate spirit
*Mare, Marien, Marrion, Mary,
Maryen, Maryian, Maryon*

Mariposa
(Spanish) butterfly
Mari, Mariposah, Maryposa

Mariquita
(Spanish) form of Margaret;
party-loving
*Marikita, Marrikita,
Marriquita*

Maris
(Latin) sea-loving
Mere, Marice, Meris, Marys

Marisa
(Latin) sea-loving; (Spanish)
combo of Maria and Luisa
*Marce, Maressa, Marissa,
Marisse, Mariza Marsie,
Marysa, Maryssa, Merisa*

Marisela
(Spanish) hearty
Marisella, Marysela

Mariska
(American) endearing
Mareska, Marisca, Mariskah

Marisol
(Spanish) stunning
*Mare, Mari, Marizol,
Marrisol, Marzol, Merizol*

Maritza
(Place name) St. Moritz,
Switzerland

Marixbel
(Spanish) pretty
Marix

Marjie
(Scottish) short for Marjorie
Marji, Marjy

Marjorie
(Greek, English, Scottish)
bittersweet; pert
*Marg, Marge, Margerie,
Margery, Margorie, Marjie,
Marjori*

Marky
(American) mischievous
Marki, Markie

Marla
(German) believer;
easygoing
Marlah, Marlla

Marlaina
(American) form of Marlene;
dramatic
Marlaine, Marlane

Marlana
(Hebrew, Greek) vamp
Marlanna

Marleal
(American) form of Mary;
desired
Marle, Marleel, Marly

Marlee
(Greek) guarded
Marleigh, Marley, Marli, Marlie, Marly

Marlen
(American) desired
Marl, Marla, Marlin

Marlena
(German) pretty; bittersweet
Marla, Marlaina, Marleena, Marlina, Marlyna, Marlynne, Marnie

Marlene
(Greek) high-minded; attractive;
(English) adorned
Marlean, Marlee, Marleen, Marleene, Marley, Marline, Marly, Marlyne

Marley
(English) form of Marlene
Mar, Marlee, Marlie, Marly

Marlis
(German) combo of Maria and Elisabeth; religious
Marl, Marlice

Marlise
(English) considerate
Marlice, Marlis, Marlys

Marlo
(American) vivacious
Marloe, Marloh, Marlow, Marlowe

Marlycia
(Spanish) desired
Lycia, Marly, Marlysia

Marna
(French) from Marlene; rejoices

Marnie
(Hebrew) storyteller
Marn, Marnee, Marney, Marni, Marny

Marnina
(French) from Marlene; joyful
Marneena, Marnyna

Marnita
(American) worrier
Marneta, Marni, Marnite, Marnitta, Marny

Marolyn
(Invented) form of Marilyn; desired; precious
Maro, Marolin, Marolinne

Maromisa
(Japanese) combo of Maro and Misa; warm
Maromissa

Marquise
(French) noble-spirited
Markeese, Marquees, Marquisa, Mars

Marquisha
(African American) form of Marquise
Marquish

Marquita
(Spanish) happy girl
Marqueda, Marquitta, Marrie

Marrie
(American) variant of Mary; desired
Marry

Marsala
(Italian) of Marseille, Italy; rambunctious
Marse, Marsela, Marsie

Marsha
(Latin) light-haired; combative
Marcia, Mars, Marsie

Marshay
(American) exuberant
Marshae, Marshaya

Marta
(Danish) treasure
Mart, Marte, Marty, Merta

Marterrell
(American) changeable
Marte, Marterill, Martrell

Martha
(Aramaic) lady
Marta, Marth, Marti, Marty, Mattie

Marthe
(Aramaic) ladylike

Marti
(English) short for Martha; dreamy
Martee, Martey, Martie, Marty

Martina
(Latin, German) combative
Marteena, Martene, Marti, Martinna, Martyna, Tina

Martine
(French) combative

Martivanio
(Italian) form of Martina; feisty; fighter
Mart, Marti, Tivanio

Martonette
(American) form of male name Martin; feisty little girl
Martanette, Martinette, Martonett

Marty
(English) from Martha; hopes
Marti

Marusya
(Slavic) soft-hearted

Marvel
(French) astounding; marvelous

Marvella
(French) marvelous woman
Marva, Marvelle, Marvie, Mavela

Mary
(Hebrew) bitter; in the Bible, the mother of Jesus
Maire, Mara, Mare, Maree, Mari, Marie, Mariel, Marlo, Marye, Merree, Merry, Mitzie

Marya
(Arabic) white and bright
Marja

Maryalice
(American) combo of Mary and Alice; friendly
Marialice, Maryalyce

Maryann
(English, American) combo of Mary and Ann; special
Mariann, Marianne, Maryan, Maryann, Maryanne

Mary-Catherine
(American) combo of Mary and Catherine; outgoing
Maricatherine, Marycatherine, Mary-Kathryn

Maryellen
(American) combo of Mary and Ellen; satisfied
Maryellin, Maryellyn

Mary-Elizabeth
(American) combo of Mary and Elizabeth; kind
Marielizabeth, Mary Elizabeth, Maryelizabeth

Maryjo
(American) Marijo; combo of Mary and Jo; likable
Marijo

Marykate
(American) combo of May and Kate; splendid
Marikate, Mary-Kate

Marykay
(American) combo of Mary and Kay; adorned
Marikay, Marrikae

Maryke
(Dutch) kind; desired
Mairek, Marika, Maryk, Maryky

Mary-Lou
(American) combo of Mary and Lou; athletic
Mary Lou, Marylou

Mary-Marg
(American) dramatic
Marimarg

Mary-Margaret
(American) combo of Mary and Margaret; dramatic, kind
Marimargaret, Mary Margaret, Marymarg, Marymargret

Marypat
(American) combo of Mary and Pat; easygoing
Mary-Pat, Mary Pat

Marysue
(American) combo of Mary and Sue; country girl
MariSue, Merrysue, Mersue

Masha
(Russian) child who was desired

Mashonda
(African American) believer
Masho, Mashonde

Masina
(Last name as first) charming; delightful

Mason
(French) diligent; reliable

Massey
(German) confident
Massi, Massie

Massiel
(American) giving
Masie, Masiel, Massey, Massielle

Massim
(Latin) great
Massima, Maxim, Maxima

Matia
(Hebrew) a God-given gift
Matea, Mattea, Mattie

Matilda
(German) powerful fighter
Mat, Mathilda, Mattie, Tilda, Tillie, Tilly

Mattie
(English) most honored
Matt, Matte, Mattey, Matti, Matty

Matylda
(Polish) strong fighter
Matyld

Maude
(English) old-fashioned
Maud, Maudie

Maudeen
(American) countrified
Maudie, Mawdeen, Mawdine

Maudisa
(African) sweet
Maudesa, Maudesah

Mauna
(American) attractive
Maune, Mawna, Mon

Maura
(Latin, Irish) dark
Moira, Maurie

Maureen
(Irish, French) night-loving
Maura, Maurene, Maurine, Moreen, Morene

Maurelle
(French) petite
Maure, Maurie, Maurielle

Maurise
(French) dark
Morise, Maurice

Mauve
(French) gentle
Mauvey, Mauvie

Mave
(French) bird; melodic

Mavis
(French) singing bird
Mauvis, Mav, Mave

Maxeeme
(Latin) form of Maxime; maximum

Maxie
(Latin) fine
Maxee, Maxey, Maxy

Maxime
(Latin) maximum
Maxey, Maxi, Maxim

Maxine
(Latin) greatest of all
Max, Maxeen, Maxene, Maxie, Maxy

May
(Old English) bright flower
Mae, Maye

Maya
(Latin, Hindi, Mayan) creative; mystical
Maia, Maiya, Mayah, Mya, Myah, Mye

Maybelle
(American) combo of May and Belle; lovely May
Mabelle, Maebelle, Maybell, May-Belle

Maybelline
(Latin) variation of Mabel; lovable
Mabie, May, Maybeline, Maybie, Maybleene

Mayella
(American) combo of May and Ella; jolly
Ella, Maella, May, Mayela, Mayell, Mella

Mayghaen
(American) fortunate

Mayim
(Origin unknown) special
Mayum

Maykaylee
(American) ingenious
Maykayli, Maykaylie, Maykayly

Mayo
(Irish) place name; vibrant
Mayoh

Mayra
(Spanish) flourishing; creative
Mayrah

Mayrant
(Spanish) industrious
Maya, Mayrynt

Mazel
(American) form of Hazel; shining; (Hebrew) lucky girl
Masel, Mazil, Mazal

Mazie
(Scottish) form of Maisie

Mazu
(Chinese) goddess of the sea

McCanna
(American) ebullient
Maccanna, McCannah

McCauley
(Irish) feisty
Mac, McCauly, McCawlie

McCay
(Irish) creative
Mackaylee, McCaylee

McCormick
(Irish) last name as first name
MacCormack, Mackey

McGown
(Irish) sensible
Mac, MacGowen, Mackie, McGowen

McKenna
(American) able
Mackenna, Makenna

McKenzie
(Scottish) form of Mackenzie
Mackie, McKinzie, Mickey

McMurtry
(Irish) last name as first name
Mac, McMurt

Mead
(Greek) honey-wine-loving
Meade, Meed, Meede

Meadhoh
(Irish) joyful

Meadow
(English) place name; calm
Meadoh

Meagan
(Irish) joyous; precious
Maegan, Meaghan, Meegan, Meg, Meganne, Meggie, Meggye, Meghan

Meara
(Irish) happy girl

Meashley
(American) charmer
Meash, Meashlee

Meatah
(American) athletic
Mea, Mia, Miata, Miatah

Meave
(Irish) sings

Medalle
(American) pretty
Medahl, Medoll

Medardo
(Spanish) pretty

Medea
(Greek) ruling; cruel
Medeia

Medusa
(Greek) contriver; temptress

Meena
(Hindi) fish

Meera
(Hindi) rich

Meg
(Greek) able; lovable
Megs

Megan
(Irish) precious, joyful
Meagan, Meaghen, Meggi, Meghan, Meghann

Meggie
(Greek) best
Meggey, Meggi, Meggy

Megha
(Welsh) pearl

Meghan
(Welsh) pearl
Meghen, Meghyn

Mehetabel
(Hebrew) won by faith
Mehitabel

Mehul
(Hindi) rain girl

Meirion
(Hebrew) light

Meissa
(Hindi) from Mesha; moonlike
Meisa, Meysa, Meyssa

Mel
(Greek) sporty
Mell

Melada
(Greek) from Melanie; dark
Mel, Melli

Melana
(Greek) giving; dark

Melanna
(Greek) dark

Melancon
(French) dark beauty; sweet
Mel, Melance, Melaney, Melanie, Melanse, Melanson, Melonce, Melonceson

Melania
(Italian) giving; philanthropic
Mel, Melly

Melanie
(Greek) dark; sweet
Melanee, Melaney, Melani, Melany, Meleni, Melenie, Meleny

Melantha
(Greek) dark-skinned; sweet
Melanthah

Melba
(Australian) talented; light-hearted
Melbah

Meleda
(Spanish) sweet
Meleeda, Melida, Melyda

Melia
(German) dedicated
Meelia, Meleea, Melya, Melyah

Melicent
(English) variant of Millicent; strong
Melisent

Melina
(Greek) honey; sweet
Meleena, Melena, Melinah, Melyna

Melinda
(Latin) honey; sweetheart
Linda, Linnie, Linny, Lynda, Mellie, Melynda, Milinda, Mindy, Mylinde

Melisande
(French) strong
Melisenda

Melissa
(Greek) honey
Melisa, Melysa, Melyssa, Melyssuh

Mellicent
(German) from Millicent; royal born
Melicent, Mellycent, Melycent

Mellie
(Greek) bee; busy

Melody
(Greek) song; musical
Mel, Mellie, Melodee, Melodey, Melodie

Meloney
(American) form of Melanie; dark and sweet
Mel, Melone, Meloni

Melora
(Latin) good
Meliora, Melorah, Melourah

Melosa
(Greek) variant of Melissa; bee; never rests
Melossa

Melrose
(Place name) sweet girl
Mellrose, Melrosie

Melvia
(American) leader; dark
Mel, Mell, Melvea

Melvina
(Irish) prepared to lead
Malvina

Mena
(Egyptian) pretty
Meenah, Menah

Meosha
(African American) talented
Meeosha, Meoshe, Miosha

Merary
(American) merry
Marary, Meraree, Merarie

Mercedes
(Spanish) merciful; rewarded
Mercedez, Mercides, Mersadez, Mersaydes

Mercia
(English) variant of Marcia; combative

Mercy
(English) forgiving
Merce, Mercee, Mercey, Merci, Mercie

Meredith
(Welsh) protector
Mer, Meredithe, Meredyth, Merridith, Merry, Merydith, Merydithe

Meri
(Irish) by the sea
Merrie

Meridian
(American) perfect posture
Meredian, Meridiane

Merie
(French) secretive; blackbird
Mer, Meri, Myrie

Meriel
(Irish) girl who shines like the sea
Meri, Merial, Merri, Merriyl, Merry

Merilyn
(English, American) combo of Merry and Lynn
Marilyn, Mer, Meralyn, Merelyn, Meri, Merill, Merilynn, Merilynne, Merri, Merrill, Merrylyn

Meris
(Latin) variant of Merissa; the sea girl
Meriss, Merris, Merrys, Merys

Merissa
(Latin) ocean-loving
Merisa, Meryssa

Merit
(American) deserving
Merite, Meritt, Meritte, Meryt, Merytt, Mirit

Merle
(Irish) shining girl
Merl, Murl, Murle

Merribeth
(English) cheerful
Merri-Beth, Merrybeth

Merrilee
(American) combo of Merri and Lee; happy
Marilee, Merilee, Merrylee, Merry-Lee

Merrill
(Irish) shines
Merril

Merry
(English) cheerful
Mer, Meri, Merie, Merree, Merrey, Merri, Merrie, Mery

Merryjane
(English) combo of Merry and Jane; happy
Merijane, Merrijane, Merrijayne, Merryjaine, Merryjayne

Mersaydes
(Invented) variant of Mercedes
Mercy, Mersa, Mersy

Mersey
(English) River Mersey; rich
Merce, Merse

Mersia
(Hebrew) variant of Mersera; princess
Mercy, Mers, Mersea, Mersy

Meryl
(German) well-known; (Irish) shining sea
Mer, Merel, Merri, Merrill, Merryl, Meryll

Mesa
(Place name) earthy
Mase, Maysa, Mesah

Mesha
(Hindi) born in lunar month; moon-loving
Meshah

Meta
(Scandinavian) short for Margaret; devoted

Mhari
(Scottish) from Mary; religious
Mhairi

Mi
(Chinese) obsessive
My, Mye

Mia
(Scandinavian, Italian) blessed; girl of mine
Me, Mea, Meah, Meea, Meya, Mya

Miaka
(Japanese) influential

Miana
(American) combo of Mi and Ana
Mianna

Micah
(Hebrew) religious
Mica, Mika, My, Myca

Micala
(Hebrew) from Michaela; wonders
Micalah, Michala, Michalah, Mikala, Mikalah, Mycala, Mycalah, Mychala, Mychalah, Mykala, Mykalah

Michaela
(Hebrew) God-loving
Meeca, Micaela, Micela, Michael, Michal, Michala, Michalla, Michela, Mikaela, Mikala, Mikela, Mycaela, Mycaela, Mycela, Mychaela, Mychela, Mykaela, Mykela

Michaelannette
(American) combo of Michael and Annette; spirited
Annette, Michelannet

Michaele
(Hebrew) loving God

Michele
(Italian, French, American) God-loving
Machele, Machelle, Mechele, Mia, Michell, Michelle, Mischel, Mischell, Mischelle, Mish, Mishell, Mishelle

Michelin
(American) lovable
Michalynn, Mish, Mishelin

Micheline
(French) form of Michele; delightful
Mishelinne

Micki
(American) quirky
Mick, Mickee, Mickey, Micky, Miki, Mikie, Mycki

Mickley
(American) form of Mickey; fun-loving
Mick, Mickaella, Micklee, Mickley, Mickli, Miklea, Miklee, Mikleigh, Mikley, Myk, Mykkie

Micole
(American) combo of Micha and Nicole; happy-go-lucky girl
Macole, Micolle

Mid
(American) middle child
Middi, Middy

Migon
(American) precious
Mignonne, Migonette, Migonn, Migonne

Mignon
(French) cute
Migonette, Mim, Mimi, Minyon, Minyonne

Miguelinda
(Spanish) combo of Miguel and Linda; strong-willed beauty
Miguel-Linda, Miguelynda

Mika
(Hebrew) wise and pious
Micah, Mikah, Mikie

Mikaela
(Hebrew) God-loving
Mik, Mikayla, Mike, Mikhaila, Miki

Mila
(Russian, Italian) short for Camilla; dearest
Milah, Milla, Millah, Mimi

Milagros
(Spanish) miracle
Mila, Milagro

Milantia
(Panamanian) calm
Mila

Mildred
(English) gentle
Mil, Mildread, Mildrid, Millie, Milly

Milena
(Greek) loving girl
Mela, Mili, Milina

Miliani
(Hawaiian) one who caresses
Mil, Mila

Milissa
(Greek) softspoken
Melissa, Missy

Milla
(Polish) gentle; pure
Mila, Millah

Millay
(Literature) soft

Millicent
(Greek, German) soft-hearted
Melicent, Melly, Milicent, Millie, Millisent, Milly, Millycent, Milycent, Missy

Millie
(English) short for Mildred and Millicent
Mil, Mili, Millee, Milley, Milli, Milly

Mim
(American) short for Miriam; cute
Mimm, Mym, Mymm

Mima
(Burmese) feminine

Mimi
(French) short for Camilla; willful
Meemee, Mim, Mims, Mimsie

Mimosa
(Botanical) sensitive; tree

Min
(Chinese) sensitive; soft-hearted

Mina
(German, Polish) resolute protector; willful
Meena, Mena, Min, Minah, Myna, Mynah

Mindy
(Greek) short for Melinda; breezy
Mindee, Mindey, Mindi, Mindie, Myndee, Myndi

Minerva
(Latin, Greek) bright; strong
Menerva, Min, Minnie, Myn

Minette
(French) loyal woman
Min, Minnette, Minnie

Ming
(Chinese) shiny; hope of tomorrow

Minhtu
(Asian) light and clear

Mini
(Scandinavian) mine

Miniver
(English) assertive
Meniver, Minever, Miniverr

Minna
(German) sturdy
Mina, Minnie, Mynna

Minnie
(German) short for Minerva
Mini, Minni, Minny

Minta
(English) memorable
Minty

Mira
(Latin, Spanish) wonderful girl
Meara, Mirror

Mirabel
(Latin) marvelous; beautiful reflection
Marabelle, Mira, Mirabell, Mirabelle

Mirabella
(Italian) marvelous
Mira, Mirabellah

Mirabelle
*Mirabell, Myrabell,
Myrabelle*

Miraclair
(Latin) combo of Mira and
Clair; wonderful; gentle
*Mira-Clair, Miraclaire,
Miraclare*

Miracle
(American) miracle baby
Merry, Mira, Mirakle, Mirry

Miranda
(Latin) unique and amazing
*Maranda, Meranda, Mira,
Mirrie, Myranda*

Mirella
(Spanish) wonderful
*Mira, Mirel, Mirela, Mirell,
Mirelle, Myrela, Myrella*

Mirelle
(Latin) wonder
Mirell, Myrell, Myrelle

Mireya
(Hebrew) form of Miriam;
melancholy

Mireyli
(Spanish) wondrous;
admirable
Mire, Mirey

Miri
(Gypsy) bittersweet
*Meeri, Miree, Mirey, Mirie,
Miry*

Miriam
(Hebrew) living with
sadness
*Mariam, Maryam, Meriam,
Miri, Miriame, Miriem,
Mirriam, Miryam, Miryem,
Mitzi, Myriam, Myriem,
Myryam, Myryem*

Mirit
(English) variant of Merit;
deserving
Miritt, Miryt, Mirytt

Mirka
(Polish) glorious
Mira, Mirk

Mirtha
(Greek) burdened
Meert, Meerta, Mirt, Mirta

Mischanna
(Hebrew) form of Miriam;
desired
*Misch, Mischana, Mish,
Mishanna, Mishke*

Mishelene
(French) form of Micheline;
pretty; believer
Mish, Misha, Mishlene

Missy
(English) short for Melissa
*Miss, Missee, Missey, Missi,
Missie*

Misty
(English) dreamy
*Miss, Missy, Mistee, Mistey,
Misti, Mistie, Mysti*

Mitten
(American) cuddly
Mitt, Mittun, Mitty

Mittie
(American) short for
Matilda and Mitten; darling
Mittee, Mittey, Mitti, Myttie

Mitzi
(German) dancer
*Mitsee, Mitzee, Mitzie,
Mitzy*

Miya
(Japanese) peaceful as a
temple
Miyah

Mnemosyne
(Greek) goddess of memory

Mo
(Irish) form of Maureen;
night-loving

Mobley
(Last name as first name)
beauty queen
*Moblee, Mobli, Moblie,
Mobly*

Mocha
(Arabic) coffee with
chocolate
Mo, Moka, Mokka

Modesty
(Latin) modest
Modesti, Modestie

Moeshea
(African American) talented
*Moesha, Moeesha, Moeshia,
Moisha, Mosha, Moysha*

Mohana
(Hindi) enchants; siren

Moina
(Hawaiian) also Moana;
ocean-loving
Moyna

Moira
(English, Irish) pure; great
one
*Maura, Moir, Moirah, Moire,
Moyrah*

Moire
(Irish) great girl

Moirin
(Irish) excellent

Mokysha
(African American) dramatic
*Kisha, Kysha, Mokesha,
Mokey*

Moll
(Literature) *Moll Flanders*;
outgoing
Mol, Molly

Molly
(Irish) jovial
*Moli, Moll, Molley, Molli,
Mollie*

Momo
(Japanese) peaches

Mona
(Greek) short for Ramona;
shining-cheeked
Monah, Mone

Monday
(American) born on
Monday; hopeful
Mondae

Moneek
(Invented) form of
Monique; saucy; advisor
Moneeke

Monet
(French) artistic
Mon, Monae, Monay

Monica
(Greek) seeking company of
others
*Mon, Mona, Monicka,
Monika, Monike, Monique*

Monical
(American) combo of
Monica and L; lively
*Monecal, Moni, Monicle,
Monikal*

Monika
(Polish) advisor

Monique
(French) saucy; advisor
*Mon, Mone, Monee,
Moneeqe, Moneeque, Moni,
Moniqe*

Monroe
(Last name as first) orderly
Monro, Monrow, Monrowe

Monserrat
(Latin) tall
Monserat

Montana
(Place name) U.S. state
Montayna, Montie, Monty

Montenia
(Spanish) climber
Monte, Montenea, Montynia

Monya
(American) confident
Mon, Monyeh

Moon
(American) dreamy
*Monnie, Moone, Moonee,
Mooney, Moonny, Moonnye*

Moon Unit
(Invented) universal appeal
Moon-Unit

Mor
(Irish) sweet

Mora
(Spanish) sweet as a
blueberry

Morag
(Scottish) goddess
Morrag

Moraima
(Spanish) forgiving
Mora, Morama

Moran
(French) dark

More
(American) bonus
Moore, Morie

Moreen
(English) good friend

Morgan
(Welsh) girl on the seashore
*Mor, Morey, Morgane,
Morgannna, Morgen,
Morgyn*

Morgander
(American) soft-spoken;
divine

Moriah
(French) dark girl;
(Hebrew) God-taught
*Mareyeh, Mariah, Moorea,
More, Moria, Morie, Morria,
Morya*

Morine
(American) form of
Maureen; fond of night
Morri

Moritza
(Place name) St. Moritz,
Switzerland; playful

Morla
(American) form of Marla;
easygoing
Morley, Morly

Morna
(French) dark

Morta
(Mythological) one of the
Roman Fates; the cutter

Morven
(American) magical
Morvee, Morvey, Morvi

Morwenna
(Welsh) seamaiden
Mo, Morwen

Morwyn
(Welsh) maiden
*Morwen, Morwenn,
Morwynn, Morwynna*

Moselle
(Hebrew) uplifted
Mose, Mozelle, Mozie

Moya
(Scandinavian) mother
Moiya, Moy

Moyra
(Irish) excellent

Muadhnait
(Irish) little noble girl

Mudiwa
(African) beloved
Mudewa

Muirne
(Irish) affectionate

Muna
(Arabic) hopes
Moona

Munira
(Irish) wishful

Murali
(Irish) seagoing

Murdina
(Slavic) dark spirit
Murdi, Murdine

Muriel
(Celtic) shining
*Meriel, Mur, Murial,
Muriele, Muriell, Murielle,
Muryel, Muryell, Muryelle*

Murphy
(Irish) spirited
*Murphee, Murphey, Murphi,
Murphie*

Murray
(Last name as first name)
brisk
Muray, Murraye

Musa
(African) child; muse

Musetta
(French) instrument;
musical
Museta

Musette
(French) instrument;
musical
Musett

Musique
(French) musical
Museek, Museke, Musik

Mussie
(American) musical
Muss, Mussi, Mussy

Mwazi
(Israeli) type of fig

Myeshia
(African American) giving
Meyeshia, Mye, Myesha

Myfanwy
(Welsh) water baby

Mykala
(Scandinavian) giving
Mykaela, Mykela, Mykie

Mykelle
(American) generous
Mykell

Myla
(English) forgiving
Miela, Mylah

Mylene
(Greek) dark-skinned girl
Myleen

Mylie
(German) forgiving
Miley, Mylee, Myli

Myna
(English) talkative
Mina, Minah

Mynola
(Invented) smart
*Minola, Monoa, Mynolla,
Mynolle*

Myra
(Latin) fragrant
Mira, Myrah

Myriam
(French) bittersweet life

Myrischa
(African American) fragrant
doll
*Myresha, Myri, Myrish,
Myrisha, Rischa*

Myrka
(Slavic) great
Mirk, Mirka, Myrk

Myrna
(Irish) loved
Merna, Mirna, Murna

Myrtle
(Greek) loving
Mertle, Mirtle, Myrt, Myrtie

Mysha
(Russian) form of Misha;
protective
Mischa, Mish, Misha, Mysh

Mysta
(Invented) mysterious
Mista, Mystah

Mystique
(French) intriguing woman
*Mistie, Mistik, Mistique,
Misty, Mystica*

Naama
(Hebrew) sweet
Naamah, Naamit

Naamah
(Biblical) sweet
Nanay, Nayamah, Naynay

Naarah
(Aramaic) bright light
Naara

Naava
(Hebrew) delightful girl
Naavah, N'Ava

Nabiha
(Arabic) noble
Naihah

Nabila
(Arabic) noble
Nabeela, Nabilah, Nabilia

Nabulungi
(African) of nobility

Nada
(Arabic) morning dew;
giving

Nadelie
(American) form of Natalie;
Christmas-born; beauty
Nadey

Nadeline
(Invented) born on
Christmas
Nad, Nadelyne

Nadette
(French) darling girl

Nadezda
(Russian) hopeful
Nadeia

Nadia
(Slavic) hopeful
*Nada, Nadea, Nadeen,
Nadene, Nadi, Nadie,
Nadina, Nadine, Nady*

Natka
(Russian) wonders; hopes

Nadidaa
(Slavic) hopes
Nadidah

Nadine
(Russian, French) dancer
*Nadeen, Nadene, Nadie,
Nadyne, Naidyne*

Nadira
(Arabic) precious gem
Nadirah, Nadra

Nadya
(Russian) optimistic; life's
beginnings

Nadyan
(Hebrew) pond; reflective
Nadian

Nadzieja
(Greek) water nymph
Nadzia, Nata, Natia, Natka

Naeemah
(African) breathtaking

Nafshiya
(Persian) precious girl

Nagida
(Hebrew) thrives
*Nagia, Nagiah, Nagiya,
Najiah, Najiya, Najiyah,
Negida*

Nagisa
(Japanese) from the shore

Nahara
(Aramaic) light
Nehara, Nehora

Nahida
(Hebrew) rich
Nahid

Nahla
(Arabic) succeeds

Nahtanha
(African) warm

Nai
(Japanese) intelligent
Nayah

Naia
(Hawaiian) water nymph

Naida
(Greek) nymph-like
Naiad, Naya, Nayad, Nyad

Nailah
(African) successful
Naila

Naimah
(Arabic) happy
Naeemah, Naima

Naja
(Greek) form of Nadia

Najat
(Arabic) safe
Nagat

Najiba
(Arabic) safe
Nagiba, Nagibah, Najibah

Najla
(Arabic) large-eyed

Najwa
(Arabic) confidante
Nagwa

Nakesha
(African American) combo
of Na and Kesha
*Naka, Nakeisha, Nakie,
Nakisha*

Nakia
(Arabic) purest girl
Nakea

Nakita
(Russian) precocious
*Nakeeta, Nakeita, Nakya,
Naquita, Nikita*

Nala
(African) loved
Nalah, Nalo

Nalani
(Hawaiian) calming
Nalanie, Nalany

Nalin
(Native American) serene
maiden

Nallely
(Spanish) friend
Nalelee, Naleley, Nallel

Nalukea
(Hawaiian) sky girl

Nami
(Japanese) rides a wave
Namiko

Namisha
(African) content with life

Namono
(African) twin

Nampeyo
(Native American) female
snake; sly
Nampayo, Nampayu

Nan
(German, Scottish, English)
bold; graceful
Na, Nana, Nannie, Nanny

Nana
(Hebrew) from Ann;
graceful

Nanabah
(Hebrew) from Ann; full of
grace

Nanala
(Hebrew) from Ann; grace

Nanalie
(American) form of Natalie;
graceful; Christmas-born
Nan, Nana, Nanalee

Nance
(American) giving
Nans

Nancy
(English, Irish) generous
woman
*Nan, Nancee, Nanci,
Nancie, Nansee, Nonie*

Nandana
(Hindi) delightful; challenges
Nandini, Nandita

Nanek
(Hebrew) from Nancy;
moves with grace
Naneka, Naneki, Naneta

Nanette
(French) giving and
gracious
Nanet

Nani
(Greek) charming beauty
Nan, Nannie

Nanice
(American) open-hearted
*Nan, Naneece, Naneese,
Naniece*

Nanise
(American) variant of Nan;
mercurial

Nanna
(Scandinavian) brave
Nana

Nanon
(French) slow to anger
Nan, Nanen

Nanvah
(African) God's gift, an
infant

Nao
(Japanese) truthful; pleasing

Naola
(American) from Naomi;
truthful

Naoma
(Hebrew) lovely

Naomi
(Hebrew) beautiful woman
*Naoma, Naomia, Naomie,
Naomy, Naynay, Nene,
Neoma, Noami, Noemi,
Noemie, Noma, Nomah,
Nomi*

Nara
(Greek, Japanese) happy;
dreamy
Narah, Nera

Narcissa
(Greek) narcissistic
*Narcisa, Narcisse, Narkissa,
Nars*

Narcissie
(Greek) conceited; daffodil
*Narci, Narcis, Narcissa,
Narcisse, Narcissey, Narsee,
Narsey, Narsis*

Narda
(Latin) fragrant

Narelle
(Australian) of the sea

Naresha
(Hindi) ruler; wise

Nari
(Japanese) thunders loudly

Narilla
(Gypsy) boisterous
Narrila, Narrilla

Nascha
(Native American) owl;
watchful

Naseem
(Hindi) breezy

Nashota
(Native American) second
twin

Nashan
(Origin unknown) miracle
child

Nasia
(Hebrew) miraculous child
*Naseea, Naseeah, Nasiah,
Nasya, Nsayah*

Nasnan
(Native American) miracle
child; mystical

Naspa
(Hebrew) form of Nasia;
wondrous
Nasia, Nasya

Nasrin
(Hindi) wild rose
Nasreen

Nastasia
(Greek, Russian) gorgeous
girl
Nas, Nastasha, Natasie

Nasya
(Hebrew) God's miracle
Nasia

Nat
(American) short for
Natalie; Christmas baby
Natt

Nata
(Latin) saving

Natalia
(Russian, Latin) born on
Christmas; beauty
*Nat, Nata, Natala, Natalea,
Natalee, Natalie, Natalya,
Nati, Nattie, Nattlee, Natty*

Natalie
(Latin) born on Christmas
*Natala, Natalee, Natalene,
Natalia, Natalina, Nataline,
Natalka, Natalya, Natelie,
Nathalia, Nathalie*

Natane
(Native American)
daughter; giving

Nataniah
(Hebrew) God's gift
*Natania, Nataniela,
Nataniella, Natanielle,
Natanya, Nathania,
Nathaniella, Nathanielle,
Netana, Netanela, Netania,
Netaniah, Netaniela,
Netaniella, Netanya,
Nethania, Nethanisah,
Netina*

Natarsha
(American) splendid
Natarsh, Natarshah

Natasha
(Latin, Russian) glorious;
born on Christmas
*Nastasia, Nastassia,
Nastassja, Nastassya,
Nastasya, Natacha,
Natashah, Natashia,
Natassia, Nitasha, Tashi,
Tashia, Tasis, Tassa, Tassie*

Natesa
(Hindi) goddess

Nathadria
(Hebrew) form of Nathan;
gift of God
*Natania, Nath, Nathe,
Nathed, Nathedrea, Natty,
Thedria*

Nathalie
(French) born on Christmas
Natalie

Nathitfa
(Arabic) unflawed
*Nathifa, Nathifah, Natifa,
Natifah*

Nation
(American) spirited; patriotic
Nashon, Nayshun

Natividad
(Spanish) Christmas baby

Natka
(Polish) hope for tomorrow

Natosha
(African American) form of
Natasha; born on Christmas
Nat, Natosh, Natoshe, Natty

Natsu
(Japanese) summer's child
Natsuko, Natsuyo

Nauasia
(Latin) variant of Nausicaa
(kind princess in *The
Odyssey*)

Naveen
(Spanish) snowing

Navita
(Hebrew) pleasure;
(Hispanic) original
Nava, Navité

Navy
(American) daughter of a
member of the Navy; dark
blue

Nawal
(Arabic) gifted

Nayana
(Irish) form of Neala; winner

Nayeli
(African) of beginnings

Nayo
(African) joy baby

Nazihah
(Arabic) truthful

Nazira
(Arabic) equality
Nazirah

Nazly
(American) idealistic
Nazlee, Nazli, Nazlie

Neal
(Irish) spirited
Neale, Neel, Neil

Neala
(Irish) spirited
*Neal, Nealie, Nealy, Neeli,
Neelie, Neely, Neila, Neile,
Neilla, Neille*

Nealy
(Irish) winner
Nealee, Nealey, Neali, Nealie

Neary
(English) variant of Nerissa;
snail; slow
*Nearee, Nearey, Neari,
Nearie, Neeree, Neerey,
Neeri, Neerie, Neery*

Neata
(Russian) from Nataliya;
born on Christmas
Neeta

Neba
(Latin) misty
Neeba, Niba, Nyba

Necedah
(Native American) yellow
hair

Nechama
(Hebrew) comforts others
*Nachmi, Necha, Neche,
Nehama*

Neche
(Spanish) pure

Nechona
(Spanish) pure

Neci
(Hungarian) intense

Necie
(Hungarian) intense
Neci

Neda
(Slavic) Sunday baby
Nedda, Neddie, Nedi

Nedaviah
(Hebrew) generous girl
Nedavia, Nedavya, Nediva

Nedda
(English) born to money
Ned, Neddy

Nedra
(English) secretive
Ned, Nedre

Neely
(Irish) sparkling smile
Nealy, Neelee, Neilie, Nelie

Neema
(Hebrew) melodious

Neenah
(Native American) flowing water

Nefris
(Spanish) glamorous
Nef, Neff, Neffy, Nefras, Nefres

Neh
(Hebrew) from Nehara; light

Neha
(Hindi) loves
Nehali, Nehi

Nehanda
(Hebrew) comforter

Neia
(African) promising

Neiley
(Irish) winner
Neelee, Neeley, Neeli, Neelie, Neely, Neilee, Neili, Neilie, Neily

Neima
(Hindi) growing; tree

Neith
(Egyptian) feminine
Neit, Neithe

Neka
(Native American) wild

Nekeisha
(African American) bold spirit
Nek, Nekeishah, Nekesha, Nekisha, Nekkie

Nekoma
(Native American) uninhibited; new moon

Nelda
(American) friend
Neldah, Nell, Nellda, Nellie

Nelia
(Spanish) short for Cornelia; yellow-haired
Neelia, Neely, Nela, Nelie, Nene

Nelka
(Spanish) yellow hair
Nela

Nell
(English) sweet charmer
Nelle, Nellie

Nellie
(English) short for Cornelia and Eleanor
Nel, Nela, Nell, Nelle, Nelli, Nelly

Nelliene
(American) form of Nellie; charming
Nell, Nelli, Nellienne

Nelvia
(Greek) brash
Nell, Nelvea

Nemera
(Hebrew) leopard; exotic

Nemesis
(Mythological) goddess of justice and retribution

Nemoria
(American) crafty
Nemorea

Nenet
(Egyptian) sea goddess

Neola
(Greek) new baby
Neolah

Nepa
(Arabic) talented

Nera
(Hebrew) candlelight
Neria, Neriah, Neriya

Nereida
(Spanish) sea nymph
Nere, Nereide, Nereyda, Neri, Nireida

Neressa
(Greek) coming from the sea
Narissa, Nene, Nerissa, Nerisse

Nerida
(Greek) sea nymph
Nerice, Nerina, Nerine, Nerisse, Neryssa, Rissa

Nerissa
(English) snail; moves slowly
Nerisa, Nerise

Nerthus
(Scandinavian) masterful

Nerys
(Welsh) ladylike
Neris, Neriss, Nerisse

Nesiah
(Greek) lamb; meek
Nesia, Nessia, Nesya, Nisia, Nisiah, Nisva

Nessa
(Irish) devout
Nessah

Nessie
(Greek) short for Vanessa
Nese, Nesi, Ness

Nest
(Welsh) pure
Nesta

Nestora
(Spanish) she is leaving
Nesto, Nestor

Neta
(Hebrew) growing and
flourishing

Netia
(Hebrew) from Neta; plant;
growing

Netira
(Spanish) flourishing

Netis
(Native American)
worthwhile

Netra
(American) maturing well
Net, Netrah, Netrya, Nettie

Netta
(Scottish) champion
Nett, Nettie

Nettie
(French) gentle
*Net, Neta, Netta, Netti,
Nettia, Netty*

Nettiemae
(American) combo of Nettie
and Mae; small-town girl
*Mae, Netimay, Nettemae,
Nettie, Nettiemay*

Neva
(Russian, English) the
newest; snow
Neeva, Neve, Niv

Nevada
(Spanish) place name; girl
who loves snow
Nev, Nevadah

Neve
(Irish) promising princess

Neviah
(Irish) from Nevina;
worshipful
Nevia

Nevina
(Irish) she worships God
Nev, Niv, Nivena, Nivina

Newlin
(Last name as first name)
healing
*Newlinn, Newlinne, Newlyn,
Newlynn*

Neyda
(Spanish) pure
Ney

Neza
(Slavic) from Agnes;
prayerful
Neysa

Ngabile
(African) aware; knowing

Ngozi
(African) fortunate

Ngu
(African) peaceful

Nguyet
(Vietnamese) moon child

Nia
(Greek) priceless
Niah

Niabi
(Native American) fawn;
docile

Niamh
(Irish) promising

Niandrea
(Invented) form of
Diandrea; pretty
Andrea, Nia, Niand, Niandre

Nibal
(Arabic) completed

Nicelda
(American) industrious
Niceld, Nicelde, Nicey

Nichele
(American) combo of Nicole
and Michele; dark-skinned
Nichel, Nichelle, Nishele

Nichole
(French) light and lively
Nichol

Nichols
(Last name as first name)
smart
*Nick, Nickee, Nickels,
Nickey, Nicki, Nickie, Nicky,
Nikels*

Nick
(American) short for Nicole
Nik

Nicki
(French) short for Nicole
Nick, Nickey, Nicky, Niki

Nicks
(American) fashionable
*Nickee, Nickie, Nicksie,
Nicky, Nix*

Nico
(Italian) victorious
Nicco, Nicko, Nikko, Niko

Nicola
(Italian) lovely singer
Nekola, Nick, Nikkie, Nikola

Nicolasa
(Spanish) spontaneous;
winning
Nico, Nicole

Nicole
(French) winning
Nacole, Nichole, Nick, Nickie, Nikki, Nikol, Nikole

Nicolette
(French) a tiny Nicole; little beauty
Nettie, Nick, Nickie, Nicoline, Nikkolette, Nikolet

Nicolie
(French) sweet
Nichollie, Nikolie

Nida
(Greek) sweet girl

Nidia
(Latin) home-loving
Nidie, Nidya

Niemi
(Origin unknown) beauty
Nyemi

Niesha
(African American) virginal
Neisha, Nesha, Nesia, Nessie

Nieves
(Spanish) snows
Neaves, Ni, Nievez, Nievis

Nihal
(Greek) from Nicole; victor

Nike
(Greek) goddess of victory; fleet of foot; a winner

Nikeesha
(American) from Nikita; joyful
Niceesha, Nickeesha, Nickisha, Nicquisha, Nykesha

Niki
(American) short for Nicole and Nikita
Nick, Nicki, Nicky, Nik, Nikki, Nikky

Niki-Lynn
(American) combo of Niki and Lynn
Nicki-Lynn, Nicky-Lynn, Nikilinn, Nikilyn

Nikita
(Russian) daring
Nakeeta, Niki, Nikki, Niquitta

Nikithia
(African American) winning; frank
Kithi, Kithia, Nikethia, Niki

Niko
(Greek) from Nikola; winning
Neeko, Nyko

Nikole
(Greek) winning
Nik, Niki

Nili
(Hebrew) plant; flourishes

Nilsine
(Scandinavian) wine; ages well

Nima
(Arabic) blessed
Neema, Neemah, Nema, Nimah

Nimesha
(American) combo of Nima and Mesha; skeptical

Nina
(Russian, Hebrew, Spanish) bold girl
Neena, Nena, Ninah

Nina-Lina
(Spanish) combo of Nina and Lina; lovely
Nina Lina, Ninalena, Ninalina

Ninetta
(American) from Nanette; cloud
Nineta

Ninette
(American) from Nanette; cloud

Nini
(Hungarian) forgiving
Ninee, Niney, Ninie, Ninnee, Ninney, Ninni, Ninnie, Niny

Ninon
(French) feminine
Ninen

Ninovan
(American) combo of Nina and Van; fast runner

Niobe
(Greek) vain

Nipa
(Hindi) stream

Nira
(Hindi) night
Neera, Nyra

Niranjana
(Hindi) full moon

Nirel
(Hebrew) light of knowledge

Nirvana
(Hindi) completion; oneness with God
Nirvahna, Nirvanah

Nirveli
(Hindi) water babe

Nisha
(Hindi) nighttime
Nishi

Nishi
(Japanese) from the west; sincere
Nishie, Nishiko, Nishiyo

Nissa
(Hebrew) symbolic
Nisa, Niss, Nissah, Nissie

Nissie
(Scandinavian) pretty; elf
Nisse, Nissee

Nita
(Hebrew) short for Juanita
Neeta, Nitali, Nite, Nittie

Nitara
(Hindi) well grounded

Nitsa
(Greek) from Helen; lovely face

Nituna
(Native American) sweet daughter

Niu
(Chinese) girlish; confident

Niva
(Spanish) variant of Neva; snowy
Neva

Nixi
(German) mystical
Nixee, Nixie

Niy
(American) lively
Nye

Nizana
(Hebrew) from Nitzana; budding beauty
Nitza, Nitzana, Zana

Noa
(Hebrew) chosen
Noah

Noami
(Hebrew) variant of Naomi; attractive
Noamee, Noamey, Noamie, Noamy

Nobantu
(African) able

Noel
(Latin) born on Christmas
Noela, Noelle, Noellie, Noli

Noelan
(Hawaiian) Christmas girl

Noelle
(French) Christmas baby
Noel, Noell

Noga
(Hebrew) light of day

Nohelia
(Hispanic) kind
Nohelya

Noicha
(African) light heart
Nolcha

Noirin
(Irish) from Norin; honored

Nokomis
(Native American) moon child

Noksu
(African) princess

Nola
(Latin) sensual
Nolah, Nolana, Nole, Nolie

Nolan
(Latin) bell; from Nola; laughing
Nolen, Nolyn

Noleta
(Latin) reluctant
Nolita

Nomalanga
(Hawaiian) lingers

Nombeko
(African) honored child

Nombese
(African) wonder girl

Nomble
(African) beautiful
Nombi

Nomusa
(African) goodhearted

Nona
(Latin) ninth; knowing
Nonah, Noni, Nonie, Nonn, Nonna, Nonnah

Noni
(Latin) ninth child

Noor
(Hindi) lights the world
Noora

Nora
(Greek, Scandinavian, Scottish) light; bright; from the north
Norah, Noreh

Noranna
(Irish) combo of Nora and Anna; honorable
Anna, Nora, Norana, Norannah, Noranne, Noreena

Norazah
(Malaysian) light

Norberta
(German) famous girl from the north

Noreen
(Latin) acknowledging others
Noreena, Norene, Noire, Norin, Norine, Norinne, Nureen

Norell
(Scandinavian) northern girl
Narelle, Norelle

Nori
(Japanese) normal

Noriko
(Japanese) follows tradition

Norika
(Japanese) athletic
Nori, Norike

Norlaili
(Asian) northern

Norma
(Latin) gold standard
Noey, Nomah, Norm, Normah, Normie

Norna
(Scandinavian) time goddess

Norris
(English) serious
Nore, Norrus

Nota
(American) negative
Na, Nada, Not

Notaku
(Asian) dealing with grief

Noula
(Irish) from Nuala; white
Noulah

Noura
(Arabic) light girl
Nourah

Nourbese
(African) wonderful

Nova
(Latin) energetic; new
Noova, Novah, Novella, Novie

Novak
(Last name as first name) emphatic
Novac

Novella
(Latin) new

Novena
(Latin) blessing; prayerful
Noveena, Novina, Novyna

Novia
(Spanish) sweetheart
Nov, Novie, Nuvia

Nowell
(American) variant of Noelle; gives
Nowel, Nowele, Nowelle

Nu
(Vietnamese) confident
Niu

Nudar
(Arabic) golden girl

Nueva
(Spanish) new; fresh
Nue, Nuey

Nuha
(Arabic) great mind

Numa
(Spanish) delightful
Num

Numa-Noe
(Spanish) combo of Numa and Noe; delight
Numanoe

Nuna
(Native American) girl of the land

Nunia
(Native American) girl of the land

Nunibelle
(American) combo of Nuni and Belle; pretty
Nunibell, Nunnibelle

Nunu
(Vietnamese) friendly

Nur
(Arabic) bright light
Nura, Nuri, Nurya

Nura
(Aramaic) light-footed
Noora, Noura, Nurrie

Nuria
(Arabic) light
Noor, Noura, Nur, Nuriah, Nuriel

Nurit
(Hebrew) from Nurita; flower
Nurice, Nurita

Nurlene
(American) boisterous
Nerlene, Nurleen

Nuru
(African) light of day

Nusi
(Hungarian) from Hannah; blessed girl

Nutan
(Native American) variant of Nutah; heart

Nuvia
(American) new
Nuvea

Nydia
(Latin) nest-loving; home and hearth woman
Nidia, Nidiah, Ny, Nydiah, Nydie, Nydya

Nyla
(Arabic) successful; astounding
Nila

Nylene
(American) shy
Nyle, Nylean, Nyleen, Nyles, Nyline

Nyree
(Asian) seagoing

Nysa
(Greek) life-starting
Nisa, Nissa, Nissie, Nysa, Nyssa

Nyura
(African) light

Nyx
(Greek) lively
Nix

Oba
(Mythology) river goddess

Obala
(African) from Oba; river goddess
Oballa, Obla, Obola

Obede
(English) obedient
Obead

Obedience
(American) obedient
Obey

Obelia
(Greek) needle; cautious
Obellia, Obel, Obiel

Obey
(American) obedient

Obioma
(African) kind

Oceana
(Greek) ocean-loving; name given to those with astrological signs that have to do with water
Oceonne, Ocie, Oh

Ocin
(Origin unknown) comes into life

Octavia
(Latin) eighth child; born on eighth day of the month; musical
Octave, Octavie, Octivia, Octtavia, Ottavia, Tave, Tavi, Tavia, Tavie

Oda
(Hebrew) praises the Lord

Odalis
(Spanish) humorous
Odales, Odallis, Odalous, Odalus

Oddrun
(Scandinavian) secret love
Oda, Odd, Oddr

Oddveig
(Scandinavian) woman with spears

Ode
(African) born on a road

Odeda
(Hebrew) strength of character

Odeen
(Hebrew) praises

Odele
(Hebrew, Greek) melodious
Odela, Odelle, Odie

Odelette
(Greek) melodic; rich
Odelet, Odette

Odelia
(Hebrew, Greek) singer of spiritual songs
Odele, Odelle, Odie, Odila, Odile, Othelia

Odelinda
(Hebrew) praises

Odelita
(Spanish) vocalist
Odelite

Odera
(Hebrew) works the soil

Odessa
(Place name) traveler on an odyssey
Odessah, Odie, Odissa

Odette
(French) good girl
Oddette, Odet, Odetta

Odhairnait
(Irish) little and green; elfin-like

Odile
(French) sensuous
Odyll

Odilia
(Spanish) wealthy
Eudalia, Odalia, Odella, Odylia, Othilia

Odina
(Native American) mountain girl

Odine
(Scandinavian) rules

Odiya
(Hebrew) God's song

Ofa
(Polynesian) loving

Ofira
(Hebrew) golden girl

Ogin
(Native American) rose

Ohara
(Japanese) meditative
Oh

Ohela
(Hebrew) tent; nature-loving

Oheo
(Native American) beauty

Oira
(Latin) from Ora; prays

Okalani
(Hawaiian) heavenly child

Okei
(Japanese) from Oki; ocean girl

Oki
(Japanese) born mid-ocean; loves the water

Oksana
(Russian) praise to God
Oksanah, Oksie

Ola
(Scandinavian) bold
Olah

Olabisi
(African) joy

Olaide
(American) lovely; thoughtful
Olai, Olay, Olayde

Olaug
(Scandinavian) loves her ancestors; loyal

Oldriska
(Czech) ruling noble
Olda, Oldra, Oldrina, Olina, Oluse

Oleda
(Spanish) audacious

Oleia
(Greek) smooth

Olena
(Russian) generous
Olenya

Olenka
(Russian) from Helen; lovely

Olenta
(Origin unknown) sweet

Olesia
(Greek) regal

Oleta
(Greek) true
Oletta

Olga
(Russian) holy woman
Ola, Olgah, Ollie

Oliana
(Polynesian) oleander; beautiful

Olida
(Spanish) lighthearted
Oleda

Olidie
(Spanish) light
Oli, Olidee, Olydie

Olina
(Hawaiian) joy
Oleen, Oline

Olinda
(Latin) fragrant

Oline
(Hawaiian) happy
Olina

Olino
(Spanish) scented
Olina, Oline

Olisa
(African) loves God

Olive
(Latin) subtle
Olyve

Olivia
(English) flourishing
*Olive, Olivea, Oliveah,
Oliviah, Ollie*

Olubayo
(African) resplendent

Olufemi
(African) God loves her

Olva
(Latin) from Olivia; olive
tree; natural girl

Olvyen
(Welsh) footprint in white;
lasting impression

Olwen
(Welsh) magical; white
Olwynn

Olya
(Latin) perfect
Olyah

Olympia
(Greek) heavenly woman
*Olimpia, Ollie, Olympe,
Olympie*

Olynda
(Invented) form of Lynda;
fragrant; pretty
*Lyn, Lynda, Olin, Olinda,
Olynde*

Oma
(German) grandmother;
(Hebrew) pious
Omah

Omana
(Hindi) womanly

Omanie
(Origin unknown) exuberant
Omanee

Omayra
(Latin) fragrant
(Spanish) beloved
Oma, Omyra

Omega
(Greek) last is best

Omemee
(Native American) dove;
peaceful

Omesha
(African American) splendid
Omesh, Omie, Omisha

Omie
(Italian) homebody
Omee

Ominotago
(Native American) sweet
sound

Omolara
(African) birth timed well;
welcome baby

Omora
(Arabic) red-haired

Omorose
(African) lovely

Omri
(Arabic) red-haired

Omusa
(African) adored

Omusupe
(African) precious baby

Ona
(Latin) the one
Oona

Onatah
(Native American) earth
child

Onawa
(Native American) alert

Ondina
(Latin) water spirit
Ondi, Ondine, Onyda

Ondrea
(Czech) from Andrea; svelte
Ondra

Ondreja
(Czech) from Andrea; pretty
girl

Oneida
(Native American)
anticipated
*Ona, Oneeda, Onida, Onie,
Onyda*

Oneshia
(American) combo of Oney
and Neshia; one who waits

Oni
(African) desired child

Onia
(Latin) one and only

Onie
(Latin) flamboyant
Oh, Oona, Oonie, Una

Onora
(Latin) honorable
Onoria, Onorine

Ontina
(Origin unknown) an open
mind
Ontine

Onyx
(Latin) pretty shine

Oona
(Latin) one alone
Oonagh, Oonah

Opa
(Native American) owl;
stares

Opal
(Hindi) the opal; precious
Opale, Opalle, Opie

Opalina
(Sanskrit) gem
Opaline

Ophelia
(Greek) helpful woman;
character from
Shakespeare's *Hamlet*
*Ofelia, Ofilia, Ophela,
Ophelie, Ophlie, Phelia,
Phelie*

Ophira
(Hebrew) fawn; lovable
Ofira

Opportina
(Italian) sees opportunity;
successful
Opportuna

Oprah
(Hebrew) one who soars;
excellent
*Ophie, Ophrie, Opra, Oprie,
Orpah*

Ora
(Greek) glowing
Orah, Orie

Orabel
(Latin) believes in prayer
*Orabelle, Oribel, Oribella,
Oribelle*

Oraleyda
(Spanish) light of dawn
Ora, Oraleydea, Oralida

Oralie
(Hebrew) light of dawn
Oralee, Orali, Orla

Orange
(Color name) sparkly

Orbelina
(American) excited, dawn
*Lina, Orbe, Orbee, Orbeline,
Orbey, Orbi, Orby*

Ordella
(Latin) from Ora; prays

Orea
(Latin) from Ora; prays

Oreille
(Latin) from Oriel; gold

Orela
(Latin) from Oriel; golden girl

Orella
(Latin) golden girl
Oralla

Orenda
(Place name) Orinda,
California; lovely gold

Orene
(French) nurturing
Orane, Orynne

Orfelinda
(Spanish) pretty dawn
Orfelinde, Orfelynda

Orianna
(Latin) sunny; dawn
*Oria, Orian, Oriana, Oriane,
Orianna, Oriannah, Orie*

Orin
(Irish) dark-haired
Oren, Orinn

Oringa
(Invented) variant of
Orinda; golden

Orino
(Japanese) works outside
Ori

Oriole
(Latin) golden light
*Oreilda, Oreole, Oriel,
Oriella, Oriol, Oriola*

Oritha
(Greek) motherly

Orithna
(Greek) natural

Orla
(Irish) gold

Orlain
(French) famed

Orlanda
(German) celebrity

Orlaith
(Irish) golden lady

Orlena
(Russian) sharp-eyed

Orlenda
(Russian) eagle-eyed
Orlinda

Orly
(French) busy
Orlee

Ormanda
(Latin) noble
Ormie

Orna
(Irish) dark-haired
Ornah, Ornas, Ornie

Ornice
(Irish) pale face

Orpah
(Hebrew) escapes; fawn
*Ophra, Ophrah, Orpa,
Orpha, Orphy*

Orsa
(Greek) from Ursula;
stubborn

Orseline
(Latin) bearlike

Ortensia
(Italian) from Hortense; joiner

Orthia
(Greek) straightforward

Ortrud
(Scandinavian) variant of Gertrude; fresh
Ortrude

Orva
(French) golden girl
Or, Orvan, Orvah

Orya
(Origin unknown) forthcoming

Osana
(Latin) praises the Lord

Osarma
(Origin unknown) sleek

Osen
(Japanese) one in a thousand

Oseye
(African) happy

Osithe
(Place name) variant of Ostia, Italy; together
Osyth

Osyka
(Native American) eagle-eyed

Otha
(German) excels

Otilie
(Czech) fortunate girl

Otina
(Origin unknown) fortunate

Ottavia
(English) from Octavia; eighth

Otthild
(German) prospers
Ottila, Ottilia, Ottilie, Otylia

Ottilie
(Czech) lucky omen

Ottolee
(English) combo of Otto and Lee; appealing
Ottalie, Ottilie

Otylia
(Polish) rich
Oteelya

Ouida
(Literature) romantic

Ourania
(Greek) heavenly

Ovalia
(Spanish) helpful
Ova, Ove, Ovelia

Ovida
(Hebrew) worships

Ovyena
(Spanish) helps

Owena
(Welsh) feisty
Oweina, Owina, Owinne

Oya
(Africa) invited to earth

Oyama
(African) called out

Oza
(African) strong

Ozara
(Hebrew) treasured
Ozarah

Ozera
(Hebrew) of merit

Ozioma
(Origin unknown) strength of character

Ozora
(Hebrew) rich

Paavna
(Hindi) pure

Paavani
(Hindi) purity of the river

Pabiola
(Spanish) small girl
Pabby, Pabi, Pabiole

Paca
(Spanish) free girl

Pace
(Last name as first name) charismatic
Pase

Pacifica
(Spanish) peaceful
Pacifika

Padgett
(French) growing and learning; lovely-haired
Padge, Padget, Paget, Pagett, Pagette

Padma
(Hindi) lotus blossom

Page
(French) sharp; eager
Pagie, Paige, Paje, Payge

Pageant
(American) theatrical
Padg, Padge, Padgeant, Padgent, Pagent

Paili
(Irish) wished-for child

Paisley
(Scottish) patterned
Paislee, Pazley

Paiton
(English) from a warring town; sad

Paka
(African) kitty cat

Pal
(American) friend; buddy

Pala
(Native American) water

Palakika
(Hawaiian) much loved

Palemon
(Spanish) kind
Palem, Palemond

Paley
(Last name as first name) wise
Palee, Palie

Palila
(Polynesian) bird; free flight

Palla
(Greek) from Pallas; wise

Pallas
(Greek) wise woman
Palace, Palas

Palma
(Latin) successful
Palmah, Palmeda, Palmedah

Palmer
(Latin) palm tree; balmy

Palmira
(Spanish) palm-tree girl
Palmyra

Paloma
(Spanish) dove
Palloma, Palometa, Palomita, Peloma

Pamela
(Greek) sweet as honey
Pam, Pamala, Pamalia, Pamalla, Pamee, Pamelia, Pamelina, Pamelinn, Pamella, Pamelyn, Pamilla, Pammee, Pammela, Pammi, Pammie, Pammy, Pamyla, Pamylla

Pana
(Native American) partridge; small

Pandita
(Hindi) learned

Pandora
(Greek) a gift; curious
Pan, Pand, Panda, Pandie, Pandorah, Pandorra, Panndora

Pang
(Chinese) innovative

Pangiota
(Greek) all is holy

Panna
(Hindi) emerald; knowing

Panola
(Greek) all

Panphila
(Greek) all loving
Panfila, Panfyla, Panphyla

Pansy
(Greek) fragrant
Pan, Pansey, Pansie, Panze, Panzee, Panzie

Panthea
(Greek) loves all gods

Panther
(Greek) wild; all gods
Panthar, Panthea, Panthur, Panth

Panya
(Greek) she is crowned

Panyin
(African) the older twin

Paola
(Italian) firebrand

Paolabella
(Italian) lovely firebrand

Papina
(African) vine; clings

Paradise
(Word as name) dream girl

Paris
(French) capital of France; graceful woman
Pareece, Parie, Parice, Parisa, Parris, Parrish

Parker
(English) noticed; in the park
Park, Parke, Parkie

Parminder
(Hindi) attractive

Parnelle
(French) small stone
Parn, Parnel, Parnell, Parney

Parslee
(Botanical) complementary
Pars, Parse, Parsley, Parsli

Parthenia
(Greek) from the Parthenon;
virtuous
*Parthania, Parthe, Parthee,
Parthena, Parthene,
Parthenie, Parthina,
Parthine, Pathania, Pathena,
Pathenia, Pathina, Thenia*

Parthenope
(Greek) siren

Parvani
(Hindi) full moon
Parvina

Parvati
(Hindi) mountain child

Parvin
(Hindi) star
Parveen

Pascale
(French) born on a religious
holiday
*Pascal, Pascalette,
Pascaline, Pascalle,
Paschale, Paskel, Paskil*

Pascasia
(French) born on Easter
Paschasia

Paschel
(African) spiritual
Paschell

Pash
(French) clever
Pasch

Pasha
(Greek) lady by the sea
Passha

Passion
(American) sensual
*Pashun, Pasyun, Pass,
Passyun*

Pasua
(French) Easter child

Pat
(Latin) short for Patricia;
tough
Patt, Patty

Paterekia
(Hawaiian) patrician
Pakelekia

Pati
(African) gathers fish

Patia
(Latin) short for Patricia;
hard-minded

Patience
(English) woman of patience
*Pacience, Paciencia, Pat,
Pattie*

Patrice
(French) form of Patricia;
svelte
*Pat, Patreas, Patreece,
Pattie, Pattrice, Trece, Treecc*

Patricia
(Latin) woman of nobility;
unbending
*Pat, Patreece, Patreice,
Patria, Patric, Patrica,
Patrice, Patricka, Patrizia,
Patrisha, Patsie, Patsy,
Patti, Pattie, Patty, Tricia,
Trish, Trisha*

Patrina
(American) noble; patrician
*Patryna, Patrynna, Tryna,
Trynnie*

Patsy
(Latin) short for Patricia;
brassy
*Pat, Patsey, Patsi, Patsie,
Patti, Patty*

Patty
(English) short for Patricia
and Patrice; sweet
Pat, Pati, Patti, Pattie

Paula
(Latin) small and feminine
*Paola, Paolina, Paulah,
Paule, Pauleen, Paulene,
Pauletta, Paulette, Paulie,
Paulina, Pauline, Paulita,
Pauly, Paulyn, Pavla,
Pavlina, Pavlinka, Pawlah,
Pawlina, Pola*

Paulette
(French) form of Paula; little
Paula
*Paula, Paulett, Paulie,
Paullette*

Paulina
(Latin) small; (Italian) lovely
Paula, Paulena, Paulie

Pauline
(Latin) short for Paula;
precocious
Pauleen, Paulene

Pausha
(Hindi) lunar month;
moonlike

Pavana
(Origin unknown) from
Paulina; ravishing
Pavani

Pax
(Latin) peace goddess

Paxton
(Latin) peaceful
Pax, Paxten, Paxtun

Payton
(Last name as first name)
aggressive
*Pay, Paye, Payten, Paytun,
Peyton*

Paz
(Hebrew, Spanish)
sparkling; peaceful
*Paza, Pazia, Paziah, Pazice,
Pazit, Paziya, Pazya*

Paza
(Hebrew) golden child
Paz

Pazzy
(Latin) peaceful
Paz, Pazet

Peace
(English) peaceful woman
Pea, Peece

Peaches
(American) outrageously
sweet
Peach, Peachy

Peakalika
(Hawaiian) happiness

Pearl
(Latin) jewel from the sea
*Pearla, Pearle, Pearaleen,
Pearlena, Pearlette, Pearley,
Pearlie, Pearline, Pearly,
Perl, Perla, Perle, Perlette,
Perley, Perlie, Perly*

Pecola
(American) brash
Pekola

Pedzi
(Origin unknown) gold

Pefilia
(Spanish) profile

Pega
(Greek) from Peggy; happy

Peggy
(Greek) pearl; priceless
Peg, Peggi, Peggie

Pegma
(Greek) happy

Pei
(Place name) village; from
Tang Pei, China

Peigi
(Scottish) pearl; priceless

Peke
(Hawaiian) from Bertha;
gives

Pela
(Polish) loves the sea;
special

Pelagia
(Polish) sea girl
*Pelage, Pelageia, Pelagie,
Pelegia, Pelgia, Pellagia*

Pelagla
(Greek) girl of the sea
*Pelagie, Pelagi, Pelagia,
Pelagias, Pelaga*

Pele
(Hawaiian) volcano;
conflicted

Peleka
(Hawaiian) strong; marvel

Pelham
(English) thoughtful
*Pelhim, Pellam, Pellham,
Pellie*

Pelia
(Hebrew) marvelous
Peliah, Pelya, Pelyia

Pelika
(Hawaiian) strong

Pelipa
(African) loves horses
Phillipa

Pelulio
(Hawaiian) sea treasure

Pemba
(African) powerful

Penda
(African) beloved

Pendant
(French) necklace; adorned
Pendan, Pendanyt

Penelope
(Greek) patient; weaver of
dreams
*Pela, Pelcia, Pen, Penalope,
Penelopa, Penina, Penine,
Penna, Pennelope, Penni,
Pennie, Penny, Pinelopi,
Popi*

Peni
(Greek) thinker

Peninah
(Hebrew) pearl; lovely
*Peni, Penie, Penina, Penini,
Peninit, Penny*

Penny
(Greek) short for Penelope;
spunky
Pen, Penee, Penni, Pennie

Penthea
(Spanish) orchid; lovely
*Fentheam, Fentheas, Pentha,
Pentheam, Pentheas*

Peony
(Greek) flowering; giving praise
Pea, Peoni, Peonie

Peoria
(Place name) poised

Pepita
(Spanish) high-energy
Pepa, Peppita, Peta

Pepper
(Latin) spicy
Pep, Peppie, Peppyr

Peppy
(American) cheerful
Pep, Peppey, Peppi, Peps

Perach
(Hebrew) flowering
Perah, Pericha, Pircha, Pirchia, Pirchit, Pirchiya, Pirha

Perdita
(Latin) wanders away

Perel
(Latin) tested
Perele

Perfecta
(Spanish) perfection
Perfekta

Peril
(Latin) victor

Periwinkle
(Botanical) blue-eyed; flower girl

Perla
(Latin) substantial
Perlah

Peridot
(Arabic) green gem; treasured
Peri

Perlace
(Spanish) small pearl
Perl, Perlahse, Perlase, Perly

Perlette
(French) pearl; treasured
Pearl, Pearline, Peraline, Perl, Perle, Perlett

Perlie
(Latin) form of Pearl
Perli, Purlie, Perly

Perlina
(American) small pearl
Pearl, Perl, Perlinna, Perlyna

Pernella
(Scandinavian) rock; dependable
Pernelle, Parnella, Pernilla

Pernille
(Scandinavian) rock; safe

Peron
(Latin) travels

Perouze
(Armenian) turquoise gemstone
Perou, Perous, Perouz, Perry

Perpetua
(Spanish) lasting

Perri
(Greek, Latin) outdoorsy
Peri, Perr, Perrie, Perry

Persephone
(Greek) breath of spring
Pers, Perse, Persefone, Persey

Persis
(Latin) from Persia; exotic
Perssis

Pesha
(Hebrew) flourishing
Peshah, Peshia

Peshe
(Hebrew) saved

Pershella
(American) philanthropic
Pershe, Pershel, Pershelle, Pershey, Persie, Persy

Persia
(Place name) colorful
Persha, Perzha

Peta
(English) saucy
Pet, Petra, Petrice, Petrina, Petrona, Petty

Petra
(Slavic) glamorous; capable
Pet, Peti, Petrah, Pett, Petti, Pietra

Petrine
(Scandinavian) rock

Petronilla
(Greek) form of Peter; rock; dependable
Petria, Petrina, Petrine, Petro, Petrone, Petronela, Petronella, Pett

Petula
(Latin) petulant song
Pet, Petulah, Petulia

Petunia
(American) flower; perky
Pet, Petune

Pfeiffer
(Last name as first) lovely blonde; talented

Phaedra
(Greek) bright
Faydra, Faydrah, Padra, Phae, Phedra

Phan
(Asian) shares

Phashestha
(American) decorative
Phashey, Shesta

Pheakkley
(Vietnamese) faithful

Pheba
(Greek) smiling
Phibba

Phedra
(Greek) bright child
Faydra, Fedra, Phadra, Phaedra, Phedre

Phemia
(Greek) language

Phenice
(Origin unknown) enjoys life
Phenicia, Pheni, Phenica, Venice

Pheodora
(Greek) God's gift to mankind

Phernita
(American) articulate
Ferney, Phern

Phia
(Irish) saint

Phila
(Greek) loving
Phil, Philly

Philadelphia
(Greek) loving one's fellow man
Fill, Phil, Philly

Philana
(Greek) loving
Filana, Filly, Philly

Philantha
(Greek) loves flowers

Philberta
(English) intellectual

Philene
(Greek) loving others

Philida
(Greek) loving others
Philina, Phillada, Phillida

Philippa
(Greek) horse lover
Feefee, Felipa, Phil, Philipa, Philippe, Phillie, Phillipina, Phillippah, Pippa, Pippy

Philise
(Greek) loving
Felece, Felice, Philese

Philly
(Place name) from Philadelphia, Pennsylvania
Filly, Philee, Phillie

Philomena
(Greek) beloved
Filomena, Filomina, Mena, Phil, Phillomenah, Philomen, Philomene, Philomina

Phiona
(Scottish) variant of Fiona; special
Phionna

Phira
(Greek) loves music

Phoebe
(Greek) bringing light
Febe, Fee, Feebe, Feebs, Pheabe, Phebe, Phebee, Pheby, Phobe, Phoeb, Phoebey, Phoebie, Phoebs

Phoenix
(Place name) U.S. city; (Greek) rebirth
Fee, Fenix, Fenny, Phenix, Phoe

Phonsa
(Origin unknown) jubilant

Photina
(Origin unknown) fashionable

Phylicia
(Greek) fortunate girl
Felicia, Phillie, Phyl, Phylecia

Phyllida
(Greek) lovely; leafy bough
Filida, Phyll, Phyllyda

Phyllis
(Greek) beautiful; leafy bough; articulate; smitten
Fillice, Fillis, Phil, Philis, Phillis, Philliss, Phillisse, Phyl, Phylis, Phyllys

Pia
(Latin) devout
Peah, Piah

Picabo
(American) place name
Peekaboo

Piedad
(Spanish) devout

Pier
(Greek) form of Peter; rock; reliable
Peer

Pierette
(Greek) reliable
Perett, Perette, Piere

Pierina
(Greek) dependable
Peir, Per, Perina, Perine, Pieryna

Pilar
(Spanish) worthwhile; pillar of strength

Pili
(Spanish) pillar; strength

Pililani
(Hawaiian) strong one

Pilisi
(Hawaiian) simple life

Piluki
(Hawaiian) little leaf; small

Pilvi
(Italian) cheerful
Pilvee

Pineki
(Hawaiian) peanut; tiny girl

Pinga
(Hindi) dark

Pingjarje
(Native American) shy; little doe

Pink
(American) blushing
Pinkee, Pinkie, Pinky, Pinkye, Pynk

Pinquana
(Native American) fragrant girl

Piper
(English) player of a pipe; musical

Pippa
(English) ebullient; horse-lover
Pip, Pipa

Pippi
(English) blushing; (French) loving horses
Pip, Pippie, Pippy

Pirene
(French) rock; dependable

Pirouette
(French) ballet term
Piro, Pirouet, Pirouetta

Pita
(English) comforting

Pitana
(Origin unknown) accented

Pitarra
(American) interesting
Pitarr Peta, Petah

Pity
(American) sad
Pitee, Pitey, Pitie

Pixie
(American) small; perky
Pixee, Pixey, Pixi

Placida
(Latin) serenity
Plasida

Platinum
(English) from the Spanish Platinal; fine metal
Plati, Platnum

Platona
(Spanish) good friend

Pleasance
Pleasant, Pleasants, Pleasence

Pleshette
(American) plush
Plesh

Pleun
(Origin unknown) wordsmith

Plum
(Botanical) fruit; healthy

Po
(Italian) effervescent
Poe

Pocahontas
(Native American) joyful
Poca, Poka

Poe
(Last name as first name) mysterious

Poetry
(Word as name) romantic
Poe, Poesy, Poet

Polete
(Hawaiian) small; kind
Poleke, Polina

Polina
(Russian) small
Po, Pola, Polya

Polly
(Irish) devout; joyous
Pauleigh, Paulie, Pol, Pollee, Polley, Polli, Pollie

Pollyanna
(American, English) combo of Polly and Anna; happy-go-lucky
Polianna, Polliana, Pollie-anna, Polly

Polyxena
(Mythology) very hospitable
Pomona
(Latin) apple of my eye
Pomonah
Pompa
(Last name as first name)
pompous
Pompy
Pompey
(Place name) lavish
Pomp, Pompee, Pompei,
Pompy
Poni
(African) second daughter
Pony
(American) wild west girl
Poney, Ponie
  Poodle
  (American) sweet; curly-
  haired
  Poo, Pood, Poodly
Poonam
(Hindi) kind soul
Poppy
(Latin) flower; bouncy girl
Pop, Poppi, Poppie
Pora
(Hebrew) fertile
Porsche
(Latin) giving; high-minded
Porsh, Porsha, Porshe,
Porshie, Portia
Porsha
(German) giving
Porshea

Portia
(Latin) a giving woman
Porcha, Porscha, Porsh,
Porsha, Porshuh
Posala
(Native American) good-bye
to spring
Posh
(American) fancy girl
Posha
Posy
(American) sweet
Posee, Posey, Posie
Poupée
(French) doll
Pou
Powder
(American) gentle; light
Pow, Powd, Powdy, Powdyr,
PowPow
Pragyata
(Hindi) knowledgeable
Prarthana
(Hindi) prays
Pratibha
(Hindi) understanding
Precia
(Latin) important
Preciah, Presha, Presheah,
Preshuh
Precious
(English) beloved
Precia, Preciosa, Preshie,
Preshuce, Preshus
Prema
(Hindi) love
Premlata
(Hindi) loving

Prescilian
(Hispanic) fashionable
Pres, Priss
Presencia
(Spanish) presents well
Presley
(English) talented
Preslee, Preslie, Presly,
Prezlee, Prezley, Prezly
Pribislava
(Polish) glorifed; helpful
Pribena, Pribka, Pribuska
Price
(Welsh) loving
Pri, Prise, Pry, Pryce, Pryse
Prima
(Latin) first; fresh
Primalia, Primetta, Primia,
Primie, Primina, Priminia,
Primma, Primula
Primalia
(Spanish) prime; first
Primavera
(Italian) spring child
Primola
(Botanical) flower; from
primrose; first
Prim, Prym, Prymola
Primrose
(English) rosy; fragrant
Prim, Primie, Rosie, Rosy
Princess
(English) precious
Prin, Prince, Princesa,
Princessa, Princie, Prinsess

Prinscella
(American) combo of
Princess and Priscilla;
princess
*Princella, Prins, Prinsce,
Prinscilla, Prinsee, Prinsey*

Prisca
(Latin) old spirit

Prisciliana
(Spanish) wise; old
Cissy, Priscili, Priss, Prissy

Priscilla
(Latin) wisdom of the ages
*Cilla, Precilla, Prescilla,
Pricilla, Pris, Priscella,
Priscila, Prisilla, Priss,
Prissie, Prissilla, Prissy,
Prysilla*

Prisisima
(Spanish) wise and feminine
Priss, Prissy, Sima

Prisma
(Hindi) cherished baby

Prissy
(Latin) short for Priscilla;
wise; feminine
Prisi, Priss, Prissie

Priti
(Hindi) lovely

Pristina
(Latin) pristine

Priya
(Hindi) sweetheart
Preeya, Preya, Priyah

Prochora
(Latin) leads

Promise
(American) sincere
Promis

Proserpine
(Mythology) queen of the
underworld; secretive

Prospera
(Latin) does well

Protima
(Hindi) dancing girl

Prova
(French) place name;
Provence
Pro, Proa, Provah

Pru
(Latin) short for Prudence
Prudie, Prue

Prudence
(Latin) wise; careful
*Perd, Pru, Prudencia,
Prudie, Prudince, Pruds,
Prudu, Prudy, Prue*

Prunella
(Latin) shy
Pru, Prue, Prune, Prunie

Pryor
(Last name as first name)
wealthy
Prieyer, Pryar, Prye, Pryer

Psyche
(Greek) soulful
Sye, Sykie

Pua
(Hawaiian) flower

Pulcheria
(Italian) chubby; curvy
Pulchia

Puma
(American) cougar; wild
spirit
*Poom, Pooma, Poomah,
Pumah, Pume*

Purity
(English) virginal
Puretee, Puritie

Purnima
(Hindi) full moon baby

Pyera
(Italian) sturdy; formidable;
rock
Pyer, Pyerah

Pyllyon
(English) enthusiastic
Pillion, Pillyon, Pillyun

Pyrena
(Greek) fiery temper

Pyria
(Origin unknown) cherished
Pyra, Pyrea

Pyrrha
(Latin) fire

Pythia
(Greek) prophet

Qadira
(Arabic) wields power
Kadira

Qamra
(Arabic) moon girl
Kamra

Qing
(Origin unknown) quick

Qitarah
(Arabic) aromatic

Qiturah
(Arabic) aromatic
Qeturah, Quetura, Queturah

Q-Malee
(American) form of Cumale;
open-hearted
*Cue, Q, Quemalee, Quemali,
Quemalie*

Quan
(Chinese) goddess of
compassion

Quanda
(English) queenly
*Kwanda, Kwandah,
Quandah, Qwanda*

Quanella
(African American)
sparkling
Kwannie, Quanela

Quanesha
(African American) singing
*Kwaeesha, Kwannie,
Quaneisha, Quanisha*

Quanika
(American) combo of Quan
and Nika; joyful
*Quanikka, Quanikki,
Quanique, Quawanica*

Quantina
(American) brave queen
*Kwantina, Kwantynna,
Quantinna, Quantyna, Tina*

Qubilah
(Arabic) easygoing

QueAnna
(American) combo of Que
and Anna; genuine
*Keana, KeAnna, KeeAnna,
Queana*

Queen
(English) regal; special
*Quanda, Queena,
Queenette, Queenie*

Queenie
(English) royal and dignified
*Kweenie, Quee, Queen,
Queeny*

Queenverlyn
(Invented) combo of Queen
and Verlyn; lady
Queenee, Queenie

Queisha
(American) contented child
Queysha, Queshia

Quenby
(Swedish) feminine
*Quenbee, Quenbey, Quenbi,
Quenbie, Quinbee, Quinbie,
Quinby*

Quenna
(English) feminine
Kwenna

Querida
(Spanish) dear one

Questa
(French) looking for love
Kesta

Queta
(Spanish) head of the
house
Keta

Quiana
(Origin unknown) from
Hannah; practical
*Qiana, Qianna, Quianna,
Quiyanna*

Quilla
(English) writer
*Kwila, Kwilla, Quila, Quillah,
Quyla, Quylla*

Quinby
(Scandinavian) living like
royalty
*Quenby, Quin, Quinbie,
Quinnie*

Quinceanos
(Spanish) fifteenth child
Quin, Quince, Quincy

Quincy
(French) fifth
*Quince, Quincey, Quinci,
Quincie, Quincy, Quinsy*

Quincylla
(American) popular; fifth
child
Cylla, Quince, Quincy

Quinella
(Latin) a girl who is as
pretty as two
Quinn

Quinn
(English, Irish) smart
Quin, Quinnie

Quinta
(Latin) fifth day of the month

Quintana
(Latin) fifth; lovely girl
Quentana, Quinn

Quintessa
(Latin) essential goodness

Quintina
(Latin) fifth child
Quentina, Quintana,
Quintessa, Quintona,
Quintonette, Quintonice

Quintilla
(Latin) fifth girl
Quintina

Quintona
(Latin) fifth

Quintwana
(American) fifth girl in the
family
Quintuana

Quinyette
(American) likeable; fifth
child
Kwenyette, Quiny

Quirina
(Latin) contentious

Quisha
(African American) beautiful
mind
Keisha, Kesha, Key

Quita
(Latin) peaceful
Keeta, Keetah

Rabab
(Origin unknown) different

Rabiah
(Arabic) breezy

Rabbit
(American) lively; energetic
Rabit

Rabia
(Arabic) wind

Rachael
(Hebrew) peaceful as a lamb
Rach, Rachaele, Rachal,
Rachel, Rachie, Rae,
Raechal, Rasch, Ray, Raye

Racheline
(American) combo of Rachel
and Line
Rachelene

Rachelle
(French) calm
Rach, Rachell, Rashell,
Rashelle, Rochelle

Racquel
(French) friendly
Racquelle, Raquel

Rada
(Polish) glad

Radha
(Hindi) successful
Radhika

Radmilla
(Slavic) glad; hardworking

Rae
(English) raving beauty
Raedie, Raena, Ray, Raye

Raegan
(French) delicate
Reagan, Regan, Regun

Raelene
(American) combo of Rae
and Lene; smart

Rafa
(Arabic) joyful girl
Rafah

Rafaela
(Hebrew) spiritual
Rafayela

Rafferty
(Irish) prospering
Raferty, Raff, Raffarty, Rafty

Ragnild
(Scandinavian) goddess of
war
Ragnhild, Ragnhilda,
Ragnhilde, Ragnilda,
Ranillda, Reinheld, Renilda,
Renilde, Reynilda, Reynilde

Raheel
(Hebrew) from Rachel;
sheep; meek
Raheela

Rahela
(Hawaiian) lamb

Rahil
(Hebrew) from Rachel;
sheep; meek

Rahima
(Pakistani) loving
Raheema, Raheema

Rain
(English) falling water
Rainie, Reign

Raina
(German) dramatic
Raine, Rainna, Rayna

Rainbow
(American) bright
Rain, Rainbeau, Rainbo, Rainie

Raine
(Latin) helpful friend
Raina, Rainie, Rana, Rane, Rayne

Rainey
(Last name as first name) giving
Rainee, Rainie, Raney

Rainey-Anne
(American) combo of Rainey and Anne; languid
Rainee, Raineeann, Rainee-Anne, Rainey, Raneyann, Raneyanne

Raisa
(Russian) embraced
Rasa

Raissa
(Russian) from Rose; rosy cheeks

Raja
(Arabic) optimist

Rajani
(Hindi) dark; hopeful

Raji
(Hindi) royal

Rajni
(Hindi) dark night

Raka
(Hindi) royal

Raleigh
(Irish) admirable
Raileigh, Railey, Raley, Rawleigh, Rawley

Ralphina
(American) from Ralph; simplistic
Ralphine

Rama
(Hindi) godlike; good

Ramona
(Teutonic) beautiful protector
Rae, Ramonah, Ramonna, Raymona

Ramsay
(English) from the isle of rams; country girl
Ramsey

Rana
(Hebrew) fresh;
(Hindi) beauty

Randa
(Latin) admired
Ran, Randah

Randall
(English) protective of her own
Rand, Randal, Randi, Randy

Randelle
(American) wary
Randee, Randele

Randi
(English) audacious
Randee, Randie, Randy

Rane
(Scandinavian) queen-like
Rain, Raine, Ranie

Rani
(Hebrew) joyous; (Hindi) queen
Rainie, Ranie

Rania
(Sanskrit) regal
Ranea, Raneah, Raney, Ranie

Ranielle
(French) royal; frank

Ranita
(Hebrew) musical
Ranit, Ranite, Ranitra, Ranitta

Raoule
(Spanish) from Raoul; wild heart
Raoula, Raula

Rapa
(Hawaiian) lovely by moonlight

Raphaela
(Hebrew) helping to heal
Rafaela, Rafe

Raquel
(Spanish) sensual
Racuell, Raquelle, Raqwel

Rasheeda
(Hindi) pious
Rashee, Rashida, Rashie, Rashy

Rashidah
(Arabic) on the right path
Rashida

Rashinique
(African American) rash
Rash, Rashy

Raven
(English) blackbird
Ravan, Rave, Ravin

Ravenna
(English) blackbird

Rawnie
(Slavic) ladylike
Rawani, Rawn, Rawnee

Ray
(American) simplistic approach
Rae, Raymonde

Rayleen
(American) popular
Raylene, Raylie, Rayly

Rayna
(Scandinavian) strong girl

Raynelle
(American) giving hope; combo of Ray and Nelle
Nellie, Rae, Raenel, Raenelle

Raynette
(American) ray of hope; dancer
Raenette, Raynet

Razia
(Hebrew) secretive
Razeah, Raziah

Razina
(African) nice

Rea
(Polish) flowing
Raya

Reagan
(Last name as first name) strong
Regan, Reganne, Reggie

Reannah
(English) combo of Rae and Annah; divine
Reana, Reanna, Rennie

Reanne
(American) happy
Reann, Rennie, Rere, Rianne

Reba
(Hebrew) fourth-born
Rebah, Ree, Reeba

Rebecca
(Hebrew) loyal
Becca, Becki, Beckie, Becky, Rebeca, Rebeka, Rebekah

Rebi
(Hebrew) friend who is steadfast
Reby, Ree, Ribi

Rebop
(American) zany
Reebop

Reed
(English) red-haired
Read, Reade, Reid, Reida

Reenie
(Greek) peace-loving
Reena, Reeni, Reeny, Ren, Rena

Reese
(American) style-setting
Ree, Reece, Rees, Rere

Reeve
(Last name as first name) strong

Regan
(Irish) queenly
Reagan

Regeana
(American) form of Regina; queen
Rege, Regeanah, Regeane

Regina
(English, Latin) thoughtful
Gina, Rege, Regena, Reggie, Regine

Regine
(Latin) royal
Regene, Rejean

Rehema
(African) well-grounded
Rehemah, Rehemma, Rehima

Reiko
(Japanese) appreciative

Reine
(Spanish) from Reina; queen

Rela
(German) everything
Reila, Rella

Reina
(Spanish) a thinker
Rein, Reinie, Rina

Reith
(American) shy
Ree, Reeth

Rella
(Origin unknown) rogue

Remah
(Hebrew) pale beauty
Rema, Remme, Remmie, Rima, Ryma

Remedios
(Spanish) helpful

Remember
(American) memorable
Remi, Remmi, Remmie, Remmy

Remi
(French) woman of Rheims; jaded
Remeè, Remie, Remy

Rena
(Hebrew) joyful singer
Reena, Rinah, Rinne

Renae
(French) form of Renee; born again
Renay, Rennie, Rere

Renard
(French) fox; sly
Ren, Renarde, Rynard, Rynn

Renata
(French) reaching out
Renie, Renita, Rennie, Rinata

Rene
(Greek) hopeful
Reen, Reenie, Reney

Renea
(French) form of Renee; renewal
Renny

Renee
(French) born again
Rene, Rennie, Rere

Renetta
(French) reborn
Ranetta, Renette

Renie
(Latin) renewal

Renita
(Latin) poised
Ren, Renetta, Rennie

Renite
(Latin) stubborn
Reneta, Renita

Renzia
(Greek) form of Renee; peaceful
Renze

Resa
(Greek) productive; laughing
Reesa, Reese, Risa

Reseda
(Spanish) helpful; (Latin) fragrant flower
Res, Reseta

Reshauna
(African American) combo of Re and Shauna
Reshana, Reshawna, Reshie

Reshma
(African) compassionate

Reta
(African) shakes up
Reda, Reeda, Reeta, Rheta, Rhetta

Reva
(Hebrew) rainmaker
Ree, Reeva, Rere

Reveca
(Spanish) form of Rebecca; charming
Reba, Rebeca, Reva

Rexanne
(English) combo of Rex and Anne; gracious
Rexan, Rexann, Rexanna

Rexella
(English) combo of Rex and Ella; lighthearted
Rexalla, Rexel, Rexela, Rexell, Rexey, Rexi, Rexy

Rexie
(American) confident
Rex, Rexi, Rexy

Reyna
(English) elegant; (Greek) peaceful woman
Raina, Rayna, Rey

Reynalda
(German) wise
Raynalda, Rey, Reyrey

Reynolds
(Scottish) wispy
Rey, Reye, Reynells, Reynold

Reza
(Czech) from Theresa; playful
Rezi, Rezka, Riza

Rhea
(Greek) earthy; mother of gods; strong
Ria

Rheta
(American) form of Rita; intelligent

Rhianna
(Welsh) pure
Rheanna

Rhiannon
(Welsh) goddess; intuitive
Rhian, Rhiane, Rhianen, Rhiann, Rhianon, Rhyan, Rhye, Riannon

Rhoda
(Greek) rosy
Rhodie, Roda, Rodi, Rodie, Rody, Roe

Rhodanthe
(Greek) from Rhodes; thinker
Rhodante

Rhona
(Scottish) power-wielding
Rona, Ronne

Rhonda
(Welsh) vocal;
quintessential
Rhon, Ron, Ronda, Ronnie

Rhondie
(American) perfect
Rond, Rondie, Rondy

Rhonwen
(Welsh) lovely
*Rhonwenne, Rhonwin,
Ronwen*

Ria
(Spanish) water-loving;
river
Reah, Riah

Riana
(Irish) frisky
Reana, Rere, Rianna, Rinnie

Riane
(American) attractive
Reann, Reanne

Riannon
(Irish) free spirit
Rianna

Rica
(Spanish) celestial
*Ric, Ricca, Rickie, Rieka,
Rika, Ryka*

Ricarda
(German) has power

Richelle
(French) strong and artistic
*Chelle, Chellie, Rich, Richel,
Richele, Richie*

Richenda
(German) rules

Richesse
(French) wealthy
Richess

Ricki
(American) sporty
*Rici, Rick, Rickie, Ricky, Rik,
Riki, Rikki*

Rickma
(Hindi) from Rukmi; golden

Rico
(Italian) sexy
Reko, Ricco

Rida
(Arabic) satisfied
Ridah

Rihana
(Irish) pretty

Riley
(Irish) courageous; lively
*Reilly, Rylee, Ryleigh, Ryley,
Rylie*

Rilla
(German) lives by the brook

Rima
(Arabic) graceful; antelope
*Rema, Remmee, Remmy,
Rimmy, Ryma*

Rimona
(Hebrew) pomegranate;
small

Rina
(Hebrew) joy
Renah

Rinda
(Scandinavian) loyal
Rindah

Ring
(American) magical
Ringe, Ryng

Riona
(Irish) regal
*Rina, Rine, Rionn, Rionna,
Rionne*

Ripley
(American) unique
Riplee, Ripli, Riplie

Riquette
(French) feminine form of
Richard

Rissa
(Latin) laughing
*Resa, Risa, Riss, Rissah,
Rissie*

Rita
(Greek) precious pearl
Reda, Reita, Rida

Ritalinda
(Spanish) combo of Rita
and Linda; treasured
*Linda, Retalinda, Retalynde,
Rita, Ritalynd, Ritalynda*

Ritsa
(Greek) short for Alexandra;
noteworthy

Ritz
(American) rich
Rits

Riva
(Hebrew) joining; sparkling
Reva, Revi, Revvy

Rivalee
(Hebrew) combo of Riva
and Lee; joined
Rivalea, Riva-Lee

River
(Latin) woman by the stream
Riv

Rivers
(American) trendy
Riza
(Greek) dignified
Reza, Rize
Roanna
(Spanish) brown skin
*Ranna, Roanne, Ronni,
Ronnie, Ronny*
Roberta
(English) brilliant mind
*Robbie, Robby, Robertah,
Robi*
Robin
(English) taken by the wind;
bird
*Robbie, Robby, Robinn,
Robinne, Robyn*
Robina
(Scottish) birdlike; robin
Robena
Robinetta
(American) combo of Robin
and Etta; graceful dancer
*Robbie, Robineta,
Robinette*
Rochelle
(French) small and strong-
willed; (Hebrew) dream-like
beauty
*Roch, Roche, Rochel, Rochi,
Rochie, Rochy, Roshelle*
Rockella
(Invented) rocker
Rockell, Rockelle
Rocky
(American) tomboy
*Rock, Rockee, Rockey,
Rockie*

Roda
(Polish) intelligent
Roddy
(German) well-known
*Rod, Roddee, Roddey,
Roddi, Roddie*
Roderica
(German) princess
*Rica, Roda, Roddie,
Rodericka, Rodrika*
Rogertha
(American) form of Roger;
substantial
Rodge
Rohan
(Hindi) sandalwood; pretty
Rohana
(Hindi) sandalwood;
textured
Rohanna
Roisin
(Irish) rose
Roksana
(Polish) dawn
Roksanna, Roksona
Rolanda
(German) rich woman
Rolane, Rollande, Rollie
Rolandan
(German) form of Roland;
from a famous land
*Roland, Rolanden, Rollie,
Rolly*
Roline
(German) destined for fame
*Roelene, Roeline, Rolene,
Rollene, Rolleen, Rollina,
Rolline, Rolyne*

Roma
(Italian) girl from Rome;
adventurous
Romy
Romaine
(French) daredevil
*Romain, Romane, Romayne,
Romi*
Roman
(Italian) adventurous
*Romi, Romie, Rommie,
Rommye, Romyn*
Romey
(Latin) sea-loving
Romy
Romilda
(Latin) striking
*Romelda, Romey, Romie,
Romy*
Romilla
(Latin) from Rome; she who
wanders
*Romella, Romi, Romie,
Romila*
Romilly
(Latin) wanderer
Romillee, Romillie, Romily
Romney
(Welsh) winding river
Romola
(Latin) from Rome; dark-
haired
Romona
(Spanish) form of Ramona
Mona, Rome, Romie, Romy
Romy
(French) short for Romaine;
roaming
Roe. Romi, Romie

Rona
(Scandinavian, Scottish) powerful
Rhona, Ronne, Ronni

Ronat
(Scandinavian) from Rhona; smiles

Ronda
(Welsh) form of Rhonda; a standout
Ronni

Ronelle
(English) winner
Ronnie

Roney
(Scandinavian) form of Rona; lively
Roneye, Roni

Ronneta
(English) go-getter
Roneda, Ronnete, Ronnette, Ronnie

Ronni
(American) energetic
Ron, Ronee, Roni, Ronnie, Ronny

Rori
(Irish) spirited; brilliant
Rory

Ros
(English) from Rosalind; rosy and pretty
Roz

Rosa
(Italian) rose; (German) blushing beauty
Rose, Rossah, Roza

Rosabella
(Italian) combo of Rosa and Bella; beautiful rose

Rosabelle
(French) combo of Rosa and Belle; beautiful rose
Belle, Rosa, Rosabel, Rosa-Belle

Rosalba
(Latin) glorious as a rose
Rosalbah, Rosey, Rosi, Rosie, Rosy

Rosalia
(Italian) hanging roses
Rosa, Rosalea, Rosaleah, Rosaliah, Roselia, Rosey, Rosi, Rosie, Rossalia, Rosy

Rosalie
(English) striking dark beauty
Leelee, Rosa, Rosalee, RosaLee, Rosa-Lee, Rosie, Rossalie, Roz, Rozalee, Rozalie

Rosalind
(Spanish) lovely rose
Lind, Ros, Rosa, Rosalyn, Rosalynde, Rosie, Roslyn, Roslynn, Roz

Rosalinda
(Spanish) lovely rose
Rosa-Linda, Rosalynda

Rosaline
(Spanish) a rose
Rosalyn, Rosalynne, Roslyn

Rosalvo
(Spanish) rosy-faced
Rosa, Rosey

Rosamaria
(Italian) combo of Rosa and Maria; rose; devout
Rosa-Maria

Rosamond
(English) beauty
Rosa, Rosamun, Rosamund, Rose, Rosemond, Rosie, Roz

Rosanna
(English) lovely
Rosannah

Rosaoralia
(Spanish) combo of Rosa and Oralia; rosy
Rosa Oralia, Rosa-Oralia, RoseyO

Rose
(Latin) rose; blushing beauty
Rosa, Rosey, Rosi, Rosie, Rosy, Roze, Rozee

Roseandrea
(Invented) combo of Rose and Andrea

Roseanna
(English) combo of Rose and Anna
Rosana, Rosannah, Rose, Roseana, Rosie

Roseanne
(English) combo of Rose and Anne
Rosann, Rosanne, Rose Ann, Rosie

Rosebud
(Latin) flowering

Roselle
(Latin) rose

Rosellen
(English) pretty
Roselinn, Roselyn

Rosemarie
(Latin, Scandinavian)
combo of Rose and Marie
Rose-Marie, Rosemary

Rosemary
(English) combo of Rose
and Mary; sweetheart
Ro, Rose Mary, Rose, Rosie

Rosenda
(Spanish) rosy
*Rose, Rosend, Rosende,
Rosey, Rosie, Senda*

Rosetta
(Italian) longlasting beauty
Rose, Rosy, Rozetta

Rosette
(Latin) flowering; rosy
Rosett, Rosetta

Roshall
(African American) form of
Rochelle; dreamy
Rochalle, Roshalle

Roshawna
(African American) combo
of Rose and Shawna
*Rosh, Roshanna, Roshie,
Roshona, Shawn*

Rosheen
(Latin) rose

Roshell
(French) form of Rochelle;
small and strong-willed
Rochelle, Roshelle

Roshni
(Sanskrit) light

Roshumba
(African American)
gorgeous
Rosh, Roshumbah

Roshunda
(African American)
flamboyant
*Rosey, Roshun, Roshund,
Rosie, Roz*

Rosie
(English) bright-cheeked
Rose, Rosi, Rosy

Rosina
(English) rose

Rosita
(Spanish) pretty
Roseta, Rosey, Rosie, Rositta

Roslyn
(Scottish) combo of Rose
and Lyn; lovely girl

Ross
(Scottish) peninsula is home
Rosse

Rotella
(American) smart
Rotel, Rotela

Roth
(American) studious
Rothe

Rotnei
(American) bright
Rotnay

Rowan
(Welsh) blonde
Rowanne

Rowena
(Scottish) blissful; beloved
friend
Roe, Roenna, Rowina

Roxanna
(Persian) bright
Roxana, Roxie

Roxanne
(Persian) lovely as the sun
*Roxane, Roxann, Roxie,
Roxy*

Roxy
(American) sunny
Rox, Roxi, Roxie

Royale
(English) of royal family
*Royalla, Royalene,
Roayalina, Royall, Royalle,
Royalyn, Royalynne*

Royce
(English) king's child
Roice

Royetta
(American) combo of Roy
and Etta; cowgirl
*Etta, Roy, Roye, Royett,
Royette*

Roynale
(American) motivated
Roy, Royna, Roynal

Roz
(French) short for Rosalind
Ros, Rozz, Rozzie

Rozena
(American) form of Rosena;
pretty
Roze, Rozenna

Rozonda
(American) pretty
Rosonde, Rozon, Rozond

Rube
(Hawaiian) ruby; gem

Rubena
(Hebrew) sassy
Rubyn, Rubyna, Rueben

Rubianney
(American) combo of Rubi and Anney; shining
Rubi, Rubianey, Rubianne, Rubi-Anney, Rubyann

Rubilee
(American) combo of Ruby and Lee; shining
Ruby Lee, Rubylee

Rubina
(Pakistani) gem
Rubi

Rubra
(French) from Ruby; jewel
Rube, Rue

Ruby
(French) precious jewel
Rubi, Rubie, Rue

Ruby-Jewel
(American) combo of Ruby and Jewel; sassy
Rubijewel, Rubyjewel, Ruby-Jule

Ruchi
(German) brash

Rudelle
(English) ruddy skin
Rudella

Rudy
(German) sly
Rudee, Rudell, Rudie

Rue
(English, German) looking back
Ru

Rufina
(Italian) red-haired
Rufeena, Rufeine, Ruffina, Ruphyna

Ruelynn
(American) combo of Rue and Lynn; smart and famous
Rue Lynn, Ruelin, Ruelinn, Rue-Lynn, Rulynn

Rufaro
(African) happy

Rula
(American) wild-spirited
Rue, Rulah, Rewela

Rumer
(English) unique
Ru, Rumor

Runa
(Scandinavian) secret

Rupli
(Hindi) beautiful

Ruri
(Japanese) emerald
Rure, Rurrie, RuRu

Rusbel
(Spanish) beautiful girl with reddish hair
Rusbell, Rusbella

Russo
(American) happy
Russoh

Rusty
(English) red-haired girl
Rustee, Rusti

Ruta
(Lithuanian) practical
Rue, Rudah, Rutah

Ruth
(Hebrew) loyal friend
Rue, Ruthie, Ruthy

Ruthanne
(American) combo of Ruth and Anne
Ruthann

Ruthemma
(American) combo of Ruth and Emma
Routhemma, Ruthema

Ruthie
(Hebrew) friendly and young
Ruth, Ruthey, Ruthi, Ruthy

Ryan
(Irish) royal; assertive
Ryann, Ryen, Ryunn, Rian

Ryanna
(Irish) leader
Rianna, Rianne, Ryana, Ryanne, Rynn

Ryba
(Hebrew) traditional
Reba, Ree, Riba, Ribah

Rylee
(Irish) brave
Rilee, Rili, Ryelee, Ryley, Ryli, Ryly

Ryn
(American) form of Wren
Ren, Rynn

Ryne
(Irish) form of Ryan; divine; special
Rynea, Ryni, Rynie

Rynie
(American) loves the woods
Rinnie, Ryn

Rynn
(American) outdoorsy woman
Rin, Rynna, Rynnie, Wren

Rynnea
(American) sun-lover
Rynnee, Rynni, Rynnia

Saba
(Arabic) morning star
Sabah

Sabella
(English) spiritual
Bella, Belle, Sabela, Sabell, Sabelle, Sebelle

Sabina
(Latin) desirable
Sabeena, Sabine, Sabinna, Sabyna, Say

Sabine
(Latin) tribe in ancient Italy
Sabeen, Sabienne, Sabin, Sabyne

Sable
(English) chic
Sabelle, Sabie

Sablette
(American) luxurious
Sable, Sablet

Sabra
(Hebrew) substantial
Sabe, Sabera, Sabrah

Sabrina
(Latin) place name; passionate
Breena, Brina, Brinna, Sabe, Sabreena, Sabrinna

Sacha
(Greek) helpful girl
Sachie, Sachy

Sachi
(Japanese) girl
Sachee, Sachey, Sachie, Sachy, Sashi, Shashie

Sadie
(Hebrew) charmer; princess
Sade, Sadee, Sady, Sadye, Shaday

Saffron
(Indian) spice
Saffrone, Safron

Saga
(Scandinavian) sensual
Sagah

Sagal
(American) action-oriented
Sagall, Segalle

Sage
(Latin) wise
Saige

Sahara
(Place name) desert; wilderness
Saharra

Sahare
(American) loner

Sahila
(Hindi) guides others

Sahri
(Arabic) giving

Saida
(Hebrew) happy girl
Sada, Sadie

Sailor
(American) outdoorsy
Sail, Saile, Sailer, Saylor

Sajah
(Hindi) meritorious
Sajie, Sayah

Sakura
(Japanese) wealthy

Sal
(Italian) short for Salvador; (American) short for Sally

Salama
(African) safe

Salena
(Latin) needed; basic
Salene, Sally

Salima
(Arabic) healthy
Salma

Salina
(French) quiet and deep
Sale, Salena

Sally
(Hebrew) princess
Sal, Salli, Sallie

Salma
(Hebrew) peaceful; (Spanish) ingenious; (Hindi) safe
Sal, Sali, Sallee, Salley, Salli, Sally, Salmah, Salwah

Salome
(Hebrew) sensual; peaceful
Sal, Salohme, Salomey, Salomi

Salowmee
(Invented) form of Salome; peaceful
Sal, Salomee, Salomie, Salomy, Slowmee

Salvadora
(Spanish) saved
Sal, Salvadorah

Salvia
(Spanish) healthy

Sam
(Hebrew) God leads

Samantha
(Hebrew) good listener
Sam, Samath, Sammi, Sammie

Samara
(Hebrew) God-led; watchful
Sam, Samora

Samarantha
(Invented) combo of Samara and Samantha

Sami
(Hebrew) insightful
Sam, Sammie, Sammy

Samia
(Hindi) joyful
Sameah, Samee, Sameea, Samina, Sammy

Samimah
(Hebrew) praised

Samuela
(Hebrew) selected
Samm, Sammi, Sammy, Samula

Samyrah
(African American) music-loving
Samirah, Samyra

Sana
(Arabic) quintessential beauty

Sancha
(Spanish) sacred child
Sanchia

Sandi
(Greek) defends others
Sand, Sanda, Sandee, Sandie, Sandy

Sandip
(Hindi) knowing

Sandra
(Greek) helpful; protective
Sandrah, Sandy

Sandrea
(Greek) selfless
Sandreea, Sandie, Sanndria

Sandreen
(American) great
Sandrene, Sandrin, Sandrine

Sandy
(American) playful
Sandee, Sandey, Sandi, Sandie

Sanila
(Indian) full of praise
Sanilla

Saniyya
(Hindi) a special moment in time

Sanjuana
(Spanish) from San Juan; God-loving
Sanwanna

Sanjuanita
(Spanish) from San Juan; combo of San Juan and Juanita; believer
Juanita, Sanjuan

Sanna
(Scandinavian) truthful
Sana

Santa
(Latin) saint

Santana
(Spanish) saintly
San, Santanne, Santie, Santina

Santeene
(Spanish) passionate
Santeena, Santene, Santie, Santina, Santine, Satana

Santia
(African) lovable
Santea

Santonina
(Spanish) ardent

Sapphire
(Greek) precious gem
Safire, Saphire, Sapphie, Sapphyre

Sappho
(Greek) blue

Sara
(Hebrew) God's princess
Sae, Sarah, Saree, Sarrie

Sarafina
(Hebrew) angelic
Seraphina

Sarah-Jessica
(American) combo of Sarah and Jessica; charismatic
Sarah Jessica, Sara-Jess, Sarajessee, Sarajessica

Sarai
(Hebrew) contentious
Sari

Saraid
(Irish) best

Sarajane
(American) combo of Sara and Jane
Sarahjane

Saralee
(American) combo of Sara and Lee

Saramay
(American) combo of Sara and May
Sarah-May, Saramae

Saree
(Hebrew) woman of value
Sarie, Sary

Sari
(Hebrew, Arabic) noble
Saree, Sarey, Sarie, Sarree, Sarrey, Sarri

Sarika
(Hindi) thrush; sings

Sarilla
(Spanish) princess
Sarella, Sarill, Sarille

Sarina
(Hebrew) strong
Sareena, Sarena, Sarrie

Sarit
(Hebrew) form of Sarah; majestic
Saritt, Saryt, Sarytt

Sarita
(Spanish) regal
Sareeta, Sarie, Saritah

Sasha
(Russian) beautiful courtesan; helpful
Sacha, Sachie, Sascha, Sasheen, Sashy

Saskia
(Dutch) dramatic
Saskiah

Sassy
(Irish) Saxon girl; flirtatious
Sass, Sassi, Sassie

Satchel
(American) unusual
Satchal

Satin
(French) shiny
Saten

Saturine
(American) form of Saturn
Saturenne, Saturinne, Saturn, Saturyne

Saundra
(Greek) defender
Sandi, Sandra, Sandrah

Savannah
(Spanish) place name; open heart
Sava, Savana, Savanah, Savanna, Seven

Savina
(Latin) form of Sabina
Saveena, Savyna

Sawyer
(Last name as first name) industrious
Sawya, Sawyar, Sawyhr, Sawyie, Sawyur

Sayde
(American) form of Sadie; charming
Saydey, Saydie

Sayo
(Japanese) born at night
Saio, Sao

Scally
(Last name as first) introspective
Scalley, Scalli

Scarlett
(English) red
Scarlet, Scarletta, Scarlette

Schae
(Irish) variation of Shea; fairy place
Schay

Schemika
(African American) form of Shameka
Schemi, Schemike

Scherry
(American) form of Sherry
Scherri, Scherrie

Schmoopie
(American) baby; sweetie
Schmoopee, Schmoopey, Schmoopy, Shmoopi

Schulyer
(Dutch) form of Skyler; protective
Schulyar, Sky, Skye

Schylar
(Dutch) sheltering
Schylarr, Schyler, Schylerr, Schylur, Schylurr

Scooter
(American) wild-spirit
Scooder, Scoot

Scotty
(Scottish) girl from Scotland
Scota, Scotti, Scottie

Scout
(French) precocious
Scouts

Scully
(Irish) strong
Scullee, Sculleigh, Sculley, Sculli, Scullie

Scyllaea
(Greek) mythological monster; menace
Cilla, Scylla, Silla

Sea
(American) sea-loving; flowing
Cee, See

Sealy
(Last name as first name) fun-loving
Celie, Seal, Sealie

Sean
(Hebrew, Irish) God is giving

Seana
(Irish) giving
Seane, Seanna, Suannea

Seandra
(American) form of Deandra; intuitive
Seandre, Seandreah, Seanne

Season
(Latin) special; change
Seas, Seasee, Seasen, Seasie, Seasun, Seazun, Seezun

Seaton
(English) from the coast
Seaten, Seeten, Seeton, Seten, Seton

Sebastiane
(Latin) respected female
Sebastian, Sebbie

Seely
(English) bright
Sealee, Sealey, Seali, Sealie, Sealy, Seelee, Seeley, Seeli, Seelie

Seema
(Hebrew) treasured; soft-hearted
Seem

Seine
(French) river; flowing
Sane

Sejal
(Origin unknown) together

Sela
(Hebrew) short for Cecilia; substantial
Cela, Celia, Selah, Selia

Selda
(German) sure-footed
Seda, Seldah, Selde, Seldee, Seldey, Seldi, Seldie

Selena
(Greek) like the moon; shapely
Celina, Sela, Seleene, Selene, Selina, Sylena

Selene
(Greek) goddess of the moon
Seleene, Seline, Selyne

Selima
(Hebrew) peacemaker
Selema, Selemmah

Selin
(Turkish) calm

Selina
(Greek) moon
Celina

Sella
(English) from Selena; glowing
Sela

Selma
(German) fair-minded female
Selle, Sellma, Selmah, Zele, Zelma

Selona
(Greek) form of Selena; goddess
Celona, Sela, Seli, Selo, Selone

Selsa
(Hispanic) enthusiastic
Sel, Sels

Sema
(Greek) earthy
Semah, Semale, Semele

Semele
(Mythology) needs proof

Semilla
(Spanish) earth mother
Samilla, Sem, Semila, Semillah, Semmie, Semmy, Sumilla

Semiramis
(African) meets goals

Semone
(American) sentimental
Semonne

Sendy
(American) form of Cindy
Sendee, Sendie

Seneca
(Italian, Native American)
leader
Seneka

September
(Latin) serious; month
Seppie, Sept

Septima
(Latin) seventh child
Septimma, Septyma

Sequoia
(Cherokee) giant redwood;
formidable
Sekwoya

Serafina
(Hebrew) ardent
*Serafeena, Serafeenah,
Serafinah, Serafyna,
Serafynah, Serifina,
Seraphina, Seraphine*

Seraphina
(Latin) angel
*Serapheena, Serapheenah,
Seraphinah, Seraphyna,
Serphynah*

Seren
(Latin) serene
Ceren, Seran

Serena
(Latin) calm
*Sarina, Sereena, Serenah,
Serina*

Serendipity
(Invented) mercurial; lucky
*Sere, Seren, Serendipitee,
Serin*

Serenity
(American) serene
Sera, Serenitee, Serenitie

Sesame
(American) inventive
Sesamee, Sezamee

Seth
(Hebrew) set; appointed;
gentle
Sethe

Seville
(Place name) from Seville,
Spain
Sevill, Sevyll, Sevylle

Seymoura
(Invented) form of male
name Seymour; calm
Seymora

Shade
(English) cool
Shadee, Shadi, Shady

Shadow
(English) mysterious
Shado, Shadoh

Shae
(Hebrew) shy
Shay

Shaela
(Irish) pretty
Shae, Shaelie, Shala

Shaelin
(Irish) pretty
*Shae, Shaelyn, Shaelynn,
Shalyn*

Shaeterral
(African American) well-
shaped
Shatey, Shatrell, Shayterral

Shail
(American) pretty
Shale

Shaina
(Hebrew) beauty

Shaine
(Hebrew) pretty girl
Shanie, Shay, Shayne

Shainel
(African American) animated
Shainell, Shainelle, Shaynel

Shakira
(Arabic, Spanish) pretty
movement
*Shak, Shakeera, Shakeerah,
Shakeira, Shakie, Shakyra,
Skakarah*

Shakonda
(African American) lovely

Shalanda
(African American) vivid
Shalande, Shally, Shalunda

Shaleah
(Hebrew) combo of Sha and
Leah; funny
Shalea, Shalee, Shaleeah

Shaleina
(Turkish) humorist
Shalina, Shalyna, Shalyne

Shalene
(Hindi) giving

Shalonda
(African American)
enthusiastic
Shalie, Shalondah,
Shalonna, Shelonda

Shamara
(Arabic) assertive
Shamarah, Shemera

Shameena
(Arabic) beautiful
Shamee, Shameenah,
Shamina, Shaminna

Shamika
(African American) loving
Shameika, Shameka,
Shamekah, Shamika,
Shemeca

Shamsa
(Pakistani) adorable

Shan
(Chinese) coral

Shana
(Hebrew) pretty girl
Shaina, Shan, Shanah,
Shane, Shannah, Shanni,
Shannie, Shanny, Shayna,
Shayne

Shanae
(Irish) generous
Shan, Shanea, Shanee

Shandee
(English) hopeful
Shandi, Shandie, Shandy

Shandilyn
(American) not forsaken
Shandi, Shandy

Shandra
(American) fun-loving
Chandra, Shan, Shandrie

Shane
(Irish) soft-spoken
Shain, Shaine, Shanee,
Shanie, Shayne

Shaneka
(African American) perky;
pretty
Chaneka, Shan, Shanekah,
Shanie, Shanika

Shanelle
(African American) variant
of Chanel; stylish
Shanel, Shannel, Shannell,
Shanny

Shani
(African) great

Shania
(African) ambitious; bright-
eyed
Shane, Shaniah, Shanie,
Shaniya, Shanya

Shanice
(African American) bright-
eyed
Chaniece, Shaneese, Shani,
Shaniece

Shanika
(African American) pretty;
optimistic
Shan, Shane, Shanee,
Shaneeka, Shaneika,
Shaneikah, Shanequa,
Shaney, Shaneyka

Shaniqua
(African American) outgoing
Shane, Shaneekwa,
Shaneequa, Shanequa,
Shanie, Shanikwa,
Shaniquah, Shanneequa

Shanique
(African American) outgoing

Shanisha
(African American) bright
Chaneisha, Chanisha, Shan,
Shanecia, Shaneisha, Shanie

Shanna
(Irish) lovely
Shanah, Shanea, Shannah

Shannon
(Irish) smart
Shann, Shanna, Shannen,
Shannyn, Shanon

Shanny
(Irish) bubbly
Shannee, Shanni, Shannie

Shanta
(French) singing
Shantah, Shante, Shantie

Shantara
(French) bright-eyed
Shantay, Shantera, Shantie

Shante
(French) from Chantal; song
Shantae, Shantay

Shantell
(American) bright singer
Chantel, Shantal, Shantel

Shanti
(Hindi) calm

Shaquan
(American) fine
Shak, Shaq, Shaquanda,
Shaquanna, Shaquie,
Shaquonda

Shaquita
(African American) delight
Shaq, Shaqueita, Shaqueta,
Shaquie

Shara
(Hebrew) form of Sharon; open
Sharah, Sharra, Sherah

Shardae
(Arabic) wanderer
Chardae, Sade, Shaday, Sharday, SharDay

Sharee
(American) dear
Sharie

Shari
(French) beloved girl
Shar, Sharee, Sharree, Sher, Sherri

Sharice
(French) graceful
Cherise, Shar, Shareese, Shares

Sharif
(Russian) mysterious
Shar, Shareef, Sharey, Shari, Sharrey, Shary

Sharine
(Hebrew) from Sharon; open heart
Shareen, Shareene, Sharyne

Sharissa
(Hebrew) flat plain; quiet

Sharita
(French) charitable
Shar, Shareetah, Shareta

Sharla
(American) friendly
Sharlah

Sharlene
(German) form of Charlene
Charleen, Charlene, Shar, Sharl, Sharleen, Sharline, Sharlyne

Sharlott
(American) variant on Charlotte; feminine
Charlotte

Sharmaine
(American) from Charmaine; song

Sharmeal
(African American) exhilarating
Sharm, Sharma, Sharme, Sharmele

Sharna
(Hebrew) broad-minded
Sharn, Sharnah

Sharnea
(American) quiet
Sharnay, Sharnee, Sharney

Sharnelle
(African American) spiritual
Sharnel, Sharnie, Sharny

Sharnette
(American) fighter
Chanet, Charnette, Shanet, Sharn, Sharnett, Sharney

Sharon
(Hebrew) open heart; desert plain
Shar, Sharen, Shari, Sharin, Sharren, Sharron, Sharry, Sharyn, Sheron, Sherron

Sharona
(Hebrew) from Sharon; desert plain
Sharonah, Sharonna, Sharonnah

Sharonda
(African American) open
Sharondah, Sheronda

Sharrona
(Hebrew) open
Sharona, Sharonne, Sherona, Shironah

Sharterica
(African American) beloved
Sharter, Sharterika, Shartrica, Sharty

Shasta
(American) majestic mind
Shastah

Shatoya
(African American) spirited
Shatoye, Shay, Shaytoya, Toya

Shauna
(Hebrew, Irish) giving heart
Shauhna, Shaunie, Shaunna, Shawna

Shaune
(American) wide smile
Shaun, Shaunie, Shawn

Shauntee
(Irish) dancing eyes
Shaun, Shawntey, Shawntie, Shawnty

Shavon
(Irish) devout; energetic
Chavon, Chavonne, Shavaun, Shavon, Shavonne

Shawana
(African American) dramatic
Shavaun, Shawahna, Shawanna, Shawnie

Shawandreka
(African American) gutsy
Shawan, Shawand, Shawandrika, Shawann, Shawuan

Shawn
(American) smiling
Shawne, Shawnee, Shawnie, Shawny

Shawna
(Hebrew, Irish) form of Sean; God is gracious
Shawnna

Shawnda
(Irish) helpful friend
Shaunda, Shaundah, Shona

Shawneequa
(African American) loquacious
Shauneequa, Shawneekwa

Shawnel
(African American) audacious
Shaune, Shaunel, Shaunelle, Shawn, Shawnee, Shawnelle, Shawney, Shawni

Shawnie
(American) playful
Shaunie, Shawni

Shay
(Irish) fairy place
Shaye

Shayjuana
(African American) combo of Shay and Juana; cheerful
Shajuana, Shajuanna, Shay

Shayla
(Irish) fairy palace

Shaylie
(Latin) playful
Shaleigh, Shaylea, Shaylee, Shealee

Shayne
(Hebrew) form of Shane; pretty
Shaine, Shane, Shay, Sheyne

Shayonda
(African American) regal
Shay, Shaya, Shayon, Shayonde, Sheyonda, Yona, Yonda

Shea
(Irish) soft beauty
Shae, Shay

Sheba
(Hebrew) short for Bathsheba; queenly
Chebah, Sheeba, Sheebah

Sheddreka
(African American) dynamo
Shedd, Sheddrik, Shedreke

Sheela
(Hindi) gentle spirit
Sheelah, Sheeli, Sheila

Sheelyah
(Irish) form of Shelia; woman
Sheel, Sheil

Sheena
(Hebrew) shining
Sheen, Sheenah, Shena

Sheeneva
(American) combo of Sheena and Eva; shiny
Shee, Sheen, Sheena, Sheeny

Sheila
(Irish) vivacious; divine woman
Shaylah, Sheela, Sheilia, Sheilya, Shel

Shelagh
(Irish) fairy princess

Shelby
(English) dignified
Chelby, Shel, Shelbee, Shelbi, Shelbie

Sheldon
(English) farm on the ledge
Shelden

Shelia
(Irish) woman; gorgeous
Shelya, Shelyah, Shillya

Shelita
(Spanish) little girl
Chelita, Shelite, Shelitta

Shell
(English) meadow; (French) from Michelle
Shel

Shelley
(English) outdoorsy; meadow
Shelee, Shelli, Shelly

Shelton
(English) farm on a ledge
Shelten

Shena
(Irish) shining
Shenae, Shenea, Shenna

Sheneeka
(African American) easygoing
Shaneeka, Shaneka, Sheneecah, Sheneka

Shepard
(English) vigilant
Shep, Sheperd, Shepherd, Sheppie

Shera
(Hebrew) light-hearted
Sheera, Sheerah, Sherah

Sheray
(French) saucy
Cheray, Sherayah

Sherael
(American) form of Sherry; distinctive
Sheraelle, Sherelle, Sherryelle

Sheree
(French) dearest girl
Sheeree, Sher, Shere

Sherele
(French) bouncy
Sher, Sherell, Sherrie

Sheresa
(American) dancer
Sher, Sherisa, Sherissa, Sherri

Sheretta
(American) sparkling
Shere, Sherette

Sheri
(French) sparkling eyes
Sher, Sherri, Sherrie

Sherice
(French) artistic
Cherise, Sher, Shereece, Sherisse

Sheridan
(Irish) free spirit; outstanding
Cheridan, Cheridyn, Sheridyn, Sherridan

Sherilyn
(American) combo of Sheri and Lyn
Sharilyn, Sheralyn, Sheri-Lyn, Sheri-Lynn, Sherry-Lynn

Sherita
(French) stylish
Cherita, Sheretta

Sherleen
(American) easygoing
Sherl, Sherlene, Sherline, Sherlyn, Shirline

Sherlitha
(Spanish) feminine
Sherl, Sherli

Sherolynna
(American) lovely
Cherolina, Sher, Sheralina, Sherrilina

Sherrill
(English) bright
Cheril, Cherrill, Sherelle, Sheril, Sherrell, Sheryl

Sherrunda
(African American) free spirit
Sharun, Sharunda, Sherr, Sherrunde, Sherunda

Sherry
(French) outgoing
Sher, Sheri, Sherreye, Sherri, Sherrie, Sherye

Sherrylynn
(American) combo of Sherry and Lynn
Sharolyn, Sher, Sherilyn, Sherry, Sherylyn

Sheryl
(French) beloved woman
Cheryl, Sharal, Sher, Sheral, Sheril, Sherill

Sherylin
(American) combo of Sheryl and Lynn
Sherylinn, Sherylyn, Sherylynn

Shevonne
(Gaelic) ambitious
Shavon, Shevaune, Shevon

Sheyenne
(Native American) form of Cheyenne; audacious
Shey, Shianne, Shyann, Shyanne, Shyenne

Sheyn
(Hebrew) beauty

Shibhan
(Irish) variation of Siobhan; God is gracious
Shiban, Shibann, Shibhann

Shiela
(Irish) blind

Shifra
(Hebrew) beautiful woman
Sheefra, Shifrah

Shikendra
(African American) spirited
Shiki, Shikie, Skikend

Shiloh
(Hebrew) gifted by God
Shilo, Shy

Shine
(American) shining example
Shena, Shina

Shiney
(American) glowing
Shine, Shiny

Shinikee
(African American) glorious
*Shinakee, Shinikey,
Shynikee*

Shira
(Hebrew) song; singer
Shirah, Shiree

Shireen
(English) charmer
*Shareen, Shiree, Shireene,
Shirene, Shiri, Shiry,
Shoreen, Shureen, Shurene*

Shirleen
(American) nature-loving
Shirlene, Shirline

Shirley
(English) bright meadow;
cheerful girl
*Sherlee, Sherley, Sherly,
Shir, Shirl, Shirly*

Shlonda
(African American) bright
Londa, Schlonda, Shodie

Shola
(Hebrew) spirited
Sholah

Shon
(Irish) from Shona;
gracious; loving
Shonn

Shona
(Irish) open-hearted
Shonah, Shonie

Shonda
(Irish) runner
*Shondah, Shonday,
Shondie, Shounda,
Shoundah*

Shonta
(Irish) fearless
*Shauntah, Shawnta, Shon,
Shontie*

Shony
(Irish) shining
*Shona, Shonee, Shoni,
Shonie*

Shoshana
(Hebrew) beautiful; lily
*Shoshanna, Shoshannah,
Shoshauna*

Shula
(Arabic) flaming

Shulamit
(Hebrew) serene

Shulondia
(African American) dynamic
*Shulee, Shuley, Shuli,
Shulonde, Shulondea,
Shulondiah*

Shuntay
(African American; Irish) a
form of Shonta; goodness
Shuntae

Shura
(Greek) protective

Shyama
(Native American) variant of
Cheyenne; thinker

Shyanne
(Native American) form of
Cheyanne
Shy

Shyla
(English) creative
Shila, Shy, Shylah

Shyne
(American) standout
Shine

Sia
(Welsh) calm; believer
Cia, Seea

Sian
(Welsh) believer

Siana
(Welsh) ebullient
Sian, Siane

Sib
(Anglo-Saxon) from Sibley;
friendly
Sibb

Sibley
(Anglo-Saxon) related
Siblee, Sibly

Sibyl
(Greek) intuitive
*Cibyl, Cyb, Cybil, Cybill,
Cybyl, Sib, Sibbi, Sibbie,
Sibby, Sibella, Sibil, Sibill,
Sibyll, Sibylla, Sybela, Sybil,
Sybyl*

Sid
(Place name) from Saint-
Denis, France; from Sidney
Sidd

Sidney
(Place name) from Saint-
Denis
Sidnee, Sidni, Sidny

Sidonia
(French) spiritual
Sid, Sidoneah, Sydonya

Sidonie
(French) appealing
Sidonee, Sidony, Sydoni

Sidra
(Latin) star
Cidra, Siddey, Siddie, Siddy, Sidi, Sidrie, Sydra

Sienna
(Place name) delicate; reddish-brown
Siena, Siene

Sierra
(Place name) peaks; outdoorsy
Cierra, Searah, Searrah, Siera, Sierrah, Sierre

Sigfrid
(German) peacemaker
Sig, Sigfred, Sigfreid, Siggy

Signe
(Latin) symbol
Sig, Signie, Signy

Sigourney
(English) leader who conquers
Sig, Siggie, Signe, Signy, Sigournay, Sygourny

Sigrid
(Scandinavian) lovely
Segred, Sig, Siggy, Sigrede

Sigrun
(Scandinavian) winning
Cigrun, Segrun

Sikita
(American) active
Sikite

Sile
(Turkish) misses home

Siline
(Greek) from Selene; moon
Sileen, Sileene, Silyne

Silvanna
(Spanish) nature-lover
Sil, Silva, Silvana, Silvane, Silvanne, Silver

Silver
(Anglo-Saxon) light-haired
Silva, Silvar, Sylver

Silvia
(Latin) deep; woods-loving
Sill, Silvy, Siviah, Sylvia

Simcha
(Hebrew) joyful
Simchah

Simi
(Lebanese) soft
Sim

Simica
(American) tender
Sim, Simika, Simmy

Simona
(American) form of Simon; wise
Sim, Simon, Sims

Simona
(Hebrew) svelte
Simonah, Symmie, Symona, Syms

Simone
(French) wise and thoughtful
Sim, Simonie, Symone

Sinai
(Place name) Mt. Sinai

Sinclair
(French) person from St. Clair; admired
Cinclair, Sinclare, Synclair, Synclare

Sindy
(American) left behind
Cindy

Sine
(Irish) God's gift

Sinead
(Irish) singer; believer in a gracious God
Shanade

Siobhan
(Irish) believer; lovely
Chevon, Chevonne, Chivon, Shavonne, Shevon

Siphronia
(Greek) sensible
Ciphronia, Sifronea, Sifronia, Syfronia

Siren
(Greek) enchantress
Syren

Sirena
(Greek) temptress
Sireena, Sirenah, Sirine, Sisi, Sissy, Syrena

Sirene
(Greek) enchantress
Sireen, Sireene, Siryne

Sisley
(Last name as first name) able

Sissy
(Latin) short for Cecilia or little sister; immature; ingenue
Cissee, Cissey, Cissy, Sis, Sissi, Sissie

Sistene
(Italian) spiritual
Sisteen, Sisteene

Sita
(Hindi) divine
Seeta, Seetha

Sivana
(Irish) from Sivney; easygoing
Sivanah

Sive
(Scandinavian) Siv, wife of Thor; she matters

Skye
(Scottish) place name; high-minded; head in the clouds

Skyler
(Dutch) protective; sheltering
Schuyler, Skieler, Skilar, Skiler, Skye, Skyla, Skylar, Skylie, Skylor

Slane
(Irish) form of Sloane; striking
Slaine

Slaney
(Last name as first name) selective

Slava
(Russian) glory

Sloane
(Irish) strong
Sloan, Slone

Sly
(American) from Slyvestra

Slyvestra
(American) feminine form of Slyvester

Smiley
(American) radiant
Smile, Smilee, Smiles, Smili, Smily

Snooks
(American) sweetie
Snookee, Snookie

Snow
(American) quiet
Sno, Snowy

Snowdrop
(Botanical) white flower

Socorro
(Spanish) helpful
Socoro

Sofie
(Greek) wise

Sofya
(Russian) wise
Sofi, Sofie, Sofiya

Solana
(Spanish) sunny
Solanah, Soley, Solie

Solange
(French) sophisticated
Solie

Soledad
(Spanish) solitary woman
Saleda, Solada, Solay, Sole, Solee, Solie, Solita

Soleil
(French) sun

Soline
(French) solemn
Solen, Solenne, Souline

Solita
(Latin) alone
Soleeta, Solyta

Soloma
(Hindi) from Soma; lunar

Sommer
(English) warm
Sommie, Summer, Summi

Sona
(Hindi) from Sonal; sunshine

Sonal
(Hindi) golden girl of the sun

Sonay
(Asian) bright-eyed
Sonnae

Sondra
(Greek) defender of mankind

Sonel
(Hindi) from Sonal
Sonell

Song
(Chinese) independent

Sonia
(Slavic) effervescent
Soni, Sonnie, Sonny, Sonya

Sonja
(Scandinavian) bright woman

Sonnet
(American) poetic
Sonnett, Sonni, Sonny

Sonoma
(Place name) wine-loving
Sonomah

Sonora
(Place name) easygoing
Sonorah

Sonseria
(American) giving
Seria, Sonsere, Sonsey

Sonya
(Greek) wise
Sonia, Sonje

Soo
(Korean) gentle spirit

Soon-Yi
(Chinese) delightful;
assertive

Soozi
(American) form of Suzy;
friendly
*Soos, Sooz, Souz, Souze,
Souzi*

Sophia
(Greek) wise one
*Sofeea, Sofi, Sofia, Sofie,
Sophea, Sopheea, Sophie,
Sophy*

Sophie
(Greek) from Sophia;
intelligent
*Sophee, Sophey, Sophi,
Sophy*

Sora
(Native American) chirping
bird
Sorra

Sorangel
(Spanish) heavenly
Sorange

Soraya
(Persian) royal

Sorcha
(Irish) bright
Shorshi, Sorsha, Sorshie

Sorele
(French) reddish-brown hair

Sorrel
(English) delicate
*Sorel, Sorell, Sorie, Sorree,
Sorrell, Sorri, Sorrie*

Sosannah
(Hebrew) from Susannah;
rose
Sosana, Sosanah, Sosanna

Soshana
(Hebrew) from Shoshanah;
lily
Soshanah

Sozos
(Hindi) clingy
Sosos

Spaulding
(English) divided field
Spalding

Spencer
(English) sophisticate
Spence, Spenser

Spirit
(American) lively; spirited
Spirite, Spyrit

Sprague
(American) respected
Sprage

Spring
(English) springtime; fresh
Spryng

Sri
(Hindi) glorious
Shree, Shri, Sree

Stacey
(Greek) hopeful and
spiritual
*Stace, Staci, Stacie, Stacy,
Staycee*

Stacia
(English) short for
Anastasia; devout
*Stace, Stacie, Stasia,
Stayshah*

Stanise
(American) darling
*Stanee, Staneese, Stani,
Stanice, Staniece*

Star
(English) a star
Starr

Starla
(American) shining
Starlah, Starlie

Starling
(English) glossy bird

Starlite
(American) extraordinary
Starlight, Starr

Stasia
(Greek, Russian)
resurrection
Stacie, Stasie, Stasya

Stefanie
(Greek) regal;
(German) crowned
*Stafanie, Stefannye,
Stefany, Steff, Steffany,
Steffie, Stephanie*

Steff
(Greek) short for Stephanie; crowned

Steffi
(Greek) short for Stephanie; crowned; athletic
Steffie, Steffy, Stefi

Stefnee
(American) form of Stephanie/Stefanie; regal
Stef, Steffy

Stella
(Latin) bright star
Stele, Stelie

Stephanie
(Greek) regal
Stefanie, Steff, Steffie, Stephenie, Stephney

Stephene
(French, Greek) dignified
Steph, Stephie, Stephine

Stephney
(Greek) crowned
Stef, Steph, Stephie, Stephnie

Sterla
(American) quality
Sterl, Sterlie, Stirla

Stevie
(Greek, American) jovial
Steve, Stevee, Stevey, Stevi

Stockard
(English) stockyard; sturdy
Stockerd, Stockyrd

Storelle
(Invented) legend
Storee, Storell, Storey, Stori

Storm
(English) powerful

Stormy
(American) impulsive
Storm, Stormi, Stormie

Story
(American) creative
Stori, Storie, Storee, Storey

Suanne
(American) combo of Sue and Anne
Suann, Sueann, Sueanne

Sue
(Hebrew) flower-like; lily
Susy, Suze, Suzy

Suellen
(American) combo of Sue and Ellen
SueEllen, Sue-Ellen

Sugar
(American) sweet
Shug

Sugy
(Spanish) short for the name Sugar; sweet
Sug, Sugey, Sugie

Suki
(Japanese) beloved
Suke, Sukie, Suky

Sula
(Greek) sea-going
Soola, Sue, Suze

Sullivan
(Last name as first name) brave-hearted
Sulli, Sullie, Sullivin, Sully

Summer
(English) summery; fresh
Somer, Sommer, Sum, Summie

Sun
(Korean) obedient girl
Suna, Suni, Sunnie

Sundancer
(American) easygoing
Sunndance

Sunday
(Latin) day of the week; sunny
Sun, Sundae, Sundaye, Sundee, Sunney, Sunni, Sunnie, Sunny, Sunnye

Sunila
(Hindi) blue sky

Sunita
(Hindi) Dharma's child
Suniti

Sunna
(American) sunny
Sun, Suna

Sunny
(English) bright attitude
Sonny, Sun, Sunni, Sunnye

Sunshine
(American) sunny

Suprina
(American) supreme
Suprinna

Surbhi
(Indian) sweet smelling

Surrender
(Word as name) dramatic
Surren

Susan
(Hebrew) lily; pretty flower
Soozan, Sue, Susahn, Susanne, Susehn, Susie, Suzan

Susannah
(Hebrew) gentle
*Sue, Susah, Susanna,
Susie, Suzannah*

Susette
(French) from Susan;
flowering
Susett

Susie
(American) short for Susan
*Susey, Susi, Susy, Suze,
Suzi, Suzie, Suzy*

Sutton
(Last name as first name)
southern town
Suten, Sutten, Suton

Suz
(American) short for Susan;
lily; pretty flower
Suze

Suzan
(American) from Susan;
flower
Suzen

Suzanne
(English) fragrant
*Susanne, Suzan, Suzane,
Suzann, Suze*

Suzette
(French) pretty little one
Sue, Susette, Suze

Svea
(Swedish) patriotic
Svay

Svetlana
(Russian) star bright
Sveta, Svete

Swan
(Scandinavian) swan-like

Swanhildda
(Teutonic) swan-like;
graceful
*Swan, Swanhild, Swann,
Swanney, Swanni, Swannie,
Swanny*

Sweeney
(Irish) young and
rambunctious
Sweenee, Sweeny

Sweetpea
(American) sweet
Sweet-Pea, Sweetie

Swell
(Invented) good
Swelle

Swift
(word as name) bold
Swiftie, Swifty

Swoosie
(American) unique
Swoose, Swoozie

Syb
(Greek) from Sybil
Sybb

Sybil
(Greek) future-gazing
*Sibel, Sibyl, Syb, Sybill,
Sybille, Sybyl*

Syd
(French) from Sydney
Sydd

Sydel
(Hebrew) princess

Sydlyn
(American) quiet
Sidlyn, Sydlin, Sydlinne

Sydney
(French) enthusiastic
Sidney, Syd, Sydnee, Sydnie

Syl
(Latin) loves the woods
Sill

Sylvan
(Latin) from the forest
*Silvan, Silven, Silvyn,
Sylven, Sylvyn*

Sylvana
(Latin) forest; natural woman
Silvanna, Syl, Sylvie

Sylvestra
(English) lives in the woods

Sylvia
(Latin) sylvan; girl of the
forest
Syl, Sylvea

Sylvie
(Latin) sylvan; peacefulness
*Sil, Silvie, Silvy, Syl, Sylvey,
Sylvi, Sylvy*

Sylwia
(Polish) serene; in the woods
Silwia

Symira
(American) enthusiastic
Sym, Symra, Syms, Symyra

Symone
(Hebrew) good listener
Sym

Symphony
(American) musical
*Simphony, Symfonie,
Symfony, Symphonee,
Symphonie*

Syna
(Invented) sweet
Sina

Synora
(American) languid
Cinora, Sinora, Synee, Syni, Synor, Synore

Synpha
(American) capable
Sinfa, Sinpha, Synfa

Syreta
(American) assertive
Sireta

Tabia
(African) talented girl

Tabina
(Arabic) follower of Muhammed

Tabitha
(Greek) graceful; gazelle
Tabatha, Tabbatha, Tabbi, Tabytha

Tabla
(Native American) wears a tiara; regal

Tacey
(American) precious
Tace, Tacita

Tacha
(American) form of Tasha (from Natalie); born on Christmas
Tach

Tacho
(American) form of Tasha (from Natalie); born on Christmas

Taci
(American) strong

Tacie
(American) healthy
Tace, Taci, Tacy

Tadewi
(Native American) wind

Tadi
(Native American) variation of Tadewi

Tadita
(Native American) runner
Tadeta

Taesha
(American) sterling character
Tahisha, Taisha, Taisha, Tisha

Taeshawna
(American) combo of Tae and Shawna; glamorous
Taeseana, Taeshauna, Taeshona, Tayseana, Tayshauna, Tayshawna, Tayshona

Taffeta
(American) shiny
Tafeta, Taffetah, Taffi, Taffy

Taffy
(Welsh) sweet and beloved
Taffee, Taffey, Taffi

Taft
(English) loved
Tafte

Taghrid
(Arabic) singing bird

Tahcawin
(Native American) doe

Tahira
(Arabic) pure
Tahirah

Tahiyya
(Arabic) welcome
Tahiyyah

Tahnee
(English) little one

Tai
(American) fond
Tie, Tye

Taima
(Native American) thunder
Taimah, Taiomah

Tain
(Native American) new moon

Tainee
(Native American) variation of Tain

Taipa
(Native American) quail

Taiwo
(African) firstborn of twins

Tajudeen
(Spanish) clingy
Taj, Tajjy, Taju

Taka
(Japanese) honorable

Takala
(Native American) cornstalk
Takalah

Takara
(Japanese) beloved gem
Taka, Taki

Takayren
(Native American)
commotion

Takeko
(Japanese) child of the
bamboo

Takenya
(Native American) falcon in
flight

Takeya
(African American) knowing
Takeyah

Taki
(Japanese) waterfall

Takia
(Arabic) spiritual
Taki, Tikia, Tykia

Takira
(American) combo of Ta and
Kira; prayerful
Kira, Takera, Tikiri

Takisha
(African American) combo
of Ta and Kisha; joyful
*Takeisha, Takish, Tekisha,
Tykisha*

Takuhi
(Armenian) queen

Tala
(Native American) wolf

Talal
(Hebrew) dew

Talila
(Hebrew) dew

Talasi
(Native American)
cornflower

Tale
(African) green

Talent
(American) self-assured
Talynt

Talesha
(African American) friendly
*Tal, Taleesh, Taleisha,
Talisha, Tallie, Telesha*

Tali
(Hebrew) confident

Talia
(Greek) golden; dew from
heaven
*Tahlia, Tali, Tallie, Tally,
Talya, Talyah*

Talibah
(African) intellectual
Tali, Talib, Taliba

Talisa
(African American) variation
of Lisa
Telisa

Talise
(Native American) beautiful
creek

Talitha
(African American) inventive
*Taleetha, Taleta, Taletha,
Talith, Tally*

Tallis
(English) forest

Tallulah
(Native American) leaping
water; sparkling girl
*Talie, Talley, Tallula, Talula,
Talulah*

Talluse
(American) bold
Talloose, Tallu, Taluce

Tally
(Native American) heroine
Tallee, Talley, Talli, Tally, Taly

Talma
(Hebrew) hill

Talou
(American) saucy
Talli, Tallou, Tally

Talutah
(Native American) red

Talya
(Hebrew) lamb
Talia

Tam
(Japanese) decorative
Tama

Tamah
(Hebrew) marvel
Tama

Tamaka
(Japanese) bracelet;
adorned female

Tamaki
(Japanese) bracelet

Tamala
(American) kind
*Tam, Tama, Tamela,
Tammie, Tammy*

Tamanna
(Hindu) desire

Tamar
(Hebrew) palm; breezy
Tama, Tamarr

Tamara
(Hebrew) royal female
Tamera, Tammy, Tamora, Tamra

Tamas
(Hindu) palm tree
Tamasa, Tamasi, Tamasvini

Tamasine
(English) twin; feminine of Thomas
Tamasin, Tamsin, Tamsyn, Tamzen, Tamzin

Tamay
(American) form of Tammy; soft
Tamae, Tamaye

Tambara
(American) high-energy
Tam, Tamb, Tambra, Tamby, Tammy

Tamber
(American) combo of T and Amber; energetic
Amber, Tam, Tambey, Tambur

Tambusi
(African) frank
Tam, Tambussey, Tammy

Tame
(American) calm

Tamefa
(African American) form of Tameka
Tamefah, Tamifa

Tamesha
(African American) open face
Tamesh, Tamisha, Tammie, Tammy

Tamesis
(Spanish) name for the Thames River
Tam, Tamey

Tami
(Japanese) people
Tamie, Tamiko

Tamia
(Japanese) little gem
Tameea, Tamya

Tamika
(African American) lively
Tameca, Tameeka, Tameka, Tamieka, Tamikah, Tammi, Tammie, Tammy, Temeka

Tamiko
(Japanese) the people's child
Tami, Tamico, Tamika

Tamirisa
(Indian) night; dark
Risa, Tami, Tamirysa, Tamrisa, Tamyrisa

Tammi
(American) sweetheart
Tam, Tammie, Tammy, Tammye

Tamohara
(Hindu) the sun

Tamony
(Hebrew) from Tamara; palm tree; warm
Tamanee, Tamaney, Tamani, Tamanie, Tamany, Tamonee, Tamoney, Tamoni, Tamonie

Tamra
(Hebrew) sweet girl
Tammie, Tamora, Tamrah

Tamrika
(African) newly created
Tamreeka

Tamsin
(English) benevolent
Tam, Tami, Tammee, Tammey, Tammy, Tammye, Tamsa, Tamsan, Tamsen

Tamyrah
(African American) vocalist
Tamirah

Tana
(Slavic) petite princess
Taina, Tan, Tanah, Tanie

Tanaka
(Japanese) swamp dweller

Tanay
(African American) new
Tanee

Tanaya
(Hindu) daughter

Tandy
(English) team player
Tanda, Tandi, Tandie

Tane
(Polynesian) fertile

Tanesha
(African) strong
Tanish, Tanisha, Tannesha, Tannie

Tangela
(American) combo of Tan and Angela
T'Angela

Tangelia
(Greek) angel
Gelia, Tange, Tangey

Tangenika
(American) form of former
country Tanganyika
Tange, Tangi, Tangy

Tangi
(American) tangerine
Tangee

Tango
(Spanish) dance
Tangoh

Tangyla
(Invented) form of Tangela;
special
Tange, Tangy

Tani
(Slavic) glorious
Tahnie, Tanee, Tanie

Tania
(Russian, Slavic) queenly
Tannie, Tanny, Tanya

Tanina
(American) bold
Tan, Tana, Tanena, Taninah,
Tanney, Tanni, Tannie,
Tanny, Tanye, Tanyna

Tanis
(Slavic) from Tania; fairy
queen
Taniss, Tanys, Tanyss

Tanise
(American) unique
Tanes, Tanis

Tanish
(Greek) eternal
Tan, Tanesh, Tanny

Tanisha
(African American) talkative
Taniesha, Tannie, Tenisha,
Tinishah

Tanith
(Irish) estate
Tanita, Tanitha

Tansy
(Latin) pretty
Tan, Tancy, Tansee, Tanzi

Tanuneka
(African American) gracious
Nuneka, Tanueka, Tanun

Tanvi
(Hindu) young woman

Tanya
(Russian) queenly bearing
Tahnya, Tan, Tanyie,
Tawnyah, Tonya

Tanyanika
(African American) combo of
Tayna and Nika; wild spirit
Nike, Tanya, Tanyani, Yanika

Tanyav
(Slavic) regal
Tanyev

Tanyette
(Italian) talkative
Tanye, Tanyee, Tanyett

Tanze
(Greek) form of Tansy;
eternal
Tans, Tansee, Tanz, Tanzee,
Tanzey, Tanzi

Tao
(Vietnamese) apple

Tapa
(Spanish) little snack
Tapas

Tapasya
(Hindu) bitter

Tapice
(Spanish) covered
Tapeece, Tapeese, Tapese,
Tapiece, Tapp, Tappy

Taquanna
(African American) noisy
Takki, Takwana, Taquana,
Taque, Taquie

Taquesha
(African American) joyful
Takie, Takwesha

Taquilla
(American) from the
Spanish word tequila; lively
Takela, Takelah, Taque,
Taquella, Taqui, Taquile,
Taquille

Tara
(Gaelic) towering
Tarah, Tari, Tarra

Taral
(Hindu) rippling

Taran
(American) earthy
Taren, Tarran, Tarren, Tarryn,
Taryn

Tarani
(Hindu) light

Taree
(Japanese) tree branch

Tarika
(Hindu) star

Tarlam
(Hindu) flowering

Taro
(Invented) card name; farsighted
Taroh

Tarsha
(American) combo of Tasha and Tara
Tarsh, Tay

Tarub
(Arabic) cheerful

Taryn
(American) combo of Tara and Karyn; exuberant; (Irish) bright; combo of Tara and Erin
Taran, Taren, Tarran, Tarrin, Tarron

Tasha
(Russian) Christmas-born baby
Tacha, Tahshah, Tash, Tashie, Tasia, Tasie, Tasy, Tasya

Tashanah
(African American) spunky
Tash, Tashana

Tashanee
(African American) lively
Tashaunie

Tashawndra
(African American) bright smiling
Tasha, Tashaundra, Tashie

Tashel
(African American) studious
Tasha, Tashelle, Tashelle, Tochelle

Tashina
(African American) sparkles
Tasheena, Tasheenah, Tashinah

Tashka
(Russian) together
Tashca, Tashcka

Tashza
(African American) form of Tasha; bright
Tashi, Tashy, Tashzah

Tasida
(Native American) rides a horse

Tasma
(American) twin
Tasmah

Tasmind
(American) twin

Tasmine
(English) twin
Tasmin

Tassi
(Slavic) bold
Tassee, Tassey, Tassy

Tate
(English) short

Tateeahna
(Invented) form of Tatiana; snow queen

Tatiana
(Russian) snow queen
Tanya, Tatania, Tatia, Tatianna, Tatiannia, Tatie, Tattianna, Tatyana, Tatyanna

Tatsu
(Japanese) dragon

Tatum
(English) cheery; high-spirited
Tata, Tate, Tatie, Tayte

Taura
(Latin) bull-like; stubborn

Tavia
(Latin) short for Octavia; light
Tava, Taveah, Tavi

Tawannah
(African American) talkative
Tawana, Tawanda, Tawanna, Tawona

Tawanner
(American) loquacious
Tawanne, Twanner

Tawanta
(African American) smart
Tawan, Tawante

Tawia
(African) born after twins

Tawny
(American) tan-skinned
Tawn, Tawnee, Tawni, Tawnie

Tawnya
(American) form of Tonya; tan
Tawnie, Tawnyah, Tonya, Tonyah

Tawyn
(American) reliable; tan
Tawenne, Tawin, Tawynne

Tayanita
(Native American) beaver

Tayla
(American) doll-like
Taila, Taylah

Taylor
(English) tailor by trade; style-setter
Tailor, Talor, Tay, Taye, Taylar, Tayler

Tazmin
(American) from Jasmine;
zany
Tazminn, Tazmyn, Tazmynn

Tazmind
(American) from Jasmine;
outgoing

Tazu
(Japanese) stork

Teagan
(Irish) worldly; creative
Teague, Teegan, Tegan

Teague
(Irish) creative
Tee, Teegue, Tegue

Teah
(Greek) goddess
Tea

Teale
(English) blue-green; bird
Teal, Teala

Teamhair
(Irish) hill

Teamikka
(African American) form of
Tamika; lively
Teamika

Teana
(American) form of Tina;
high-energy
Teanah, Teane

Tecoa
(American) precocious
Tekoa

Teddi
(Greek) cuddly
Ted, Teddie, Teddy

Tedra
(Greek) outgoing
Teddra, Tedrah

Tegvyen
(Welsh) lovely

Tehara
(Native American) darling
Tihara, Tyhara

Tejuana
(Place name) Tijuana, Mexico
T'Juana, Tijuana

Tekira
(American) legendary
Tekera, Teki

Tekla
(Greek) legend; divine glory
*Tekk, Teklah, Thekla, Tikla,
Tiklah*

Tela
(Greek) wise
Tella

Teleri
(Welsh) variation of Eleri

Teleza
(African) slippery

Telina
(American) storyteller
Teline, Telyna, Telyne, Tilina

Telma
(Greek) ambitious

Telsa
(American) form of Tessa;
successful
Telly

Temetris
(African American)
respected
*Teme, Temi, Temitris,
Temmy*

Temira
(Hebrew) tall
Temora, Timora

Temperance
(Latin) moderation

Tempest
(French) tempestuous;
stormy
Tempeste, Tempie, Tempyst

Templa
(Latin) spiritual; moderate
Temp, Templah

Tenesha
(African American) clever
*Tenesia, Tenicha, Tenisha,
Tennie*

Tennille
(American) innovative
*Tanielle, Tanile, Ten, Teneal,
Tenile, Tenneal, Tennelle,
Tennie*

Tenuvah
(Hebrew) fruit and
vegetables

Tenuva
(Hebrew) variation of
Tenuvah

Teo
(Spanish) from Spanish male
name Teodoro; God's gift
Teeo, Teoh

Teodora
(Scandinavian) God's gift
Teo, Teodore

Tequila
(Spanish) alcoholic
beverage
*Tequela, Tequilla, Tiki,
Tiquilia*

Terena

(English) feminine version of Terence
Tereena, Terenia, Terina, Terrena, Terrina, Teryna

Teresa

(Greek) gardener
Taresa, Terese, Terhesa, Teri, Terre, Tess, Tessie, Treece, Tressa, Tressae

Terese

(Greek) nurturing
Tarese, Therese, Treece

Tereso

(Spanish) reaper
Tere, Terese

Teri

(Greek) reaper
Terre, Terri, Terrie

Terilyn

(American) combo of Teri and Lynn
Terelyn, Terrelynn, Terrilynn, Terri-Lynn

Terlah

(Arabic) of the earth

Terolyn

(American) combo of Tere and Carolyn; harvesting; flirtatious
Tarolyn, Tero, Terolinn, Terolinne

Terra

(Latin) earthy; name for someone born under an astrological earth sign
Tera, Terrie

Terrell

(Greek) hardy
Ter, Teral, Terell, Terrelle, Terrie, Teryl

Terrena

(Latin) smooth-talking
Terina, Terrina, Terry

Terry

(Greek) short for Theresa
Teri, Terre, Terrey, Terri, Tery

Tertia

(Latin) third
Ters, Tersh, Tersha, Tersia

Teshuah

(Hebrew) reprieve
Teshua, Teshura

Tess

(Greek) harvesting life
Tesse

Tessa

(Greek) reaping a harvest
Tesa, Tessie, Teza

Tessella

(Italian) countess
Tesela, Tesella, Tessela

Tessica

(American) form of Jessica; friendly
Tesica, Tess, Tessa, Tessie, Tessika

Tessie

(Greek) form of Theresa; wonderful
Tessey, Tessi, Tezi

Tetsu

(Japanese) iron

Tevy

(Cambodian) angel

Thada

(Greek) appreciative
Thadda, Thaddeah

Thadyne

(Hebrew) worthy of praise
Thadee, Thadine, Thady

Thalassa

(Greek) sensitive
Talassa, Thalassah, Thalasse

Thalia

(Greek) joyful; fun
Thalya

Thana

(Arabic) thanksgiving

Thandiwe

(African) affectionate

Thanh

(Vietnamese) brilliant

Thao

(Vietnamese) respect

Tharamel

(Invented) form of the word caramel; dedicated
Thara

The

(Vietnamese) pledged

Thea

(Greek) goddess
Teah, Teeah, Theah, Theeah, Theo, Tiah

Theda

(American) confident
Thada, Thedah

Theia

(Greek) divine one

Thia

(Greek) goddess

Thekia

(Greek) famous

Thekla
(Greek) famous; divine
Tecla, Tekla, Thecla

Thelma
(Greek) giver
Thel

Thema
(African) queen

Themba
(African) trusted

Theodora
(Greek) sweetheart; God's gift
Dora, Teddi, Teddie, Teddy, Tedi, Tedra, Tedrah, Theda, Theo, Theodorah, Theodrah

Theola
(Greek) excellent
Theo, Theolah, Thie

Theone
(Greek) serene
Theona, Theonne

Theophania
(Greek) god's features
Theophanie

Theophila
(Greek) loved by God
Theofila

Theora
(Greek) God's gift
Theorah, Theorra, Theorrah

Theresa
(Greek) reaping a harvest
Reza, Teresa, Terri, Terrie, Terry

Therese
(Greek) bountiful harvest
Tereece, Terese, Terise, Terry

Therna
(Greek) wild
Thera

Theta
(Greek) letter in Greek alphabet; substantial
Thayta, Thetah

Thetis
(Greek) mother of Achilles

Thi
(Vietnamese) poem

Thim
(Thai) ice cream; sweet

Thirzah
(Hebrew) pleasant
Thirza, Thursa, Thurza

Thocmetony
(Native American) flower
Tocmetone

Thomasina
(Hebrew) twin
Tom, Toma, Tomasa, Tomasina, Tomina, Tommie, Toto

Thora
(Scandinavian) like thunder
Thorah

Thu
(Vietnamese) autumn

Thuy
(Vietnamese) gentle

Thyra
(Scandinavian) loud
Thira

Tia
(Greek) princess; (Spanish) aunt
Teah, Tee, Teia, Tiah

Tian
(Greek) lovely
Ti, Tiane, Tiann, Tianne, Tyan, Tyann, Tyanne, Tye

Tiana
(Greek) highest beauty
Tana, Teeana, Tiane, Tiona

Tianth
(American) pretty and impetuous
Teanth, Tia, Tian, Tianeth

Tiara
(Latin) crowned goddess
Teara, Tearra, Tee, Teearah, Tierah, Tira

Tibby
(American) frisky
Tib, Tibb, Tybbee

Tiberia
(Latin) majestic;
(Place name) Tiber River
Tibbie, Tibby

Tibisay
(American) uniter
Tibi, Tibisae

Tichanda
(African American) stylish
Tichaunda, Tishanda

Tiena
(Spanish) earthy
Teena

Tierah
(Latin) jeweled; ornament
Tia, Tiarra, Tiera

Tiernan
(English) lord

Tierney
(Irish) wealthy
Teern, Teerney, Teerny, Tiern

Tifara
(Hebrew) festive
Tiferet, Tifhara

Tifaya
(Greek) form of Tiffany
Tifaya, Tifayane, Tiff, Tiffy

Tiffany
(Greek) lasting love
Tifanie, Tiff, Tiffanie, Tiffenie, Tiffi, Tiffie, Tiffy, Tiphanie, Tyfannie

Tigress
(Latin) wild
Tigris, Tye, Tygris

Tigris
(Irish) tiger

Tiki
(Polynesian) ancestor; image
Tekee

Tilda
(German) short for Matilda; powerful
Telda, Tildie, Till, Tylda

Tilla
(German) industrious
Tila

Tilly
(German) cute; strong
Till, Tillee, Tillie

Timmie
(Greek) short for Timothie; honorable
Tim, Timi, Timmy

Timothea
(Greek) honoring God
Timaula, Timi, Timie, Timmi, Timmie

Timothie
(Greek) honorable
Tim, Timmie, Timothea, Timothy

Tina
(Latin, Spanish) little and lively
Teena, Teenie, Tena, Tiny

Tionne
(American) hopeful
Tionn

Tiponya
(Native American) owl; watchful

Tippah
(Hindi) from Tipo (tiger); ferocious

Tipper
(Irish) pourer of water; nurturing
Tip, Tippy, Typper

Tippett
(American) giving

Tippie
(American) generous
Tippi, Tippy

Tira
(Hebrew) camp

Tirion
(Welsh) gentle

Tirrza
(Hebrew) sweet; precious
Thirza, Thirzah, Tirza, Tirzah

Tirtha
(Hindu) ford

Tirza
(Hebrew) kindness
Thirza, Tirza, Tirzah

Tisa
(African) ninth child
Tesa, Tesah, Tisah

Tish
(Latin) happy
Tysh

Tisha
(Latin) joyful
Tesha, Ticia, Tishah, Tishie

Tishra
(African American) original
Tishrah

Tishunette
(African American) happy girl
Tish, Tisunette

Tita
(Greek) giant; large

Titania
(Greek) giant

Tivona
(Hebrew) lover of nature

Tiwa
(Native American) onion

Tobago
(Place name) West Indies island; islander
Bago, ToTo

Tobi
(Hebrew) good
Tobie, Toby

Toffey
(American) spirited
Toff, Toffee, Toffi, Toffie, Toffy

Tohuia
(Polynesian) flower

Toinette
(Latin) wonderful
Toin, Toinett, Toney, Tony, Toynet

Toireasa
(Irish) strong
Treise

Toki
(Japanese) chance

Tokiwa
(Japanese) steady

Tolikna
(Native American) coyote ears

Tollie
(Hebrew) confident
Toll, Tollee, Tolli, Tolly, Tollye

Toloisi
(French) from Toulouse; ingenious

Toma
(Latin) short for Tomasina
Tomas, Tomgirl, Tommi, Tommie, Tommy

Tomazja
(Polish) twin

Tomeka
(African American) form of Tamika
Tomeke

Tomiko
(Japanese) wealthy
Miko, Tamiko, Tomi

Tomitria
(African American) form of Tommy
Tomi

Tommie
(Hebrew) sassy
Tom, Tomi, Tommy

Tomo
(Japanese) intelligence

Tonaya
(American) valuable
Tona, Tone

Tonia
(Latin) a wonder
Toneah, Tonya, Tonyah, Toyiah

Tonietta
(American) combo of Toni and Etta; valuable
Toni, Toniett, Toniette

Tonisha
(African American) lively
Nisha, Tona, Toneisha, Tonesha, Tonie, Tonish

Toni
(Latin) meritorious
Tone, Tonee, Tonie, Tony

Tonia
(Latin) daring
Tonni, Tonnie, Tony, Tonya

Tooka
(Japanese) ten days

Topaz
(Latin) gemstone; sparkling
Tophaz

Topekia
(American) form of Topeka
Topeka, Topeke, Topekea

Topsy
(English) topnotch
Toppie, Toppsy, Topsey, Topsi, Topsie

Tora
(Scandinavian) thunder

Torborg
(Scandinavian) thunder
Thorborg, Torbjorg

Tordis
(Scandinavian) Thor's goddess

Tori
(Scottish) rich and winning
Toree, Torri, Torrie, Torry, Tory

Torill
(Scandinavian) loud
Toril, Torille

Torrance
(Place name) confident
Torr, Torri

Torunn
(Scandinavian) loved by Thor

Tosha
(Slavic) priceless
Tosh, Toshia

Toshala
(Hindu) satisfied

Toshio
(Japanese) year-old child
Toshi, Toshie, Toshiko, Toshikyo

Toski
(Native American) bug

Totsi
(Native American) moccasins

Tova
(Hebrew) good woman
Tovah

Toy
(American) playful
Toia, Toya, Toye

Trace
(French) takes the right
path
Traice, Trayce

Tracey
(Gaelic) aggressive
*Trace, Tracee, Traci, Tracie,
Tracy*

Tracilyn
(American) combo of Tracy
and Lynn; combative
*Trace, Tracelynn, Tracilynne,
Tracy-Lynn*

Tracy
(English) summer
*Trace, Tracee, Tracey, Traci,
Tracie, Trasey, Treacy, Treesy*

Tranell
(American) confident
*Tranel, Tranelle, Traney,
Trani*

Trang
(Vietnamese) smart

Traniqua
(African American) hopeful
*Tranaqua, Tranekwa,
Tranequa, Trani, Tranikwa,
Tranney, Tranniqua, Tranny*

Trava
(Czech) grass

Traviata
(Italian) woman who
wanders

Trazanna
(African American) talented
Traz, Trazannah, Traze

Tree
(American) sturdy

Treece
(American) short for Terese
Treese, Trice

Treena
(American) form of Trina
Treen

Trella
(Spanish) star; sparkles
Trela

Tremira
(African American) anxious
Tremera, Tremmi

Treneth
(American) smiling
Trenith, Trenny

Trenica
(African American) smiling
Trenika, Trinika

Trenise
(African American) songbird
*Tranese, Tranise, Trannise,
Treenie, Treneese, Treni,
Trenniece, Trenny*

Trenyce
(American) smiling
Trienyse, Trinyce

Tressa
(Greek) reaping life's harvest
Tresa, Tresah, Tress, Trisa

Tressie
(American) successful
*Tress, Tressa, Tressee,
Tressey, Tressi, Tressy*

Treva
(English) homestead by the
sea

Trevina
(English) variation of Treva;
feminine Trevor

Tricia
(Latin) humorous
*Treasha, Tresha, Trich,
Tricha, Trish, Trisha*

Trilby
(English) literary
Trilbie, Trilby

Trina
(Greek) perfect; scintillating
Tina, Treena, Trine, Trinie

Trinh
(Vietnamese) virgin

Trinidad
(Place name) island off of
Venezuela; spiritual person
Trini, Trinny

Trinity
(Latin) triad
Trini, Trinita

Trinlee
(American) genuine
Trinley, Trinli, Trinly

Trish
(American) short for
Patricia; funny
Trysh

Trisha
(American) short for
Patricia: funny
Tricia

Trishelle
(African American)
humorous girl
*Trichelle, Trichillem, Trish,
Trishel, Trishie*

Trissy
(American) tall
Triss, Trissi, Trissie

Trista
(Latin) pensive; sparkling love
Tresta, Trist, Tristie, Trysta

Tristen
(Latin) bold
Tristan, Tristie, Tristin, Trysten

Tristica
(Spanish) form of Trista; pretty
Trist, Tristi, Tristika

Trixie
(Latin) personable
Trix, Trixi, Trixy

Trixiebelle
(American) combo of Trixie and Belle; sweet personality
Belle, Trix, Trixeebel, Trixiebell, Trixybell

Tru
(English) from Truly; true
True

Truc
(Vietnamese) desire

Trudy
(German) hopeful
Trude, Trudi, Trudie

True
(American) truthful
Truee, Truie, Truth

Truette
(American) truthful
Tru, True, Truett

Truffle
(French) delicacy
Truff, Truffy

Trulencia
(Spanish) honest
Lencia, Tru, Trulence, Trulens, Trulense

Truly
(American) honest
True, Trulee, Truley

Trusteen
(American) trusting
Trustean, Trustee, Trustine, Trusty, Trusyne

Truth
(American) honest
Truthe

Try
(American) earnest
Tri, Trie

Tryna
(Greek) form of Trina
Trine, Tryne, Trynna

Tsifira
(Hebrew) crown

Tsomah
(Native American) rose

Tsonka
(American) capricious
Sonky, Tesonka, Tisonka, Tsonk

Tsuhgi
(Japanese) second daughter

Tsula
(Native American) fox

Tua
(Polynesian) outdoors

Tualau
(Polynesian) outdoors

Tucker
(English) tailor
Tukker

Tuenchit
(Thai) mysterious

Tuesday
(English) weekday

Tuhina
(Hindu) snow

Tuki
(Japanese) moon

Tula
(Native American) moon

Tulia
(Spanish) glorious
Tuli, Tuliana, Tulie, Tuliea, Tuly

Tully
(Irish) powerful; dark spirit
Tull, Tulle, Tulli, Tullie

Tulsi
(Hindu) basil

Turin
(American) creative
Turan, Turen, Turrin, Turun

Turney
(Latin) wood worker
Turnee, Turni, Turnie, Turny

Turquoise
(French) blue-green
Turkoise, Turquie, Turrkoise

Tursha
(Slavic) warm
Tersha

Tusa
(Native American) prarie dog

Tuwa
(Native American) earth

Tuyen
(Vietnamese) angel
Tuyet

Twaina
(English) divided
Twayna

Tweetie
(American) vivacious
Tweetee, Tweetey, Tweeti

Twiggy
(English) slim
Twiggie, Twiggee, Twiggey

Twyla
(English) creative
Twila, Twilia

Twynceola
(African American) bold
Twin, Twyn, Twynce

Tyana
(African American) new

Tye
(American) talented

Tyeoka
(African American) rhythmic
Tioka, Tyeo, Tyeoke

Tyesha
(African American)
duplicitous
*Tesha, Tisha, Tyeisha,
Tyiesha, Tyisha*

Tyisha
(African American) sweet
Isha, Tisha, Ty, Tyeisha, Tyish

Tyler
(American) stylish; tailor
Tielyr, Tye

Tymitha
(African American) kind
*Timitha, Tymi, Tymie,
Tymith, Tymy, Tymytha*

Tyndall
(Irish) dark
*Tyndal, Tyndel, Tyndell,
Tyndyl, Tyndyll*

Tyne
(American) dramatic; (Old
English) sylvan
Tie, Tine, Tye

Tyneil
(African American) combo
of Ty and Neil; helpful
Tyne, Tyneal, Tyniel

Tynisha
(African American) fertile
Tinisha, Tynesha, Tynie

Tyra
(Scandinavian) assertive
woman
Tye, Tyrah, Tyre, Tyrie

Tyrea
(African American) form of
Thora; thunder
Tyree, Tyria

Tyrina
(American) ball of fire
*Tierinna, Tye, Tyreena,
Tyrinah*

Tyronna
(African American) combo
of Tyronne and Anna;
special
*Tierona, Tye, Tyrona,
Tyronnah*

Tyson
(French) son of Ty
Ty, Tysen

Tyzna
(American) ingenious,
assertive
Tyze, Tyzie

Tzadika
(Hebrew) loyal
Zadika

Tzafra
(Hebrew) morning
Tzefira, Zafra, Zefira

Tzahala
(Hebrew) happy
Zahala

Tzeira
(Hebrew) young

Tzemicha
(Hebrew) in bloom
Zemicha

Tzeviya
(Hebrew) gazelle
*Civia, Tzevia, Tzivia, Tzivya,
Zibiah, Zivia*

Tzigane
(Hungarian) gypsy
Tsigana, Tsigane

Tzila
(Hebrew) darkness
Tzili, Zila, Zili

Tzina
(Hebrew) shelter
Zina

Tzipiya
(Hebrew) hope
Tzipia, Zipia

Tziyona
(Hebrew) hill
Zeona, Ziona

Tzofi
(Hebrew) scout
Tzofia, Tzofit, Tzofiya, Zofi, Zofia, Zofit

Tzuriya
(Hebrew) God is powerful
Tzuria, Zuria

Uberta
(Italian) bright

Uchechi
(African) God's will

Udavine
(American) thriving
Uda

Udele
(English) prospering woman
Uda, Udela, Udell, Udella, Udelle

Uela
(Unknown) dedicated to God
Uella

Uganda
(Place name) African nation

Ula
(Celtic) jewel-like beauty
Eula, Ulah, Ule, Ulla, Ylla

Ulanda
(American) confident
Uland, Ulandah, Ulande

Ulani
(Hawaiian) happy;
(Polynesian) happy
Ulanee

Ulda
(Unknown origin) prophetess

Ule
(Unknown origin) burdens

Ulielmi
(Unknown origin) intelligent

Ulima
(Unknown origin) smart

Ulla
(German) powerful and rich

Ulphi
(Unknown origin) lovely
Ulphia, Ulphiah

Ulrika
(Teutonic) leader
Rica, Ulree, Ulric, Ulrica, Ulrie, Ulry, Urik

Ultima
(Latin) aloof

Ulva
(German) wolf; courage

Ulyssia
(Invented) from Ulysses; wanderer
Lyss, Lyssia, Uls, Ulsy, Ulsyia

Uma
(Hebrew) nation; worldview
Umah

Umberlina
(Unknown origin) feminine form of Umberto

Umeko
(Unknown origin) blossom

Umnia
(Arabic) desirable
Umniah, Umniya, Umniyah

Una
(Latin) unique
Ona, Oona, Unah

Undine
(Latin) from the ocean
Ondine, Undene, Undyne

Undra
(American) one; longsuffering

Unice
(English) sensible
Eunice, Uniss

Unique
(Latin) singular
Uneek

Unity
(English) unity of spirit
Unitee

Unn
(Scandinavian) loving
Un

Ural
(Place name) Ural Mountains
Ura, Uralle, Urine, Uris

Urania
(Greek) universal beauty
Ranie, Uraine, Urana, Uraneah, Uranie

Urbai
(Unknown origin) gentle

Urbana
(Latin) born in the city
Urbani, Urbanna, Urbannai

Urbi
(Egyptian) princess

Uria
(Hebrew) God is my flame
Ria, Uri, Uriah, Urial, Urissa

Uriela
(Hebrew) God's light
Uriella, Uriyella

Urith
(Hebrew) bright
Urit

Ursa
(Greek, Latin) star; bear-like
Urs, Ursah, Ursie

Ursula
(Latin) little female bear
Ursa, Urse, Ursela, Ursila

Urta
(Latin) spiny plant

Usha
(Indian) dawn; awakening

Usher
(Word as name) helpful
Ush, Ushar, Ushur

Uta
(Teutonic) battle heroine

Utas
(Unknown origin) glorious

Ute
(German) rich and powerful

Utica
(Native American)
Uticas, Uttica

Utopia
(American) idealistic
Uta, Utopiah

Uttasta
(Unknown origin) from the homeland

Uzbek
(Place name) for Uzbekistan
Usbek

Uzetta
(American) serious
Uzette

Uzia
(Hebrew) God is my strength
Uzial, Uzzia, Uzzial

Uzma
(Spanish) capable
Usma, Uz, Uzmah

Uzoma
(African) the right way

Vacla
(Origin unknown) vain

Vaclava
(Origin unknown) conceited

Vada
(German) form of Valda; winner
Vaida, Vay

Vadnee
(Origin unknown) gives

Val
(Latin) short for Valerie; strong

Vala
(German) chosen one

Valarie
(Latin) strong
Val, Valaria, Valerie

Valborg
(Scandinavian) from power mountain
Valborga

Valda
(German) high spirits
Val, Valdah, Valida, Velda

Vale
(English) valley; natural
Vail, Vaylie

Valeda
(Latin) strong woman
Val, Valayda, Valedah

Valencia
(Spanish) place name; strong-willed
Val, Valecia, Valence, Valenica, Valensha, Valentia, Valenzia, Valincia

Valene
(Latin) strong girl
Valaine, Valean, Valeda, Valeen, Valen, Valena, Valeney, Vallen, Valina, Valine, Vallan, Vallen

Valentina
(Latin) romantic
Val, Vala, Valantina, Vale Valentin, Valentine, Valiaka, Valtina, Valyn, Valynn

Valeny
(American) hard
Val, Valenie

Valeria
(Spanish) having valor
Valeri, Valerie, Valery

Valerie
(Latin) robust
*Vairy, Val, Valarae, Valaree,
Valarey, Valari, Valarie, Vale,
Valeree, Valeri, Valeriane,
Valery, Vallarie, Valleree,
Valleri, Vallerie, Vallery,
Valli, Vallie, Vallirie, Valora,
Valry, Veleria, Velerie*

Valerta
(Invented) form of Valerie;
courageous
Valer, Valert

Valeska
(Polish) joyous leader
*Valese, Valeshia, Valeske,
Valezka, Valisha*

Valetta
(Italian) feminine
Valettah, Valita, Valitta

Valkie
(Scandinavian) from
Valkyrie; fantastic
*Val, Valkee, Valki, Valkry,
Valky*

Vallie
(Latin) natural
Val, Valli, Vally

Vallie-Mae
(Latin) from Valentina and
Mae; romantic
*Valliemae, Vallimae,
Vallimay*

Valma
(Scandinavian) loyal

Valonia
(Scandinavian) loyal
Vallon, Valona

Valora
(Latin) intimidating
*Val, Valorah, Valori, Valoria,
Valorie, Valory, Valorya*

Valore
(Latin) courageous
Val, Valour

Valoria
(Spanish) brave
Vallee, Valora, Valore

Value
(Word as name) valued
Valu, Valyou

Valyn
(American) perky
Valind, Valinn, Valynn

Vamia
(Hispanic) energetic
Vamee, Vamie

Vanda
(German) smiling beauty
*Vandah, Vandana, Vandelia,
Vandetta, Vandi, Vannda*

Vanessa
(Greek) flighty
*Nessa, Van, Vanassa,
Vanesa, Vanesah, Vanesha,
Vaneshia, Vanesia,
Vanessah, Vanesse,
Vanessia, Vanessica,
Veneza, Vaniece, Vaniessa,
Vanisa, Vanissa, Vanita,
Vanna, Vannessa, Vanneza,
Vanni, Vannie, Vanny,
Varnessa, Venesa, Venessa*

Vani
(Russian) from Vania;
hospitable

Vania
(Hebrew) gifted
Vaneah, Vanya

Vanille
(American) from vanilla;
simplistic
*Vana, Vani, Vanila, Vanile,
Vanna*

Vanity
(English) vain girl
Vanita, Vaniti

Vanna
(Greek) golden girl
*Van, Vana, Vanae, Vannah,
Vannalee, Vannaleigh*

Vanora
(Welsh) wave; mercurial
Vannora

Vanthe
(Greek) variant of Xanthe;
yellow-haired

Vantrice
(American) combo of Van
and Trice; retreats
Vantrece, Vantricia, Vantrisa

Vanya
(American) form of Vanna;
self-assured
Vani, Vanja, Vanni, Vanyuh

Vara
(Greek) strange
Varah, Vare

Varda
(Hebrew) rosy
*Vadit, Vardah, Vardia,
Vardice, Vardina, Vardis,
Vardit*

Varaina
(Invented) form of Loraine

Varina
(Czech) from Barbara; strange

Varna
(Origin unknown) no trace of vanity

Vashti
(Persian) beauty
Vashtee, Vashtie

Vasta
(Persian) pretty
Vastah

Vasteen
(American) capable
Vas, Vastene, Vastine, Vasty

Vaughan
(Last name as first name) smooth talker
Vaughn, Vawn, Vawne

Vaydell
(American) combo of Vay and Dell; jokester

Veata
(Cambodian) smart; organized
Veatah

Veda
(Sanskrit) wise woman
Vedad, Vedah, Vedis, Veeda, Veida, Vida, Vita

Vedette
(French) watchful
Veda, Vedett, Vedetta

Vedi
(Sanskrit) wisdom

Vega
(Scandinavian) star
Vay, Vayga, Vegah, Veguh

Velacy
(Origin unknown) delicate

Velda
(German) famous leader
Veleda, Valeda

Veleda
(German) intelligent
Vel, Veladah, Velayda

Velika
(Slavic) wonder

Velinda
(American) form of Melinda; practical
Vel, Velin, Velind, Vell, Velly, Velynda

Vell
(American) short for Velma; practical
Vel, Velly, Vels

Velma
(German) hardworking
Valma, Vel, Vellma, Velmah, Vilma, Vilna

Velonie
(American) combo of V and Melonie; smooth
Val, Vallonia, Valoniah, Valonia

Velore
(Origin unknown) poised

Velvet
(French) luxurious
Vel, Vell, Velvete, Velvett

Venecia
(Italian) girl from Venice; sparkles
Vanecia, Vanetia, Veneise, Venesa, Venesha, Venesher, Venesse, Venessia, Venetia, Venette, Venezia, Venice, Venicia, Veniece, Veniesa, Venise, Venisha, Venishia, Venita, Venitia, Venize, Vennesa, Vennice, Vennisa, Vennise, Vonitia, Vonizia

Veneradah
(Spanish) honored; venerable
Ven, Venera, Venerada

Veneranda
(Spanish) venerated; respected

Venetia
(Latin) girl from Venice

Venice
(Place name) city in Italy; coming of age
Vanice, Vaniece, Veneece, Veneese

Venitia
(Italian) forgiving
Esha, Venesha, Venn, Venney, Venni, Vennie, Venny

Venke
(Polish) from Venice

Vennita
(Italian) from Venice, Italy; having arrived
Nita, Vanecia, Ven, Venesha, Venetia, Venita, Vennie, Vinetia

Ventura
(Spanish) fortunate

Venus
(Latin) loving; goddess of love
Venis, Venise, Vennie, Venusa, Vinny

Vera
(Russian) faithful friend
Vara, Veera, Veira, Veradis, Verah, Vere, Verie, Vira

Verbena
(Latin) natural beauty

Verda
(Latin) breath of spring
Ver, Vera, Verdah, Verde, Verdi, Verdie, Viridiana, Viridis

Verdad
(Spanish) verdant; honest
Verda, Verdade, Verdie, Verdine, Verdite

Verdie
(Latin) fresh as springtime
Verd, Verda, Verdee, Verdi, Verdy

Verena
(English) honest
Veren, Verenah, Verene, Verenis, Vereniz, Verina, Verina, Verine, Virena, Virna

Verenase
(Swiss) flourishing; truthful
Ver, Verenese, Verennase, Vy, Vyrenase, Vyrennace

Verity
(French) truthful
Verety, Verita, Veritee, Veriti, Veritie

Verla
(Latin) truthful

Verlene
(Latin) vivacious
Verleen, Verlena, Verlie, Verlin, Verlina, Verlinda, Verline, Verlyn, Verlynne

Verlita
(Spanish) growing

Vermekia
(African American) natural
Meki, Mekia, Verme, Vermekea, Vermy, Vermye

Verna
(Latin) springlike
Vernah, Verne, Vernese, Vernesha, Verneshia, Vernessa, Vernetia, Vernetta, Vernette, Vernia, Vernice, Vernis, Vernisha, Vernishela, Vernita, Verusya, Viera, Virida, Virna, Virnell

Verneta
(Latin) verdant
Vernita, Verna, Virena, Virna

Vernice
(American) natural
Verna, Vernica, Vernicca, Vernie, Verniece, Vernique

Vernicia
(Spanish) form of Vernice; springtime
Vern, Verni, Vernisia

Vernita
(Latin) of the spring

Verona
(Place name) a city in Italy; flourishes; honest

Veronica
(Latin) girl's image; real
Nica, Ronica, Varonica, Veron, Verhonica, Verinica, Verohnica, Veron, Verone, Veronic, Veronice, Veronika, Veronne, Veronnica, Vironica, Vonni, Von, Vonni, Vonnie, Vonny, Vron, Vronica

Veronique
(French) realistic woman; form of Veronica
Veroneek, Veroneese, Veroniece

Versperah
(Latin) evening star
Vesp, Vespa, Vespera

Vertrelle
(African American) organized
Vertey, Verti, Vertrel, Vetrell

Vesela
(Origin unknown) open
Vess

Vespera
(Latin) evening star

Vesta
(Latin) home-loving; goddess of the home
Vess, Vessie, Vessy, Vest, Vestah, Vesteria

Veste
(Latin) keeps home fires burning
Esta, Vesta

Vetaria
(Slavic) regal woman

Vevay
(Latin) form of Vivian; lively
*Vevah, Vi, Viv, Vivay, Vivi,
Vivie*

Vevila
(Irish) vivacious

Vevina
(Latin) sweetheart

Vi
(Latin) short for Viola; kind
Vy, Vye

Vianca
(American) from Bianca;
white

Vianey
(Spanish) form of Vivian;
alive
*Via, Viana, Viane, Viani,
Vianne, Vianney, Viany*

Vianna
(American) combo of Vi and
Dianna; special
Viana, Viann, Vianne

Vianne
(French) striking
Vi, Viane, Viann

Vibeke
(Hindi) vibrant

Vicky
(Latin) short for Victoria
*Vic, Viccy, Vick, Vickee,
Vickey, Vicki, Vickie, Vikkey,
Vikki, Viky*

Victoria
(Latin) winner
*Vic, Vicki, Vicky, Victoriah,
Victoriana, Victorie,
Victorina, Victorine, Victory,
Vikki, Viktoria, Vyctoria*

Victory
(Latin) a winning woman
Vic, Viktorie

Vida
(Hebrew) short for Davida
Veeda

Vidella
(Spanish) life
Veda, Vida, Videline, Vydell

Vidette
(Hebrew) loved
*Viddey, Viddi, Viddie,
Vidett, Videy*

Vidonia
(Portuguese) vine; winding

Vienna
(Latin) place name, a city in
Austria
*Veena, Vena, Venna, Viena,
Viennah, Vienne, Vienette,
Vina*

Viennese
(Place name) from Vienna
Vee, Viena, Vienne

Viera
(Spanish) smart; alive

Viet
(Place name) form of
Vietnam
Vee, Viette

Vigdis
(Scandinavian) war goddess

Vigilia
(Latin) vigilant

Vignette
(American) special scene

Vilhelmina
(Scandinavian) from
Wilhelmina; perseveres
Velma, Vilhelmine, Vilma

Villette
(French) little village girl
Vietta

Vilma
(Spanish) form of Velma;
industrious
Vi, Vil

Vimala
(Hindi) attractive

Vina
(Hindi) musical instrument
*Veena, Vena, Vin, Vinah,
Vinesha, Vinessa, Vinia,
Viniece, Vinique, Vinisha,
Vinita, Vinna, Vinni, Vinnie,
Vinny, Vinora, Vyna*

Vinah
(American) up-and-coming
Vi, Vyna

Vincentia
(Latin) winner
*Vicenta, Vin, Vincenta,
Vincentena, Vincentina,
Vincentine, Vincenza, Vincy,
Vinnie*

Vincia
(Spanish) forthright; winning
Vincenta, Vincey, Vinci

Vinefrida
(Scandinavian) from
Winnifred; bold

Vinia
(Spanish) vineyard woman

Vinita
(Hindi) she comes home

Vinne
(American) from the vineyard

Viola
(Latin) violet; lovely lady
Vi, Violah, Violaine, Violanta, Viole, Violeine

Violanth
(Latin) from the purple flower violet
Vi, Viol, Viola, Violanta, Violante

Violet
(English, French) purple flower
Vi, Viole, Violette, Vylolet, Vyoletta, Vyolette

Violyne
(Latin) from the purple flower violet
Vi, Vio, Viola, Violene, Violine

Virgilee
(American) combo of Virgi and Lee; pure girl
Virge, Virgee, Virgi, Virgilea, Virgileigh, Virgy, Virgylee

Virgilia
(Latin) bears all; stoic
Virgillia

Virginia
(Latin) pure female
Giniah, Verginia, Verginya, Virge, Virgen, Virgenia, Virgenya, Virgie, Virgine, Virginio, Virginnia, Virginya, Virgy, Virjeana

Viridas
(Latin) green; growing
Viridis

Viridiana
(Spanish) combo of Viri and Diana; ostentatious
Di, Diana, Diane, Viri, Viridi, Viridiane

Viridis
(Latin) green and verdant
Virdis, Virida, Viridia, Viridiana

Virtue
(Latin) strong; pure

Vision
(Word as name) visionary

Vita
(Latin) animated; lively; life
Veda, Veeta, Veta, Vete, Vitaliana, Vitalina, Vitel, Vitella, Vitia, Vitka, Vitke

Viv
(Latin) short for Vivian; vital

Viva
(Latin) alive; lively
Veeva, Vivan, Vivva

Vivecca
(Scandinavian) lively; energetic
Viv, Viveca, Vivecka, Viveka, Vivica, Vivie, Vyveca

Vivi
(Hindi) vital
Viv

Vivian
(Latin) bubbling with life
Viv, Viva, Vive, Vivee, Vivi, Vivia, Viviana, Viviane, Vivie, Vivien, Vivienne, Vivina, Vivion, Vivyan, Vyvyan

Vivianna
(American) inventive
Viviannah, Vivianne

Vivilyn
(American) vital
Viv, Vivi

Vix
(American) short for Vixen
Vixa, Vixie, Vyx

Vixen
(American) flirt
Vix, Vixee, Vixie

Vlasta
(Slavic) likeable

Voila
(French) attention; seen
Vwala

Volante
(Italian) veiled

Voletta
(French) mysterious
Volette, Volettie

Vona
(French) pretty woman

Vonda
(Czech) loving; talented
Vondah, Vondi

Vondrah
(Czech) loving
Vond, Vonda, Vondie, Vondra, Vondrea

Voneisha
(American) combo of Von and Neisha; precocious
Voneishia, Vonesha, Voneshia

Vonese
(American) form of
Vanessa; pretty
*Vonesa, Vonise, Vonne,
Vonnesa, Vonny*

Voni
(Slavic) affectionate
Vonee, Vonie

Vonna
(French) graceful
*Vona, Vonah, Vonne, Vonni,
Vonnie, Vonny*

Vonnala
(American) sweet
*Von, Vonala, Vonnalah,
Vonnie*

Vonshae
(American) combo of Von
and Shae; confident
Von, Vonshay

Vontricia
(American) combo of Von
and Tricia; thinks
*Vontrece, Vontrese,
Vontrice, Vontriece*

Voyage
(Word as name) trip;
wanderer
Voy

Vyera
(Spanish) variant of Viera;
lively; smart

Wade
(American) campy

Wafa
(Arabic) loyal

Wakana
(Japanese) plant; thriving

Wakanda
(Native American) magical
Wakenda

Wakeen
(American) spunky
Wakeene, Wakey, Wakine

Wakeishah
(African American) happy
Wake, Wakeisha, Wakesha

Walburga
(German) protective
*Walberga, Wallburga,
Walpurgis*

Walda
(German) powerful woman
*Waldah, Waldena, Waldette,
Waldina, Wallda, Wally,
Welda, Wellda*

Waleria
(Polish) sweet

Waleska
(Last name as first name)
effervescent
Wal, Walesk, Wally

Walker
(English) active; mover
Wallker

Walkiria
(Mythology) from Valkyrie;
woodland nymph

Wallis
(English) from Wales; open-
minded
*Walis, Wallace, Walless,
Wallie, Walliss, Wally,
Wallys*

Wanda
(Polish) wild; wandering
*Vanda, Wahnda, Wandah,
Wandie, Wandis, Wandy,
Wannda, Wenda,
Wendaline, Wendall,
Wendeline, Wendy,
Wohnda, Wonda, Wonnda*

Wanetta
(English) fair
Waneta, Wanette, Wanita

Warda
(German) guards her own
Wardia, Wardine

Warma
(American) warmth-filled
Warm

Warna
(German) defends her own

Warner
(German) outgoing; fighter
Warna, Warnar, Warnir

Waverly
(English) wavers in the
meadow of swaying aspens
Waverley

Waynette
(English) makes wagons;
crafts wood
Waynel, Waynelle, Waynlyn

Weeko
(Native American) pretty

Wehilani
(Hawaiian) heaven

Wenda
(German) adventurer
Wend, Wendah, Wendy

Wendell
(English) has wanderlust
*Wendaline, Wendall,
Wendelle*

Wendy
(English) friendly; childlike
*Wenda, Wendaline, Wende,
Wendee, Wendeline,
Wendey, Wendi, Wendie,
Wendye*

Weslee
(English) girl from meadows
of the west
*Weslea, Weslene, Wesley,
Weslia, Weslie, Weslyn*

Weslia
(English) meadow in the
west
Wesleya, Weslie

Weslie
(English) woman in the
meadow
Wes, Weslee, Wesli

Wheeler
(English) inventive
Wheelah, Wheelar

Whitley
(English) outdoorsy
*Whitelea, Whitlea, Whitlee,
Whitly, Whittley, Witlee*

Whitman
(English) white-haired
Whit, Wittman

Whitney
(English) white; fresh
*Whit, Whiteney, Whitne,
Whitnea, Whitnee,
Whitneigh, Whitni, Whitnie,
Whitny, Whittaney,
Whittany, Whittney, Whytnie*

Whitson
(Last name as first) white
Whits, Whitty, Witte, Witty

Whittier
(Literature) distinguished
Whitt

Whoopi
(English) excitable
*Whoopee, Whoopie,
Whoopy*

Whynesha
(African American) kind-
hearted
*Whynesa, Wynes, Wynesa,
Wynesha*

Wibeke
(Scandinavian) vibrant
Wiebke, Wiweca

Wiktoria
(Polish) victor
Wikta

Wilda
(English) wild-haired girl
Willda, Willie, Wylda, Wyle

Wile
(American) coy; wily
Wiles, Wyle

Wilfreda
(English) goal-oriented
Wilfridda, Wilfrieda

Wilhelmina
(German) able protector
*Willa, Willhelmena, Willie,
Wilma*

Willa
(English) desirable
Will, Willah

Willette
(American) open
Wilet, Wilett, Will, Willett

Willine
(American) form of Will;
willowy
Will, Willene, Willy, Willyne

Willis
(American) sparkling
Wilice, Will, Willice

Willow
(American) free spirit;
willow tree
Willo

Wilona
(English) desirable
*Wilo, Wiloh, Wilonah,
Wylona*

Wilma
(German) sturdy
*Willma, Wilmah, Wilmina,
Wylm, Wylma*

Wilmot
(English) from William;
prissy; God-fearing

Wilona
(English) desired child
Willonoa, Willone, Wilone

Win
(German) flirty
Winnie, Wyn, Wynne

Wind
(American) breezy
*Winde, Windee, Windey,
Windi, Windy, Wynd*

Winda
(African) hunts for prey

Windy
(English) likes the wind
*Windee, Windey, Windi,
Windie, Wyndee, Wyndy*

Winema
(Native American) leader

Winetta
(American) peaceful;
country girl
*Winette, Winietta, Wyna,
Wynette*

Winifred
(German) peaceful woman
*Win, Wina, Winafred, Windy,
Winefred, Winefride,
Winefried, Winfreda,
Winfrieda, Winifryd, Winne,
Winnie, Winniefred,
Winnifreed, Wynafred,
Wynifred, Wynn, Wynne,
Wynnifred*

Winkie
(American) vital
Winkee, Winky

Winna
(African) friendly
Winnah

Winner
(American) outstanding

Winnie
(English) winning
Wini, Winny, Wynnie

Winnielle
(African) victorious female
*Winielle, Winniele,
Wynnielle*

Winola
(German) vivacious

Winona
(Native American) firstborn
girl
*Wenona, Wenonah, Winnie,
Winnona, Winoena,
Winonah, Wye, Wynnona,
Wynona, Wynonah,
Wynonna*

Winsome
(English) nice; beauty
Wynsome

Winter
(English) child born in
winter
Wynter

Wisdom
(English) discerning

Wistar
(German) respected
Wistarr, Wister

Wisteria
(Botanical) vine; entangles
Wistaria

Wonder
(American) filled with
wonder
*Wander, Wonda, Wondee,
Wondy, Wunder*

Wonila
(African American) swaying
Waunila, Wonilla, Wonny

Wood
(American) smooth talker
*Woode, Woodee, Woodie,
Woody, Woodye*

Wova
(American) brassy
Whova, Wovah

Wren
(English) flighty girl; bird
Renn, Wrin, Wryn, Wrynne

Wyanda
(American) form of Wanda;
gregarious
Wyan

Wyanet
(Native American) lovely
Wyanetta, Wyonet, Wyonetta

Wyetta
(French) feisty
Wyette

Wylie
(American) wily
Wylee, Wyley, Wyli

Wymette
(American) vocalist
*Wimet, Wimette, Wymet,
Wynette*

Wynne
(Welsh) fair-haired
*Win, Winne, Winnie, Winny,
Winwin, Wyn, Wynee, Wynn,
Wynnie*

Wynstelle
(Latin) chaste; star
*Winstella, Winstelle,
Wynnestella, Wynnestelle*

Wyomie
(Native American) horse-rider on the plains
Why, Wyome, Wyomee, Wyomeh, Wyomia

Wyoming
(Native American) U.S. state; cowgirl
Wy, Wye, Wyoh, Wyomia

Wysandra
(Greek) fair; protects

Wyss
(Welsh) spontaneous; fair
Whyse

Xanadu
(Place name) an idyllic, exotic, fictional place
Zanadu

Xandra
(Greek) protective
Xandrae, Zan, Zandie, Zandra

Xanthe
(Greek) beautiful blonde; yellow
X, Xanth, X-Anth, Xantha, Xanthie, Xes, Zane, Zanthie

Xanthippe
(Greek) form of Xanthe; wife of Socrates

Xaverine
(Invented) combo of Katherine and Xanthe

Xavia
(Origin unknown) feminine form of Xavier; familiar

Xaviera
(French) smart
Zavey, Zavie, Zaviera, Zavierah, Zavy

Xara
(Hebrew) form of Sara

Xena
(Greek) girl from afar
Xenia, Zen, Zena, Zennie

Xeniah
(Greek) gracious entertainer
Xen, Xenia, Zenia, Zeniah

Ximena
(Greek) greets

Ximenia
(Spanish) form of Serena; peaceful

Xiomara
(Spanish) congenial

Xylene
(Greek) outdoorsy
Leen, Lene, Xyleen, Xyline, Zylee, Zyleen, Zylie

Xylia
(Greek) woods-loving
Zylea, Zylia

Xylophila
(Greek) lover of nature

Yadira
(Hindi) dearest

Yael
(Hebrew) strength of God
Yaele, Yayl, Yayle

Yaeshona
(American) combo of Yae and Shona; worries
Yaeseana, Yaeshauna, Yaeshawna, Yayseana, Yayshauna, Yayshawna, Yayshona

Yaffa
(Hebrew) beautiful girl
Yafa, Yafah, Yaffah, Yapha

Yahaira
(Hebrew) precious
Yajaira

Yahnnie
(Greek) giving
Yahn, Yanni, Yannie, Yannis

Yaki
(Japanese) tenacious
Yakee

Yakira
(Hebrew) adored baby

Yale
(English) fertile moor
Yaile, Yayle

Yamileth
(Spanish) girl of grace
Yami

Yamilla
(Arabic) form of
Jamila/Camilla; beautiful
Yamila, Yamyla, Yamylla

Yamille
(Arabic) beautiful
Yamill, Yamyl, Yamyle,
Yamylle

Yana
(Slavic) lovely
Yanah, Yanna, Yanni,
Yannie, Yanny

Yancy
(Native American) Yankee;
sassy
Yancee, Yancey, Yanci,
Yancie

Yanessa
(American) form of
Vanessa; smooth
Yanesa, Yanisa, Yanissa,
Yanysa, Yanyssa

Yanisha
(American) combo of Yanis
and Nisha; high hopes
Yaneesha, Yanysha

Yannette
(American) combo of Y and
Annette; melodic
Yanett, Yannett, Yanny

Yaquelin
(Spanish) form of Jaqueline
Yackie, Yacque, Yacquelyn,
Yaki, Yakie, Yaque,
Yaquelinn, Yaquelinne

Yara
(Spanish) expansive;
princess
Yarah, Yare, Yarey

Yardena
(Hebrew) flows naturally

Yardley
(English) open-minded
Yardlee, Yardleigh, Yardli,
Yardlie, Yardly

Yarine
(Russian) peaceful
Yari, Yarina

Yarita
(Spanish) flashy

Yarkona
(Hebrew) growing

Yashona
(Hindi) rich
Yaseana, Yashauna,
Yashawna, Yeseana,
Yeshauna, Yeshawna,
Yeshona

Yasmine
(Arabic) pretty
Yasmeen, Yasmen, Yasmin,
Yasminn, Yasmyn, Yasmynn

Yasmina
(Hindi) from Jasmine;
blossoms
Yasmeena, Yasmyna

Yaura
(American) desirous
Yara, Yaur, YaYa

Yazmin
(Persian) pretty flower
Yazmen, Yazminn, Yazmyn,
Yazmynn

Yeardley
(English) home enclosed in
meadow
Yeardlee, Yeardleigh,
Yeardli, Yeardlie, Yeardly

Yebenette
(American) little
Yebe, Yebey, Yebi

Yelena
(Russian) friendly

Yelisabeta
(Russian) form of Elizabeth
Yelizabet

Yemaya
(African) smart; quirky
Yemye

Yenny
(American) combo of Y and
Jenny; happy
Yen, Yeni, Yenney, Yenni

Yessenia
(Spanish) devout
Jesenia, Yesenia

Yetta
(English) head of home

Yeva
(Russian) lively; loving
Yevka

Yina
(Spanish) winning
Yena

Ynez
(Spanish) from Inez; pure

Yoanna
(Hebrew) form of John;
believer
Yoana, Yoanah, Yoannah

Yodelle
(American) old-fashioned
Yode, Yodell, Yodelly, Yodette, Yodey

Yoella
(Hebrew) loves Jehovah
Yoela, Yoelah, Yoellah

Yohanna
(Greek) violet; textured
Yohana, Yohanah, Yohannah

Yoko
(Japanese) good; striving
Yokoh

Yola
(Spanish) form of Yolanda; violet
Yolanda, Yoli

Yolanda
(Greek) pretty as a violet flower
Yola, Yolana, Yolandah, Yolie, Yoyly

Yolie
(Greek) violet; flower
Yolee, Yoley, Yoli, Yoly

Yon
(Korean) lotus; lovely
Yonn

Yona
(Hebrew) dove; calm
Yonah, Yonna, Yonnah

Yonaide
(American)
Yonade, Yonaid

Yonina
(Hebrew) dove; calm
Yonyna

Yonit
(Hebrew) passive
Yonitt, Yonyt, Yonytt

Yordaine
(French) from Jorden; descends
Yordane, Yordayne

Yordan
(Hebrew) from Jordan; descends
Yorden, Yordyn

Yordana
(Hebrew) humble
Yordanah, Yordanna, Yordannah

Yori
(Japanese) dependable
Yoree, Yorey, Yorie, Yory

York
(English) forthright
Yorkie, Yorkke

Yosepha
(Hebrew) from Josephine; pleasure

Yoshe
(Japanese) from Yoshi; good girl
Yoshee, Yoshey, Yoshi, Yoshie, Yoshy

Young
(Korean) forever

Yovona
(African American) from Yvonne; joy
Yovaana, Yovanna, Yovhana, Yovhanna, Yoviana, Yovianna

Ysabel
(Spanish) from Isabel; clever
Ysabell, Ysabelle, Ysebel, Ysebell, Ysebelle, Ysybel, Ysybell, Ysybelle

Ysabella
(Spanish) smart and witty
Ysabela, Ysebela, Ysebella, Ysybela, Ysybella

Ysanne
(English) graceful
Esan, Esanne, Essan, Ysan, Ysann

Yseult
(Irish) prettiness
Yseulte

Yu
(Asian) jade; a gem

Yue
(Asian) happy

Yuette
(American) capable
Yue, Yuete, Yuetta

Yuki
(Japanese) snow child

Yulan
(Spanish) splendid

Yule
(Spanish) from Yulene; competitive

Yuliana
(Invented) combo of Y and Juliana
Ana, Yuli, Yuliann, Yulianne

Yuna
(African) gorgeous
Yunah

Yurianna
(Invented) combo of Yuri and Anna; royal
Yuri, Yuriann, Yurianne

Yuta
(American) dramatic
Uta

Yves
(French) male name; clever girl

Yvette
(French) lively archer
Yavet, Yevette, Yvete, Yvett

Yvonne
(French) athletic
Vonne, Vonnie, Yavonne, Yvone, Yvonna

Yzabel
(Hebrew) variant of Isabel; clever
Yzabell, Yzabelle, Yzebel, Yzebell, Yzebelle, Yzybel, Yzybell, Yzybelle

Zabrina
(American) from Sabrina; clever; fruitful
Zabreena, Zabryna

Zachah
(Hebrew) Lord remembered; brave-hearted
Zach, Zacha, Zachie, Zachrie

Zada
(Arabic) fortunate
Zaida, Zayda

Zafira
(Arabic) successful
Zafirah

Zahara
(African) flower
Zahari, Zaharit

Zahavah
(Hebrew) golden girl
Zahava, Zeheva, Zev

Zahira
(African) flower
Zahara, Zahirah, Zahrah, Zara, Zuhra

Zahra
(African) blossoming
Zara, Zarah

Zaida
(Spanish) peacemaker
Zada, Zai

Zainab
(Arabic) brave

Zaira
(Arabic) flower
Zara, Zarah, Zaria, Zayeera

Zaire
(Place name) country in Africa
Zai, Zay, Zayaire

Zakah
(African) smart
Zaka, Zakia, Zakiah

Zakiya
(Arabic) chaste
Zakiyah

Zale
(Greek) strong force of the sea
Zaile, Zayle

Zalika
(African) born to royalty

Zaltana
(Native American) high mountain

Zambee
(Place name) from Zambia
Zambi, Zambie, Zamby, Zamby

Zamilla
(Greek) strong force of the sea
Zamila, Zamyla, Zamylla

Zamir
(Hebrew) intelligent leader
Zameer, Zamyr

Zan
(Greek) supportive; (Chinese) praiseworthy
Zander, Zann

Zana
(Greek) defender; energetic
Zanah

Zandra
(Greek) shy; helpful
Zan, Zondra

Zane
(Scandinavian) bold girl
Zain

Zaneta
(Spanish) God is good

Zanita
(American) gifted
Zaneta, Zanetta, Zanette, Zanitt, Zeneta

Zanna
(Hebrew) lily
Zana, Zanah, Zannah

Zanth
(Greek) leader
Zanthe, Zanthi, Zanthie, Zanthy

Zara
(Hebrew) dawn; glorious
Zahra, Zarah, Zaree

Zarena
(Hebrew) dawn
Zareena, Zarina, Zaryna

Zarifa
(Arabic) successful

Zarina
(Hebrew) form of Sarika

Zarita
(Hebrew) form of Sarah; princess

Zarmina
(Origin unknown) bright
Zar, Zarmynna

Zashawna
(American) combo of Zasha and Shawna; spontaneous
Zaseana, Zashauna, Zashona, Zeseana, Zeshauna, Zeshawna, Zeshona

Zawadi
(African) gift

Zayit
(Hebrew) olive

Zaylee
(English) heavenly
Zay, Zayle, Zayley, Zayli, Zaylie

Zayna
(Arabic) wonderful
Zayne

Zaynab
(Iranian) child of Ali
Zainab

Zaza
(Hebrew) golden

Zazalesha
(African American) zany
Lesha, Zaza, Zazalese, Zazalesh

Zazula
(Polish) outstanding

Zdenka
(Czech) one from Sidon; winding sheet
Zdena, Zdenicka, Zdenina, Zdeninka, Zdenuska

Zdeslava
(Czech) present glory
Zdevsa, Zdisa, Zdiska, Zdislava

Zea
(Latin) grain
Zia

Zeandrea
(American) from Deandrea; noticed
Zeandraea, Zeandraya, Zeandria, Zeandrya

Zeb
(Hebrew) Jehovah's gift

Zeborah
(Invented) combo of Deborah and Zea

Zef
(Polish) moves with the wind
Zeff

Zeffa
(Origin unknown) breezy

Zefiryn
(Polish) a form of Zephyr; windlike

Zehara
(Hebrew) light

Zehava
(Hebrew) gold
Zahava, Zehovit, Zehuva, Zehuvit

Zehira
(Hebrew) careful

Zel
(Persian) cymbal

Zela
(Greek) blessed; smiling

Zelda
(German) practical
Zell, Zellie

Zelenka
(Czech) fresh

Zelfa
(African American) in control

Zelia
(Spanish) sunshine
Zeleah

Zella
(German) resistant

Zelma
(German) divine

Zemira
(Hebrew) song

Zemorah
(Hebrew) tree branch
Zemora

Zenae
(Greek) helpful
Zen, Zenah, Zennie

Zenaida
(Greek) daughter of Zeus

Zenana
(Hebrew) woman
Zena, Zenia

Zenda
(Hebrew) holy

Zenia
(Greek) open
*Zeniah, Zenney, Zenni,
Zennie, Zenny, Zenya*

Zenobia
(Greek) strength of Zeus

Zephyr
(Greek) the west wind;
wandering girl
*Zefir, Zeph, Zephie, Zephir,
Zephira, Zephyra*

Zeppelina
(English) beautiful storm

Zera
(Hebrew) seeds

Zeraldina
(Polish) spear ruler

Zerafina
(Greek) the west wind;
zephyr
Zerafeena, Zerafyna

Zerdali
(Turkish) wild apricot

Zerena
(Turkish) golden woman
Zereena, Zerina, Zeryna

Zerlinda
(Hebrew) dawn
Zerlina

Zerren
(English) flower

Zesiro
(African) first of twins

Zesta
(American) zestful
Zestah, Zestie, Zesty

Zeta
(English) rose; Greek letter
Zetah, Zetta

Zett
(Hebrew) olive; flourishing
Zeta, Zetta

Zevida
(Hebrew) current
Zevuda

Zhane
(African American) feminine
of Shane

Zhen
(Chinese) pure

Zhenia
(Latin) bright
Zennia, Zhen, Zhenie

Zhi
(Chinese) of high character;
ethical

Zho
(Chinese) character

Zhong
(Chinese) honorable

Zhuo
(Chinese) smart; wonderful
Zuo

Zi
(Chinese) flourishing; giving

Zia
(Latin) textured
Zea, Ziah

Zigana
(Hungarian) gypsy

Zihna
(Native American) spinning

Zila
(Hebrew) shadowy
Zilah, Zilla, Zillah, Zylla

Zilias
(Hebrew) shadow
Zillia, Zillya, Zilya

Zilpah
(Hebrew) dignity
*Zillpha, Zilpha, Zulpha,
Zylpha*

Zimbab
(Place name) from
Zimbabwe, country in Africa
Zimbob

Zimriah
(Hebrew) songs
Zimria, Zimriya

Zina
(Greek) hospitable woman
Zena, Zinah, Zine, Zinnie

Zinnia
(Botanical) flower
*Zenia, Zinia, Zinny, Zinnya,
Zinya*

Ziona
(Hebrew) symbol of good
Zionah, Zyona, Zyonah

Zipporah
(Hebrew) bird in flight
*Ziporah, Zippi, Zippie,
Zippora, Zippy*

Ziracuny
(Native American) water

Zirah
(Hebrew) coliseum
Zira

Zita
(Spanish) rose;
(Arabic) mistress
Zeeta, Zitah

Ziva
(Hebrew) brilliant
Zeeva, Ziv

Ziz
(Hungarian) dedicated
Zizz, Zyz, Zyzz

Zlata
(Czech) golden

Zoa
(Greek) life; vibrant

Zoann
(American) combo of Zo
and Ann; alive
Zoan, Zoanne, Zoayn

Zocha
(Polish) wisdom

Zoe
(Greek) lively; vibrant
Zoee, Zoey, Zoie, Zooey

Zofia
(Polish) skilled

Zofie
(Czech) wise

Zoheret
(Hebrew) shining

Zola
(French) earthy
Zolah

Zolema
(American) confessor
Zolem

Zona
(Latin) funny; brash
Zonah, Zonia, Zonna

Zonia
(English) flower

Zonta
(Native American) honest

Zooey
(Greek) life

Zoom
(American) energetic
Zoomi, Zoomy, Zoom-Zoom

Zora
(Slavic) beauty of dawn
*Zara, Zorah, Zorrah, Zorre,
Zorrie*

Zoralle
(Slavic) ethereal
Zoral, Zoralye, Zorre, Zorrie

Zore
(Slavic) dawn of day

Zorianna
(American) combo of Zori
and Ann; practical
Zoree, Zori, Zoriannah, Zory

Zorina
(Slavic) golden
Zorana

Zorka
(Slavic) dawn
Zorke, Zorky

Zorna
(Slavic) golden

Zosa
(Greek) lively
Zosah

Zowie
(Irish) vibrant
Zowee, Zowey, Zowi, Zowy

ZsaZsa
(Hungarian) wild-spirited
Zsa, Zsaey

Zuba
(English) musical

Zubaida
(Arabic) laborer
Zubaidah, Zubeda

Zudora
(Sanskrit) laborer

Zulah
(African) country-loving
Zoola, Zoolah, Zula

Zuleyka
(Arabic) brilliant; sparkling
Zelekha, Zue, Zuleika, Zuley

Zulema
(Arabic) lovely
Zulima

Zulma
(Arabic) vibrant
Zul, Zule, Zulmah

Zuma
(Arabic) vital

Zuni
(Native American) creative
Zu

Zuri
(African) beautiful

Zuriel
(American) from Ariel;
special

Zuwena
(African) good

Zuzanna
(Polish) misunderstood
Zu, Zue, Zuzan, Zuzana

Bibliography

"America's 40 Richest Under 40." *Fortune* Online. 16 Sept. 2002
    <http://www.fortune.com>.

"The American States." Collin, P.H., ed. *Webster's Concise Desk Dictionary*. New York:
    Barnes & Noble Books, 2001.

"The Animal Kingdom." Collin, P.H., ed. *Webster's Concise Desk Dictionary*. New York:
    Barnes & Noble Books, 2001.

Baby Center Baby Name Finder Page. 1 Dec. 2002
    <http://www.babycenter.com/babyname>.

Baby Chatter Page. 1 Dec. 2002 <http://www.babychatter.com>.

Baby Names/Birth Announcements Page. 1 Oct. 2002
    <http://www.princessprints.com>.

Baby Names Page. 1 Dec. 2002 <http://www.yourbabysname.com>.

Baby Names Page. 1 Nov. 2002 <http://www.babynames.com>.

Baby Names Page. 1 Oct. 2002 <http://www.babyshere.com>.

Baby Names World Page. 15 Jan. 2003 <http://www.babynameworld.com>.

Baby Zone Page. "Around-the-World Names." 15 Jan. 2003
    <http://www.babyzone.com/babynames>.

"Biographical Names." Collin, P.H. ed. *Webster's Concise Desk Dictionary*. New York:
    Barnes & Noble Books, 2001.

"Biographical Names." *The Merriam-Webster Dictionary*. Springfield, Mass: Merriam
    Webster, Inc., 1998.

"Books of the Bible." Collin, P.H., ed. *Webster's Concise Desk Dictionary*. New York:
    Barnes & Noble Books, 2001.

Celebrity Names Page. 1 Nov. 2002 <http://www.celebnames.8m.com>.

"Common English Given Names." *The Merriam-Webster Dictionary*. Springfield, Mass: Merriam Webster, Inc., 1998.

Death Penalty Info Page. 1 Feb. 2003 "Current Female Death Row Inmates." <http://www.deathpenaltyinfo.org/womencases.html>.

Dunkling, Leslie. *The Guinness Book of Names*. Enfield, UK: Guinness Publishing, 1993.

eBusinessRevolution Page. 1 Nov. 2002 <http://www.ebusinessrevolution.com/babynames/a.html>.

ePregnancy Page. 1 Dec. 2002 <http://www.Epregnancy.com/directory/Baby_Names>.

"Fifty Important Stars." Gove, Philip Babcock, ed. *Webster's Third New International Dictionary of the English Language Unabridged*. Springfield, Mass: Merriam-Webster, Inc., 1981.

"Gambino Capos Held in 1989 Mob Hit." Jerry Capeci. This Week in Gangland, The Online Column Page. 1 Aug. 2002 <http://www.ganglandnews.com/column289.htm>.

Hanks, Patrick, and Flavia Hodges. *A Dictionary of First Names*. Oxford: Oxford University Press, 1992.

Hanley, Kate and the Parents of Parent Soup. *The Parent Soup Baby Name Finder: Real Advice from Real Parents Who Have Named Their Babies and Lived To Tell About It— with More Than 15,000 Names*. Lincolnwood, Illinois: Contemporary Books, 1998.

Harrison, G.B. ed. *Major British Writers*. New York: Harcourt, Brace &World, Inc., 1959.

HypoBirthing Page. "Baby Names." 1 Oct. 2002 <http://www.hypobirthing.com>.

Indian Baby Names Page. 1 Nov. 2002
    <http:// www.indiaexpress.com/specials/babynames>.

Irish Names Page. 15 Jan. 2003 <http://www.hylit.com/info>.

Jewish Baby Names Page. 15 Jan. 2003 <http://www.jewishbabynames.net>.

Lansky, Bruce. *The Mother of All Baby Name Books: Over 94,000 Baby Names Complete with Origins and Meanings.* New York: Meadowlark Press (Simon and Schuster), 2003.

Kaplan, Justin, and Anne Bernays. *The Language of Names: What We Call Ourselves and Why It Matters.* New York: Simon & Schuster, 1997.

"Months of the Principal Calendars." Gove, Philip Babcock, ed. *Webster's Third New International Dictionary of the English Language Unabridged.* Springfield, Mass: Merriam-Webster Inc., 1981.

"Most Popular Names of the 1990s." Social Security Administration Online. 1 Nov. 2002 <http://www.ssa.gov/OACT/babynames>.

"Most Popular Names of the 1980s." Social Security Administration Online. 1 Nov. 2002 <http://www.ssa.gov/OACT/babynames>.

"Most Popular Names of the 1970s." Social Security Administration Online. 1 Nov. 2002 <http://www.ssa.gov/OACT/babynames>.

"Most Popular Names of the 1960s." Social Security Administration Online. 1 Nov. 2002 <http://www.ssa.gov/OACT/babynames>.

"Most Popular Names of the 1950s." Social Security Administration Online. 1 Nov. 2002 <http://www.ssa.gov/OACT/babynames>.

"Most Popular Names of 2001." Social Security Administration Online. 1 Nov. 2002 <http://www.ssa.gov/OACT/babynames>.

"Most Powerful Women in Business." *Fortune* Online. 14 Oct. 2002
    <http://www.fortune.com>.
"Movie-Star Names." Internet Movie Database online. 1 Nov. 2002
    <http://www.imdb.com>.

Norman, Teresa. *A World of Baby Names: A Rich and Diverse Collection of Names from Around the World.* New York: Perigee (Penguin Putnam), 1996.

Origins/Meanings of Baby Names from Around the World Page. 1 Nov. 2002
    <http:// www.BabyNamesOrigins.com>.

Oxygen Page. "Baby Names." 1 Nov. 2002 <http://www.oxygen.com/babynamer>.

Parenthood Page. 1 Nov. 2002
    <http:// www.parenthood.com/parent_cfmfiles/babynames.cfm>.

"The Plant Kingdom." Collin, P.H., ed. *Webster's Concise Desk Dictionary.* New York: Barnes & Noble Books, 2001.

Popular Baby Names Page. 1 Nov. 2002 <http://www.popularbabynames.com>.

"Presidents of the United States." Collin, P.H. ed. *Webster's Concise Desk Dictionary.* New York: Barnes & Noble Books, 2001.

"Prime Ministers of the U.K." Collin, P.H. ed. *Webster's Concise Desk Dictionary.* New York: Barnes & Noble Books, 2001.

Racketeering and Fraud Investigations Page. 4 Feb. 2003
    <http://www.oig.dol.gov/public/media/oi/mainz01.htm>.

Rick Porelli's AmericanMafia.com Page. 21 June 2002
    <http://www.americanmafia.com/news/6-21-02_Feds_Bust.html>.

Rosenkrantz, Linda, and Pamela Redmond Satran. *Baby Names Now.* New York: St. Martin's Press, 2002.

Rosenkrantz, Linda, and Pamela Redmond Satran. *Beyond Charles and Diana: An Anglophile's Guide to Baby Naming.* New York: St. Martin's Press, 1992.

Rosenkrantz, Linda, and Pamela Redmond Satran. *Beyond Jennifer and Jason.* New York: St. Martin's Press, 1994.

Ryan, Joal. *Puffy, Xena, Quentin, Uma: And 10,000 Other Names for Your New Millenium Baby.* New York: Plume (Penguin Putnam), 1999.

Schwegel, Janet. *The Baby Name Countdown.* New York: Marlowe & Company (Avalon), 2001.

Shaw, Jessica. *The Everything Baby Names Book.* Massachusetts: Adams Media Corporation, 1996.

"Signs of the Zodiac." Gove, Philip Babcock, ed. *Webster's Third New International Dictionary of the English Language Unabridged.* Springfield, Mass: Merriam-Webster Inc. Publishers, 1981.

Television-show credits. 1 Oct. 2002–25 Feb. 2003.

Texas Department of Criminal Justice Page. "Offenders on Death Row." 1 Feb. 2003 <http://www.tdcj.state.tx.us/stat/offendersondrow.htm>.

Trantino, Charlee. *Beautiful Baby Names from Your Favorite Soap Operas.* New York: Pinnacle Books, 1996.

20,000+ Names Page. "20,000+ Names from Around the World." 1 Nov. 2002 <http:// www.20000-names.com>.

United Kingdom Baby Name Page. 15 Jan. 2003 <http://www.baby-names.co.uk>.

Wallace, Carol McD. *The Greatest Baby Name Book Ever,* New York: Avon, 1998.

About the Author

Diane Stafford

Author of the wildly popular book *40,001 Best Baby Names,* magazine editor (five times running), and creative-agency writer, Diane Stafford has 25 years' experience in writing and editing—but nothing has rivaled the indecent amount of fun involved in turning out a second edition, called *50,001 Best Baby Names*, with 10,000 more names for readers.

Adding names from numerous sources, including radio-talk-show listeners who called in when Stafford did first edition interviews, this high-energy author gamely enlarged the scope of a book already filled with great names, fun anecdotes, and baby-naming tips.

"Today people are more creative than ever when it comes to naming their babies," notes Stafford. "Though it may be hard to believe, the fact is, every name in this book belongs to someone out there—even ones as off-the-wall as Dijonaise, Zero, and Oddrun. Although the traditional favorites like Emma and Joshua still reign supreme, lots of people enjoy making up names for their kids, thus adding to the huge universe of options. While name inventing *is* controversial—people even talk about it at cocktail parties—my feeling is that you have every right to relish choosing a name for your baby. Sure, take it seriously, but not too seriously."

Stafford adds, "Having a baby is absolutely the most wonderful thing that can happen to a person, and I hope this book reflects my enormous respect for parents and my celebration of the special privilege of parenting."

Living in sunny Newport Beach, California, Stafford —a transplant from Houston, Texas—writes books and works for a creative agency. Her published books include: *Migraines For Dummies, Potty Training For Dummies, The Encyclopedia of STDs, No More Panic Attacks, 1000 Best Job-Hunting Secrets*, and her latest, *50,001 Best Baby Names*. Four of these books were co-authored with Stafford's daughter, Jennifer Shoquist, M.D.; her job-hunting book co-author was Moritza Day.

Dad's Picks

_____

_____

_____

_____

_____

_____

_____

_____

_____

_____

_____

_____

Mom's Picks

_____

_____

_____

_____

_____

_____

_____

_____

_____

_____

Our Picks

Notes

Notes

Notes

Notes

Notes

_____

_____

_____

_____

_____

_____

_____

_____

_____

_____

_____

Notes

Notes

Look for these titles from Sourcebooks

101 Things Every Kid
Should Do Growing Up
$12.95 U.S./$19.95 CAN
hardcover • 1-57071-861-X
$9.95 U.S./$15.95 CAN
paper • 1-57071-862-8
288 pages • 5¾ x 6½

301 Bright Ideas
for Busy Kids
$12.95 U.S./$19.95 CAN
paper • 1-4022-0050-1
384 pages • 4¼ x 9

The New Mom's
Companion
$13.95 U.S./$21.95 CAN
paper • 1-4022-0014-5
320 pages • 6½ x 8

On the Go with Baby
$14.95 U.S./$23.50 CAN
paper • 1-57071-952-7
336 pages • 4¼ x 9

The Parenting Bible
$14.95 U.S./$23.50 CAN
paper • 1-57071-907-1
464 pages • 7 x 9

Preschool for Parents
$12.95 U.S./$19.95 CAN
paper • 1-57071-172-0
192 pages • 6 x 9

The Secret Language
of Children
$14.95 U.S./$23.95 CAN
paperback • 1-4022-0242-3
368 pages • 6 x 9

What Every Parent Needs
to Know about 1st, 2nd &
3rd Grades
$12.95 U.S./$19.95 CAN
paper • 1-57071-156-9
184 pages • 6 x 9

Look for the 365 Series from Sourcebooks

365 Games Babies Play
$12.95 U.S./$19.95 CAN
paper • 1-4022-0108-7
408 pages • 5¼ x 8

365 Games Toddlers Play
$12.95 U.S./ $19.95 CAN
paper • 1-4022-0176-1
408 pages • 5¼ x 8

365 Afterschool Activities
$12.95 U.S./$19.95 CAN
paper • 1-57071-080-5
416 pages • 5¼ x 8

365 Days of Creative Play
$12.95 U.S./$19.95 CAN
paper • 1-57071-029-5
384 pages • 5¼ x 8

365 Foods Kids Love to Eat
$12.95 U.S./$19.95 CAN
paper • 1-57071-030-9
416 pages • 5¼ x 8

365 Ways to
Raise Great Kids
$12.95 U.S./$19.95 CAN
paper • 1-57071-398-7
416 pages • 5¼ x 8